MEDIA ENVIRONMENTS

Using Movies and Texts to Critique Media and Society

Fourth Edition

EDITED BY BARRY VACKER

SAN DIEGO

Bassim Hamadeh, CEO and Publisher
John Remington, Managing Executive Editor
Carrie Baarns, Senior Manager, Revisions and Author Care
Kaela Martin, Project Editor
Rachel Kahn, Production Editor
Jess Estrella, Senior Graphic Designer
Alexa Lucido, Licensing Manager
Ursina Kilburn, Interior Designer
Natalie Piccotti, Director of Marketing
Kassie Graves, Senior Vice President, Editorial
Jamie Giganti, Director of Academic Publishing

3970 Sorrento Valley Blvd., Ste. 500, San Diego, CA 92121

Contents

PART 01 | MODELS FOR ANALYZING TECHNOLOGIES, SYSTEMS, AND CONTENT

Recommended Films

The Hunger Games: Catching Fire 2013
2001: A Space Odyssey 1968
Blade Runner 1982
Ghost in the Shell 1995
Akira 1998
Star Trek 2009
The Walking Dead 2010–
Inception 2010
Her 2013

** The editor's recommended films are listed first for each chapter.

Acknowledgments

As with any textbook, this anthology would not have been possible without the efforts of many people. My thanks: To Johanna Marcelino, former acquisitions editor at Cognella who initially approached me about doing an "innovative" anthology. To be honest, I was very skeptical about her interest because virtually all textbook publishers are ultraconservative in their approach and methodologies. That is why the media and society textbooks have hardly changed in style and structure over the past forty years, despite the proliferation of media in our culture. Much to my surprise, Johanna immediately grasped the essence of my vision for this volume and paved the way for the first edition of this book to happen. Thanks for getting it, Johanna!

To Carrie Baarns (revisions acquisitions editor) and Kaela Martin (project editor) at Cognella, who saw the merits in a revised and updated fourth edition of this book and were a pleasure to work with on this edition. Thank you to production editors Alia Bales and Rachel Kahn.

To Jess Estrella, Emely Villavicencio, and Ursina Kilburn, the designers at Cognella who made the cover and interior design look so great. Thank you for making it all work together.

To Alexa Lucido at Cognella, who negotiated all the licensing agreements with the variety of publishers and authors.

To all my colleagues in the Klein College of Media and Communications and the Department of Media Studies and Production at Temple University: thanks to all of you who shared your ideas and offered useful suggestions for improving this anthology concept, especially Jan Fernback and Sherri Hope Culver. Thanks to Senior Vice Provost Elizabeth Leebron Tutelman for providing me with the opportunity to teach so many of the large lecture courses in media theory at Temple and for supporting my experiments with different teaching styles and methods in these classes. Thanks to Paul Swann, Matthew Lombard, Nancy Morris, and Pamela Barnett, all of whom provided helpful feedback for teaching large and small theory-based courses. Thanks to everyone!

To Julia Hildebrand and Angela Cirucci for sharing their valuable insights about teaching with this book.

To Jarice Hanson at the University of Massachusetts Amherst for sharing many ideas and insights during our numerous conversations.

To Gail Bower for her enthusiastic support of this anthology. Your patience and thoughtful advice was invaluable in helping me navigate the complexities of this project.

To all the teaching assistants and undergraduate students in my courses for your enthusiastic responses to the ideas of the films and readings that prove the educational thesis of this book.

Finally, my thanks go to the many filmmakers and writers included in this anthology. Their knowledge and artistry have furthered our understanding of the evolution and effects of the global media environments. We all see further because of their visions.

We become what we behold.

—Marshall McLuhan

Introduction
Media Theory, Four Models for Analysis, and Four Unifying Narratives

by Barry Vacker

BEGINNINGS AND ENDS

*G*reenlights—that's the title of Matthew McConaughey's *New York Times* best-selling book, which peaked at #1 in 2020. The title of the book is a "meme." In fact, McConaughey himself is a meme. You've likely never met him, but you know who he is: the Academy Award–winning actor with the Texas twang and sexy smile. McConaughey has replicated throughout our global media environments to become a household name, one of the most famous movie stars in the world. As of this writing, reports are that McConaughey is considering a run for the governor of Texas.[1] That's no surprise, as movie stars have long been getting elected as president and governor in America. That McConaughey is included in this book has nothing to do with his political views, whatever they may be, and everything to do with the power of media, fame, celebrity, and the clever metaphors in *Greenlights*—all of which is an inviting way to introduce students to media theory and analysis.

About greenlights, McConaughey writes:

> In our lives, they are an affirmation of *our* way. They're approvals, support, praise, gifts, gas on our fire, attaboys, and appetites. They're cash money, birth, springtime, health, success, joy, sustainability, innocence and fresh starts. ...
>
> Greenlights can also be disguised as yellow and red lights. A caution, a detour, a thoughtful pause, an interruption, a disagreement, sickness and pain. A full-stop, a jackknife, an intervention, failure, suffering, a slap in the face, death.

The first passage expresses our hope and optimism, our dreams and desires for new beginnings. You are just beginning this college course and you surely have many hopes and desires for what you will learn about our media environments, just as you know that college offers a new beginning for the rest of your life. Greenlights are not only *an affirmation of our way* but are also an affirmation of our worldviews and belief systems. That's how memes spread, that's how things go viral, that's how belief systems persist for hundreds or thousands of years. Memes spread best when they reinforce or reflect what we already believe, our hopes and dreams, our yearnings for beginnings over ends.

The second passage expresses our concerns and worries, our fears and nightmares about what might be happening presently or what the future might bring. A given light may still seem green, but embedded in it are yellow and red lights, directing us to slow down or stop. That's why, even though the traffic light is green, we also look both ways before going through the intersection.

Evidence-based theory gets the greenlight in this book, along with greenlight for clear reasoning, philosophical insights, and powerful metaphors for understanding our media environments. This includes technologies and their messages, the form and content that shapes our media usage and consumption.

---

1   Marianne Garvey, "Matthew McConaughey Is Considering a Texas Governor Run," *CNN*, March 12, 2021.

MEDIA AND COMMUNICATION THEORY

Traditional media and communication theory begins with this basic model.

BASIC COMMUNICATION MODEL

Sender →→ → Message →→ → Receiver

Sender: The person who initiates the communication

Message: The specific collection of words, images, or gestures used to convey the message

Receiver: The audience for the message, from whom the sender usually expects a response

---

Here's an obvious example. When you send a text to a friend, you are the *sender*, the text content is the *message*, and your friend is the *receiver*. Let's make it slightly more complex. If you were in a classroom or campus auditorium (for large courses) during a typical class session, then the professor would be the *sender*, the lecture content would be the *message*, and you, the student, would be the *receiver*. But we know class lectures do not work exactly like that. That's too simple. Why? One reason is *noise*.

BASIC COMMUNICATION MODEL

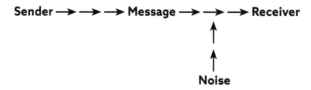

Sender →→ → Message →→ → Receiver
↑
↑
Noise

Noise: Anything that interferes with the audience receiving or comprehending the message

---

While the professor is giving the lecture or leading the discussion, there may be distractions impacting your ability to process or understand the message. Maybe it is the student behind you smacking on gum or the student next to you playing *Candy Crush* or watching TikTok videos. Maybe the noise is that you are texting with a friend, thinking about your job, worrying about an exam you'll be taking later that day, or daydreaming about heading to the beach during summer vacation.

In general, the *senders* in media include individuals (like you), corporations, governments, movie studios, athletes and celebrities, news and media organizations, and business, political, and religious leaders—and so on. Their messages are the *content* of the media and include all the email messages, text messages, status updates, press releases, films and TV shows, tweets and videos, news and entertainment, and advertisements and propaganda. As in the realm of art and music, all content is created and expressed in a specific medium and form. In communication theory, that form is called the *channel*.

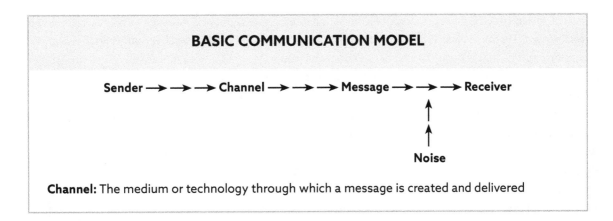

BASIC COMMUNICATION MODEL

Sender → → → Channel → → → Message → → → Receiver

↑ ↑ Noise

Channel: The medium or technology through which a message is created and delivered

The channel (or medium) is the *technological form* through which the message is delivered and received. In traditional communication theory, the channel is usually inserted between the message and the receiver. In my view, the channel should be placed between the sender and the message—precisely because the channel (the medium and technology) inherently shapes the creation, construction, delivery, and reception of the message. The sender shapes the message to fit within the selected medium. As discussed in chapter 1, this is what is meant by theorist Marshall McLuhan's famed phrase "The medium is the message."

Consider the classroom setting. Is the professor talking, reading from notes, using PowerPoint slides, or showing a video or a film? Does the professor talk in a way that increases your interest, or decreases your interest? Do the PowerPoints have engaging images and content, or is the content (message) all words on a slide? Is the font large enough to easily read? Is the video or film relevant and does it help illustrate the content and message? Is the screen bright enough or large enough to be seen from the back of the room?

Different media technologies transform the form and style of messages. For example, art can use paintings on canvases, sculptures in marble or steel, or images on screens or on old buildings (graffiti). Print media, such as books and newspapers, use words on paper. Electronic media combine words and images on television screens, laptops, and mobile phones. Of course, e-books combine words and screens. What's important is that each of these channels is not merely a neutral conveyor of messages—each channel transforms the messages and affects how the messages are received. In other words, the media form shapes the media content.

All of the above have a significant impact on another aspect of the media and communication process: *feedback*.

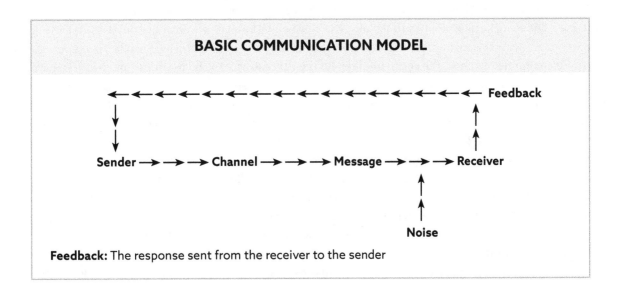

BASIC COMMUNICATION MODEL

← ← ← ← ← ← ← ← ← ← ← ← ← ← Feedback

Sender → → → Channel → → → Message → → → Receiver

↑ ↑ Noise

Feedback: The response sent from the receiver to the sender

In a college course, the most prominent feedback is exams, papers, and projects such as presentations, videos, or works of art. During a class lecture, the feedback may come from the students verbally contributing to the discussion or giving hot takes in Twitter or the Zoom chat room. Maybe the students are merely sitting in silence, taking notes, and thinking about the messages coming from the professor.

In a movie theater, the feedback might be the laughter, tears, or applause. Let's not forget the all-important ticket sales at the box office or revenues from streaming. At a music concert, the feedback might be the cheers and dancing among the fans. Of course, there might be boos if the band or artists are playing below fan expectations. During a new product launch, such as for a soft drink or a mobile phone app, the most important feedback is sales and downloads. During an election, the most important feedback is the vote totals for the respective candidates. Of course, the channels and media technologies also shape the feedback—hence flame wars, Twitter threads, and battles between trolls, keyboard warriors, or internet tough guys. Finally, the entire communication process is happening within the surrounding culture, which includes the many artistic, technological, philosophical, ideological, and personal factors that shape media, messages, and their effects.

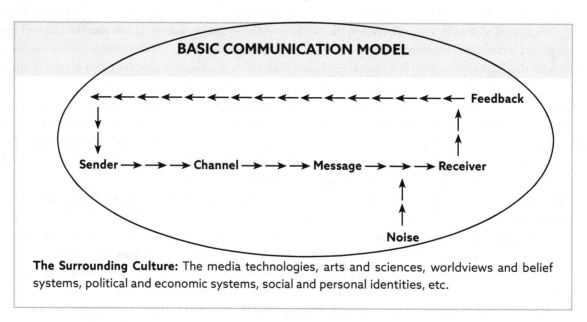

BASIC COMMUNICATION MODEL

Feedback

Sender → → → Channel → → → Message → → → Receiver

Noise

The Surrounding Culture: The media technologies, arts and sciences, worldviews and belief systems, political and economic systems, social and personal identities, etc.

This traditional model has long proven to be useful for breaking down the basic media and communication processes. The model can be applied to the topics in this book. However, we don't live our lives in a situation where communication is easily segmented for analysis. In fact, we live our entire lives inside a planetary media environment, home to almost the entire totality of our culture. Given the increasing (though still imperfect) accessibility of media technologies and the internet, we are all senders and receivers of messages and feedback, in a global culture filled with screens, technologies, distractions, and incessant noise. All of that is why the traditional model must be integrated into larger theories and models—*models that reflect the local and global, the personal and social, the technological and ecological, and the planetary and interstellar.*

We inhabit a 24/7, online, omnipresent, globally networked media system. Virtually all media technologies, industries, content, and usages have converged to shape human consciousness and culture as technological environments. Media-as-environments is the existential reality of the twenty-first century. As explained in chapter 1, all messages are *memes* that replicate within the planetary media ecologies, which are comprised of *layers of media technologies* (channels) that extend from our consciousness to surround the planet and reach deep into space.

Rather than examine communication in separate segments and media as separate industries (news, radio, television, social media, etc.), *Media Environments* explores these media in their totality and provides four *broad and deep* models for understanding and interrogating many universal themes that span media and global culture. These topics are highly interdisciplinary, situating media theory and media effects within the realms of science, philosophy, aesthetics, and cultural studies. That is why we combined art (movies) with theory and science: precisely because we need a mix of the arts, sciences, and humanities to better understand the world.

FOUR MEDIA MODELS: SUPERPOWERS FOR SEEING AND UNDERSTANDING MEDIA ENVIRONMENTS

The first three chapters of *Media Environments* provide "models" for understanding broad and deep patterns in media, technology, and communication. By *model*, we mean a smaller thing to explain the larger thing that is difficult to see or too large to grasp. For example, no one has ever seen the solar system as a totality, but via models we know how it looks and works. No one has seen all the data in a DNA molecule, but we know how it looks from the helix model. Simply put, a model is something small-scale that explains the large-scale, the micro that explains the macro. For this book, we will use four media models supported by a variety of theories: memes, networks, the spectacle, and hyperreality.

Chapter 1: **Memes** replicating in media ecologies

—These are the messages and overall environment for global communication; the media ecologies are filled with an accelerating complexity of messages, noise, and feedback.

Chapter 2: **Networks** and platforms spanning the planet

—These are homes to the various global channels, through which messages and feedback are shaped, sent, and received.

Chapter 3: The **Spectacle** as a way of life and **Hyperreality** as a media-generated reality we inhabit

—Both the spectacle and hyperreality are the content and messages shaped by the channels: the forms of media and technology.

Once you grasp each model, you will have a much deeper understanding of media, technology, society, and why you believe what you believe. And having a richer, deeper understanding of things is central to higher education in universities around the world. It's like you will have superpowers, like X-ray eyes for decoding the world around you. Grasping and using these media models will empower you in your future life and career. You'll be a bit more like the superheroes in your favorite comics, films, video games, or graphic novels. In the remaining chapters, these four models will be applied across a variety of topics:

Chapter 4: News and Entertainment

Chapter 5: Social and Mobile Media

Chapter 6: Freedom and Protest

Chapter 7: Capitalism and Consumption

Chapter 8: Media, the Anthropocene, and Planetary Consciousness

Chapter 9: Media and Science

FOUR UNIFYING NARRATIVES

The aim of this book is to empower you with a *unifying and connecting narrative* for understanding and living in our planetary media environments, with the purpose of uniting your fellow students and you in discourse of topics that span cultures, identities, and demographics. Why unifying truths and universal themes? Because no matter how many tribes we split into, humans remain a single species on a tiny planet in a vast universe. Given the events happening on Planet Earth, we need to get our act together and become far more enlightened. Central to becoming enlightened is *transcending* our own individuality and subjectivity, learning to think in terms of the universal that connects us all to our shared origins and destiny.

These narratives are grounded in our actual place on our planet and in the universe, not in artificial borders, nations, theisms, or other constructs and cultural walls that divide us from each other and from our own humanity. Every beginning has it ultimate starting point, the green light that gets things rolling. Let's begin at the ultimate beginning.

1. OUR COSMIC ORIGINS: WE ARE MADE OF STARDUST

All humans are made of the most common elements of the cosmos, which have emerged and evolved across 13.75 billion years, the estimated age of the observable universe. One of the best summaries I've read is from *New Scientist* magazine:

> The human body contains around 20 different elements, mostly made inside ancient stars. If you deconstructed an 80kg human into atoms, you would get about the following amounts of the different elements[2]:
>
> **Oxygen—52kg**
> This element makes up more than half the mass of your body but only a quarter of its atoms.
>
> **Carbon—14.4kg**
> The most important structural element, and the reason we are known as carbon-based life forms. About 12 per cent of your body's atoms are carbon.
>
> **Hydrogen—8kg**
> The hydrogen atoms in your body were formed in the Big Bang. All the others were made inside a star long ago and were flung into space by a supernova explosion. So, though you may have heard that we are all stardust, that isn't strictly true.
>
> **Nitrogen—2.4kg**
> The four most abundant elements in the human body—hydrogen, oxygen, carbon and nitrogen—account for more than 99 per cent of the atoms inside you. They are found throughout your body, mostly as water but also as components of biomolecules such as proteins, fats, DNA and carbohydrates.[3]

---

2   Note that 80 kg equals about 175 lbs. One kilogram (kg) equals about 2.2 pounds, and one gram (g) equals 0.03 ounces.

3   "What Is the Body Made Of?," *New Scientist*, n.d., https://www.newscientist.com/question/what-is-the-body-made-of/. Other elements primarily include calcium (1.12 kg), phosphorous (880 g), sulphur (200 g), potassium (200 g), and sodium (120 g). Of course, there are others.

We know the composition of the stars from our telescopes and the composition of our bodies from microscopes, perhaps the two most profound media technologies we have ever created. As discussed in the final reading in chapter 1, telescopes are "exo-media" that look away from humanity, while microscopes are "endo-media" that peer inside things. Our phones are mostly "ego-media": humans looking at humans, where we see ourselves as members of tribes and nations, which we see as unique and often divisive. The direction of the gaze of media technologies is crucially important, for different directions tell very different stories.

2. OUR EVOLUTIONARY ORIGINS: WE ARE A SINGLE SPECIES

All humans share 99.5–99.9 percent of the same DNA, and we share 98 percent of the same DNA with our nearest simian ancestors. There is only one existential and cultural conclusion to draw from these facts: Humanity is a single evolutionary species, and inside our cells is the origins for our *universality* and *diversity*—as individuals and as members of the human species.

That we know our cosmic and evolutionary origins is a tribute to our curiosity, creativity, and desire to understand our place in the universe. As discussed in chapter 9 ("Media and Science"), these discoveries and the technologies that made them possible are utterly awe-inspiring and transformative.

3. OUR SHARED HOME: A TINY PLANET IN A MAJESTIC UNIVERSE

Given our cosmic and evolutionary origins, there is another conclusion that must be drawn. We are members of a single species sharing a tiny planet that is about 4.7 billion years old. Our planet orbits an energy-providing star in the Milky Way, a galaxy of 400 billion stars in a vast and wondrous universe populated with untold numbers of stars, planets, black holes, and possible life-forms. The observable universe stretching across 100 billion light years is populated with two trillion galaxies and vast voids of empty space.

That we share this planet with each other and with all the other life-forms on it is an evolutionary and ecological fact. That the universe is vast and majestic shows, at least for the foreseeable future, that all we have to save ourselves is ourselves. The only way out of our ecological crisis and cultural conflicts is to acknowledge another conclusion to be drawn from these facts: that we need true equal rights, inclusivity, a mix of cooperation and competition, and ecological protections and alternative energies for a sustainable civilization that minimizes its impact on the living systems of Planet Earth.

4. SHARING THE PLANET:
CULTURES OF DIVERSITY, EQUALITY, AND INCLUSIVITY

Given the three unifying narratives above, the only philosophical and political conclusion is that every human on Planet Earth possesses universal equal rights—regardless of age, gender, ethnicity, class, ability, sexuality, or gender orientation. And that means everyone! Black, White, brown, indigenous, persons of all colors, LGBTQ+, and persons in any city, nation, homeland, territory, or continent—each one of us possesses these rights precisely because we are members of a single species. That we share these rights on a tiny planet is why our societies need to be inclusive and welcoming. No ethnicity is superior or super-special. With equal rights and inclusivity should come mutual respect and understanding, embracing our diversity and universality as central to living as enlightened human beings. An inclusive society creates a sense of belonging, the very thing we all need as members of the human species.

Sharing our planet means we must learn to cooperate locally, nationally, and globally to address the human future, short-term and long-term—as individuals and as members of the species. Embedded in the future we face are numerous political challenges and a complexity of issues involving, to name just a few, inequality and inequity, racism and nationalism, religious bigotry and supremacist intolerance, police brutality and the prison-industrial complex, and nuclear weapons and the militarization of society. As history has shown, these issues are extremely important and must be studied and corrected. In fact, these issues are analyzed in numerous books and college courses. All of these behaviors and phenomena need to be stopped, and they need a permanent red light, signaling their eventual demise in the long arc of reason, morality, and justice.

Of course, the four unifying narratives offer an idealistic hope, which is precisely why they are necessary, now and for the long term. It is a hope grounded in our shared existential and scientific reality. It is my belief that the four unifying truths collectively offer a unifying starting point for addressing and analyzing media and society (and all the issues named above). That's a beginning worthy of a green light.

COMBINING MOVIES AND TEXTS

The overall goal of *Media Environments* is to inspire you to think creatively and critically based on a broad cultural literacy that includes media and society, theory and technology, and the arts and sciences. Critical thinking and cultural literacy require learning at a deeper level, beyond the latest media trends and techno-gizmo, and they require being open to exploring the wider range of patterns in technological and cultural evolution. *Media Environments* explores themes and issues that are universal to students, media, and society in the twenty-first century.

In addition to the shared narratives and media models, this book embraces a simple concept: combine movies with texts to critique media and society. If you are a student, you might be thinking, "Cool. This will be a fun class." But remember, you are reading this in a book. If you are a professor, you might be thinking, "Oh, no! More edutainment!" But like the students, you are reading this in a book packed with critical theory. The idea is to use the movies to introduce students to critical thinking about media and society. The process is simple:

1. View any of the films (or key scenes from the films) that go with the chapter. This can be done in class or by the students on their own time.
2. Read the introduction and essays in the chapter.
3. Discuss the film and readings together in class.

It's that simple. Entertainment and enlightenment do not have to be in opposition, though they surely are in most of popular culture. "Fun" and "critical thinking" can coexist in a classroom. Art and theory can work together to enlighten and educate in ways that are entertaining and empowering. Consider the following.

BLACK MIRROR AND BLADE RUNNER 2049

Black Mirror and *Blade Runner 2049*—a hit TV anthology and a blockbuster Hollywood sequel. Set in the near future, both are works of science fiction that offer striking visions of our species immersed in the 24/7 media environments that surround our planet, permeate our society, and transform our consciousness. No one is immune to the cognitive and cultural effects of the technologies—not you, not your professor, not your fans, friends, or followers.

Like all species that have ever existed on Earth, we have adapted to our environments, the technological and cultural environments of human civilization in the twenty-first century. As the most advanced species on our planet, we have created radically new environments for living together—the electrified, mechanized, and mediated metropolises we inhabit and share on a daily basis. We have migrated from nature to culture. Like nature, our cities, towns, and suburbs are always evolving and changing, yet we exist within these technological and cultural environments and stay busy adapting to what our species has created. Once we grasp these existential conditions, then we can truly begin to understand the role of media in our society and our daily lives.

Black Mirror (2011–) and *Blade Runner 2049* (2017) are powerful examples of storytelling and visual art, each dramatizing key issues involving media, technology, and society while providing warnings of plausible futures for life in the mediated metropolis. By setting the stories in the future, the artists' goal is to allow us to think more clearly about where we are going today, individually as humans and collectively as a species. Though made primarily for television, *Black Mirror*'s episodes are more like short films, each varying in length, with unique storylines. The episodes provide science fiction scenarios delving into how our beliefs and behaviors are being shaped by the current array of media technologies and how they might develop and function in the future—a future to come in five years or five minutes.

OTHER MOVIES ABOUT MEDIA AND SOCIETY

Of course, films about media and society are not limited to science fiction. Most recently, films like *The Circle* (2017) and *Money Monster* (2016) examine the effects of media and media technology on daily life while posing questions about surveillance, celebrity, entertainment, artificial intelligence, economic power, and our electronic-digital financial systems.

Meanwhile, *The Post* (2017) looks at the recent past, showcasing the role of the press in the Pentagon Papers scandal, showing how US presidents and the Pentagon lied to the American public about the war in Vietnam. In contrast, *Arrival* (2016) offers a sci-fi venture into a possible future, cleverly showing how the roles of media and language might impact humanity's encounter with peaceful extraterrestrials. Though set in the past and the future, *The Post* and *Arrival* also offer insights about today's world, raising questions about truth, democracy, freedom of the press, political power, mass opinion, and tribalism and nationalism. Even the James Bond film *Spectre* (2015) raises profound questions about surveillance and security in our mediated democratic societies.

The point here is that movies need not be mere entertainment. The use of movies to investigate media, technology, and society is not new. *His Girl Friday* (1940) and *Meet John Doe* (1941) show that movies have long attempted to offer insight and criticism about the increasing role of media and technology in society. Such efforts continued across the decades with *Ace in the Hole* (1951), *A Face in the Crowd* (1957), *Fahrenheit 451* (1966), *Privilege* (1967), *Network* (1976), *The China Syndrome* (1979), *Blade Runner* (1982), *Tron* (1982), *Videodrome* (1983), *Quiz Show* (1994), *Contact* (1997), *The Truman Show* (1998), *The Matrix* (1999), *The Insider* (1999), *Fight Club* (1999), *V for Vendetta* (2005), *Good Night, and Good Luck* (2005), *WALL-E* (2008), *The Social Network* (2010), *Her* (2013), *The Fifth Estate* (2013), *The Hunger Games* series (2012–2015), *Black Panther* (2018), *Ready Player One* (2018), *Avengers: Infinity War* (2018), and many others. Of course, there are fictional TV series, such as *The Twilight Zone* (1959–1964), *Black Mirror* (2011–), and *The Feed* (2019–). No doubt future filmmakers will continue such efforts.

THESE FILMS ARE NOT MEANT TO BE YOUR FAVORITES; THEY ARE MEANT TO GET YOU TO THINK BEYOND THE LATEST HOT TAKE

Collectively, these films survey how are we using and adapting to our media technologies, many of which seem to be evolving at ever-accelerating rates in the twenty-first century. Are our media technologies functioning more to bring us together as a peaceful and enlightened species? Or are social media turning us into tweeting tribes inhabiting echo chambers? What role do media technology and corporations—Apple, Google, Facebook, Netflix, Disney, Amazon, Comcast, Time-Warner, News Corp—play in our society? What about news, fake news, protest and resistance, capitalism and consumerism, celebrities and superheroes, social and mobile media, and even artificial intelligence such as Siri and Alexa? What about the other environments we inhabit—the ecosystems of Planet Earth? What about science, telescopes, and knowing our true place in the universe?

These are some of the topics and questions explored in *Media Environments*. The most important thing is not that you love or hate any of the films mentioned or discussed in this book, but that you understand what they are saying about your world—a world lived inside 24/7 media environments.

Most of the recommended media films are fictional, though there are some documentaries listed that are also artful and creatively produced. In our view, the artful fictional or documentary film is more powerful than the standard "talking head" documentary. Of course, we are not saying that every fictional film on the list is a masterpiece. What we are saying is that the combination of films and texts provides a way to creatively and critically map the "environments" of media—the mental, material, and cultural environments. The aim is not to watch all the films; rather, we hope that professors will choose the films that they believe best align with the readings and their own teaching expertise. Each introduction and essay provides plenty of issues to discuss within the chapter topic.

UNDERSTANDING AND DISAGREEMENT

Another goal of this book is to generate understanding, not necessarily universal agreement among all readers, students, or professors. It would be incredibly arrogant on our part to assume that everyone should believe everything in this book immediately. Our beliefs and worldviews are woven deeply into our neurons, and it is not easy to "change" the beliefs of anyone, including you or your fellow students. So we do not assume the readings in the book will transform your consciousness or change your mind about anything. Though this book presents many great ideas to empower you in your use and understanding of media, the only person who can change your beliefs is *you*. At the end of the semester, you might have the exact same beliefs as you had before.

Since there is no way to cover the entirety of the theories and effects of media in society, it's likely that you'll disagree with something in the book. That's natural. Understanding is the key. As with everything in this book, you can agree or disagree with what is discussed in the following readings. That's your choice. If you disagree, there are two things you should do: (1) make sure you have a thorough understanding of the claim or theory with which you disagree, and (2) make sure your alternative claim or media theory correlates to empirical reality, embraces verifiable evidence, expresses consistent logic, and applies universally as much as possible. That makes for great class discussions and helps enlighten everyone. Plus, that is how knowledge adapts and evolves.

THE EVOLUTION OF OUR KNOWLEDGE

This anthology presents you with new theory to better explain the conditions created by our media environments. All our knowledge and understanding should be thought of as contextual and evolutionary, not timeless or static. What we know may be subject to revision when we're presented with new facts, new conditions, or new theories. That science and theory evolve is their virtue, and it need not imply naive relativism. That this is the fourth edition of *Media Environments* shows that this book has evolved, revising and adding to the knowledge presented on the following pages. Let's begin.

PART 01

MODELS FOR ANALYZING TECHNOLOGIES, SYSTEMS, AND CONTENT

ACE IN THE HOLE (1951)

"The curse of the seven vultures" is a newspaper headline that sets off a national media spectacle about a man trapped in a cave.

NETWORK (1976)

"We're mad as hell and we're not gonna take this anymore!" yell the followers of Howard Beale. They shout this out their windows and collectively in TV studios, thus showing the viral power of the media spectacle.

FIGHT CLUB (1999)

"The first rule of Fight Club is, you do not talk about Fight Club," commands Tyler Durden to his "space monkeys," who want to overthrow consumerism, capitalism, and the modern world.

THE HUNGER GAMES (2012)

"Katniss" and the "three-finger salute" become symbols to rally the citizens of Panem.

ARRIVAL (2016)

The circular symbols of the alien language baffle, are beautiful, and quickly become memes online.

MEMES AND MEDIA ECOLOGIES
The Basic Units of Information and Their Technological Environments

By Barry Vacker and Julia M. Hildebrand

J ulia M. Hildebrand coauthored the section of this introduction on "Media Ecologies."

RED LIGHTS, YELLOW LIGHTS, AND GREEN LIGHTS

Stop. Slow down. Go. The fact that we know which directive goes with which color of light is a perfect example of a meme.

Matthew McConaughey's poetic description of all the symbolism in "green lights" not only shows the power of language and human imagination but also illustrates how ideas get copied, modified, and passed along to create new uses, new meanings, and new purposes for the original idea. That's what memes do. They replicate. *Greenlights* is a meme, McConaughey is a meme, and so is *Media Environments*.

Apple and Amazon are two of the most successful companies on Earth. They have replicated on a planetary scale. They are global memes. Apple and Amazon give us the green light to download, buy, and consume pretty much whatever we want, whenever we want, *seemingly* in endless quantities. Meanwhile, environmental destruction and the science of climate disruption are giving us bright yellow and red lights. These lights are flashing all over the ecosystems of our planet.

If the mention of climate disruption hit your hot button, welcome to the power of memes. Memes do not care what you believe, only that you *believe*. Memes want you to copy them and pass them along—regardless of whether they are true or not. Memes replicate like viruses.

COVID-19 does not care whether you believe it is real or a hoax, only that for the virus to get passed along, it helps tremendously if you do not wear a mask, properly fitted and hopefully with an N95 level of protection. As McConaughey writes, "death" is the ultimate red light, the ultimate end. As of this writing, the total deaths of Americans from COVID-19 now exceeds one million, a significant portion of the six million total deaths from COVID-19 around the world.[1] Being vaccinated, properly wearing masks, and social distancing can help bring an end to the mass death happening around the world. That's a fact. Still hitting a hot button? That's the power of memes (and of "hot media," discussed in the third reading in chapter 1).

---

1   For a detailed explanation of probable case counts and total death counts, see: https://www.worldometers.info/coronavirus/country/us/ and https://www.worldometers.info/coronavirus/about/.

WHAT IS A MEME?

In addition to being a famous movie star, Matthew McConaughey is a professor of practice at The University of Texas at Austin, where he received his Bachelor of Science degree in Radio-Television-Film (1993). He teaches a course on the film industry and shares his ideas, insights, expertise, and experiences with the students enrolled in one of the largest film programs in the United States. McConaughey is doing what all professors do, which is to pass along knowledge to the students in their courses. All the knowledge and ideas that professors impart are memes. With my PhD from McConaughey's alma mater, I was educated to pass along knowledge/memes as a professor, writer, and media theorist, and later I taught myself (with assistance from another artist) to be a mixed-media artist. In our idealism as professors, we hope the knowledge/memes we pass along will stay with the students long after the final exam, even informing and shaping their lives.

That's not easy and it may well be impossible, though students might remember McConaughey's memes far better than they remember mine. Getting the memes to stay in your mind and impact your life is a profound challenge, precisely because all memes compete with each other in a vast, always evolving ecosystem that we inhabit and must adapt to—the 24/7 media environments. That's the challenge this book accepts: media environments packed with memes encountering red, yellow, and green lights.

MEMES: THE BASIC UNITS OF INFORMATION

In its simplest terms, a meme (rhymes with cream) is a basic unit of information and communication; it's any idea, image, belief, or behavior that can be copied and passed along. By this, I do *not* mean mere "internet memes," clever GIFs, or viral videos, though all of those are also memes. In this context, memes have a much larger and more profound meaning.

As basic units of information, memes refer to anything that humans do, share, and pass along—from selfies to social systems, cat videos to artworks created throughout humanity, fashion to the architecture in our cities, sound bites to the sciences that explain life and the cosmos, and TED Talks to the philosophies that seek to explain our meaning and purpose in NASA's universe of two trillion galaxies stretching across 100 billion light-years. That's right: *Everything* you know and believe about the world and universe is a meme, as are *all* your clothes, hairstyles, and favorite music, movies, and sports teams. Everything in this book is a meme.

Your brain is home to your mind—the vessel for knowledge, ideas, values, and worldviews. You most likely inherited many of your beliefs from your parents or from the area where you grew up. In *Greenlights*, McConaughey discusses the influence of his parents and growing up in Texas. Similarly, you have acquired other ideas from your friends, the media, and maybe even some professors. The units of information you acquire are the product of mutations of or competitions between previous units of information—especially if those new ones seem to offer better or clearer explanations of the world and your place in it.

The meme serves as the first media model in this book. The concept of the "meme" was coined by biologist Richard Dawkins in his book *The Selfish Gene*, in which he presented his explanation of genetic evolution.[2] Dawkins observed that culture evolves in many ways similar to genes, and he created "meme" as a term for explaining cultural evolution in new ways. Since then, the concept of memes has become the object of study for multiple thinkers, as illustrated in the various definitions provided in Richard Brodie's book *Virus of the Mind*.[3]

---

2 Richard Dawkins, *The Selfish Gene* (Oxford, UK: Oxford University Press, 1976), 189–201. *Meme* is a hybrid term, derived and condensed from the word *mimeme*, which has roots in the Greek word for *imitation*; Dawkins also thought *meme* could be related to "memory" and the French word *même* (p. 192).
3 Richard Brodie, *Virus of the Mind* (New York: Hay House, 2009), 5–11.

- Biological definition: The *meme* is the basic unit of cultural transmission, or imitation.
- Cognitive definition: A *meme* is an idea, the kind of complex idea that forms itself into a distinct memorable unit. It is spread by *vehicles* that are physical manifestations of the meme.
- Brodie's definition: A *meme* is a unit of information in a mind whose existence influences events such that more copies of itself get created in other minds.

These definitions provide a method for thinking about the transmission of ideas from consciousness to consciousness. Across the millennia of cultural evolution, memes have survived and flourished because they managed to replicate, mutate for survival advantage, and continue to be selected within the minds of their hosts. Some memes are simple; some are highly complex.

HOW MEMES SPREAD TO YOUR CONSCIOUSNESS

As mentioned, memes are not new. They go back to the beginning of human communication. Some of the origins of memes are indicated in Werner Herzog's film *Cave of Forgotten Dreams*, in which humans used art to create representations (or copies) of their world. The beautiful artworks were created with paint on cave walls, both of which we can understand as early "media." Memes and media help us think about how knowledge, ideas, beliefs, and worldviews spread across time and space.

For example: Why are you a fan of Beyoncé, LeBron James, Tom Brady, or any other pop or sports star? Why are you a fan of the local sports team? Why do you use social media sites? How did you come to know of *The Big Bang Theory*, *The Incredibles*, or *Avengers: Infinity War*? What do you know and believe about the world, the universe, the role of media in human existence? Where did you get those units of information? Think it over.

Can you say you consciously chose those thoughts and beliefs? Or did the thoughts and beliefs choose you? That may sound like a strange question, but it is not. It is based on a very powerful idea. Maybe the units of information in media replicate like genes and spread like a virus, face-to-face or via our communication technologies. Can activities, beliefs, and worldviews be thought of as contagions passed among minds? The spread of information (via media) is depicted in several classic media films discussed in this book.

MEMES IN *ARRIVAL*

Consider the 2016 science-fiction film *Arrival*, in which peaceful extraterrestrials arrive on Earth seeking to communicate with humans. Their language—when converted to symbols for humans to see and "read"—takes the form of complex patterns based on circles. Humans have never seen these forms of language but must decode them in order to communicate with the extraterrestrials. The aliens' language is a *new meme* that must be understood and eventually replicated among humans for communication to occur.

Among the several things about media and society to learn from *Arrival*, here are three:

1. Art and language are media.
2. Symbolic language is a meme that replicates and serves as a primary mode of communication.
3. Clear communication is needed for peaceful cooperation among and between species, peoples, and nations.

Just as the heroic professors (played by Amy Adams and Jeremy Renner) learned how to communicate in the new language of the aliens in *Arrival*, you learned how to communicate on Facebook, Twitter, and various other social media. Though easier to learn than the alien language, social media are new forms of communication that you adopted.

MEMES IN *CONTACT*

A similar example takes place in *Contact*, the 1997 science-fiction classic starring Jody Foster and Matthew McConaughey. In this thoughtful film, an advanced extraterrestrial civilization receives television signals from Earth and beams the signals back to Earth, along with the designs for building an interstellar transportation machine to "contact" the civilization. In effect, the extraterrestrials have discovered memes from Earth and replicated the memes by sending them back to our planet as a way of saying "hello." Humans then build the machine, itself a meme that is replicated, to establish contact with the extraterrestrial civilization. (*Contact* is discussed in greater detail in chapter 9.) Like the extraterrestrials finding humans in *Arrival* and *Contact*, it is likely that social media found you on the internet. That's how memes work. They *arrive* and they make *contact*. They find you.

DID YOU FIND TWITTER, OR DID TWITTER FIND YOU?

Facebook has friends and fans, Twitter has followers, and YouTube and TikTok have viral videos. Let's think about these popular online communities by asking some questions:

- Did you find Facebook, or did Facebook find you? Was it through the recommendation of a "friend"? Did you actively choose to become a "fan" of something or someone—let's say Lady Gaga—on Facebook, or did it seem as if the Lady Gaga fan club chose you?
- Did you find Twitter, or did Twitter find you? Did you actively choose to become a follower, or did the practice of following on Twitter find you?
- Did you choose to find that viral video on YouTube, or did it seem as if the viral video found you?

Of course, these questions are rhetorical, yet they also are meant to be seriously thought-provoking. It is likely that you "found" Facebook, Twitter, and YouTube through a friend, long before your parents and grandparents ever heard of these media. Once you found them, they were easy to use because it was easy to *imitate* what others were doing in these online communities. That is why these communities grew so quickly. As of 2021, Facebook had 2.8 billion users, approaching one-third of the world's population. YouTube has 2 billion users. As of this writing, TikTok has almost 1 billion users and is spreading rapidly. Consider that some music videos on YouTube have been viewed billions of times, often within a relatively short time frame. The current YouTube champs are the music videos "Baby Shark Dance" (by Pinkfong, with 8.8 billion views), "Despacito" (by Luis Fonsi, with 7.4 billion views), and "The Shape of You" (by Ed Sheeran, with 5.3 billion views). Of course, videos by Beyoncé, Adele, Lady Gaga, Wiz Khalifa, and many others have more than a billion views as well.

THE JOURNEY OF A MEME ACROSS TIME AND SPACE

Kat Oleary, a former student in my courses at Temple University, has six hundred thousand followers who like her witty and wacky videos in TikTok. Some of Kat's videos have had millions of viewers. In 2019, Temple's social media team asked Kat to do a one-day "takeover" of the Temple Instagram account, wherein Kat streamed and posted about what she did on campus. Kat dropped by my office during that day and we livestreamed our walk to the classroom auditorium (for 225 students) in another building, passing by many of the popular food and coffee trucks. As we approached a coffee truck, Kat asked me what I wanted students to get from my media class. I replied that I wanted students to experience an "explosion of awareness" (accompanied by my making a cheesy "swooshing" sound).

In that phrase, I was echoing a meme started by Apollo 14 astronaut Edgar Mitchell, who said that the view of Earth from the moon effected an "explosion of awareness" in his consciousness. Mitchell's meme echoed from the moon to Earth in 1972, found my consciousness in a 1990s documentary about the moon landings, and then made its way into Kat's livestream on Instagram in 2019. That's the power of memes.

IS SPORTS FANDOM RANDOM?

Let's extend our analysis to sports teams and fans. If you are a fan of a certain American football team, why are you a fan of *that* football team? Is it because it is intrinsically superior to all other football teams? If so, your team would never lose a game or fire its coach. More likely, you are a fan because of sheer chance rather than pure choice. Maybe your fan preferences were determined by where you were born and/or raised by your parents; perhaps you grew up in a city that has a professional football team, such as Dallas, Philadelphia, or San Francisco.

Sports "fans" are perfect examples of how memes can shape thoughts and beliefs, elicit behaviors, and generate potentially undying love and reverence. McConaughey is a superfan for all things about the Texas Longhorns, especially the football team. Of course, some teams, such as the Dallas Cowboys and the New York Yankees, find fans outside their regional areas. They develop followings because of their success. The process is simple: when teams win, they get more fans. Breathless sportscasters remind us that momentum changes, but winning is *contagious*! It's a meme.

Teams and fans have identifying slogans and regional nicknames, such as "How 'bout them Cowboys?" for the Dallas Cowboys and "Hook 'em Horns" for the Texas Longhorns. Fans often wear their team's logo or jersey. Imitation is flattery. I live in downtown Philadelphia, and when the Eagles won the 2018 Super Bowl, the celebration parade drew almost two million fans, all wearing green Eagles jerseys, sweaters, and hoodies on the chilly day. From the balcony of my loft on the parade route, I watched the joyous fans stream in from every street; it looked like a species migration one might see on the National Geographic TV channel.

Cities and colleges build magnificent stadiums, temples, and coliseums for their teams and fans. If you cannot attend the game, you can always migrate to the neighborhood sports bar or view the game on your 72" flat-screen TV in your dwelling. This explains how money is made off fans—many billions of dollars, in fact. To survive as economic and cultural entities, teams need fans and television needs viewers. They function together, always trying to acquire more fans.

And what better way to gain fans than to be celebrated on television in the annual rituals and spectacles of the Super Bowl and the Bowl Championship Series? "Super" games and "championships" are attractive and seductive, as are game-winning plays, heroic quarterbacks, and glamorous cheerleaders. The spectacle of televised sports is part of the world symbolically illustrated in *The Hunger Games* films.

YOUR BELIEFS: CHOICE OR CHANCE?

So, did you *consciously* choose to be a fan because of the unique virtues of your team? Be honest. Or is your preference the product of chance (your parents and where you were born), the team, and the media, all of which combine in trying to choose you to be a fan? As for me, I inherited the meme of where my father went to college—The University of Texas at Austin. That's where I went to graduate school. So it seems natural to me that my favorite college team is the Texas Longhorns, the team we watched on TV while we lived in Austin and the suburbs of the Dallas area. Yet, if my father had chosen another university, my favorite team might be different. That's why, as a professor of media studies, I realize that my fandom is, in part, random. It's a mix of chance and choice. Mostly chance.

Much like your fan preferences, many of your thoughts and beliefs may have been passed down to you from your parents. Political, philosophical, and, especially, religious ideas strongly correlate to your parents' beliefs and/or the area, nation, or region of the world in which you were born. Simply put, religious followers born in North America are more likely to be Christian, while those born in the Middle East are more likely to be Muslim, and those born in Southeast Asia are more likely to be Buddhist or Hindu. This means your initial worldviews are more likely the product of chance than your personal conscious choice. Just like teams need fans and TV needs viewers, political parties need voters and philosophies and religions need followers.

When you agree with your parents in these realms, it likely makes them quite happy. On the other hand, you may have expressed beliefs or behaviors significantly different from those of your parents, perhaps causing them much consternation. At some point, you decide to discard a previous belief or behavior of your parents in favor of a new idea and activity. You are no longer a fan or a follower of the previous belief, which is no longer being passed on through you. Beliefs die out when they are no longer passed on to the succeeding generations.

All these examples—Facebook, Twitter, YouTube, sports fans, following parents, and chance over choice—raise essential questions about the spread of memes across time and space, especially via communication technologies. So, are you the master of your thoughts or are you mostly the host of various mind viruses? McConaughey's passages say you're in charge. Are you? Yellow light?

FROM GENES TO MEMES TO TEMES

Genes were the first replicators, fueling the biological evolution of life across billions of years, including the evolution of the human mind. That's a scientific fact. Emerging from our minds, memes can be seen as the second replicators, fueling the cultural evolution of humans around the world. In the words of meme scholar Susan Blackmore, humans are "gene machines and meme machines." The most complex memes—such as sports or religions or worldviews or ecology or consumerism or counterculture—can be thought of as metamemes or memeplexes. As explained by Blackmore, a *metameme* is an overarching meme that contains many lesser memes, while a *memeplex* refers to a complexity of memes, or clusters of smaller memes, that replicate together in a manner that furthers the survival of the memes, collectively and individually.[4]

Blackmore's insights help us understand why Apple and Amazon are metamemes—they collectively embody many memes that make up a larger meme. Apple and Amazon symbolize capitalism, corporate power, convenience, entertainment, and so on. Similarly, many of the superhero films are memeplexes—the *Avengers* universe includes memes such as Iron Man, Thor, Hulk, Black Widow, Black Panther, Captain America, and Spiderman. The various superheroes replicate singularly and collectively in the movies, comic books, and multimedia environments.

It is important to understand that the popularity of a meme, metameme, or memeplex has nothing to do with truth or with a term's true value, but rather with its ability to survive by saying something about the world that ensures its replication in the hosts—including you. In other words, any given meme may be true or may be false. While a meme could be popular because it speaks to reality, a meme might be unpopular precisely because it is true and challenges a widely held belief system. The most powerful of memes, metamemes and memeplexes, are believed because they provide a model of the world—however accurate or inaccurate—that provides a sense of meaning, a sense of understanding, and a sense of destiny and purpose. This is why it is important to verify what you believe and discard what is untrue.

Blackmore also identified a "third replicator," for which she coined the term *teme*. It is any technology that gets itself copied, improved, and replicated. The internet, for example, is the evolutionary combination of the telegraph, telephone, radio, cinema, television, satellites, fiber optics, computers, and other memes and media. To borrow from McConaughey, we could say the internet is "the autobahn of life," a global network where memes and temes encounter green, yellow, and red lights—all day, every day.

MEDIA ECOLOGIES

The same way that memes can shape our thoughts, feelings, and actions, so can temes. An entire intellectual tradition is dedicated to studying the technologies that impact us on individual and societal levels: media ecology. Media ecologists understand "media"—that is, human-made artifacts—as environments. Likewise, any human-made environment can be approached as a "medium." We create, then inhabit, and adapt to these environments similar to other species in their specific ecologies. Hence, when we're exploring culture and society across time

---

4   Susan Blackmore, *The Meme Machine* (Oxford, UK: Oxford University Press, 1999), 19.

and space, we should not only study memes (the "what") but also study media (the "how") and the sociotechnical environments they come into and out of.

One key thinker in media studies is Marshall McLuhan, who understood and pointed to the relevance of media in our lives. Although most of his ideas come from the 1950s and 1960s, many of them remain highly applicable today. For example, McLuhan essentially predicted the World Wide Web thirty years before it was invented. He also used the phrase "the matrix" long before Neo, Morpheus, and Trinity battled it in *The Matrix*. Most notably, McLuhan coined a phrase that you may have heard elsewhere before: "global village." The global village is what we live in today.[5] But what did he mean exactly?

"THE GLOBAL VILLAGE"

In one of his most famous books, *Understanding Media* (originally published in 1964), McLuhan argues that electric media (such as television and now the internet) allow information and images to traverse the globe, bringing us closer together.[6] The "global village" is instant communication—as if face-to-face, yet spanning the planet.

Remarkably, the global village is not a utopian state of society, as he explains in the short reading included in this chapter. While we get closer to each other, we also become more involved in each other's lives. We start to live in utmost proximity to each other. What happens when people and things are too close? Friction, fights, frustration. This observation seems even more accurate today in this age of always-on hyperconnectivity and information overload. Our exposure to and engagement with digital media become increasingly intense.

The global village is the technological subtext for many episodes of *Black Mirror*, featuring the on-screen collision of ideas, images, people, things, and events, all linked and simultaneously visible on local, national, and global scales. This is especially evident in the episodes "National Anthem," "Fifteen Million Merits," "The Waldo Moment," "White Christmas," "Nosedive," "Hated in the Nation," and "Arkangel." The global village is also the world Mae navigates in the social media film *The Circle* (2017). McLuhan explains how the world contracted to a village means "fission, not fusion." We (Vacker and Hildebrand) expand on this idea of the global village and give some of McLuhan's other approaches a fresh look in the experimental essay "Hot and Cool in the Media(S) cene"—which was honored with the 2019 John Culkin Award for Outstanding Praxis in the Field of Media Ecology.

MEDIA AS EXTENSIONS OF US

Let's briefly return to this notion of "media" as *any* human-made technology. This means that the clock and the car are as much media as the television and the smartphone. Furthermore, McLuhan speaks of media as *extensions of human faculties*—in other words, extensions of the human body and mind.[7] According to him, for example, the alphabet extends the eyes. The printing press extends the alphabet. Similarly, clothing extends the skin, just as buildings extend our clothing.[8] Cars and trains extend our feet, helping us move faster and further. However, living within and surrounded by these technologies, we have become numb to their effects on us. We are unable to clearly see our media environments for what they are and how they work us. What kind of media ecology are you in right now? Are you aware of the effects it has on your body and your mind?

---

5   Marshall McLuhan, *Understanding Media: The Extensions of Man* (New York: McGraw-Hill, 1964).

6   McLuhan, *Understanding Media.*

7   McLuhan, *Understanding Media.*

8   Marshall McLuhan, "Clothing–'Extension of Our Skin,'" Marshall McLuhan, June 30, 2016, https://mcluhanlives.wordpress.com/2016/06/27/clothing-extension-of-our-skin/#:~:text=Marshall%20McLuhan%20states%20that%20%E2%80%9Ctechnologies,kinds%20of%20technologies%20like%20wheels%E2%80%9D.&text=Clothing%20is%20also%20a%20way,%E2%80%9D%20(McLuhan%2C%201964).

"THE MEDIUM IS THE MESSAGE"

McLuhan describes the important role of media in our lives in his famous aphorisms "the medium is the message"[9] and "the medium is the massage" (the latter phrase comes from a typo on the cover of his 1967 book, but McLuhan liked it and developed it further).[10] With those playful phrases, he means that we need to pay attention to the form of a medium rather than merely its specific contents. To him, what information is being sent via satellite at any given moment is less relevant than the fact that we can send information via satellite. To understand past, present, and emerging media environments, it is less important where you drive your car to and what apps you use on your smartphone than the fact that you are driving a car and using a smartphone. Too often, we pay attention only to *what* we communicate and do with our tech, tools, and toys instead of *how* we communicate with them and what effect their form has on us and others. Media—as our extensions and environments—impact how we think, feel, and act, how we conceive and perceive the world around us. In other words, technology can "massage" our consciousness into modes of thinking about and viewing the world in certain ways. Of course, this does not mean that the contents have no importance, for they surely do. But it is the medium that conditions us for the message.

You are extending your consciousness into media environments with your status updates on Facebook, your images on Instagram, and your videos on YouTube. Yet, beyond this ability to put information online, there are many effects of our technological extensions. Ultimately, such media can reorder our perceptions of the world, causing us to understand the world in different ways. The films and readings in this anthology illustrate this profound point.

MEDIA AND THEIR MESSAGES

McLuhan, furthermore, argued that the content of each medium is another medium.[11] The printed word contains the written word, which contains the spoken word, which contains human thought. Television contains film and radio, with film containing the camera and the vision of the eye while radio contains the telephone and the spoken word. With media convergence via digitalization, many computers now contain all previous media, all migrating into cyberspace and connected via the internet. As a result, computers and cyberspace function as containers for the contents of the human mind and consciousness. Those containers vary, and "the medium is the message."

Let's consider some examples of such media messages:

Social message of the printing press: Mechanized mass society. The written word was exponentially amplified in the fifteenth century with the printing press, the first true mass medium. As McLuhan explains in *The Gutenberg Galaxy*, first published in 1962, the printing press helped usher in the modern civilization that surrounds us. This includes the spread of mass society and mechanized lifestyles fueled by mass production; sacred texts and secular revolutions; individualism and nationalism; free speech and human rights; and the industrial systems of capitalism and communism, along with democracy and socialism.[12] More than five centuries later, the book you are now reading was born of the printing press. Kindle and e-books likewise have their origins in papyrus and the printing press.

Social message of television: Society of the spectacle. Our thoughts and perceptions extended into visual forms with photography and film and electronic forms with the telegraph and telephone, both of which went wireless with radio and digital technologies. Instant messages and iPhones are the latest incarnation of communication across distances. Radio and motion picture cameras combined to produce television, from which we get NBC, CNN, YouTube, Hulu, Netflix, and much more. As with the printing press, television has massaged our senses to get us accustomed to the effects of the screen—a "society of the spectacle" in which images are commodified as forms of economic power and social influence.[13] According to philosopher Guy Debord, the essential stance of television and the screen is that *viewing is doing*. This leads to the society of spectacle and the triumph of image

---

9   McLuhan, *Understanding Media*.
10   Marshall McLuhan and Quentin Fiore, *The Medium Is the Massage* (San Francisco: HardWired, 1997).
11   McLuhan, *Understanding Media*.
12   Marshall McLuhan, *The Gutenberg Galaxy*, Reprint ed. (Toronto: University of Toronto Press, 2011).
13   Guy Debord, *Society of the Spectacle* (Oakland, CA: AK Press, 2005).

along with the cultures of hype, celebrity, consumerism, sports, surveillance, voyeurism, televisual politics, shrinking attention spans, sound-bite thinking, lack of exercise, and declining book reading. Enlightenment may appear on television, but it must obey what media ecologist Neil Postman calls the bias of TV: entertainment.[14] And it is television that made the global village seem so real.

Social message of the car: Mobile consumer society. The automobile is a technology that transports us from point A to point B. In taking us places, the car generated the media environments of suburbia, malls, fast food, and the highway system, which amplified tourism and transformed distribution systems (via trucking); all of this caused massive fossil fuel consumption and carbon emissions, which have shaped US domestic and foreign policies. The medium of the car has a much larger message than transporting people from point A to point B. Over time, the car has massaged individuals, communities, and societies into embracing an entire mode of being—the mobile consumer society, dependent on fossil fuels.

Social message of the computer: Network society. Now think of the computer as a medium that transports information from various points. The need to connect mainframe and personal computers generated the hyper-medium of the internet. Once the computers were connected, the need to access and transmit increasing amount of information on them generated the World Wide Web, invented in 1990 by Tim Berners-Lee at the CERN nuclear research facility near Geneva, Switzerland. The World Wide Web then made possible the kind of user-friendly websites, web browsers (Safari), search engines (Google), video sites (YouTube), and social media (Facebook) we know today. In transporting information, the computer helped generate the internet, the World Wide Web, and social media, all of which are combining to change our public policies, economy, social organization, distribution systems, the spread of knowledge, and the very way we communicate and represent ourselves to the world. The medium of the computer has a much larger message than containing and sending information from point A to point B. The computer has massaged our body and mind into embracing the 24/7 networked society that spans the globe and links people with information, entertainment, and one another.

FIGURE 1.0.1 An artist and former student, Sara Falco (The W?ldCard) created this striking graphic artwork to illustrate our species' immersion in electric light. @wildcardpro

---

14 Neil Postman, *Amusing Ourselves to Death: Public Discourse in the Age of Show Business* (New York: Viking, 1985).

Social message of electric light: A 24/7/365 always-on society. Electric light is central to the global village. We take electric light for granted as a neutral technology with little or no effect on how we think or view the world. Yet, electric light massages our consciousness every day and night. When night arrives, we flip the light switch, and the light bulb immediately glows in our homes, as if we have our own personal star to illuminate the darkness. Electric light has produced a nonstop planetary civilization that displaces the Milky Way with an electric galaxy of light bulbs, floor lamps, streetlights, neon signs, LED lights, and proliferating screens. Electric light makes possible the electronic screen, which is central to all the computers we use today. Your computer or mobile phone screen is made of thousands of tiny electric lights. Without these tiny electric lights, the computers and the internet would be of little practical value. Without these lights, the global village would hardly exist.

Existential message of electric light: We are the center of everything. In our metropolises, who is still able to look at the night sky with awe and wonder? Electric light and the digital screens it fuels have, in effect, returned us to "the center of the universe," a vast and expanding media universe that shapes our nighttime practices and rituals. Not only have our industrial cities mostly removed us from nature, but our electric lights and electronic screens make the cosmos disappear from the everyday lives of humanity. In this sense, social media and electronic screens are the continuation of electric light, allowing us to pretend to be at the center of our universe. In this way, the electric light and its extension via digital screens unintentionally counter the effects of the telescope.

EGO-, ECO-, ENDO-, AND EXO-MEDIA

As probed in this chapter in the reading titled "Hot and Cool in the Media(S)cene," social media tend to make us look inward at each other and at ourselves. We call those "ego-media." In contrast, "exo-media"—such as telescopes and some satellites—are those that help us look out and away from humankind, far into deep space. Operating in between those two extremes, eco-media—such as camera drones and Earth-facing satellites—bring attention to the surfaces of our planet. Finally, "endo-media"—such as microscopes and MRI machines—peer inside atoms, molecules, and our cells. What are the sociocultural effects of these different types of technologies? In the example of exo-media, for instance, it is the discovery that we are not the center of the universe, neither in space nor in time. This profound insight is on display across four decades of the *Star Trek* films and TV shows, which include the perpetual discovery of "new life-forms and new civilizations." Prior to the invention of the telescope, the universe of *Star Trek* was largely unknowable.

Thus, our technologies have a great impact on our perceptions and how we organize ourselves into societies and cultures. If we think of media only as vehicles of content, then we are missing the larger effects. Many of these effects are utterly unintended and unforeseen.

LAWS OF MEDIA

Later in his career, McLuhan and his son Eric developed a tool for applying McLuhan Sr.'s media theories. They call it the "laws of media" or the tetrad (see the figure below). To understand media and media messages, the McLuhans suggest approaching any human-made technology with four questions: (1) What does it enhance? (2) What does it make obsolete? (3) What does it retrieve from the past? and (4) What does it turn into when pushed to an extreme? According to McLuhan and McLuhan, using these four questions illuminates the larger sociocultural powers of a given medium. Exploring a medium through this lens can produce multiple different tetrads depending on the context and your focus.[15]

---

15   Marshall McLuhan and Eric McLuhan, *Laws of Media: A New Science* (Toronto: University of Toronto Press, 1988).

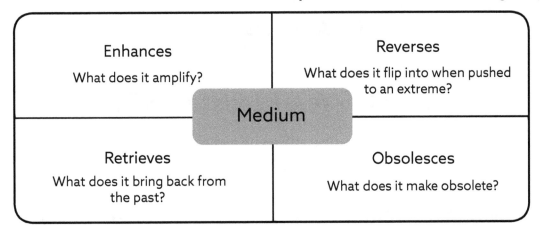

| FIGURE 1.0.2   Medium Diagram

Each medium extends our body and senses in certain ways, displaces something (another technology or condition), retrieves something previously lost, and reverses into something else when overextended or overheated. Here are a few examples for such enhancement, obsolescence, retrieval, and reversal afforded by different media:[16]

The Car: The car extends mobility into the highway system, but its overextension created traffic jams and overdependence on fossil fuels, thus triggering a return to bicycle riding and pedestrian culture. The acceleration of the car generated speed and fast food, thus triggering reversals into the movements of the slow city and slow food.

Radio and Mobile Phone: Both extend our voice, ears, and consciousness around the world while retrieving town criers and oral traditions lost to print media.

Satellites: Satellites extend our eyes and consciousness around the planet, thus putting Earth inside its own technological sphere and helping to retrieve ecology and environmentalism.

Telescopes: Telescopes and space probes extend our eyes and consciousness into deep space. Telescopes dislodged humans from the center of the universe, triggering for many people a reversal that seeks to return us to the center of the universe—in the form of electronic screens, social media, and creation myths.[17]

Several more extensions and reversals are outlined in "Hot and Cool in the Media(S)cene." In this reading, we also *redefine* McLuhan's concepts of "hot" and "cool," discussing how certain media (e.g., the smartphone and social media) can "heat us up" while others (the space telescope) "cool us down." Ultimately, memes and media have subtle, yet profound, effects on us individually and collectively living in the 24/7 global village of the twenty-first century.

Here is a "green light" for diving more deeply into these topics.

---

16   The tetrad can be applied not only to human-made technologies but indeed to anything from electric screens to beaver dams and even to the Sun as a medium. See Nicholas C. Grodsky, Julia M. Hildebrand, and Ernest A. Hakanen, "Screens as Human and Non-Human Artefacts: Expanding the McLuhans' Tetrad," *Explorations in Media Ecology* 17, no. 1 (March 2018): 23–39.

17   Barry Vacker and Genevieve Gillespie, "Yearning to Be the Center of Everything When We Are the Center of Nothing: Parallels and Reversals at Chaco, Hubble, and Facebook," *Telematics and Informatics*, Special Edition: The Facebook Phenomenon 30, no. 1 (February 2013): 35–46.

WHAT'S A GREENLIGHT?

MATTHEW MCCONAUGHEY is an Academy Award-winning actor, number 1 best-selling author (*Greenlights*), and professor of practice in the Department of Radio-Television-Film at the University of Texas at Austin.

Greenlights mean go—advance, carry on, continue. On the road, they are set up to give the flow of traffic the right of way, and when scheduled properly, more vehicles catch more greenlights in succession. They say proceed.

In our lives, they are an affirmation of *our* way. They're approvals, support, praise, gifts, gas on our fire, attaboys, and appetites. They're cash money, birth, springtime, health, success, joy, sustainability, innocence, and fresh starts. We love greenlights. They don't interfere with our direction. They're easy. They're a shoeless summer. They say yes and give us what we want.

Greenlights can also be disguised as yellow and red lights. A caution, a detour, a thoughtful pause, an interruption, a disagreement, indigestion, sickness, and pain. A full stop, a jackknife, an intervention, failure, suffering, a slap in the face, death. We don't like yellow and red lights. They slow us down or stop our flow. They're hard. They're a shoeless winter. They say no, but sometimes give us what we need.

Catching greenlights is about skill: intent, context, consideration, endurance, anticipation, resilience, speed, and discipline. We can catch more greenlights by simply identifying where the red lights are in our life, and then change course to hit fewer of them. We can also earn greenlights, engineer and design for them. We can create more and schedule them in our future—a path of least resistance—through force of will, hard work, and the choices we make. We can be responsible for greenlights.

Catching greenlights is also about timing. The world's timing, and ours. When we are in the zone, on the frequency, and with the flow. We can catch greenlights by sheer luck, because we are in the right place at the right time. Catching more of them in our future can be about intuition, karma, and fortune. Sometimes catching greenlights is about fate.

Navigating the autobahn of life in the best way possible is about getting relative with the inevitable at the right time. The inevitability of a situation is not relative; *when* we accept the outcome *of a* given situation as inevitable, then *how* we choose to deal with it *is* relative. We either persist and continue in our present pursuit of a desired result, pivot and take a new tack to get it, or concede altogether and tally one up for fate. We push on, call an audible, or wave the white flag and live to fight another day.

The secret to our satisfaction lies in *which* one of these we choose to do *when*.

This is the art of livin.

I believe everything we do in life is part of a plan. Sometimes the plan goes as intended, and sometimes it doesn't. *That's* part of the plan. Realizing *this* is a greenlight in itself.

The problems we face today eventually turn into blessings in the rearview mirror of life. In time, yesterday's red light leads us to a greenlight. All destruction eventually leads to construction, all death eventually leads to birth, all pain eventually leads to pleasure. In this life or the next, what goes down will come up.

It's a matter of how we see the challenge in front of us and how we engage with it. Persist, pivot, or concede. It's up to us, our choice every time.

A DIALOGUE

McLuhan Hot and Cool

MARSHALL MCLUHAN, one of the most famed media theorists of 20th century, is author of *Understanding Media, The Medium is the Massage*, and *War and Peace in the Global Village*.

The global village absolutely insures maximal disagreement on all points. It never occurred to me that uniformity and tranquillity were the properties of the global village. It has more spite and envy. The spaces and times are pulled out from between people. A world in which people encounter each other in depth all the time.

The tribal-global village is far more divisive—full of fighting—than any nationalism ever was. Village is fission, not fusion, in depth. People leave small towns to *avoid* involvement. The big city *lined* them with its uniformity and impersonal milieu. They sought propriety and in the city, money is made by uniformity and repeatability. Where you have craftsmanlike diversity, you make art, not money. The village is not the place to find ideal peace and harmony. Exact opposite. Nationalism came out of print and provided an extraordinary relief from global village conditions. I don't *approve* of the global village. I say we live in it.

It's like the universe. Margaret Fuller said, "I accept the universe," and Carlyle said, "Yes, you'd better."

I accept media as I accept cosmos. They assume I'm for or against Gutenberg. Bunk! I think of technologies as highly identifiable objects made by our own bodies. They feel that technologies are strange, alien intruders from outer space.

STEARN: When you say that technologies are extensions of man, are they as well extensions of man's will?

McLUHAN: In the ordinary sense of subliminal wish and drive—yes. Man, however, intends the cultural consequences of any extension of himself.

STEARN: What are we to do with all this information? How does it affect our consciousness?

McLUHAN: When man is overwhelmed by information, he resorts to myth. Myth is inclusive, time-saving, and fast. Children are driven today into mythic thinking. When environmental effects shift beyond a certain point, everybody agrees on a new strategy.

To be conscious or unconscious is to make a certain order of experience. I possess no theory of consciousness. But that says nothing. Throughout my work, however, I am saying that awareness is being pushed more and more out into the environment. Technology pushes human awareness out into the environment. Art becomes environment. Our environments are made of the highest levels of human consciousness. ...

Literally, *Understanding Media* is a kit of tools for analysis and perception. It is to *begin* an operation of discovery. It is not the completed work of discovery. It is intended for practical use. Most of my work in the media is like that of a safecracker. In the beginning I don't know what's inside. I just set myself down in front of the problem and begin to work. I grope, I probe, I listen, I test—until the tumblers fall and I'm in. That's the way I work with all these media.

Depth operations are natural to modern studies in all fields including psychiatry and metallurgy and structural analysis. In order to inspect any situation structurally you have to inspect it from all sides simultaneously, which is a sort of cubist gimmick. A structural approach to a medium means studying its total operation, the *milieu* that it creates—the environment that the telephone or radio or movies or the motorcar created. One would learn very little about the motorcar by looking at it simply as a vehicle that carried people hither and thither. Without understanding the city changes, suburban creations, service changes—the environment it created—one would learn very little about the motorcar. The car then has never really been studied structurally, as a form.

If you look at print not as a conveyer belt of data but as a structure somewhat different from the spoken word, somewhat different from manuscript culture, then you are at once in a world where you have to repeat yourself furiously in order to capture all facets simultaneously. The literary form is truly not adapted to simultaneity and structural awareness and this of course is inherent in the very first acts of writing in early times when a vast amount of human awareness was tossed out. Very little of the qualities of speech can be captured by written form, very little of nuance, very little of the drama and action of speech can be captured by written form whatever. But today, with the oscillograph, tape recorder, and various electronic devices, speech is being felt in depth and discovered in structural multi-facet-ness for the first time in human history. So naturally anybody who has become vividly aware of the many, many structural facets of speech, when confronted with the literary form, is aghast at its impoverished character. It's very abstract—it has eliminated most language and speech from its medium. The moment you begin to look at speech as a structure you quickly understand why writing as a structure really cannot deal with much speech. ...

McLuhan: Communication, in the conventional sense, is difficult under any conditions. People prefer *rapport* through smoking or drinking together. There is more communication there than there ever is by verbal means. We can share environments, we can share weather, we can share all sorts of cultural factors together but communication takes place only

inadequately and is very seldom understood. For anybody to complain about lack of communication seems a bit naïve. It's actually very rare in human affairs. This has been studied in our time by F. C. Bartlett in his book *Remembering* or I. A. Richards, and others. The most skilled students of poetry, when their reading and understanding of a poem are checked, are found to be monstrously mistaken. It isn't only country bumpkins who have difficulty reading good poems—it is the professors of literature. They too have a very inadequate relation to the world of poetry and prose. Practical criticism created a mortal terror in the academic world in 1929 because it revealed that the best students and professors were quite incapable of reading ordinary poems.

There is a kind of illusion in the world we live in that communications is something that happens all the time, that it's normal. And when it doesn't happen, this is horrendous. Actually, communication is an exceedingly difficult activity. In the sense of a mere point-to-point correspondence between what is said, done, and thought and felt between people—this is the rarest thing in the world. If there is the slightest tangential area of touch, agreement, and so on among people, *that* is communication in a big way. The idea of complete identity is unthinkable. Most people have the idea of communication as something matching between what is said and what is understood. In actual fact, communication is *making*. The person who sees or heeds or hears is engaged in making a response to a situation which is mostly of his own fictional invention. What these critics reveal is that the mystery of communication is the art of making. What they make in difficulties, confusions, vague responses is natural. It goes on all the time in all human affairs as between parents and children, for example. We are always improvising interpretations of everything we do, see, feel, and hear. With ingenuity, with great skill, we improvise responses in order to enable us to continue our relations with our fellows.

Platonic dialogues come out of an oral rather than a literary culture. In a highly literate culture, the dialogue form becomes repugnant. It came back with radio and panel shows. Highly literate people speak on one level, in a monotone. "Good" prose is spoken this way. A level of form, one plane. You cannot discuss multi-relationships on a single plane, in a single form. That's why the poets of our time have broken all the planes and sequences, forming a cubist prose. "I don't follow you"—as if that had anything to do with reasoning. It has to do with lineality and visuality. Logical or connected discourse is highly visual and has very little to do with human reasoning. ...

In the sense that these media are extensions of our-selves—of man—then my interest in them is utterly humanistic. All these technologies and the mechanisms they create are profoundly human. What does one say to people who cannot see extensions of their own bodies and faculties, who find their environments invisible? They call these same environments alien, nonhuman and search for a "point of view." This is simply the inabil-ity to observe ordinary data. Content analysis divorces them from reality.

They are talking about art as a blood bank, as stored precious moments of experience. The idea that art's job is to *explore* experience too never dawned on them. The job of art is not to store moments of experience but to explore environments that are otherwise invisible. Art is not a retrieval system of precious moments of past cultures. Art has a live, ongoing function. Milton's phrase—"A great book is the precious life-blood of the master spirit." The humanist fault, since the Renais-sance, has been to sell art totally short. Since Gutenberg, art has become a retrieval system. Before, art was a means of merging with the cosmos. My critics' notion of art is incredibly defective and feeble. Blake regarded art as exploratory. He thought of it as a means of unit-ing all the human faculties, aspiring to the unity of the imagination. Art-as-probe is survival. They are saying: "Without art, what impoverished lives we would lead." ...

Now the satellite or space capsule world is only pos-sible as a result of intense study of consequences. This is a new stress in our time. To build a capsule you must foresee all the possible effects on the human form. Buck-minster Fuller has remarked that the space capsule is the first completely designed human environment. Up to the present, we have not been designing environments. We have been designing things to put into the envi-ronment. It's like finding the right picture for the right room. Now one says, "What kind of a room will grow out of this picture?" The space capsule is an extension of the planet. ...

McLUHAN: It seems to me that the great advantage in understanding the operational dynamics of various media is to quiet them down, not exploit them. If you understand these dynamics, you can control media, eliminate their effects from the environment. And this is most desirable. I think we would do ourselves a con-siderable kindness if we closed down TV operations for a few years. If TV was simply eliminated from the United States scene, it would be a very good thing. Just as radio has a most malignant effect in Africa or Alge-ria, or China—in highly auditory cultures, radio drives these people nearly mad with paranoia and tribal inten-sity—TV, in a highly visual culture, drives us inward in depth into a totally nonvisual universe of involvement. It is destroying our entire political, educational, social, institutional life. TV will dissolve the entire fabric of society in a short time. If you understood its dynamics, you would choose to eliminate it as soon as possible. TV changes the sensory and psychic life. It is an oriental form of experience, giving people a somber, profound sense of involvement.

HOT AND COOL IN THE MEDIA(S)CENE

JULIA M. HILDEBRAND is Assistant Professor of Communication at Eckerd College in St. Petersburg, Florida. Her publications explore mobile technologies and digital culture, and they have appeared in such journals as *Media, Culture & Society, Mobile Media & Communication*, and *Explorations in Media Ecology*.

BARRY VACKER

INTRODUCTION

Anthropocene—Mediacene.

Layers of fossils—Layers of media technology.

Ways of living—Ways of seeing.

If we are in the Anthropocene, then how can we not be in the Mediacene? If technological civilization has transformed the **eco**systems on its host planet, Earth, then how can mediated civilization have not transformed the **ego**-systems in its host species, human consciousness? If we have extended visual technologies into the tiniest particles, into our bodies, around the planet, and into deep space, then how can our visions have not been transformed?

Mediacene. Mediaseen. **Media(S)cene.**

We do not mean "Mediacene" in a strict scientific sense. Rather, we mean it as a techno-philosophical concept related to how media technologies make us **see**

and, in turn, how we can **see** them. Hence, the playful term "Media(S)cene." The goal is to creatively combine theory and art. Rather than to explain, the goal is to explore, expand, explode.

As such, we are inspired by media theorist Marshall McLuhan, who claims that "Scientists make their discoveries as 'artists,' not specialists. Such scientists construct experiments as 'works of art' to probe the environment."[1] With the Media(S)cene, we want to present an imaginative probe into our contemporary media environment. It's like McLuhan's approach upgraded for the twenty-first century—"McLuhan 21.0."

More concretely, the Media(S)cene is a model for a **visual media ecology** and a call for art for this media epoch, a project for this seeing, this accelerating media evolution—on Earth, in space, into the Hubble universe of the twenty-first century. Why? Because it's the media epoch. We're in it. There is no exit. We need a fresh understanding. We agree, theory needs art. Now.

---

1   Marshall McLuhan and Eric McLuhan, *Media and Formal Cause* (NeoPoiesis, 2011), 55.

*This essay received a prestigious international aware: The 2019 John Culkin Award for Praxis from the Media Ecology Association.

LOVE AND THE VOID

The year 1967 saw the publication of McLuhan's classic art text *The Medium Is the Massage*, exploring how media—human-made technologies—"massage" our senses, our ways of feeling, thinking, and being. Its original cover featured a woman wearing a LOVE dress. Fittingly, that year also saw the release of the Beatles's classic song "All You Need Is Love"—which was created as Britain's contribution to *Our World*, the very first live international satellite television broadcast that literally reached around the globe. A prophetic forerunner to YouTube, *Our World* featured programming about everyday life in nineteen nations and reached four hundred million to seven hundred million people, the largest television audience ever up to that date. The program was broadcast on June 25 during the famed Summer of Love. As an expression of the utopian optimism of the moment, the Beatles performed "All You Need Is Love" to close the broadcast.

Five decades later, it seems as if "All You Need Is Like" in Our World, with media infrastructures and mobile technologies spanning the globe, further massaging our senses—our ways of seeing, moving, doing, being. At the same time, our media technologies have extended deeper into outer space, making Our World seem like an utter speck amid the voids of the Milky Way and the expanding universe. *We face the paradox of our civilization's greatest discovery: the universe is vast and majestic, and our species is insignificant and might be utterly meaningless.* We've found two trillion galaxies but no aliens, no gods, and no universal meaning for human existence. Zero, nada, zip.

Is that why, every day, most of us fill an empty hand with a mobile phone and fill our eyes with an electronic screen roaming that world? McLuhan's "global village," jam-packed with online tribes vying for more followers and fans but also feuds? Media massages that help us feel special in an immense universe? Our tech consolation for our cosmic insignificance? Media building, loving, liking, shaming, hating … sensory massaging to fill existential voids?

We are facing voids in the universe, our philosophies, our knowledge, and our everyday. We create theories, technologies, practices, and relationships that help us distract from, close in, or fill those voids. Yet, in the ever-expanding universe, the voids, too, are expanding. More massages, please!

By juxtaposing the LOVE with a VOID dress (and yes, of course, there is a smartphone), we want to zoom in on a macro-level media theory that connects the small with the big, the inner with the outer, the finite with the infinite. How we make that visible and how, in turn, we are affected by those visibilities. Media scenes and Media seen. The idea is to think about contemporary media massages on a larger scale. A big strata.

BIG STRATA

Our different ways of seeing span eons. Petroglyphs to photographs, movies to TVs, phones to drones, supercolliders to space telescopes—technologies of sight all now made visible on screens, made mobile and global via networks that traverse the planet, made interstellar by leaving the solar system and peering into deep space.

Extending from inside the human body, into society, across and above Earth's surface and into outer space are layered networks of media technologies—**a media strata**. The contemporary physical layers are obvious: fiber optics and phone lines are underground and under the oceans, while mobile phones are above ground and drones are in the air and satellites are in space; the Large Hadron Collider is buried underground, while the Hubble Telescope is orbiting the planet and *Voyager* has exited the solar system.

Within those media layers are other media layers spanning the planet, permeating our cities, propelling data through our devices. A central infrastructure is the internet, within which is the World Wide Web, within which are social media. Data centers, databases, software, code. Layers of tweets, timelines, and status updates. Cell towers and satellite dishes. Streetlights, electric lights, and LED signs. There are platform layers, interface layers, address layers, and user layers. "Grids" on the surface, "clouds" above, housing and being housed by Google, Facebook, Apple, Amazon, the National Security Agency, and endless other firms

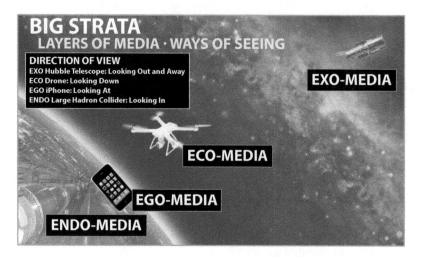

FIGURE 1.3.1   Big Strata

and government agencies around the world.[2] Big strata, big data, Big Brother.

Extending in multiple directions from within the big strata are several overarching types of visual media technologies—each unique yet overlapping and interconnected. **Each positions the view and viewer**, the gaze and gazer, the sight and seer in particular ways, shaping both subject and object, the visualizer and the visualized. As McLuhan argued, individually and collectively, media technologies "massage" our consciousness toward media-specific ways of seeing, ways of knowing, ways of believing.[3] We recognize four major types of visual and visualizing media technologies:

ENDO-MEDIA

These **look into** the inner workings of things in the universe, be it human or nonhuman. Current examples include the Large Hadron Collider, microscopes, digital X-ray imaging, magnetic resonance imaging, and many genetic technologies.

EGO-MEDIA

These **look at** humanity's sociocultural activities, the individual and the collective, the self and the other, the profane and the sacred. Examples include cave paintings, drawings, photographs, cinema, television, computers, smartphones, and, of course, social media.

ECO-MEDIA

These **look down** upon Earth's surface, landscapes, architectures, infrastructures, oceans, and continents. Here, we are using "eco" in the broad sense of technologies that look at geographies, ecologies, habitats, and environments, both natural and human-made. Current examples are aerial imaging technologies such as satellites and drones.

EXO-MEDIA

These **look away** toward the planets and stars, into the interstellar and intergalactic, attempting to reach farthest out into the universe. Current examples are the Hubble Space Telescope, the Atacama Array, Voyager, the Mars rover, and any other telescopes and space probes.

Each visual technology is a specific "vision machine," to use Paul Virilio's term, with its "vision" shaped by the direction of the gaze and the distance it travels. Each vision machine opens up novel abilities to see and visualize (along with monitoring and control).[4] Differentiating between those four types and exploring the direction of their gazes opens up new avenues for understanding our current visual media environment and its effects on us, individually and collectively.

The types of visual media technologies can overlap and are interconnected. The electric light, McLuhan's medium without a specific content, is the ground for

2   Benjamin Bratton, *The Stack: On Software and Sovereignty* (Cambridge, MA: MIT Press, 2015).
3   Marshall McLuhan, *Understanding Media: The Extensions of Man* (New York: McGraw-Hill, 1964), vii–viii; Marshall McLuhan, *The Medium Is the Massage* (San Francisco: Hardwired, 1996 [1967]), 68; Marshall McLuhan, *Counterblast* (New York: Harcourt, Brace, & World, 1969), 85.
4   Paul Virilio, *The Information Bomb* (London: Verso, 2000).

all screen media, be it endo, ego, eco, or exo. It illuminates paths, streets, and cities and can thus function as an eco-medium while also visualizing ego-media on digital screens. One can argue that the glowing lights from screens and cities spanning the planet, effecting a 24/7 civilization, have become a spectacle that erases nature and the night sky from our daily consciousness. Exo-media images (galaxies, black holes) circulate via ego-media (Facebook, Twitter, YouTube), while all four media types are linked via the internet. Operated at a distance, the civilian drone is an eco-medium capturing beaches and sunsets, treating humans as mostly surface phenomena. Yet the closer the drone to the human, the more ego becomes the medium. Ego-media and exo-media in particular can conflict easily. Why? One is hot and the other is cool.

HOT VS. COOL

In the 1960s, McLuhan developed a hot-cool binary based on how much human involvement is needed when engaging with a medium. A hot or high-definition medium, such as film, requires little participation and involvement from us to make sense of the information provided. Think: a movie audience watching in the theater. In contrast, a cool or low-definition medium, such as a landline telephone, asks for much more sensory investment from someone conversing on the phone, filling in mental images around the words of the person on the other end of the line.

Intrigued by the poetics of the hot and cool, we retheorize McLuhan's binary toward a different hot-cool scale that spans our endo-, ego-, eco-, and exo-media. This hot-cool scale allows us to home in on how those layers of visual media operate and why.

HOT MEDIA

Endo- and ego-media are hot media that promote an **inward gaze**, with viewing subject and viewed objects in **close proximity** to each other. Hot media deal with higher densities of matter, molecules, atoms, events, energy, humans, and, thus, high friction. In proximity, entities can rub or smash against one another. Acceleration, quick reactions, short attention spans, instant feedback loops. **Temperatures are higher; tempers are hotter.**

As such, endo-media reveal atoms and molecules billions of years old along with tight clusters of subatomic particles, protons, neutrons, electrons, hadrons, leptons, muons, and ever smaller things. Ancient rocks, precious metals, light metals, heavy metals, radiation. Inside our bodies, we see cells and neurons, diseases and antibodies, replicating viruses and mutating DNA. At and below Earth's surface, we see our ways of living conflict with Earth, humanity's ego-systems disrupting the planet's ecosystems—layers of our fossils, detritus, pollution, leftover radiation from atomic bombs along with increasing carbon dioxide in the atmosphere. In the oceans, there are warmer waters, rivers of nitrogen, increasing acidification, dead zones, bleached coral, gyres of plastic garbage. In the Anthropocene, hot endos and egos fuel the global warming of eco.

Hence, heat and friction also lie in our global layers of ego-media, giant clusters of networks and webs, all jammed with ever more contents and contexts. Platforms, websites, services, affordances. Google, Facebook, Twitter, Snapchat, Instagram, YouTube, Netflix. Social media sharing, caring, shaming, connecting. Hashtags and emojis, clickbait and catfishers. Hot takes, hive minds, eHarmony. YOLO. Tinder love, tribal chieftains, internet trolls, TV realities, Twitter gods. Fake news, false flags, and filter bubbles. FOMO. Cute cat videos and candy crushes. LOL. Meming and mining. Copies of copies of copies. Reduce, remix, redact. Colliding echo chambers. Siri and Alexa. Firewalls and border walls. Breaking news, Streetviews, Times Square. Screens and screening. TSA, NSA, MI6, MSS. Governments, corporations, and capitalism. Democracy, socialism, and fascism. Arab Spring. Occupy. Women's March. #MeToo. Superheroes, Super Bowls, and World Cups. Empowerment, domination, entertainment, distraction. Tribe rubs against tribe. **Proximity, friction, and heat in hot ego-media.**

COOL MEDIA

Eco- and exo-media are cool media: those technologies with mostly an **outward gaze**, with objects **further apart** or **moving away**. Earth is below us, the stars are beyond us, and galaxies are moving away. Cool media deal with lower densities, lower friction—with distance, drift, wander, wonder, wow. Temperatures are lower,

FIGURE 1.3.2 Hot Media

tempers are cooler. Whatever is hot out there—stars, black holes, supernovas—is surrounded by the cool, the void, the entropy toward absolute zero. From the big bang to the big chill. Deep space, deep time, deep futures.

In the cool gaze, events slow, attention spans grow, reflection trumps reaction, the species supersedes the tribe, and borders and wars become artificial and absurd. Micro-particularities and hot affective conditions are not visible, but large-scale patterns, movements, and locations become more apparent. The more distant, aerial, and heightened perspective—beyond the thick, hot, reactive layers closer to us—opens up larger views and visions. Google Earth, Hubble Deep Fields, Sloan Digital Sky Survey. The cosmic web of galaxies in a universe getting less crowded by the moment, with all galaxies destined to disappear beyond all horizons. Thrust apart by ever-expanding voids of space, the universe is expanding in all directions, likely forever, across trillions of trillions of years, toward thermodynamic exhaustion, zero energy. Voids, holes, and emptiness in outer space and in our philosophies become visible. We are the center of nothing. Nihilism and enlightenment are the challenge. The universal over the tribal. **Terrestrial heat replaced by the cosmic chill.** There are no widely accepted politics or political

narratives in the cool. Hot politics freeze in the cosmic background temperature.

Can hot and cool overlap? Yes. That's why this is a hot-cool scale and *not* a typology with fixed categories and clear-cut boundaries. Google Earth gets hotter the closer it zooms in toward Street View but gets cooler the further it zooms out to show Earth as a planet in its totality. The Large Hadron Collider is a hot endo-medium, but its intense heat and energy might help us understand the expansion of the universe mapped by cool media. Deep Field images appear in hot Twitter, but we know the Hubble Telescope is peering into an ancient universe expanding from the heat of the big bang toward the deep cool of infinite entropy. Deep space, deep cool. **The void.** Also, atoms are mostly empty, with vast spaces of mostly nothingness. In voids and vastness, hot meets cool.

Moreover, there seems to be a traceable dynamic between ego- and exo-media of one countering the other (see the following Extensions-Reversals graphic). Hot and cool collide and conflict. Hot prevails over cool when we focus on ourselves and consume ego-media's endless spectacles, shares, and status updates. Extensions into the **cool trigger reversals** into the hot. It's more comfy in the warm.

FIGURE 1.3.3   "Cool Media," printed and stretched canvas. 4' x 5'.
Concept: Julia Hildebrand and Barry Vacker. Graphic design: Vacker,
Hildebrand, and Sara Falco, 2019.

EXTENSIONS AND REVERSALS

Over the past century, exo-media and ego-media tech-nologies have coevolved in a strange dance of extensions and reversals. Since Edwin Hubble's unveiling of the expanding universe, there has been a long line of dual discoveries and innovations—scientific discoveries revealing a vast universe of which we are not the center, as well as technological innovations that place us at the center of the mediated universe. *It seems as if ego-media might be our consolation for exo-media, for not being the center of the universe.*

Drawing from Marshall and Eric McLuhan, this coevolution can be theorized in terms of enhancement, retrieval, obsolescence, and reversal, as detailed in *Laws of Media* (1988). Each media technology simultaneously extends our senses and retrieves something previously lost. At the same time, each technology contains the genetic code of its own **reversal**, the point when the technology is pushed to an extreme—or overextended—flipping its original functions and benefits. For example, the car is an extension of our feet, enabling a more mobile society, but its overuse and proliferation resulted in traffic congestion and accidents, thus less or no movement. The development of the car engine and the phenomenon of mechanical acceleration resulted in cultural byproducts such as "fast" food and increased waste, which eventually reversed into the "slow" food and city movements.

TELEVISION

Let's consider an ego-medium. Television is an extension of our eyes, ears, and consciousness around the planet, while the light shining through the screen retrieves cave paintings and campfire tales (television programming). By retrieving images and information from around the planet and outer space, TV's glowing screen (the light shining through toward us) effects a reversal of the vanishing point in mirroring the world—thus placing human consciousness at the center of everything. A similar process is visible with social media. In a sense, Facebook is television by other means.

TELESCOPES

As an exo-medium, telescopes extend our eyes and expand our awareness, enabling us to increase our knowl-edge of the universe as well as further understand our own planet. By gaining this knowledge, we've encountered both the cosmic sublime and cosmic nihilism. Terrified, we reverse and seek refuge in anything—such as theism, television, or social media technologies—that would return us to the center of the universe.

Like all telescopes, the Hubble Space Telescope—along with the television, the microchip, and the computer—extends the electronic eye and consciousness into deep space while retrieving the petroglyph, the campfire, and the night sky lost to electric light in the metropolises. As with television, the visual vanishing point is still reversed, but the additional information provided by spectral photography challenges the centrality of the human viewer by showing a universe of vast size, scale, and age.

Since telescopes and other exo-technologies have allowed us to see we're not the center of the universe, we argue that a massive McLuhan-like reversal has been underway. The technologies of the Space Age were greeted with global enthusiasm in the 1960s, yet the very meanings of the vast universe lacked such global attention and passion when those sights and insights challenged previous cosmologies, ideologies, and theologies. We had to rethink or reverse. *For the most part, we have reversed toward ego-centric instead of exo-centric patterns.*

As shown in the graphic below, the evolution of electronic television, hypertext, the World Wide Web,

and Facebook follows a parallel trajectory to that of Edwin Hubble, the Hubble Space Telescope, and how we see ourselves in a vast and expanding universe. Television and the electronic screen, for instance, are ego-media emerging and evolving with key moments in the use of telescopes, the central exo-media in revealing the size and scale of the universe. The graphic shows how key discoveries of exo-media are paralleled by major technological developments for ego-media. Just as exo-media show we're not the center of the universe, ego-media simulate that we are the center of the universe, at least the center of everything important.

THE SCREEN IS THE SCENE

The Media(S)cene is simultaneous explosion and implosion, taking place on our screens and in our society. Digital media are proliferating rapidly, as visible in the explosion of screens, images, and data. Yet these same

FIGURE 1.3.4   Extensions and Reversals 1

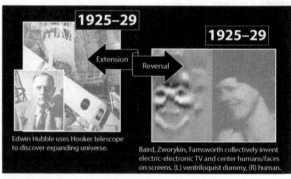

FIGURE 1.3.5   Extensions and Reversals 2: Hubble Telescope, etc.

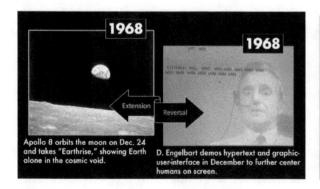

FIGURE 1.3.6   Extensions and Reversals 3: Moon and Dr. Engelbart

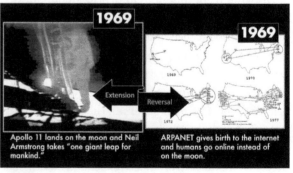

FIGURE 1.3.7   Extensions and Reversals 4: Apollo 11 and ARPANET

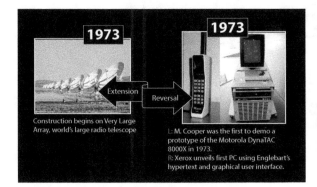

FIGURE 1.3.8   Extensions and Reversals 5:
Very large array

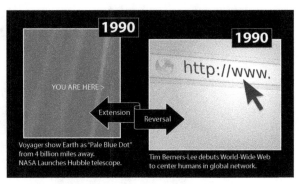

FIGURE 1.3.9   Extensions and Reversals 6:
Voyager Image with Earth as Pale Blue dot,
world-wide web

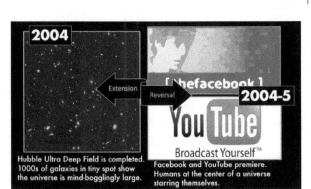

FIGURE 1.3.10   Extensions and Reversals 7:
Hubble Ultra Deep Field, Facebook and Youtube

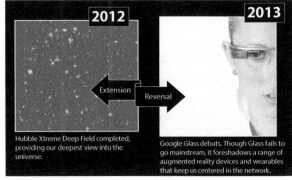

FIGURE 1.3.11   Extensions and Reversals 8:
Hubble Xtreme Deep Field and Google Glass

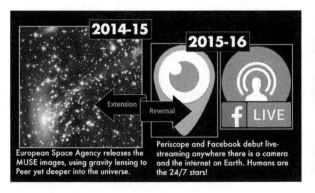

FIGURE 1.3.12   Extensions and Reversals 9:
European Space Agency Muse Image, Periscope,
Facebook live

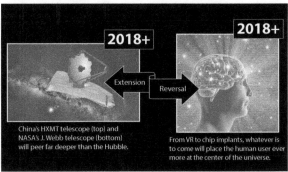

FIGURE 1.3.13   Extensions and Reversals 10:
China's HXMT telescope, NASA's J and VR to chip
implants

technologies are also causing an implosion of perception, resulting in networks of echo chambers.

As McLuhan explains in *Through the Vanishing Point* (1968), television (with its light flowing through the screens) effects a reversal in the vanishing point, which is no longer "out there" but "in here"—such as in the spectator's living room and consciousness. "Our World" is just beyond the screen, coming toward us, massaging us with a torrent of views, visions, vistas.

McLuhan's insights are even more relevant in the twenty-first century. Screens keep proliferating, through which vanishing points are reversed and images collide

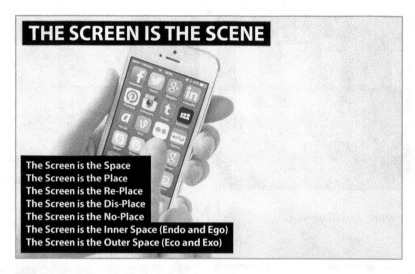

THE SCREEN IS THE SCENE

The Screen is the Space
The Screen is the Place
The Screen is the Re-Place
The Screen is the Dis-Place
The Screen is the No-Place
The Screen is the Inner Space (Endo and Ego)
The Screen is the Outer Space (Eco and Exo)

| **FIGURE 1.3.14**   The Screen is the Scene

and collapse upon human consciousness. In effect, each viewer is a vanishing point, a neural node of electronic subjectivity and cosmic centrality, point zero for echo chamber culture.

To consume the world via the screen is to let the world crash upon and into you—implosion. Simultaneously, images replicate, screens get larger, vision sees further, big data grows exponentially, and the universe along with our knowledge of it expand in all directions—explosion. The viewer is a mobile vanishing point for all things, the center of everything, the pre-Copernican in a Hubble universe. Ego-media make us the center of the universe. **iPhone, therefore I am**.

The cult show *Black Mirror* gets this, for the black mirrors are our screens reflecting us to us—we're the vanishing points, the echo chambers. With electronic screens, all points end in us, not in some external realm of universal enlightenment. It's been that way since the first black mirrors, the obsidian disks used ten thousand years ago. Cathode ray tubes. Liquid crystal display. Plasma screen. Gorilla Glass. All black mirrors. Screens.

Our electronic experiences collide, collapse, and crash into the spectacle on the screens, shooting photons into our eyes and shaping perception in our minds—ways of seeing what counts as real, true, good, valuable, and beautiful on Planet Earth hurtling through the universe.

In the Media(S)cene, both our visual media world and our media-specific world**views** demand attention. So how do processes of implosion and explosion show across endo-, ego-, eco-, and exo-media?

ENDO-MEDIA

Explosion through smashing the smallest particles in the universe, through invasion into the smallest parts of the human body. We're made of stardust, our atoms forged in stars. Teletechnologies, such as microscopes and cameras, extend the gaze ever inward, from the Human Genome Project to CRISPR, gene mapping to gene editing. Virilio warns that after teletechnologies have conquered the "territorial body" and the geological core of our planet, our own "animal body" is to be colonized in an "intraorganic intrusion of technology and its micromachines into the heart of the living."[5] The result is a new Darwinian, from natural evolution to techno-evolution. An edited and augmented human is emerging, better and worse at once.

EGO-MEDIA

Egocentric views and visions projected onto life and Earth. Implosion of the social into the virtual, explosion of the self upon the screen, implosion of the self into oneself. Self-consumption, self-absorption, and ultimately self-amputation.[6] Total tuning in leads to

---

5   Virilio, *The Art of the Motor* (Minneapolis: University of Minnesota Press, 1995), 100.
6   Marshall McLuhan, *Understanding Media: The Extensions of Man* (New York: McGraw-Hill, 1964).

sensory overload. According to McLuhan, we can't help but become numb and tune out. Amplification turns into amputation, cutting off our awareness of ego-media's impact on us. Numbed, we turn to the ego-defaults. Money. Power. Domination. Distraction. Social media: Facebook, FaceTime, Snapchat, Instagram. Twitter. Tinder. Networked narcissism, shared e-subjectivity, the search for sex and love. Mobile vanishing points. Screens spanning the abyss. The new pre-Copernicans.

ECO-MEDIA

Explosion of visual media above the planet, looking at and down, visualizing global patterns. Apollo 8's Earthrise image. Earth from space at night, cities aglow and networked around the planet. Continental drift, deforestation, ice sheets melting, CO_2 emissions, urban sprawl. Meanwhile, implosion of the earthly resources (that help build and maintain endo-, ego-, and eco-media infrastructures and ecologies).

EXO-MEDIA

Explosion of views into outer space, to the edge of reachable space and time. Two trillion galaxies, expanding outward—explosion. Photos rushing toward us, through the Hubble Space Telescope, through our screens—implosion. Deep space, deep time. As human knowledge of the exo expands, actual and potential operations cramp back into the ego; Mars colonization, moon mining. Exomedia meet endo-media at the Large Hadron Collider. Acceleration inward to recreate the big bang, smashing particles at the Large Hadron Collider—explosion and implosion.

In combination, eco- and exo-media can have profound effects on us when it comes to environmental and cosmic awareness of the self and other. Seeing Earth from space, as with Apollo 8's Earthrise image, has deeply affected not only numerous space travelers but also ecological theory more generally. While aboard the Apollo spacecraft or the International Space Station, astronauts and cosmonauts report experiencing deep feelings of awe, self-transcendence, and a primal connection to the universe. Apollo 14 astronaut Edgar Mitchell described the experience as an "explosion of awareness." This "explosion of awareness" provides an exciting and existential basis for a twenty-first-century media philosophy—for the future of the human species on Earth and in space.

CODA, OR WHY WE NEED ART

The Media(S)cene presents such a media philosophy for our contemporary visual media environment. It serves as an aesthetic and artistic framework that can be a "teaching machine for the training of perception and judgment."[7] As endo-, ego-, eco-, and exo-media shape and reshape our ways of seeing and being, we call for artistic reflection and creative action to assess and address the contemporary hot and cool, the implosive and explosive character of the Media(S)cene and its effects on us. As McLuhan presaged, "Perhaps it is time for the roles of artist and bureaucrat/entrepreneur to reverse positions. Our New World of chaos and complexity is too volatile, too precarious, too important to be left in the hands of the merely practical administrator."[8] Indeed, it is time. Time for the explosion of media to be countered by an explosion of awareness, a counter-aesthetic. **Apple, please move over for the Artist.**

---

7   Marshall McLuhan, opening of "The Emperor's New Clothes," in Marshall McLuhan and Harley Parker, *Through the Vanishing Point: Space in Poetry and Painting* (New York: Harper & Row, 1968).
8   Marshall McLuhan and Eric McLuhan, *Media and Formal Cause*, 139.

CREDITS

TRON (1982)

A computer programmer gets sucked inside a giant supercomputer, which was a stand-in for the early days of computers, video games, cyberspace, and the internet. A battle ensues between the "users" and the corporate "programs" for freedom and control of computers, networks, and video games.

Director: Steve Lisberger
Starring: Jeff Bridges and David Warner

HACKERS (1995)

Teen gamers and hackers use the internet to thwart an ecological terrorist, while staying one step ahead of the Feds. Appearing as the internet was emerging in popular consciousness, *Hackers* is not a great film, but it is an early attempt to show the potential positive power of the global computer networks.

Director: Iain Softly
Starring: Angelina Jolie and Jonny Miller

YOU'VE GOT MAIL (1998)

A romantic comedy about finding your soul mate via chat rooms and the internet. The film suggests that the network gives you a better shot at love than the streets and parties of New York. All internet dating sites owe this film a big thank you (and yearly bonus check), for Tom and Meg transformed internet dating from creepy to cute for mainstream culture

Director: Nora Ephron
Starring: Tom Hanks, Meg Ryan, and Dave Chappelle

TRON: LEGACY (2010)

The sequel to Tron, this film shows a battle for the control of the internet and the digital future. Though not as clever as *The Matrix, TRON: Legacy* clearly shows the militarization of the internet that is now being carried out by world governments. There are many clever visuals symbolizing the architecture of networks and digitalization.

Director: Joseph Kosinski
Starring: Jeff Bridges, Garrett Hedlund, and Olivia Wilde

THE FIFTH ESTATE (2013)

This film depicts the battle between WikiLeaks and the US government, which attacked WikiLeaks for using the internet to publish leaked evidence of apparent war crimes. But trying to play it safe on this hot-button topic, *The Fifth Estate* weakens its key ideas. Yet, the film still knowingly grasps that the battle is over the fate of the internet and attempts to show the actual and symbolic power of the internet. Which ideology should control the most powerful media network in human history: censorship and suppression or freedom of the press?

Director: Bill Condon

Starring: Benedict Cumberbatch and Daniel Brüh

THE CIRCLE (2017)

After graduating from college, Mae gets a job at the "The Circle," a massive internet and social media company that has permeated the networks of the global village. Later, Mae becomes a global celebrity by wearing a camera 24/7, making her life "transparent" to millions of fans and followers. But, internet fame has a downside in the global village. An underrated film sure to generate classroom discussion.

Director: James Ponsoldt

Starring: Emma Watson, Tom Hanks, and John Boyega

CHAPTER TWO

NETWORKS AND PLATFORMS
The Structure of the Global Media Ecologies

By Barry Vacker and Angela Cirucci

LIVIN' AMID THE GRIDS, WEBS, AND CLOUDS

In *Greenlights*, Matthew McConaughey plays the role of pop philosopher when he writes this:

> Navigating the autobahn of life in the best way possible is about getting relative with the inevitable at the right time. The inevitability of a situation is not relative; when we accept the outcome of a given situation as inevitable, then how we choose to deal with it is relative. We either persist and continue in our present pursuit of a desired result, pivot and take a new tack to get it, or concede altogether and tally one up for fate. We push on, call an audible, or wave the white flag and live to fight another day. …

This is the art of livin'.

We can apply McConaughey's concept of livin' to our daily lives. On a daily basis, the internet is our "autobahn of life." Back in the day, the internet was once called the "Infobahn" and the "Information Superhighway." At some point in the early 1990s, the term *internet* (international network) prevailed as the preferred choice of name, a perfect example of one meme outcompeting other memes to claim a concept.

Obviously, McConaughey is using a technological metaphor to convey a philosophical point, for the autobahn is the famed federal highway system of Germany, where there are some stretches of highway without speed limits for some vehicles. In such areas, the recommended speed limit is 130 kilometers (81 miles) per hour. That's a green light, for sure. Similarly, some of the interstate highways in the western parts of America have speed limits of 80 mph and 85 mph, though these limits are enforced. On the internet, there is little to no speed limit, as the electronic images and information travel at the speed of light. That's 186,000 miles per second. Of course, servers, computers, bandwidth, and file size impact the speeds at which we send and receive information. But the speed is still massively fast, and the computers and networks keep getting faster, while bandwidth keeps increasing to transmit ever larger files, especially videos, movies, and megapixel photos.

In 2021, the internet is where we do most of our livin'—looking at screens and processing and creating images and information. As of April 2021 the human population was 7.8 billion people, and 5.2 billion people had already migrated to the internet. Though the internet is barely more than forty years old, it was already a mediated territory frequented by 66 percent of the human population. Social media users now total 4.2 billion, or 53 percent of humanity.

**HUMAN POPULATION AND
THE TOP 15 SOCIAL MEDIA PLATFORMS***

Population: 7.8 billion humans in 100,000 years

Population: from 1 billion in 1800 to 7.8 billion in 2020

Mobile phone users: 5.2 billion in 40+ years

Internet users: 4.7 billion in 40+ years

Social media platforms: 4.2 billion users in 25 years

Platform	Year Created	Users
1. Facebook	2004	2.7 billion
2. YouTube	2005	2.3 billion
3. WhatsApp	2009	2 billion
4. Facebook Messenger	2008	1.2 billion
5. Instagram	2009	1.2 billion
6. WeChat	2011	1.2 billion
7. TikTok	2017	689 million
8. Tencent QQ	1999	617 million
9. Douyin	2016	600 million
10. Weibo	2010	511 million
11. Telegram	2013	500 million
12. Snapchat	2011	498 million
13. Kuaishou	2011	480 million
14. Pinterest	2009	442 million
15. Reddit	2005	430 million

*Karl Kangur, "Top 15 Most Popular Social Networking Sites and Apps [2021]," Dreamgrow, May 23, 2021.

As seen in the above table, the growth of the internet and social media is nothing less than staggering. The market value for mobile phones, computers and laptops, and social media firms exceeds many trillions of dollars. Humanity has evolutionary roots that reach back four million years, but the modern human and its complex brain (making tools, being able to use language, creating art and symbolic communication, copying and replicating memes) emerged about one hundred thousand years ago. Yet, in the past one hundred fifty years we have extended our consciousness to encircle the planet with our electronic media networks. That's a bright green light!

The internet is where we search for answers, seek solutions for our situations, and persist through the tsunami of information from a Google search request. We pivot, click, link, share, upload, download, give up, or push on. Apps, websites, videos, and rabbit holes. Maybe we find the answer or solution, maybe not. One thing is certain. We will be using the internet every day, for it is the autobahn of our lives. It's the art of livin'—amid grids, webs, and clouds, all part of the networks and platforms that collectively make up our planetary media ecologies.

Think of it this way. As discussed in chapter 1, memes replicate in our electric media ecologies, with layers of media technologies (endo-, ego-, eco-, and exo-media) that tell different stories depending on the direction of their gaze. Weaving throughout these ecologies and layers of technology are networks connected to platforms, which host all our blogs, tweets, and videos. These technologies are not neutral, for they massage our beliefs and behavior, while making possible unprecedented realms of power and wealth. We now have four media models to help us analyze media and society.

NETWORKS AND WEBS

You're livin' in a complexity of ever-growing and ever-evolving media ecologies. Screens and more screens; thousands of satellites surround the planet; millions of miles of fiber optics in the metropolises; computers, TVs, Kindles, iPhones, iPods, and iPads, each storing and streaming music, videos, films, websites, blogs, news, sports, opinion, art, and science—all connected via that vast network we call the internet. And there are newspapers and books, too, like the one you are reading now. Media are vast environments, ecologies of consciousness and culture, organized via the technologies of vast, global, and interplanetary networks.

TEMES: TECHNOLOGICAL REPLICATORS

Our global and interplanetary networks are never static, always evolving and expanding their domain as they extend our eyes, ears, and nervous system around the planet. Like memes, they copy, mutate, and replicate. Networks, webs, platforms, and clouds—these are all examples that perfectly illustrate Susan Blackmore's innovative insights about memes and technological evolution (chapter 1).[1] Blackmore thinks that, following genes and memes, a third replicator has emerged: the replicator of technology, or what she calls "temes."[2] All of our media technologies are mass-produced, which means they are copied and replicated, like genes and memes. The technologies also adapt and mutate with new innovations.

For example, the large mainframe computers of the 1950s became desktop personal computers in the 1970s, which became laptops in the 1990s, which became tablets and smartphones in the 2000s. Television screens migrated to computers in the 1950s and then spread to personal computers, laptops, tablets, smartphones, and drones. The concept of temes helps us understand how technologies, networks, and platforms replicate, mutate, and spread.

THE EVOLUTION OF NETWORKS

Though trade and shipping routes span the millennia, twenty-first-century media networks have their origins in the early electric networks, especially the electrical grid, along with the telegraph and telephone. The electrical grid is premised in the idea that all homes and businesses get their juice from a local or regional (yet mostly centralized) energy source—such as coal-fired plants, nuclear power plants, and hydroelectric dams. Sustainable technologies, such as solar and wind, are being added to the power grids around the world, and the sooner we move to all-sustainable energies, the better.

---

1   Susan Blackmore, *The Meme Machine* (London: Oxford University Press, 2001).
2   Susan Blackmore, "Susan Blackmore on Memes and Temes" (TED2008 conference, February 2008).

| FIGURE 2.0.1   Map of the electrical "grid" in the United States, circa 2020.

As Marshall McLuhan stated, electricity altered the entire *environment* in which we live, at once connecting peoples across nations, while also transforming and accelerating the pace of life, the rhythms of everyday existence. Without the electrical grid, contemporary civilization would not be possible, for there would be no juice for our homes, lights, screens, factories, refrigerators, heaters and air conditioners, and all the other daily miracles of science and technology that we take for granted. Obviously, there are inequalities and inequities that must be addressed in America and all around the world. But think about it. In effect, we have our own personal stars (light bulbs) in our homes and the North Pole (refrigerators) in our kitchens.

Modeled on the autobahn, the interstate highway system is another example of a network and platform, hosting cars, trucks, and motorcycles for transportation across the nation and the continent. From the car and highway system emerged suburbs, malls, fast foods, trucking, regional and national tourism (beaches, theme parks, national parks, etc.), and a host of other effects—all powered by fossil fuel consumption. As discussed in chapter 1, the car and highway system massaged our behavior in creating the mobile consumer society.

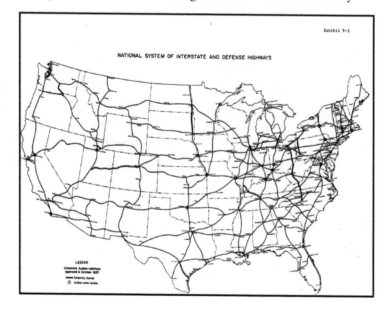

| FIGURE 2.0.2   Map of the interstate highway system, circa 1957.

Born in the mid-nineteenth century, the telegraph networks evolved into the telephone systems of the twentieth century. As with electricity and highways, the idea was to link everyone together—the same with radio and television networks, which were local, regional, and national. The telephone systems and TV networks became the prototype for cable television systems, powered by fiber optics and hosting nationally known channels like HBO, CNN, and ESPN, as well as hundreds of other channels and networks. By the end of the twentieth century, the internet was being transmitted by phone and cable systems around the world.

The original telephone system was a decentralized network, allowing point-to-point or one-to-one communication. A traditional phone call (on a land line) to your friend is an example. In contrast, radio and television were centralized networks, enabling point-to-multipoint or one-to-many communication. Think of your favorite local radio station or the Super Bowl.

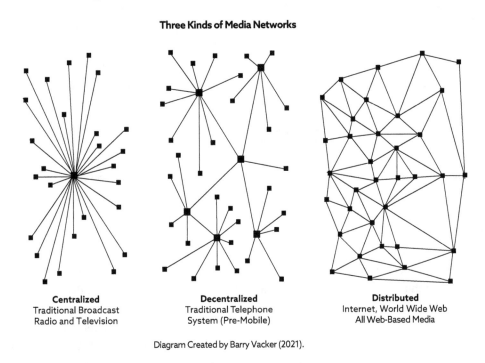

Three Kinds of Media Networks

Centralized	**Decentralized**	**Distributed**
Traditional Broadcast	Traditional Telephone	Internet, World Wide Web
Radio and Television	System (Pre-Mobile)	All Web-Based Media

Diagram Created by Barry Vacker (2021).

FIGURE 2.0.3   Diagram of three kinds of electronic media networks.

SURFING THE WEB: FROM PROFITS TO PROTESTS

Like the highway system for cars and trucks, the internet and World Wide Web permit us to transport images and information across a global network. The internet and the World Wide Web combined centralized and decentralized networks into a distributed network and massively amplified their power. This enables communication in any combination—for example, one-to-one (an email or text message), one-to-many (an email blast), many-to-one (sending emails to the White House to protest a police action), and many-to-many (a video going viral). As seen in the distributed networks, the internet has a weblike structure—hence the phrase "surfing the web."

The distributed open networks have had paradoxical effects. Following in the wake of television, the internet and social media have further decimated the newspaper industry while also wiping out video stores and most music/record stores. These are just a few examples. At the same time, the internet and social media have created huge entrepreneurial opportunities around the world.

During the "dotcom" boom of the 1990s, firms like America Online (AOL), Yahoo, and Google rose to their well-documented international fame. AOL was a subscription service that introduced the internet to mainstream America, but its paid subscriber model was not prepared for the onslaught of free services like Yahoo, Google, Facebook, and YouTube. As detailed by Charlton D. McIlwain in this chapter, Black entrepreneurs like David Ellington and Malcom CasSelle also took advantage of the early internet euphoria to create NetNoir, a pioneering website dedicated to serving the online interests of Black Americans. NetNoir was a hit and had a significant long-term cultural impact. According to McIlwain, Ellington and CasSelle cashed out very wealthy and "accomplished something truly great and consequential for black America: to think that blackness was at the center of the internet universe, something responsible for ushering the masses online."[3]

As of 2021, firms like Google, Amazon, and Facebook are worth hundreds of billions of dollars, while Apple has made hundreds of billions off its iPhones and iTunes store. Of course, there have been many other entrepreneurs and organizations taking advantage of the internet and social media platforms. Profits have been complemented by protests, as seen with various protest movements, such as the Arab Spring, Occupy Wall Street, #MeToo, Black Lives Matter, the March for Science, and the Climate Strike. *The point is that the ecologies of networks and platforms confer social and economic power around the world—local, regional, national, and international.*

PLATFORMS AND CLOUDS

You aren't just livin' in a digital world; today's society is a "platformed" one. Maybe you've heard catchphrases like "the sharing economy" or "the gig economy." These terms are meant to conjure up feelings of economic progress, technological innovation, empowerment, and neoliberalism. A platformed society is promoted as one that can bypass traditional organizational structures, regulations, and overhead costs, one that provides products directly with no offline intermediaries.[4]

This is an interesting sociocultural imaginary, considering that, in reality, the "Big Five" tech companies drive our internet livin', and thus our everyday livin'. Alphabet, Amazon, Facebook, Apple, and Microsoft function very much like the Big Five media companies (AT&T, Comcast, Disney, ViacomCBS, and Fox)—they are traditional hierarchical corporate structures that lead the way in tech standards. And "independent" digital companies rely on the Big Five to function. For example, Netflix relies on Amazon Web Services (AWS) and Airbnb relies on Google Maps.[5] Because the Big Five have such a hold on our platformed society, they also have a hold on our society more broadly, because a platformed society is one that not only uses platforms but also is constantly impacted by platform cultures. So, how does it all work?

UNDERSTANDING PLATFORMS

Platforms are defined as "programmable infrastructure[s] designed to organize interactions between users."[6] At first glance, it's easy to read this definition and think only of end-users, those of us who have the TikTok or Gmail app installed on our smartphone. This is understandable, particularly because the word *user* is thrown around in popular discourse and mainstream media to mean only end-users. But the first step in understanding what platforms really are, and thus what they have the power to do, is to recognize there are three main types of users that platforms organize interactions between: end-users, advertisers, and developers.

---

3   Charlton D. McIlwain, *Black Software: The Internet and Racial Justice, from the AfroNet to Black Lives Matter* (New York: Oxford University Press, 2020), 246.
4   José Van Dijck, Thomas Poell, and Martijn De Waal, *The Platform Society: Public Values in a Connective World* (New York: Oxford University Press, 2018).
5   Van Dijck, Poell, and De Waal, *Platform Society*.
6   Van Dijck, Poell, and De Waal, *Platform Society*, 9.

End-users are the traditional consumers of a service's final product. End-users are ultimately for whom the product has been designed. Thus, the end-user interface is the product that we see after we tap the app icon. Because this is all we see as end-users, it is easy to imagine platforms as spaces that are only about posting, DMing, sharing content, watching videos, hailing a ride, or ordering a pizza. But the processes that are necessary behind the scenes—or in the "backend"—provide a far more dynamic livin' space than what end-user interfaces reveal. As José Van Dijck, Thomas Poell, and Martijn De Waal explain,

> A platform is fueled by *data,* automated and organized through *algorithms* and *interfaces,* formalized through *ownership* relations driven by *business models,* and governed through *user agreements.*[7]

Platforms are powered by the data we create by posting or filling out profiles, but also through data we implicitly create, like GPS locations, time stamps, and battery percentages. Data are also created about us: algorithms not only sort content; they also ingest data and output inferences about who we are and what we are likely to do next. The "rules" of platforms are defined through who owns, designs, and funds the digital spaces—and the rights that end-users have, or, more specifically, the rights that end-users are granted, are shrouded in legalese within user agreements or Terms of Service (TOS) documents.

ADVERTISERS AND DEVELOPERS

Here is where the other two types of users—advertisers and developers—come in. Advertisers are still interacting with the same databases (where data are stored) that populate end-user interfaces. A common misconception is that companies like Facebook and Google sell user data to advertisers. This isn't actually the case. Instead, advertisers are given an advertiser API—application programming interface—that looks different than the end-user interface and provides a different set of tools that allows advertisers to create targeted ads to be consumed by end-users. These tools provide categories that summarize user data, allowing advertisers to create targeted ads based on categories like ZIP codes, buying habits, and levels of education reached.

Developers are another type of user, and they see a different, third type of API. Developer APIs are most often for third parties that want to create apps but need the help of established platforms to do so. For instance, maybe you have tried to play a game or take a quiz on Facebook. Before you were allowed into the app, you received a pop-up to approve that that game or quiz could access certain data from your profile. This pop-up signals that the game or quiz was built by a third party, but the third party used some of Facebook's resources so they would not have to build and maintain an entire, freestanding app themselves. As another example, you are likely familiar with the prompt to log on to an "independent" app by using your Facebook or Google username and password (known as OAuth or Open Authorization). Again, that developer is borrowing a Big Five's encryption and security process so the third-party developer doesn't have to build and maintain such a complex and important infrastructure themselves. Like advertisers, developers are not granted direct access to user data (including passwords!); instead, they are provided with the tools needed to ensure that their app functions as designed.

Why is this more thorough conception of platforms and users so masked? Tarleton Gillespie, principal researcher at Microsoft Research New England, has some ideas about it. He argues that when we hear the word *platform* we think of a technical support system that gives users a place to be heard and to find opportunities. These assumptions all, in some way, benefit the platform.[8] In other words, the ambiguity surrounding what platforms and users are gives the companies themselves, often the Big Five, an advantage.

---

7   Van Dijck, Poell, and De Waal, *Platform Society,* 9.
8   Tarleton Gillespie, "The Politics of 'Platforms,'" *New Media & Society* 12, no. 3 (2010): 347–364.

LOOKING AT THE CLOUDS

As discussed above, platforms are the programmable infrastructures that organize interactions between end-users, advertisers, and developers. These platforms, however, are reliant on "the cloud." For many, "the cloud" signifies a lightness, a floating, easy, nondescript weightless body hovering over us. Ironically, "the cloud" portion of the digital experience is both literally and figuratively the heaviest.

The National Institute of Standards and Technology defines *cloud computing* as

> a model for enabling convenient, on-demand network access to a shared pool of configurable computing resources (e.g., networks, servers, storage, applications, and services) that can be rapidly provisioned and released with minimal management effort or service provide interaction.[9]

In other words, "the cloud" enables access to data and services at any time and from almost anywhere, with little knowledge necessary regarding how the technologies actually work. Data move through "the cloud," and metadata live on "the cloud." "The cloud" allows companies to move their resources off-site, which also means no local access. This clearly details why "the cloud" is figuratively the heaviest. But why literally?

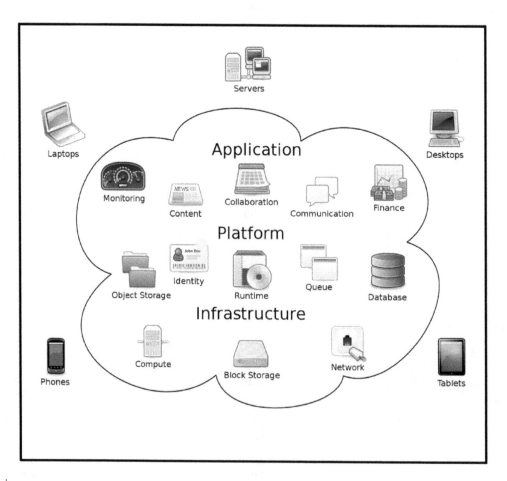

FIGURE 2.0.4   Diagram of the Cloud

Used colloquially, "the cloud" often refers to the idea that you can save data, like files or photos, somewhere else, "lightening up" your phone, tablet, or laptop. This process involves your files and photos being broken into

---

9   https://www.nist.gov/programs-projects/nist-cloud-computing-program-nccp

packets—small bits of data that, when brought back together, turn into your file or photo again—and being saved across some company's "cloud" or server farms, each packet being stored on at least two servers (computers) for the sake of redundancy (in case one server goes down). So, when you save a photo to "the cloud" you are really sending pieces of the photo across the world, destined to be livin' in computers owned by Google, Apple, or whatever company's storage space, or cloud, you are using.

In the final reading of this chapter, "Celebrities of the Cloud," Angela Cirucci explains the paradoxical effects of the "persistence" and "ephemerality" of the internet. The essay also explores the cultural parallels between our religions and our omnipresent media ecologies.

| **FIGURE 2.0.5**   Computer server room

Server farms, or the huge, often underground, areas where all these computers live, are much heavier than any other typical piece of consumer computing equipment, and they're definitely heavier than a cloud. On its website, Google touts cloud locations in twenty-four regions, seventy-three zones, and over two hundred countries and territories.[10] Clouds not only allow data to be saved off-site but also allow virtual access to applications and services. For example, Amazon Web Services (AWS) offers (1) AWS CodeBuild, a service that builds and tests digital code in the cloud, and (2) Amazon Interactive Video Service, a service that manages interactive video streams.

HOLLYWOOD NETWORKS

With the advent of the computer and the internet, Hollywood has attempted to depict the power of networks and to offer warnings about the abuse of that power. Though not masterpieces, these films do offer interesting perspectives on the ever-evolving role of computers and networks in our lives.

---

10   See https://cloud.google.com/about/locations#regions.

One other film merits mention here, though it is *not* centrally about media networks. Stanley Kubrick's *2001: A Space Odyssey* is a mind-bending masterpiece about human origins and destiny in the vastness of the cosmos. Importantly, *2001* has the single most influential and compelling cinematic vision of computer networks and artificial intelligence of the future. In the film, the main spacecraft is controlled by a 24/7 wireless computer network linked throughout the craft. Astronauts interface with the network by talking to the artificial intelligence program that runs the network—think a perfected Siri linked to the internet. Not content to merely dazzle with technofuturism, *2001* also offers serious warnings about living under total surveillance in such a powerful network. So far, all warnings have been ignored.

MOORE'S LAW

Grasping the importance of the network requires understanding digitalization and the meme of "Moore's Law." Digitalization means all words, images, and music in our media technologies are stored, manipulated, and transmitted as tiny bits of digital and electronic information. Inside the microprocessors that power our media technologies, the electronic information is coded in a binary sequence of numeric ones (1s) and zeros (0s). These 1s and 0s are "bits" of information, the genes of digital DNA, the smallest elements in the electronic universe. They have no color, no size, and no weight, and they can travel at the speed of light. Inside the microprocessors, the bits are in the form of electrical current carried via electrons through the circuitry—when the current passes through the circuit, it is "on," and when the current does not pass through, it is "off." When these on-off states are sequenced as 1s and 0s, the strings of binary code become the content of the media, with the circuitry of computers functioning as the container for the expanding global network.

The power of computers and the network is the product of continual innovations in the microprocessors, innovations that follow a pattern known as "Moore's Law." In 1965, Gordon Moore, the cofounder of Intel, observed that the number of transistors that could fit on a computer chip had doubled every year since 1959, and he predicted that the pattern would continue for at least ten more years. By 1975, the pattern revealed the doubling of transistors every eighteen months to two years—not the exact time frame Moore predicted, but still a radically fast expansion of processing power. Since then, this pattern has generally held true, with power doubling about every two years while also declining in price. This remarkable pattern has come to be known as Moore's Law and is expected to hold true for the foreseeable future.[11] Moore's seemingly modest insight has, in effect, described and predicted the explosive growth of computer and media power, an expanding global network doubling in size and power every eighteen to twenty-four months.

This may sound like jargon for technogeeks, but it is a key idea for understanding media technologies and their power. Moore's Law is an example of "period-doubling," the process by which a small system can grow enormously large by repeatedly doubling over a given period. For example, suppose you had a job offer upon graduation: the employer offered to pay you one penny on the first day but pledged to double your pay every day for the first month. Should you take the job? Yes, then retire after Day 30. Let's look at what you would earn if you began with a penny and doubled your pay every day for a month: Day 1 = 1 cent, Day 2 = 2 cents, Day 7 = 64 cents, Day 8 = $1.28, Day 15 = $164, Day 22 = $21,000, Day 29 = $2.7 million, Day 30 = $5.4 million. Your one-month total = $10.8 million. This is not a trick. Do the calculations for yourself.

If you have been in college for two years, the size and power of the global media environments have effectively doubled during that time. Have *you* doubled your power in the past two years?

The growth, power, content, and social value of our media environments are following this *exponential* pattern. And this does not include the people linking to the network. That number is increasing exponentially and now

---

11   Ray Kurzweil, *The Age of Spiritual Machines* (New York: Viking, 1999), 20–25.

exceeds 2.5 billion and counting. Of course, since there are 7.6 billion people on the planet, the internet has a long way to go before becoming accessible to everyone. But it will happen.

Moore's Law is the technological backdrop for films like *2001: A Space Odyssey*, *The Matrix*, *I Robot*, *Her*, *Ex Machina*, and *Blade Runner 2049*, in which computers and networks display artificial intelligence and simulate human consciousness. Will these sci-fi computers and electronic minds ever be realized outside a movie theater? Is Hal in *2001* the grandfather of Siri? Is Siri the grandmother of Samantha in *Her*? Will we plug our consciousness into a global computer network, as shown in *The Matrix*? Will the global village and global consciousness become the same thing? Some futurists think so.[12] Do you?

"INFORMATION WANTS TO BE FREE" (BUT BEING "FREE" HAS A PRICE)

During the 1990s and the early days of internet proliferation, the slogan "Information wants to be free" was a meme that circulated among "Libertarians" and those who wanted the internet to be an open network, free of censorship and accessible to everyone. In the first reading in this chapter, Jaron Lanier (a long-time innovator and theorist of the internet) explains that Moore's Law has indeed reduced the cost of information, but the idea of users accessing and sharing "free" information has enabled the emergence of wealthy and powerful service providers and social media platforms. In effect, most everyone supplies free labor for firms like Facebook, Twitter, and TikTok, while those firms pocket millions off our data and the clicks those data generate.

Of course, a few "influencers" many make good money by promoting products and services, but the "free" information comes with a price—total surveillance, free labor, and subtle forms of social and economic control. There are no easy solutions, but micropayment systems might be a good first step to leveling the economic playing field.

PLANETARY, INTERPLANETARY, AND INTERSTELLAR NETWORKS

When the former Soviet Union launched the *Sputnik* satellite in 1957, it was hailed as a monumental achievement and a major leap in global communications for the human species. The United States soon followed with Vanguard (1958) and Telstar (1962), signaling a new era of global communication and the possibility of greater harmony and understanding among nations.[13] *Sputnik* and Telstar signaled more than mere global communications, for satellites and all electronic media have radically transformed how we understand the organization of society and our place on the planet. As Marshall McLuhan explained, "When Sputnik went up on October 4, 1957, it put the planet inside a man-made environment for the first time. Spaceship Earth has no passengers, only crew. Sputnik transformed the planet into Spaceship Earth with a program problem."[14]

McLuhan realized that we have effected a media environment that spans our planet, making instant communication possible yet operating on a global scale. Of course, there are thousands of satellites now, linking up peoples and organizations in every nation on Spaceship *Earth*. Reports vary, but there are an estimated two thousand working satellites in orbit around Earth, with one thousand used for communication (mostly ego-media), over

---

12   Ray Kurzweil, "The Human Machine Merger: Are We Heading for *The Matrix*?" in *Taking the Red Pill: Science, Philosophy and Religion in* The Matrix, ed. Glenn Yeffeth (Dallas: Benbella Books, 2003).
13   Telstar was so remarkable for its era that it was the title of a futuristic instrumental song by the Tornadoes; in 1962, the song reached number one on the pop charts in Britain and the United States. Opening with space sounds, followed by drums, lead guitar, and organ, it's a pretty cool song that kind of exemplifies the technological optimism of the era. The song probably works for dancing the Twist or the Floss.
14   Marshall McLuhan, *Understanding Me: Lectures and Interviews* (Cambridge, MA: MIT Press, 2003), 242.

four hundred for weather, ecological, and Earth-observation purposes (eco-media), and almost one hundred for GPS purposes.[15] Obviously, many of our media networks and platforms (TV, GPS, mobile phones, etc.) are dependent on these satellites.

INTERPLANETARY: MAPPING THE PLANETS

In 1977, NASA launched *Voyager 1* and *Voyager 2*, two robotic space probes, to map the outer planets Jupiter, Saturn, Uranus, and Neptune. The images that the probes captured were spectacular, and they massively expanded our knowledge of these planets while also extending our electronic media networks to the furthest reaches of the solar system. Similarly, the various Mars rovers—*Sojourner*, *Opportunity*, *Spirit*, *Curiosity*, and *Perseverance*—have extended our eyes to the red planet. Operated by NASA's Jet Propulsion Laboratory in Pasadena, California, the rovers have the ultimate quest of discovering possible ancient life-forms in the red sands and dried-up seas and riverbeds.

So far, every planet in the solar system has been visited and studied by a space probe, including the recent *Cassini* probe, which studied Jupiter, and the *Huygens* lander, which landed (via parachute) on Titan, one of the moons of Jupiter. The list of discoveries from this mission would fill a book, but in particular the volcanoes and oceans discovered on the moons of Saturn are incredible and may yet reveal signs of ancient or current life. Notably, the Cassini-Huygens mission was an international collaboration, involving NASA, the European Space Agency, and the Italian Space Agency.

INTERSTELLAR: *VOYAGER* HAS LEFT THE SOLAR SYSTEM

As of 2021, the *Voyagers* had entered the interstellar medium beyond the solar system. Traveling at 15 kilometers per second and 16 kilometers per second, respectively, *Voyager 2* and *Voyager 1* are destined to wander the Milky Way for eternity, hurtling through the vast voids between our solar system and the nearest stars. Though not headed toward any particular star, *Voyager 1* will pass in the vicinity of the star Gliese 445 in about forty thousand years; Gliese is about 1.7 light-years from Earth. *Voyager 1* is the most remote object ever created by the human species. Via our electronic networks, we have extended our consciousness around the planets and now outside the solar system. We are an interstellar species. Isn't it time we act like an enlightened and peaceful species, too?

CREDITS

---

15 Therese Wood, "Who Owns Our Orbit: Just How Many Satellites Are There in Space?" World Economic Forum, October 23, 2020, https://www.weforum.org/agenda/2020/10/visualizing-easrth-satellites-sapce-spacex.

MOTIVATION

JARON LANIER is a scientist and musician best known for his work in Virtual Reality research, a term he coined and popularized. *Time* named him one of the "Time100" in 2010. He lives in Berkeley, California.

THE PROBLEM IN BRIEF

We're used to treating information as "free,"[1] but the price we pay for the illusion of "free" is only workable so long as most of the overall economy *isn't* about information. Today, we can still think of information as the intangible enabler of communications, media, and software. But as technology advances in this century, our present intuition about the nature of information will be remembered as narrow and short-sighted. We can think of information narrowly only because sectors like manufacturing, energy, health care, and transportation aren't yet particularly automated or 'net-centric.

But eventually most productivity probably *will* become software-mediated. Software could be the final industrial revolution. It might subsume all the revolutions to come. This could start to happen, for instance, once cars and trucks are driven by software instead of human drivers, 3D printers magically turn out what had once been manufactured goods, automated heavy equipment finds and mines natural resources, and robot nurses handle the material aspects of caring for the elderly. (These and other examples will be explored in detail later on.) Maybe digital technology won't advance enough in this century to dominate the economy, but it probably will.

Maybe technology will then make all the needs of life so inexpensive that it will be virtually free to live well, and no one will worry about money, jobs, wealth disparities, or planning for old age. I strongly doubt that neat picture would unfold.

Instead, if we go on as we are, we will probably enter into a period of hyper-unemployment, and the attendant political and social chaos. The outcome of chaos is unpredictable, and we shouldn't rely on it to design our future.

The wise course is to consider in advance how we can live in the long term with a high degree of automation.

PUT UP OR SHUT UP

For years I have presented complaints about the way digital technology interfaces with people. I love the technology and doubly love the people; it's the connection that's out of whack. Naturally, I am often asked, "What would you do instead?" If the question is framed on a

---

1   As exemplified by free consumer Internet services, or the way financial services firms can often gather and use data without having to pay for it.

personal level, such as "Should I quit Facebook?" the answer is easy. You have to decide for yourself. I am not trying to be anyone's guru.[2]

On the level of economics, though, I ought to provide an answer. People are not just pointlessly diluting themselves on cultural, intellectual, and spiritual levels by fawning over digital superhuman phenomena that don't necessarily exist. There is also a material cost.

People are gradually making themselves poorer than they need to be. We're setting up a situation where better technology in the long term just means more unemployment, or an eventual socialist backlash. Instead, we should seek a future where more people will do well, without losing liberty, even as technology gets much, much better.

Popular digital designs do not treat people as being "special enough." People are treated as small elements in a bigger information machine, when in fact people are the *only* sources or destinations of information, or indeed of any meaning to the machine at all. My goal is to portray an alternate future in which people are treated appropriately as being special.

How? Pay people for information gleaned from them if that information turns out to be valuable. If observation of you yields data that makes it easier for a robot to seem like a natural conversationalist, or for a political campaign to target voters with its message, then you ought to be owed money for the use of that valuable data. It wouldn't exist without you, after all. This is such a simple starting point that I find it credible, and I hope to persuade you about that as well.

The idea that mankind's information should be made free is idealistic, and understandably popular, but information wouldn't need to be free if no one were impoverished. As software and networks become more and more important, we can either be moving toward free information in the midst of insecurity for almost everyone, or toward paid information with a stronger middle class than ever before. The former might seem more ideal in the abstract, but the latter is the more realistic path to lasting democracy and dignity.

An amazing number of people offer an amazing amount of value over networks. But the lion's share of wealth now flows to those who aggregate and route those offerings, rather than those who provide the "raw materials." A new kind of middle class, and a more genuine, growing information economy, could come about if we could break out of the "free information" idea and into a universal micropayment system. We might even be able to strengthen individual liberty and self-determination even when the machines get very good.

This is a reading about futuristic economics, but it's really about how we can remain human beings as our machines become so sophisticated that we can perceive them as autonomous. It is a work of nonnarrative science fiction, or what could be called speculative advocacy. I'll argue that the particular way we're reorganizing our world around digital networks is not sustainable, and that there is at least one alternative that is more likely to be sustainable.

MOORE'S LAW CHANGES THE WAY PEOPLE ARE VALUED

The primary influence on the way technologists have come to think about the future since the turn of the century is their direct experience of digital networks through consumer electronics. It only takes a few years, not a lifetime, for a young person to experience Moore's Law-like changes.

Moore's Law is Silicon Valley's guiding principle, like all ten commandments wrapped into one. The law states that chips get better at an accelerating rate. They don't just accumulate improvements, in the way that a pile of rocks gets higher when you add more rocks. Instead of being added, the improvements *multiply*. The technology seems to always get twice as good every two years or so. That means after forty years of improvements, microprocessors have become *millions* of times better. No one knows how long this can continue. We don't agree on exactly why Moore's Law or other similar patterns exist. Is it a human-driven, self-fulfilling prophecy or an intrinsic, inevitable quality of technology? Whatever is going on, the exhilaration of accelerating change leads

---

2   ... though I'll make a suggestion at the end of the book.

to a religious emotion in some of the most influential tech circles. It provides a meaning and context.

Moore's Law means that more and more things can be done practically for free, if only it weren't for those people who want to be paid. People are the flies in Moore's Law's ointment. When machines get incredibly cheap to run, people seem correspondingly expensive. It used to be that printing presses were expensive, so paying newspaper reporters seemed like a natural expense to fill the pages. When the news became free, that anyone would want to be paid at all started to seem unreasonable. Moore's Law can make salaries—and social safety nets—seem like unjustifiable luxuries.

But our immediate experience of Moore's Law has been cheap treats. Yesterday's unattainably expensive camera becomes just one of today's throwaway features on a phone. As information technology becomes millions of times more powerful, any particular use of it becomes correspondingly cheaper. Thus, it has become commonplace to expect online services (not just news, but 21st century treats like search or social networking) to be given for free, or rather, in exchange for acquiescence to being spied on.

ESSENTIAL BUT WORTHLESS

As you read this, thousands of remote computers are refining secret models of who you are. What is so interesting about you that you're worth spying on?

The cloud is driven by statistics, and even in the worst individual cases of personal ignorance, dullness, idleness, or irrelevance, every person is constantly feeding data into the cloud these days. The value of such information could be treated as genuine, but it is not. Instead, the blindness of our standards of accounting to all that value is gradually breaking capitalism.

There is no long-term difference between an ordinary person and a skilled person in this scheme. For now, many kinds of skilled people do well in a software-mediated world, but if things don't change, those who own the top machines will gradually emerge as the only elite left standing. To explain why, consider how advancing

technology could do to surgery what it has already done to recorded music.

Musical recording was a mechanical process until it wasn't, and became a network service. At one time, a factory stamped out musical discs and trucks delivered them to retail stores where salespeople sold them. While that system has not been entirely destroyed, it is certainly more common to simply receive music instantly over a network. There used to be a substantial middle-class population supported by the recording industry, but no more. The principal beneficiaries of the digital music business are the operators of network services that mostly give away the music in exchange for gathering data to improve those dossiers and software models of each person.

The same thing could happen to surgery. Nanorobots, holographic radiation, or just plain old robots using endoscopes might someday perform heart surgery. These gadgets would perform the economic role that MP3 players and smartphones took on in music delivery. Whatever the details, surgery would then be reconceived as an information service. The role of human surgeons in that case is not predetermined, however. They will remain *essential,* for the technology will rely on data that has to come from people, but it isn't decided yet if they'll be *valued* in terms that lead to wealth.

Nonspecialist doctors have already lost a degree of self-determination because they didn't seize the centers of the networks that have arisen to mediate medicine. Insurance and pharmaceutical concerns, hospital chains, and various other savvy network climbers were paying better attention. No one, not even a heart surgeon, should pretend to be indefinitely immune to this pattern.

There will always be humans, lots of them, who provide the data that makes the networked realization of any technology better and cheaper. This reading will propose an alternative, sustainable system that will continue to honor and reward those humans, no matter how advanced technology becomes. If we continue on the present path, benefits will instead flow mostly to the tenders of the top computers that route data about surgery, essentially by spying on doctors and patients.

THE BEACH AT THE EDGE OF MOORE'S LAW

A heavenly idea comes up a lot in what might be called Silicon Valley metaphysics. We anticipate immortality through mechanization. A common claim in utopian technology culture is that people—well, perhaps not everyone—will be uploaded into cloud computing servers[3] later in this century, perhaps in a decade or two, to become immortal in Virtual Reality. Or, if we are to remain physical, we will be surrounded by a world animated with robotic technology. We will float from joy to joy, even the poorest among us living like a sybaritic magician. We will not have to call forth what we wish from the world, for we will be so well modeled by statistics in the computing clouds that the dust will know what we want.

Picture this: It's sometime later in the 21st century, and you're at the beach. A neuro-interfaced seagull perches and seems to speak, telling you that you might want to know that nanobots are repairing your heart valve at the moment (who knew you had a looming heart problem?) and the sponsor is the casino up the road, which paid for this avian message *and* the automatic cardiology through Google or whatever company is running that sort of switchboard decades hence.

If the wind starts to blow, swarms of leaves turn out to be subtle bioengineered robots that harness that very wind to propel themselves into an emergent shelter that surrounds you. Your wants and needs are automatically analyzed and a robotic masseuse forms out of the sand and delivers shiatsu as you contemplate the wind's whispers from your pop-up cocoon.

There are endless variations of this sort of tale of soon-to-appear high-tech abundance. Some of them are found in science fiction, but more often these visions come up in ordinary conversations. They are so ambient in Silicon Valley culture that they become part of the atmosphere of the place. Typically, you might hear a thought experiment about how cheap computing will be, how much more advanced materials science will become, and so

on, and from there your interlocutor extrapolates that supernatural-seeming possibilities will reliably open up later in this century.

This is the thought schema of a thousand inspirational talks, and the motivation behind a great many startups, courses, and careers. The key terms associated with this sensibility are *accelerating change, abundance,* and *singularity.*

THE PRICE OF HEAVEN

My tale of a talking seagull strikes me as being kitschy and contrived, but any scenario in which humans imagine living without constraints feels like that.

But we needn't fear a loss of constraints. Utopians presume the advent of abundance not because it will be affordable, but because it will be free, provided we accept surveillance.

Starting back in the early 1980s, an initially tiny stratum of gifted technologists conceived new interpretations of concepts like privacy, liberty, and power. I was an early participant in the process and helped to formulate many of the ideas I am criticizing in this reading. What was once a tiny subculture has blossomed into the dominant interpretation of computation and software-mediated society.

One strain of what might be called "hacker culture" held that liberty means absolute privacy through the use of cryptography. I remember the thrill of using military-grade stealth just to argue about who should pay for a pizza at MIT in 1983 or so.

On the other hand, some of my friends from that era, who consumed that pizza, eventually became very rich building giant cross-referenced dossiers on masses of people, which were put to use by financiers, advertisers, insurers, or other concerns nurturing fantasies of operating the world by remote control.

It is typical of human nature to ignore hypocrisy. The greater a hypocrisy, the more invisible it typically becomes, but we technical folk are inclined to seek an airtight whole of ideas. Here is one such synthesis—of

---

3 A "server" is just a computer on a network that serves up responses to other computers. Generally home computers or portable devices aren't set up to acknowledge connections from arbitrary other computers, so they aren't servers. A "cloud" is a collection of servers that act in a coordinated way.

cryptography for techies and massive spying on others—which I continue to hear fairly often: Privacy for ordinary people can be forfeited in the near term because it will become moot anyway.

Surveillance by the technical few on the less technical many can be tolerated for now because of hopes for an endgame in which everything will become transparent to everyone. Network entrepreneurs and cyber-activists alike seem to imagine that today's elite network servers in positions of information supremacy will eventually become eternally benign, or just dissolve.

In the telling of digital utopias, when computing gets ultragood and ultracheap we won't have to worry about the reach of elite network players descended from today's derivatives funds, or Silicon Valley companies like Google or Facebook. In a future world of abundance, everyone will be motivated to be open and generous.

Bizarrely, the endgame utopias of even the most ardent high-tech libertarians always seem to take socialist turns. The joys of life will be too cheap to meter, we imagine. So abundance will go ambient.

This is what diverse cyber-enlightened business concerns and political groups all share in common, from Facebook to WikiLeaks. Eventually, they imagine, there will be no more secrets, no more barriers to access; all the world will be opened up as if the planet were transformed into a crystal ball. In the meantime, those true believers encrypt their servers even as they seek to gather the rest of the world's information and find the best way to leverage it.

It is all too easy to forget that "free" inevitably means that someone else will be deciding how you live.

THE PROBLEM IS NOT THE TECHNOLOGY, BUT THE WAY WE THINK ABOUT THE TECHNOLOGY

I will argue that up until about the turn of this century we didn't need to worry about technological advancement devaluing people, because new technologies always created new kinds of jobs even as old ones were destroyed. But the dominant principle of the new economy, the information economy, has lately been to conceal the value of information, of all things.

We've decided not to pay most people for performing the new roles that are valuable in relation to the latest technologies. Ordinary people "share," while elite network presences generate unprecedented fortunes.

Whether these elite new presences are consumer-facing services like Google, or more hidden operations like high-frequency-trading firms, is mostly a matter of semantics. In either case, the biggest and best-connected computers provide the settings in which information turns into money. Meanwhile, trinkets tossed into the crowd spread illusions and false hopes that the emerging information economy is benefiting the majority of those who provide the information that drives it.

If information age accounting were complete and honest, as much information as possible would be valued in economic terms. If, however, "raw" information, or information that hasn't yet been routed by those who run the most central computers, isn't valued, then a massive disenfranchisement will take place. As the information economy arises, the old specter of a thousand science fiction tales and Marxist nightmares will be brought back from the dead and empowered to apocalyptic proportions. Ordinary people will be unvalued by the new economy, while those closest to the top computers will become hypervaluable.

Making information free is survivable so long as only limited numbers of people are disenfranchised. As much as it pains me to say so, we can survive if we only destroy the middle classes of musicians, journalists, and photographers. What is not survivable is the additional destruction of the middle classes in transportation, manufacturing, energy, office work, education, and health care. And all that destruction will come surely enough if the dominant idea of an information economy isn't improved.

Digital technologists are setting down the new grooves of how people live, how we do business, how we do everything—and they're doing it according to the expectations of foolish utopian scenarios. We want free online experiences so badly that we are happy to not be paid for information that comes from us now or ever. That sensibility also implies that the more dominant information becomes in our economy, the less most of us will be worth.

SAVING THE WINNERS FROM THEMSELVES

Is the present trend really a benefit for those who run the top servers that have come to organize the world? In the short term, of course, yes. The greatest fortunes in history have been created recently by using network technology as a way to concentrate information and therefore wealth and power.

However, in the long term, this way of using network technology is not even good for the richest and most powerful players, because their ultimate source of wealth can only be a growing economy. Pretending that data came from the heavens instead of from people can't help but eventually shrink the overall economy.

The more advanced technology becomes, the more all activity becomes mediated by information tools. Therefore, as our economy turns more fully into an information economy, it will only grow if more information is monetized, instead of less. That's not what we're doing.

Even the most successful players of the game are gradually undermining the core of their own wealth. Capitalism only works if there are enough successful people to be the customers. A market system can only be sustainable when the accounting is thorough enough to reflect where value comes from, which, I'll demonstrate, is another way of saying that an information age middle class must come into being.

PROGRESS IS COMPULSORY

Two great trends are colliding, one in our favor, and the other against us. Balancing our heavenly expectations, there are also countervailing fears about such things as global climate change and the problem of finding food and drinking water for the human population when it peaks later in this century. Billions more people than have ever been sustained before will need water and food.

We bring the great problems of our times on ourselves, and yet we have little choice but to do so. The human condition is an evolving technological puzzle. Solving one problem creates new ones. This has always been true and is not a special quality of present times.

The ability to grow a larger population, through reduced infant mortality rates, sets up the conditions for a greater famine. People are cracking the inner codes of biology, creating amazing new chemistries, and amplifying our capabilities with digital networks just as we are also undermining our climate, and critical resources are starting to run out. And yet we are compelled to plunge forward, because history isn't reversible. Besides, we must be honest about how bad things were in lower-tech times.

New technological syntheses that will solve the great challenges of the day are less likely to come from garages than from collaborations by many people over giant computer networks. It is the politics and economics of these networks that will determine how new capabilities translate into new benefits for ordinary people.

PROGRESS IS NEVER FREE OF POLITICS

Maybe the coolest technology could get very good and cheap, *while at the same time* crucial fundamentals for survival could become expensive. The calculi of digital utopias and man-made disasters don't contradict each other. They can coexist. This is the heading of the darkest and funniest science fiction, such as the work of Philip K. Dick.

Basics like water and food could soar in cost *even as* intensely sophisticated gadgets, like automated nano-robotic heart surgeons, float about as dust in the air in case they are needed, sponsored by advertisers.

Everything can't become free at once, because the real world is messy. Software and networks are messy. And the sprawling miracle of information-animated technology rests on limited resources.

The illusion that everything is getting so cheap that it is practically free sets up the political and economic conditions for cartels exploiting whatever isn't quite that way. When music is free, wireless bills get expensive, insanely so. You have to look at the whole system. No matter how petty a flaw might be in a utopia, that flaw is where the full fury of power seeking will be focused.

BACK TO THE BEACH

You sit at the edge of the ocean, wherever the coast will be after Miami is abandoned to the waves. You are thirsty. Random little clots of dust are full-on robotic interactive devices, since advertising companies long ago released plagues of smart dust upon the world. That means you can always speak and some machine will be listening. "I'm thirsty, I need water."

The seagull responds, "You are not rated as enough of a commercial prospect for any of our sponsors to pay for freshwater for you." You say, "But I have a penny." "Water costs two pennies." "There's an ocean three feet away. Just desalinate some water!" "Desalinization is licensed to water carriers. You need to subscribe. However, you can enjoy free access to any movie ever made, or pornography, or a simulation of a deceased family member for you to interact with as you die from dehydration. Your social networks will be automatically updated with the news of your death." And finally, "Don't you want to play that last penny at the casino that just repaired your heart? You might win big and be able to enjoy it."

THE BATTLE FOR BLACK CYBERSPACE

CHARLTON D. MCILWAIN is Vice Provost of Faculty Engagement & Development at New York University, and Professor of Media, Culture, and Communication at NYU's Steinhardt School. He is also the Founder of the Center for Critical Race & Digital Studies, and the co-author of *Race Appeal: How Candidates Invoke Race in U.S. Political Campaigns*, winner of the 2012 APSA Ralph Bunche Award.

Beginning on April 12, 1861, America engaged in a great civil war. On January 1, 1863, President Abraham Lincoln's Emancipation Proclamation gathered legal force. For two years, five months, and nineteen days thereafter, nothing changed for many slaves. Then, Major General George Granger and Union troops arrived in Galveston, Texas. There he read the proclamation:

> The people of Texas are informed that in accordance with a Proclamation from the Executive of the United States, all slaves are free. This involves an absolute equality of rights and rights of property between former masters and slaves, and the connection heretofore existing between them becomes that between employer and free laborer.[1]

No slave was free until all slaves were free. And so black people commemorated the day. They called it Juneteenth. The day both ended slavery and ushered in a brief period of Reconstruction.

* * *

One hundred thirty years later to the day, David Ellington and Malcolm CasSelle symbolically assumed General Granger's role. Their announcement was as revolutionary as that historic moment when that last slave received word that she was free.

It all started earlier in 1994. Timothy Jenkins worked on the sly back east to launch GoAfro. Meanwhile, Malcolm beckoned David back down to The Dungeon. There, Malcolm gave David a glimpse of the future.

That's where Jerry Yang was, ya know, and people like that. And I showed him Yahoo! for the first time. It was the early days, and Jerry was one of my classmates. We were really at the frontier. David was excited by it. Again, coming from the perspective of someone who knew nothing about computers. Coming from the world of a lawyer, who used a PC for word processing. We were accessing the Web. The Internet. So imagine going from a computer that was not connected to anything, to a computer that is connected to everything. He was like, "What? I mean, this could do so many things." You can see all of this information. You can find all this stuff. David was fascinated by it. To me, I was like, well, yeah. ... Of course. I mean, it wasn't novel to me. It was the way things were. But I said it again—the future is about connected computers.

David was savvy enough to see the future with Malcolm—even if he didn't fully understand it. But, he understood his clients. He understood that the arc of history did not always bend toward justice.

I mean, I didn't know anything about money. I was tired of seeing my black entertainment clients get burned in LA in entertainment. I saw this new medium as a new way that not only could my clients and potential future clients be a part of this distribution channel, this platform that was coming called the Internet. Because, remember, I had secret insight. My partner was at Stanford in the computer science lab in the dungeons.

I saw the kids were in on this thing, coming up with content or using it to do research. I had used LexisNexis in law school in the eighties. You're doing your dial-in, you're looking up a case and you type in the case code and the name and then you have to read cases related to the case. I could learn case law, but it was all text. What these guys were showing me was this new medium, because this thing called the World Wide Web came along, WWW, and that's what gives you audio, graphics, sound, whatever. So anyway, he and I then decided this is really interesting, maybe there's a way that you and I could work together.

* * *

America Online (AOL) started in 1983 as a gaming company, Control Video Corporation. When it reorganized toward the close of the 1980s as America Online, Steve Case, one of the company's founders, became its chief executive officer. Case quickly orchestrated a series of financial and personnel decisions designed to lift AOL high atop the Internet service provider market.

By 1994, the company was on track. But Case saw that AOL needed more aggressive marketing. It needed to capitalize on its existing market to build new ones. Case did not wait to develop the aggressive, guerilla marketing prowess that AOL needed. He bought it. In 1994, AOL acquired Redgate Communications Corporation. The computer marketing firm published magazines such as the *Amiga Buyers Guide*. As its name suggests, the magazine/marketing tool reviewed hardware and software related to Commodores Amiga computer.

Even more than the company itself, Case wanted Redgate's president, Ted Leonsis, who had made his first millions—forty to be exact—when he was just twenty-five. Leonsis did not believe the adage that "content is king." At least not in the same way that Lee Bailey had embraced the principle. Sure, he believed that you need great content to attract audiences. But Leonsis thought community was marketing's strongest foundation.

Community and providing context is what's important. We will always remain member-centric, not IP-[information provider] centric.

Leonsis started looking for people who could bring other people together. And he came up with a plan to find them. As 1994 drew to a close, Leonsis announced a bold first strategy to grow AOL's subscription-based Internet portal. The goal: get a million and more Americans online. He looked for what he called "infopreneurs." He did not imagine run-of-the-mill content producers. The magazine world he came from and the media business in general were awash with such mere mortals. Leonsis searched for people who could bring other people—by the millions—to the online community AOL was beginning to swiftly build. Leonsis named his venture The Greenhouse. Its plan was simple. Find a handful of companies, led by people who could help AOL accomplish its goal; provide them capital; take a minority share of the company in exchange; throw AOL's recently acquired marketing weight behind them; then sit back and watch the dream unfold.

* * *

David explained.

And then literally in '94, I was dating a woman who was working for a multimedia firm—so this is actually all relevant—who was working for a multimedia firm, a brand-new thing called a multimedia interactive agency, called Redgate Communications, here in the Bay Area. It was run by a man named Ted Leonsis. There was this other little company in Washington, DC, called America Online, and it had a $400 million market cap and it was trying to grow. And there were all these other online services called Prodigy, CompuServe, Genie from General Electric, Apple's E-World, and they were competing. And what they started out with, like everyone else in the entertainment business, everyone was focusing on CD-ROMs. But what Ted saw after publishing a few CD-ROMs with catalogs on it, he saw that as you put it into the computer, it could also dial the modem and connect to an online service.

He showed that to Steve Case. Steve Case then bought Redgate communications, and then Ted said, and this is in 1994, Ted said, "What I want to do is develop some infopreneurs," as the new president of America Online in 1994. "I wanted to identify different types of pure online content people. And I'd like it to be [as] diverse as possible." My girlfriend, who worked for Ted, is now an employee of America Online because Redgate got bought by America Online.

She said to Ted, "Hey, I have a boyfriend who would like to start something black and black entertainment-related.

What do you think about that?" Ted said, "I love it. Get me a business plan."

David was the approaching-middle-age lawyer. Malcolm was the young geek. David took the lead. His vision was dead on. But Malcolm was there to remind David that his execution—his proposal—lacked, well ... a kind of technological charm.

We suddenly realized that the idea of a network of black culture was an opportunity.

The two tossed around potential names for the venture that began exploding in their minds. *Afronet* was first out of the gate. They ruled it out. They discovered that a company with that name already existed—selling hairnets! Not to mention, Malcolm also pointed out that an online service named Afronet also already existed. Malcolm suggested *CyberBlack*. David squashed it. *Too hard*, he said.

I could have easily gone down the path of trying to be this blacker-than-black service. But then, I had to say, hold it—we're about to enter *the 21st Century. And it's going to be about communication. It's about creating a place for people to talk, debate, and have fun. To me the business model of the next century is about inclusion.[2]*

Then it happened, in tandem:

Net ...
     Noir.

David typed up a document that was the basic idea. Like a one-pager. Or two-pager. And it was all in like Courier font. It looked like it was done on an actual typewriter! I think it was actually a word processor. And I looked at it, and I was like, w-e-ll, yeah, okay. It was from a lawyers perspective—ya know, bullet items and, it was like an outline. And I said, "I don't think it actually works that way, but I get your point." So that's how it started. We built a team, got the business plan together.

Then, Malcolm and David walked into Redgate, sat in front of Leonsis, a young, now-larger-than-life entrepreneur who sat on top of the online world. Not fazed by celebrity, wealth, or the fact that Leonis stood to make or break their dream, David and Malcolm made their pitch.

NetNoir. What was it? What could it be? Why should it exist? How would they do it, and what made them think they could be successful? David and Malcolm laid it all out for Leonsis.

This is a cybergateway into Afrocentric Culture.[3]

We believe our content will be very appealing to universities, especially the 103 historically black colleges and universities.[4]

NetNoir will be a study in synergy. Our advertisers, our content providers and our merchandisers will all come together and mutually promote each other while focusing on Afrocentric Culture.[5]

This is a cultural imperative. The service's software will drive the purchase of hardware by people who are interested in Afrocentric information and opportunities online, but aren't already involved with technology.[6]

It is global in scope, including Afro-Caribbean, Afro-Latin, Afro-European, Continental Africa as well as African American. Anyone who has an interest in Afrocentric culture can come in and participate. You don't have to be black.

If we create software, that is, faces, entertainers, literature, you know, academic pursuits, that look and feel like things that you're comfortable with, there's a reason for you to get online.[7]

Malcolm and David walked away from the meeting confident. But they were realists. They knew theirs was a shot in the dark. They had applied to Leonis's Greenhouse program, just like seventeen hundred other individuals, teams, and companies vying for America Online's money marketing; and home within its online portal. There were seventeen hundred other people also convinced that their idea could work.

David and Malcolm had been part of many different kinds of pitch meetings across Silicon Valley. Those meetings didn't so much put them on the defensive; but they did put a chip or two on each of their shoulders. They were usually the only two black people in the room; and had to fight to get what seemed to come easily to their white competitors. But those meetings had also helped David and Malcolm realize that they worked for more than just their own personal financial hopes and dreams. NetNoir, they both firmly believed, would not just be good for them (though, to be clear, they both planned to get filthy rich). They also believed their success would translate to something significant and positive for black people. They willingly shouldered that burden. If we don't succeed, they don't succeed.

I was going to literally—Malcolm and [me]—for '93 and '94, we must have gone to eight or nine different conferences. We were always the only black guys in the room. And we were sitting there watching, and at that time it was only white guys with pocket protectors. It was truly geeks. No women at all, maybe one or two, and they're super-geeky, too. And it was just really like four or five hundred people in a room. I can remember one conference in particular, and no one was talking about anything black. They were always focusing on the Grateful Dead, the Rolling Stones, and then I heard Prince was doing something. ... And it was like, "Oh, that's nice." I was like, Oh, no, no, no. I want all of our stuff to be on here. You're not going to build this new medium and cut us out.

Determination kept them going while they put the pieces of their company together. But determination alone wasn't going to build the company. They needed AOL. They needed Ted.

* * *

With these kinds of endeavors, you bet the jockeys and not the horse they're riding. They both showed up for the pitch meeting and they were able to articulate with a gleam in their eye exactly what they're going to do. Having a gateway to the entirety of Afrocentric culture was appealing. More than that, they were more appealing as a team. They could have come in and sold us anything. I knew in the first fifteen minutes I was going to do this deal.[8]

* * *

Again, David provided details.

We were the first company funded in this thing called the Greenhouse Program that was launched by America Online. They did it as a marketing tool, as a vehicle and as, basically, it's an exercise in vision. Because what Ted got is that online content would be compelling and would drive people to use this new technology called online service, because everyone knew that CD-ROMs were purely a hybrid technology. It was going to lead to something bigger. And that bigger thing became known as the Internet.

Remember, the commercial aspect of the Internet—the Internet has been around for thirty years for university professors to talk to the DoD, the Department of Defense—but the commercial aspect—there has to be sexy and compelling content. And Ted had the vision and convinced Steve Case, the chairman of AOL, that that's what you need to do. We need to have original content and we need to identify infopreneurs and that's what he did. And this black company was the very first company funded in that vision.

To say that David and Malcolm were ecstatic would be a severe understatement. They knew they deserved the multimillion-dollar vote of support. But it's a whole different thing when the man holding the bag of money realizes it too.

Though, on a more practical level, Malcolm and David were excited because they, personally, *really* needed the cash!

David and I were starting up the company and basically we were broke. We had quit our jobs. We shook hands with AOL, but we were still negotiating the terms of our contract with AOL ... we knew that we had to get moving in order to get a jump on what we were trying to do, so that we could be the first, we didn't have much time on our hands to mess around. We had asked AOL for an advance on our financing and for it to be rolled over into our equity ... and they agreed to send us a check for $30,000.

Well, the first thing they did was FedEx the check to me in San Francisco. Mind you, I was in San Francisco and David was in Los Angeles. However, the check was made out to both Malcolm CasSelle and David Ellington. But of course at the time we did not even have a joint account together. We weren't even in the same city. David would have to come up to San Francisco or I would have to go down to Los Angeles.

We had no money. So, I borrowed money from a friend to get a one-way ticket to Los Angeles. We drove to Beverly Hills where David had a bank account at the Bank of America, and tried to deposit and cash the check. We needed access to this money. They took the check and said, "I'm sorry sir, we can't cash a check for this amount. However, since you have been such a good customer, we can advance you $1000. It will take two weeks to clear ..."

We said, "No, you don't understand. We need this check now!" So the teller walks away and comes back and then says, well okay, even though you don't have two cents in your account to your name, we will advance you $5000!

But then, the teller goes away and comes back and says, "I'm sorry, but there's insufficient funds."

We couldn't believe it. AOL gave us a rubber check! Here I am in Los Angeles on my one-way ticket, and we have this piece of paper for this check with all these zeros, and it's useless!

So we call the AOL office and it turns out that the person we did the deal with, Ted Leonsis, is out on vacation. And so we explain the story to his assistant, and she ends up calling him on this mobile phone in Florida where he's on a boat. And we said, "Ted, they just told us there are insufficient funds in this account." There was a long pause and then he screams, "What do they mean there's insufficient funds! There is $60 million in that account! Okay, I'll call you back." And it ends out working out okay. I got back up to San Francisco and we get the money.[9]

Once they got their money the NetNoir team went to work. As they did, they honed their vision. That vision was now joined in wedlock to AOL's vision.

None of us knew where the hell this was going or where it was leading. But Ted had the vision to say, "Wait a minute. This is basically a new medium." And it's the new television. There's got to be television programming. And it's not going to be just for geeks. It's going to be for the masses. And of course, Steve Case's background came from Procter & Gamble, so he obviously was always focusing on consumers, and AOL was that. But they first started with financial channels and really clunky and you click on things, and lots of text oriented, not video. I mean, we take it all for granted now, what we can do with our mobile devices, let alone what we could do with our PCs back then.

He was like, "Oh no, if there's anything about black culture, it is compelling and crossover. You guys go build that. Make that happen." He's focusing on crossover. I'm focusing on making sure my culture is a part of or is directly a dead-center part of this new media. I ain't going to lie, I had no idea where this was going. Ted, none of us. None of us knew. I know Mark. I know Chris Larson of E-Loan and Larry Page of Google when they were just getting funded. None of us knew that it was going to be this freaking big and this revolutionary.

We thought it was going to be big, but no one knows. We were just trying to build something. It was cool. We really did drink the Kool-Aid. It's going to change the world. It's going to democratize the entire planet when people have access. More ways for people to vote that couldn't vote before.

When I saw how big it was and when I saw Ted was taking me seriously, I was like—Oh. I was determined to make sure that my culture, that black culture was a part of this new media. But I was just driven by I wanted to make sure that black culture was on this medium. So I had meetings with Ebony. Black Entertainment Television tried to buy me, Bob Johnson. I was going around—Essence. Everyone was trying to watch my shit or go around me and go to AOL. And Ted, to his credit, pushed everyone back.

To his credit, rather than alienating them, David, as NetNoir s CEO, struck deals and brought them into the fold. He made allies and content partners out of the legacy black media outlets. The outlets would provide NetNoir content. NetNoir would provide what everybody needed: visibility.

* * *

It was Juneteenth, 1995. The world's black diaspora had something more to celebrate than their century-ago release from bondage. Reporting for the Associated Press, Elizabeth Weise wrote, It took until June 19, 1865 for Texas slaves to find out the Emancipation Proclamation had freed them two years earlier, an event the black community celebrates as Juneteenth. Now a new Afrocentric on-line service seeks to ensure that blacks never again have to wait that long to learn about their culture, and founders chose Juneteenth's 130th anniversary to launch NetNoir Online.[10]

David, Malcolm, and the NetNoir team used one of its primary services, a live chat room, to announce its presence to the online world. And, they did it using what would be one of NetNoir's signature content features. A celebrity live chat, or what they and others in the business called a forum. On that day, testifying to the moment's historical magnitude, David and Malcolm had invited Larry Irving, head of the US Department of Commerces National Telecommunications and Information Administration. He leveraged the moment to highlight what was most on his mind. It was less about NetNoir itself, more about encouraging more blacks to get online. NetNoir's announcement chat forum was the last time that David and Larry Irving would see themselves as allies. They ventured in separate directions to build different sections of the new information superhighway. David was an entrepreneur. Larry was a policymaker. David had one aim—make money for himself, his company and his investors. Larry concerned himself with how this new technology might positively or negatively affect all black people, and those without the financial means to find an onramp to the information superhighway.

But not everyone shared David's, Malcom's, and AOL's optimism for NetNoir. After NetNoir's Juneteenth launch, skeptical media analysts, financial speculators, stock prognosticators, and advertising industry writers alike lined up to throw shade. Could NetNoir single-handedly integrate the whitest, most expansive, and potentially most lucrative new neighborhood on earth—cyberspace? People who questioned NetNoir's ability to live up to the hype that AOL had helped to manufacture throughout the spring of 1994 didn't necessarily speak out of turn. Larry Irving's department at Commerce had already leaked the findings from its landmark study. Irving had commissioned the study in collaboration with the US Census Bureau, and it showed that blacks were far behind other computer and Internet-connected users, with 20 percent more whites owning computers than blacks.[11]

Malcolm and David had built it. And to hell with the early Web's demographics. Fuck that study. David saw through it all. Nobody really knew at the time who was online and who was not. Irving's study was already too behind the times to properly assess cyberspaces market realities. Data for the study came from the 1990 census, supplemented by a specific computer study early in 1994. And the study's conclusions were based primarily on measuring computer and computer modem home ownership. But computer ownership wasn't everything. Schools have computers. So do libraries, churches, community centers, friends, and universities—all the places that black folk congregate and share knowledge and resources. Not to mention computers, equipped with all the necessary tools to get online, had invaded the workplace.

David and Malcolm knew their people would come. They knew that whether it was in computers or online services or any other material good—we had become a market from whom many could profit. David and Malcolm knew that they would make money from NetNoir. They hoped they would be role models for future entrepreneurs. They had built and begun to develop the space

to make this happen, a platform from which other black people could launch their ventures.

FIGURE 2.2.1 Malcolm CasSelle, Cofounder of NetNoir. Courtesy of Malcolm CasSelle.

Farai Chideya had left Harvard, gone to work for *Newsweek*, then parlayed her work into freelancing. She was the first to take advantage of NetNoir's new platform to build something new—this time for journalism. It was also new for black people and those across the world who lived, understood, and recognized the ways that race, gender, sexuality, religion, and other factures shaped human experience.

Questioning the status quo was a family tradition.[12] Farai Chideya's mother had raised her daughter alone, oscillating between careers as a journalist and teacher. Farai arrived at such a question when she walked into Harvard Square in 1986. Sure, one part of that question focused inward. *Am I as sophisticated as all these kids around me?* she wondered quietly. But more important, as part of both Harvard's black and female minority, her presence at Harvard questioned the institution's business as usual. Her poignant and pointing prose challenged the status quo in the columns and stories she wrote for the *Independent*. The paper itself had begun as an alternative to the news presented by Harvard's official newspaper, the *Crimson*. Farai challenged that status quo again when she graduated with distinction in 1990: magna cum laude, with a degree in English literature.

Harvard was far enough ahead of the curve to have a computer lab on campus. Farai lived just a stone's throw away from the place where wizards still stayed up late,[13] but she never darkened its doors. As the decade of the 1990s threw open its gates, her concerns couldn't have been further away. She walked away from Harvard and began her career as a journalist at *Newsweek*. She continued to cultivate her voice and she had a platform, but it belonged to *Newsweek*. Soon she would find another; one of her own.

In the early 1990s, Farai had been invited to join an online community called the WELL (Whole Earth Tectronic Link), a BBS launched by a group of hippie technologists in the late 1980s and early 1990s. Farai was one of few non-white folks in that community, but she saw the power the platform provided.

It grew into a cultural juggernaut where you had all these journalists from across the country. I remember reading Sinbad ... he was on the WELL and he'd be online chatting. The bulletin boards got political, as people talked about everything. With WELL, anyone can create a subtopic. People could start conferences and there were also closed conferences that were membership only, dealing with specific issues. It was like friends meeting in a coffee shop.

Farai was freelancing. Websites proliferated, but she was interested in building something that was much more interactive.

What was interesting to me was bulletin boards where there was active exchange. Then, you see blogs, and I was like oh I could do this, so I did.

By late 1995 Farai had connected with Omar Wasow, a young, black, digital upstart who had built a BBS called New York Online from his Brooklyn home. That community helped to birth what became PopandPolitics.com. PopandPolitics was one of the earliest blogs ever produced.

I saw PopandPolitics as a place where I could be free and say what I wanted without editorial oversight, which again is good and bad. With solo blogging ... most successful bloggers, even ones who are solo bloggers, have someone editing them. I enjoyed the freedom. Newsweek *had rules about how much voice you could put into a particular piece.*

In her words, there was something going on—a new way of producing and distributing content. A new way

of trying to produce targeted news for both public edification and journalistic profit.

Um, is it just me or is there something going on here? Well, both. Somethings definitely going on—one of the hottest, smartest websites targeted at young Americans—and then there's me and the rest of the crew that brings you "Pop & Politics." I'm CNN political analyst Farai Chideya, and the rest of my team includes guest writers and the web design team of New York Online.

With an incredible reader response to elements including an interactive quiz, an advice column, and numerous new essays, we've already built a strong following. Now we're actively looking for sponsors to help us continue and expand one of the hottest sites on the net. Contact New York Online President Omar Wasow (omar@nyo.com) for rates and information.

Farai capitalized on the blog's visibility. Then she doubled her efforts. The same year, she authored her award-winning book, *Don't Believe the Hype: Fighting Cultural Misinformation About African Americans*. She used PopandPolitics, and NetNoir helped to catapult the book to award-winning, multiple print-run status.

FIGURE 2.2.2 Farai Chideya, Founder of PopandPolitics.com. Courtesy of Farai Chideya.

Like Farai, Lee Bailey's first foray into the new online environment was connected to the work he'd been doing his whole professional career. It began when he expanded *RadioScope*. He had created an email newsletter called the *Electronic Urban Report*. At the same time, NetNoir soon encountered a serious challenge. The black masses that arrived at NetNoir directly—through other locations on AOL, or the open Web—voraciously consumed content. They needed to be fed literally 24/7 with stuff that was relevant and new.

NetNoir was like the black component of AOL. They needed content, so they reached out to me. They were aware of me and RadioScope, and they thought I'd be interested in providing them with entertainment content. Of course I was. It was perfect timing. I was interested in the Internet and being connected with it. They needed content. It was a perfect marriage.

AOL was this closed wall garden, an Internet within Internet. The content was behind a wall. You had to be an AOL subscriber to get to their content. That was cool but I wanted to reach an even wider audience. Mike Blackstock, a Boston-based web host (globaldrum.com) found out about the newsletter and contacted him [David]. Mike would reproduce the newsletter on his website. At the time, the newsletter had complete stories.

We didn't have a website per se, but we had a newsletter and an email address. He contacted me and I thought that sounded like a good idea. At the same time new stories were set up on their own page. He wasn't that sophisticated and I wasn't either.

They repurposed the entire newsletter, with ten to fifteen stories per publication. It was one, incredibly long page of scrolling text that was primarily all text. He gave us distribution via website where people could find it online.

We found advertisers on our own. I never even thought about charging either NetNoir or GlobalDrum or anyone for the content. That came later. At that point it wasn't really a consideration.

It was a new medium, but NetNoir was playing in Lee's world: the content business, and the advertising and marketing business. Lee willingly distributed his content to NetNoir and others for free. Not to worry. Lee knew perfectly well he had to turn those eyeballs into cash.

* * *

By 1995, competition—sometimes tension—intensified. Some folks came to the game to make money, pure and simple. Others knew they had to make money, but they chased it in service of a larger, more community-, educational-, or activist-focused goal. For a short time, GoAfro made a run at NetNoir, with William at the helm.

When NetNoir was released, it was the first time someone like AOL spent money on anything like this. So they invested a half a million dollars into NetNoir. AOL themselves did it. They wanted this to be a success. So USA Today *covered it. Barbara Reynolds wrote the article on it. And Charlayne Hunter-Gault was the star. In other words, when it opened, it featured Charlayne Hunter-Gault, which at that time was like a Katie Couric kind of person.*

And so that was the draw for them, coming out of San Francisco. And it was being managed by some pretty cool black people who were very hip and sophisticated. And it was clearly designed to attract—in fact, Barbara Reynolds's words were—the urban intelligentsia, the black intelligentsia. It was designed to attract that young professional, you know, black crowd of that eighteen to thirty-four age group category. And the content they had was like lifestyle stuff, nothing serious.

Our project on CompuServe was created by PhDs, academic historians. They represented their magazine called American Visions. *It was the official magazine of the Afro-American Museum Association, closely tied to the Smithsonian. And so it had already had six years of publication and we just focused on that stuff. So if you wanted an in-depth treatment on the history of black/ white cooks, we had that material. And that was the difference between our forum on CompuServe and their forum on America Online.*

So we were competing against each other. You know, CompuServe had us to brag about and AOL had NetNoir. CompuServe was very strict. It was like being in Catholic Church. AOL had no rules. If you wanted to curse, you could curse. And so people did it. People looked out for themselves, and they preferred the more open environment of AOL. So the same person probably was on both services, because it just depended on what they came to the service for. But ultimately the glue, or what I call stickiness, was always the socialized chats.

I hosted celebrity events. I had celebrities on there and we hosted those things. It's like, you know, you have a big interview situation with like a big-name person and everybody shows up for that. We had that. We brought that. But people came every day not for that. They really came to, like, chat with the girl that's cute and just put up a picture of herself in Los Angeles. And maybe you two will get together. All that was going on the side, and that was exactly what brought people back over and over, to the point where some people became addicted. I mean I remember women who would call me up, tell me that they just got cut off. They can't connect, can I help them, talk to so-and-so. I mean that was not unusual, man, I'm telling you. That was not unusual.

And so that was really the glue, that stickiness was that chat. Those chats kind of were private. You could be sitting in the forum with the forum content, what's needed to sponsor stuff, so to speak, while simultaneously you've got three open chat windows, talking to three different people at once. And that was really what kept people there, I think, in my opinion.

Both GoAfro and NetNoir had found that more than anything else, people flocked to their respective sites because they could connect with people whom they never had the opportunity to otherwise. All those lofty platitudes that David had mentioned about strengthening democracy, increasing minority participation in politics, and saving the world and all that shit. It paled in comparison to making a love connection. It doesn't mean that both platforms didn't try. It just meant that both began to see the realities of how and why everyday black people would want to use this new medium. And unfortunately for GoAfro, NetNoir and AOL were built to capitalize on this reality. CompuServe was not.

***

Some of the Vanguard had hitched their wagons to the two corporate ISP giants, AOL and CompuServe. But others tried to edge their way into the market on their own.

Back in 1994, Derrick had given Alou "Lou" Macalou and the BGSA's tech committee the green light to pursue building the UBP. At the same time he began to channel all his energy into his own brainchild. He called it *Knowledge Base.*

15 MAR 1994—INTRODUCTION / PURPOSE & SCOPE OF BUSINESS

To take full advantage of the information superhighway and all of its educational & business resources, it is becoming increasingly necessary for families and individuals to own (or at least be familiar with) personal computers. This is because the PC is the primary link between individual users and the vast network of services available via the Internet, which is the backbone of this superhighway.

What I shall describe here is a business plan that focuses on offering consulting/teaching/development services that will cater to a broad spectrum of individuals ranging from first-time computer buyers, to those who wish to computerize their small businesses, and to those who wish to become knowledgeable of information access tools available via the Internet. To reiterate, my markets are: First-time computer buyers; Small business owners; Those interested in accessing the Internet.

These activities will be defined from my generic skill set, which currently features writing, researching & learning, and teaching. Immediate results could be obtained from the following activities (technical): freelance writing & consulting; technical; image processing & general DSP; computers in the home & small businesses; and (non-technical), negotiating the Ph.D. process; financial resources for graduate school; on-campus tutoring (mathematics & junior-senior-level Electrical Engineering courses).

Derrick proposed to counsel first-time computer buyers on their purchasing decisions by showing them what hardware and software best fit their needs, setting them up with intelligible instruction manuals, and providing them how-to books to help maximize their purchase. He would teach them how to maintain their systems, provide in-home software tutorials, and show them the real-world uses for popular software applications like Microsoft's Office suite. He thought he would offer the same services to small business owners. Some added services would be appropriate of course: consulting in business-related computer applications; setting up an office network; configuring email; and choosing an Internet service provider, like CompuServe or AOL. Maybe he could even offer a crash course in programming, using Unix tools such as vi, sed, awk, perl, yacc, and shell programming.

By 1995, Lou and others had begun building the UBP. Derrick still led Georgia Techs BGSA. And he began using it as a vehicle to launch activities consistent with Knowledge Base's vision.

Beginning in 1995, now all of us could pay attention to our research in our day job. You know, the UBP really was our research. And its 1995, so there's no major, even at Georgia Tech, no information technology. Its not mature enough yet for it to become part of the academy. So we're going on our own devices, and our advisors aren't really concerned because the advisors are walking through the labs to see those nerds on the computers, and that means research is happening. So they leave us alone, and we build it out and one day Lou tells me, "I want to make this into a company, do you mind?" I said, "Well ... no. I don't mind, that's kind of what we do in this environment." The black student office area of the Society of Black Engineers is next to [the] grad student association, which was right next door to the African American Student Union.

And when you're all in the same office space like that, you're always doing entrepreneurial things, so there are a lot of small businesses that you can run out of those offices and build into larger enterprises. But the spirit is that we're all about trying to get together and build stuff. So I tell 'em, Lou, you go 'head and do it man. I wish you guys well because I'm trying to build something too, it's called Knowledge Base. Who knows, at some point maybe we join these, because the vision of Knowledge Base is to take advantage of who I've been all my life. I'm the guy that everybody comes and says, hey, can you show me how to do this? I said, okay, I can leverage that. I can definitely leverage that.

So here's what I envision. You guys go put this UBP together. Maybe I can get together with you and Knowledge Base, and we can do outreach. Like grass-roots outreach. There's a lot of people at this school where everybody's smart. But there's a lot of people at this school that know nothing

about this. Imagine what's going on out there in the city, in the country, anywhere we go, we can introduce people to this stuff. And we can build our own office. It makes sense.

So fast-forward to the end of 1995. Lou calls me up and he says, "Hey man, I'm about to do this, and I think I'm gonna leave school. What are you gonna do?" I said, "Okay, well, I don't wanna leave school just yet ... so if you're serious, let me know how you want me to fall." So he came back and he said, "Well, I think you're the only one among us engineers who knows anything about business. So can you build this into a business?"

And so, that's what I do. I show people how to do stuff. So sure, I can build this into a business but here's the thing. I'm the architect. Seldom heard, seldom seen. I'm like the glue. I'm going to build it, hold things together, then I'm gonna disappear. And hopefully what I put together will stay together. That's gonna have a lot to do with you, and who you bring in. Because I know you. I don't know the guys you're bringing in.

Derrick fulfilled his promise. Early in 1996 he began to ink a marketing plan—the blueprint for UBP's business enterprise. He called it BGS Infosystems.

EXECUTIVE SUMMARY

BGS Infosystems, Inc. Marketing Plan
CONFIDENTIAL

BGS Infosystems Inc. ("BGSI," "The Company"), founded in January 1996 with two employees and currently headquartered in Atlanta, GA, is seeking initial equity financing of $99,980 (9998 shares of outstanding stock at $10 per share). This funding is desired to establish BGSI's business infrastructure by allowing the purchase of computer and office equipment, the leasing of office space and communication hardware, the retention of a lawyer, accountant, and independent contractors, and the payment of employee salaries. This figure will increase significantly once all financial projections have been completed.

This desired infrastructure will support BGSI's primary business activity—the development, maintenance, and marketing of an Internet directory accessible through the World Wide Web (WWW) called the **Universal Black Pages**™ **(UBP).** The UBP is a comprehensive directory of African-related Internet resources that has been under development since July 1994. The primary purpose of the UBP is to encourage development of African-related categories and topics which are not currently available via existing WWW pages, which will result in a greater WWW presence for members of the African diaspora. BGSI's effort to motivate development of WWW content and to maintain a comprehensive directory of that content will result in the following user benefits:

- Users enjoy the time they spend browsing the page—they are *edutained* (that is, they are educated and entertained).
- It can be used as an educational resource (in conjunction with traditional media like books, periodicals, and films) by students and teachers at all levels of education.
- It can be a vehicle for promoting use of the Web and the Internet among people of African descent.
- It will serve as a networking tool for people with African interests.
- It will offer a more global perspective of African peoples and cultures.

BGSI plans to produce revenue with the UBP by selling advertisements to companies who desire exposure to the UBP's niche audience—persons of African descent who range in age from 18 to 35. The UBP currently has 18 advertising spaces available. Leasing all 18 spaces to only one advertiser apiece can generate $45,000 in gross monthly revenue ($545,000 per year). BGSI plans to utilize current WWW programming technology to develop techniques to display multiple advertisements on the same page, similar to the way advertisements rotate on the scorer's table at professional and collegiate basketball games. This could significantly increase projected revenues.

BGSI has carefully studied and researched the commercialization of the Internet and WWW for the past six months. This research has indicated that there are currently several general Internet directories who are accepting advertisers. Some of them have acquired as many as 50 customers. These general directories are accessed on the order of millions of times per day and gross monthly revenues as high as *$59,000 per advertising customer.*

The UBP is a niche product currently accessed on the order of thousands of times per day. After researching other Internet directories' advertising rates, BGSI has scaled its advertising rate in accordance with its smaller audience. The Company's research indicates, though, that the UBP is currently the largest Internet directory of its type (i.e., a directory of African-related resources), and has been in development at least nine months longer than the nearest direct competitor. As of the writing of this plan, none of the UBP's direct competitors are accepting advertisers. The UBP plans to be first.

The core technical operation of the UBP is performed by internal software modules called *engines*. Among the engines that are either currently employed or under development in the UBP are the following:

- ***Search Engine.*** The search engine is proprietary software that allows a user to locate specific entries in the UBP database using keywords.
- ***Survey Engine.*** The survey engine is not proprietary software. This software was developed by Jim Pitkow, a graduate student in the Georgia Tech College of Computing. The survey engine employs features which validate answers before terminating a survey.
- ***Registration Engine.*** The registration engine is proprietary software which steps users through the process of registering information in the database. The engine actively checks the validity of information as it is submitted. Once registered, the data is stored in a database for further processing by the administration engine.
- ***Page Builder I Engine.*** Page Builder I is proprietary software which is still in development. It dynamically "builds" HTML-coded pages at regular intervals, incorporating the most recent changes to the UBP database.
- ***Administrative Engine.*** The administrative engine is used solely by the UBP staff to maintain the UBP database, change graphical user interface (GUI) formatting, maintain sponsorship, and perform other site administrative tasks.

The core of BGSI management is comprised of two African-American males, Alou Macalou and Derrick Brown (both of whom hold advanced engineering degrees from Georgia Tech), who together possess a strong fundamental knowledge of both the technological and business aspects of the Internet and WWW. BGSI's management core is also well-versed in emerging computer technology, and contains individuals who are strong leaders, effective communicators, and have a clear vision of how the Internet and WWW can positively impact the African diaspora.

BGSI has also assembled a support team that includes directors with over 25 years of marketing experience, advisors who are at the top of their respective academic fields, a highly skilled group of individual contractors, and sound professional support personnel. A comprehensive business plan with detailed financials will be available in late May 1996. BGSI management is pleased to discuss details of this business plan or its marketing plan, and to render demos of the UBP to serious investors.

Derrick did what he promised. He was the architect, and this thirty-eight-page business plan was his blueprint. It was Derrick's time to disappear. But circumstances just wouldn't let him. And that's what began to spell the beginning of the end, not just for Derrick, but for all of the Vanguard.

A battle for black cyberspace meant there would be winners and losers. Would the Vanguard determine their own fates? Or would someone else pick who won and who lost? The answer to these questions was about to become crystal clear.

* * *

Derrick had left Lou alone to run his own show. But Lou pulled Derrick into the mix, hoping to leverage his skills to launch UBP. Once he was in, it was hard for Derrick not to take umbrage with the direction in which he saw Lou and his team taking UBP.

Lou and his people—they never fell in. And I realized that at our organizational meeting. We had assembled a board now. I assembled a board and wrote a business plan. Got us in front of Georgia Tech's business incubator. They have an incubator called the Advanced Technology Development Center. We were trying to do something and we needed resources. Because they have a place where your company can go to, and that allows you to share resources and ideas and to get on the agenda with

incubator. Everybody wants in, and so you get to go and pitch them. So I'm like, okay, I don't necessary agree with you, Lou, but this is your show.

Derrick did not think of himself as an entrepreneur or businessman. But he was certainly more of one than Lou Macalou and the other folks on his UBP team. Derrick thought that Lou's way of organizing not just UBPs work, but his management of his team, was all wrong. He seemed to fuck up everything from managing what little finances the team had, to assigning tasks and responsibility among his fellow engineers. Lou recognized as much. But he was the master coder, and from his point of view, UBP was his to own and showcase. But he still asked Derrick to pitch UBP to potential investors. Derrick agreed to do this, but not before making his concerns known to Lou.

So anyway, I pitched the material that we put together. But I said to Lou, "Let me tell you something, since you guys can't seem to get along, I understand that I'm not ... that this thing is not going to happen." But it happened. We made the presentation. But the director of the Incubator says, "Look, guys, I don't think we can get behind you. Because this team is a little shaky. But I'll tell you what, if it doesn't work out, you call me, Derrick. Because we'd like to have you over here." So I said to myself, "Well, we're in the water now." I said, all right, all right, cool.

So now were back in the organizational meeting in March of '96, and I didn't realize at the time, here's what happened. Lou—aerospace engineer, programmer extraordinaire—he's built all the code for the entire site of the Universal Black Pages. He's also written a very nice search engine that I would say rivals anything that Yahoo! had built. He wrote it back in 1994. It was very simple, very simple. So he suggests to Larry, who was an electrical engineer, like myself. But we're in different areas, I was in signal processing and Larry was in micro-electronics. So we are in the same major, but were still on different ball fields. So Lou starts this conversation.

Larry—hey, I think were going to use this type of web server.

I [Derrick] concede, Lou. Larry, that sounds like it will work.
HOW DARE YOU SUGGEST WHAT KIND OF WEB SERVER WE SHOULD USE!

The next day Larry walks into the office. I can tell by his face. ... So I'm like, o-o-o-kay, we can put the champagne—over—there.

> *Why are you quitting?*
> Well, Lou is crossing over into my lane. He is not a server person. We see him breaking the bank. I'm out!
> *Larry, come on man. Wait!*

Fortunately, Lou showed back up the next day. So we go in there and make a presentation to the national black data processing associates. The BDPA back in those days was, I guess, what you would call the older version of the Society of Black Engineers. They represented engineering and learning more on the old school data processing and computer needs. It was a great group, great group.

So we made a lot of inroads presenting there, and we were able to forge ahead, attract some more investments, which is the only way we can move forward in comfort. We had this elaborate stock agreement that Lou and Larry had put together—for a company that just raised its first capital. They've got this agreement that says they would both always have 47.62 percent of all stock. ... So if any additional stock is authorized they would both be issued, we'd be issued amounts of stock enough to maintain their respective numbers and control.

And I'm like, "Who came up with this?" The eternal question. ... Let me answer it for you—some engineers. This is crazy. So I go over to them, and I said now tell me what happened. They were at the same school. They didn't really know each other. They both come from MIT and here is the nature of the relationship. In essence there was no relationship. I go up to Larry and have the same conversation, and it's easy to see. Not only was this never gonna work. It's not gonna work now.

So I wrote to the investors, who happened to be my best friends, and I said, "Okay, guys, this is the story. ..." And they said, "Well, look, we support whatever the project is. We just want you to know we gave that money to you." That you is me. "So you need to figure out how you're going to get our money back!'

So I call Lou up.

> *Hey, Lou. I've got to tell you something.*
> You better let me go first.
> *Damn.*

Derrick is afraid of what he knows is coming.

I'm in San Diego.
> *Why are you in San Diego?*
> Well, I needed to take a job, so I'm here now. It's my first day.

And then he didn't tell me anything more. Come to find out, there's a lady involved.

FIGURE 2.2.3 Derrick Brown, inside the office of the Universal Black Pages/Knowledge Base at Georgia Tech University. Courtesy of Derrick Brown.

So now it all makes sense. But everything that we had is now in my lap. And I said, "Well, in the greater scheme of things, I guess this is what I do."

So I learned. Every part of operations. How to program, that wasn't my thing. I continue that process of reviewing the sites, writing the descriptions and building a database, because that was our capital and that's also my sweet spot of interest. So now the website has almost five thousand links. I just had no idea that there's that much stuff out there about us. Because it's still not that easy to make a webpage in 1996. Not everybody knows how to do it. It's not something people have money to do. I'm interacting every day with people all over the world and I'm smiling on the inside because I'm like, okay, these guys are walking away from all of this.

But I guess the joke was on me. The whole thing got to a point where it was such an overwhelming experience. It's information overload. You've got so much stuff coming at you, and it's all exciting you, it's stimulating you. Your mind's moving in a thousand different directions and creates stress. I was stressed. I was stressed. So I said no. I might be veering too far in this direction, and getting away from knowledge-based directions.

CELEBRITIES OF THE CLOUD

The Persistence and Ephemerality of the Internet

ANGELA M. CIRUCCI, PhD, is an assistant professor of Communication Studies at Rowan University in Glassboro, New Jersey. As a digital media scholar, she analyzes the intersection of institutional practice and user knowledge. Often focusing on identity, Angela has a passion for studying how digital spaces impact the lives of marginalized communities.

There is a tension between the persistence and the ephemerality of the internet.

I am betting you have heard the warning "What you do online lives forever." Or, maybe something more like "Whatever your post on the web stays on the web." These foreboding remarks are often used to teach students about their online reputations, warning them that digital data stick around and could impact their job search or future relationships. Your data are like memes that come back to haunt you. But this is a difficult concept to grasp—in the offline world we do not expect to be tracked as we move through physical spaces and social encounters.

At the same time, however, there is a particular ephemeral, or fleeting, feeling that the internet induces. Unlike static nouns used in early computing—trash can, recycle bin, desktop, mouse—the internet is depicted kinetically using verbs to describe what is possible—we surf, search, post, like, share, and Google.[1] Originally, this was largely because the internet, in a way, is about movement. All data accessed on the internet live somewhere else. Not on your phone, your tablet, or your laptop. Data that make up the text, images, videos, and posts you view are stored on multiple servers, or computers that serve us content, across the world. So, in a way, the internet is always moving to us, around us, through us. That is why the internet is central to the planetary media ecologies we inhabit.

This ephemeral, always shifting, nature is now amplified by contemporary social media platforms that rely on algorithmic renderings, constantly updating what an app user's feed and account display. Every time you pull down an app or refresh a social media site's page, you see something slightly different—a new algorithmically sorted News Feed appears, and posts have gained likes, comments, and shares.

In this reading, I explore the duality of the persistent and ephemeral internet. Analyzing social media, platforms, and celebrity culture, I argue that the persistence of the internet, dichotomously paired with its promise of ephemerality, makes for a new type of celebrity—users who are tracked by, and famous within, "the cloud," and are thus religiously governed by the big digital media companies—Facebook, Google, Apple, Microsoft, and Amazon.

---

1 Denis L. Jamet and Jean Moulin-Lyon, "What Do Internet Metaphors Reveal about the Perception of the Internet," *Metaphorik. de* 18, no. 2 (2010): 17–32.

PERSISTENT WEBS AND EPHEMERAL INTERFACES

In the move from the web-based internet to platforms, content became even more ephemeral. There are no longer unique URLs to take us back to any one moment in time. For example, it used to be that news sites "published" daily issues in the same way that they would release daily newspapers. Nytimes.com had unique URLs—www.nytimes.com/yr/mo/day/front—that allowed users to go back and view a previous issue, just as if they had saved that day's newspaper. In a platform culture, however, this is no longer the case. Previous articles are archived under the dates they were released on NYTimes.com, but changes through the site's platform tools may have been made to the article and the reader would likely never know.[2]

Early social media sites, like Myspace.com, allowed users to directly manipulate their stored data when they would edit profile content, add music to their page, or alter HTML/CSS code to change background and font colors.[3] These early social media sites certainly still privileged the present, but content that was altered and viewed was much more directly linked to the infrastructures, and the servers were where the user data lived. It is also not a coincidence that social media sites like Myspace did not collect data, target-advertise, or show sorted content that trapped users in positive feedback loops, displaying only what it was assumed users "wanted."

TIKTOK EPHEMERALITY

Contemporary social media—TikTok, Facebook, Twitter, Instagram, Snapchat, and so on—are built around the optimistic promises of digital ephemerality. Much of the advertised rhetoric is based in "privacy." In a 2021 Facebook post,[4] driven by data privacy concerns swarming around Facebook,[5] CEO Mark Zuckerberg outlines a more "privacy focused" platform. One of his new principles is "reducing permanence." Most of this section describes only small changes to forward-facing settings that allow users to set content to expire or to archive content. It is unclear which, if any, "cloud" content processes will be changed. Other companies, like Snapchat, have gone so far as to claim design that incorporates "intentional ephemerality"—posts that "disappear" after a chosen length of time. Yet even Snapchat was not completely honest when that company advertised "disappearing data."[6]

However, because platforms represent an automated system that is always shifting, this also means that you can never go back and view what your profile looked like two months ago or two years ago. You cannot go back to before a comment was deleted or before someone unfollowed you. But, perhaps more importantly for the purposes of my argument, there are no actual data at www.facebook.com or www.twitter.com. Just like their app counterparts, they are simply false fronts, skeletons that run platform programs that pull in certain data relevant to the logged-in user at that moment in time.

These platform facades are known as end-user interfaces (EUIs), and they exist to *interface*, or communicate, data to end-users in a way that matches the EUI design. Application programming interfaces (APIs) for developers and advertisers work in a similar manner. Interfaces, with different aesthetics, allow third-party programmers and advertisers to use platform-provided programs to create new applications and to target-advertise. EUIs are, in a way, also APIs. But perhaps users are not seen as having the power to "program" much of anything.

---

2   Using the Wayback Machine, you can see that www.nytimes.com started digitally publishing regularly in February 1999 and moved to a platform-based model—using www.nytimes.com/section/todayspaper only for previous issues—in February 2018.
3   Interestingly, the ability for users to alter profile colors began as a bug. But Myspace developers realized how much users enjoyed the feature, so instead of patching the bug, over time they made the feature increasingly easier to use.
4   Mark Zuckerberg, "A privacy-focused vision for social networking," Facebook.com, 2021, https://www.facebook.com/notes/2420600258234172/.
5   Largely due to the Cambridge Analytica scandal.
6   See, for example, Woodrow Hartzog, "Don't listen to Snapchat's excuses. Security is its job," Wired.com, 2014, https://www.wired.com/2014/10/the-snappening-is-not-your-fault/.

Platforms privilege the present, and time within them is constantly moving forward. They reveal only snapshots in time, ephemera, moments that users can never recover. Like yesterday's TikTok dances, the past seems to slip away quickly and quietly ... until the platform decides how and when the past will come back to you.

YOUR SELECTIVE AND HIDDEN PASTS

The brilliance of contemporary social media is in their ability to tout ephemerality but profit from persistence. The unavailability of past data for end-users at the front end starkly juxtaposes the reliance on metadata—data about data—at the back end. Millions of data points are collected each second, sorted into profiles, and automatically thrown into algorithms that make choices from how to sort a news feed or discover page to how a user may vote in an upcoming election.[7] Via machine learning AI, these data are what allow the platforms to keep moving, to continuously flesh out the skeletons and provide users with the expected app experiences.

To be clear, in a platform society, really no one has direct access to data anymore. Applications are used in nearly every circumstance—sophisticated programs, often automated, that reach into "the cloud" (the servers) and read data as needed. Yes, users are provided with a few tools to make small changes to how data may look at the front end, but users are not privy to any tools that can actually change the platform's infrastructure.

The important point here is that while you as the end-user are meant to always feel some kinetic social media platform experience, you are constantly bombarded with your past selves and provided with very little control of this clandestine persistence. "Privacy" tools are often provided by social media platforms, claiming to assist users with getting their content to only the people with whom the user wants to share. But take note of one important piece—these tools are always relevant to the ephemeral EUI, not the persistent cloud. There are no settings that, like an advertiser or developer API, give end-users real control over all the cloud holds.

Sometimes this uncontrollable persistence is more visible than other features. Timehop and social media features like Facebook's "Memories" flaunt platforms' abilities to design applications that are situated in persistence, oddly contrasting the promise of ephemerality on which they otherwise depend. Facebook's "Memories" became infamous for bringing up traumatic memories of expartners or deceased loved ones. Facebook's response? Not to give end-users more control, but to use platform tools to algorithmically decide which "Memories" posts are likely to conjure up negative emotions and to not display them.

Usually, however, like blocked "Memories" content, the persistence of the cloud is hidden, subtle, and, again, not for end-users to really play any part in. Targeted ads, suggested content, and sorted news feeds bordering on extreme echo chambers are all ways in which persistence reigns in a platform culture. Oddly, platforms are in the business of not collecting *too* much data; limited server space means that designers must know how to sculpt "digital voids," because knowing what data to *exclude* is critical in the development of algorithmic processes.[8] In other words, the tension around the persistence of "the cloud" is not a bug, it is a feature.

How can all this happen with so little public knowledge? It is extremely difficult to imagine the type of persistence "the cloud" provides. In the offline world, there is no expectation that information about us, in our everyday habits and social encounters, persists. It is not common to imagine that the universe is recording our every move and then using these recordings to make decisions that alter our future experience ... unless you do.

---

7   These data include information about pretty much anything you do on or with your phone—as well as data you are not actively contributing, like phone operating system, battery percentage, WiFi connection, and other installed apps.
8   Benjamin N. Jacobsen, "Sculpting Digital Voids: The Politics of Forgetting on Facebook," *Convergence: The International Journal of Research into New Media Technologies* 27, no. 2 (2021): 357–70, https://doi.org/10.1177/1354856520907390.

GODS, CELEBRITIES, AND YOU

For thousands of years, religion has offered the type of persistent, omnipresent force that "the cloud" brings. Whatever God or gods you may (or may not) believe in, a large part of most religions is that a higher being (or beings) is watching over you, remembering you, and perhaps making slight or major alterations to your life's path. This is exactly the purpose of the cloud—to save and process just as much data as necessary to keep platforms functioning and profitable.

In the second edition of *Media Environments*, I argued that social media train us to be our own paparazzi—in effect, "first-person paparazzi"—snapping pictures of ourselves and promoting our narratives with the hopes of gaining the ever-elusive attention exhibited online, validated through likes, follows, shares, comments, and subscribers.[9] This practice was born out of the inescapable celebrity culture in which we live. We look up to celebrities, aspiring to have their fame and conspicuously consuming goods with the hopes of gaining similar attention online.

In fact, some have argued that we entered this celebrity culture because celebrities are like our new gods. This is quite appealing because, unlike traditional gods, celebrities are no longer completely untouchable. They are still far beyond our reach, but they are human and allow us to feel slightly closer to becoming "god-like" ourselves. Additionally, like religion, celebrities distract us from real issues happening across the globe—issues that are particularly terrifying in what many have categorized as our currently post-god world.[10]

When celebrities became our new gods, a sort of reversal took place. While traditional religious gods watch us, we watch celebrities. We take note of what they wear, where they shop, who they are in a relationship with. Books are devoted to narrating their lives and to understanding them. News outlets follow them, updating everyday people on their current situation. We keep a running tab on celebrities, placing their importance in the universe above many others'.

FIRST-PERSON PAPARAZZI

With the arrival of social media platforms, everyday people realized they could become their own "first-person paparazzi" and craft narratives of themselves in extremely public forums. The EUI design of social media literally taps into celebrity culture, fostering a desire, often an unconscious one, to fight for ever more "eyeballs."[11] Platform tools and functionalities teach users that to be authentic is to perform some honest, consistent, corporate self that competes for attention and sacrifices anonymity in the name of visibility, attention, and fame. Social media EUIs are designed literally to support celebrity culture and to lead everyday users to unintentionally brand themselves.[12] This means that we as users are groomed to want other users to watch us and track us just as we watch and track celebrities.

In reality, few actual humans are watching us via the EUI. Maybe a few good friends or family members are keeping up, but these manageable "followers" parallel offline social expectations anyhow. Maybe your posts do show up on public feeds, or maybe not, depending on how much attention your account gets and if sorting algorithms include you in others' feeds. But the one party that is *always* watching is "the cloud." You are a celebrity of the cloud.

9   Angela M. Cirucci, "Social Media as Video Games: How We Act as First Person Paparazzi and Why It Matters," in *Media Environments*, 2nd ed., edited by Barry Vacker (San Diego, CA: Cognella Academic Publishing, 2014), 163–170.
10   Ellis Cashmore, *Celebrity/Culture* (Abingdon-on-Thames, Oxfordshire, UK: Taylor & Francis, 2006), 252.
11   Crystal Abidin, "#In$tagLam: Instagram as a Repository of Taste, a Burgeoning Marketplace, a War of Eyeballs," in *Mobile Media Making in an Age of Smartphones*, edited by Marsha Berry and Max Schleser (New York: Palgrave Pivot, 2014), 119–128.
12   Angela M. Cirucci, "Facebook and Unintentional Celebrification," in *Microcelebrity Around the Globe*, edited by Crystal Abidin and Megan Lindsay Brown (Bingley, UK: Emerald Publishing, 2018).

TWO GRAND ILLUSIONS

Social media platforms provide us with two grand illusions: control over our persistent selves and the ephemeral promise of celebrity.

The first illusion is that social media platforms provide us with a control over our persistent selves that is impossible in the offline world. We can decide we want to reword a post, block certain followers, use photo editors and filters, and so on. And all these pieces also come with the promise of ephemerality, the promise that we can keep performing online, keep working toward crafting some hoped-for identity that seems just too perfect for the offline world. Attainable offline, maybe? But attainable online? Seemingly a quicker path. Social media platforms promise both that we can truly live in the moment and that we have control over how the moment persists.

But this is not entirely how it works. EUIs are applications on top of programs run by algorithms driven by data and metadata living on and moving through "the cloud." As end-users, we actually have very little control over our data, how those data are used, and how others may view us. In addition, the persistence of our data leads to targeted content, biased assumptions, and prejudiced choices made "for us," simply because some machine learning AI said so.[13] Thus, the control still belongs to "the cloud." More specifically, the control belongs to the digital media conglomerates.

The second illusion that social media platforms promise is one of importance, celebrity status, and fame. Because EUI design taps into and makes visible the tropes of celebrity culture, it is easy to believe that using social media leads to, in one way or another, a better, more important, and more attention-deserving self. Through the control promised, users see themselves as their own public relations team or paparazzi, carefully sculpting their identities for mass consumption.

GODS IN THE CLOUD

In reality, it is rare that massive numbers of people see an everyday user's content. Instead, "the cloud" itself is our biggest fan. It is the one party that sees all our content, tracks each of our moves, remembers what we have done, and continues to "personalize" experiences just for us. Our reliance on the cloud reverses the religious model back to a god-centric model wherein one, overarching, omnipresent force knows everything about us, tracks us, and alters our experiences. Just like in the offline world, we have power over our ephemeral selves, but the digital gods—Facebook, Apple, Microsoft, Amazon, and Google—have the true power, the power over persistent identities.

Oddly, my argument here is highlighted by the ways in which loyalty to specific tech companies has become known as "religious" or "cultlike." Often, for example, Apple users buy only Apple products, sticking to the Apple "belief system" and relying on it to guide them through life. Of course, the companies themselves exploit this religious parallel, making it nearly impossible, or at least extremely difficult, to pair hardware and software from competing companies.

Broadly, religion is the idea that there is some persistent layer, some greater power, that tracks all that we do as we move through the offline world. This is exactly the uncanny tension that exists around the persistent and ephemeral internet. We love that we can feel a bit of power over ourselves, but we hate that there is some new omnipresent force that controls cultural norms and presents new "rules" for how to live. Just like the universe, or wherever your god(s) lives, "the cloud" is inaccessible. We cannot destroy it, but we also cannot recover it.

---

13   See, for example, Safiya Umoja Noble, *Algorithms of Oppression: How Search Engines Reinforce Racism* (New York: New York University Press, 2018).

NETWORK (1976)

A brilliant satire and critique of the media spectacle, where news and entertainment merge to produce high ratings, huge profits, and TV terrorists. Perhaps the greatest media film ever, no one is innocent: corporate execs, news anchors, programmers, and the audiences who are "mad as hell and not going to take it anymore."

Director: Sidney Lumet

Starring: Peter Finch, Faye Dunaway, William Holden, and Robert Duvall

QUIZ SHOW (1994)

Based on the real-life "quiz show" scandals of the 1950s, the film offers a powerful critique of the media spectacle and celebrity system, both of which devour the career of a college professor. Who survives the scandal? NBC and television—key forces of the spectacle.

Director: Robert Redford

Starring: Ralph Fiennes and John Turturro

THE TRUMAN SHOW (1998)

Truman Burbank grows up living his entire life inside a vast television studio, where he is the star of the 24/7 reality TV show, *The Truman Show*. Eventually, Truman grows suspicious of his surroundings and makes a break for freedom outside the TV universe. Obviously inspired by Plato's Cave, *The Truman Show* poses a subtle question: who is the real "prisoner"? Is it Truman or the audience gazing upon his daily life?

Director: Peter Weir

Starring: Jim Carrey, Laura Linney, and Ed Harris

THE MATRIX (1999)

Another retelling of Plato's Cave, *The Matrix* borrows from Jean Baudrillard to portray a future in which humans are enslaved to a global computer network, where the mediated world has become the "real world" for everyone except Morpheus and his band of rebel hackers. Note the reference to Baudrillard's book, *Simulacra and Simulation*, which Neo opens to retrieve a computer disk for his late-night visitors. Then, take the red pill and read the book. Or at least read Baudrillard's reading in this chapter.

Director: The Wachowski Brothers

Starring: Laurence Fishburne, Carrie-Anne Moss, and Keanu Reeves

INVICTUS (2009)

Can television and the spectacle unite a country and help overcome apartheid? Nelson Mandela thought so and used the 1995 Rugby World Cup and success of the South African team to unite South Africans in the aftermath of the end of apartheid.

Director: Clint Eastwood

Starring: Morgan Freeman and Matt Damon

MONEY MONSTER (2016)

On a popular TV talk show called "Money Monster," the host gives stock market investment advice to millions of viewers while also dressing like a boxer and grooving with dancers. A disgruntled investor (who lost his life savings) takes over the show and threatens to kill the host live on TV, unless the host explains how billions disappeared from the stock market. Soon the events go viral on social media and the world gazes upon the media spectacle

Director: Jodie Foster

Starring: Julia Roberts and George Clooney

CHAPTER THREE

THE SPECTACLE AND HYPERREALITY
How Technology and Content Generate Our "Realities"
*Barry Vacker and Colby Chase**

COLBY CHASE served as the research assistant for this book. She received her MA in Media Studies from Temple University and her BA in Creative Writing from Emerson College. Her research explores the effects of the consolidation of media ownership, as well as the commercialization of countercultural movements.

"I'M A BELIEVER"

Peter Tork passed away in 2019. Who was Peter Tork? He was a member of "the Monkees," the band that starred in *The Monkees*, the hit TV show from the 1960s. *The Monkees* saw the future coming.

With all the charm and catchy tunes, it is easy to overlook that *The Monkees* (the show) and "the Monkees" (the band) represent a profound shift in contemporary culture and consciousness. *The Monkees* prophesied how TV would come to generate the reality to which the world conforms—*the screen reality of which the world dreams, worships, and becomes.* As media theorist Marshall McLuhan once said, "We become what we behold." Two Monkees songs reached #1 on the *Billboard* Hot 100 charts: "Daydream Believer" and "I'm a Believer." Believers are we all.

"MONKEE MUSIC"

With a name that merged Darwin and pop culture, *The Monkees* was the early-stage evolution of *the simulacrum—* the copy for which there is no original. After all, the Monkees did not exist prior to the TV show, which ran from 1966 to 1968. The Monkees were actors and characters assembled to play a fictitious band invented for the show, a fake band that cranked out hyperreal hits and even toured for a brief period. *The Monkees* won two Emmy Awards and the Monkees sold 75 million records.

In the 2000s, the Monkees toured again, prompting Peter Tork to tell the UK's *Telegraph*, "This is not a band, it's an entertainment operation whose function is Monkee music." Mickey Dolenz added, "It's a misnomer to even call it a group. The Monkees was the cast of a television show. If you approach it with those goggles on, everything just makes so much more sense." Of course, Tork and Dolenz are correct with regard to the music. But *The Monkees* show has a philosophical legacy that permeates popular culture and consciousness—a legacy seen in the power of TV and screens to transform reality into a mirror of television.

MEDIA CONTENT: SIMULACRA AND THE HYPERREAL

Media ecologies, networks, and platforms are technologies within which the content of media are created and replicated. The content of media is all the memes circulating around us and through us, all the images, tweets, selfies, news, podcasts, movies, videos, TV shows, football games, video games, celebrity talk shows, and so on. The list is endless. What happens when this "content" becomes the "reality" it is supposed to represent, when the images of the real substitute for the real?

The Monkees and "the Monkees" show how signs and symbols of the real generate the new real. The Monkees are the simulacra, copies in which the original is not present, no longer desired, no longer even existing, or never existed in the first place. Simulacra fill what Jean Baudrillard called the hyperreal—a world of copies, clones, celebrities, replicas, reproductions, fakes, facades, screens, spectacles, simulations, staged events, social media, and so on.

This world is a hot media hyperreal, filled with hot takes and hotter tribes, all vying for recognition and domination on the stages of staged events, our world of endless entertainment and instant infamy. TV does not merely reflect reality, for reality reflects TV such that *reality and TV are now the same thing*, completely indistinguishable in the 24/7 spectacle of the internet. That's our world today, online and off, the hyperreal world, and *The Monkees* saw it coming, no less than Disneyland, Las Vegas, Hollywood, or Silicon Valley, whose entire *raison d'etre* is to stockpile endless copies of the world and our lives, made by computers and for the screens.

It's no coincidence that *The Monkees* debuted the year before the first Super Bowl, a staged event for TV, now a massive spectacle permeating pop culture and changing the perceived destiny of cities. The hyperreal is the new *real* world, a reality-TV world writ large, leaping from the screens to the streets, to the suburbs, to the skyscrapers, to the highest positions of corporate and political power. The hyperreal extends from the TV screens of 1966 all the way to the reality-TV simulacrum taking the White House in 2016. Across 50 years, America and the world became the believer!

What do we believe? We believe in the spectacle and hyperreality. That's the content of our daily existence. As Christof told a global television audience in *The Truman Show*, "We accept the reality of the world with which we're presented."

THE SOCIETY OF THE SPECTACLE

In Paris in 1967, Guy Debord authored *The Society of the Spectacle*, the seminal book that explains the internal logic and social effects of the spectacle. According to Debord,

> In societies where modern conditions of production prevail, all of life presents itself as an immense accumulation of spectacles. Everything that was directly lived has moved away into a representation.

Hence, the spectacle describes a technological and cultural shift to replace lived experience with representations of lived experience. This shift was primarily facilitated by the advent of screen media—namely, television and film. It now extends all throughout the internet and social and mobile media. Debord argues that screen media divorce the public from their humanity by turning active experience into mediated experience for passive consumption. The spectacle is not merely a way of watching television or scrolling through Twitter; rather, it ultimately becomes a way of thinking and interacting with the world at large. Viewing becomes doing. We become imitators of a mediated life rather than actors in a real life. Or, our real life will be shaped and ordered within our mediated life. In the spectacle, viewing is as powerful as doing. In fact, viewing *is* doing, perfectly illustrated by video games, sports fandom, and celebrity worship.

Debord believes that the spectacle will swell larger and larger and ultimately absorb all facets of lived experience, while colonizing consciousness with the endless glowing images. The spectacle will become the primary means that the public uses to understand all things political, economic, social, cultural, and artistic. This shift is evident in a screen culture that represents the world through stylized visuals and sleek narrative devices, which problematically makes entertainment the norm for representing even serious and social and intellectual issues. From the moment that senator John F. Kennedy looked dashing on television in 1960 and won the election, the electronic media spectacle has steadily expanded its domain to encompass political consciousness in America and elsewhere. This includes the election system and entertainment culture that produced the following people as president: a B-movie actor and TV host (Ronald Reagan), a Major League Baseball team owner (George W. Bush), and a reality-TV star and beauty pageant owner (Donald Trump).

For nearly a decade before the publication of *Society of the Spectacle*, Debord had been affiliated with collectives such as the Situationist International, which was concerned with renegotiating the relationship between art, technology, and the public. Considering art from a top-down approach allows us to think about it as being something that a select few are given the resources to produce, while the rest of us are destined to be mere spectators and consumers. In the production systems of Hollywood, a select few executives, producers, directors, screenwriters, and actors are given the money and opportunity necessary to produce multimillion-dollar films, such as *Interstellar* and *Star Wars: The Force Awakens*. In general, these films represent the ideas and motivations of the select few and are distributed across the country and globe. The rest of us are tasked with merely being the audience of ticket buyers and overpriced-popcorn munchers. Of course, we can buy or stream the movies via Amazon and Netflix or perhaps download bootleg copies from BitTorrent or other sites.

For Debord, individuals can reclaim their agency by denouncing art as a product to be viewed on the screen and instead considering art as something that should be lived in daily life. Entertainment is derived from real life, and according to this logic, screen culture takes lived experience and makes it unidimensional. There are several means through which the spectacle takes hold:

> **Images:** Television and film are visual media, which means that these modes can effectively captivate audiences only by transforming the vibrancy of lived experience into images that convey lived experience to audiences.
>
> **Distraction:** Consider, when you tune in your television, all of the other things you are tuning out: your thoughts, ambitions, relationships, politics, and general engagement with the world around you. The spectacle is a means to make audiences passive and complacent.
>
> **Entertainment:** Bright lights, loud music, computer-generated imagery, professional actors with wardrobe specialists and teams of hair stylists and makeup designers. The media does not present real life; it presents to us a heightened, glamorous type of life meant to dazzle us and keep us as interested viewers. The spectacle is a representation of this life. The only way to combat and negotiate the spectacle is to reimagine how we spend our leisure and intellectual time.

LIFE IMITATES MEDIA

Given the amount of time we spend with ego-media, it follows that as a society we would internalize the logic of each medium. As Marshall McLuhan explains, each medium massages our consciousness to accept its messages. A mind massaged by the spectacle will come to embrace the spectacle, uncritically and often with love and awe.

The spectacle describes how modes of entertainment have become the means to understand lived experience. The more we become accustomed to being audience members, the more we identify as members of an audience and, ultimately, the more the logic of the entertainment spectacle becomes the primary means through which we engage with the physical world. We begin to crave amusement and entertainment.

Still not sold on the idea that the spectacle and screens shape your life? Then consider the narrative function of social networks. The Facebook timeline allows us to tell our story the way we want it to be told. By creating a chronology of our lives, the timeline allows us to tell our life stories using all the familiar plot devices of the literary and film traditions: the story begins at birth, and updates about new friends or relationship details serve as minor plot arcs through our stay on the network. Even adding pictures and updating statuses allows us to characterize ourselves in whatever manner we desire. We are audiences for our own lives and the lives of others. Without audiences giving us "likes" for our daily activities, we may feel sad, lonely, or less worthy.

To counter these feelings, we arm ourselves with personal cameras and digital recording devices. These allow us to represent ourselves as the bodies on the screen, ready for the gaze of the audience and ourselves. The popularity of these devices is evident in the fact that they are standard features in cell phones and computers, and they indicate our willingness to climb inside the spectacle. Home editing equipment like Photoshop, Final Cut, or the filters on Instagram allow us to present stylized versions of ourselves, using the technologies of the spectacle to present ourselves as glamorously as our onscreen idols.

Perhaps the old saying "life imitates art" needs a status update. For the age of the spectacle, the new maxim is "life imitates media." For many, *life* is media. This is the ego-media spectacle inside the *Black Mirror* episodes "Fifteen Million Merits" and "Nosedive."

THE SPECTACLE SHAPES OUR ECONOMY AND SOCIETY

The spectacle is exploited by capitalism, corporations, advertisers, politicians, religions, televangelists, pseudo-scientists, conspiracy theorists, and world militaries. The goal is to make a profit and accrue power by generating viewers and seducing consumers and citizens into buying products, cultural values, lifestyle choices, political candidates, evidence-free belief systems, and endless wars. Major corporations and institutions use branding tactics to get customers to remember their names even without selling any particular product. This explains why logos are everywhere. Perhaps there's a logo on your clothes or baseball cap right now. If so, are you a walking billboard? Did you get paid for wearing that message? Or did you pay for the privilege of wearing someone else's message? Have you internalized the logic of the spectacle?

What about your tattoos? Have you converted your skin into a screen for displaying images? Are tattoos the way people participate in the spectacle? In a society of spectacle, are tattoos a way for people to show their tribal affiliation, brand themselves, or advertise their mating possibilities?

In "Media Culture and the Triumph of the Spectacle," Douglas Kellner examines the impact of the spectacle on American popular culture.[1] Media products are vehicles for the transmission of social values and are therefore specific to the historical moment and culture in which they were created. Thus, a television show is not simply a good way to kill a half hour; instead, it is a representation of a society's dominant fears, goals, values, norms, ambitions, prejudices, behavior, and identity. Kellner also uses the spectacle to explain trends in politics, fashion, architecture, technology, and, ultimately, every facet of society. The sheer scale of the spectacle could make it an overwhelming concept to critique and deconstruct. Kellner takes a more optimistic approach, however, arguing that understanding how messages are constructed empowers us to be smarter critics of media and have keener eyes to decode the world around us.

What could be happening just below the surface that could account for the popularity of televised sports? What values are explored through sports? Conquest, competition, and cooperation: the games simulate tribal conquest, while the passion of competition is a stand-in for Darwinian evolution, and the cooperation and "game plans" mirror the cooperative planning that humans must do to survive as individuals and as a species. Individual greatness: the fans celebrate the players' athletic skills, hard work, and quick thinking. The athletes become heroes, local gods for local fans. Of course, when athletes cause a team to lose, the fans turn on them with boos and jeers, transforming the athletes from gods to goats. Global events such as the Olympics and the

---

1 Douglas Kellner, "Media Culture and the Triumph of the Spectacle," https://pages.gseis.ucla.edu/faculty/kellner/essays/mediaculturetriumphspectacle.pdf.

World Cup are celebrations of nationalism, patriotism, local cultures, and technological pageantry. For people who may have grown up playing sports or watching sports with their families, there are elements of nostalgia and intergenerational celebration.

THE HUNGER GAMES AND DALLAS COWBOYS STADIUM

One of the most spectacular scenes in *The Hunger Games: Catching Fire* is when Katniss (Jennifer Lawrence) and Peeta (Josh Hutcherson) enter the massive stadium in a chariot, with flames emerging from the back of their striking black uniforms. Of course, these uniforms are not unlike the sleek black fashions often worn by the rebels in *The Matrix*. The crowd erupts upon seeing the spectacle of Katniss and Peeta, the fire symbolizing District 12, home to coal miners and a key energy source for Panem. In this clever scene, *The Hunger Games* points us toward understanding our fourth media model: hyperreality.

In *The Hunger Games: Catching Fire*, we see how the spectacle evolves into hyperreality in much the same way that memes and temes evolve. You might also think of hyperreality as the spectacle on steroids. Hyperreality is where the signs and symbols of the real have replaced the real, thus creating an artificial reality that consumers and users consider superior to the real reality. Hyperreality is not merely a "fake reality," for it exists in many forms: theme parks, hotels in Las Vegas, football stadiums, virtual reality, and video games; even Facebook and much of social media can be understood in terms of hyperreality. To paraphrase Jean Baudrillard, hyperreality is more real than real, more true than true, more beautiful than beautiful.

Like Delos in *Westworld* and the TV studio in *The Truman Show*, the stadium in *The Hunger Games* is a simulacrum (a copy where the original is no longer present) of the stadiums one might have found in ancient Rome, sites of gladiatorial battles that entertained the masses, very much like football in America. We could say the same about the more popular kind of "football" (what Americans call "soccer") played around the world. In all team sports, teams have names that reflect the memes and traditions from their territory on our planet. In Panem's District 12, the black uniforms and flames signify coal and energy. In Texas, the silver helmet and single blue star signify the Dallas Cowboys.

COWBOY SIMULACRA

The Dallas Cowboys are the simulacrum for real cowboys, who once existed and became part of American mythology but are no longer present in industrialized cities like Dallas. Of course, there are still many guys wearing big cowboy hats, big belt buckles, and big boots and driving big trucks in the big state of Texas, but they are not real cowboys. Such urban and suburban cowboys illustrate the power of memes while showing how the spectacle and hyperreality have permeated our consciousness and society. In Texas and elsewhere, there are few real cowboys or cowgirls but many hyperreal cowboys and cowgirls.

Completed in 2009, Cowboys Stadium (now branded as "AT&T Stadium") is a monumental steel-and-glass cavern. It is the largest domed stadium in the world. In addition to football games, there are rock concerts and other spectacles; music performances have included U2, George Strait, and Paul McCartney, whose concert was the first event in the stadium. Like all stadiums, Cowboys Stadium serves the celebrity system. The many (the fans) watch the few (the players, cheerleaders, and musicians). Plus, the wealthy and nouveau riche get to view the game and concerts from the exclusive luxury suites, just like the royalty in *Gladiator* and the corporate elite in *Rollerball*, the overlooked 1975 film that anticipated many major trends in media and sports. *Rollerball* also showed how professional team sports is a powerful form of social control powered by television and disposable athlete-heroes.

Even while attending a game in Cowboys Stadium, you can also watch it on high-definition television screens. Mounted above the playing field is a massive flat-screen TV, sixty yards long and shining *very* brightly with thirty million LEDs (See "Welcome to the Desert of the Red Pill" in this chapter). It's the largest and brightest screen at any athletic venue, though some team is likely to top it in the future. Running throughout the stadium are three thousand flat screens of varying sizes that are mounted everywhere you look. It's like attending a football game in Times Square. The architecture of the stadium is very sleek and somewhat futuristic, looking like a spacecraft (especially when aglow at night) sitting next to the original Six Flags theme park, which was built in 1961, just six years after Disneyland.

So, the new stadium features football in Times Square inside a spacecraft, all sitting next to a theme park! Welcome to hyperreality.

With a screen that is 60 percent the size of the playing field, it ought to be obvious that the map is overtaking the territory. Yet even the football field itself is a map, with lines marking the territories of each team, highlighted by the colors in the end zone—an end zone that signals not only where a touchdown is scored but also the end of the "reality" that is the field. With football and many other sports, the map has far exceeded the territory.

So what's happening in Cowboys Stadium? Just take the media virus, the spectacle, and the hyperreal, combine them with Moore's Law, and add one hundred thousand fans wearing team jerseys watching on television the action that is happening right in front of them, and you've got it! That's NFL and college football. The meme of territorial conquest is simulated in a hyperreal environment, experienced as a spectacle by the tribes of fans. The map is the territory. Beginning in 2013, AT&T now spends almost $25 million per year for the naming rights for the stadium, but that does not change any of these conditions. In fact, it only illustrates the corporate and cultural immersion into hyperreality.

THE "VALUE" OF THE DALLAS COWBOYS

A reality-TV star was president of the United States from 2017 to 2021. That's a fact. Regardless of your political views, it is important to realize that Donald Trump's election was not an anomaly or an aberration—it's symbolic of a longer and deeper trajectory in America's ego-media consciousness.

Consider the case of Jerry Jones, the owner of the Dallas Cowboys. The Dallas Cowboys football team is worth $5.5 billion, making it the most valuable sports franchise in the world. Jones purchased the Cowboys for $140 million in 1989, which is the equivalent of $295 million in 2021. The Cowboys promptly won three Super Bowls by 1996, primarily because Jimmy Johnson (the first coach that Jones hired) built a powerhouse team.

Since then, the Cowboys have won two playoff games and have not sniffed a Super Bowl. Jerry Jones has been the owner and general manager the entire time. Yet, despite such a colossal failure, the Cowboys franchise has skyrocketed in value all the way to the top. How can continual failure still generate rewards in the billions of dollars?

The answer (in large part) is the spectacle and hyperreality, where you can go twenty-five years without winning a Super Bowl. Those facts hit your hot button? Don't forget the power of memes, while also realizing the seductive allure of the spectacle and hyperreality. In the spectacle and hyperreality, no one has to be competent at anything except making promises and entertaining the echo chambers packed with true believers, also known as fans, friends, and followers. Just ask Jerry Jones, one of the kings of *The Matrix*.[2] The same is true for Q and many other celebs and politicians.

Like the Monkees, Jean Baudrillard saw it coming.

---

2   Recall the near-complete collapse of the Texas power grid during the major winter storm in February 2021. Millions of Texans were without power for several days, amid a massive ice storm, with temperatures between zero and twenty degrees. Jerry Jones is the major shareholder in a natural gas company that price-gouged Texans during the crisis, raising prices by 600 percent to 7,500 percent over precrisis levels. See Michael Rosenberg, "As Texas Freezes, Jerry Jones Does What He Always Does," *Sports Illustrated*, February 18, 2021. Jones's moral bankruptcy drew widespread media criticism, inside and outside of Texas, but I bet very few Cowboys fans in Texas will turn their back on cheering for the Cowboy simulacra. Like Monkees fans, they are believers.

NEO'S BOOK IN *THE MATRIX*

Since we humans first peered out of our caves, we have sought to represent the world to ourselves via art, language, symbols, architecture, metamemes, media technologies, models of the universe, and so on. With cave paintings, there is a simple and direct relation between representation and reality, as shown in Werner Herzog's *Cave of Forgotten Dreams*. Hidden in a cave for thirty thousand years, these cave paintings are astonishing and powerful works of art. Over time, every era or age creates new methods and models to represent the world, from paintings to movies to video games and virtual realities. For Jean Baudrillard, the way we represent the world to ourselves has evolved over time, changing with the technologies of the eras and increasing exponentially in complexity such that representations of reality have become the reality. *Think of it this way: The maps have overtaken the territories.*

In the *Matrix* trilogy, there is only one book shown, and it is in Neo's apartment. Early in the *The Matrix*, Neo (Keanu Reeves) opens a dark green book called *Simulacra and Simulation*; the book is a hollowed shell containing computer disks and other items. In that scene, the Wachowskis are referencing the key book of media philosopher Jean Baudrillard, the main theorist of "hyperreality." The second reading in this chapter is a brief excerpt from *Simulacra and Simulation*, where we see the origins of Morpheus's line "Welcome to the desert of the real" and the concept of "maps overtaking territories." In this chapter, you get to read the key passages from Neo's book in *The Matrix*. How cool is that?

HYPERREALITY: WHERE MAPS OVERTAKE TERRITORIES

In *Simulacra and Simulation*, Baudrillard argues that the "real world" has largely disappeared from consciousness, having been displaced by models, copies, and simulations—what Baudrillard terms the "hyperreality" now indistinguishable from the original reality being displaced. This is the cumulative effect of Disneyland, Hollywood, television, social media, and the proliferation of electronic media. On the first page of Neo's book, Baudrillard writes (as if anticipating the power of Facebook and social media) this:

> Today abstraction is no longer that of the map, the double, the mirror, or the concept. Simulation is no longer that of a territory, a referential being, or a substance. It is the generation by models of a real without origin or reality: a hyperreal. The territory no longer precedes the map, nor does it survive it. It is nevertheless that map that precedes the territory. ... The real is produced from miniaturized cells, matrices, and memory banks, models of control—and it can be reproduced an indefinite number of times from these. ... It is no longer a question of imitation, nor duplication, nor even parody. It is a question of substituting the signs of the real for the real.[3]

In effect, Baudrillard is saying that electronic media have departed on their own trajectory of reprogramming or reproducing the world, as embodied in the world of Disneyland and Cowboys Stadium. We like to think of media as *maps* for our world, as suggested by Google Maps and by Facebook status updates. But, in many ways, the situation is reversed—*the media maps are generating the territories to which our culture and consciousness conform.* Rather than represent reality, the media, Hollywood, and Disneyland anticipate and generate reality. The real and the fictional are no longer dualities but rather cloned models in an endless series of reproduction, thus blurring distinctions between the fictional and the authentic—between the symbol and what it stands for. *We live in a world where the signs and symbols of the real have largely replaced the real.* That's the real meaning of Disneyland and Cowboys Stadium in our mediated culture and consciousness. The maps have replaced the territory; the maps are the territory. *That's how we got a reality-TV star as president.*

---

3   Jean Baudrillard, *Simulacra and Simulation* (Ann Arbor: University of Michigan Press, 1994), 1–2.

Hyperreality and simulacra do not refer to simplistic illusions that do not exist, for they can be very real things. Once you grasp the concept of hyperreality and the simulacrum, you will see that they are everywhere in our society, often being the very things we consider most real. After all, the Super Bowl is one giant hyperreality, yet it is watched as if it is the realest and most important thing in our part of the Milky Way.

Times Square, Disneyland, Cowboys Stadium, and the Super Bowl are all microcosms of the hyperreality first theorized by Jean Baudrillard. In fact, Baudrillard is sort of hyperreal himself, kind of like Plato and Marshall McLuhan on steroids, with some occasional Jean-Paul Sartre as his energy drink to wash it down. That helps explain why Baudrillard is a controversial and complex thinker whose explanations of the hyperreal are often vague or obscure. For many people, the concept of the hyperreal might be the most difficult media model to understand. Yet if you're a fan of *Black Mirror*, then you can see variations on hyperreality in "Fifteen Million Merits," "Nosedive, "Playtest," "White Christmas," "USS Callister," and, finally, "San Junipero," which is one of the most popular and hopeful episodes in the series.

One of Baudrillard's essential memes is that much of hyperreality is a hollow world of surfaces, facades, and replicas: a world of reproductions, of cloned realities, of mediated existence. If we think of media as maps, then the media maps have overtaken the territories of reality. Better yet, the maps are generating the territories as a substitute reality. Consider how many hours people spend in front of electronic screens, supposedly to put their lives and reality in order. If the screens are maps and we spend most of our time staring at the screens, then hasn't the map become the territory? Aren't the proliferating maps generating the territory? Isn't this condition perfectly exemplified by Times Square, Disneyland, Las Vegas, Facebook, TikTok, the NFL, Jerry Jones, President Trump, and the QAnon conspiracy theories?[4]

THE SELF-DRIVING SPECTACLE

The self-driving automobile is another example of how our lives are transformed under the imperatives of the spectacle and hyperreality. Sure, we're told that self-driving cars are safer and less likely to be involved in an accident, thus reducing insurance costs. At least, that is what we're told. An extension of our feet, the automobile was once a symbol for freedom and autonomy—two of the key traits that contributed to the evolution of the human species as it migrated around the world. Mobility was essential to the survival of our species, from walking to riding horses and on stagecoaches, to driving in cars and traveling in trains and planes. What made the horse and car unique is that we were in individually in control. While driving a car, especially on the open highway, one was actually using the car as a technological expression of will, mobility, and autonomy.

The self-driving car ends that experience and converts the car into a media environment, where "driving" and traveling become an entertainment and consumer experience. After all, won't our eyes be glued to screens while Apple and Google track us and shapes our experience as they direct us and sell to us? Consider the insights of Matthew Crawford:

> Arguably, the first and fatal development was that cars became boring to drive, starting in the 1990s.... With no shifter and no clutch, you don't really feel that you are *doing* anything. This lack of involvement is exacerbated by features that partially automate the task, such as cruise control. Nor, with GPS navigation, are you much required to notice your surroundings, and to actively convert what you see into an evolving mental picture of your route. Between the quiet

---

4   I will be frank: If your mind has been colonized by the memes of Q, then there is likely nothing I can write that will open your mind to the power of memes and the seductions of spectacle and hyperreality, the very ecologies in which you are immersed. QAnon is discussed in appendix C.

smoothness, the passivity, and the sense of being carried for by some surrounding entity you can't quite identify, driving a modern car is a bit like returning to the womb.

The smartphone arrived in 2007. Now we had something to keep boredom at bay while getting around in the new manner, and it proved irresistible. This irresistibility became a new business model in Silicon Valley: harvesting and selling our attention. This is not hard to do when the road is a distant and dimly felt thing, as it is when one is serenely cocooned in four thousand pounds of plushness. The windshield begins to seem like one more screen, and it cannot compete with the dopamine candy offered on the other screens. So now Silicon Valley is going to solve the problem of distracted driving that it helped create, by removing us from the driver's seat. ...

We catch a glimpse of one possible future in the animated film WALL-E, in which we see ... people ferried about a hovering grid in their car-like pods. Finally relieved of the burden of paying attention to their surroundings, they slurp from enormous cup holders and gaze raptly at their screens, untroubled by the overdetermination of their world. Their faces beam, in a slackened sort of way, with the opiate pleasure of novelties piped into their cockpit from afar. These beings are safe and content, and somehow less than human.[5]

Though Crawford does not use the terms "spectacle" or "hyperreality," that is the world he is describing. Championed by Google, Elon Musk, governments, politicians, and just about every techie "futurist" in the world, the self-driving car represents "progress" only on a hyperreal highway that passes through Disneyland, Times Square, and Las Vegas, all charted by GPS, Facebook, Instagram, and other social media platforms. Driving, freedom, and autonomy will be reduced to mere simulacra while the maps obliterate the territories and effect the physical devolution of the human species. Welcome to *WALL-E* and *The Matrix*.

IS THERE A RED PILL?

In a poetic and powerful scene in *The Matrix*, the rebel-philosopher Morpheus offers Neo a "red pill." If swallowed, it will allow one to liberate or transform oneself to see the "Matrix" for what it is—a system of illusion to keep society under control and disconnected from empirical reality. The Matrix separates us from the authentic real world, from our authentic real selves, and from each other as individual members of the collective human species, all in a shared journey on a tiny planet in a vast and awe-inspiring universe. As explained in the reading "Welcome to the Desert of the Red Pill," red pills have proliferated among rebel simulacra, like copies of copies of copies, just as Baudrillard would have predicted. Is there a true red pill? Is there an exit?

In the reading "Hope and Identity in the Hyperreal: *The Matrix* and 'San Junipero,'" Meesh Cosares offers an optimistic take on how the trans narrative in *The Matrix* can empower marginalized peoples to confront systems of inequality and injustice. As explained by codirector Lilly Wachowski, *The Matrix* symbolized a "trans narrative" in a "world that wasn't quite ready for it yet" in 1999.[6] No doubt *The Matrix* and "red pill" inspired possibilities for personal transformation, cultural empowerment, and philosophical enlightenment, as is often symbolized by the best of science fiction. The key is to make sure the maps and territories actually contribute to a more just, fair, equal, sane, and sustainable society—*situated in the actual territory*! All of this takes passion, courage, and long-term effort.

---

5   Matthew B. Crawford, *Why We Drive: Toward a Philosophy of the Open Road* (New York: William Morrow, 2020), 5–6.
6   Netflix Film Club, "Why *The Matrix* Is a Trans Story According to Lilly Wachowski" (Interview), YouTube, August 4, 2020.

In his more radical texts, Baudrillard suggests there is no exit, no red pill. That's because the real or authentic reality is no longer accessible, no longer existing outside our mediated perceptions. The remaining "real" realities, if they exist, reside in "the desert of the real," those natural deserts that exist far outside the metropolises, or maybe in the cultural deserts that exist in the fissures within the metropolises. This is *imperfectly* illustrated when Morpheus says to Neo, "Welcome to the desert of the real," and both are situated next to a rocky landscape, next to a smoldering metropolis, all inside a TV reality. *The Matrix* is a metaphor for living in our 24/7 media ecologies, the hyperreality of everyday life. We do not have to be literally plugged in to a computer network and living in a gooey pod to be in "the Matrix." Spending ten or more hours a day gazing into our electronic screens seems close enough to *The Matrix*, especially if we have little understanding of the world outside the media.

The reading "Welcome to the Desert of the Red Pill" shows that there are many levels of meaning for *The Matrix* and "red pills" in America, some of them philosophically hopeful and liberating, though the overall hyperreal condition we inhabit is very dystopian. Amid the shreds of reality there are glimmers of hope, even as "Red Pill America" remains suspended in the night sky, hovering above the desert of the real, held aloft by the light beams radiating out from Hollywood, Las Vegas, and Silicon Valley.

SCIENCE IN THE SPECTACLE AND HYPERREALITY

If there are red pills, science is one of them, along with evidence-based thinking and worldviews and philosophies anchored in the existence that surrounds us. Can science-based media and programming flourish in hyperreality and the 24/7 media spectacle? After all, Carl Sagan's documentary series *Cosmos: A Personal Voyage* (1980) and Neil deGrasse Tyson's reboot of it, *Cosmos: A Spacetime Odyssey* (2014), were monumental efforts to use television to present a scientific account of the universe to viewers around the world.

According to the *New York Times*, *Cosmos: A Spacetime Odyssey* received the largest rollout for a series in television history. Created by Tyson, Ann Druyan (widow of Carl Sagan), and Seth MacFarlane (creator of *Family Guy*), the *Cosmos* reboot aired in one hundred seventy countries and forty-five languages.[7] The opening episode aired on March 9, 2014, on ten networks simultaneously, including Fox, FX, and National Geographic. At the beginning of the opening episode, US president Barack Obama offered viewers this introduction:

> America has always been a nation of fearless explorers, who dreamed bigger and reached farther than others imagined. That's the spirit of discovery that Carl Sagan captured in the original *Cosmos*. Today, we're doing everything we can to bring that same sense of possibility to a new generation, because there are new frontiers to explore and we need Americans eager to explore them. There are no limits. So open your eyes and open your imagination. The next great discovery could be yours.[8]

Any assessment of the size of the audience shows some good news and some less-than-good news. The good news: the opening episode reached about 5.8 million viewers on Fox and about 8 million total viewers across all ten networks, while Fox hoped to reach 40 million worldwide.[9] A count of 8 million is fabulous compared to the

---

7   Dennis Overbye, "A Successor to Sagan Reboots *Cosmos*," *New York Times*, March 3, 2014, website accessed June 10, 2017.

8   "President Obama's COSMOS Introduction | Cosmos: A Spacetime Odyssey," *National Geographic*, YouTube, March 9, 2014.

9   Scott Collins, "Neil deGrasse Tyson's 'Cosmos' Ratings Not So Stellar on Fox," *Los Angeles Times*, March 10, 2014, website accessed March 24, 2014; Michael O'Connell, "TV Ratings: Fox's 'Cosmos' Pulls 8.5 Million Viewers Across 10 Networks," *Hollywood Reporter*, March 10, 2014, website accessed April 20, 2014.

ratings of the Science Channel, which attracts an average of 284,000 viewers in prime time. The less-than-good news: *Cosmos* was not able to retain the audience from the first episode.

During the thirteen episodes broadcast on Fox in 2014, *Cosmos* lost almost 50 percent of the viewers from the first week. This means that 98–99 percent of Americans chose not to view the series on Fox. Only 1 percent tuned in for the final episode. Surely, the audience will grow with the repeat airings on the National Geographic Channel and online access via Hulu, Amazon, and the *Cosmos* site.

Judging by the ratings and the echo chamber of tweets, the series was largely ignored by most everyone except the science geeks or those people who already embrace a scientific account of the universe. Just think: the most heavily promoted popular science education program in *human history* is ignored by 98–99 percent of the citizens in the nation in which it was produced. Tyson led the creation of a second series, *Cosmos: Possible Worlds* (2020), but it was promoted with far less fanfare than *Cosmos: A Spacetime Odyssey*.

None of this is the fault of Tyson, Druyan, or MacFarlane. The low ratings are an indictment of America, its failing science education, and the echo chambers and pseudoscientific hyperrealities provided by Hollywood and the internet (for more, see the discussion of "Media and Pseudoscience" in appendix B). Outside of a few films and the *Cosmos* series, Hollywood and the news media have not tried very hard to increase scientific literacy and enlighten the populace. There is but one channel in America devoted to science: the Science Channel. And even it has abundant infotainment and "science" shows filled with pseudoscience and various antics, such as the series *Outrageous Acts of Science*. Hollywood and mainstream television would rather crank out an endless supply of movies and TV shows catering to every paranormal and pseudoscientific belief. Recent examples include *Ghost Hunters*, *House on Haunted Hill*, *Reincarnation*, *Hereafter*, *Dead Famous*, *Celebrity Ghost Stories*, *Resurrection*, and *Psychic Kids: Children of the Paranormal*. The proliferation of these shows helps explain why there were so few viewers for *Cosmos*. Welcome to hyperreality and Plato's Cave.

PLATO'S CAVE

In a philosophical sense, *The Matrix* is a retelling of Plato's Cave. So are Guy Debord's *Society of the Spectacle* and Jean Baudrillard's *Simulacra and Simulation*. In Plato's epic allegory, the prisoners were forced to view the shadows and images on the wall, shadows caused by sunlight and fires outside the cave entrance. They were unable to exit and discover the real reality outside the cave. Even when a freed prisoner returns to tell them about the real reality, they do not believe it, for the freed prisoner appears as just another shadow on the wall.[10] Of course, this is a metaphor for our current mediated hyperreality. Yet, Plato's allegory also illustrates why it is much easier to fool people than to show them that they have been fooled. To show them they have been fooled requires them to confront the shadows in their minds, so it is much easier to just incorporate the truth-teller into their shadow reality. Should we be surprised that supporters of QAnon are winning elections in America?

In *The Truman Show* (1998), Peter Weir updates Plato's cave for hyperreal conditions, where Truman Burbank (Jim Carrey) inhabits a "reality" that exists entirely within a massive TV studio. His territory is entirely on the map. Truman (the true man of television) might have escaped his hyperreality at the end of the movie, though it is not 100 percent certain. But what is clear is that the viewers merely changed channels, remaining prisoners on the map of television, still wedded to the hyperreal consciousness. As the maps proliferate, is there an exit, an outside territory that can be accessed? As for Truman, he had spent his entire life in a mediated universe customized to him.

---

10   There is a great claymation version of Plato's Cave on YouTube (search: "The Cave: An Adaptation of Plato's Allegory in Clay").

BILLIONS OF "TRUMAN SHOWS"—INCLUDING YOURS

How is Plato's Cave or *The Truman Show* any different than your Facebook, Twitter, or TikTok feeds? Powered by algorithms that send you links that echo your worldview, social media platforms make possible billions of daily Truman Shows, billions of echo chambers, billions of maps generating territories, billions of caves with shadows dancing on the screens. Social media firms get rich while you click ever deeper into hyperreality. No wonder QAnon has millions of followers, even though none of its predictions ever come close to being true. No wonder Americans and most of the world cannot even agree on the basic facts of reality. Our common territories and shared destinies are being obliterated by the billions of hot media maps, all designed to make us feel like champs of *The Matrix*, stars of our daily Truman Shows.

Variations on the Cave abound in films about media and culture: *Money Monster*, *The Circle*, *The Hunger Games*, *Wag the Dog*, *Quiz Show*, *eXistenZ*, *Fight Club*, *Vanilla Sky*, *V for Vendetta*, *Waking Life*, and the classics like *Ace in the Hole*, *Fahrenheit 451*, *Westworld*, and *Network*. In many ways, the hyperreal model is a postmodern spin on Plato's Cave. Hyperreality was central to making possible a reality-TV star as president—the presidential simulacrum worshipped and despised across America. You can bet that more celebrities, media moguls, movie stars, and various other kinds of "stars" will seek the presidency in the future. Should we be surprised that Matthew McConaughey is considering (as of this writing) a run for governor of Texas?[11]

---

11   Marianne Garvey, "Matthew McConaughey is Considering a Texas Governor Run," *CNN*, March 12, 2021.

THE PRECESSION OF SIMULACRA

from *Simulacra and Simulation*

JEAN BAUDRILLARD (1929–2007) was a French sociologist and cultural theorist. Author of numerous books on media and culture, his most famous work is *Simulacra and Simulation*—the mysterious green book opened by Neo in *The Matrix*.

The simulacrum is never what hides the truth—it is truth that hides the fact that there is none.

The simulacrum is true.

— *Ecclesiastes*

If once we were able to view the Borges fable in which, the cartographers of the Empire draw up a map so detailed that it ends up covering the territory exactly (the decline of the Empire witnesses the fraying of this map, little by little, and its fall into ruins, though some shreds are still discernible in the deserts—the metaphysical beauty of this ruined abstraction testifying to a pride equal to the Empire and rotting like a carcass, returning to the substance of the soil, a bit as the double ends by being confused with the real through aging)—as the most beautiful allegory of simulation, this fable has now come full circle for us, and possesses nothing but the discrete charm of second-order simulacra.[1]

Today abstraction is no longer that of the map, the double, the mirror, or the concept. Simulation is no longer that of a territory, a referential being, or a substance. It is the generation by models, of a real without origin or reality: a hyperreal. The territory no longer precedes the map, nor does it survive it. It is nevertheless the map that precedes the territory—*precession of simulacra*—that engenders the territory, and if one must return to the fable, today it is the territory whose shreds slowly rot across the extent of the map. It is the real, and not the map, whose vestiges persist here and there in the deserts that are no longer those of the Empire, but ours. *The desert of the real itself.*

In fact, even inverted, Borges's fable is unusable. Only the allegory of the Empire, perhaps, remains. Because it is with this same imperialism that present-day simulators attempt to make the real, all of the real, coincide with their models of simulation. But it is no longer a question of either maps or territories. Something has disappeared: the sovereign difference, between one and the other, that constituted the charm of abstraction. Because it is difference that constitutes the poetry of the map and the charm of the territory the magic of the concept and the charm of the real. This imaginary of representation, which simultaneously culminates in and is engulfed by the cartographer's mad project of the ideal coextensivity of map and territory, disappears in the simulation whose operation is nuclear and genetic, no longer at all specular or discursive. It is all of metaphysics that is lost. No more mirror of being and appearances, of the real and its concept. No more imaginary coextensivity: it is genetic miniaturization

---

1 Cf. J. Baudrillard, "L'ordre des simulacres" (The order of simulacra), in *L'échange symbolique et la mort* (Symbolic exchange and death) (Paris: Gallimard, 1976).

that is the dimension of simulation. The real is produced from miniaturized cells, matrices, and memory banks, models of control—and it can be reproduced an indefinite number of times from these. It no longer needs to be rational, because it no longer measures itself against either an ideal or negative instance. It is no longer anything but operational. In fact, it is no longer really the real, because no imaginary envelops it anymore. It is a hyperreal, produced from a radiating synthesis of combinatory models in a hyperspace without atmosphere.

By crossing into a space whose curvature is no longer that of the real, nor that of truth, the era of simulation is inaugurated by a liquidation of all referentials—worse: with their artificial resurrection in the systems of signs, a material more malleable than meaning, in that it lends itself to all systems of equivalences, to all binary oppositions, to all combinatory algebra. It is no longer a question of imitation, nor duplication, nor even parody. It is a question of substituting the signs of the real for the real, that is to say of an operation of deterring every real process via its operational double, a programmatic, metastable, perfectly descriptive machine that offers all the signs of the real and short-circuits all its vicissitudes. Never again will the real have the chance to produce itself—such is the vital function of the model in a system of death, or rather of anticipated resurrection, that no longer even gives the event of death a chance. A hyperreal henceforth sheltered from the imaginary, and from any distinction between the real and the imaginary, leaving room only for the orbital recurrence of models and for the simulated generation of differences.

*   *   *

THE HYPERREAL AND THE IMAGINARY

Disneyland is a perfect model of all the entangled orders of simulacra. It is first of all a play of illusions and phantasms: the Pirates, the Frontier, the Future Worlds, etc. This imaginary world is supposed to ensure the success of the operation. But what attracts the crowds the most is without a doubt the social microcosm, the *religious,* miniaturized pleasure of real America, of its constraints and joys. One parks outside and stands in line inside, one is altogether abandoned at the exit. The only phantasmagoria in this imaginary world lies in the tenderness and warmth of the crowd, and in the sufficient and excessive number of gadgets necessary to create the multitudinous effect. The contrast with the absolute solitude of the parking lot—a veritable concentration camp—is total. Or, rather: inside, a whole panoply of gadgets magnetizes the crowd in directed flows—outside, solitude is directed at a single gadget: the automobile. By an extraordinary coincidence (but this derives without a doubt from the enchantment inherent in this universe), this frozen, childlike world is found to have been conceived and realized by a man who is himself now cryogenized: Walt Disney, who awaits his resurrection through an increase of 180 degrees centigrade.

Thus, everywhere in Disneyland the objective profile of America, down to the morphology of individuals and of the crowd, is drawn. All its values are exalted by the miniature and the comic strip. Embalmed and pacified. Whence the possibility of an ideological analysis of Disneyland (L. Marin did it very well in *Utopiques, jeux d'espace* [Utopias, play of space]): digest of the American way of life, panegyric of American values, idealized transposition of a contradictory reality. Certainly. But this masks something else and this "ideological" blanket functions as a cover for a *simulation of the third order:* Disneyland exists in order to hide that it is the "real" country, all of "real" America that *is* Disneyland (a bit like prisons are there to hide that it is the social in its entirety in its banal omnipresence, that is carceral). Disneyland is presented as imaginary in order to make us believe that the rest is real, whereas all of Los Angeles and the America that surrounds it are no longer real, but belong to the hyperreal order and to the order of simulation. It is no longer a question of a false representation of reality (ideology) but of concealing the fact that the real is no longer real, and thus of saving the reality principle.

The imaginary of Disneyland is neither true nor false, it is a deterrence machine set up in order to rejuvenate the fiction of the real in the opposite camp. Whence the debility of this imaginary, its infantile degeneration. This world wants to be childish in order to make us believe that the adults are elsewhere, in the "real" world, and to conceal the fact that true childishness is everywhere—that it is that of the adults themselves who come here to act the child in order to foster illusions as to their real childishness.

Disneyland is not the only one, however. Enchanted Village, Magic Mountain, Marine World: Los Angeles is surrounded by these imaginary stations that feed reality, the energy of the real to a city whose mystery is precisely that of no longer being anything but a network of incessant, unreal circulation—a city of incredible proportions but without space, without dimension. As much as electrical and atomic power stations, as much as cinema studios, this city which is no longer anything but an immense scenario and a perpetual pan shot, needs this old imaginary like a sympathetic nervous system made up of childhood signals and faked phantasms.

Disneyland: a space of the regeneration of the imaginary as waste-treatment plants are elsewhere, and even here. Everywhere today one must recycle waste, and the dreams, the phantasms, the historical, fairylike, legendary imaginary of children and adults is a waste product, the first great toxic excrement of a hyperreal civilization. On a mental level, Disneyland is the prototype of this new function. But all the sexual, psychic, somatic recycling institutes, which proliferate in California, belong to the same order. People no longer look at each other, but there are institutes for that. They no longer touch each other, but there is contactotherapy. They no longer walk, but they go jogging, etc. Everywhere one recycles lost faculties, or lost bodies, or lost sociality, or the lost taste for food. One reinvents penury, asceticism, vanished savage naturalness: natural food, health food, yoga. Marshall Sahlins's idea that it is the economy of the market, and not of nature at all, that secretes penury, is verified, but at a secondary level: here, in the sophisticated confines of a triumphal market economy is reinvented a penury/sign, a penury/simulacrum, a simulated behavior of the underdeveloped (including the adoption of Marxist tenets) that, in the guise of ecology, of energy crises and the critique of capital, adds a final esoteric aureole to the triumph of an esoteric culture. Nevertheless, maybe a mental catastrophe, a mental implosion and involution without precedent lies in wait for a system of this kind, whose visible signs would be those of this strange obesity, or the incredible coexistence of the most bizarre theories and practices, which correspond to the improbable coalition of luxury, heaven, and money, to the improbable luxurious materialization of life and to undiscoverable contradictions.

HOPE IN HYPERREALITY

Exploration of Identity in *The Matrix* and "San Junipero"

MEESH COSARES graduated in 2021 from the Klein College of Communication at Temple University, where they majored in Media Studies and Production and minored in Theater. They were a peer teacher and a guest lecturer in Dr. Vacker's undergraduate media class in fall 2020. Meesh has a variety of academic interests, including queer theory, children's media, interactive media, storytelling, and new media. This is their first published paper, and they are excited to publish more in the future.

OPENING THE BOX

In Greek myth, Pandora was created by the gods to punish Prometheus, the trickster god who stole fire and gave it to humanity. On Pandora's wedding day, the powerful god Zeus gave her a beautiful box (or in some translations a jar) and told her that she could not open it under any circumstances. For a while Pandora listened, but over time her curiosity got the better of her. When she opened the box, terrible evils were let out into the world. These evils have been translated into ideas like greed, disease, hunger, poverty, war, sadness, and in some cases death itself. But in all the stories the last thing to be found at the bottom of the box is "Hope."

In some stories, Hope is too weak to fly out of the box and remains trapped inside. It is viewed as the most horrible thing in the box, weighed down by malice and pain. In some cases, Hope is even translated to "deceptive expectation." In other tellings of the story, however, Hope takes on a different form. It is seen as the most beautiful thing in the world. Pandora keeping Hope in the box is seen as a metaphor for "holding on to hope," even in the darkest of days. There are even some retellings where Hope flies out of the box, to spread itself to the rest of the world.

The Matrix (1999)[1] and *Black Mirror*'s episode "San Junipero" (2016) are two pieces of media that in a way echo the myth of Pandora's box. Many analysts use these films to highlight the fears, dangers, and morally gray areas of hyperreality and the advancement of technology in our society. While these interpretations are important and valid, we can also see these films as hopeful stories of individuals being able to explore and develop their identities and self-expression in the presence of a virtual hyperreality.

UNDERSTANDING WHAT'S INSIDE

The hopeful vision of *The Matrix* and "San Junipero" can be better understood if readers are familiar with some basic terms and concepts—hyperreality, cisheteronormative, queer, and transgender. *Hyperreality* is Jean Baudrillard's term for the state of our technological society wherein

---

1   While this reading deals with only the first *Matrix* film, many of the themes of transformation permeate the series.

the signs and symbols of the real replace the real. The Matrix and San Junipero are hyperreal places. All "real" experiences have been replaced by simulated experiences.

Cisheteronormative is an important term when we're considering the state of society. A *cis* or *cisgender* individual identifies with the gender they were assigned at birth, and a *heterosexual* is someone who is attracted to the opposite sex. There is a social mindset present that this is the norm for how someone should identify. Therefore, when someone does not identify with either of these labels, they are seen as outcasts or "others." Whether or not an individual perpetuates these ideas, the ideas are deeply rooted in the fabric of our society.[2]

Queer in this context is used as an umbrella term to refer to the LGBTQ+ (Lesbian, Gay, Bisexual, Transgender, Queer+) community, as well as looking at and reading media with a queer lens.[3] In general, the term *transgender* (or *trans*) refers to someone who does not identify as the gender they were assigned at birth. What is unique and important when it comes to the discussion of gender and sexuality is that there is no universal experience. Every individual has their own journey and gets to determine their own identity and the labels that make them most comfortable.

THE TRANSFORMATION MATRIX

The Matrix tells the story of a dystopian future where individuals are unknowingly living in a simulated reality called the "Matrix," while their bodies are enslaved by intelligent machines who use them as an energy source. The story focuses on Thomas Anderson, an individual who was born and raised inside the Matrix and discovers the truth about his reality. Using the alias Neo, he joins up with a group of rebels and can free his mind and fight against the machines for the sake of humanity. *The Matrix* is a rich film, with ideas and concepts that continue to resonate now, more than twenty-two years after its release. At its core, the film is about transformation

and breaking free of a false reality. Despite the dystopian nature of *The Matrix*, we see people who can transform themselves and battle the systems that oppress them—not only from the outside but also from the inside.

In the context of identity formation, the story of *The Matrix* has a very profound and important meaning for many members of the LGBTQ+ community, and notably for individuals who identify as transgender. We can make direct comparisons between the journey of Neo throughout the movie and the journey that queer people take in our society.

"SPLINTER IN YOUR MIND"

When Neo first expresses that he feels that something is off, Morpheus says to him, "You've felt it your whole life, felt that something is wrong with the world. You don't know what, but it's there like a splinter in your mind, driving you mad."

In our cisheteronormative society, most individuals are raised with certain expectations for how they should behave based on their sex. These expectations sometimes start even before a child is born, with gender-reveal parties making an extravagant show of pink or blue. A quick search for baby onesies for boys and girls makes this very clear. Girl's onesies are light-colored and tout phrases like "Dream big" and "I don't drool, I sparkle," while onesies for boys are often in darker colors and have phrases like "Always seek adventure" and "I'd flex but I like this onesie."

These expectations of gender behavior also extend to expectations of sexuality. Many people have their own stories of family members grilling them from a very young age about having boyfriends or girlfriends. For individuals who identify as cisgender and/or straight, these things may not mean much. However, for those who identify otherwise, these things can cause that splinter in the mind to grow. From there, the only way out or through is by escaping the expectations that are set forth for you, or in a way escaping from your own Matrix.

---

2   Definition inspired by Julia Serano: http://juliaserano.com/terminology.html.
3   I acknowledge the history and derogatory uses of the word *queer* in the past and encourage further reading on its reclamation.

THE TRANSGENDER MATRIX

One notable publication on this topic is "Taking the Red Pill: Using *The Matrix* to Explore Transgender Identity Development."[4] The authors detail how the main character's evolution from Mr. Anderson to Neo aligns with multiple stages of transgender identity development. This has led to the authors and many other thinkers seeing the "red pill" that Neo takes in order to begin his journey as a direct parallel to the HRT (hormone replacement therapy) pills that many transgender people take to affirm their identities.

In a YouTube interview produced by Netflix, Lilly Wachowski, the cowriter and codirector of the film, came forward to celebrate the ways in which *The Matrix* is now being seen as a trans story.[5] Wachowski said,

> I'm glad that people are talking about the movies with a trans narrative. I love how meaningful these films are to trans people. Because when you talk about transformation ... and the idea of the seemingly impossible becoming possible I think that's why it speaks to them so much.

Lilly and her sister/cowriter and codirector Lana Wachowski are both transgender women who came out of the closet after *The Matrix* and its sequels were released. They are accomplished writers, filmmakers, directors, and producers who have had continued success in Hollywood. Lilly says the films were "all about the desire for transformation, but it was all coming from a closeted point of view."

Lilly also speaks about the original characterization of Switch, a member of the resistance. When Lana and Lilly were writing the character, they wanted Switch to be female in the Matrix and male in the real world. However, Warner Brothers decided that the character would be played by one actress with a slightly more androgynous look. Lilly goes on to say,

I don't know how present my transness was in the background of my brain as we were writing it, but it all came from that same sort of fire. Because trans people exist in this, especially me and Lana, we were existing in a space where the words didn't exist, so we were always living in a world of imagination. That's why I gravitated toward sci-fi and fantasy and played Dungeons and Dragons. It was all about creating worlds. It freed us up as filmmakers because we were able to imagine stuff at that time that you didn't necessarily see onscreen.

THE HOPEFUL MATRIX

At first glance, the phrase "hopeful dystopia" might seem paradoxical. Dystopias are stories of worlds gone wrong, often showing how hubris and technological advancements lead to the downfall of society. Freedom is often replaced with control and oppression by a larger power. Yet, many of the dystopian stories of our time are also stories of hope. They may not have a positive outlook when it comes to the future of our society, but they wouldn't become cultural touchstones if all they did was make us feel like the future is doomed and there is nothing we can do about it. These stories are about the characters who undermine the system and fight for a better future. Their role within the story shows us that humanity is resilient, even in the most trying of times.

Neo and the resistance are beacons of hope in *The Matrix*. Some may argue that by the end of the movie the group has failed—since much of the resistance has died, the machines now know where they are, and nobody other than Neo was able to be freed from the Matrix. However, the goal of the resistance was never to destroy the Matrix in one fell swoop. We can see the struggle that Neo had to go through to fully understand his situation

4   Joseph M. Currin, Fallyn M. Lee, Colton Brown, and Tonya R. Hammer, "Taking the Red Pill: Using *The Matrix* to Explore Transgender Identity Development," *Journal of Creativity in Mental Health* 12, no. 3 (2017): 402–409, https://doi.org/10.1080/15401383.2016.1249815.

5   Netflix Film Club, "Why *The Matrix* Is a Trans Story According to Lilly Wachowski" (2020), https://www.youtube.com/watch?v=adXm2sDzGkQ

and come into his own, and if everyone were to be pulled out of the Matrix at once the result would be mass chaos. All we need to do in order to see their success is listen to what Neo says at the end of the movie: "I believe that the Matrix can remain our cage or it can become our chrysalis, that's what you helped me to understand. That to be free, you cannot change your cage. You have to change yourself."

This final plea is not just for the machines or for the people of the Matrix, but for the audience. This sentiment resonates from both a queer perspective and a hyperreal perspective. When many queer people discover their identities, they often feel as though they are broken or wrong. But by acknowledging that we live in a society that is deeply rooted in cisheteronormativity, we find that it is not queer people who are unfit for society, but society that is unfit for queer people. So queer people must go through their own journeys to find a place in society. Many have created their own spaces within, both physically and online, where they can move away from these ideas and express themselves more comfortably. For some, it is about advocating and educating, trying to build understanding in the people around them so they do not perpetuate these damaging ideas. Others just exist as themselves, not aiming to teach but simply aiming to be another member of society.

From a hyperreal perspective, it is about acknowledging that as a society we are trending toward the hyperreal: that virtual experiences or manipulated realities like Disneyland are becoming more normal, and in some cases are preferred to the authentic experience. While our society may be transforming radically and quickly, we have to acknowledge that our humanity—our emotions, our desires, and our opinions—can never be replaced by signs and symbols of the real. We have to find or create experiences in our world that feel real and authentic. What is important for both of these perspectives is that everyone's journey is individual and happens in its own time. As Morpheus says multiple times throughout the movie, "I'm trying to free your mind, Neo, but all I can do is show you the door. You're the one that has to step through."

SAN FREEDOM

"San Junipero" is an episode of *Black Mirror*, a British sci-fi anthology series created by Charlie Brooker and currently owned by Netflix. Each episode of the series features a movie-length story about possible media futures and the societal consequences of advancing technology. "San Junipero" was released in 2016 as part of *Black Mirror*'s third season and has received much critical acclaim, including two primetime Emmy awards.

The episode follows two women, Yorkie and Kelly, as they form a romantic relationship with each other in the beach resort town of San Junipero. As the story progresses, we learn that San Junipero is not actually a real place, but rather a simulated reality that the elderly can visit once a week. Users of San Junipero can also choose to live there "full time" as residents, meaning that after their body dies, their consciousness remains in the simulated reality.

Users of the simulation inhabit younger versions of their bodies, so they can modify their appearances in traditional ways and do not face the same physical limitations. Death is not possible in the virtual space, and social taboos are not as present because there is a communal understanding that this space exists for its users to explore and have fun.

Yorkie is able to live a life in San Junipero that she never had the privilege of living in the real world. She was paralyzed at the age of twenty-one in a car crash, but in San Junipero she is not limited by her physical condition and can walk and talk like everyone else. In the real world, Yorkie also deals with an oppressive family, whose negative reaction to her coming out was the catalyst for her car crash. She is being kept alive despite her wish to be euthanized and live full-time in San Junipero. When she is able to visit San Junipero, Yorkie is empowered to be herself and love whomever she wants to love without any fear of repercussion. This doesn't mean that she is a reckless character. In fact, Yorkie is quite introverted due to her lack of experiences both in San Junipero and in real life due to her injury.

Kelly, on the other hand, has a very different story. In the real world, Kelly lived a full life with a husband and a daughter who have both passed away. She is a party girl, outgoing, and not afraid to be a little reckless.

She confides in Yorkie that despite knowing that she was bisexual for most of her life, she never acted on her feelings in the real world. Much of her attitude stems from the fact that she initially had no intention of living full-time in San Junipero but instead expected to die naturally like her daughter and her husband. Her goal was to have no roots, so that it would be easier for her when she eventually had to leave. As she begins to spend more time in San Junipero and falls in love with Yorkie, she realizes that her decision might not be so cut-and-dried.

Kelly and Yorkie are not stock characters. They are well-rounded and unique, and their differences create an interesting dynamic in their relationship. Their love for one another is not a set piece in the story or a catalyst for something bigger to happen; their love is the story. It subverts the traditional *Black Mirror* episode, which usually focuses on technology creating a dark and dystopian landscape.

SAN ESCAPISM

San Junipero—as a hyperreal space—provides its visitors a temporary escape from the real world. In other stories of virtual hyperreality, there is a fear that virtual life will take over real experiences. However, the living users of San Junipero have strict limitations so that they stay connected to the real world. The ideas of "San Junipero" are not so far-fetched in our current society. In an interview about the episode, Charlie Brooker said he was inspired by nostalgia therapy, a form of mindful reflection on the past used to help older folks be more connected in the present.[6] In San Junipero, Kelly and Yorkie don't merely reflect on their past; they inhabit an alternative past and get to create a new future.

"San Junipero" also allows us to think more deeply about the role of escapism in society. To say that life is hard is an understatement. We all struggle, and we all deserve to have space to step away from our troubles. How each individual does that is their own choice to make. It can be binge-watching a television series, going

to a museum, working out, or doing drugs. Some people play video games to escape into an artificial world that's different from our own, and they may even use that world to connect with others. We should not feel shame for taking time to escape, and we should not shame the visitors of San Junipero for doing the same.

An analysis of "San Junipero" would be incomplete without a discussion of the element of death that is present within the episode. What happens after death is one of the defining questions of life, and we may never have a concrete answer for it. For many people, not knowing creates great existential anxiety that permeates everyday life. However, San Junipero provides an alternative to the unknown. It is an answer and an assured place to go. Whether or not we feel that this decision is incorrect or immoral, we should not judge Kelly or Yorkie for their choice.

SAN LOVE

The episode also subverts the traditional queer love story, which more often than not ends in death and tragedy. This has been a problem in queer storytelling for a very long time, and it continues to be a problem. Some attention was brought to this issue in 2016, a few months before the release of "San Junipero," when four lesbian or bisexual female characters on primetime television died within thirty days of each other. It reignited a conversation about this trope, known as "Bury Your Gays" of "Dead Lesbian Syndrome." An early example of this comes from the 1976 soap opera *Executive Suite,* where a lesbian character chases her love interest into the street and is hit by a truck. As of March 2016, 146 lesbian or bisexual characters had died on television, with only about sixteen television shows granting around eighteen couples happy endings.[7]

What is unique about the love story of Yorkie and Kelly is that while it caused the body count to go up to 148, these characters were granted a happy ending even in death. They subvert the tragic ending that we have

---

6   Brian Formo, "*Black Mirror*: Charlie Brooker and Gugu Mbatha-Raw Talk "San Junipero" in Our Spoiler Interview (October 2016), Collider, https://collider.com/black-mirror-san-junipero-explained-netflix-interview/.
7   Dorothy Snarker, "Bury Your Gays: Why 'The 100,' 'Walking Dead' Deaths Are Problematic," *Hollywood Reporter*, March 21, 2016, https://www.hollywoodreporter.com/live-feed/bury-your-gays-why-100-877176.

come to expect. We can imagine, as in all relationships, that as a couple they may have their problems over time. But we aren't forced to see a montage of them fighting or yelling at each other as Belinda Carlisle plays in the background. We see them happy together, enjoying their new lives and loving each other. As Yorkie says in the episode, "It's not a trap."

There is no denying that San Junipero is a hyperreal place, and yet Kelly and Yorkie's love for one another is not hyperreal. We can see, through the characters' actions inside and outside of San Junipero, that they care about one another deeply. It is important to remember that the presence of a hyperreality does not mean that nothing can be authentic. Hyperreality is only an environment; your state of mind and your relationship to the world are what determine how you act in said environment. "San Junipero" is an undeniable story of queer love, resilience, and real emotion in an artificial world.

FROM THE DESERT OF THE REAL TO THE BEACHES OF SAN JUNIPERO

Neo and Yorkie, as the protagonists of their stories, are born into worlds that oppress them. Neo lives under the rule of oppressive machines. The Matrix exists solely for the purpose of control. While its inhabitants are able to live a life, it is not a full life but merely a simulation of what could be. Yorkie, on the other hand, lives under the control of her parents. Even after her accident, no part of what physical life she has left is hers to control. Neo and Yorkie are held to certain expectations regarding their behavior, and they are taught not to question things. But when they eventually ask these seemingly forbidden questions about reality and cisheteronormative society, they are offered the chance for validation and escape.

Morpheus offers Neo the red pill or the blue pill, and Kelly offers to buy Yorkie a drink on her first night in San Junipero. Neither of them knew what would happen if they said yes, but they took a leap of faith anyway in the hope that their choice would lead them down a more authentic path. Like Pandora herself, they couldn't

help but open the box. From then on, they were able to begin personal journeys to define themselves outside of oppression. While these are individual experiences focused on self-identity, neither of them takes the journey alone. Neo has Morpheus and the resistance behind him, teaching and guiding him inside and outside of the Matrix. Yorkie has Kelly, who shows her that she is not broken and that she deserves to be loved for who she is, both inside and outside of San Junipero.

This is where the two stories find a major point of contrast. Neo must escape from hyperreality to find himself, and Yorkie must escape to hyperreality to find herself. This illustrates the malleability of a hyperreal environment and the adaptability of humanity. Hyperreality is a tool; its presence doesn't inherently mean good or bad. That is why it is the perfect playground for stories about transformation and exploration.

While the Matrix may be a site of control, we see hope for transformation and a brighter future. And while San Junipero may be a place for escape, there we see true love and hope for a more authentic life. These hopes and desires bring about change not just in hyperreality, but in the real world of these stories as well. *The Matrix* and "San Junipero" remind us that humanity will always keep things real, even in the most artificial of places.[8]

---

8   A special thank you to Hazel Boston and Barry Vacker for their assistance in editing this paper.

"WELCOME TO THE DESERT OF THE RED PILL"

BARRY VACKER teaches media and cultural studies at Temple University in Philadelphia, where he is an associate professor in the Klein College of Media and Communication. Professor Vacker has taught media studies courses for over 20 years and authored many articles and books on art, media, culture, and technology. His newest works include: *Black Mirror and Critical Media Theory* (2018), an anthology co-edited with Angela Cirucci; *Media(S)cene* (2019), an ongoing art and media theory project co-developed with Julia Hildebrand; and *Specter of the Monolith* (2017), a critique of space exploration inspired by the classic *2001: A Space Odyssey*. Professor Vacker earned his PhD from the University of Texas at Austin.

FIGURE 3.4.1   Desert of the red pill

This is a slightly modified version of an essay published in *Curious*, an online publication inside *Medium*, 2020.

Red Pill America. On May 17, 2020, Elon Musk tweeted "Take the red pill." Soon the same day, Ivanka Trump tweeted "Taken." Flashback. Exactly seventeen years earlier, on May 17, 2003, I was interviewed by Anderson Cooper on CNN about the meanings of *The Matrix*.

Flash-forward. Elon's tweet has 554K hearts, while Ivanka's has 91K hearts. Red pills are proliferating—copies of copies of copies!

As Morpheus said to Neo at the philosophical climax of *The Matrix*: "Welcome to the desert of the real." Now it's a desert basin littered with red pills.

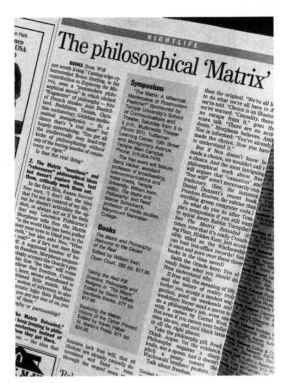

| **FIGURE 3.4.2** Coverage of *The Matrix Reloaded* and *The Matrix* "philosophy" in the *Philadelphia Inquirer*

FLASHBACK: "MAPPING THE MATRIX" IN 2003

So why was I being interviewed by Anderson Cooper about *The Matrix*? The occasion was the opening weekend of *The Matrix Reloaded* and a small symposium called "Mapping the Matrix," which I hosted on a Sunday afternoon at Temple University. ***What happened that morning is much like what is happening around America now.***

Mostly forgotten is that *The Matrix Reloaded* generated massive buzz in the media, even rivaling current *Star Wars* openings. This was before Facebook and Twitter. Front-page stories in newspapers, huge sections in the weekend guides, and coverage in radio and TV talk shows. Speakers at the symposium were interviewed on local radio stations. Among the speakers and panelists, there were two authors of works related to *The Matrix*: William Irwin, editor of *The Matrix and Philosophy* (2002), one of the best-selling philosophy books of all time, and Read Mercer Schuchardt, contributor to *Taking the Red Pill: Science, Philosophy and Religion in*

The Matrix (2003). Other panelists included Temple film professor Jeff Rush, Cal-Berkeley media scholar Theresa Geller (then a PhD student at Rutgers), and my long-time friend Elisa Durrette (then the chief "Futurist" at FedEx/Kinkos), who is now the head of legal-commercial transactions at Cloudflare, a global internet powerhouse.

In the cover imagery (Figure 3.4.2a, left), the *Philadelphia Inquirer* reflects some of the striking imagery of *The Matrix* films. This was state-of-the-art newspaper design in 2003. Yet, to college students of 2021 (and beyond), the static nature of the printed paper cover cannot match the moving images on glowing electronic screens. The inability of paper to match the *spectacle* of screens is one key reason for the demise of newspapers on paper, along with the loss of classified ads and the lack of interactivity. There is no way to reverse this process. The only hope for newspapers is to successfully adapt to the spectacle and online networks, while exploring alternative and sustainable funding models, which is exactly what the *Philadelphia Inquirer* is doing by operating under the direction of a non-profit institute—The Lenfest Institute for Journalism.[1]

---

1   Christine Schmidt, "Three Years Into Non-Profit Ownership, the Philadelphia Inquirer is Still Trying to Chart its Future," *Nieman Lab*, Nieman Foundation at Harvard, August 22, 2019.

FIGURE 3.4.3 *Simulacra and Simulation* book

Today abstraction is no longer that of the map, the double, the mirror, or the concept. Simulation is no longer that of a territory, a referential being, or a substance. It is the generation by models of a real without origin or reality: a hyperreal. The territory no longer precedes the map, nor does it survive it. It is nevertheless the map that precedes the territory—*precession of simulacra*—that engenders the territory, and if one must return to the fable, today it is the territory whose shreds slowly rot across the extent of the map. It is the real, and not the map, whose vestiges persist here and there in the deserts that are no longer those of the Empire, but ours. *The desert of the real itself.*

FIGURE 3.4.4 Photo of page 1 from my copy of *Simulacra and Simulation* (1994)

The photo on the right (Figure 3.4.2b, right) features information about the symposium, again reflective of newspaper design circa 2003. Yet, by the standards of 2021, the listing seems radically incomplete compared to online news and media, which would feature links to the presenters' bios, personal websites, and/or Twitter feeds. The online media (newspapers included) must obey the rules of the spectacle and screens, along with the links demanded by planetary networks and social media platforms. Collectively, online news sites are now part of the spectacle and hyperreality—i.e., the very realm described by Morpheus as "The Matrix."

EVERYONE HAS THEIR "MATRIX"

That Sunday morning, the atmosphere in the auditorium was electric, with more energy than I have personally experienced in any symposium—across thirty years as a grad student and a professor. Since the semester was over, there was no extra credit for students to artificially populate the room. The auditorium was packed, standing room only, with people sitting in the aisles. The crowd was diverse across age, gender, and ethnicity. Some Morpheus fans were in trench coats, others in Trinity-inspired shiny black pants, most just there because they were stoked about the ideas in *The Matrix*. *It was like Comic Con meets philosophy symposium.* Red pills everywhere, with differing effects. In the vibrant Q&A, it was clear that "the Matrix is everywhere"

and everyone had their own version of what it was and who was in control. Just like 2020.

NEO'S BOOK

In the *Matrix* trilogy, only one book is shown and it is in Neo's apartment. Early in the *The Matrix*, Neo opens a dark green book called *Simulacra and Simulation*; the book is a hollowed shell containing computer disks and other items. With the facade of a book, the Wachowskis are referencing the key concept of controversial philosopher Jean Baudrillard.

Baudrillard is often misunderstood, both by "postmodernist" followers and by "political" critics, who don't get the metaphorical style of his writings. I'm not a follower who agrees with everything written by Baudrillard, who disavowed postmodernism. So do I, as an existentialist in the vein of Jean-Paul Sartre. *But I embrace the aesthetic role of powerful metaphors to highlight our cultural conditions and contradictions, as presented in* **Simulacra and Simulation.** That's what art (like *The Matrix* or Sartre's *No Exit*) and poetic theorists (like Baudrillard) can do—make something visually clear that is often lost in the dry writings of most thinkers. Obviously, Lana and Lilly Wachowski got that when they were cowriting and codirecting *The Matrix*.

As depicted on the the first page of Neo's book (Figure 3.4.4), Baudrillard offered a complex metaphorical passage. We like to think of media technology as "maps" for our world, as suggested by Google Maps, Facebook status updates, and endless social media pics and posts. But, almost always, over time, the situation is paradoxically reversed—*the media maps are generating the territories to which our culture and consciousness conform.* Obviously, that seems insane, or at least radically counterintuitive. But bear with me. Simply put, Baudrillard argued that society mirrors the dominant media technologies, just like cities mirror the technologies of cars, suburbs, highways, and skyscrapers. If those technologies can transform cities with models of *mass production*, then why can't media tech transform consciousness with models of *mass reproduction*?

That's often a hard thing to grasp, but it is the "reality" we faced in 2020. After all, America had a reality-TV star for president. Below are three key concepts from the passage. A shot of tequila might help wash down the following sections. Or your fave drink.

1. THE MAP IS THE TERRITORY

Baudrillard believed that the map has overtaken the territory it is supposed to represent, such that *the map is the territory*. It's a metaphor. The "map" is media technology, the "territory" is reality.

What's the dominant media now? Screens and cameras connected via networks spanning the planet. Total screen and media usage (home, work, coffeehouses, TV, internet, news, video, music, gaming, etc.) now averages ten to fourteen hours per day, which means the screens are our daily maps and territories. Following the rise of television, the media maps no longer merely "represent" reality; in fact, they generate the realities we recreate in society, realities old and new.

"The map is the territory" is an updated take on **Marshall McLuhan's "the medium is the massage."** McLuhan first used the term *matrix* when discussing "automation" in his 1964 book *Understanding Media* (p. 364). Baudrillard's and McLuhan's phrases both mean that technology massages and shapes consciousness in the image of the technology's forms, rules, and realities. Here are some brief examples.

Television produces some great shows, but it reduces book reading and it leads to Las Vegas and 24/7 entertainment culture.

Hollywood produces some mind-blowing films, but it also leads to celebrity worship, Disneyland, and dreamworlds as the preferred daily existence—the dream "reality" of *Keeping Up with the Kardashians* consumed on screens across the planet.

Social media curate news for us, but they also shrink attention spans and reproduce the "global village"—with everyone in utmost proximity, everyone in everyone's face, flame wars, hot takes, and tribal conflict.

Social media reproduce the **screen worlds** of television and Hollywood, where everyone is a star, super-special, with a "truth" to entertain or enrage us. From influencers to internet tough guys to Twitter gods. That's how a reality-TV star becomes a celebrity president. That's the map overtaking the territory.

2. HYPERREALITY AND SIMULACRA

Powered by screens, we live in a "hyperreal" world where the signs and symbols of the real have largely transformed the real or replaced it. The real and fictional are no longer dualities. *Simulacra* is plural for *simulacrum*, the copy in which the original is no longer present, needed, or desired.

Morpheus taps into Baudrillard when he says, *"The Matrix is a system."* As the technological "system" advances through innovation, it produces model after model of the new desired "reality." The models then crank out endless copies and clones, replicas and reproductions, fakes and facades, substitutes and simulacra. They are all reliant on each other for meaning and value. It is models that generate the brands of mass production, from Big Macs to Grande Lattes, Jeeps to Teslas, 501s to Dos Equis, Pradas to Ray-Bans—all of which are empirically real, but are presented as if original or authentic, special or sexy, or just super-cool. Even the high-rises and suburbs were generated in models.

Media and advertising generate endless models for lifestyles (goth, gangsta, hipster, etc.), music styles (rock, rap, country, electronic, etc.), and sports fandom (Cowboys, Patriots, Longhorns, Trojans, etc.). The models proliferate, which is why there is a fervent quest for *meaning and authenticity,* in a world filled with brands, logos, flags, religions, and spectacles—the Oscars, the World Cup, megachurches, and so on.

The planetary sprawl of hyperreality is the cumulative effect of Las Vegas, Disneyland, Hollywood, television, social media, and the proliferation of screens. Cleverly, the "fake" worlds of Vegas and Disneyland mask the fact that the rest of society and "reality" are bound up in copies and simulacra. The Super Bowl is one giant hyperreality, a staged event, a simulacrum of tribal conquest—yet it is watched as if it is the realest and most macho thing in our part of the Milky Way. That's why celebrities, footballers, and presidents generate such loyalty.

In a world of fakes and facades, these three groups are the most hyperreal things to love, to worship, to obey—***they're more real than real, more true than true, more beautiful than beautiful.*** No wonder the real territory of Earth is pillaged and polluted to power the maps and models.

The system is perfected with capitalism, but it also works with fascism, socialism, and religion because "the system" is the mass production of goods and mass reproduction of images—which are done in any political system for profit or propaganda.

For Baudrillard, all life is absorbed and reproduced within the system, including all resistance to the system. Rebels are reproduced and red pills proliferate. As shown with Elon and Ivanka, rebel simulacra are everywhere. Copies of copies of copies.

That's why being a real rebel is so damn hard. The copies replicate, the copies gain power, any real rebellion is neutralized or marginalized, and "the system" stays intact, in control.

Lady Gaga's Hyperreal Halftime

Hyperreality presents a media universe that is "better" than the real "universe," especially in America's biggest events. A perfect example is Lady Gaga's halftime performance during the 2017 Super Bowl in Houston. Gaga begins the performance atop the open roof in the stadium.

Behind and below her, we can see the glowing sprawl of Houston in the background—not a star above is visible. The Milky Way is erased in the skyglow of electric lights, the nighttime Matrix for our cities. As Gaga begins singing "God Bless America," the white lights of drones appear behind her in the night sky—the simulacra of the stars no longer visible, no longer necessary, no longer desirable.

The drones soon turn into a red, white, and blue American flag, prompting Lady Gaga (suspended by a cable) to drop into the stadium and its total hyperreal spectacle. Cheers erupt. In America, patriotism and nationalism are religions now dominant in the other universe of illusion—hyperreality. For many Americans, there is no worthy universe beyond mythical "America," no worthy reality beyond hyperreality—the glowing Matrix suspended by fiber optic cables above the "desert of the real."

3. THE DESERT OF THE REAL

Shreds of reality are scattered across our screens, distant territories beneath our glowing maps, powered by silicon sands. The "desert" is no longer merely "out there" in the American Southwest or in Saharan Africa, but is also just below our screens, just beyond our mediated perceptions of the world. The remaining "real" realities—***if they exist according to Baudrillard***—reside in "the desert of the real." Those are the natural deserts that exist far outside the metropolises, or maybe the cultural deserts that exist in the fissures within the metropolises. In the voids, the shreds, the cracks, the fragments, there might be openings for new territories, new autonomous zones, new moments of adventure and liberation for daily life, as with the "Situationist International" movement of the 1960s.

FIGURE 3.4.5 Like all NFL stadiums, Cowboys Stadium (now AT&T Stadium) is pure hyperreality.

FIGURE 3.4.6 The New York-New York Hotel, Las Vegas

This is where the **real rebellion** can begin, getting a foothold in the voids and fissures in the system, to address the social injustices, the equity imbalances, the ecological impacts. Like lava flowing from a volcano that makes new land on Earth, new territories can erupt and emerge amid the maps, lands seeking to be more just, fair, equal, peaceful, factual, and sustainable—as with Occupy Wall Street, Black Lives Matter, #MeToo, the Women's March, the March for Science, the George Floyd protests, and the Climate Strike, or with the Apollo 8 "Earthrise" image and the first Earth Day fifty years ago. *The existential and social challenge is to keep the new territory from being checked by "the system" (in all its forms), from being lost or buried in the glowing maps of hyperreality and consumer society.* Any changes must be real, not hyperreal, not simulacra, not another map filled with the signs and symbols of change.

THERE IS NO EXIT

For Baudrillard, there was no conspiracy, no secret cabal, no mysterious puppet masters. Hyperreality was the evolutionary consequence of technological civilization, coupled with humanity's perpetual unhappiness and emptiness—which it seeks to fill with ever more consumer goods, ever more gods, ever more technological wizardry, ever more maps that are territories. This is where capitalism and tech innovation merge to create the endless consumer-entertainment-celebrity society, which continues to expand despite its devastating impact on the environment.

In his more radical texts, Baudrillard asserts that the real (or authentic) reality is no longer available or accessible, no longer existing outside hyperreality. All that was left was to try to hack it with nihilistic theory. That's why he thought *The Matrix* ultimately missed the real meaning of hyperreality and his works. The movie offered hope. But, for Baudrillard, there is no exit—*there is no red pill.*

THE MATRIX HAS MANY READINGS

Like all great art and science fiction, *The Matrix* can be read on multiple metaphorical levels. Historically, *The Matrix* is a powerful retelling of "Plato's Cave." In Plato's famed allegory, the prisoners were forced to view the shadows on the cave walls, unable to exit and discover the real reality in the sunlight outside the cave. In another reading, *The Matrix* presents a deep-state conspiracy theory about an artificial reality—"pulled over our eyes" —that is patrolled by armies of artificial intelligence, the Agent Smith clones.

In an August 2020 interview on YouTube, codirector Lilly Wachowski said *The Matrix* is a metaphor for a "trans narrative" in a "world that wasn't quite ready for it yet." As Wachowski explained, "The Matrix stuff was all about the desire for transformation but it was all coming from a closeted point of view, and so we had the character of Switch who was like a character who would be a man in the real world and then a woman in the Matrix." Wachowski added, "I love how meaningful those films are to trans people. ... I'm glad that it has gotten out that, you know, that was the original intention."

Add to that Wachowski's reference to Baudrillard's *Simulacra and Simulation* and it clear that *The Matrix* is a complex and multilayered film that many find inspiring. That's why the film belies any shallow reading that suggests there is an easy, surefire way to break out and find "freedom."

THE DESERT OF THE RED PILL

In *The Matrix*, there is a famous scene in which the rebel-philosopher Morpheus offers Neo a choice of taking the red pill or the blue pill. Swallowing the blue pill allows one to stay in "the Matrix" and live life surfing the images of the mediated reality that substitutes for the real reality, which remains unknown and inaccessible or simply undesirable and irrelevant. If we take the blue pill, we remain in the realm of the simulacra. Of course, as fans of *The Matrix* know, Neo swallows the red pill, which liberates his mind to see the Matrix for what it is: a vast system of technology designed to keep society under control and detached from the authentic reality, separate from our authentic selves, and disconnected from our destiny as collective members of the human species. In other words, the blue pill keeps us on the maps, while the red pill gets us to the underlying territories.

Naturally, the Matrix has produced its own red pill simulacra, just as Baudrillard would have predicted. Since the release of *The Matrix* in 1999, the meaning of the red pill has evolved, just as one would expect from a meme. The red pill symbolized "freedom," "transformation," and "independent thinking," but it has been appropriated to stand for *freedom from evidence* and liberation from empirical reality, as in the case of QAnon (to name one powerful example). The Matrix has produced a red pill simulacrum to keep the dominant systems and ideologies intact, especially in politics, religion, conspiracy, and pseudoscience.

"Red pills" now proliferate among conspiracy theorists—"the Matrix" of new world orders, deep states, false flags, Flat Earth, Young Earth, UFO cover-ups, Area 51, fake moon landings, ancient aliens, Bill Gates, and so on. The evil conspirators' goals supposedly are coup d'états to establish one-world governments in which they will maintain power, impose tyranny, take away freedoms, and implant chips to track us (even though our phones already do that quite well).

Deep-state theorists scour the internet for conspiracies, yet they seem to rarely bother researching the real science of pandemics, vaccinations, evolution, and climate disruption. These rebels complain about their freedoms being lost, yet they fail to grasp that the internet and social media provide them a global platform to shout their theories worldwide—albeit inside the Matrix like this essay. So they take their red pills and bring their semiautomatics to the state house, threatening legislators, like the heroes they were trained to be at Fort YouTube. The Matrix needs heroes and it reproduces them. Real, fake, and everything in between.

Whereas the original "red pill" in *The Matrix* was more about discovering a philosophical liberation in a *new worldview*, it seems current red pills now are about reinforcing *existing worldviews* of power and profit—nationalism, patriotism, militarism, theism, racism, unchecked capitalism, and hyperreality everywhere. Rather than reinforcing those ideologies, it seems

real rebels should be challenging them—the existing "Matrix" of massive power, profit, and domination.

THINKING REASONABLY IN HYPERREALITY

Given the layers of social media and the internet, it's no wonder "deep states" and conspiracy theories are proliferating, spiraling beyond reason and right into Baudrillard's hyperreality. The conspiracy maps overtake the factual territories—*conspiracies more real than real, more true than true.*

I don't blindly trust governments, corporations, or political parties, for all deceive or mislead far too often. The US government lied about atomic radiation, lied about Vietnam, and lied about Iraq, to name a few. Institutions and organizations often conspire, but we have to be reasonable in how we take on that problem.

It's not easy, especially amid hyperreality. In thinking about alleged conspiracies, I do my best to apply reason and logic to known evidence, while realizing the constructs of hyperreality. That's why I know Apollo 11 landed on the moon, why there is no "ancient alien" conspiracy, and why the "Flat Earth" and "Young Earth" theories are scientifically bogus.

MAPPING A CHAOTIC WORLD

In a fully mediated world, the bigger the horror, the bigger the map. JFK was shot down in broad daylight, thus a massive conspiracy theory. Jetliners caused the Twin Towers to implode, thus the 9/11 "truther" movement. The universe is vast and doesn't care about us, thus creationism and the "Young Earth" and "Flat Earth" theories, with evidence supposedly denied in a giant conspiracy by world scientists. Big horror, big map, the Matrix.

But, what if the massive maps mask the real horror—fears of chaos and events being "out of control." Perhaps the world is, indeed, chaotic? Wasn't that the lesson of "chaos theory" in the 1980s and 1990s? Science shows that small singular events can trigger huge aftermaths, what is known as "the butterfly effect." The universe and Earth are filled with chaotic unpredictability, with sudden singularities triggering massive effects. But, the human mind fears chaos, evolving a massive pattern-recognition processor in our brains. To cover for the chaos, we create ever larger maps.

We fear a chaotic world with things "out of control," so we want to believe that someone or some being is in control with a perfect plan. So we map massive conspiracies. We know we can't solve our big problems in a vast universe, so we invent gods and superheroes, to comfort us, to make us feel special, to show we deserve to exist in what might be a meaningless universe.[2] All of the above are why the 2017 "March for Science" may end up as little more than a glitch in the Matrix, a momentary gust of sand in the desert of the real.

RED PILL AMERICA

Death Valley and Las Vegas are inseparable; you have to accept everything at once;

the unchanging timelessness and the wildest instantaneity.

Jean Baudrillard, America (1988)

America is ground zero for the Matrix and red pills, with rebel simulacra everywhere in hyperreality. Technology has erased the night sky and pushed nature far away, leaving humanity as cosmic narcissists and the center of everything, buying and battling inside hyperreality while we ravage the planet and effect a sixth extinction event. The universal narrative has dissolved into tribal warfare, the timeless into the electronic instant, such that a common bond and a shared destiny seem impossible on the territories of Planet Earth. Yet, it is the common bond that humanity so desperately needs.

Empirical reality exists in fragmented and polluted shreds, far too often buried by the glow of electronic screens, where hot prevails over cool, heat over chill. Are truth and reality mere subjective power constructs inside hyperreality, or do the images of Earth from space or the Hubble telescope images suggest there is an objective universal existence we all inhabit?

FIGURE 3.4.7 Left: Luxor Hotel, Las Vegas (2013); Right: Badwater Sign, 85.5 meters below sea level, Death Valley (2007).

2   Yet, it is a vast universe still filling us with awe and wonder to inspire us in our physical insignificance, if only we will use our big brains to develop a new philosophy to unite the human species with a shared destiny on our tiny planet. So far, such a philosophical map is absent from our popular culture.

In his book *The Perfect Crime*, Baudrillard wrote that technology and the hyperreal have murdered reality and gotten away with it—"the perfect crime." Is not something similar happening in America, with more than one million total deaths from COVID (as of March 29, 2022), a pandemic that millions think is a typical flu exaggerated by scientists, doctors, and the "lamestream" media to take away their freedoms?[3]

In the spirit of Baudrillard's metaphors and *The Matrix*, poetics work best to sum up America. A second shot of tequila might help finish this up!

Lady Gaga leapt off the roof in the Super Bowl against a drone-filled night sky, symbolizing an "America" suspended in the darkness above Badwater only by the light beams shooting skyward from Las Vegas—and radiating throughout the vectors of Hollywood, Disneyland, and Silicon Valley. Are there enough lights on to prevent the fall? Like a once-mighty Atlantis, America, the simulacrum of freedom and democracy, is imploding inside the Matrix, seemingly poised to plunge into the *Death Valley of the real*—a final philosophical resting point in the Badwater Basin, the carnage of America 282 feet below sea level, the lowest point in North America.

500 miles south across the desert, Trump's Wall is baking in the desert sun.

Welcome to the desert of the red pill.

CREDITS

---

3   For a detailed explanation of probable case counts and total death counts, see: https://www.worldometers. info/coronavirus/country/us/ and https://www.worldometers.info/coronavirus/about/.

PART 2

SELECT TOPICS FOR MEDIA ANALYSIS

QUIZ SHOW (1994)

Based on the real life "quiz show" scandals of the 1950s, the film offers a powerful critique of the media spectacle and celebrity system, both of which devour the career of a college professor. No one really survives the scandal, except NBC and television—key forces of the spectacle.

Director: Robert Redford

Starring: Ralph Fiennes and John Turturro

WAG THE DOG (1997)

To help an incumbent president win reelection, a super-secret group of propagandists manipulate the media spectacle to make it seem war with Albania is necessary to prevent an act of nuclear terrorism. With Americans rallied to support the (illusion of a) war, the president is reelected, and no one is the wiser—except the Hollywood big shot who "produced" the war and now wants "credit."

Director: Barry Levinson

Starring: Robert de Niro, Anne Heche, and Dustin Hoffman

GOOD NIGHT, AND GOOD LUCK (2005)

The famed broadcast journalist, Edward R. Murrow, plays a key role in exposing the hypocrisies and propaganda tactics of Sen. Joseph McCarthy during the Communist scare of the Cold War. Murrow and fellow journalists must battle political power and corruption while resisting CBS's overall corporate interests—which are drawing large audiences to uncontroversial shows that keep advertisers happy and make profits for CBS.

Director: George Clooney

Starring: David Strathairn, Patricia Clarkson, and Robert Downey Jr.

THE POST (2017)

When a former Pentagon employee leaks information about the Vietnam War and reveals a government cover-up spanning four presidencies, the editors and owner of the *Washington Post* face tough decisions in going face-to-face with the White House and US government. At stake are the First Amendment and freedom of press.

Director: Steven Spielberg
Starring: Meryl Streep and Tom Hanks

SELECT FILMS ABOUT NEWS AND CELEBRITIES

CHAPTER FOUR

NEWS AND CELEBRITIES

The Form and Content of News: From Facts to Fame to Fake News

Barry Vacker

W hat's more important? Fake news or fake celebs? Fabricated stories or modified bodies? In the realms of ego-media and hyperreality, it's hard to tell. When it comes to real stars or movie stars, the answer is clear—Hollywood trumps the Milky Way.

After all, these celebrity entertainers have been elected to high office in America: a movie star president (Ronald Reagan, 1981–1989), a reality-TV star president (Donald Trump, 2017–2021), a pro-wrestler governor of Minnesota (Jesse Ventura, 1999–2003), and a movie star governor of California (Arnold Schwarzenegger, 2003–2011). The partial owner of a baseball team was elected president (George W. Bush, 2001–2009), after being elected governor of Texas. As of this writing, movie star Matthew McConaughey may run for governor of Texas, though he has not declared a party affiliation. None of this should surprise us. Though Reagan, Trump, Schwarzenegger, and Bush were all Republicans, and Ventura was a member of the conservative Reform Party, it's only a matter of time before the celeb president is a Democrat.

The point here is to offer insights for media analysis, not political analysis (which is important, but beyond the scope of this book). After all, we live inside a planetary media ecology filled with memes, spectacle, and hyperreality, and celebs and entertainers are the gods of spectacle and hyperreality. And most humans worship their Gods and gods, regardless of whether there is empirical evidence or a plausible rationale for their worship.

Just as the *forms* of news media technology have evolved from newspapers to electronic screens, the *content* of news has evolved (or devolved) from information to entertainment, from facts to fame to fake news. For a TV screen or a computer screen to function, we must be in front of the screen, staring at, watching, or gazing at what is on the screen. Screens convert us into viewers and present an ethos where *viewing is doing*. For example, if we ask friends what they have been doing, they might say they were watching a movie on Netflix, playing the *Call of Duty* video game, or scrolling through some Twitter or Instagram feeds. In all these examples, they are viewing what is on a screen. Viewing is what they are doing.

Who do we like to view the most on a screen? Celebrities! We like to watch celebs and we expect them to entertain us. Many of us expect celebs to be founts of enlightenment and even to serve as our political leaders. As Ellis Cashmore explains in this chapter's reading "Answering/The Big Question," celebs are secular gods and goddesses, our public symbols of capitalism, democracy, and individualism. They are icons of our hopes, dreams, and destinies.

In a culture of screens and entertainment, that's why celebrities rule and truth is just the latest hot take. That's why you might well reject the following analyses, precisely because your brain has evolved amid a hot media hyperreality. That's the power of memes.

THE ROLE OF THE NEWS MEDIA

Many people think the role of the news media is to cheerlead for Team America, support their favorite political leader, or overlook criminal activities of high-ranking officials anywhere in America or the rest of the world. The same is true for the news media in any city or nation. This belief is deeply flawed. Journalists and the news media should report both the good and the bad. The role of journalism and news media is not to merely report "facts," for facts without context and analysis can be incomplete, misleading, or downright deceptive. *The role of journalism and the news media is to uncover evidence, explain events, find the truth, and report it all in a cohesive and meaningful manner—always taking the side of truth.* Sadly, in today's hot media world of TV talking heads and Twitter gods, truth is too often swept asunder in a tsunami of rants, factoids, bogus assertions, and conspiracy theories, all more aligned with ideology than with the actual reality they claim to describe.

THE DISH AND DIRT

Why do so many people want the dish on their fave celebs yet deny the dirt on their fave political and military leaders? Is it popularity versus patriotism? Paparazzi swarm the celebrities, while the Pentagon and the White House hide dirty secrets that few citizens care to know and few journalists bother to investigate. Worse, millions of Americans now routinely dismiss facts as "fake news," unable or unwilling to comprehend a world beyond the hyperreality constructed in their echo chambers.

So, what about the real news that is forgotten or denied? What about when the Pentagon and presidents deceive the public about wars or war crimes? If you think that American "national security" needs protection, the Supreme Court long ago rejected that argument when it comes to war and the public's right to know what the military is doing in our nation's name. *It's time to set aside being a joystick general or naive patriot and think critically about the role of news, especially news involving war, death, and destruction.* It's great that Harvey Weinstein and his ilk are brought down via #MeToo, but what about generals and presidents who may have committed or permitted war crimes? After all, the United States signed the Geneva Conventions, which forbid torture and the inhumane treatment of captured soldiers and civilians as well as the "carpet bombing" of villages, towns, and cities. Is this mentioned in any of the Hollywood movies that glorify warfare? Think about it.

HOLLYWOOD AND THE NEWS

Hollywood has produced several excellent films that critique the complex roles of news media in society. There are three general approaches taken in these films:

1. Portray journalists and the news media as heroic pursuers of truth in the challenging of political and economic power, most notably *All the President's Men (1976), Good Night, and Good Luck (2005),* and, most recently, *The Post* (2017). All three films are based on real historical events.
2. Show how the news media can be manipulated by powerful political and corporate interests, as portrayed in *Meet John Doe* (1941), *The China Syndrome* (1979), and the satiric dark comedy *Wag the Dog* (1997). Ahead of their time, *Meet John Doe* and *Wag the Dog* both show how "fake news" can be created.
3. Provide a dystopian portrayal of the news media succumbing to the sheer power of the spectacle and entertainment, as shown in *Ace in the Hole* (1951), *Network* (1976), and *Wag the Dog.*

These films show there is a long history of debate and criticism about the effects of print, electronic, and digital media on the dissemination of news, information, knowledge, and understanding in society. On one hand, we are living amid an information explosion, yet we face information overload as much of the enlightening information is overwhelmed by entertainment. How media and society have adapted to these conditions is shown in the popularity of *The Colbert Report* and *The Daily Show* (with Trevor Noah), along with more recent comedy news shows like *Full Frontal* (starring Samantha Bee) and *Last Week Tonight* (starring John Oliver). That these shows appear on Comedy Central, HBO, and YouTube seems to confirm the overall vision of media ecologist Neil Postman and attorney/professor Marty Kaplan. We apparently need court jesters to help us handle the corruption of our political leaders and the stupidity of a dumbed-down society, wedded to entertainment, echo chambers, and cults of arrogant ignorance.

FACTS, TRUTH, AND NEWSPAPERS

As dramatized in Steven Spielberg's *The Post*, the struggle between government secrets and freedom of the press is a crucial issue facing democratic society. Facts and truth matter, then and now.

The publisher of the *Washington Post*, Kay Graham (Meryl Streep), and her editor, Ben Bradlee (Tom Hanks), faced complex challenges in deciding to publish stories based on documents leaked by a military analyst working for the Pentagon. The documents revealed that US military leaders were clearly deceiving the American public about the results of the war in Vietnam. In fact, they were flat-out lying, including hiding war crimes and unnecessary death and destruction among civilian populations. The deception spanned *twenty* years. This was real news involving real events, and it deserves to be remembered just as much as *Keeping Up with the Kardashians*. Real dirt on presidents is probably more important than dish on celebs.

What many people do not realize is that news reporters often base their stories on leaked documents or leaked information. How else to ferret out crime and corruption among the superpowerful? Leaking and publishing is key to a free press, an informed electorate, and an open society. In fact, leaked information is central to two of America's greatest and most famous examples of investigative journalism:

- Using a copy machine, Daniel Ellsberg (an analyst with the RAND Corporation, which consulted with the Pentagon) provided copies of classified materials to the *Washington Post*, the *New York Times,* and other newspapers, which published information about the lies and corruption involving the US war in Vietnam. Even the Pentagon's own reports documented the falsehoods.
- Using tips and leaked information from an inside source, Bob Woodward and Carl Bernstein unraveled the Watergate criminal conspiracy that brought down the Richard Nixon administration.

As shown in *The Post*, the Pentagon Papers events represent high points in the media's role of countering government power and helping preserve democracy and representative government.

During the Vietnam War, Ellsberg worked for the Pentagon and became concerned when he learned that the US military was misrepresenting what was happening in the war, especially the secret expansion of the war and the bombing of Cambodia and Laos.[1] The Johnson administration and military deceived the US Congress; none of this had been reported in the mainstream media. Ellsberg used a copy machine to make copies of the Pentagon's detailed secret report, which came to be known as the "Pentagon Papers."[2] In 1971, Ellsberg leaked the papers to select newspapers and they began reporting on the information, which contradicted what the military had

---

1   See the documentary film *The Most Dangerous Man in America: Daniel Ellsberg and the Pentagon Papers* (2009).
2   The official title of the report was *United States–Vietnam Relations, 1945–1967: A Study Prepared by the Department of Defense.*

been telling US citizens and their political representatives. Keep in mind, the military and democratically elected political representatives are supposed to be subordinate to the citizens.

Ellsberg was eventually identified and charged with felony crimes under the Espionage Act of 1917. President Nixon and the White House were unable to convince the news media not to publish the stories, so the US government sued the *New York Times* in an attempt to set a precedent and prevent publication of the documents. President Nixon sought executive authority to silence the press on grounds of national security. In other words, the government's plan B was censorship, buttressed by fears of damaging "national security."

THE SUPREME COURT AND THE PUBLIC'S RIGHT TO KNOW

The legal battle between a free press and government censorship quickly reached the US Supreme Court. On June 30, 1971, the court issued its landmark verdict in favor of the *New York Times* and freedom of the press. In a 6–3 vote, the court struck down the injunction that prohibited the press from publishing the stories. The court ruled that the press had the First Amendment right to publish the articles without "prior restraint," a censorship doctrine that the United States has since abandoned, going back to the famous trial of John Peter Zenger in the eighteenth century.

The Supreme Court's opinion was crafted by Hugo Black and William O. Douglas, two of America's greatest free-speech jurists in the twentieth century. Because of the controversy surrounding WikiLeaks, the Terror War, and so-called fears of damaging "national security," it is necessary to quote at length from the court's opinion:

> Both the history and language of the First Amendment support the view that the press must be left free to publish news, whatever the source, without censorship, injunctions, or prior restraints.
>
> In the First Amendment the Founding Fathers gave the free press the protection it must have to fulfill its essential role in our democracy. The press was to serve the governed, not the governors. *[The Government's power to censor the press was abolished so that the press would remain forever free to censure the Government. The press was protected so that it could bare the secrets of government and inform the people. Only a free and unrestrained press can effectively expose deception in government. And paramount among the responsibilities of a free press is the duty to prevent any part of the government from deceiving the people and sending them off to distant lands to die of foreign fevers and foreign shot and shell.]* In my view, far from deserving condemnation for their courageous reporting, the *New York Times*, the *Washington Post*, and other newspapers should be commended for serving the purpose that the Founding Fathers saw so clearly. In revealing the workings of government that led to the Vietnam war, the newspapers nobly did precisely that which the Founders hoped and trusted they would do. ...
>
> To find that the President has "inherent power" to halt the publication of news by resort to the courts would wipe out the First Amendment and destroy the fundamental liberty and security of the very people the Government hopes to make "secure." No one can read the history of the adoption of the First Amendment without being convinced beyond any doubt that it was injunctions like those sought here that Madison and his collaborators intended to outlaw in this Nation for all time.
>
> *[The word security is a broad, vague generality whose contours should not be invoked to abrogate the fundamental law embodied in the First Amendment. The guarding of military and diplomatic*

secrets at the expense of informed representative government provides no real security for our Republic.][3] [Italics mine.]

Along with the Supreme Court's decision, the Watergate and Pentagon Papers events represent high points in the mass media's role of helping end an increasingly unpopular war while preserving some features of democratic society. Five decades later, many of America's newspapers and mass media do not have the vision (or they lack the courage) to challenge military and political authority when it is most necessary. And it seems that many citizens do not care, either, or that they feel hopeless in effecting any change. Nevertheless, sites like WikiLeaks are filling the media void with digital media, thus representing the next phase in the technological evolution of news and journalism.[4] This evolution cannot be stopped without destroying freedom of the press and the power of the internet.

Ellsberg used a copy machine to copy the documents, to replicate the memes of the Pentagon's reports. Back in 1970, photocopying was a relatively new technology and was considered powerful, though the paper documents still had to pass from hand to hand. Today, WikiLeaks and other organizations use the internet, an exponentially more powerful technology, perfect for replicating memes on a global scale, from one computer to billions of computers.

Four decades after the Vietnam War and the Pentagon Papers, the United States found itself in another controversial war. In the Vietnam War, American citizens were told that the US soldiers and bomber pilots were fighting, dying, and killing to contain communism. In the war in the Middle East, citizens were told that soldiers were fighting, dying, and killing to contain terrorism by invading Iraq, even though the evidence suggests Iraq posed no threat to the United States and did not mastermind the terrorist attacks of September 11, 2001.

The Manning leaks. In 2010, Chelsea Manning, a soldier in the US Army, leaked a large collection of classified documents to WikiLeaks. Much of the information in the documents was subsequently published in 2010 and 2011 by WikiLeaks, the *Guardian, Der Spiegel*, and the *New York Times*. Known as the Iraq War logs and Afghan War logs, some of these documents reveal deceit, misinformation, and apparent *war crimes perpetrated by the US military.*[5] Manning was eventually identified, arrested, and convicted in a military court of violating the Espionage Act and was sentenced to thirty-five years in prison. In 2017, US president Obama commuted Manning's sentence to seven years of confinement.

The Snowden leaks. In 2013, Edward Snowden, an intelligence agent with the National Security Agency (NSA), leaked classified documents regarding the surveillance abuses by the NSA. Fearful of facing a long prison term like Manning, Snowden fled to Russia, where he remains in exile (as of this writing). In sum, Manning and Snowden are whistleblowers who "leaked" information about military and government activities that they thought citizens of the United States and the world should know about. Though their leaks surely violate their contracts or oaths to the military and the NSA, the leaks to the media follow well-established precedents.

In the wars in Vietnam and the Middle East, the presidents and Pentagon officials deceived the American public, and more than one million people were killed in the destruction. As with the My Lai massacre in Vietnam, evidence surfaced regarding American soldiers committing war crimes in Iraq. Shouldn't the American public know the activities of its military and political leaders, especially when war is involved?

---

3   *New York Times Co. v. United States*, 403 US 713 (1971).
4   Charlie Beckett and James Ball, *WikiLeaks: News in the Networked Era* (Cambridge, UK: Polity, 2012).
5   Perhaps the most famous of the leaked documents is the video of US Apache helicopter pilots shooting down about a dozen people on the streets of Baghdad, at times bragging and laughing while they did it. Two of the dead were journalists for Reuters News. Reuters requested to see the video, but those requests were denied. Eventually, the video was among the documents leaked to WikiLeaks, which then made the video available to the media. Dan Froomkin, "WikiLeaks VIDEO Exposes 2007 'Collateral Murder' in Iraq," *Huffington Post*, June 5, 2010. As of this writing, the video is available on YouTube and Vimeo, listed under "Collateral Murder."

In principle, Ellsberg, Manning, and Snowden are whistleblowers. They copied information—about deceitful and controversial war tactics, strategies, and policies—and released it to the media. It is instructive that the Watergate scandal and the Pentagon Papers case both emerged while America was involved in a controversial war. Many media critics make the case that the press should be muzzled in times of war; this meme spreads uncritically among many minds, especially the talking heads on television and their tribes of viewers. Muzzling the press and the news media is dangerous and counterfactual to legal precedent clearly established by the US Supreme Court. It is when a nation is at war, especially a controversial war, that the press must remain courageous and free, at least in an open and democratic society.

If we want the dish on celebs, then we should get the dirt on the military and political leaders. Or should we just put our heads in the sand about war crimes while making sure NFL players stand for the national anthem (chapter 6)? Meanwhile, the perpetrators of the war crimes have yet to face any charges in court.

Similarly, the White House and Senate cheerleaders of the violent insurrection on January 6, 2021, have yet to face any changes or penalties for supporting the overthrow of a free and fair election. Yes, antidemocratic forces sought to overthrow a presidential election and now seek to suppress voting in the United States while setting the stage for overturning future elections. Sadly, those are facts. Did all that hit your hot button? Those sensations and emotional reactions are your mind utterly conditioned by hot media and hyperreality to react and respond with tribal warfare and conspiracy theory (See appendix C).

WHY TV IS LIKE LAS VEGAS AND DISNEYLAND

It's no surprise that the first Disneyland was built just as television began its proliferation across America, putting entertainment at the center of our living rooms and our brains. After all, no one buys a "reading center" for their homes, but many people have "entertainment centers" in their houses, where their television, stereo, and video games are integrated into a site for the consumption of spectacle. Apple and Best Buy make billions of dollars in profit, while Barnes & Noble struggles and Borders Books goes out of business. Of course, Amazon sells books and e-books, but that barely dents the proliferation of entertainment technology.

Across the decades, TV screens have transformed the news from being mostly about information to being about entertainment, from a shared daily reality provided by local newspapers to fragmented echo chambers on screens networked across cities, nations, and the planet. As seen at your local Best Buy or Apple store, TV screens and computer screens are proliferating and getting ever larger in size. In contrast, daily newspapers are struggling to merely survive, their relevance, revenues, and readership shrinking every day.

"THE AGE OF SHOW BUSINESS"

In his book *Amusing Ourselves to Death: Public Discourse in the Age of Show Business*, Neil Postman explains that the technology of television has never been neutral and its very nature amplifies the pleasure of entertainment, with little room for the power of enlightenment. It is naive to think that television can produce an overall enlightened society. A student of Marshall McLuhan, Postman explains it like this:

> Such a hope represents what Marshall McLuhan used to call "rear-view mirror" thinking; the assumption that a new medium is merely an extension or amplification of an older one; that an automobile, for example, is only a fast horse, or that electric light is a powerful candle. To make such a mistake in the matter at hand is to misconstrue entirely how television redefines the meaning of public discourse. Television does not extend or amplify literate culture. It attacks it.[6]

---

6 Neil Postman, *Amusing Ourselves to Death: Public Discourse in the Age of Show Business* (New York: Viking, 1985), 83–84.

As explained in chapter 1 of this book, no media technology is neutral. The medium is the message, with each technology massaging our consciousness to embrace the dominant worldview—the essential way of seeing the world—presented by the technology. As Postman explains, the dominant worldview of television is entertainment:

> Entertainment is the supra-ideology of all discourse on television. No matter what is depicted or from what point of view, the overarching assumption is that it is there for our amusement and pleasure. That is why even on news shows which provide us daily with fragments of tragedy and barbarism, we are urged by broadcasters to "join them tomorrow." What for? One would think that several minutes of murder and mayhem would suffice as material for a month of sleepless nights. ... Everything about a news show tells us this—the good looks and amiability of the cast, their pleasant banter, the exciting music that opens and closes the show, the vivid film footage, the attractive commercials—all these and more suggest that what we have just seen is no cause for weeping. A news show, to put it plainly, is a format for entertainment, not for education, reflection or catharsis.[7]

Postman was writing in the 1980s, just as cable TV was spreading in America, yet his insights have become even more true with the proliferation of cable news, the internet, and social media like Facebook and Twitter. Entertainment has moved deep into our electric consciousness, creating a performative culture seeking the endless attention of audiences. And who best grabs attention? It is celebrities, movie stars, and reality-TV stars, along with their online extended family of microcelebrities, influencers, and bloggers and vloggers. Marty Kaplan, director of the Norman Lear Center, dedicated to the study of entertainment on society, at the University of Southern California, explains this process:

> In contemporary America, and arguably in most industrial democracies, the imperative of practically every domain of human existence is to grab and hold the attention of audiences. In politics, it is now more important for a candidate to have big name recognition, and the money to buy big media, than it is to have big ideas. In news, it is essential to have high ratings, but it only optional to have high accuracy.[8]

This drive to entertain and perform for audiences has transformed journalism and the news business. Kaplan writes,

> Communication, rather than striving to convey truth and meaning, now prizes informing an audience less than having an audience. The public interest has been redefined as what the public is interested in; the public sphere has become a theater, where citizenship is performance. ... Journalism, whose practitioners in high-end newspapers and early broadcast outlets once saw their tasks as recording the truth, now largely functions to hold up a mirror to our funhouse reflection. ... The fairness of the contemporary journalism resembles not the fairness of a judge and jury weighing evidence within a framework of rules, but rather the fairground of the carnival midway, where barkers shout out on behalf of their wares. ... Like it or not, our species is a sucker for novelty; sex, fear, pictures, motion, noise scatology; fin; we can't stop our eyes from turning toward spectacle and celebrity.[9]

---

7 Postman, *Amusing Ourselves*, 87–88.
8 Marty Kaplan, "Welcome to the Infotainment Freak Show," in *What Orwell Didn't Know: Propaganda and the New Face of American Politics*, ed. András Szántó (New York: PublicAffairs, 2007), 138.
9 Kaplan, 139–40, 142.

What are the biggest testaments to these conditions? Twitter, Instagram, Facebook, and almost every other social media platform. Shakespeare wrote that "all the world's a stage," but now that stage is within the hyperreality radiating across the world from Disneyland and Las Vegas. Kaplan writes,

> Commerce, once about goods and services, is today about experiences and aspirations; every store promises a little bit of Disneyland. Even our interior lives are played out through the tropes of entertainment.[10]

And Postman writes,

> For Las Vegas is a city entirely devoted to the idea of entertainment, and as such proclaims the spirit of a culture in which all public discourse increasingly takes the form of entertainment. Our politics, religion, news, athletics, education and commerce have been transformed into congenial adjuncts of show business, largely without protest or even much popular notice. The result is that we are a people on the verge of amusing ourselves to death.[11]

Though Kaplan and Postman are not referencing Jean Baudrillard, the connection of television to Disneyland and Las Vegas is perceptive and accurate. Baudrillard writes,

> Disneyland is presented as imaginary in order to make us believe the rest is real, whereas all of Los Angeles and the America that surrounds it are no longer real, but belong to the hyperreal order and the order of simulation.[12]

As long we believe that Disneyland is fake and what's outside is "real," then television and social media will exert their power to surround us with spectacle and hyperreality, the very signs and symbols that substitute for the real (chapter 3). Given the expanding size of TV screens and computer screens, it is no surprise that ego-driven, hot media conditions prevail. We live in a hyperreal ecology filled with gods, celebs, and fake news vying for power and domination.

DEALING WITH FAKE NEWS

Knowing facts is crucial to democracy and a sane daily existence. So are real news and real journalists. Sadly, we now have millions of Americans who do not care what the facts are about their favorite celebs and political leaders. Obvious lies are embraced as truths, serial liars are worshipped as gods, and democracy is now in serious danger in America. Entertainment and echo chambers dominate, while QAnon conspiracy theories present "truths" and "prophecies"—no more valid than nonsense of Nostradamus and astrology charts of Co–Star, all supposedly predicting the events of nations and the destinies of people (see appendix C). Real news is denounced as "fake news," while fake news and fake realities proliferate. Simulacra are everywhere, as signs and symbols substitute for reality and authenticity. Welcome to hyperreality, where there are no easy solutions.

In addition to the overall ecology of hot media and hyperreality, fake news (and propaganda) replicates for a complex variety of reasons. As detailed by Justin McBrayer in the book *Beyond Fake News*, these reasons include

- Being overwhelmed by information glut and by cheap access to endless streams of "news" and "information," especially misinformation;

---

10   Kaplan, 138.
11   Neil Postman, *Amusing Ourselves to Death: Public Discourse in the Age of Show Business* (New York: Viking Penguin, 1986), 3.
12   Jean Baudrillard, *Simulacra and Simulation* (Ann Arbor: University of Michigan Press, 1994), 12.

- Our personal biases to consume *what we want*, an intrinsic drive that has been amplified by consumer society and the customization of all products and services (see chapter 7);
- Intellectual blind spots to which our species has yet to adapt;
- The drive for simple answers to complex questions, especially the *big questions*: Why are we here? How and why did this event happen? Who is running the world? and so on; and
- The reluctance to have our worldview challenged, no matter how convincing the logic and evidence for another worldview or belief system.[13]

McBrayer likens the proliferation of fake news and misinformation to pollution and litter that need to be cleaned up, thus suggesting that you "pick up a rake and clean up your own yard," "ask your neighbors not to litter," and "support the clean-up effort of professionals" to "keep America beautiful." Other collective and social steps include boycotting misinformation, making companies more responsible, and providing "carrots" and "sticks" for preventing the creation and replication of fake news.[14]

However, we must keep in mind that all news stories and pieces of information are memes, and memes want to replicate! In a 24/7 media ecology, countering that power is a profound challenge. In the book *The Anatomy of Fake News*, Nolan Higdon recommends ten steps for detecting fake news, given in the exhibit below.

TEN STEPS FOR DETECTING FAKE NEWS AND SAVING DEMOCRACY[15]

1. DO I WANT TO BE INFORMED OR A FAKE NEWS DISSEMINATOR?

- Given the massive amount of online news, sharing new content does not make us informed or enlightened. It's far better to investigate rather than hit the share button for our echo chambers.

2. SHOULD I REACT OR INVESTIGATE?

- Hot media conditions generate instant reactions, and fake news is designed to elicit emotional reactions—tapping to what you already believe, regardless of whether it is true or not.
- As Higdon writes, "When we slow down, we can investigate the content and its underlying evidence."

3. WHY WAS MY ATTENTION DRAWN TO THIS CONTENT?

- When we encounter news content, we need to realize it is was programmed for our echo chamber. To counter this, we all need to practice self-reflection, recognize our personal biases, and limit our attraction to content that has been designed for us to share before thinking.

4. WHO IS THE PUBLISHER OF THIS CONTENT?

- We need to identify the source of the news content. Different creators have different motives, including legitimate news organizations, political parties, government agencies, celebrity PR agents, and many other self-interested actors.

---

13   Justin McBrayer, *Beyond Fake News: Finding the Truth in a World of Misinformation* (New York: Routledge, 2021). These reasons are discussed across chapters 1–6 of McBrayer's book.
14   McBrayer, *Beyond Fake News*, 164–181.
15   Note: In the bullet points, I have paraphrased Higdon and sometimes added my own thoughts to correlate with themes in this book.

5. WHO IS THE AUTHOR OF THIS CONTENT?

• Is the author with a legitimate publisher, news organization, or institution? Of course, this does not prevent news organizations from making mistakes or intentionally presenting falsehoods, but asking this question is a key step in detecting fake news.

6. DO I UNDERSTAND THIS CONTENT?

• Be honest. Do you really understand what you are reading and sharing? Pseudoscience and antiscience proliferate by relying on the presumption of knowledge, when the "knowledge" is bogus, incorrect, or an outright falsehood.
• For any story you believe and share, you should know the following: Who? What? When? Where? Why? How? Otherwise, you do not *know* the truth of the story.
• Reliable fact-checking organizations exist: Media Matters, Fairness & Accuracy in Reporting (FAIR), Snopes, PolitiFact, and FactCheck.

7. DOES THE EVIDENCE HOLD UP UNDER SCRUTINY?

• Is there any empirical evidence for the news claim? Does the evidence hold up when analyzed?
• Is the claim based on a fallacy, such as ad hominem (attacking the speaker, not the message), straw person, non sequitur (conclusion does not follow), false equivocation, red herring, appeal to questionable authority, ad populum (bandwagon), begging the question (circular reasoning), glittering generality (sounds so great), slippery slope, oversimplification, appeal to perfection (the utopian fallacy), wishful thinking, magical beliefs (theology, astrology), and virtually all conspiracy theories (see appendix C).

8. WHAT IS MISSING FROM THIS CONTENT?

• Keep in mind, the *absence* of information is often just as important as the information present in the news story. Fake news preys on lack of evidence and missing information. One way to see what is missing is to cross-check the story with other news stories on the same topic.

9. WHO MIGHT BENEFIT FROM OR BE HARMED BY THIS MESSAGE?

• History provides numerous examples of fake news, propaganda, and misinformation generating support for wars, social division, and dictatorial regimes. Often the goal is to generate moral panics and outrage, radicalize citizens and consumers, marginalize the legitimate press, and manipulate democracy to install an authoritarian regime.

10. DOES THIS CONTENT QUALIFY AS JOURNALISM?

• Does the news and information serve any of these democratic functions: aiding the marketplace of ideas, setting the public agenda, serving as a watchdog against powerful interests (such as governments and corporations), and disseminating truthful information to mobilize the public to effect legal social change? Most importantly, we must recall that the prime function of journalists and legitimate news organization is to promote truth and accuracy and fairness and impartiality, to be accountable, and to uphold humanity.

Note: The bullet points paraphrase Higdon and sometimes include Professor Vacker's own thoughts to correlate with themes in this book.
Source: Nolan Higdon, *The Anatomy of Fake News: A Critical News Literacy Education* (Oakland: University of California Press, 2020), 144–158.

CELEBRITIES AND POP CULTURE

Judging by the popularity of celebrities and entertainers, we might conclude that their world and their lives are very important to most of society. People worry about fake news, yet celebs get all kinds of cosmetic surgery and have their bodies and faces digitally enhanced in Hollywood films. You don't really think all those hunky actors are that ripped, do you? Do all those six-pack abs came solely from diet and exercise, from personal chefs and personal trainers? Modified celebrities are part of the spectacle and hyperreality discussed in chapter 3.

Celebrities are famous people—that much is obvious. Many make lots of money and seem to live glamorous lives among "the beautiful people." Celebrities are the royalty of media culture, the aristocrats of pop culture. We like to gaze upon celebrities, the gods and goddesses of our dreams and desires. They star in our movies, TV shows, and sporting events. Two celebrities have starred as president of the United States: Ronald Reagan (movie star) and Donald Trump (reality-TV star).

Many people like to watch celebrities talk to other celebrities on TV talk shows. Many people just like to watch celebrities, whatever they are doing, for a variety of reasons. That's the whole point of *Keeping Up with the Kardashians*: watching them embody the consumer-celebrity lifestyle of which most of us can only dream. The Kardashians validate the Hollywood-American dream of everyday glam and sprawling luxury, along with the narcissism and voyeurism of social media culture. And our voyeurism is powered by paparazzi and the internet.

THE PAPARAZZI AND THE INTERNET

The term *paparazzi* entered global pop culture with Federico Fellini's *La Dolce Vita*, the 1960 masterpiece about the emerging mores of celebrity culture in post–World War II Rome. Sixty years later, the paparazzi fuel the replication of celebrity culture around the world via the media environments. In effect, the paparazzi keep celebrities under surveillance, functioning like guards we place on the celebrities to watch their every move. The paparazzi surround them, stalking them, hoping to get the money shot that will appear on the covers of all the celebrity magazines (*People*), the gossip tabloids (*National Enquirer*), and the up-to-the-minute scandal sites (TMZ.com). Celebrities are memes, with their images replicating throughout the network. So it's no surprise that getting the dish on them is very profitable.

The internet enables celebrities to bypass the paparazzi and traditional news media to communicate with their followers via Twitter, Facebook, YouTube, and other social media platforms. As of this writing, Barack Obama, Katy Perry, and Justin Bieber all have over one hundred million Twitter followers. Perry's YouTube channel has forty million followers, while her anthem "Roar" has been viewed over 3.4 billion times. Of course, the internet also empowers microcelebrities, those who have used social media to attain fame outside the traditional Hollywood and mass media systems.

In *The Circle*, Mae becomes a worldwide celebrity when she volunteers to go "fully transparent" and wear the SeeChange camera 24/7. Portrayed by Emma Watson, Mae has millions of fans and followers who text about her every move and mood. Social media and Moore's Law make it possible for Mae to be a celebrity. In the world of *The Hunger Games*, Katniss instantly becomes a celebrity because of her triumph with Peeta in the Hunger Games. Winners of the Hunger Games become famous and revered, like the winners of the World Cup, the Super Bowl, *American Idol*, and a host of other shows in which people compete for awards, ratings, and the possibility of being a celebrity.

Keep in mind that just because you follow these celebrities on Twitter or Instagram does not mean that you know them. You are viewing a crafted, mediated version of them, located in the realm of the spectacle and hyperreality. In effect, you are viewing their memes and simulacra, their signs and symbols absent the original person, who is not present.

CELEBRITY SCIENTISTS

Celebrities are not limited to movie stars and super-rich people. After all, Stephen Hawking was a celebrity, likely the most famous scientist in the world at the time of his death. His fame was amplified enormously by *A Brief History of Time*, the fabulous documentary based on his book of the same name. Directed by Errol Morris, this documentary was a hit movie at the box office, and I recall it playing to packed theaters the two times I saw it. When I was a professor at SMU in Dallas, I had the good fortune to see Hawking talk on campus in 1999. He was treated as if he was a visiting rock star. The campus was abuzz, and local radio stations and newspapers covered his visit with excitement.

In the era of electronic mass media, the first celebrity scientists were probably Albert Einstein, Jane Goodall, and Carl Sagan. Sagan was famed for the epic thirteen-part documentary series *Cosmos: A Personal Voyage* (1980). *Cosmos* completely blew me away when I saw it as a rerun in the late 1980s. Goodall, one of the most important scientists of the twentieth century, was featured in the 2017 documentary *Jane*. With the proliferation of cable television, social media, and online streaming, celebrity scientists are proliferating. These include Neil deGrasse Tyson, Brian Cox, Lisa Randall, Jim Al-Khalili, Andrea Ghez, Michio Kaku, Mae Jemison, Steven Pinker, Amy Mainzer, and Jill Tarter, who was the real-life role model for Ellie Arroway, the character portrayed by Jodie Foster in the 1997 hit movie *Contact*. Tyson hosted *Cosmos: A Spacetime Odyssey* (2014), while Cox has hosted several documentary series for the BBC, most notably *Wonders of the Universe* (2011). The key to being a celebrity scientist is the ability to work well with electronic media, conveying wit, charm, and charisma, especially in documentaries and social media.[16]

Certainly, it is nice that scientists can be celebrities like movie stars, explain scientific concepts in sound bites for entertainment consciousness, and have millions of followers on Twitter. But it's one thing to write a popular book about science and be hip with tweets and quite another thing to integrate the big bang and the majestic universe into a meaningful cosmic and cultural narrative that will be embraced by the human species. Science alone is not enough, for it must be complimented by art and philosophy.

CELEBRITY ARTISTS

As Pablo Picasso, Frida Kahlo, and Andy Warhol showed, artists can also become huge celebrities. Celebrity artists today include Damien Hirst, James Turrell, Jenny Holzer, Kehinde Wiley, Jean-Michel Basquiat, Michael Heizer, and many others. Those artists who do become celebrities are masters of the artistic spectacle and the use of media technologies and mediated images. For Warhol, it was his silk screens of celebrity photos, while Wiley often portrays Black celebrities or Black youth in settings that reference the classical paintings of pre-1800 European artists. Basquiat's "neo-expressionist" paintings were inspired by Black American, African, and Aztec cultural histories, along with the celebrity culture of musicians and athletes.

Hirst creatively appropriates signs and symbols (simulacra) that are circulating in art and mediated pop culture, most famously a dead shark floating in formaldehyde in a glass case. It's *Jaws* conquered for you to experience as an aesthetic object. For several decades, Holzer has deployed images of written language in multiple visual forms, especially the glowing electronic scrolls with various phrases.

Turrell uses electric light as a pure art form to illuminate installations in sites ranging from the Guggenheim Museum to the epic Roden Crater, a dormant volcano in a remote area of northern Arizona. Google it. Roden Crater is home to a mind-blowing collection of naked-eye observatories—integrating nature, the stars, and the viewer in an aesthetic experience. Cool media as art.

Heizer's specialty is monumental land art, and his media are the elements of Earth itself, which he uses to great effect in contrast with skies, space, and technological civilization. His most recent popular work is *Levitated Mass*, the megalithic 340-ton boulder astride a 400-foot-long concrete trench on the grounds of the Los Angeles County Museum of Art. You experience the art by walking under the boulder situated against the skies of LA. That *Levitated Mass* is the subject of its own documentary film attests to the celebrity status of Heizer. As the film shows, the boulder was carried on a gigantic truck (biggest truck I've even seen, by far) that snaked through LA at 1–2 miles per hour while generating a media spectacle. Cheering crowds gathered and street parties were held at night as the boulder passed by, with many people recording it on their phones—showing that the boulder was, indeed, a rock star!

---

16   Declan Fahey, *The Celebrity Scientists: Out of the Lab and into the Limelight* (Lanham, MD: Rowman and Littlefield, 2015).

THE AGE OF SHOW BUSINESS

from *Amusing Ourselves to Death*

NEIL POSTMAN (1931–2003) was an American critic and educator who taught at New York University. *Amusing Ourselves to Death* was not only a best-selling book, but it inspired the concept album, *Amused to Death* (1992), by Roger Waters, former bassist for Pink Floyd.

A dedicated graduate student I know returned to his small apartment the night before a major examination only to discover that his solitary lamp was broken beyond repair. After a whiff of panic, he was able to restore both his equanimity and his chances for a satisfactory grade by turning on the television set, turning off the sound, and with his back to the set, using its light to read important passages on which he was to be tested. This is one use of television—as a source of illuminating the printed page.

But the television screen is more than a light source. It is also a smooth, nearly flat surface on which the printed word may be displayed. We have all stayed at hotels in which the TV set has had a special channel for describing the day's events in letters rolled endlessly across the screen. This is another use of television—as an electronic bulletin board.

Many television sets are also large and sturdy enough to bear the weight of a small library. The top of an old-fashioned RCA console can handle as many as thirty books, and I know one woman who has securely placed her entire collection of Dickens, Flaubert, and Turgenev on the top of a 21-inch Westinghouse. Here is still another use of television—as bookcase.

I bring forward these quixotic uses of television to ridicule the hope harbored by some that television can be used to support the literate tradition. Such a hope represents exactly what Marshall McLuhan used to call "rear-view mirror" thinking: the assumption that a new medium is merely an extension or amplification of an older one; that an automobile, for example, is only a fast horse, or an electric light a powerful candle. To make such a mistake in the matter at hand is to misconstrue entirely how television redefines the meaning of public discourse. Television does not extend or amplify literate culture. It attacks it. If television is a continuation of anything, it is of a tradition begun by the telegraph and photograph in the mid-nineteenth century, not by the printing press in the fifteenth.

What is television? What kinds of conversations does it permit? What are the intellectual tendencies it encourages? What sort of culture does it produce?

These are the questions to be addressed in the rest of this book, and to approach them with a minimum of confusion, I must begin by making a distinction between a technology and a medium. We might say that a technology is to a medium as the brain is to the mind. Like the brain, a technology is a physical apparatus. Like the mind, a medium is a use to which a physical apparatus is put. A technology becomes a medium as it employs a particular symbolic code, as it finds its place in a particular social setting, as it insinuates itself into economic and political contexts. A technology, in other words, is merely a machine. A medium is the social and intellectual environment a machine creates.

Of course, like the brain itself, every technology has an inherent bias. It has within its physical form a predisposition toward being used in certain ways and not others. Only those who know nothing of the history of technology believe that a technology is entirely neutral. There is an old joke that mocks that naive belief. Thomas Edison, it goes, would have revealed his discovery of the electric light much sooner than he did except for the fact that every time he turned it on, he held it to his mouth and said, "Hello? Hello?"

Not very likely. Each technology has an agenda of its own. It is, as I have suggested, a metaphor waiting to enfold. The printing press, for example, had a clear bias toward being used as a linguistic medium. It is *conceivable* to use it exclusively for the reproduction of pictures. And, one imagines, the Roman Catholic Church would not have objected to its being so used in the sixteenth century. Had that been the case, the Protestant Reformation might not have occurred, for as Luther contended, with the word of God on every family's kitchen table, Christians do not require the Papacy to interpret it for them. But in fact there never was much chance that the press would be used solely, or even very much, for the duplication of icons. From its beginning in the fifteenth century, the press was perceived as an extraordinary opportunity for the display and mass distribution of written language. Everything about its technical possibilities led in that direction. One might even say it was invented for that purpose.

The technology of television has a bias, as well. It is conceivable to use television as a lamp, a surface for texts, a bookcase, even as radio. But it has not been so used and will not be so used, at least in America. Thus, in answering the question, What is television?, we must understand as a first point that we are not talking about television as a technology but television as a medium. There are many places in the world where television, though the same technology as it is in America, is an entirely different medium from that which we know. I refer to places where the majority of people do not have television sets, and those who do have only one; where

only one station is available; where television does not operate around the clock; where most programs have as their purpose the direct furtherance of government ideology and policy; where commercials are unknown, and "talking heads" are the principal image; where television is mostly used as if it were radio. For these reasons and more television will not have the same meaning or power as it does in America, which is to say, it is possible for a technology to be so used that its potentialities are prevented from developing and its social consequences kept to a minimum.

But in America, this has not been the case. Television has found in liberal democracy and a relatively free market economy a nurturing climate in which its full potentialities as a technology of images could be exploited. One result of this has been that American television programs are in demand all over the world. The total estimate of U.S. television program exports is approximately 100,000 to 200,000 hours, equally divided among Latin America, Asia and Europe.[1] Over the years, programs like "Gunsmoke," "Bonanza," "Mission: Impossible," "Star Trek," "Kojak," and more recently, "Dallas" and "Dynasty" have been as popular in England, Japan, Israel and Norway as in Omaha, Nebraska. I have heard (but not verified) that some years ago the Lapps postponed for several days their annual and, one supposes, essential migratory journey so that they could find out who shot J.R. All of this has occurred simultaneously with the decline of America's moral and political prestige, worldwide. American television programs are in demand not because America is loved but because American television is loved.

We need not be detained too long in figuring out why. In watching American television, one is reminded of George Bernard Shaw's remark on his first seeing the glittering neon signs of Broadway and 42nd Street at night. It must be beautiful, he said, if you cannot read. American television is, indeed, a beautiful spectacle, a visual delight, pouring forth thousands of images on any given day. The average length of a shot on network television is only 3.5 seconds, so that the eye never rests,

---

1 On July 20, 1984, *The New York Times* reported that the Chinese National Television network had contracted with CBS to broadcast sixty-four hours of CBS programming in China. Contracts with NBC and ABC are sure to follow. One hopes that the Chinese understand that such transactions are of great political consequence. The Gang of Four is as nothing compared with the Gang of Three.

always has something new to see. Moreover, television offers viewers a variety of subject matter, requires minimal skills to comprehend it, and is largely aimed at emotional gratification. Even commercials, which some regard as an annoyance, are exquisitely crafted, always pleasing to the eye and accompanied by exciting music. There is no question but that the best photography in the world is presently seen on television commercials. American television, in other words, is devoted entirely to supplying its audience with entertainment.

Of course, to say that television is entertaining is merely banal. Such a fact is hardly threatening to a culture, not even worth writing a book about. It may even be a reason for rejoicing. Life, as we like to say, is not a highway strewn with flowers. The sight of a few blossoms here and there may make our journey a trifle more endurable. The Lapps undoubtedly thought so. We may surmise that the ninety million Americans who watch television every night also think so. But what I am claiming here is not that television is entertaining but that it has made entertainment itself the natural format for the representation of all experience. Our television set keeps us in constant communion with the world, but it does so with a face whose smiling countenance is unalterable. The problem is not that television presents us with entertaining subject matter but that all subject matter is presented as entertaining, which is another issue altogether.

To say it still another way: Entertainment is the supra-ideology of all discourse on television. No matter what is depicted or from what point of view, the overarching presumption is that it is there for our amusement and pleasure. That is why even on news shows which provide us daily with fragments of tragedy and barbarism, we are urged by the newscasters to "join them tomorrow." What for? One would think that several minutes of murder and mayhem would suffice as material for a month of sleepless nights. We accept the newscasters' invitation because we know that the "news" is not to be taken seriously, that it is all in fun, so to say. Everything about a news show tells us this—the good looks and amiability of the cast, their pleasant banter, the exciting music that opens and closes the show, the vivid film footage, the attractive commercials—all these and more suggest that what we have just seen is no cause for weeping. A news show, to put it plainly, is a format for

entertainment, not for education, reflection or catharsis. And we must not judge too harshly those who have framed it in this way. They are not assembling the news to be read, or broadcasting it to be heard. They are televising the news to be seen. They must follow where their medium leads. There is no conspiracy here, no lack of intelligence, only a straightforward recognition that "good television" has little to do with what is "good" about exposition or other forms of verbal communication but everything to do with what the pictorial images look like.

I should like to illustrate this point by offering the case of the eighty-minute discussion provided by the ABC network on November 20, 1983, following its controversial movie *The Day After*. Though the memory of this telecast has receded for most, I choose this case because, clearly, here was television taking its most "serious" and "responsible" stance. Everything that made up this broadcast recommended it as a critical test of television's capacity to depart from an entertainment mode and rise to the level of public instruction. In the first place, the subject was the possibility of a nuclear holocaust. Second, the film itself had been attacked by several influential bodies politic, including the Reverend Jerry Falwell's Moral Majority. Thus, it was important that the network display television's value and serious intentions as a medium of information and coherent discourse. Third, on the program itself no musical theme was used as background—a significant point since almost all television programs are embedded in music, which helps to tell the audience what emotions are to be called forth. This is a standard theatrical device, and its absence on television is always ominous. Fourth, there were no commercials during the discussion, thus elevating the tone of the event to the state of reverence usually reserved for the funerals of assassinated Presidents. And finally, the participants included Henry Kissinger, Robert McNamara, and Elie Wiesel, each of whom is a symbol of sorts of serious discourse. Although Kissinger, somewhat later, made an appearance on the hit show "Dynasty," he was then and still is a paradigm of intellectual sobriety; and Wiesel, practically a walking metaphor of social conscience. Indeed, the other members of the cast—Carl Sagan, William Buckley and General Brent Scowcroft—are, each in his way, men of intellectual bearing who are not expected to participate in trivial public matters.

The program began with Ted Koppel, master of ceremonies, so to speak, indicating that what followed was not intended to be a debate but a *discussion*. And so those who are interested in philosophies of discourse had an excellent opportunity to observe what serious television means by the word "discussion." Here is what it means: Each of six men was given approximately five minutes to say something about the subject. There was, however, no agreement on exactly what the subject was, and no one felt obliged to respond to anything anyone else said. In fact, it would have been difficult to do so, since the participants were called upon seriatim, as if they were finalists in a beauty contest, each being given his share of minutes in front of the camera. Thus, if Mr. Wiesel, who was called upon last, had a response to Mr. Buckley, who was called upon first, there would have been four commentaries in between, occupying about twenty minutes, so that the audience (if not Mr. Wiesel himself) would have had difficulty remembering the argument which prompted his response. In fact, the participants—most of whom were no strangers to television—largely avoided addressing each other's points. They used their initial minutes and then their subsequent ones to intimate their position or give an impression. Dr. Kissinger, for example, seemed intent on making viewers feel sorry that he was no longer their Secretary of State by reminding everyone of books he had once written, proposals he had once made, and negotiations he had once conducted. Mr. McNamara informed the audience that he had eaten lunch in Germany that very afternoon, and went on to say that he had at least fifteen proposals to reduce nuclear arms. One would have thought that the discussion would turn on this issue, but the others seemed about as interested in it as they were in what he had for lunch in Germany. (Later, he took the initiative to mention three of his proposals but they were not discussed.) Elie Wiesel, in a series of quasi-parables and paradoxes, stressed the tragic nature of the human condition, but because he did not have the time to provide a context for his remarks, he seemed quixotic and confused, conveying an impression of an itinerant rabbi who has wandered into a coven of Gentiles.

In other words, this was no discussion as we normally use the word. Even when the "discussion" period began, there were no arguments or counterarguments, no scrutiny of assumptions, no explanations, no elaborations, no definitions. Carl Sagan made, in my opinion, the most coherent statement—a four-minute rationale for a nuclear freeze—but it contained at least two questionable assumptions and was not carefully examined. Apparently, no one wanted to take time from his own few minutes to call attention to someone else's. Mr. Koppel, for his part, felt obliged to keep the "show" moving, and though he occasionally pursued what he discerned as a line of thought, he was more concerned to give each man his fair allotment of time.

But it is not time constraints alone that produce such fragmented and discontinuous language. When a television show is in process, it is very nearly impermissible to say, "Let me think about that" or "I don't know" or "What do you mean when you say ...?" or "From what sources does your information come?" This type of discourse not only slows down the tempo of the show but creates the impression of uncertainty or lack of finish. It tends to reveal people in the *act of thinking*, which is as disconcerting and boring on television as it is on a Las Vegas stage. Thinking does not play well on television, a fact that television directors discovered long ago. There is not much to *see* in it. It is, in a phrase, not a performing art. But television demands a performing art, and so what the ABC network gave us was a picture of men of sophisticated verbal skills and political understanding being brought to heel by a medium that requires them to fashion performances rather than ideas. Which accounts for why the eighty minutes were very entertaining, in the way of a Samuel Beckett play: The intimations of gravity hung heavy, the meaning passeth all understanding. The performances, of course, were highly professional. Sagan abjured the turtle-neck sweater in which he starred when he did "Cosmos." He even had his hair cut for the event. His part was that of the logical scientist speaking in behalf of the planet. It is to be doubted that Paul Newman could have done better in the role, although Leonard Nimoy might have. Scowcroft was suitably military in his bearing—terse and distant, the unbreakable defender of national security. Kissinger, as always, was superb in the part of the knowing world statesman, weary of the sheer responsibility of keeping disaster at bay. Koppel played to perfection the part of a moderator, pretending, as it were, that he was sorting out ideas while, in fact, he was merely directing the performances. At the end, one could only applaud those performances, which is what a good television program always aims to achieve; that is to say, applause, not reflection.

I do not say categorically that it is impossible to use television as a carrier of coherent language or thought in process. William Buckley's own program, "Firing Line," occasionally shows people in the act of thinking but who also happen to have television cameras pointed at them. There are other programs, such as "Meet the Press" or "The Open Mind," which clearly strive to maintain a sense of intellectual decorum and typographic tradition, but they are scheduled so that they do not compete with programs of great visual interest, since otherwise, they will not be watched. After all, it is not unheard of that a format will occasionally go against the bias of its medium. For example, the most popular radio program of the early 1940's featured a ventriloquist, and in those days, I heard more than once the feet of a tap dancer on the "Major Bowes' Amateur Hour." (Indeed, if I am not mistaken, he even once featured a pantomimist.) But ventriloquism, dancing and mime do not play well on radio, just as sustained, complex talk does not play well on television. It can be made to play tolerably well if only one camera is used and the visual image is kept constant—as when the President gives a speech. But this is not television at its best, and it is not television that most people will choose to watch. The single most important fact about television is that people *watch* it, which is why it is called "*television*." And what they watch, and like to watch, are moving pictures—millions of them, of short duration and dynamic variety. It is

in the nature of the medium that it must suppress the content of ideas in order to accommodate the requirements of visual interest; that is to say, to accommodate the values of show business.

Film, records and radio (now that it is an adjunct of the music industry) are, of course, equally devoted to entertaining the culture, and their effects in altering the style of American discourse are not insignificant. But television is different because it encompasses all forms of discourse. No one goes to a movie to find out about government policy or the latest scientific advances. No one buys a record to find out the baseball scores or the weather or the latest murder. No one turns on radio anymore for soap operas or a presidential address (if a television set is at hand). But everyone goes to television for all these things and more, which is why television resonates so powerfully throughout the culture. Television is our culture's principal mode of knowing about itself. Therefore—and this is the critical point—how television stages the world becomes the model for how the world is properly to be staged. It is not merely that on the television screen entertainment is the metaphor for all discourse. It is that off the screen the same metaphor prevails. As typography once dictated the style of conducting politics, religion, business, education, law and other important social matters, television now takes command. In courtrooms, classrooms, operating rooms, board rooms, churches and even airplanes, Americans no longer talk to each other; they entertain each other. They do not exchange ideas; they exchange images. They do not argue with propositions; they argue with good looks, celebrities and commercials. For the message of television as metaphor is not only that all the world is a stage but that the stage is located in Las Vegas, Nevada.

ANSWERING/THE BIG QUESTION

from *Celebrity Culture*

ELLIS CASHMORE is a professor of culture, media and sport at Staffordshire University. Author of numerous books, his most recent include *Beyond Black: Celebrity and Race in Obama's America* (2012) and *Martin Scorsese's America* (2009).

WHY?

April, 2005: Reese Witherspoon says she's been chased across town from her gym by paparazzi who encircled her in the Hollywood Hills and only retreated after she appealed to a private security guard at the entrance to a gated community. A photographer is later charged with child endangerment and battery after allegedly hitting a five-year-old child with his camera and pushing away another to take pictures of Witherspoon and her children.

June, 2005: Driving her Mercedes-Benz, Lindsay Lohan is in collision with a pursuant minivan driven by a photographer who is subsequently charged with assault with a deadly weapon—the vehicle. The photographer is later cleared, though the case encourages Governor Arnold Schwarzenegger to sign legislation allowing celebrities to collect large damage awards from paparazzi who harass them.

August, 2005: Several cars follow Scarlett Johansson as she leaves her Hollywood home for Disneyland in her Mercedes. In her attempt to escape them, she bumps a Daihatsu carrying a mother and daughter to whom she apologizes. Johansson's agent tells the *Los Angeles Times*: "At least two or three of them [paparazzi] had been camping outside of her house for five days … she's left Los Angeles. You can't deal with it any more."

September, 2005: The *Daily Mirror* newspaper carries a story based on a 45-minute video that purports to show Kate Moss preparing and snorting five lines of cocaine in a London recording studio, where her boyfriend Pete Doherty—who has a well-documented history of drug dependency—was working with his band. Earlier, the *Daily Mirror*'s sister paper, the *Sunday Mirror*, had paid out "substantial damages" after publishing a story claiming that Moss had collapsed after taking coke in Barcelona in 2001.

October, 2005: After disappearing in 1993, Kate Bush re-emerges from her self-imposed exile to release a new album. She became a recluse to escape the media and to raise a family away from the glare of the kind of publicity to which she had become accustomed since her first single "Wuthering Heights" became an international hit in 1978.

When Kate Bush receded from the public view, we let her. When I say "we" I mean everybody, not just the paparazzi, the television crews, and the other members of the media, but everybody who licensed them, however unwittingly. Despite avoiding scandals, she must have sensed that it was going to be hard to slide between professional and personal lives. The membrane separating them was getting evermore permeable. She opted for the personal. By the time she decided to return to her recording career, things had changed appreciably. It's likely that had she started her recording career today, she would be pursued as vigilantly—and in Moss's case, the pursuit was downright vengeful—as any of the other female celebrities in the vignettes that opened this reading.

It could be argued that it's a small price to pay. After all, celebrities earn serious money and, much as some deny it, they wallow in the admiration if not outright adoration. Having your home staked out and having a perpetual tail of media personnel, as they say, goes with the territory. My purpose in this book is not to put the case for or against the celebrities. Rather, it's to understand the changes that have led to the collective preoccupation with them. The vignettes are not untypical. On the contrary, they are representative illustrations of the lengths to which the media will go just to satisfy our appetites for pictures and news of, or just gossip about, people whom we don't know but feel we do know. When all's said and done, celebrities should make no lasting impact on most of our lives, apart from prompting the occasional emotion: like the joy we take in listening to their music; or the contentment in watching their acting; or the thrill of just seeing them; or maybe the ecstasy in fantasizing about them. But there's more. We spend an inordinate amount of time and money reading about them, staring at pictures of them, discussing them, and, in some cases, obsessing over them. All of which leads us to our final question. Why?

Why? is a loaded question, of course. On what grounds? Under what conditions? In what circumstances? For what reason? With what purpose? [...]

Celebrity culture has been with us just about long enough to generate a body of literature. [...] Like any other subject-based literature, there is a branch devoted to theorizing. This is where the Why? question gets answered, though, as we will see, in a number of different, sometimes contrasting ways. We shouldn't expect anything less: celebrity culture, like any other aspect of study, defies any once-and-for-all answers. Instead, there are perspectives, models, accounts, and conceptual approaches, all of which offer a way of answering questions and asking a few more.

[...]

THE NEW ECCLESIASTES

Religion. It enchants us. I mean this literally. We are caught in a spell we either can't break or don't want to break because we have faith. Faith replaces the need for evidence. Our belief in whatever particular complex of beliefs we call our religion dictates that we believe *in* it rather than believing it conditionally. Adherents of religions don't, for example, say: "I'm prepared to accept that there is a superhuman, controlling power such as god and that god should be worshipped, but only on the condition that, at some stage, I'll be supplied with proof of this." More typically, we devote ourselves and organize our mental outlook and conduct accordingly without ever needing even a sign. Those who do search for signs usually find them in the quotidian, that is, the common everyday things that most people take for granted.

Religion has been under threat since before the eighteenth-century Enlightenment, which used reason and individualism to challenge traditions of prejudice and superstition. Science and technology addressed many of the questions asked and answered by religion and poured them into a different mould. It reshaped them in a way that invited answers, without any recourse to faith. Science offered proof.

This occasioned a gradual decline not so much in religious belief but in the significance religion had in society, especially Western European societies. Secularization spread, though perhaps not as universally as enthusiasts of science would like. Religion has held fast and still dominates the politics and culture in some parts of the world. In others, it's retreated temporarily, only to return with renewed influence. But science meant that religion's power to bewitch had been weakened. The overall project started by the Enlightenment brought with it disenchantment. This has led some writers to conclude that celebrities have served to re-enchant a world in which deities have either been abandoned or emptied of their power, leaving a "post-God world."

"Celebrities are our myth bearers; carriers of the divine forces of good, evil, lust and redemption," declared Jill Neimark, marshaling the historical work of Leo Braudy to bolster her claim (1995: 56). Braudy's *The Frenzy of Renown: Fame and its history*, was, as its subtitle indicates, a historian's perspective on fame (1997). First published in 1986, just before the changes that animated our intense interest in celebrities, it examined the triumphs of famous figures long before the age of celebrity. In fact, Braudy identifies Alexander the Great as the first truly famous person. As long ago as the third century BCE Alexander regarded himself as no other human: more a deity or a hero of Homeric legend. With no media in the sense we understand it today, Alexander made use of an alternative apparatus for spreading news of himself and his achievements. He commissioned authors to chronicle his battles, artists to depict his likeness, and engravers to design, shields, coins, and other artifacts bearing his profile. Alexander actively encouraged worship and exaltation by fashioning himself after the gods and demigods of ancient Greece.

Alexander may be a prototype of the godlike human, but he certainly wasn't a celebrity (at least, only when played by Colin Farrell, in the movie *Alexander*). All of his efforts at immortality and indeed those of the many Roman emperors, who vaingloriously followed his example, were aimed at separating themselves from their subjects. They deliberately flouted legal and moral rules as a way of confirming their extraordinary status: rules applied to humans, not gods. In a similar way, the Pharaohs of ancient Egypt, such as Akhenaten and his wife Nefertiti, ordered the building of edifices to commemorate their existences and the European aristocracy of the Middle Ages commissioned portraits of themselves to ensure their posterity. They cultivated the popular conception that their world was not that of ordinary mortals; they were untouchable.

There are remnants of this type of behavior in today's celebrity temple. For example, Mariah Carey's famous refusal "to do stairs" assisted her elevation above both her audience and the rest of her entourage. Outlandish demands worked for the likes of Cleopatra, so presumably today's celebs think they will work for them. But, no one seriously thinks the celebrities are deities. Or do they?

"Post-God celebrity is now one of the mainstays of organizing recognition and belonging in secular society," writes Chris Rojek (2001: 58). Celebrities appear as gods in human form or simulacra of departed deities. Celebrity culture, in this view, becomes a functional equivalent of religion, with beliefs and practices associated with religion "converging" with those of celebrity culture.

[...] What was once a vast gulf between Them and Us has been narrowed to the point where celebrities have become touchable. The likes of Lohan, Johannson, and indeed Carey appear on celluloid, but hawkish photographers make sure that most of the widely circulated images show them tracksuited on their way to the shopping mall, often bedraggled, and sometimes annoyed enough to greet their watchful media with all-too-human gestures (Cameron Diaz was famously photographed giving the finger to paparazzi). So it appears to make little sense to regard them as godlike beings rather than ordinary people who have bad hair days like everyone else. Rojek suggests that the "glut of mass-media information" which personalizes the celebrity has turned them from being distant figures, not just into ordinary people but "significant others." "They are also symbols of belonging and recognition that distract us in positive ways from the terrifying meaninglessness of life in a post-God world" (2001: 95).

This might strike some readers as decaf phenomenology, with the "terrifying meaninglessness" in fact being a resignation to the mundane monotony of everyday life, and with the "positive ways" in which celebrities distract us being retail therapy. But there is more complexity to the argument. "Celebrities offer peculiarly powerful affirmations of belonging, recognition, and meaning in the midst of the lives of their audiences" (2001: 53).

Secularization may have been overstated, but religion has certainly had to adapt in order to survive in many parts of the world. In some important respects, it has reconfigured so that it can respond to the "uprooting effect of globalization." In striving to meet the needs of the rootless flock, religion has borrowed the style of celebrity culture. Its leaders are charismatic tv personalities, its sermons arrive in people's homes via television or the internet, and it elevates its showbusiness devotees into standard bearers. This is part of a convergence. The other part is celebrity culture's ability to supply experiences that, for fans, are every bit as meaningful as religious experiences. This is why fans spend more time reading tabloids than they do the Good Book. As Rabbi Shmuley Boteach put it: "MTV and Access Hollywood has supplanted Ecclesiastes and Proverbs" (2002: 1).

While Rojek describes this as a "hypothesis," other writers have put it to the test. Lynn McCutcheon and John Maltby are part of a team of psychological researchers who have explored the manner in which consumers engage with celebrities. [...] We covered several of their research projects, many of which explore what the researchers call "celebrity worship." The term makes clear allusions to religion, though we should remain mindful that the word worship derives from the Old English *weorthescipe*, meaning, basically, worthy. To worship someone or something means to show respect or acknowledge merit. Paying reverence to deities is but one meaning of the term. Celebrity worship sounds less profound once this is borne in mind, though the research of McCutcheon *et al.* delivers a somewhat surprising conclusion: many of those who follow celebrities do so with a zeal that actually does resemble religious fervor (2002, 2003; Maltby *et al.* 2004).

Celebrity worship is measurable on a Celebrity Worship Scale, low worship describing what many of us do: watch and read about celebrities. At the other extreme, there is the level at which worshipful followers show "a mixture of empathy with the celebrity's successes and failures, over-identification with the celebrity, compulsive behaviours, as well as obsession with details of the celebrity's life" (McCutcheon *et al.* 2002: 67). This is the kind of uncompromising and extreme disposition we might regard in a different context as religious zealotry

or fanaticism (remember: some trace the origins of the word fan to fanatic, which has religious connotations, [...].

Adoring or even obsessing over celebrities as idols or role models is a "normal part of identity development in childhood and adolescence," according to McCutcheon *et al.* (2003: 309). It's a form of parasocial interaction. We may identify with cartoon characters or the fictional characters played by actors, rather than the actors themselves. But we may also idolize rock stars, movie stars, and any other kind of celeb that attracts us. It becomes a psychologically abnormal state when it continues into adulthood, perhaps leading to the worshipper's neglect of everyday duties. It may lead to the believer's having deluded conceptions about the nature of his or her relationship with one or more celebrities. Or even what the researchers call "addiction to a celebrity."

McCutcheon and her colleagues are specifically interested in the psychological origins and effects of celebrity worship on the individual, rather than its cultural sources or its wider ramifications. As such, they don't address the question of whether celebrity worship has converged with or even replaced religious worship, as Rojek suggests. Their evidence is, however, persuasive: the intensity of emotional involvement, the impact on the life of the believer, the pattern of engagement with the rest of the world (from sociability to withdrawal) are all features of celebrity worship that have religious counterparts. [...] The scholars question the usual separation of stalkers from other devotees: "The distinction between pathological and nonpathological worship is somewhat tenuous" (2002: 69).

The team's findings are complemented by those of Susan Boon and Christine Lomore, also psychologists, who discovered that fans were not simply influenced by the way celebrities dressed, made up, wore their hair, or by their overall demeanor: "they took note of their attitudes and values, especially on issues of morality" (2001). Such a finding invites comparisons not only with prophets, preachers, or sages, but with priests, pastors, and ordained ministers responsible for the spiritual leadership of a church or other religious organization.

THE WORLD THROUGH A LENS

In the 1960s, when Daniel Boorstin was completing the first edition of his *The Image: A guide to pseudo-events in America*, he wondered about the effects of living in an "illusory" world of created characters. Mediated, two-dimensional images were becoming as important to us as real people: we only needed to flick a switch or open a magazine and we were in the alternative world. Compared to this, our own world must have seemed colorless and uninteresting. In Boorstin's world, people exchanged ideas and gossiped about stars and tv characters rather than learning about each other and, by implication, about themselves.

The early 1960s: the Beatles, Martin Luther King, Motown, George Best, *Cleopatra*. The names seem to be from a different age. They are. Yet we know them all. And they're all comprehensible and not just as historical entities. The media supports a vivid imagination. We may be detached observers, but we feel we know, perhaps do actually know, all about the Beatles and the story of Motown without having to delve into the history books. The media is just *there* like a Greek chorus, different voices singing different things simultaneously and continuously.

This is where our story of celebrity began, of course. The early 1960s witnessed the beginning of our new enchantment. Our senses were massaged or manipulated by a newly tenacious media that fed on the real people behind the image. Of course, what they were doing was delivering new images to replace the old.

There were potent images that lingered in the mind long after the early 1960s: the first live transatlantic television broadcast via the Telstar satellite in 1962; the assassination of John F. Kennedy in 1963; the first spacewalk in 1964; England's World Cup win in 1966 (watched by about 400 million tv viewers). These were delivered by television. The "illusory" world grew both bigger and smaller to viewers watching "live" transmissions of events 250,000 miles away.

Essentially the same media that delivered the first moon landing delivered celebrities. To be precise, images of celebrities. David Giles provides an illustration, inviting his readers to put themselves in the shoes of a famous female recording artist. After a harrowing experience with the paparazzi, she is summoned to the studios by her record company to make a second album, a single from which is going to be released ahead of the album. When the single becomes available (downloads are typically around before the cd), the press office arranges over 100 interviews and the singer is whisked around the country to make tv and radio appearances. "You are replicated furiously," Giles assures the hypothetical singer/reader. "Dozens of newspapers and glossy, full-colour magazines carry photographs of you ... The video, for a start, receives heavy 'rotation' on specialist TV channels and several plays on terrestrial TV" (2000: 52).

The single sells well, prompting another few weeks of "saturation media coverage" and every time the song is played whether on radio, tv, iPod, or whatever, "you stroll into their living room ... you are *there*" (2000: 52).

The singer obviously isn't physically there: Giles means that her presence is summoned by a visual or audile representation that registers in the imagination. Jessica Evans tenders a phrase to capture this: "Mediated persona is a useful term in that it reminds us how celebrity as a category is *absolutely dependent on the media* to create and disseminate a persona to an audience" (2005: 19).

Evans's emphasis reveals the colossal importance she places on the role of the media in the creation and perpetuation of celebrity. Giles is equally convinced of the media's efficacy in bringing celebrity culture into being, though his inflection is on the way in which technology has taken matters to a new level.

Braudy's history of fame alerts readers to the manner in which primitive media were used not only to circulate news but to glorify and lionize rulers, whether kings, generals, priests, or saints. "So it can be argued that there is much continuity between the representations of the famous in the past and the present," writes Evans (2005: 20).

Citing examples from history, Evans argues that even the "pseudo-events" Boorstin believed were stage-managed episodes specific to the twentieth century have much older precedents. Louis XIV (the seventeenth-century French king, not the San Diego band) was adept at making carefully designed public rejoicings appear spontaneous. The point is: public relations is not as new as we think and the media, even before the age of print, were used as promotional vehicles. Fame then has always involved some mediating agency that represents and disseminates news and images. Edited collections, such as James Monaco's 1978 *Celebrity: The media as image makers* and Lisa Lewis's 1992 *The Adoring Audience: Fan culture and popular media*, as their titles suggest, concentrated on the power of the media both in governing the depiction of celebrities and influencing the experience of consumers through the twentieth century.

While her approach accentuates historical continuity, Evans identifies the period 1890–1930 as "crucial" when "the mass media invented a particular kind of 'star' persona" (2005: 23). [...] In making the private lives of entertainers a part of their overall public persona, the emerging media in concert with the film industry nurtured a new kind of relationship between the famous and their audiences. Between them, there were texts, defined by Evans's collaborator Frances Bonner as "socially constructed assemblages of items such as spoken or written words, or pictures" (2005: 59). (An "assemblage" is something made of unrelated things joined together, so the text is basically anything that's intelligible to the consumer, or the person doing the "reading.")

In Evans's model then, there are three conceptual elements: the production, text, and reception. While each contributes to making celebrity a meaningful social entity, the relationship between them is variable. Culture industries may produce a particular set of images or personae of celebrities, but there is no guarantee that audiences will interpret them in the way intended: the texts may be quite different. "Reception" is perhaps a poor choice of words in that it implies passivity, whereas consumers are seen as discriminately selecting and decoding media messages in a way that resists manipulation.

Although the media and the elaborate organizations that augment them drive celebrity production and, as such, remain the engine of the model, the texts that circulate in a way have a life of their own once in the public discourse (actually "in" the public discourse isn't quite appropriate as the discourse is actually constituted or made by the public).

Giles sees less historical continuity. New media technologies rupture developments, opening up unanticipated opportunities for aspiring celebrities. They did so in the fourteenth century when the modern theater became popular, providing a "vehicle ... for creating fame." Then again in the fifteenth century with the invention of the printing press; engravings were a popular way of portraying the human face before photography. "Celebrity is essentially a media production, rather than the worthy recognition of greatness," says Giles, echoing Evans and naming hype as its "purest form."

Hype has no object of any value: it just implies "that a phenomenon can be made to appear valuable, even when its value is non-existent" (2000: 20). While he doesn't go into the etymology of the term, note that its root is *huperbole*, Greek for excess, from which we get hyperbole, an exaggerated statement. Giles cites P. T. Barnum as the pioneer of hyping: the techniques he used for publicizing the exhibits of his shows were much the same as those used today. The Hollywood film industry's publicity machine refined and perfected what was an art for Barnum into something resembling a science. After the 1950s, domestic television became a new medium for creating celebrities *par excellence*. There had been nothing to compare with tv: it served to shrink the distance between viewers and events and the people who featured in the events; but it also began to create events of its own—shows, performances, competitions, and even news items specifically made by and for television. The video recorder pushed things further, allowing viewers to play events over and over again. As with Evans, Giles's stress is on the media as the engine that drives celebrity culture. The actual celebrities are almost incidental to the theory.

Giles believes that there is a long-standing and even desperate desire for fame among human populations. Changing forms of media have effectively made it possible for more and more people to gain the kind of mass exposure that brings fame. Myriad media around the globe rapidly and exponentially reproduce images of people. "The proliferation of media for publicizing the individual has been reflected in a proliferation of celebrated individuals," writes Giles. "As the mass media has expanded, so individuals have had to do less in order to be celebrated" (2000: 32).

The process copies itself like a replicating DNA. Technological developments in the media have enabled humans to reproduce images of themselves "on a phenomenal scale, thus providing an evolutionary rationale for the obsessive pursuit of fame" (2000: 53).

While both Evans and Giles acknowledge that other writers (and I need to include myself in this group) see something qualitatively distinctive and exceptional about contemporary celebrity culture, they highlight the continuity in the role of the media. Admittedly, Giles pinpoints the bewilderingly fast reproductive properties of today's media as crucial to the fleeting celebrities that flit across our screens today and disappear next week. But celebrity culture is continuance masquerading as uniqueness. The media were always pivotal: their forms have changed; their effects haven't.

IN THE SERVICE OF CAPITAL

The Roman poet Juvenal might have been reflecting on the way his countryman in the first century of the common era assigned celebrity status to gladiators when he coined the phrase *panem et circenses*. Translated as "bread and circuses" it describes the way in which ancient Roman leaders would provide food and entertainment to the underprivileged plebeians, allowing them access to the spectacular gladiatorial contests and chariot races at the Colosseum and other vast stadiums. Without the agreeable distractions and a full stomach, the masses might have grown discontented and started to wonder why they had little money, lived in inadequate accommodation, and, unlike their rulers, could never afford life's luxuries. Immersing themselves in the excitement of the contests and cheering on their champions diverted their attention away from more mundane matters.

Juvenal was alluding to power, specifically the uneven distribution of it and how this imbalance was maintained. The sections of the populations that had little power and no real chance of gaining the advantages that go with it had to be placated somehow. If not, they might have grown restless and begun to ask searching questions that could destabilize power arrangements. Keeping them satisfied maximized the chances that they wouldn't notice. The entertainment may have been good wholesome fun—well, as wholesome as pitching humans against lions can be—but it also served an ideological purpose. It fostered a style of popular thinking that was compatible with a particular type of political and economic system.

Critics of sports such as Paul Hoch (1972) and Jean-Marie Brohm (1978) wrote challenging polemics in the 1970s, identifying athletics events as key amusements that kept the working class preoccupied. Too preoccupied, it turned out, to oppose capitalist systems that were designed to exploit them. Drawing on Marx's opiate thesis, in which he likened religion to a drug that dulls the senses and provides a temporary sensation of well-being, critics saw sports as a kind of functional equivalent of religion, commanding the attention of millions of fans without delivering any tangible improvements to their lives. Sports and, by implication, other types of popular entertainment have ideological utility: they reinforce the status quo.

This invites [...] images [...] [of] heads of mega-corporations gathered around a table to hatch plots designed to keep the working classes from noticing how the system works against them. Neither Hoch, Brohm, nor any of the other theorists who followed their leads pictured the scene so melodramatically. Sports and entertainment today may be overpraised and soak up too much of our time and money; but they haven't been designed to assist society's ruling power-holders. They are best viewed as convenience rather than connivance.

Celebrities do ideological work too. This is hardly profound: more a statement of the obvious. They massage our senses in a way not totally dissimilar to the gladiators. Like the citizens of ancient Rome, we are captivated, enthused, and thrilled by people we don't know and who probably don't care about us. Maybe we don't have the same deprivations from which we have to be distracted, but there are serious issues that impact on everybody: climate change, globalization, war, for instance. These and other issues already provoke widespread dissent and, often, outright protest. The prospects for even more forceful protests might be great were it not for the diverting power of celebrities. At least, that's what theorists of the bread and circuses school would argue. They'd find an ally in the comic Chris Rock who offered his own take on celebrity culture in 2004: "It's a trick to get your mind off the [Iraq] war. I think [George] Bush sent that girl to Kobe's room. Bush sent that little boy to Michael Jackson's house. Bush killed Laci Peterson [whose mysterious disappearance stirred up widespread curiosity] ... all to get your mind off the war!" (quoted in *Maclean's*, June 21, 2004).

Even those who are not persuaded by the basic version have converted its premise into a more sophisticated model, the engine of which is still ideology. The title of P. David Marshall's book *Celebrity and Power: Fame in contemporary culture* is a clue to his approach (1997). He sees the concept of individuality as vital to both contemporary capitalist democracy and consumerism. Celebrities are not just people; they are influential representatives. They represent "subject positions that audiences can adopt or adapt in the formation of social identities" (1997: 65). There is a "celebrity-function" which is to "organize the legitimate and illegitimate domains of the personal and the individual within the social" (ibid.: 57).

Matt Hills interprets this: "The celebrity or star appears to give rise to, and anchor their very own authenticity and individuality. But what appears as a natural property of the charismatic celebrity is actually produced by discourses of celebrity" (2005: 151). Giles pares this down to basics: "The capitalist system uses celebrities to promote individualism and illusions of democracy (the 'anyone can do it' myth) [...] capitalism retains its hold on society, by reducing all human activity to private 'personalities' and the inner life of the individual" (2000: 19 and 72).

Multiplying numbers of celebrity escapees of the *Big Brother* house and other reality television shows have appeared since the publication of Marshall's book, though he would surely use the "ordinary" celebrities as further proof of his thesis. And, despite the attempts of the previously mentioned Mariah Carey and the others who strive to keep the purdah that separates Them from Us intact, consumers have seen through the veil.

Graeme Turner has adopted Marshall's framework in his book *Understanding Celebrity*. In particular, he points to Marshall's potentially useful "spin": "His proposition [is] that the celebrity-commodity provides a very powerful form of legitimation for capitalism's models of exchange and value by demonstrating that the individual has a commercial as well as a cultural value" (2004: 25).

Celebrities then have social functions. Like the proto-celebrity gladiators, they serve political ends as well as providing pleasure for the masses. They participate, however unwittingly, in a process that entices—some might say inveigles—Us into thinking about ourselves and

Them in a particular way: as freestanding individuals living in a merit-rewarding society; and one, we might add, in which the good life advertised by celebrities is open to anyone with enough money. This is, for Turner, the primary function: "Celebrities are developed to make money" (2004: 34). In the kind of competitive market system fostered by capitalism, only ever-increasing consumption can keep the system running.

Vertical integration features in Turner's analysis. This describes the tendency of large corporations, especially media corporations, to incorporate a range of industrial processes in its portfolio. News Corp., for example, can produce the content of tv, film, and other media, market it through its agencies and distribute it to consumers through its multimedia networks. It can also promote its own films or programs through its print media and cross-promote other products. Straightforward product placement is commonplace in all media, though the movie *Tomorrow Never Dies* took it to a new level. 007 used an Ericsson JB988 phone, which was advertised using the movie as a frame, while the movie was promoted in a complementary process of brand integration [...].

While Turner doesn't mention this movie, nor its star Pierce Brosnan, whose own value was elevated by the cross-promotion, he seems to have something like them in mind when he writes: "The celebrity's usefulness to the cross-media expansion of the major media and entertainment industry conglomerates has translated into an enhanced value for the celebrity as a commodity" (2004: 34).

Turner would find evidence for this in the way celebrities are used to transfer brand "values." Mercedes-Benz, for example, linked up with TAGHeuer, a global brand in its own right endorsed by, among others, Brad Pitt and Tiger Woods. Figures like these may not represent Mercedes directly, but their associations with the watch company that produced the Mercedes watch were useful in establishing credibility. Turner would surely find this kind of cross-brand development complementary to the cross-media expansion he cites.

So, when we learn about the kind of situations presented at the start of this reading and either sympathize with, abhor, or just laugh at the celebs' displeasure, we should remain mindful of how: "The expression of interest, in turn, provides them with the power to elicit an adulatory photo feature in *Hello!* or to demand approval of the writer assigned to prepare a profile on them for *Vanity Fair*" (2004: 36). (Within two months of her coke exposé, Kate Moss appeared on the cover and across eleven pages of this very publication.)

Celebrities perform important functions in a mature capitalist economy in which consumer demand is paramount. A competitive market needs ever-increasing consumption to keep the system moving. The "accelerator of consumer demand," to use the phrase we took from Zygmunt Bauman [...], has to be kept hard down at all times. Turner himself uses a similar analogy when he writes of the constant, urgent need for new celebrities to whet the appetites of consumers: "The industrial cycle of use and disposal ... does seem to have radically accelerated in response to the demand created by new media forms" (2004: 85).

Celebrities and the culture they epitomize are products themselves. They can be bought and sold, much like the merchandise they advertise. As such, they are parts of an industrial process that maintains our spending levels while keeping us pleasantly occupied. Turner doesn't dismiss other purposes the celebrities may have in, for instance, the fan's sense of self and individuality. He even quotes Rojek who believes that celebrities offer "peculiarly powerful affirmations of belonging, recognition, and meaning" (2001: 94).

Yet, with Marshall, Turner insists that any account of celebrities must be predicated on the recognition that "the interests served are first of all those of capital." Capitalism's growing dependence on what some call hyper-consumerism has led to an ethic of hedonism and health, excess and extravagance. Prudence, self-denial, deferred gratification, and all manner of frugality have been rendered old-fashioned by a culture that continually tries to develop discontents that can be salved only by buying commodities. Celebrities have to be understood in this context: they operate with the advertising industry—almost *as* an advertising industry—to persuade, cajole, and convince consumers that dependence is nothing to be ashamed of. If we depend on commodities, so what? As long as we have money enough to assuage the urge to consume, there is no problem.

None of the contemporary theorists on celebrity culture subscribes to the crude bread and circuses explanation. If that were so, celebrities would be no more

that eye-catching diversions that prevent us noticing more pressing issues. Yet, there is a sense in which both Marshall and Turner understand the utility of celebrities to the capitalist enterprise and believe that this is their *raison d'être*—the purpose that accounts for their very existence.

So, we return to a question asked by all the writers covered in this reading: what are celebrities for? Are they new replacement gods, media-born creations, or commodity representatives of a capitalist system that thrives on consumption? This is not an either/or question, of course. The media [...] have become increasingly obsessed with the young and prosperous, with glamour, money, and the kind of power that they confer. We, the consumers, have become fascinated, often to the point of prurience, with their well-chronicled lives. Celebrities have become godlike objects to us and we seem to delight in their sense of self-importance, their scandalous behavior, and their eagerness to deplore the media's intrusions, while inciting their interest with any device available.

The sometimes fanatical devotion we show has tempted several writers into seeing celebrity culture as a secular religion; impulse seems to dictate the behavior of some consumers more certainly than calculation. As we've seen, there is empirical support for this perspective: as there is for the other perspectives that attribute the rise of celebrities to the media and to capitalist consumerism. Neither secularization, the media, nor capitalism can be absolved; but nor can they be burdened with the whole shebang.

Celebrity culture is guided by the logic of consumerism and the celebrities are guided by this basic message: enjoy novelty, change, excitement, and every possible stimulant that can be bought over a shop counter or an internet website. The message falls on receptive ears. Consumers thrill to the sight and sound of celebrities, not because they're dupes, suckers, airheads, or simpletons, but because they have become willing accomplices in the enterprise. They too are guided by the logic of consumerism.

Appetites that were once damned as the cause of unhappiness and instability are extolled. An expansion of demand for commodities and a continuous redefining cycle of what's luxury and what's necessity has led to the elevation of new groups into the sphere of consumption we know as celebrity culture.

SUPREMELY CULTIVATED

As the first wave of theories of celebrity culture arrived, much of the critical impulse concerned its democratizing effect. The pronouncement of death for the old-style stars and egalitarian promises of fame for all seemed to herald a new continuous communion in which celebrity status was available to everyone, regardless of talent, if only for short periods. Reality television [...] seemed to confirm the promise.

Accompanying this and integral to it was what we could call a democratization of taste. Consumer items that may once have been associated with the rich and famous became widely available. Everyone could participate in a version of the good life. The once-unbreachable wall between Them and Us was replaced by gossamer-thin gauze that was thin enough to be seen through and occasionally torn. Consumers defined themselves by the commodities they bought. As we noted before, Derek Layder alludes to this in his *Understanding Social Theory* when he observes: "The pervasive effects of consumerism link identity and social status to the market for commodities" (2006: 53). "The compulsive buying of new fashions and new products" is one manifestation of this.

In 1991, Christopher Lasch wrote of the kind of society he dreaded, one in which abundance would appear to be available to everyone, while in reality being restricted to the wealthy: "The progressive conception of history implied a society of supremely cultivated consumers" (1991: 531). We now have them. In this sense, celebrity culture has been successful: the seamless unity occasioned by the end of the traditional Them and Us has brought delirious pleasure to billions the world over. Consumers devour magazines, movies, downloads, and practically everything else bearing the image, signature, or just aura of celebrities. And celebrity culture has been even more successful than Lasch could have imagined. It thrives in painlessly easing money away from people who, in a genuine sense, feel themselves part of the communion, which is less about spiritual unity, more about market harmony.

Celebrity culture does not, of course, come with a free pullout panacea for all the problems that afflict us in the early twenty-first century. For all the well-intentioned efforts of the campaigning celebrities [...], we have to conclude that they have prompted big questions, though without answering them. But there may still be opportunities: after all, there has probably never been a comparable time in history when so many people have held the ability to influence, inspire, and perhaps incite others to action. We've seen glimpses of this when celebrities confront particular issues, such as global warming, globalization, or debt relief. But, so far, no wide-ranging vision shapes the way in which people view the world.

This is probably asking too much: what celebrity is prepared to risk rearranging the thoughts of his or her fans in a way that will undermine their devotion? "Stop buying my cds, don't rent dvds, or go to the movies. And don't buy clothes or the jewelry just 'cause you see celebs wearing something similar. But, above all, become interested in people who say things that enlighten or do things that matter!" This would be like trying to stop a car with no brakes while driving it.

Celebrity culture has offered us a distinctive vision, a beguiling one too: one in which there are few limits, an expanding range of opportunities, and inexhaustible hope. Celebrities themselves are, as I've stressed throughout, the living proof of this. Ideas like restraint, prudence, and modesty have either been discredited or just forgotten. Celebrity culture has replaced them with impetuosity, frivolity, prodigality. Human impulses like these were once seen as vices; now they are almost virtuous.

Universal consumption, the promise of luxury for all, and an endless cycle of insatiable desire have been introduced not through political discourse but through the creation of a new cultural group. Celebrities have energized our material expectations, helping shape a culture in which demand is now a basic human experience. What were once luxuries are now regarded as necessities. What was once improvement is now replaced by upgrading. For all the fantasy and escapist tendencies it radiates, celebrity culture's most basic imperative is material: it encourages consumption at every level of society.

Celebrity culture's paradoxical feat is not in advancing a worldview in which social discontents have their causes in the scarcity of material commodities, so much as promoting an idea that we shouldn't think about this long enough to distract ourselves from what we do best—consume even more of those very commodities.

KATHLEEN KELLY, YOU'VE GOT MAIL (1998)

"Sometimes I wonder about my life. I lead a small life. Well, not small, but circumscribed. And sometimes I wonder, do I do it because I like it, or because I haven't been brave? So much of what I see reminds me of something I read in a book, when shouldn't it be the other way around? (...) I don't really want an answer. I just want to send this cosmic question out into the void. So goodnight, dear void."

MARK ZUCKERBERG, THE SOCIAL NETWORK (2010)

"This is what drives life at college. Are you having sex or aren't you. It's why people take certain classes, and sit where they sit, and do what they do, and at its, um, center, you know, that's what the Facebook is gonna be about."

HER (2013)

MALE VOICE IN ADVERTISEMENT: We ask you a simple question. Who are you? What can you be? Where are you going? What's out there? What are the possibilities? Elements Software is proud to introduce the first artificially intelligent operating system. An intuitive entity that listens to you, understands you, and knows you. It's not just an operating system, it's a consciousness. Introducing OS ONE—a life changing experience, creating new possibilities. (...)

FEMALE OS VOICE (Scarlett Johansson): Hello, I'm here.
THEODORE (Joaquin Phoenix): Oh, hi.
FEMALE OS VOICE Hi, how are you doing?
THEODORE: I'm well. How is everything with you?
FEMALE OS VOICE: Pretty good, actually. It's really nice to meet you.
THEODORE: Yeah, it's nice to meet you, too. What should I call you?
Do you have a name?
FEMALE OS VOICE: Yes. Samantha.

CHAPTER FIVE

MOBILE AND SOCIAL MEDIA

Is There an Inherent Need to Share Our Lives?
And to Unplug?

By Angela M. Cirucci

SHARING STORIES: CAVE PAINTINGS TO DIARIES TO TIKTOK

1973 – First mobile phone debuts in NYC.
1994 – Motorola introduces the first digital mobile phone.
2001 – Apple releases the First Generation iPod.
2003 – MySpace launches.
2004 – Facebook is introduced.
2006 – Twitter enters the social media scene.
2007 – The first iPhone is released.
2009 – WhatsApp launches.
2010 – Instagram is introduced.
2011 – Snapchat goes live.
2017 – TikTok launches.
2020 – Clubhouse goes live.[1]

In less than fifty years, especially in the last twenty-five years, social and mobile technologies have altered our media environments. This is a remarkable timeline with profound implications, as Mark Deuze explains in this chapter. While some of you may not have even been born when Motorola released the very first digital mobile phone, fifty years is a brief period in comparison to the age of the Earth (about 4.5 billion years). It's not even that long compared to the age of the United States (about 240 years). From the universe's perspective, in just the blink of an eye, mobile and social media have become important parts of our lives.

It is completely normal, in fact expected, that we always carry with us these small but powerful computers everywhere we go. We rely on mobile devices for the time; for directions, definitions, and news updates; and, of course, to stay socially connected. We look to social media apps—Facebook, Instagram, Snapchat, WhatsApp, and so on—to help us share our lives with others. Through tweets, snaps, and selfies, we have the unprecedented ability to broadcast our lives to millions of other users, who, just like us, are sharing their narratives.

---

1   For a full social media timeline see https://en.wikipedia.org/wiki/Timeline_of_social_media.

Popular news outlets deem these new patterns of media use narcissistic, inward-facing, and even solipsistic. But, as Lee Humphreys explains, sharing who we are is not a new phenomenon.[2] In fact, sharing small stories about ourselves has always been an essential piece of the human experience, reaching back to the earliest cave paintings, as shown in Werner Herzog's *Cave of Forgotten Dreams*. In the 1700s, it was commonplace for people to document their everyday lives in diaries. When away from family and friends, people would send their diaries home so that their loved ones could follow their travels. In the second half of the twentieth century, stereotypical housewife duties included keeping track of their children's lives, taking photos, and creating scrapbooks that they could share with others, including their children as they grew older.

Only in the context of traditional mass media, like television and film, where normal audience members don't produce content, does sharing small snippets about the self seem weird or narcissistic. So, if socially sharing mundane life experiences is not the problem, what positions new media to be so easily labeled "bad"? Humphreys has two ideas.

First, she notes the obvious difference in publicness. Sure, diaries were shared with family back home and scrapbooks with friends in the neighborhood, but mobile and social media allow us to make our lives truly public. Utilizing platforms with millions of users means that we also have a potential audience of millions. Prior to the rise of platforms like Facebook, Twitter, and TikTok, this was a privilege reserved for the select few television producers and film directors. In addition, as Jan Fernback introduces later in this chapter, there is a new cultural norm that encourages users to feel like all personal information *should* be made public, as we saw with the insurrection in Washington, DC, on January 6, 2021.

Second, diaries and scrapbooks are not infinite. There is only so much space to fill, and there is always some foreseeable end—baby books track the first year, diaries eventually fill up, photo albums have only so many slots. Social media, on the other hand, seemingly reach out into infinity. There is always more life to share, and, powered by Moore's Law, social media platforms always give us more space to share it.

These differences in what mobile and social media afford users begin to uncover the tensions that arise when people discuss the "problems" with contemporary media use. It's not "bad" that people want to share their stories; we've been doing that for some time. It's that we share so widely and with no imaginable end. Because mobile media never leave our side, we are always ready to post more, photograph more, and share more.

SOCIAL MEDIA TERRITORIES

Indeed, as Jean Baudrillard discusses in *Simulacra and Simulation*, as a mobile- and social-mediated people we increasingly rely on representations of the self, instead of the corporeal self. Quoting the great Argentine writer Jorge Luis Borges, Baudrillard tells the story of an emperor and his cartographer. The emperor wanted a map that perfectly represented the territory of the kingdom—so perfect, beautiful, and glorious was the map that it replaced the territory. The map was more desirable than the territory it represented. The copy was preferred over the real. The moral of this story is that when we attempt to replicate our lives via media, we begin to care more about the simulations than the real, so much so that we create simulacra, or images and copies that have no corporeal referents. Baudrillard argues that the true danger comes when we can longer distinguish the difference between the real, simulations, and simulacra. Instead, all is just hyperreal; no longer can we compare right to wrong, good to bad, heroic to evil, real to fake.

The local and finite nature of previous media helped us to remain aware of the distinction between images of people and the people themselves. As mobile and social media evolve into ever more global and omnipresent forms, it becomes progressively more difficult to know what is a 1:1 representation of the real and what is a

---

2 Lee Humphreys, *The Qualified Self: Social Media and the Accounting of Everyday Life* (Cambridge, MA: MIT Press, 2018).

simulacrum. This is especially dangerous when the technologies are used and developed with specific economic or political goals in mind.

BLACK MIRROR AND SOCIAL-MOBILE MEDIA

The popular Netflix series *Black Mirror* taps into these ideas, displaying what could happen when the extreme publicness and omnipresence of mobile and social media are taken to the extreme. In the episode "Nosedive," mobile devices are used as a social utility to decide, through user ratings (like Yelp or Tripadvisor), who deserves the best car rental, flight, job, and even friend. Indeed, the main character, Lacie Pound, is invited by a childhood friend to be her maid of honor only because she has a 4.4-out-of-5 rating. Once Lacie's rating drops below 3.0, due to a series of increasingly unpleasant events, her "friend" wants Lacie nowhere near her and her "high 4" friends. In "Nosedive," the publicness and ubiquity of mobile and social media technologies are integral to everyday life. It is as if people no longer share their lives because they want to, but because, if they wish to be a part of society, they must.

Likewise, in the *Black Mirror* episode "The Entire History of You," most people have a Grain implanted behind one ear that catalogs everything they experience. The main character, Liam, not only uses the Grain's rewind feature to continuously evaluate how he performed during an interview, but he also becomes obsessed with minute details of a dinner party, fearing his wife is having an affair. What's more, the Grain's recordings are also used at the institutional level, namely for a TSA-like screening process before Liam can board public transportation and travel home. The guard can see Liam's entire history and asks him to "share" his past week.

SOCIAL MEDIA SIMULACRA

In these two episodes, Baudrillard's warning—that the real danger of simulacra is our decreasing ability to "distinguish the difference"—rings true. The society in which Lacie lives relies heavily on mobile devices and the social media app that allows users to post about their lives and rate each other. This ubiquitous app doesn't just structure social life; it also, seemingly without much protest, dictates institutional life. Most of the characters whom we as viewers meet buy into the social rating system completely, viewing scores as so objective and real that people are denied flights, rental cars, and even basic human kindness. Similarly, Liam is so caught up in the ability to rewind his, and his wife's, life that he gets drunk, threatens to kill a man, crashes his car, and ultimately is separated from his wife and daughter.

The characters, and societies, are shown just as Baudrillard feared: unable to realize that they are privileging simulacra and subjective representations of the real, instead of the real itself. Lacie's life is ruined because she believes so deeply in bettering herself through social media posts and others' clicks. Liam relies on the Grain to "catch" his wife in a cheating scandal, but in the end, he perhaps realizes that the microtargeting afforded by the technology extends beyond what natural social evolution has prepared us for.

Beyond deep changes to our social lives, the two *Black Mirror* examples above highlight a third way in which mobile and social media differ from diaries and scrapbooks: they are becoming ever more vital to *institutional* life. In both "Nosedive" and "The Entire History of You," personal content is used not just for social relations, but for institutional ones as well. Diaries and scrapbooks were not, by and large, used to judge who should get a loan[3] or determine who is not fit to board an airplane.[4] Yet, mobile and social media provide strong new paths for corporate and governmental bodies to learn unparalleled details about digital users. The more we share, the more we open ourselves up to institutional control and profit.

---

3   http://fortune.com/2015/08/04/facebook-loan-approval-network/
4   http://fortune.com/2016/06/29/foreign-visitors-social-media-accounts/

FROM VIEWERS TO USERS TO VOTERS

If you know your tech history, you know that the World Wide Web was invented by Tim Berners-Lee in 1989. Berners-Lee had the idea that making a decentralized, hyperlinked internet experience would drastically increase the possibilities of the internet—and he was right. The introduction of the web in the early 1990s brought personal computers and the internet into many American homes. Through the 1990s, and into the new millennium, "surfing the web" and "being online" were slowly normalized.

Interestingly, during the early periods of the web, companies found it difficult to make advertising profits. Online ads were originally based on television's successful advertising model, but with one addition—a rolling log could be kept of how many people clicked on any given banner ad! It was quickly realized, however, that this process of counting clicks was shaky at best. It was unclear how to define what a click meant and, thus, how to report the "success" of an ad.[5] Like television, early models relied on webpage content to dictate what "type," or demographic, of visitor was viewing the page. Yet there was no way to know who clicked the link and what clicks, if any, led to actual purchases.

It turns out that those who first ventured to advertise on the web were still thinking of people as audience members, not as *users*. Instead of passively viewing, like with television or film, when we go online we are actively *using* a space. At first, we were typing in forums and clicking on links. Now we are uploading photos, liking posts, and sharing videos. Sure, we view Snap stories and read news updates, but we are never *just* audience members.

Soon, companies and advertisers realized that the inventions of mobile and social media were brilliant, not just because we can keep up with our social lives no matter where we go, like a ramped-up version of sending your diary home, but also because of digital companies' ability to keep up with our lives. Mobile and social media not only allow our friends and family to follow us around the globe; they also, often implicitly, allow companies to track us as well.

As *Black Mirror* episodes often display, beyond how our social lives have changed, there are also the ways in which our institutional lives have changed. Digital companies realized that thinking of us as users instead of audience members leads to the realization that we are *always* producing data. These data include the things that we, ourselves, input—name, email address, gender, photos, tweets, snaps, messages, and so on. But we also produce data unintentionally. Indeed, most digital companies, apps, and websites collect data about what we are doing, who we are with, and where we are at any given time.

In perhaps a *Black Mirror*–like incident, these state-of-the-art tracking and microtargeting technologies were used by the data firm Cambridge Analytica to craft very specific Facebook ads that attempted to tap into people's fears and neuroses, particularly those related to racism and sexism. A previous employee of the firm, Christopher Wylie, claims not only that data from ninety million Facebook users' profiles were obtained unethically but also that these data were turned against their users, employed to train algorithms that then shared targeted ads focused on compelling users (by tapping into their fears) to vote for Donald Trump in the 2016 US presidential election, for the Brexit vote, and for Ireland's anti-abortion vote.[6]

THINK ABOUT YOUR PHONE, FOR YOUR PHONE "THINKS" ABOUT YOU

Yep, that's right: *think* about your phone. Right now, your phone is probably sitting next to you. Maybe you are at home with your three roommates. Maybe you are in class, in the same building you go to every Tuesday and Thursday at 3 p.m., surrounded by roughly the same thirty or three hundred people. Maybe as you are reading

---

5   Joseph Turow, *The Daily You: How the New Advertising Industry Is Defining Your Identity and Your Worth* (New Haven, CT: Yale University Press, 2011).

6   Laura Sydell, "Whistleblower: Cambridge Analytica Aimed to Trigger Paranoia and Racial Biases," May 16, 2018, KPBS/NPR, https://www.npr.org/2018/05/16/611412562/whistleblower-cambridge-analytica-aimed-to-trigger-paranoia-and-racial-biases.

this you are also scrolling through TikTok and Snapchat. Maybe you replied to a professor's email. Maybe you just ordered some food from Uber Eats. Your phone knows *all* of this. In effect, it is "thinking" about you, or thinking of you and what you say, like, and do.

Your phone knows where you are because of GPS technology. In fact, it probably knows that you are "at home" or "in class." It begins to recognize your patterns, where you usually are on certain days and at certain times. Your phone also knows who you are around, so it can guess, with pretty high accuracy, who your roommates probably are, by pairing GPS technologies with phone IDs. Cookies and other footprints you leave are all thrown into databases, meaning that, through cross-referencing abilities, your phone knows that while you were at home, around certain people, you ordered a pizza.

Maybe you downloaded Instagram a few years back and created a profile. Now, you want to start anew. So, you completely uninstall the app, reinstall, and create a new profile, thinking you have wiped away your Instagram past. Nope. Your phone ID still links your new profile to your previous one.

Of course, to say "your phone knows" is a bit misleading. Most apps on your mobile device, as well as your operating system (iOS, Android, etc.), are constantly tracking all the data you intentionally and unintentionally create, storing them in huge databases that take up acres of land across the globe. They construct profiles about you, much fuller than any profile you have ever created for yourself, and they use *these* data to construct targeted ads that "guess" what you will buy or view at any given time. As users, we are extending our ability to share our stories, just as Humphreys explained. But, also as users, we are extending companies' abilities to commoditize these stories and make money. It behooves scrapbooks and photo albums to be finite—once one is full, the companies hope you'll buy another. But mobile and social media reverse this trend: companies that track you want to ensure they design their spaces so that you feel like you can never, and should never, stop adding to your story.

FEARS OF BEING NOTHING

As general users—wrapped up in mobile and social media's abilities to extend, as Marshall McLuhan would say, our ever-present desire to share our life stories—we are often quite unaware of the other ways our usage and data extend institutional, economic, and political gain. Evolving from passive viewer to active user and producer, you may constantly expect there to be increasing abilities to broadcast your life and to read about the lives of others. At the same time, you probably think that to be shown an ad in one app for a pair of shoes you just looked at in another app is "creepy." Yet, these activities are simply two sides of the same coin. Without us, mobile and social media would be nothing. Without mobile and social media, the fear is, of course, that we would be nothing. This is why, as Julia Hildebrand explores in this chapter, some people feel the need to "unplug."

If he were still alive today, McLuhan would perhaps warn us that the initial capabilities of mobile and social media to extend the ability to share our stories have reversed into stymieing our stories. We are now largely fixated on living our lives through very small digital boxes. Lost in amounts of likes and shares, like Lacie, and in the past, like Liam, we perhaps trust mobile and social media's imagery of ourselves more than our own.

MOBILE MEDIA LIFE

from *Moving Data*

MARK DEUZE AND THE JANNISARY COLLECTIVE (Watson Brown, Hans Ibold, Nicky Lewis, Peter Blank)

As life gets experienced not with but rather in media, the global shift toward mobile and haptic connectivity is not just a step toward natural user interfaces but also toward an increasingly seamless integration among human beings, nature, and technology. This reading explores the key components of a media life as lived through the iPhone, showing that the profound power of media can only be found in their invisibility and, ultimately, disappearance. Today's mobile phone in general—and the iPhone in particular—can arguably be seen as the ultimate device when it comes to communication and conversation, especially as it includes modalities of other media, such as television and film, games, photography, and the computer. Access to mobiles is so much more widespread than usage of the World Wide Web that James Katz, for example, suggests the device deserves the subtitle of "the real world's Internet."[1] Considering the near-universal adoption of mobile communication and the rapid growth of wireless broadband connectivity (especially in developing countries), a certain mobility afforded by small portable artifacts can be considered to be at the heart of what it means to live a media life.

Although the mobile phone as we know it has been in development for at least fifty years, and (trans-)portable phones were used by telephone companies in the United States and in the British army in the South African Anglo-Boer War (1899–1902), only since the 1980s have the devices become widely available.[2] Gerard Goggin describes how during the mid-twentieth century the combination of computer code automating many aspects of the communication process, a shift to organically shaped cells (specific areas around a transmitter tower) to send and receive mobile communication signals, and reducing otherwise rather bulky features of the artifacts involved laid the groundwork for mobile telephony.[3] In terms of size, the world's first mobile telephone call was made in 1973 with what is called the Brick: a 1,134 gram analog model manufactured by Motorola.[4] With the switch to digital networks, a new generation of mobile phones emerged: much smaller and smarter, at least according to industry rhetoric. All that intelligence refers to the contemporary cell phone's ability to learn just about everything from and about its user and how the industries catering to it—telecommunications companies, ISPs, software studios, marketing and advertising agencies, and all

---

1 James Katz, ed., *Handbook of Mobile Communication* (Cambridge, Mass.: MIT Press, 2008), 434.
2 The blog *Webdesigner Depot* has an excellent overview of cell phone design between 1983 and 2009: http://www.webdesignerdepot.com/2009/05/the-evolution-of-cell-phone-design-between-1983-2009 (15 February 2011).
3 Gerhard Goggin, *Cell Phone Culture: Mobile Technology in Everyday Life* (London: Routledge, 2006).
4 See http://en.wikipedia.org/wiki/Motorola_DynaTAC (15 February 2011).

kinds of other businesses—can adapt their products and services accordingly.

Over the past thirty-five years, the bulky and solo-use mobile phone has transformed into a sleek and multifaceted device; the iPhone 4 in fact only weighs 136 grams. This transformation continues as the mobile device morphs from a distinct technological phenomenon to an artifact of increasingly seamless media and everyday life integration. As mobile media advance, previous technologies and practices are remediated. The journey of the mobile phone's integration into modern society has left in its wake a myriad of bypassed and remediated devices. Shortly after the publication of Charles Darwin's *On the Origin of Species* (1859), the British novelist Samuel Butler, for example, responded with a satirical op-ed piece for the New Zealand newspaper *The Press,* titled "Darwin Among the Machines," published in mid-June 1863. In this piece, Butler wonders out loud about the direction of mechanical evolution, or what he calls "mechanical life," awestruck as he is "at the gigantic strides with which it has advanced in comparison with the slow progress of the animal and vegetable kingdom." Applying the principle of natural selection to machines, Butler notes how the ongoing diminution in the size of technological devices attends their development and progress toward ever-increasing independence from humans. To Butler, the emergence of wristwatches is an example of how smaller technologies may replace larger ones—clocks—and thus render them extinct.[5]

[...]

TECHNOLOGY FADING INTO OUR LIVES

The process toward the media we know today was not necessarily linear or uncontested—yet, as Gerard Goggin notes, the key to the future of cell phones seems their irrevocable (and inevitably messy) metamorphosis into mobile media, "infiltrating into and reworking all sorts of old and new media forms."[6] With that, argues Paul Levinson, comes a process whereby new media devices

"become even smaller and lighter than they are now, following Buckminster Fuller's 'dymaxion principle', which holds that new technologies get ever smaller and more powerful."[7] In the original prescient words of Fuller—an early-twentieth-century American inventor, architect, and futurist—his size-based standard is "an attitude and interpretive principle ... of doing the most with the least in consideration of a mobilizing, integrating society."[8] The architect would probably be thrilled about current attempts to reduce the size and integrate the multimodal connectedness of technologies even further.

And indeed, the iPhone seems not just to be taking over other technologies but to be entering into all kinds of reciprocal relationships with the way we live, organize, and give meaning to our lives. Summarizing the situation in the United States in 2009, the *Pew Internet and American Life Project* concludes that "mobile connectivity is now a powerful differentiator among technology users. Those who plug into the information and communications world while on-the-go are notably more active in many facets of digital life."[9] This digital life is to a large extent based on a mobile lifestyle, according to market research based on international comparative studies of attitudes and behaviors related to wireless devices and communication. Or, as one such report claimed in 2002, "constant awareness of wireless finally wanes when people are truly living a mobile lifestyle," ultimately seamlessly integrating wireless in everyday life "where people find it difficult to live a life without wireless."[10] Combining qualitative and quantitative data from Asia, Europe, and the United States, numerous researchers have mapped a globally emerging mobile communication society where what people do with mobile technology serves to reinforce, maintain, and create collective identity while at the same time functioning as an expression of a distinctly personal style and way of life. How far this process plays out in everyday life is evident in the work of media anthropologists, such as Daniel Miller, studying the various roles social and mobile media play in the lives of a variety of

5 Samuel Butler, "Darwin Among the Machines," *The Press* (New Zealand), 13 June 1863.
6 Goggin, *Cell Phone Culture.*
7 Paul Levinson, *New New Media* (New York: Allyn & Bacon, 2009), 191.
8 Buckminster Fuller, *Nine Chains to the Moon* (1938; Philadelphia: Lippincott, 1964), 340.
9 See http://www.pewinternet.org/Reports/2009/5-The-Mobile-Difference-Typology.aspx (15 February 2011).
10 Report available at http://www.contextresearch.com/context/study.cfm (15 February 2011).

groups in society: students, migrant workers, and the homeless. Miller and Mirca Madianou conclude that people around the world, coming from a wide variety of social and economic backgrounds, increasingly live in a situation of "polymedia": exposed to a plurality of media that change the relationships between communication technology and society by the mere fact of their omnipresence and seemingly effortless integration into the social and emotional realm of people's everyday existence.[11] As they state in their work, for Filipino and Caribbean people living in London and Cambridge and the families they have left behind, media are their "technologies of love." In his fieldwork, Miller finds that people spend so much time living with media that media become their life, in effect treating media as their home.[12] This results in typical "home" idioms being translated into media contexts, for example, by incessantly decorating one's online social network profile or by constantly rearranging and tidying up the files, applications, and icons of one's personal computer or smartphone. Just as the home gets infused with (and reshaped through) media, our media become domesticated spaces typified by a mass personalization effort: customized ringtones, individualized screensavers and wallpaper, fine-tuned arrangements of favorite websites and television stations, tailor-made carrying pouches and various forms of wearable media.

The central role of the mobile phone in processes of personal transformation toward greater individualization and transnational connectivity reveals its nature as a "charismatic" technology; it was originally designed for work and business but changed identity quickly as it entered the domestic sphere. Once inseparable from that sphere, the telephone in general and mobile media in particular become part of the day-to-day coordination of both family and personal life. In doing so, media add a certain dynamism and mobility to the daily rhythm of life while at the same time they should be seen as extending or even amplifying existing networks and ways of doing things. With the iPhone, boundaries between media and life blur beyond meaningful distinction. Yes,

we are overtly aware of the latest and greatest in devices and apps. At the same time, our lived experience with ubiquitous, always-on, mobile media makes these same technologies, paradoxically, disappear into our lives.

Computer scientists have long emphasized this vanishing. As Mark Weiser put it in 1991, the ideal-typical goal for engineers should be "to conceive a new way of thinking about computers, one that takes into account the human world and allows the computers themselves to vanish into the background."[13] Considering our haptic (iPhone) and kinetic (Wii and Kinect) intimate technologies today, this mission indeed seems accomplished. Weiser and his colleagues, then at the Xerox Palo Alto Research Center, envisioned devices that fit the human environment, not devices that force humans to enter mediated worlds. Next-generation tablet and smartphone technologies point to ways that the technology is indeed fading into our lives. Readers may already own an iPhone that either includes or works in harmony with other personalized machines in our lives—the refrigerator, the washer and dryer, the television, the automobile, the coffee maker.

The idea that our selves can extend into devices and "be" even when "we" are not there is by now familiar. Facebook, Twitter, and other Web-based awareness tools allow us to present multiple selves online that connect and share statuses with others (and ourselves). Today, these cherished tools prompt engagement by posing questions like *what are you doing?* and *what's on your mind?* And we oblige with a passion for sharing that has driven awareness tools to the forefront of the mobile Web. What if we could ask of our devices, *what should I do?*—or maybe even, *what should I think?* That capability is more than hypothetical. Among the darlings of Silicon Valley right now are social question and answer services. Such "answer sites" flourish around the world, providing a form of information discovery that is social and potentially more personalized than search engine results. Social Q&A sites like Quora and ChaCha thrive on mediated communities built around information sharing. The appeal is hard to deny: instead

11   See http://blogs.nyu.edu/projects/materialworld/2010/09/polymedia.html.
12   Daniel Miller and Mirca Madianou, *Migration and New Media. Transnational Families and Polymedia* (London: Routledge, 2011).
13   Mark Weiser, "The Computer for the Twenty-first Century" (1991), available at http://www.ubiq.com/hypertext/weiser/SciAmDraft3.html (15 February 2011).

of a keyword search on a search engine, answer sites allow us to express information needs as questions and answers are provided in narrative form, rather than as a list of documents, as in search engine results.

THE IPHONE ALIVE

Apple's April 2010 acquisition of Siri, a mobile personal assistant, signals the direction of next-generation Q&A for the iPhone. Siri emerged from Stanford Research Institute International, the Menlo Park research institute that is contracted by global governments and corporations. Siri drew initial funding from the Defense Advanced Research Projects Agency under its Personalized Assistant That Learns program. The goal: build a smart assistant that seamlessly shares our media life, learns from it, and guides us. Much of the interest swirling around Siri and other so-called cognitive assistants focuses on speech recognition and voice-activated search, not on the learning, bonding, and co-creative decision-making capabilities. Siri and its cohort are capable of developing what could prove to be a tantalizing intimacy with us. Additionally, one could consider the rising prominence of augmented-reality applications for the iPhone and Android platforms, which are charismatically changing how we view and interact with the world around us. Programs like the Dutch system Layar or Google's Goggles digitally overlay a multitude of information about the contents of the camera view of a smartphone in real time. The iPhone's Type'n'Walk application allows the user to literally never avert her attention from the screen by providing a camera view of the surroundings while texting or e-mailing.

Scientists working for Apple, Facebook, Google, Microsoft, and other media giants push the limits of mobile search, bringing haptic and audiovisual connectivity together with dynamic artificial intelligence. It is in this context perhaps unsurprising that a famous book on the evolution of a global artificial intelligence by George Dyson carried as its title the same name as Butler's original essay: *Darwin Among the Machines* (1998).[14] As Dyson assumed, humanity, nature, and technology coevolve. In his 2009 work *The Nature of Technology*, Brian Arthur

similarly suggests that nature and technology coevolve to the point of not just mirroring but even subsuming each other—while indeed also citing Butler's thesis.[15] Given the developments in multimodal convergence, life- and workstyle integration, social-media tools (including answer sites, mobile personal assistants, and augmented-reality applications), as well as broader trends toward human-machine osmosis, it is not too far-fetched to suggest that the iPhone is alive. Its materiality draws on the power of social and artificial intelligence. It learns from experience. It reasons. It gets to know us. It follows commands. And, if we want the iPhone to, it issues commands.

It is striking to find in many of these accounts of the history and adoption of mobile media a certain seamlessness; a way of describing and analyzing the technology strictly in terms of its success as defined by market penetration and its gradual reworking from a presumably lifeless machine into a generally reproductive yet potentially transformative social tool. Such a perspective reflects a barely implicit emphasis on how media become life—where "becoming" refers to media extending the communication and conversation capabilities of their users, embedding themselves physically with people through forms of wearable computing, and finally becoming part and parcel of every aspect of daily life and one's sense of self.

Considering the ubiquity of mobile communication and increasing migratory behaviors of people and things worldwide, researchers (such as John Urry) have made a rallying cry for a "mobility turn" in our thinking about (media and) life today. In a less ambitious but similar vein, Rich Ling and Jonathan Donner advocate the adoption of what they call a "mobile logic" as determined by mobile and increasingly ubiquitous devices around the world. The implications of such a logic governing people in their daily life, they suggest, are that individuals compartmentalize and apportion "their activities to a greater extent than previously possible," which also means that we interlace "multiple tasks with multiple actors and multiple venues, competing and jostling for time and attention." All of this seemingly frantic

---

14   George Dyson, *Darwin Among the Machines: The Evolution of Global Intelligence* (New York: Helix Books, 1998).
15   Brian Arthur, *The Nature of Technology: What It Is and How It Evolves* (New York: Free Press, 2009).

activity is premised, according to Ling and Donner, on permanent reachability or the expectation thereof. At the heart of such mobility-inspired considerations of the contemporary human condition are concerns about the structure and consequences of constant communication, and the public/private-boundary-erasing activities associated with the portability of mobile media. Mobile devices and wireless access enable constant communication, making people instantly accessible and therefore burdened with the expectation of availability. There is no alternative to the "always-on" paradigm of media life, or so it seems.[16]

Urry goes as far to consider mobile devices "lifelines" as the loss of a cell phone could throw a person into "a no-man's land of nonconnectivity."[17] Considering the widespread popularity of "Lost My Cell Phone—Give Me Your Number" groups on social networking sites like Facebook, he certainly has a point. Given the charismatic nature of media in our lives, it is perhaps safe to say that the passing of a mobile device does not just inspire the need to reclaim one's electronic address book but extends feelings of loss to the safety of one's home and community, and therefore in a very real way affects people's sense of belonging. For all their technological groundlessness and rootlessness, mobile media provide us with a space where we in effect feel connected, planted firmly in a community of peers—a sense of communal living based on our own terms and biographized experiences. Mobility in general and mobile media in particular do not necessarily uproot but, more exactly, continuously repot the plants of communal life.

CONCLUSION

An archaeology of mobile media suggests that these technologies, their uses, and how they fit into the daily lives of people around the world amplify media life's complexity in two directions. On the one hand, today's tiny yet quietly powerful mobile media can be seen as "intrinsically solipsistic" technologies, enabling the ongoing retreat of people into quasi-autonomous "personal information spaces."[18] On the other hand, this individualized mobile immersion instantly and haptically connects people with people anywhere else, thus turning their own societal bubbles of space into a fully mediated space of global coexistence. This space—or mediaspehere, to use Peter Sloterdijk's term—forms an invisible electronic shell around us whereby our entire experience of others becomes mediated. Yet life in a mediasphere can also leave people blind to coexistence.

Considering the evolution of portable communication technologies it is perhaps better to replace the "soundscapes" of cell phones with the "mediascapes" of mobile media more broadly conceived. Arjun Appadurai introduces the concept of mediascapes by way of suggesting how media are central to constituting shared imagined worlds by people and groups spread around the globe. Appadurai's analysis brings home the connection among media, daily life, and issues that world society faces on a daily basis by stressing how an ongoing deterritorialization of people through global labor and family migration contributes to the production and maintenance of symbolic ties with "imagined" homelands through media.[19] Such diasporic communities get sustained through local networks as well as transnational media connections; meeting fellow expatriates at the downtown community center while calling family members back in the homeland on the way over. The mobile phone in particular is a powerful instrument for maintaining close ties within and across otherwise geographically dispersed communities, considering their widespread popularity and the abundance of relatively cheap international calling rates. At the same time, all this mediated global connectivity does not exclude or necessarily limit local interactions. In fact, media above all seem to contribute to a process of ongoing "glocalization" of communities.

To some extent this explains the growth and success of diasporic media in general and "new" or mobile media

---

16   Rich Ling and Jonathan Donner, *Mobile Phones and Mobile Communication* (Cambridge: Polity Press, 2009), 28–29.

17   John Urry, *Mobilities* (Cambridge: Polity Press, 2007), 178.

18   David Morley, *Media, Modernity, and Technology: The Geography of the New* (London: Routledge, 2007), 211; Mark Deuze, *Media Work* (Cambridge: Polity Press, 2007), 30.

19   Arjun Appadurai, "Disjuncture and Difference in the Global Cultural Economy," in *Global Culture*, ed. Mark Featherstone (London: Sage, 1990), 295–310.

in particular, while this conclusion at the same time amplifies concerns about speed, scale, and volume in the transnational circulation of images and ideas. A glocalized world society is provincial in the sense of Sloterdijk's assumptions about people turning increasingly to the inner world of a modern individuality, supported by a complex media environment, while it is also markedly part of Appadurai's observations of an accelerating global flow of "people, machinery, money, images, and ideas."[20] The same information and communication technologies support and supercharge these seemingly different trajectories. What remains at the heart of our mobile media life—unless we wage war on it—is the gradual disappearance of media from our awareness. With media, we become invisible, perhaps both to others as to ourselves.

As the iPhone and mobile media in general pervade people's lives, such devices are rapidly being transformed from cutting-edge gadgets into a seamless integrated and multifunctional necessity of everyday life. Perhaps the most telling facet of devices contributing to this transformation is the ever-increasing ease of interaction between the technology of the device and the user. The general trend of mobile technology has been towards a haptic interface, and one cannot contest the ease with which touch-screen technology can be manipulated. In the case of the iPhone, one can navigate a dizzying maze of icons giving way to even more icons; one page sliding away to reveal yet another page—in short, a myriad of applications all accessible with simple taps and flicks of the finger.

An irony of the trend toward hapticity is these devices' loss of their tactile qualities. From the inception of the cellular phone, mobile technology has functioned via the presence of plastic or rubber keys used to navigate the device, the physical depression of the buttons and the ever-present *clacking* of the keys providing assurance to the user that her command is being processed. This tactile interface is rapidly becoming obsolete as it makes the user acutely aware of the device's presence by drawing attention to its form. Considering our earlier observations, the popularity of and corresponding shift toward ubiquitous computing, natural user interfaces, and an overall increasingly immersive engagement with

our media can possibly be explained by the realization of how media both operate as a McLuhanian extension of our bodies and must be seen as altogether fused with bodies. By drawing less attention to itself, the transition from physical keypads via touch screens to kinectic interfaces allows users to become immersed in their devices (and what they do with them). Assuming for a moment how hapticity and kinectivity will benchmark lived experience in media, this trend necessitates the assumption that for people in everyday contexts, the channel of communication evaporates.

The current and potential influence mobile media possess in how we socially and culturally navigate our environment point toward their existence as what Jean Baudrillard famously called a "simulacrum to hyperreality." As discussed earlier in this reading, there is a veritable laundry list of artifacts, activities, and arrangements that become fused in mobile media life. As reality shrinks into the palm of our hand, augmented by applications such as Layar and Goggles, mobile media amplify our bodies into a state of complete mediation. We become media, and media become us. This insight was originally voiced quite literally by the French physician Julien Offray de La Mettrie in his essay "L'homme machine" (translated as "Man a Machine" or "Machine Man"), written in 1748, where he argued against Descartes's distinction between matter and soul, instead suggesting that our bodies are like machines in that they influence the way we think and express ourselves. In his essay, La Mettrie suggests that our expressions in (and use of) media not only set us apart from primates but also introduce an element of plasticity into our lives—making ourselves and our experience of reality malleable. Before Butler's prescient take on media's (r)evolution, short stories such as E. T. A. Hoffman's "Der Sandmann" (published in 1816) and Edgar Allen Poe's "The Man That Was Used Up" (first published in 1839) explored the potential consequences of real-time man-machine fusion. Poe describes in his work an encounter with a "singularly commanding" and "remarkable man—a very remarkable man": Brevet Brigadier-General John A. B. C. Smith. After thoroughly investigating the source of Smith's unrivaled perfection and enthusiasm for "the rapid

---

20 Ibid.

march of mechanical invention" he eventually is confronted in terror with Smith as nothing but "a large and exceedingly odd-looking bundle of something," with arms, legs, shoulders, bosom, eyes, tongue and palate mechanically attached. Inspired by such work—and in particular with the uncanniness exemplified by the confrontation with a real that seems not to be—Sigmund Freud navigates similar territory in his essay "Das Unbehagen in der Kultur" (translated as "Civilization and Its Discontents" and published in 1930). In this piece (and with direct reference to Hoffman's tale about a man falling in love with what turns out to be a mechanical doll), Freud considers man a "prosthetic" God, inventing and deploying all kinds of tools and appliances that overcome the imperfections of man's own body and mind. In doing so, human beings surround themselves with technologies that put them at farther removes from direct, unmediated experience. The lived experience of being both what Freud calls "a feeble animal organism" as well as some kind of "prosthetic God" can therefore be seen as filled with ambivalence and uncertainty—necessary byproducts of life's newfound plasticity (or what Zygmunt Bauman would describe as our liquid modern lifestyle of being "permanently impermanent").

This exploration of the iPhone in the context of a perspective of life as lived *in* rather than *with* media, thus, allows us to wage war on our machines, even though our machines are us. It is a way to look at media differently while at the same recognizing that they become (like) us more and more and through our immersion in them we become like (our) media. We are concurrently confronted with real or perceived expectations of being connected at all times (and costs), constantly changing (and upgrading), instantly reachable yet always on the move, qualities we tend to anticipate in our media. Seen as such, the iPhone can be considered to be the embodiment of our life as we experience it now.

UNPLUGGING: FIVE THINGS WE SHOULD KNOW ABOUT SOCIAL MEDIA

JULIA M. HILDEBRAND is Assistant Professor of Communication at Eckerd College in St. Petersburg, Florida. Her publications explore mobile technologies and digital culture, and they have appeared in such journals as *Media, Culture & Society, Mobile Media & Communication,* and *Explorations in Media Ecology.*

Silicon Valley, we have a problem! It concerns the things we look at first in the morning. And the things we look at last before we go to sleep. And sometimes when we wake during the night. It's the devices and services that psychotherapist Nancy Colier suggests calling "relational technology": our smartphones, laptops, tablets, and smart watches, along with the socially networked services they provide.[1] In chapter 1 of this book, Barry Vacker and I conceptualize such technologies, applications, and platforms as "ego" and "hot" media. For the purposes of this chapter, I will refer to them as "social media."

Now, don't get me wrong. Plenty of positive things have come from social media and will continue to emerge. The way I can use WhatsApp to call my parents in Germany, send a snap to my sister in Denmark, and message friends and colleagues across the globe is amazing every single time. The fact that we can access the daily headlines in Mongolia, Bolivia, and the Seychelles is just as fantastic. Moreover, current international movements for social justice and other causes illuminate the tremendous value of social media for organizing change. And of course, social media have given us the opportunity to "broadcast ourselves," to

participate in public discourse, to build and promote businesses, and so on.

The benefits of Google, Facebook, Instagram, Twitter, and so on are countless, and this chapter is not about diminishing them. Instead, I want to focus on some of the issues. The harm of social media spans the *intrapersonal* (our relationships with ourselves), the *interpersonal* (our relationships with others), and the *societal.* Some of these problems are brought to light in Netflix's *The Social Dilemma* (2020).[2] The docudrama presents some of the former minds behind Google, Facebook, and Instagram's key features, along with several key scholarly thinkers. None of them seem particularly happy with our current situation. So, what is it about social media that causes concern?

To make money, social media platforms such as Google and Facebook decided to implement an advertising-based system. While this is about us seeing more relevant products, it's also about us, the users, *turning into the product.* What we like, love, hate, and have is part of the data and metadata that social media service providers harvest to sell to advertisers. Those in turn will sell to us. Algorithms that get to know us and then start making predictions about our needs,

---

1 Nancy Colier, *The Power of Off: The Mindful Way to Stay Sane in a Virtual World* (Boulder, CO: Sounds True, 2016), xii.
2 Jeff Orlowski, *The Social Dilemma,* documentary-drama (Netflix, 2020).

wants, and wishes are part of what is driving this system. Such "big-data algorithms can predict our behaviors with startling accuracy," notes media theorist Douglas Rushkoff. [3] This results in us "being hypnotized little by little by technicians we can't see, for purposes we don't know. We're all lab animals now," adds computer scientist Jaron Lanier. [4] Or to use Harvard professor Shoshana Zuboff's words, we are entering "a new economic order that claims human experience as free raw material for hidden commercial practices of extraction, prediction, and sales." [5] She calls it *surveillance capitalism*: "a marketplace that trades exclusively in human futures." [6]

We need to be plugged in and online for algorithms to keep spinning. As the apps and their media grammar keep calling us back and tying us into the social media universe, our decisions seem less and less of our own making. Who has not experienced sessions of involuntary scrolling and wondered where the last one, two, three hours went? And, it is not just the advertising-based model that extracts our attention and exploits our weaknesses. It is also the social comparison, the fear of missing out, the hyperavailability and other effects of our social media lives that can lead to addiction, depression, and isolation.

"The medium is the message," argues media scholar Marshall McLuhan. [7] This famous aphorism can help us make sense of the contemporary workings of social media. One of McLuhan's students—an equally noteworthy media theorist named Neil Postman—built on this approach and offered five things we should know about technological change more generally. [8] In the following, I apply his five ideas to the context of social media to further unpack the current dilemma. What can we learn from this approach, and how do we move forward?

SOCIAL MEDIA ARE A TRADE-OFF

"All technological change is a trade-off," argues Postman. [9] It is akin to a "Faustian bargain," a deal with the devil, in which we gain some things but lose others. Whenever technology enters our lives, there are advantages and disadvantages. Sometimes the benefits outweigh the risks, other times they don't. A clear example of this is social media. The advantages are obvious, so let's take a closer look at the disadvantages.

First, there is the problem with the *intrapersonal*. The Netflix docudrama calls it a mental health dilemma. We are facing increasing addiction, anxiety, and depression in correlation with the psychological environments that social media create. There is the tinkering with emotional states that Facebook itself admitted to, but also the unreasonable standards for beauty, fitness, popularity, and status as well as vulnerability to shaming, trolling, and cyberbullying. [10] All of this happens in an always-on context in which that hateful tweet or FOMO-inducing post finds you in the middle of the night. "Since negative emotions can be utilized more readily, of course such a system is going to tend to find a way to make you feel bad," [11] argues Lanier in relation to advertising-based platforms. Moreover, in surveillance capitalism, those ways of making you feel bad may be *tailored to you*. [12] How do we feel about this trade-off now?

Second, social media present advantages and disadvantages in the context of the *interpersonal*, meaning how you and I engage with each other. Who hasn't experienced the "lottery brain" [13] kicking in when we automatically reach for the phone at the dinner table

---

3 Douglas Rushkoff, *Team Human* (New York: W.W. Norton, 2019), 68.
4 Jaron Lanier, *Ten Arguments for Deleting Your Social Media Accounts Right Now* (New York: Picador, 2018), 5.
5 Shoshana Zuboff, *The Age of Surveillance Capitalism: The Fight for a Human Future at the New Frontier of Power* (New York: Public Affairs, 2019).
6 Orlowski, *The Social Dilemma*.
7 Marshall McLuhan, *Understanding Media: The Extensions of Man* (New York: McGraw-Hill, 1964).
8 Neil Postman, "Five Things We Need to Know About Technological Change" (1998), https://web.cs.ucdavis.edu/~rogaway/classes/188/materials/postman.pdf.
9 Postman, "Five Things," 1.
10 Lanier, *Ten Arguments*.
11 Lanier, *Ten Arguments*, 88.
12 Lanier, *Ten Arguments*.
13 Colier, *The Power of Off*, 17.

or when we're hanging out with friends? We like checking, because "new mail is a happy sound; no mail is a sad one."[14] We've become addicted gamblers regularly pulling the lever of the slot machine in the hopes of winning the big prize. But what is the big prize? What are we looking for? Are the social media messages that reach us always more relevant than what is going on in the here and now? "What's certain," cautions Colier, "is that the more we check, the more enslaved we become."[15]

Could this new normal be making us less social in our organic world? Do our in-person conversations still have the same level of depth with the smartphone at hand versus without it? Moreover, are we as committed to face-to-face relationships in a culture in which we will "maybe" attend an event, wait until the last minute for something better to come around, and then cancel with a quick and impersonal text? "Last-minute-itis,"[16] meaning the inability or unwillingness to commit, is just one symptom of a media environment that allows us "to act out of our baser qualities," making many of us, according to Colier, "more self-involved, disrespectful and undisciplined."[17] "Social media is destroying your capacity for empathy," agrees Lanier.[18] Meanwhile, "engagement through digital media is just a new way of being alone," claims Rushkoff.[19]

Third, there is the trade-off regarding the *societal*. Orlowski's *Social Dilemma* vividly explains this issue. Political polarization and divisiveness in relation to algorithmic echo chambers threaten democratic structures around the world. Roger McNamee, an early investor in Facebook, explains this phenomenon thus:

> The way to think about it is as 2.5 billion Truman Shows. Each person has their own reality with their own facts. Over time you have the false sense that

everyone agrees with you because everyone in your news feed sounds just like you. Once you're in that state, it turns out you're easily manipulated.[20]

On the one hand, we are not seeing the same information, but we get the impression that we know what's going on. On the other, the more outrageous and deceptive the content, the faster it will spread. This is how some people—including the ones close to us—may end up in a vortex of online conspiracy theories. Ultimately, not unlike Truman, we also risk losing a sense of what is true. So, the first idea to keep in mind is that social media are a trade-off.

SOCIAL MEDIA CREATE WINNERS AND LOSERS

Postman's second idea is about how "the advantages and disadvantages of new technologies are never distributed evenly among the populations."[21] This means there are winners and losers when it comes to social media. Since users become the product in surveillance capitalism, we could argue that it is first the masses that are on the shorter end of the stick. This is nothing new. Rushkoff reminds us that "the people—the masses—have always remained one entire media revolution behind those who dominate them."[22] Whenever the masses have caught up with the technological changes of their time (learning how to read, learning how to write, and then learning how to code), the elites "had moved up another level"[23] and are now controlling the hidden digital infrastructures that allow us to post, share, follow, and like. Despite this sense of agency, we remain the product.

---

14 Rushkoff, *Team Human*, 64.
15 Colier, *The Power of Off*, 19.
16 Colier, 61.
17 Colier, 63.
18 Lanier, *Ten Arguments*, 77.
19 Rushkoff, *Team Human*, 73.
20 Orlowski, *The Social Dilemma*.
21 Postman, "Five Things," 2.
22 Rushkoff, *Team Human*, 59.
23 Rushkoff, 60.

The unevenness that social media produce goes further. Discrimination due to algorithmic biases and the amplification of hate on social media disproportionately impact members of marginalized communities.[24] Princeton University professor Ruha Benjamin, for example, calls the racism coded into many of our new technologies, including social media, the "New Jim Code." Such technologies "often pose as objective, scientific, or progressive" but too often "reinforce racism and other forms of inequity."[25] McLuhan argues that technologies are *extensions of us*—along with our biases if you will.[26] According to Benjamin, implicit and explicit bias can manifest itself in robotics, "default" designs, surveillance practices, and more-harmful-than-helpful technological fixes.[27] Social media present a special paradox: They provide more opportunities to expose blatant racism, but may similarly insert insidious forms of inequity in their designs and products (for example, the "gamification of hate").[28] Even seemingly well-meaning and "neutral" functions of social media and other emerging technologies produce disenfranchisement and injustice. Hence, the second point we need to keep in mind about social media is that while some benefit, others may be harmed.

SOCIAL MEDIA ARE NOT NEUTRAL

The biases of social media warrant a bit more unpacking. Here is where McLuhan's famous aphorism "the medium is the message" comes to full light. Postman draws on this principle when arguing, "Embedded in every technology is a powerful idea, sometimes two or three powerful ideas."[29] In other words, no human-made artifact is truly *neutral*. Each tool encourages us to think, feel, and act in a certain way. So, what are the messages of social media?

Let's take a look at some of their media grammar. First, there are the algorithms: the engine of social media. By definition, *algorithms* are a set of calculations, a mathematical process. As you can imagine, however, this is not the full story. Interviewed in *The Social Dilemma*, data scientist Cathy O'Neil echoes McLuhan and Postman when saying, "I'd like to say that algorithms are opinions embedded in code. And that algorithms are not objective. Algorithms are optimized to some definition of success. … It's usually profit."[30]

Hence, one "powerful idea" inherent to social media algorithms is profit.

For those companies to make a profit, we need to stay engaged. One clever way to keep us plugged in is the infinite scroll. Rushkoff argues, "Designers have discovered that "bottomless feeds" tend to keep users swiping down … consuming more than they intend to because of that unsatiated feeling of never reaching the end."[31] The bias of bottomless feeds is thus dissatisfaction, prompting us to look for more, seeking closure without success.

Finally, what about the "like"-button as a key ingredient of social media? Could even this function have a hidden philosophy with problematic effects? Justin Rosenstein, formerly an engineer at Facebook and Google, remembers this:

> When we were making the 'like'-button, our entire motivation was 'Can we spread positivity and love in the world?' The idea that fast forward to today and teens would be getting depressed when they don't have enough likes, or it could be leading to political polarization, was nowhere on our radar.[32]

---

24 Orlowski, *The Social Dilemma*.
25 Ruha Benjamin, *Race After Technology: Abolitionist Tools for the New Jim Code* (Cambridge, UK: Polity, 2019), 2.
26 McLuhan, *Understanding Media*.
27 Benjamin, *Race After Technology*, 47.
28 Benjamin, *Race After Technology*, 23.
29 Postman, "Five Things," 3.
30 Orlowski, *The Social Dilemma*.
31 Rushkoff, *Team Human*, 66.
32 Orlowski, *The Social Dilemma*.

As this example shows, the powerful idea hidden in a technology may not necessarily be the same idea that helped create it. The effect that Rosenstein and his codevelopers anticipated from the "like"-button diverges from some of the effects we are seeing now.

Interestingly, design ethicist Tristan Harris brings up the neutrality of technologies in *The Social Dilemma*:

> If something is a tool, it genuinely is just sitting there, waiting patiently. If something is not a tool, it's demanding things from you. It's seducing you, it's manipulating you, it wants things from you. ... Social media isn't a tool waiting to be used. It has its own goals, and it has its own means of pursuing them by using your psychology against you.[33]

McLuhan and Postman would likely disagree with part of this statement. We could argue that *any human-made artifact*, even when seemingly "just sitting there, waiting patiently" has a medium-specific bias. The intensity of the manipulation may vary, with the bottomless scroll likely having a stronger hold on us than a bicycle. However, while the bicycle is not considered "persuasive technology," its presence may inconspicuously "demand" that we use it every so often. Moreover, it contains ideas about human mobility based on users having two legs, for example. Would a bicycle be a bias-free device to a person with no legs? Based on Postman's third idea, social media—like all technologies—have certain biases.

SOCIAL MEDIA CHANGE EVERYTHING

Postman's fourth idea, in particular, frames an entire school of thought: media ecology. It is the study of media, meaning *any* human-made artifacts, as environments and environments as media. Media ecologists don't think of technology as something we merely *add* to our culture, but as something that can change its very fabric. Postman compares technological change to a drop of red dye in clear water.[34] The result is not just red dye and water as separate entities. Instead, the water turns red. It changes completely.

Social media are similarly *ecological*. Not only have they been added to our daily lives, but also they've changed it. "Going online went from an active choice to a constant state of being," observes Rushkoff.[35] The goal of advertising-based social media to modify our behavior and form our habits brought about these fundamental changes. In the process of acting more consistently with our profiles and aligning with the human futures algorithms calculated for us, "our irregular edges are being filed off," warns Rushkoff.[36] It is those unpredictable, creative, and innovative ways of being human. Because of this, too, social media create new intrapersonal, interpersonal, and societal environments.

WHEN SOCIAL MEDIA BECOME UNQUESTIONED— UNPLUG

Finally, consider Postman's fifth idea: "Media tend to become mythic,"[37] meaning that eventually we take technologies for granted. Like the air we breathe and the alphabet we use, we tend to stop questioning them once they've become part of our everyday lives. To avoid viewing human-made artifacts "as gifts of nature,"[38] Postman wants us to view them "as a strange intruder"— that is, with a good dose of critical awareness.[39]

When social media and their persuasive biases have such a tight hold on us, how do we cultivate such critical awareness? Lanier suggests a simple but drastic solution: "To free yourself, to be more authentic, to be less

---

33 Orlowski.
34 Postman, "Five Things."
35 Rushkoff, *Team Human*, 62.
36 Rushkoff, 70.
37 Postman, "Five Things" 4.
38 Postman, 4.
39 Postman, 5.

addicted, to be less manipulated, to be less paranoid ... for all these marvelous reasons, delete your accounts."[40] This idea of the exit, the power of off, is valuable. Zuboff, too, argues, "To exit the hive means to enter that territory beyond, where one finds refuge from the artificially tuned-up social pressure of the others."[41]

If you think the kind of exit that Lanier and Zuboff promote goes too far, there are other ways of assessing how social media may have taken over in your life. A forty-eight-hour digital detox, for example, in which one abstains from any screen-based media, has proven to be eye-opening, indeed "life-changing," for many students in my digital media classroom. Similarly, award-winning author Tiffany Shlain advocates for a technology shabbat. One day a week, her family unplugs:

> Living 24/6 feels like magic, and here's why: it seems to defy the laws of physics, as it both slows down time and gives us more of it. I laugh a lot more on that day without screens. I notice everything in greater detail. I sleep better. It strengthens my relationships and makes me feel healthier. It allows me to read, think, be more creative, and reflect in a deeper way. Each week I get a full reset.[42]

At minimum, try creating screen-free spaces and times to be alone or with others. The goal of such and other measures is to create freedom *in* technology as opposed to freedom *from* technology.[43] While we wait for top-down data regulation, justice, and dignity to catch up, detoxing every so often can wake us from our sleep-walking in social media and benefit our intrapersonal, interpersonal, and societal well-being. That technology tends to become mythic and that we need critical awareness is Postman's fifth and final idea: "Breakdown becomes breakthrough."[44] Time to unplug?

---

40   Lanier, *Ten Arguments*, 26.
41   Zuboff, *The Age of Surveillance Capitalism*, 474.
42   Tiffany Shlain, *24/6: The Power of Unplugging One Day a Week* (New York: Gallery Books, 2019), xii.
43   Colier, *The Power of Off*, 15.
44   Marshall McLuhan and Bruce R. Powers, *The Global Village: Transformations in World Life and Media in the 21st Century* (New York: Oxford University Press, 1989), 20.

SURVEILLANCE ENVIRONMENTS: LIVESTREAMING THE INSURRECTION

JAN FERNBACK is an associate professor in the Department of Media Studies and Production at Temple University. Author of numerous articles about the internet and digitial media, her current work examines issues of privacy and surveillance, the impact of media technologies in urban revitalization, and the meaning of virtual community in contemporary culture.

For decades, the mass media have contributed to the environment of surveillance in which we exist. Communications research pioneer Harold Lasswell described how the mass media perform a surveillance function by collecting and distributing news of events, thereby allowing an individual to look over the horizon in order to know about events in the broader world. But the implication of media as devices of surveillance and for voyeurism has gone far beyond Lasswell's vision. As media technologies become cheaper and simpler to use, they become more democratized.

Anyone can use phone cameras to document and observe, and facial recognition technologies are deployed routinely by law enforcement as well as individuals with technical know-how. As antidemocratic forces converged on the US Capitol on January 6, 2021, to protest violently at the seat of democracy, they livestreamed the event on various social media platforms. In an age of transparency and access, these data streams were captured and analyzed by the very forces of democracy they sought to overthrow, resulting in identification and arrest of some rioters. This reading focuses on the role of digital technologies in creating the surveillance environment, with emphasis on social media technologies as both purposeful and inadvertent devices of image and data capture and what this means for privacy.

THE EVOLUTION OF SURVEILLANCE

We form perceptions about surveillance environments through the media in novels (George Orwell's *1984*), in film (*Enemy of the State*), online (spyware, targeted advertising), and through virtual assistants (Amazon Echo). But we both perform the watching and succumb to being watched through the media (social media, CCTV, online gaming, the television show *Big Brother*). Digital media technologies, in particular, are agents of surveillance because of their ubiquity in contemporary life and because they permit users to produce content. As our lives become utterly entwined with digital technologies, we must consider the nature of the surveillance environment and its ramifications, both dangerous and innocuous, for individuals and for society.

Surveillance is a process of concentrated monitoring of human details—at times clandestinely and at times openly—for the purposes of control. Communication technologies serve as obvious devices for surveillance

153

and control. Orwell warns in *1984* of the dangers of total state surveillance enabled by communication technologies. Michel Foucault's (1977) ideas about technologies as tools of discipline and regulation are articulated in his description of Jeremy Bentham's panopticon. In the panopticon, a prison designed for control of the mind, an unseen observer monitors all inmates simultaneously, thus assuring that inmates would assume constant surveillance and behave in a self-disciplining manner. For Foucault, the control warranted by surveillance expanded beyond prisons to other social institutions— including workplaces, hospitals, and schools—and functioned to dehumanize individuals.

Oscar Gandy's (1993) "panoptic sort" describes an elaborate system of information gathering, filtering, and dispersion enabled by information technologies. This system operates as a panopticon that uses accumulated personal data to assign individuals an economic value and sorts them into categories determined by that value. The "panoptic sort" is routine in Western society—for example, in the issuance of credit scores—and thus is a powerful element of social discipline. Roger Clarke (1988) defines "dataveillance" as the use of individual data in tracking personal behaviors or communications. Dataveillance is so widespread, according to Clarke, that it has become the prevailing form of surveillance. Examples of dataveillance include radio-frequency identification (RFID) chips embedded in consumer goods, cell phone tracking, biometric identification, computer surveillance software (keystroke and data capture programs), online data mining programs and big data analytics, databases, and consumer-supplied tracking (loyalty cards, sharing of personal information on social media, the Internet of Things).

David Lyon (1997) sees communication networks of information collection and distribution as the contemporary counterpart to Foucault's theories on control and discipline through surveillance. For Lyon, however, the panopticon is a limiting way to view surveillance; the internet and other digital technologies aid the surveillance enterprise as databases link together and expose more and more personal information. But such monitoring does not have to be overtly visible as the panopticon is. Much digital surveillance is decentralized, invisible, and even voluntary. Also, there are means to resist or evade some aspects of monitoring.

Not all perspectives on surveillance environments reflect its sinister intrusiveness. Lyon (2007) theorizes a type of "caring" surveillance exhibited by means such as security cameras that identify criminals, forensic scrutiny that bolsters law enforcement efforts, lifeguards who ensure water safety. Store loyalty cards provide customer discounts. Reality-TV shows provide entertainment around surveillance activities—what Robertson (2007, 410) calls "engaging in the publication of privacy." Citizen-gathered "news" video finds its way to legitimate news organizations. Voyeurism finds an outlet in surveillance activities as amateur porn is distributed online. Lyon (2018) cautions, however, that even "caring" surveillance has contributed to what he terms "the culture of surveillance"—a way of life that naturalizes surveillance as a practice in which we all engage and enable.

We are targets of consumer and government surveillance that expose us as big data subjects, yet we track ourselves and our loved ones using the same technologies as a form of play and entertainment. Online social networking flaunts surveillance environments by embracing the watchers; users willingly succumb to surveillance to assert identities or viewpoints within the digital technological landscape. The revelation of personal information on social media is a type of ritualized identity formation and expression.

Livestreaming political events such as protests, rallies, activism, violence, and insurrections is a type of self-surveillance that may ultimately contribute to the larger public discourse about weighty political matters. Such livestreams have become powerful symbols of and contributors to the surveillance environment. That the surveillance environment exists is understood; but what engineers this environment? How has it flourished?

Whether surveillance has protective elements or intrusive ones, its growth and vigor have resulted from the powerful interplay among military, economic, political, corporate, technological, and legal institutional bureaucracies. As surveillance tactics and modes became integrated across these bureaucracies (think ID cards, basic recordkeeping), similarities emerged that allowed surveillance to become a natural part of everyday life. In colonial America, meticulous slave records were kept, slaves were required to hold "passes" when moving about town, and slave patrols were organized to detect and capture runaways. The US military issued identification passes to soldiers during the Civil War, and military bureaucratization led to further governmental surveillance and disciplinary measures (citizen passports, census, Social Security numbers), criminal surveillance, workplace surveillance for purposes of controlling immigrant labor, and ultimately, consumer surveillance (Parenti 2003).

In all of these sectors, the emergence of computers and the digital revolution made surveillance more complete, more profound, and more ubiquitous. As surveillance is catalyzed by desires for efficiency, for global power consolidation, and for general control and discipline in each sector, the surveillance environment expands (Lyon 2007). Thus, computers and the digital revolution enable monitoring through interlinked IDs, swipe cards, databases, video patrols and CCTV, and through the integrated data repositories found on Google.

COVEILLANCE

Livestreams on social media add to the surveillance environment by promoting coveillance—a form of omnidirectional monitoring where everyone sees one another. Enacting a case of coveillance, an anonymous web developer (Greenberg 2021) created a collection of the livestreams of the January 6 Capitol insurrection (www.facesoftheriot.com) and employed facial recognition technology to [take] screen captures of participants in order to aid in their identification by law enforcement. Together, these types of surveillance, self-surveillance, and coveillance represent a type of power and control that is all-seeing, leaving individuals with little agency to combat the exposure of personal information, the corporate profit that may be made from it, and the potential consequences—whether economic, personal, political, or even medical—of so much information and misinformation being traded in the surveillance environment.

ANALYSIS: BENEFITS AND HAZARDS

The impact of the surveillance environment is manifold. There are implications for individuals, for society, for privacy, and for democracy. Lyon (2007) reminds us that digital surveillance technologies can aid the storage and sorting of personal data in ways that are harmless as well as insidious to individuals and to democracy. But, as technologies become more sophisticated, the dangers may increase. The capacities of monitoring devices and agencies are increasing, creating linkages among detailed datasets, including biometric data (passports, fingerprints, facial scans, retinal scans); locational data (GPS, cell phone tracking, RFIDs, satellite photos); medical data (records, genomic data); and criminal, consumer, military, educational, and employment data. The data flows are now global as the boundaries between nations and national policies are blurring. Thus, the bounty of data gathered via surveillance can be shunted toward so-called data havens—countries that do not recognize data protection laws that exist in the European Union or the United States.

LOSS OF PRIVACY

Some citizen groups and scholars worry about a surveillance state fostered by government and corporate monitoring of private citizens. For example, government investigators, litigators, corporate data brokers, or identity thieves might monitor you based on information traces left online that Google or social media sites might store. In the United States, the government relies on corporate data mining operations such as Experian or Axiom as a means to monitor individuals without adhering to Amendment IV to the US Constitution, which prohibits law enforcement from conducting unreasonable searches of persons or property. These companies sell data to foreign and domestic government agencies, direct marketers, and law enforcement.

Privacy advocates and other groups claim that surveillance is a threat to privacy because it intrudes upon our freedom, dignity, and integrity. Defined by Samuel Warren and Louis Brandeis in an 1890 *Harvard Law Review* article as the "right to be let alone," privacy encompasses the concepts of territory (environmental intrusion); information (personal data); body (physical intrusions such as drug testing); and communication (wiretapping or hacking) (Warren and Brandeis 1890). Our private thoughts and private lives are what make us free and dignified individuals; surveillance threatens to expose those private thoughts—our private selves—by allowing access to the bits and pieces that constitute our behaviors and our selves.

Privacy is also about controlling information about ourselves. We may attempt to control our information against corporate or governmental monitors, but we also willfully engage in providing information without recognizing that we are being surveilled. For example, social media are seen as social intimacy through information sharing. We use Instagram, TikTok, or Twitter as a form of voluntary "personal expression" that showcases our identities in the datasphere, but social media's exhibitionistic tendencies open us to the downside of being watched. We expect freedom online—freedom to be me—but the surveillance impinges on that freedom.

Social media users define their identity in part through consumer goods, thereby submitting to self-marketing, self-disclosure, and self-surveillance (and mass surveillance). As another example, Facebook quizzes "scrape" information gleaned from the quizzes for whoever authors the quiz, so that a person/company/group can view your profile, regardless of your profile's privacy rating. And livestreams amplify our voices in the public sphere but subject us to increased scrutiny from bad actors as well as good actors. Facial recognition surveillance allows law enforcement (and everyone) to search images without warrants or guarantees of upholding our rights. Ultimately, we invite self-surveillance through mediated outlets.

DEHUMANIZATION

For Foucault (1977), the type of knowledge construed through the surveillance environment results in a boundless control that can be used to dehumanize individuals. This dehumanization can be seen in the impact of surveillance on the psychology of the watchers as well as the watched. Philip Zimbardo's classic Stanford Prison Experiment (http://www.prisonexp.org) used student volunteers to perform the roles of prison guards and prisoners. The students embodied their roles: the guards treated the prisoners with contempt and brutality; the prisoners experienced emotional trauma (as seen in their crying and rage).

What parallels exist in the surveillance environment? Does being watched imply that we *should* be watched? Could that same brutality emerge when the watchers

of society observe the rest of us? Do modes of surveillance encourage the emergence of a social contract of altered behavior or conformity (among the watched) and empowerment and discrimination (among the watchers)? A power divide is created between the groups as rights and privileges are questioned. Distrust, fear, and hatred can result, and the freedom to engage in social life with dignity may be lost. The more watchers are able to construct people by virtue of an electronic dossier or by ID tracking or by CCTV images, the more reductive we become as entities. We become compilations of data, bodily movements, consumer purchases, geographic location. Not only is humanity potentially sacrificed, but we also may become *deindividuated*, a psychological term for feeling anonymous, disconnected, and overwhelmed in the crowd. Ultimately, the surveillance environment can be examined as a moral issue in addition to a political one.

TRANSPARENCY

But not all believe that surveillance threatens to create an atmosphere of totalitarianism, either in terms of privacy or in terms of dignity or freedom. Surveillance practices have entertainment value (online gaming, social media "stalking," playing with virtual assistants like Siri and Amazon Echo, even television shows comprised of surveillance video). Some people view certain types of surveillance as a comfort (for example, antiterrorism policies, nanny cams, lifeguards, public security cameras, medical supervision, citizen video of police actions, even Google Street View); hence a movement toward a transparent society (Brin 1998; Lyon 2007) has developed in which information in all spheres is completely open for all to access. Transparency provides the watched with knowledge of the types, means, and purposes of surveillance. Essentially, transparency is the idea that government and corporations can watch citizens, but citizens can watch back. If we all know one another's secrets, those secrets can no longer be used as weapons.

The notion of transparency supposedly neutralizes arguments about security versus privacy. Thus the appetite for total information has cultivated the movement toward transparency in all aspects of information as a means to combat the consequences of surveillance, with the motto "Nothing to hide, nothing to fear." Advocates claim that transparency is a necessity because the sheer accumulation of data acquired through surveillance results in profiling and discrimination against groups and individuals. This discrimination could take the form of curtailed lending or differential pricing for consumer goods, or denial of insurance to population segments deemed too risky based on "data categories" assigned to individuals under surveillance. Is transparency a tool to quash discrimination, or could transparency harm oppressed groups that rely on secrecy to flourish (such as religious minorities)?

ISSUES POSED BY "FACES OF THE RIOT"

"The Faces of the Riot" site illustrates the potential downside of transparency in its use of facial recognition technology. Evan Greer, deputy director for the online civil liberties group Fight for the Future, claims, "It would be an enormous mistake if we come out of this moment by glorifying or lionizing a technology that, broadly speaking, disproportionately harms communities of color, low-income communities, immigrant communities, Muslim communities, activists … the very same people that the faces on this website stormed the Capitol for the purpose of silencing and disenfranchising" (Greenberg 2021, para. 5). Does transparency really correct power imbalances between the watchers and the watched? Is transparency merely an excuse to legitimize more sophisticated surveillance techniques? Facial recognition technology is largely unregulated, and everyday people can cheaply harness this technology to identify faces from publicly available security camera images and social media feeds to create databases or just entertain themselves (Chinoy 2019).

If, indeed, the surveillance environment has become so entrenched in everyday life that citizens and institutions have no ability to negotiate a state of nonsurveillance, then transparency seems to be the only means toward ensuring some dignity and freedom.

- But would transparency then become a technologically mandated solution to a technologically derived problem?
- Should citizens allow the march of technological development to inflict its will upon the human

spirit, which needs its own private core and its own sense of dignity and freedom?

David Brin (1998) argues that technological evolution will modify human behavior such that transparency is the only means of recourse. However, critics might respond that Brin assigns technology too central a role in determining the course of human freedom and equality.

- Might the reliance on technology for enhanced security simply encourage reliance on technology for enhanced surveillance?
- Might openness and transparency encourage further escalation of spying in the name of security?
- Is it realistic to suppose that citizens can ever acquire the same type of surveillance capabilities and power that government and corporate institutions have?

RESISTANCE

There are both nontechnological and technological means to resist the surveillance environment. Measures of resistance include these:

- Exhibitionism
- Citizen protests
- Anonymizing or falsifying data
- Hacking surveillance technologies
- Refusal to participate in online shopping, blogging, social media, or loyalty clubs

Lorna Rhodes (2004) researched prisoners who mutilate themselves when subjected to the gaze of maximum security guards. She theorizes that, rather than demonstrating insanity, the prisoners make themselves more visible in a subversive act of rebellion against surveillance.

SOUSVEILLANCE

Another technique of resistance is *sousveillance*, literally "watching from below," a type of inverse surveillance in which the public sector monitors the security sector. Examples include citizen video, keeping tabs on various authorities (government, corporations, doctors, law enforcement, etc.), maintaining "watchdog" web sites or social media, or recording telephone conversations or police actions.

Sousveillance usually requires a response from surveillors in the form of acknowledgment, power shifting, or even the development of new, more powerful surveillance mechanisms. For example, participants in the 1999 World Trade Organization protests in Seattle recorded their own interaction with law enforcement, which spurred security organizations to reconceive surveillance and control mechanisms (mostly in the form of increasingly sophisticated CCTV).

Black Lives Matter protestors have also recorded law enforcement in an act of sousveillance, but have found that they've become targeted by law enforcement and other entities through social media and through police body-worn cameras. And the participants in the January 6, 2021, insurrection at the US Capitol have been subjected to facial recognition identification (and misidentification) through "Faces of the Riot" and other data streams. While speculation remains that the security sector's response to citizen resistance could ultimately change the power dynamic between the watchers and the watched, the complex interplay of surveillance, coveillance, and sousveillance is a force that may stunt any power equalization.

CONCLUSION

The surveillance environment is a product of the evolution of the information society from other types of social orders based on punishment, discipline, and control. Surveillance is a sociotechnical system; it is enabled by technology but defined by sociocultural realities, and those technologies are socially shaped. Big data reservoirs, facial recognition technology, and troves of corporate or governmental data mirror those realities in contemporary culture. As we are increasingly defined by the data profiles constructed from the harvest of the surveillance machine, we must examine the nature of surveillance, its consequences, and potential responses to it. Because digital technologies progress so rapidly, and because they contribute to and enable the surveillance environment in which we live, citizens must consider the impact of this environment on identity, freedom, dignity, and democracy.

REFERENCES

Brin, D. 1998. *The Transparent Society: Will Technology Force Us to Choose Between Privacy and Freedom?* Reading, MA: Addison-Wesley.

Chinoy, S. 2019. "We Built an 'Unbelievable' (but Legal) Facial Recognition Machine." *New York Times*, April 16. https://www.nytimes.com/interactive/2019/04/16/opinion/facial-recognition-new-york-city.html.

Clarke, R. 1988. "Information Technology and Dataveillance." *Communications of the ACM* 31 (5): 498–512.

Foucault, M. 1977. *Discipline and Punish: Birth of the Prison*. Translated by A. Sheridan. New York: Pantheon.

Gandy, Oscar. 1993. *The Panoptic Sort*. Boulder, CO: Westview Press.

Greenberg, A. 2021. "This Site Published Every Face from Parler's Capitol Riot Videos." *Wired*, January 28, 2021. *https://www.wired.com/story/faces-of-the-riot-capitol-insurrection-facial-recognition/*.

Lyon, David. 1997. "Surveillance Systems: Towards an Electronic Panoptical Society? Interview with Christian Höller for Telepolis," May 22, 1997. http://www.telepolis.de/english/special/pol/8026/1.html.

Lyon, David. 2007. *Surveillance Studies: An Overview*. Cambridge, UK: Polity.

Lyon, David. 2018. *The Culture of Surveillance: Watching as a Way of Life*. Cambridge, UK: Polity.

Parenti, Christian. 2003. *The Soft Cage: Surveillance in America from Slavery to the War on Terror*. New York: Basic Books.

Rhodes, Lorna. 2004. *Total Confinement: Madness and Reason in the Maximum Security Prison*. Berkeley: University of California Press.

Robertson, Roland. 2007. "Open Societies, Closed Minds? Exploring the Ubiquity of Suspicion and Voyeurism." *Globalizations* 4 (3): 399–416.

Warren, S. D., and Brandeis, L. D. 1890. "The Right to Privacy." *Harvard Law Review* 4: 193, 195–196.

1984 (1984)

This film provides a realistic depiction of George Orwell's classic dystopian novel, showing how "telescreens" (televisions that watch you while you watch them) can be used as tools of propaganda and thought control in service to a totalitarian regime. The concepts of "Newspeak" and "doublethink" are even more relevant in 2021. Richard Burton is chilling as he explains doublethink and the destruction of rational thought.
Director: Michael Radford
Starring: John Hurt, Suzanne Hamilton, and Richard Burton

MINORITY REPORT (2002)

Loosely based on Philip K. Dick's dystopian short story, this film depicts a future Washington, DC, where a network of total surveillance is used to prevent violent crime. Called "Precrime," the surveillance agency seeks to predict violent crimes before they happen, creating situations in which people are imprisoned for crimes they have thought, but not committed. Actual crimes drop to near zero, but human corruption remains the same, and that is one of the flaws in any system of total surveillance. Excellent symbolic depictions of the (networked) panopticon, the circular prison theorized by Jeremy Bentham.
Director: Steven Spielberg
Starring: Tom Cruise, Colin Farrell, and Max von Sydow

V FOR VENDETTA (2005)

Set in a dystopian future in London, V is a masking-wearing rebel who seeks to overthrow the authoritarian government that has seized power in Great Britain. To inspire the revolutionaries, V engages in many tactics, including hacking into the British Television Network to deliver a speech advocating revolution and committing terrorist activities like blowing up Parliament. In the end, the revolution supposedly succeeds as the masses take to the streets, all wearing V's "Guy Fawkes mask."
Director: James McTeigue
Starring: Hugo Weaving and Natalie Portman

TRON: LEGACY (2010)

In the sequel to the 1983 hit film, Jeff Bridges reprises his role as "Flynn," the brilliant computer coder and game designer who is trapped in the Grid by the evil corporation that wants their operating system to dominate the users of the internet. Far from a masterpiece, the film still does a good job of raising issues that are becoming ever more relevant—the militarization of the internet versus the beauty of "a system where all information is free and open."
Director: Joseph Kosinski
Starring: Jeff Bridges, Garrett Hedlund, and Olivia Wilde

THE CIRCLE (2017)

Fresh out of college and seeking meaningful employment, Mae gets a job at the "The Circle," the hippest internet-social media company on Planet Earth. When she agrees to wear a camera 24/7 to place herself under total global surveillance for millions of followers, she discovers there's a dark side to the promises of going fully "transparent" in the spectacle. An underrated film sure to generate classroom discussion.
Director: James Ponsoldt
Starring: Emma Watson, Tom Hanks, and John Boyega

CHAPTER SIX

FREEDOM AND PROTEST

The Semiotics of Protest in the Age of the Spectacle

By Barry Vacker, Tauheedah Shukriyyah Asad,

Kelly Bartsch, and Gail Bower

TRIGGERS AND POLITICS

You might be "triggered" by something in this chapter, though we hope you can keep your cool. Combine media with memes and politics, and the embers are ready to burst into flames. Hot takes and tribal conflict. Will it ever end? Not any time soon, it seems.

The point here is not to persuade you to change your political beliefs or worldviews. We know that is utterly impossible, and to pretend otherwise would be delusional. That's because there are few memes that reach deeper into our psyche than tribal affiliation and political beliefs. However, we hope this chapter provides you with a deeper and richer understanding of the power of symbols in our 24/7 media environments. *This chapter also hopes to provide you with a better understanding of the First Amendment and the right to protest, both of which are crucial to democracy, while keeping in mind that the First Amendment and freedom of expression (in all its forms) are complex and wide-ranging topics that extend far beyond the scope of a single chapter.*[1] So, while we cannot cover every issue here, let's do our best to move beyond triggers into a richer understanding of symbols, freedom, and protests.

SIGN AND SYMBOLS: FLAGS, FISTS, HASHTAGS, AND ATOMS

Flags, raised fists, hashtags like #MeToo and #BlackLivesMatter, and electrons orbiting the neutrons of atoms—all of these are signs and symbols deployed to inspire patriotism, protest movements, and public demonstrations to show mass support. Raised fists were symbols of power and resistance used by the Black Panther Party in the 1960s and, decades later, by the Black Lives Matter protest movement in the 2010s–2020s, which went global in the wake of the 2020 murder of George Floyd by Derek Chauvin, a Minneapolis police officer. Social media and hashtags have amplified the power of protest movements to spread around the world, such as "#BlackLivesMatter" to protest police killings of unarmed Black people, "#MeToo" to protest sexual assault and harassment in America

---

1 For example, see Stephan A. Smith, *Freedom of Expression* (Oxford, UK: Oxford Research Associates, 2019), and Douglas M. Fraleigh and Joseph S. Tuman, *Freedom of Expression in the Marketplace of Ideas* (Los Angeles: Sage, 2010).

and around the world, the Women's March to support women's rights, and "#climatestrike" to empower the Global Climate Strikes led by Greta Thunberg. The famed atomic symbol (three electrons orbiting a neutron) was deployed by the organizers of the March for Science, along with the hashtag "#marchforscience."

The creation and deployment of symbols is the figurative way we construct and understand the world, the way we assemble reality and understand its meaning(s). Social media technologies (the media) have changed the conditions under which the populace receive and interpret symbols (the messages). These technologies imbue objects, images of objects, and simulacra of images of objects with persuasive power throughout the media ecologies and environments. In a world of spectacle and hyperreality, one of the ways to analyze the power and meaning of symbols is through *semiotics*.

In a nutshell, semiotics is the study of signs and symbols, including their objects and systems of meanings, which replicate throughout the networks and social media platforms. Semiotic theory includes both the object/ image and its "sign" within an overall message and the meaning it conveys to the message's recipients. Semiotic theory can be quite complex, even overly complex, but here is a simple way to think about it for the purposes of this chapter:

- The Object: The physical existence of *the thing*, such as a nation, fist, atom, or event.
- The Symbol: The *image* or *representation* used to convey the object, such as the stars and stripes on a flag (to represent America), a raised fist by a person or in a graphic design, the electrons orbiting the neutrons in an atom in diagram.
- The Sign: The *meaning* associated with the thing and its symbol, which are integrated into a single concept in the minds of the viewers or the audience. Raised fist equals protest, flag equals patriotism, and atom equals science.

Other simple examples include

- The "golden arches" (symbol) for McDonald's hamburgers (object), with McDonald's being a place for families to eat and bond (sign/meaning).
- The swoosh (symbol) on Nike apparel (objects), which symbolize fitness, exercise, sports, and "Just Do It" (signs/meanings).
- The large star (symbol) on the Dallas Cowboys helmet (object associated with the city of Dallas), which symbolizes the "Lone Star State" of Texas and "America's Team" (meanings).[2]

For college teams and professional sports teams, their names often reference something from the past that has taken on mythic qualities, such as the Southern Cal Trojans, the San Francisco 49ers, the New England Patriots, the Texas Longhorns, or the Dallas Cowboys. The names "49ers," "Longhorns," and "Cowboys" all reference mythologies of the American West. Of course, many teams reference mythic pasts ("Trojans" and "Patriots"), which is a powerful way for symbols to convey emotional meaning for fans. Fans, citizens, and everyday patriots want to feel that their teams, cities, states, and nations are grounded in something profound, with deep roots in history.

For example, there are very few actual cowboys in Dallas, precisely because the *real* cowboys are on the farms and ranches outside the big cities of Texas. Dallas is a sprawling cosmopolitan metropolis and home to many major corporations, employing people who work in offices sitting at desks and managing information—not on ranches riding horses and herding cattle. Though the name "Dallas Corporations" or "Dallas Office Workers" would more accurately reflect the city, such names are far less mythic than "Dallas Cowboys." This is how symbols

---

2   The Cowboys earned the moniker "America's Team" because their games generally had higher TV ratings, at least when they were regularly in the playoffs and winning Super Bowls in the 1970s through the 1990s.

work, especially in hyperreality. The name "Cowboys" (symbol) stands for the football team (object referencing the city), which is fused in the concept "Dallas Cowboys" (sign/meaning).[3]

Billions of dollars in advertising across decades of retailing shapes the "meaning" of the signs for McDonald's and Nike. Advertising and marketing shape the meaning of numerous popular brands, such as Levi's, Jeep, Chanel, Corona, Uniqlo, Coca-Cola, Burger King, Whole Foods, Doc Martens, and any other brand with which you might be familiar. In all these cases, there are things (cars, clothes, food) with symbols (logos and ads) that convey signs (systems of meanings) that generate responses, beliefs, and behaviors. The senders are the corporations, the messages are the ads and their meanings, and the receivers are the audiences.

We must keep in mind that all signs and symbols are memes and they replicate like memes. In the spectacle, signs and symbols may stand for something that still exists somewhere and is celebrated in the images. In the hyperreal, the signs and symbols have replaced that which they stand for, such that the real thing may no longer exist. The copies have supplanted the originals, the map has overtaken the territory, and the simulacrum reigns supreme. All of this makes us easy prey for the emotional appeals of tribalism, nationalism, propaganda, fake news, celebrities (chapter 4), and consumerism (chapter 7).

FLAGS: STARS AND TRIBES

Since the beginning of fabrics and textiles, flags have been used to symbolize tribal affiliation, now seen in the flags for nations, states, and belief systems. Consider the stars and stripes on the American flag or the lone star on the California and Texas flags. The stars on the flags are signs meant to convey a tribal connection to the starry skies and to symbolize a cosmically ordained validation of that nation or state—to show that the universe approves. On one hand, this connection is completely invented, as if the universe really "approves" of what one tribe is doing on a tiny planet in a random galaxy among two trillion galaxies. Yet, science shows that our bodies and brains are all made of star stuff—yet, that fact counters the tribalism that dominates our signs, beliefs, behaviors, and identities.

Flags might be the sign that generates the deepest reactions—pro and con, love and hate. That's because flags tap into deep primal emotions related to tribal loyalties and affiliations, which are the roots of patriotism and warfare. Most everyone loves to see their favorite flag flapping in the wind, as if the air is cheering on our beliefs and worldviews. Consider the American flag, a symbol for the actual America, which conveys an array of positive meanings: freedom, opportunity, capitalism, greatness, diversity, and so on. These meanings are what draw immigrants and refugees to America from around the world. However, given the hypocrisy of American policies since its founding, the very same flag is also seen as a symbol of racism, slavery, colonization, ethnic cleansing, military empire, and many others. Depending on your political perspective, these meanings will generate a variety of emotions.

BURNING THE FLAG AND TORCHING A SYMBOL

Hot media generate hot takes, fueled by instant reactions and emotional responses. Few things generate hotter media conditions than burning a flag, especially the American flag. Considering the wide variation in meanings conveyed by the flag (about America and its policies), it's no surprise that burning an American flag (symbolic

---

3   As for those would-be macho dudes wearing cowboy hats and driving big pickup trucks across the asphalt prairies of Dallas, they are the simulacra of cowboys, the copies in which the original is no longer present. In contrast, cowboy boots have morphed into a more universal fashion accessory; those who wear cowboy boots in the metropolis are not seen as trying to be "cowboys," unlike those wearing cowboy hats. Welcome to the complexity of semiotics and hyperreality.

protest) generates such anger and vitriol, along with cheers and celebration. Burning a flag means that a sign and symbol are being torched, usually to convey another sign (message) that is counter to the symbolic meanings cherished by the dominant social regime.

During the 1984 Republican National Convention in Dallas, which was a coronation calling for four more years of Ronald Reagan as president, a protestor named Gregory Johnson burned an American flag at the Dallas City Hall.[4] As you might imagine, the torched flag triggered reactions and emotions spanning the political spectrum. Johnson's flag-burning set off a long and emotionally charged controversy that eventually led to the US Supreme Court ruling that flag-burning was a form of "symbolic" protest and "expressive" speech protected by the First Amendment.[5] Justice Anthony Kennedy perfectly summarized the issue in his concurring opinion:

> Though symbols often are what we ourselves make of them, the flag is constant in expressing beliefs Americans share, beliefs in law and peace and that freedom which sustains the human spirit. The case here today forces recognition of the costs to which those beliefs commit us. It is poignant but fundamental that the flag protects those who hold it in contempt.[6]

In the aftermath of the Supreme Court's ruling, various groups proposed the creation and passage of the "Flag Desecration Amendment" (also known as the "Flag Burning Amendment"), an amendment to the Constitution designed to outlaw flag-burning. So far, the amendment has yet to generate enough votes in the US Congress to become law.

DO YOU KNOW WHAT RIGHTS ARE PROTECTED BY THE FIRST AMENDMENT?

Protest, rebellion, and the struggle for freedom are celebrated in films such as *The Matrix*, *V for Vendetta*, and *The Hunger Games*. In all three movies, we see noble heroes—Morpheus, Neo, and Trinity in *The Matrix*, V and Evey in *V for Vendetta*, and Katniss and Cinna in *The Hunger Games*—leading rebellions against the dominant systems of control in the societies of the future. *The Matrix* was the rebel film for freedom in the internet era, while *V for Vendetta* is the rebel film for freedom during the War on Terror; *The Hunger Games* is the rebel film for a society that consumes entertainment about freedom.

Perhaps these films helped inspire Occupy Wall Street, the Arab Spring, Black Lives Matter, the Women's March, and other protests and rebellions around the world. After all, protestors wearing the V mask appeared at Occupy Wall Street protests, and the mask seems to have been embraced by the hacker movement known as Anonymous. It is because of this anonymity that we really do not know who is wearing the masks, online or in person.[7] Would it be surprising to discover that some mask wearers were government agents seeking to infiltrate and befriend the protestors, even though they were exercising their universal human rights, or their First Amendment rights protected in the Constitution of the United States? History has yet to record the outcome of these rebellions in the twenty-first century.

---

4 Johnson and the demonstrators were protesting the Reagan administration and various Texas firms based in Dallas. The flag was apparently removed from a nearby flagpole and Johnson set it aflame at the Dallas City Hall. No one was hurt, but many nondemonstrators were offended, and Johnson was charged with violating a Texas law that forbid desecration of sacred objects. He was convicted, fined $2000, and sentenced to a year in prison.

5 Johnson's conviction was overturned by the Texas Court of Appeals, which asserted that flag-burning was considered "symbolic speech" and protected by the First Amendment. The State of Texas appealed the decision to the US Supreme Court. In *Texas v. Johnson* 491 U.S. 397 (1989), the Supreme Court agreed with the Texas Court of Appeals and ruled that flag-burning was "symbolic" and "expressive" speech protected by the First Amendment.

6 *Texas v. Johnson*, 491 U.S. at 420–21 (Kennedy, J., concurring).

7 Of course, one might find the names of some of the protestors with V masks by accessing Amazon's sales records for V masks, where the names and addresses of purchasers would be archived.

THE FIRST AMENDMENT: SIX RIGHTS AND FREEDOMS

The First Amendment is perhaps the greatest political idea to emerge from America, and it has been copied and spread to many parts of the world, surely inspiring the UN's declaration of freedom of speech, belief, and expression. The First Amendment is supposed to protect six overlapping rights. Here is the breakdown.

The First Amendment's Six Rights and Freedoms	
"Congress shall make no law ..."	
(1) "respecting the establishment of religion"	(1) freedom from religious belief
(2) "prohibiting the free exercise thereof"	(2) freedom of religious belief
(3) "abridging the freedom of speech"	(3) freedom of speech
(4) abridging "the press"	(4) freedom of the press
(5) abridging "the right of the people to peaceably assemble"	(5) right to peacefully assemble in groups
(6) abridging the right "to petition the Government for a redress of grievances"	(6) right to seek redress or protest

These six rights mean—or should mean—that without fear of prosecution and imprisonment, you and/or the media can do the following:

1. Have and express your lack of belief in any religion or whatever you believe about the origins of the cosmos and humankind;
2. Believe and express whatever religion you choose;
3. State whatever idea you want;
4. Disseminate information to society via multiple forms of media;
5. Peacefully organize in a group; and
6. Peacefully protest, complain, and/or critique politicians, government, corporations, religions, and any other institution with which you disagree without fear of arrest or harassment.

Obviously, the application of these rights is complicated by the complexities of history and contemporary society, our many media technologies and platforms, and the varieties of personal tastes and social styles.[8] Other issues involve private property and various restrictions involving times (political rallies at 3:00 in the morning), places (blocking entrances to public or private buildings), and manners (issues of harassment, offensiveness, obscenity, loud music, symbolic speech, and so on).[9] Again, the complexities of these issues extend far beyond the scope of this chapter.

---

8   Jonathan W. Emord, *Freedom, Technology, and the First Amendment* (San Francisco: Pacific Research Institute for Public Policy, 1991); Edward de Grazia, *Girls Lean Back Everywhere: The Law of Obscenity and the Assault on Genius* (New York: Random House, 1992).

9   To pass the Supreme Court's First Amendment test, the government's proposed "time, place, and manner" restrictions must be neutral to the content of the speech or expression, narrowly tailored to serve a well-defined public interest, and leave open ample alternative channels of communication. See *Frisby v. Schultz*, 487 U.S. 474, 481 (1988).

"FREEDOM OF EXPRESSION"

The rights to freedom of speech and freedom of the press were eventually extended to include an umbrella of rights under the term "freedom of expression."[10] In general, these freedoms also include political speech, commercial speech (advertising), political protest, religious belief, symbolic expression (such as flag burning), and artistic expression in many forms.[11] Freedoms were also extended to various forms of electronic media, including radio and television.[12] Regarding online free speech, the Supreme Court unanimously ruled that the "anti-indecency" regulations of the Communications Decency Act (1996) violated the First Amendment.[13] Justice John Paul Stevens authored the Court's opinion and concluded it with this philosophical statement:

> The record demonstrates that the growth of the Internet has been and continues to be phenomenal. As a matter of constitutional tradition, in the absence of evidence to the contrary, we presume that governmental regulation of the content of speech is more likely to interfere with the free exchange of ideas than to encourage it. The interest in encouraging freedom of expression in a democratic society outweighs any theoretical but unproven benefit of censorship.[14]

Indeed, the growth of the internet has spread across the planet, and billions of people have access to the "free exchange of ideas" as encouraged by Justice Stevens. Since the Court's ruling, social media platforms have emerged and proliferated around the planet. As with the flag-burning cases, so with the internet—it might not be as easy as you think to silence views that you disagree with or find offensive.

It's no surprise that many people have used the internet and social media to express their views about people and society, including art, movies, sports, fashion, celebrities, religion, science, politics, economics, the environment, and endless other topics. There are numerous examples of people building large audiences with their hot takes and cultural critiques. As detailed by Christiana Dillard in this chapter, social media influencer and YouTube vlogger Jackie Aina has built a following of more than one million with her mix of beauty advice and critiques of racism and discrimination in society. Aina's online success is just what the First Amendment protects.

Humans should have a right to express these beliefs in whatever form they choose, as long as it is nonviolent and noncoercive. We respect these rights as humane individuals, because censorship, suppression, and coercion are never the path to discovering truth or producing an enlightened and empowered society. Freedom, persuasion, and toleration are always preferable to censorship, suppression, and coercion, precisely because prohibiting memes and beliefs is rarely the answer to a question. These are among the reasons we prevent governments, corporations, and other institutions from *passing laws* and *establishing rules* in order to control what books we read or websites we access, what movies or TV shows we watch, or what we believe about religion, science, and the universe.

Freedom of expression and the First Amendment represent humanist memes born of the idea that art, science, reason, and mass media could lead to a more informed, knowledgeable, peaceful, and humane society. Of course, such ideals have not been fulfilled, but that does not mean we should abandon those ideals. Otherwise, society regresses and becomes intolerant and barbarian.

---

10   Douglas M. Fraleigh and Joseph S. Tuman, *Freedom of Expression in the Marketplace of Ideas* (Los Angeles: SAGE, 2010); C. Edwin Baker, *Human Liberty and Freedom of Speech* (New York: Oxford University Press, 1989); Thomas I. Emerson, *The System of Freedom of Expression* (New York: Vintage Books, 1970).
11   Stephan A. Smith, *Freedom of Expression* (Oxford, UK: Oxford Research Associates, 2019); Rodney A. Smolla, *Free Speech in an Open Society* (New York: Alfred A. Knopf, 1992); Edward de Grazia, *Girls Lean Back Everywhere*.
12   Lucas A. Powe Jr., *American Broadcasting and the First Amendment* (Berkeley: University of California Press, 1987).
13   *Reno v. American Civil Liberties Union*, 521 U.S. 844 (1997).
14   *Reno v. American Civil Liberties Union*, 885.

HUMAN RIGHTS AND OPEN NETWORKS

In the Universal Declaration of Human Rights, the United Nations recognizes the following rights to freedom of speech and expression:

> Article 18: Everyone has the right to freedom of thought, conscience and religion; this right includes freedom to change his religion or belief, and freedom, either alone or in community with others and in public or private, to manifest his religion or belief in teaching, practice, worship and observance.

> Article 19: Everyone has the right to freedom of opinion and expression; this right includes freedom to hold opinions without interference and to seek, receive and impart information and ideas through any media and regardless of frontiers.[15]

These rights and freedoms have not always been recognized and embraced in human history, arising from a centuries-long struggle that emerged over the political and theocratic control of the ideas of books, newspapers, and various periodicals being mass-produced by the printing press.[16] Despite many successes, the struggle for freedom of speech and expression continues today in many parts of the world, including the United States.[17] Much as the printing press generated a battle between censorship and freedom, today the internet fuels a battle over censorship and freedom (speech, press, thought, and so on), access, dissent, and even the preservation of democracy.[18]

In general, freedom of expression and open networks are protected and encouraged for several overlapping reasons. These reasons are all interrelated and cannot be completely separated from each other.

1. INDIVIDUAL AND HUMAN RIGHTS

Individuals and social groups should have certain human rights. At the core of those rights is the freedom to speak, read, hear, express, and determine one's own beliefs. This also includes the right to dissent and critique any and all aspects of one's society. These rights include the uses of all previous media and the emerging media technologies to come.

2. THE PUBLIC'S RIGHT TO KNOW

Citizens in a free and open democratic society should have the intellectual and political rights to know what their elected leaders, government workers, and corporations are doing in the name of that society at home and abroad. This is even truer in our increasingly complex global society. Freely elected democratic governments are supposed to be transparent to their citizens and thus the world. To the extent that their activities impact public welfare, lands, and ecosystems, corporations also face legitimate demands to be transparent to stockholders and stakeholders. The media should be free and empowered to provide this information.

3. THE DISCOVERY OF TRUTHS VIA THE OPEN EXCHANGE OF IDEAS

The commitment to freedom of speech and openness remains the best way for truths and enlightenment to emerge in any society, anywhere, at any time. Not the perfect way, but the best way. Ideas are best exchanged and

---

15　The United Nations Universal Declaration of Human Rights.
16　Leonard Levy, *Emergence of a Free Press* (New York: Oxford University Press, 1985).
17　Jonathan Rauch, *Kindly Inquisitors: The New Attacks on Free Thought*, Expanded Edition (Chicago: University of Chicago Press, 2014).
18　Evgeny Morozov, *The Net Delusion: The Dark Side of Internet Freedom* (New York: Public Affairs, 2011).

understood in conditions of freedom, openness, and criticism, not compulsion, suppression, or coercion. Criticism is central to the evolution of memes and the pursuit of truths. Without criticism, all beliefs and memes become dogmatic and destructive. It is enlightened criticism that paves the way toward new and improved memes.

COLIN KAEPERNICK, THE NATIONAL ANTHEM, AND THE BATTLE OF THE ALAMO

In the fall of 2017, Jerry Jones and the players for the once-mighty Dallas Cowboys locked arms and knelt on the football field *for a few seconds* to show team unity in the face of President Trump's exhortation that NFL owners fire players who kneel during the playing of the national anthem. A few minutes later, a massive American flag covered the entire football field, and pop star Jordin Sparks sang "The Star-Spangled Banner," the national anthem that glorifies tribal warfare presented as a symbol of freedom and bravery. All of this was broadcast live on national television. If Jones and the Dallas Cowboys (players, coaches, and owners) had knelt *during the national anthem*, that would mean something other than an apparent shallow gesture. It was not the real thing. Welcome to the hyperreal.

After all, the entire NFL protest movement began when former San Francisco quarterback Colin Kaepernick courageously knelt during the national anthem to protest the systemic and institutional racism that exists in America, especially the unchecked police brutality exercised by militarized police who go unpunished for killing unarmed Black people. Kaepernick's protest recalled the powerful gesture by American sprinters Tommie Smith and John Carlos on the medal stand at the 1968 Olympics in Mexico City, when they raised gloved fists while "The Star-Spangled Banner" played in the stadium. The fists symbolized "Black power" at the height of the civil rights conflicts in America, which was also reeling from the 1968 assassinations of Martin Luther King Jr. and Senator Robert Kennedy.

Kaepernick exercised his right to protest by taking a knee during the national anthem. But there was a risk. The San Francisco 49ers and Dallas Cowboys owners also have the right to fire or dismiss any player for almost any reason. Technically, it falls under freedom of association, a complex legal concept beyond the scope of our discussion here. But when billionaires like Jerry Jones take a knee *before* the national anthem, then let's not pretend it was anything more than a cynical and hypocritical gesture, a simulation of support for the players. The map overtakes the territory.

If the NFL owners really respected the players and grasped the facts of American history and hypocrisy, then they would let the players take the knee without reprisal. But the NFL owners are beholden not to justice or history but to the patriotic fans and TV viewers. Plus, the advertisers want happy fans consuming their products, not contemplating social issues. It's pizza and propaganda, not politics and philosophy.

Patriotic Americans get very upset when there is a protest involving the flag, such as flag-burning (protected by the First Amendment) or kneeling during the national anthem. But should they be surprised? After all, the "Spangled Banner" has flown over the horrific injustices of slavery and ethnic cleansing of the lands occupied by forty-eight of the states in the continental US. Americans and Texans are taught to "remember the Alamo"—where two hundred Texans held off eighteen hundred Mexican soldiers for thirteen days before succumbing in heroic defeat. The battle cry of "Remember the Alamo" inspired the Texan defeat of the Mexican army one month later at the Battle of San Jacinto, which is mostly forgotten in American history.

The victory at San Jacinto led to the subsequent founding of Texas as an independent nation (1836–1845). Nevertheless, "Remember the Alamo" is the powerful symbol remembered in Texas and America, and the Alamo mission (located in San Antonio) is one of the most popular tourist destinations in Texas. The "Battle of the Alamo" is a great story perfect for Hollywood propaganda and mythmaking in films such as *The Alamo*—both the original starring screen legend John Wayne and the pathetic remake with Dennis Quaid and Billy Bob Thornton. The Battle of the Alamo and the Dallas Cowboys are products of that myth.

But what about the near-genocide of Native Americans that soon followed in Texas?[19] Native Americans were slaughtered by the thousands (including women and children) and their lands were taken, some of which are among the most beautiful lands in America. All of this was glorified in endless Hollywood westerns, which were little more than propaganda justifying conquest, colonization, and "manifest destiny." Do any of the superpatriotic Americans and Texans care to remember the near-genocide? Having grown up in Texas, I know most Texans are in denial about what happened, especially because it conflicts with Texas mythology. Denying or ignoring America's bloody and racist history is why the US flag is seen by many to be a symbol of hypocrisy.

All the above are key reasons the protests are happening now and will continue to happen in the future. And those protests will use images and symbols to convey their ideas, inspire followers, and let the opposition know they are not going away. After all, the right to protest is enshrined in the First Amendment to the Constitution of the United States. What social media have made possible is the globalization of protest movements, extending ideas of the First Amendment and human rights far beyond the borders of America. Let's consider four recent protest movements or marches: Black Lives Matter, the Women's March, the Global Climate Strikes, and the March for Science.[20]

BLACK LIVES MATTER

The Black Lives Matter movement emerged following the 2013 acquittal of George Zimmerman in the shooting death of Trayvon Martin in 2012. Replicating throughout social media, the hashtag #BlackLivesMatter helped build global awareness and solidarity in demonstrations resisting an onslaught of police violence resulting in the killing of African Americans, including Michael Brown (in Ferguson, Missouri) and Eric Garner (in New York City) in 2014.

Of course, the struggle for racial justice is deeply embedded in US history. BLM follows the Black protest tradition of the civil rights movement and other efforts for freedom and equality. These connections are illustrated in many ways. Consider the chants and symbols adopted by the movement. BLM protesters use the iconic raised Black Power fists on artwork and as a physical gesture of resistance and solidarity. This symbol was popularized by the Black Panther Party in the 1960s during the Black Power era.

SO, HOW DOES BLACK LIVES MATTER DIFFER FROM PAST RACIAL JUSTICE MOVEMENTS?

In the 1960s, the major civil rights groups used tangible materials such as pamphlets, pins, and posters to promote their messaging. Black Lives Matter is one of the most powerful examples of how social justice movements are shaped in digital spaces. It's also a remarkable illustration of how technology is used to fuel social change. Through this movement we witness protest taking shape in many forms—most notably, online activism and political expression. Throughout the movement, millions of BLM symbols, messages, and images have replicated through hashtags, viral videos, and internet memes, creating global awareness of violence against Black people in America. The rise of BLM and the convergence of social justice and social media are detailed in Tauheedah Shukriyyah Asad's reading in this chapter.

---

19   Garry Clayton Anderson, *The Conquest of Texas: Ethnic Cleansing in the Promised Land, 1820–1875* (Norman: University of Oklahoma Press, 2005).
20   Note: Topics and issues discussed in these marches are up to date as of May 21, 2021. Events after that date may not be reflected in the text.

Some of the most iconic BLM slogans and symbols of resistance have spread to virtually every aspect of our current society, from popular culture to politics. The movement has made significant waves in celebrity and entertainment culture, garnering support from public figures who supported and joined protest actions, using

---

BLM SYMBOLS IN PROFESSIONAL SPORTS

- On the night of the 2012 NBA All-Star Game, Florida teenager Trayvon Martin was shot and killed. A photo of his hometown team, The Miami Heat, wearing hoodies to protest his killing went viral. Hoodies became a symbol of protest surrounding his untimely death.
- In 2014, Cleveland Cavaliers stars LeBron James and Kyrie Irving wore T-shirts with "I Can't Breathe" on them while warming up. "I can't breathe" were the last words of Eric Garner, who died in July after a confrontation with a New York Police Department officer.
- During the reopening of the 2020 NBA season, players and coaches knelt during the playing of the national anthem, wearing "Black Lives Matter" shirts. The global protest meme "Hands Up, Don't Shoot" (sometimes altered to "Hands Up, Fight Back") became a popularized chant following the 2014 killing of Michael Brown, who was said to have taken the hands-up position, commonly understood to be nonthreatening and a sign of submission, when approaching police officers.
- In the 2021 NBA season, the league is allowing players to include social-awareness messages on their uniforms. The NBA approved twenty-nine messages, including "Equality," "Say Their Names," "I Can't Breathe," "Black Lives Matter," and "Power to the People."
- The BLM protest memes continue to replicate. Major US cities, including Charlotte, Brooklyn, Los Angeles, and Washington, DC, have painted murals of "Black Lives Matter" in large letters on their streets.

---

their popularity to amplify the cause. Following the lead of Colin Kaepernick, professional athletes and organizations became prominent actors in exercising freedom of speech and the right to protest in support of Black lives.

THE WOMEN'S MARCH

On January 21, 2017, nearly seven million women (and some men) participated in more than 420 marches in 81 countries on all seven continents. From Latvia to Los Angeles, Philadelphia to the Philippines, women came out in full force to celebrate women's rights and protest sexual assault and harassment. The march's website said the main goal was to "send a bold message to our new administration on their first day in office, and to the world that women's rights are human rights."[21] The Women's Marches also featured a sea of pink hats with special symbolic meaning.

---

21   Alejandra Maria Salazar, "Organizers Hope Women's March on Washington Inspires, Evolves," NPR website, December 21, 2016.

WHAT FUELED THIS PARTICIPATION AROUND THE WORLD? AND WHAT CAN WE LEARN FROM THE SIGNS AND SYMBOLS?

Imagine being at your job and a coworker or your boss corners you in a quiet office, away from all the activity of the business, and says something that has a sexual overtone. Or perhaps this person touches you inappropriately, without your consent.

You break away and report what happened to a supervisor, who laughs it off, excusing the aggressor or telling you that you must have misinterpreted what happened. Situations just like these—and far worse—have happened to women for centuries. By the twenty-first century, women stood up and said, "Enough." Actually, what we said is "#MeToo," the now universal symbol and social media hashtag that expresses to other women that "You're not imagining it. And I experienced the same kind of sexual harassment or abuse."

The first known usage of "Me Too" occurred in 2006 on MySpace when American activist and sexual harassment survivor Tarana Burke used it.[22] #MeToo picked up steam and became a powerful movement a decade later when women celebrities such as Alyssa Milano, Uma Thurman, and Jennifer Lawrence joined in, sharing their #MeToo moments with their fans and followers. The amplification of these stories and experiences on social media platforms and through more traditional news outlets led to the public ouster of many prominent men, including Hollywood megaproducer Harvey Weinstein, now serving a twenty-three-year prison sentence for sexually assaulting two women.[23]

As the cultural consciousness generated by #MeToo spread across the world, the United States was in the middle of endless campaigning for 2016's presidential election cycle. Former first lady and secretary of state Hillary Clinton was the Democratic candidate and the first woman to run for US president. Whether you preferred Clinton as a candidate or not, no one could deny the progress for women's rights that her candidacy represented. On the Republican side, among a crowded field, one person emerged as the favorite: New York City real estate magnate and reality-TV star Donald Trump.

On October 7, 2016, two days before the second televised presidential candidate debate, a new #MeToo story joined the others. No, it wasn't Mrs. Clinton's story. It was Mr. Trump's. The *Washington Post* reported that Trump had been recorded in 2005 by *Access Hollywood* telling one of its hosts about what he can do to women: "And when you're a star, they let you do it. You can do anything. Grab 'em by the pussy. You can do anything."[24]

You could practically hear the collective gasp.

To be clear, touching a person in a sexual manner without the individual's consent is considered "groping"— and in most US jurisdictions, "sexual assault." Yet Trump—along with many men and women who supported the populist candidate—dismissed the contents of the recording as "locker room banter." Trump went on to win the election, causing many women to feel that once again, on a more public platform, women's experiences of sexual harassment and assault were ignored and dismissed. But not without a fight.

The level of awareness and anger inspired boycotts and other actions, including the Women's March on January 21, 2017, one day after Trump's inauguration, and the Pussyhat Project. The Project's goal was to knit or crochet almost two million pussyhats for people to wear at the march and to convert Trump's derogatory term into a force to be reckoned with. If you attended the peaceful protest, you'd have seen a sea of pink knit hats, with floppy pussycat "ears" formed at the top corners.

---

22   Abby Ohlheiser, "The Woman Behind 'Me Too' Knew the Power of the Phrase When She Created It—10 Years Ago," *Washington Post*, October 19, 2017.

23   Shayna Jacobs, "Harvey Weinstein Sentenced to 23 Years in Prison for Sexually Assaulting Two Women in New York," *Washington Post*, March 11, 2020.

24   David A. Fahrenthold, "Trump Recorded Having Extremely Lewd Conversation About Women in 2005," *Washington Post*, October 7, 2016.

Of course, women's marches and the signs and symbols of these movements are not new. Our mothers and grandmothers burned bras in the 1960s in Freedom Trash Cans—not unlike Vietnam War protestors, who burned their draft cards.

Can we apply semiotics theory to the Pussyhats? The object is women's bodies, and the symbol is the pink knitted cap with ears like a cat. The sign is the power, dignity, strength, and even playfulness of women and the feminine energy to convert such a hateful remark by the man wearing the MAGA hat into a silly but useful and ultimately meaningful message. When seen through the spectacle of the women's march—the sea of pink hats—the sign becomes even more meaningful. Millions of women and the men who joined them standing together, shining a light on the truth of what women have endured.

THE GLOBAL CLIMATE STRIKES

Led by students from around the world, the Global Climate Strikes of 2019 were likely the largest climate protests in history, with an estimated six million participants in forty-five hundred locations across 150 nations.[25] The September 20 strike was scheduled three days before the United Nations Climate Action Summit. The strikes were also part of the School Strike for Climate, led by climate activist Greta Thunberg, who gave a speech in New York City to about 250,000 protestors. More than two thousand scientists in forty countries pledged to support the student-led strikes.[26] Obviously, the goal of the strikes was to draw awareness to climate change and demand public policies grounded in science and the overwhelming evidence that humans are impacting the ecology with our technological civilization powered by fossil fuels (chapter 8).

While the protestors displayed an amazing variety of signs, the image that was most common was that of Planet Earth, in various sizes and often in some combination of blue or green. The idea of seeing and visualizing Earth as a single object dates back to 1968 and 1970. The key moments were the Apollo 8 journey to the moon in 1968 and the first Earth Day in 1970.

The Apollo 8 astronauts became the first humans to escape the gravity of Earth in their journey to the moon. Via NASA and the Apollo program, humans had extended their technologies beyond the Earth to the moon. Once there, we turned the camera back toward our planet. Astronaut Bill Anders used his 35mm camera to capture the image of Earth beyond the horizon of the moon, floating amid the dark cosmic void. The famed photo is called "Earthrise" and is likely the most reproduced photo in human history. Visible in "Earthrise" are no borders, no nations, no signs of humanity, just its blue waters, white clouds, and brown and green continents, all on a planet floating amid the dark void, beyond which are billions of galaxies with sextillions of stars. The image is beautiful, the idea is sublime, the scientific concept is profound.

25   Matthew Taylor, Jonathan Watts, and John Bartlett, "Climate Crisis: 6 Million People Join Latest Wave of Global Protests," *The Guardian*, September 27, 2019, https://www.theguardian.com/environment/2019/sep/27/climate-crisis-6-million-people-join-latest-wave-of-worldwide-protests.

26   Julia Conley, "Students Have Led and We Must Follow: Thousands of Scientists from 40 Nations Join the Global Climate Strike," *Common Dreams*, September 20, 2019, https://www.commondreams.org/news/2019/09/19/students-have-led-and-we-must-follow-thousands-scientists-40-nations-join-global.

FIGURE 6.0.1 "Earthrise," Apollo 8, photo by Bill Anders (1968).

Not only did "Earthrise" confirm Galileo's discoveries but it also jump-started the contemporary environmental movement and inspired the annual celebration of Earth Day. With Apollo 8's "Earthrise" image and Apollo 17's "Blue Marble" image (1972), ecology and environmentalism had the symbols needed to inspire collective, planetary action and a new scientific model. As explained in chapter 8, Earthrise inspired the ecological model of "Gaia," where Planet Earth is "viewed as a singular living system, a megasystem in which its own evolution, as well as that of life, are tightly integrated, producing a self-regulating system for the biosphere over the eons of ancient time."[27]

In terms of semiotics, the object was Planet Earth, the symbol was Earthrise, and the sign was Earth as our only home, the living system we all share. This "sign" is so well-known that thousands of protest signs include drawings or photos of Earth. It's an easy idea to grasp: we humans all share this planet and need to take care of it, including minimizing our impact on the planet's **ecosystems**. Images of Earth in space are the signs that can inspire us individually and collectively. After all, there are no superheroes to save us in real life. Yet, as Kelly Bartsch explains in this chapter, Thanos and the Avengers give us key ideas to think about when imagining how best to protect the living systems on Earth and in the universe.

THE MARCH FOR SCIENCE

Like the protests and marches described above, the 2017 March for Science offered a ray of hope in a world plagued by antiscience worldviews—be it creationism, paranormalism, pseudoscience, antivaxx ideologies, beliefs in ancient aliens, or the denial of climate change. The Trump–Pence administration not only claimed that climate change was a "hoax" but also sought to cut the funding of numerous science organizations across America.[28] Seeing such antiscience ideologies at the pinnacle of political power caused millions to open their eyes to the effect of decades of decay of scientific literacy in America.

---

27 Barry Vacker and Kelly Bartsch, "Media and Earth's Ecology," in *Media Environments*, 4th ed. (San Diego, CA: Cognella Academic Publishing, 2022).
28 Science News Staff, "A Grim Budget Day for U.S. Science: Analysis and Reaction to Trump's Plan," *Science*, March 16, 2017.

The inaugural March for Science was held on April 22, 2017, which coincided with Earth Day celebrations, which happen annually on April 22. According to the March for Science website, "The March for Science champions robustly funded and publicly communicated science as a pillar of human freedom and prosperity. We unite as a diverse, nonpartisan group to call for science that upholds the common good and for political leaders and policy makers to enact evidence-based policies in the public interest."

Additionally, the principles and goals of the march included support for these issues:

- Increased cutting-edge science education throughout society;
- Diversity, equity, and inclusion within STEM (the fields of Science, Technology, Engineering, and Math);
- Open and honest science and public outreach;
- Funding of scientific research and its applications;
- Humanizing science and scientists;
- Partnering with the public;
- Advancing open, inclusive, and accessible science; and
- Affirming science as a democratic value.[29]

An estimated one million Americans participated in the march, with one hundred thousand at the main march in Washington, DC. Attendance in various cities included seventy thousand in Boston, sixty thousand in Chicago, fifty thousand in Los Angeles, fifty thousand in San Francisco, twenty thousand in Seattle, and fourteen thousand in Phoenix. The March for Science has replicated around the world, with the 2018 and 2019 marches including 230 and 150 satellite events in various countries.

As detailed in this book's appendix, America is facing an intellectual collapse of epic scale, as its educational systems have largely failed to instill scientific literacy and logical thinking skills in society. The consequence has been that pseudoscience and conspiracy theories proliferate in hyperreality, with maps of ignorance overtaking territories of reality. As the COVID pandemic has shown, this lack of literacy is a matter of life and death around the world. In America, more than one million people have died suffocating deaths from COVID-19, mainly because 30 to 40 percent of the citizenry deny the science of controlling a pandemic by wearing masks and getting vaccinated. This is despite the fact that vaccines have eliminated or massively reduced many deadly contagions—especially polio and smallpox. Vaccines have saved untold millions of lives in the past century.

Of course, one-time marches can be powerful for the emotions and symbolism, but they are not a solution for long-term action. Frankly, it seemed like the organizers could have chosen or designed a better logo than the atom. To those of us old enough to recall the Cold War, the atomic symbol generates memories that are not very inspirational. Perhaps the logo could have been some combination of telescopes and rockets? After all, telescopes have rocked the ideologies of our species.

FUTURE PROTESTS AND MARCHES

Future protests and marches will happen again in America unless there are significant cultural and political changes. For example, there are obvious ways to address police brutality and police killings of Black people:

1. Demilitarize the police forces,
2. End choke holds,

29 The principles and goals of the March for Science are detailed at http://marchforsciencepdx.org/about/principles-goals/. Of course, no one is saying that science or scientists are perfect or are without historical flaws and mistakes—the most insane being eugenics and the cooperation with the military to build tens of thousands of nuclear weapons. The principles and goals were also accompanied by acknowledgment of the long-standing shortcomings of science in various areas and of scientific organizations in terms of diversity, inclusion, equity, and accessibility.

3. End no-knock raids and searches,
4. End the qualified immunity that protects police officers from prosecution for crimes they commit, and
5. End the Drug War and decriminalize drugs to scale down the prison-industrial complex.

Similarly, solving our ecological and pollution problems requires these changes:

1. Ensure a steady transition from fossil fuels to sustainable energies;
2. Minimize energy consumption in general;
3. Quit polluting the planet's air, land, and seas;
4. Clean up our existing pollution; and
5. Develop ideologies *and* philosophies that place our technological civilization more in harmony with the natural world from which it emerged and upon which it depends.

Obviously, these issues are complex and can be resolved only with open-minded cooperation among citizens of America and the world. We must realize that we all have a deep and profound need to cooperatively address these issues. Yet, this cooperation is hard to attain because of divisions along the fault lines of political ideology and scientific worldviews, all replicating in the spectacle and hyperreality. The challenge posed by antiscience worldviews is even more complicated, precisely because antiscience and religious beliefs are protected by the First Amendment, as are scientific and atheistic worldviews. Just as Black Lives Matter increases awareness of systemic racism and the Global Climate Strike increases awareness of climate disruption, the rise of antiscience worldviews and the COVID-19 pandemic both increase awareness of the importance of science and evidence-based public policy.

TESTING THE COMMITMENT TO FREEDOM AND OPENNESS

Across the eons, the human species has crafted narratives and worldviews that seek to explain our origins and our destiny on Earth and in the universe. So sacred is this idea that protection of such beliefs is enshrined in the First Amendment to the US Constitution, which explicitly protects the right to believe in science, in a Creator, or in neither. That's as it should be. All humans should have these rights.[30]

The First Amendment protects our right to believe in whatever memes we wish—even pseudoscience, superstition, and conspiracy theory—regardless of whether the memes are true and correlate to reality. However, it is not that simple. The First Amendment applies only to restricting government agencies, not the private sector, from censorship. In general, it is best when governments, corporations, or religious institutions are not the final arbiter of truths, though leaders, workers, and the faithful can support or not support whatever beliefs and worldviews they choose. It is best when "truths" emerge from societal consensus, rather than being imposed from the top, which is often the path to an authoritarian and dictatorial society.

The real test of a *society's commitment* to political freedom and openness is when it permits expression of, and access to, ideas that many find to be offensive, profane, or heretical. The real test of a *democracy's commitment* to freedom is when it permits criticisms of and challenges to those with economic, political, cultural, military, and law enforcement power. If we want to create and protect a vibrant society and a representative democracy,

---

30 In addition, people should not be coerced or harassed because of their beliefs, whether religious, agnostic, or atheistic. See Virginia Villa, "Religiously Unaffiliated People Face Harassment in a Growing Number of Countries," Pew Research Center, August 12, 2019, https://www.pewresearch.org/fact-tank/2019/08/12/religiously-unaffiliated-people-face-harassment-in-a-growing-number-of-countries/.

then freedom of thought, debate, critique, and toleration are always preferable to coercion, suppression, and the censorship of ideas, beliefs, and news.

FREEDOM OF BELIEF DOES NOT MEAN FREEDOM FROM CRITIQUE

The above freedoms cut multiple ways. Freedom and toleration do *not* mean that some beliefs are above or beyond criticism, no matter how widely believed or cherished or sacred they are. That's especially why all political, religious, and scientific beliefs are subject to public criticism and open debate in the media, hopefully based on empirical evidence, sound hypotheses, and clear reasoning (at least this is the process championed by the scientific method). *Freedom of belief does not mean beliefs are to be free from critique.* Nor does it mean that believers can silence critics, at least not in a free and open society. Nor does it mean that freedom of expression extends to harassment, slander, or libel, three areas in which the law is always evolving. Of course, it goes without saying that discourse, debate, and criticism usually function best in a civil manner, but that is not always possible or desirable. That's why the US Supreme Court has long recognized protections for parody and expressions that some find offensive—such as flag-burning, or wearing a jacket that says "Fuck the Draft."[31]

Just as people have a right to express their belief in specific memes, others have a right to criticize those memes. Anything less than those equal freedoms—to believe and embrace or to not believe and criticize—is Orwellian "doublethink" and dangerous to intellectual freedom and the right to criticism. Additionally, it is criticism and open competition that should produce, over time, memes and beliefs that better correlate with reality. However, the proliferation of pseudoscience, conspiracy theory, and fact-free beliefs show that this may not always be the case. That's a key reason why democracy may not survive in America, and apparently millions of voters are okay with that.

It's easy to support freedom of speech and open networks when you agree with what is being said. It's easy to support freedom of expression when no one is preventing you from uploading your party pics to Flickr or Photobucket. After all, your pics likely do not challenge anyone's worldview or the dominant ideologies of society. It's easy to support freedom of expression from within an echo chamber. Hot media conditions seem to be generating a rising tide of disdain for evidence and intolerance for differing worldviews, across the political spectrum. What happens when a powerful segment of society disagrees with your ideas, precisely because they challenge the dominant worldview or dominant ideology in your organization? Should you be silenced or cancelled into submission? This is a question with no easy answers. People have a right to support or disagree with whatever ideas they prefer.

"CANCEL CULTURE"

Cancel culture is defined as "disavowing someone's expression within politics or otherwise, when it's deemed problematic, unacceptable or is no longer tolerable, resulting in the person being immediately labeled as 'canceled' from the public."[32] Being "canceled" often includes boycotting, unfollowing, or no longer supporting a person, company, or institution. Jonah Engel Bromwich describes canceling as a "total divestment in something (anything), often for 'transgressing fans' expectations.'"[33] While cancel culture is often used as a device to implement accountability and move society forward, many are concerned with how cancel culture may stifle important dialogue and the expression of valid perspectives, resulting in severe social and political consequences.

Spiral of Silence: Resistance Has Its Risks

Originally proposed by German political scientist Elisabeth Noelle-Neumann in 1974, "spiral of silence" refers to the tendency of people to remain silent when they feel that their views are in opposition to the majority view on

---

31 For parody, see *Hustler Magazine v. Falwell*, 485 U.S. 46 (1988); for flag-burning, see *Texas v. Johnson*, 491 U.S. 397 (1989); for "Fuck the Draft," see *Cohen v. California*, 403 U.S. 15 (1971).
32 Taiya Jarrett, "'Cancel Culture' Rises to Condemn Celebrity Actions," *The Rotunda Online*, November 13, 2018, http://www.therotundaonline.com/opinion/cancel-culture-rises-to-condemn-celebrity-actions/article_9ca67eca-e7c4-11e8-957b-53238285e3a6.html.
33 Johan Engel Bromwich, "Everyone Is Cancelled," *New York Times*, June 28, 2018, https://www.nytimes.com/2018/06/28/style/is-it-canceled.html.

a subject.[34] The spiral of silence posits that, motivated by fear of social isolation, people constantly examine the climate of opinion. Individuals who perceive that the majority share their opinions are more likely to share their opinions, while those in the minority conceal their opinions. Individuals will choose to remain silent (1) out of fear of isolation when the group or public realizes that the individual's opinion is different from that of the status quo, or (2) out of fear of reprisal or more extreme isolation, in the sense that voicing said opinion might lead to a negative consequence beyond that of mere isolation (such as loss of a job or loss of social status).

As stated above, the First Amendment does not apply to corporations or universities, some of which are public universities and private universities. It all depends on the facts and social contexts, a complex topic that is beyond the scope of this chapter. However, when a Twitter tribe calls for canceling someone, it is not necessarily a violation of the First Amendment, precisely because a complexity of factors may be at play. However, it may well be a violation of the *spirit of an open society* committed to the rational discussion of ideas and policies based on evidence and reasonable discourse. An open and tolerant society whose members live in fear of being canceled may not long exist as an open, tolerant, and progressive society. Plus, the cancelers never imagine that the tables could turn and they might end up canceled at a future date. Meanwhile, society devolves into some variation of the closed and authoritarian societies we've seen throughout history and in books and movies like *1984*, *Fahrenheit 451*, *V for Vendetta*, *The Hunger Games*, and *The Handmaid's Tale*.

IS A DEEPER PATTERN EMERGING?

Though protests have been around for ages, the size and scale of the above protests and marches are unprecedented in world history. There is a deeper pattern emerging. Perhaps we are seeing another moment in the early stages of an emergent *planetary civilization* made possible by global media technologies. Never in the history of our species could people unite from within countries around the world to protest the madness in their own countries and other countries.

These marches show what happens when people get out of their echo chambers and local-global tribes (at least for a while) and think in terms of the universal—the demands for universal human rights around the world and the desire for universal human rights, racial equality, environmental protections, and science-based public policies. This reflects the hopeful potential of the internet and social media to make a better world and connect a planetary civilization.

If we stay in our intellectual and technological tribes (focused on narcissism, nationalism, theism, exploitation, domination, and marginalization of the other), then we are going backward and retreating from a planetary civilization. Tribalism has always been a danger to peace, freedom, progress, and civilization. When we use global media technologies to connect and unite via a shared destiny and universal narrative, then a "planetary civilization" will naturally emerge in the future. This is the civilization that must emerge if our species is to be a long-term success on our planet.

Though Apollo 8 astronaut Bill Anders's camera was pointed toward Earth, the "Earthrise" image illustrates the power of cool media. With it we extended our science, technologies, and gaze away from ourselves, toward the moon and the universe, and we got a huge surprise—that Earth floating alone in space was a beautiful discovery that inspired a new scientific and ecological understanding of our planet's living system. This is surely one of the most powerful and influential *signs* of all time. We hope the young people of Planet Earth will take the full meaning to heart: the beauty, the ecology, the science, and the fact that humanity is one species sharing one planet in a vast and majestic universe.

CREDITS

Fig. 6.0.1: NASA, https://www.nasa.gov/multimedia/imagegallery/image_feature_1249.html. 1968.

---

34 Elisabeth Noelle-Neumann, "The Spiral of Silence: A Theory of Public Opinion," *The Journal of Communication* 24, no. 2 (June 1974): 43–51. https://doi.org/10.1111/j.1460-2466.1974.tb00367.x.

BLACK LIVES MATTER IN 2020: THE CHANGING LANDSCAPE OF BLACK MOVEMENTS IN DIGITAL CULTURE

TAUHEEDAH SHUKRIYYAH ASAD is a PhD student in the Klein College of Media and Communication at Temple University. Her research is focused on the intersections of Black media, community, and culture.

The year 2020 was a hard one.

We expect that each year will have its defining moments, but this one will forever be etched in history as a year unlike any other.

Sandro Galea (2020) had it right when she called 2020 "The Great American Trauma." She wrote, "We are living through a global pandemic unlike any since 1918, an economic collapse unlike any since 1933, civil unrest unlike any since 1968, and the greatest unexpected loss of life since 9/11."

And none of us were prepared for what was to come. In the United States, the COVID-19 virus infected millions and claimed more than one hundred thousand lives, making it the deadliest year in the nation's recorded history. The world spent the year in various states of lockdown, leading to more than twenty million people filing for unemployment. We experienced a historic uprising as millions of protests erupted in more than four hundred cities following the murder of George Floyd at the hands of the police. And all of this happened in the midst of a heated and polarizing presidential election year.

The collective trauma we faced as a nation was almost too much to bear. But what's even more disturbing is that Black Americans and people of color were hit particularly hard. Frustrations came to a head, and one message rang loudly across the globe: Black Lives Matter.

Alarming statistics illustrating the devastating impact of 2020 on Black communities marked a new phase for the BLM movement. Here's what we know:

- Studies show that Black Americans and people of color are disproportionately affected by the COVID-19 crisis (CDC 2021).
- Black people are 3.23 times more likely to be killed by a police officer while unarmed compared to a white individual (Schwartz and Jahn 2020).
- In the 2020 elections, Black Americans still faced massive disparities and inequalities in accessing their right to vote—150 years after the passage of the Fifteenth Amendment, which extended the franchise to Black men (Panetta 2020).

SCHOLARS WILL BE SCHOLARS

I was in my second year as a doctoral student at Temple University when I received the news that the university would be shutting down due to the outbreak of coronavirus. We were informed that in-person instruction was suspended, and the university, like most across the country, would be "going virtual"—transitioning to distance learning using Zoom videoconferencing software.

The world was changing before our eyes.

At the time, I was a teaching assistant for a Media and Society course developed on these twenty-first-century concepts (as discussed in chapters 1 and 2):

- We live in a 24/7, online, all-around-us, global network of media environments—displayed on electronic screens.
- Media technologies, industries, content, and usages have converged to shape consciousness and culture as technological environments centered on screens.

We spent months engaging in critical discussions to understand about media environments, media futures, and their (possible) impact on society. As we met for our last in-person class session, a student commented that it felt surreal that we would now be forced to live the very experiences we'd explored throughout the course.

We would soon find that mandates for social distancing, or keeping distance between ourselves and others outside of our home to "stop or slow down the spread of contagious diseases," would have an unprecedented global impact on media environments.

The student's words stuck with me. The impact of living in a screen-based environment deserves more research attention, especially in this current moment. As a scholar-activist who has one foot in the academic world and one foot in the Black community, I found it essential that we understand the ways in which today's media environment impacts the new phase of the Movement for Black Lives coalition.

While the world is confronted by the ongoing challenge of adjusting to "the new normal"—a life and routines that includes daily mask-wearing, battling Zoom overload, and "tele-everything"—activists faced unique challenges of their own. How do community organizers respond to the ongoing demand for justice, equality, and reform amid a global pandemic? Has the role that mediated communication plays in movement work changed in 2020?

POWER TO THE PEOPLE: SOCIAL MEDIA MEETS SOCIAL JUSTICE

March 13, 2020, was the day when life came to a screeching halt for many Americans. The Trump administration declared a state of emergency after an alarming spike in coronavirus cases. That was the same day Breonna Taylor, a twenty-six-year-old African American woman, was fatally shot in her Louisville, Kentucky, home by a plainclothes officer. A couple of months later, a video surfaced on social media showing the fatal arrest of George Floyd, an African American man who died after police officers knelt on his neck for 8 minutes and 46 seconds.

More than twenty million demonstrators flooded the streets in two thousand cities worldwide. Still, participating in frontline protests wasn't feasible for many people who identified with the cause. Quarantine restrictions and the threat of contracting coronavirus posed an increasing threat on Black protest traditions that relied on high-visibility public spaces. Fortunately, social media platforms were there to fill the gap.

SOCIAL MEDIA ACTIVISM: REAL OR PERFORMATIVE?

Does signing online petitions make a difference? Does retweeting or "liking" a socially conscious post on Facebook really advance the cause? Will changing a profile picture in support of a social or political campaign have a real-world impact?

This might sound absurd to anyone born after 1999, but there was once a time when people questioned the legitimacy of social media activism—the use of hashtags and social network technology—to organize and coordinate real-world action (Carrasco 2012).

Skeptics have expressed concern that online gestures do not translate into meaningful, offline participation. Slacktivism—or "clicktivism," as it's also known less pejoratively—means giving token support for a cause in digital spaces (Fisher 2020). Without offline engagement in a cause, acts such as "liking" or sharing socially conscious content on social media is viewed as a performative, lazy, and oversimplified form of activism.

But social media is very different today than it was back in 2005 when Myspace ruled the internet. In the past fifteen years, platforms like Facebook, Twitter, Instagram, and Tik Tok have revolutionized communication and have changed the way people live their lives. The sociotechnical affordances these platforms now offer has refashioned movement work. Now that social media have become integral to everyday life, it's become increasingly evident that small, sometimes passive acts known as clicktivism have a considerable impact on amplifying violence against Black people. #BlackLivesMatter is probably the most compelling example illustrating the power of clicktivism in recent history.

Social media has become deeply embedded in our everyday lives, causing unprecedented changes in social behavior, communication styles, and approaches to public dialogue. Through digital spaces, old concepts expand and take a new form. The technological and social affordances of these platforms introduced new possibilities to shape the future of movement work. At the height of the 2020 uprising, the #BlackLivesMatter hashtag averaged 3.7 million mentions per day, with a record of 8.8 million unique mentions on May 28 (Kelley 2020).

While many maintain that social media activism is no substitute for real-world grassroots organizing, more people are understanding its utility in our current media environment.

BLACK LIVES MATTER: A NEW TYPE OF MOVEMENT?

It started with a tweet:

> Black people. I love you. I love us. Our lives matter.

Alicia Garza shared these words on July 13, 2013, in response to the acquittal of George Zimmerman in the shooting death of Trayvon Martin, an unarmed Black teen. Hours later, Patrisse Cullors came across the post on Twitter and added the hashtag #blacklivesmatter.

Tensions were high following the verdict in one of Florida's most high-profile cases. As protesters took to the streets chanting "Justice for Trayvon," Garza and Cullors teamed up with Opal Tometi to set up #BlackLivesMatter Twitter and Tumbler accounts. The BLM cofounders encouraged supporters to share their stories of why #blacklivesmatter. The hashtag soon went viral. The #BlackLivesMatter hashtag would prove to be impactful in community organizing spaces, but the moment grew into a nationally recognized movement in 2014 following two police-involved deaths of Black

Americans: Michael Brown in Ferguson, Missouri, and Eric Garner in New York.

Today, Black Lives Matter is said to be the largest movement in US history, but it's important to understand the legacy of Black resistance. So what makes BLM so different? How did it become a global phenomenon?

We have to give credit to the power of social media.

Bijan Stephens (2015) makes the astute observation that "any large social movement is shaped by the technology available to it and tailors its goals, tactics, and rhetoric to the media of its time." The Black Panther Party created and distributed its own newspaper. Grassroots activists often organize "Call your elected official" campaigns to elicit responses from legislators. Nationally televised coverage of the civil rights movement and the LA riots had immediate and significant effects.

The devices that the Black Lives Matter movement uses to organize and resist are fundamentally different from, and more sophisticated than, anything that existed in the history of Black activism.

Let's consider the sociotechnical affordances of popular networking sites and how they have been used as tools for organizing, for resisting, and for advancing movements like BLM in recent years.

- **Generating and Sharing Content.** When social media became a part of our everyday lives, a huge paradigm shift in communication occurred. In addition to receiving messages, users can create and distribute content more quickly than ever before.

Social networks give everyday people the power to address, and counter, many of the problematic narratives about Black people seen in the mainstream media. The distribution of live videos and graphic images of police brutality and other acts of anti-Blackness are used as evidence to defend activists from criminal charges and to hold white supremacists accountable.

What would the public response have been surrounding the deaths of Michael Brown, Eric Garner, Ahmaud Arber, George Floyd, and countless others if millions of timelines weren't flooded with recordings of the incidents that led to their deaths?

During the unrest in Ferguson, and cities around the world, protesters use features like Twitter threads and live streaming to report live from the scene, often resulting in a swift public response.

- **Increasing Visibility.** Social media doesn't just afford users the ability to share content quickly; it allows users to increase their visibility and to share messages widely.

As mentioned above, #BlackLivesMatter became a global phenomenon after going *viral*—a term used to describe the rapid spread of a post, image, video, or link online (Christensson 2011).

The impact of increased visibility on social networks is not to be underestimated. One of the most fascinating things about these platforms is the ways in which they have shifted the traditional one-way communication model. Prior to social media, news outlets dictated what current events were newsworthy. These social media networks give users more agency to challenge the gatekeepers of news. In order to stay relevant, mainstream media must respond to topics that become highly visible on social media.

Activists often tag celebrities—prominent figures, companies, and organizations—to raise awareness for their cause. Following the 2020 deaths of George Floyd, Ahmaud Arbery, and Breonna Taylor, many celebrities, including Beyoncé, Drake, and Keke Palmer, posted messages on Instagram calling for their killers to be brought to justice. Many of these celebrity posts received millions of "likes" and reshares. Many prominent figures have shown their public support beyond mere clicktivism, through acts such as attending mass protests, incorporating the message of Black Lives Matter in their art, calling for their fans to sign petitions, donating money to social justice organizations and the families of victims, and paying for funeral costs of Black people who died at the hands of police.

Hashtags allow users to index content using a hash (#). This makes content easily searchable, and it often leads to increased visibility. Other successful movements centering on Black people include #SayHerName, #BlackGirlMagic, and #OscarsSoWhite, as well as the individual names of high-profile Black victims of police violence.

- **Community Building and Relationship Formation.** The evolution of BLM is a testament to the power of Black Twitter—a virtual community of active, African American Twitter users (Jones 2013). Although there is more to Black Twitter than social justice activism, members of this community often wield their collective cultural capital in the fight against oppression and racially motivated violence against Black people.

Twitter, Facebook, and Instagram bios provide a space for self-presentation where users can express their social and political views and meet and stay connected with others who share their interests and concerns.

Activists depend on these virtual communities to stay informed about social justice efforts and campaigns happening all over the world. These networks create opportunities to boost participation in protests, raise funds for campaigns, and promote and organize events.

Timelines and comment sections provide spaces for public discourse, while Facebook groups are often used as a private space for community groups to have discussions and to plan and disseminate information among themselves.

BLM: THE GREATEST MEME OF OUR TIME

Chapter 1 teaches us that *memes* are any idea, belief, or behavior that can be copied and passed along. With this in mind, I would argue that Black Lives Matter is one of the most significant memes of this generation. When Black Lives Matter was in its infancy, many people had trouble trying to make sense of the movement.

The hashtag went viral and expanded into a global phenomenon. But the spread and replication of these three words created ambiguity.

Is it a slogan? An organization? A movement, slogan, or hashtag?

The answer is simple: All of the above.

"Black Lives Matter" is a rallying cry used by millions of protesters, organizers, and everyday people around the world.

However, it's important to note that many proponents of this sentiment often have no affiliation with the Black Lives Matter Global Network Foundation. Adding to the confusion is the way "Black Lives Matter" is used in mainstream media as a catch-all label attached to efforts representing the interest of Black communities that exist independently of the organization (Adams 2020).

In fact, the Black Lives Matter Global Network Foundation is affiliated with the Movement for Black Lives (m4bl.org)—a coalition of more than fifty organizations representing the interests of Black communities in the United States. The coalition includes other high-profile social justice organizations, such as Dream Defenders and Black Youth Project 100.

The name "Black Lives Matter" is used most widely in reference to the international social movement that spawned from the hashtag. BLM's focus has been more comprehensive than just the criminal justice system; focusing on producing a cultural shift in a society wherein Black lives are free from systematic dehumanization. Opal Tometi explained that police brutality and extrajudicial killing were "a spark point, but it was very intentional for us to talk about the way that black lives are cut short across the board" (Chotiner 2020).

The phrase has permeated practically every aspect of society from politics to popular culture. BLM has been represented in hit television series such as *Black-ish*, *Empire*, *Law & Order*, and *Scandal*.

CONCLUSION

The state of Black America in 2020 resulted in a record number of protests and civil unrest across the nation. COVID-19 shut down parts of the world, but Black Lives Matter took the global stage. The movement, birthed on Twitter in 2013, was able to thrive in the new media environment largely because of the current affordances of major social media platforms such as Twitter, Facebook, Instagram, and Tik Tok. In the current screen-based culture brought on by pandemic-related restriction, Black freedom fighters used social media technology as organizing tools to resist systemic racism and anti-Black violence.

REFERENCES

Adams, C. 2020. "A Movement, a Slogan, a Rallying Cry: How Black Lives Matter Changed America's View on Race." *NBC News*, December 29, 2020. Retrieved from https://www.nbcnews.com/news/nbcblk/movement-slogan-rallying-cry-how-black-lives-matter-changed-america-n1252434.

Carrasco, E. 2012. "How Social Media Has Helped Activism." New Media Rockstars. Retrieved December 19, 2012, from https://newmediarockstars.com/2012/03/how-social-media-has-helped-activism/.

Centers for Disease Control and Prevention (CDC). 2021. "Health Equity Considerations and Racial and Ethnic Minority Groups." U.S. Department of Health & Human Services. Retrieved from https://www.cdc.gov/coronavirus/2019-ncov/community/health-equity/race-ethnicity.html.

Chotiner, I. 2020. "A Black Lives Matter Co-Founder Explains Why This Time Is Different." *The New Yorker*, June 3, 2020. Retrieved from https://www.newyorker.com/news/q-and-a/a-black-lives-matter-co-founder-explains-why-this-time-is-different

Christensson, Per. 2011. "Viral." TechTerms. Retrieved from https://techterms.com/definition/viral.

Fisher, R. 2020. "The Subtle Ways that 'Clicktivism' Shapes the World." *BBC*, September 15, 2020. Retrieved from https://www.bbc.com/future/article/20200915-the-subtle-ways-that-clicktivism-shapes-the-world.

Galea, S. 2020. "The Great American Trauma." *BU Today*. Retrieved from http://www.bu.edu/articles/2020/2020-the-great-american-trauma-sandro-galea/.

Jones, F. 2013. "Is Twitter the Underground Railroad of Activism?" *Salon*, July 17, 2013. Retrieved from https://www.salon.com/2013/07/17/how_twitter_fuels_black_activism/.

Kelley, A. 2020. "#BlackLivesMatter Hashtag Averages 3.7 Million Times per Day Following George Floyd's Death." *The Hill*, June 11, 2020. Retrieved from https://thehill.com/changing-america/respect/equality/502353-blacklivesmatter-hashtag-averages-37-million-times-per-day.

Movement for Black Lives. 2019. Retrieved from https://m4bl.org/.

Panetta, G. 2020. "How Black Americans Still Face Disproportionate Barriers to the Ballot Box in 2020." *Business Insider*, September 18, 2020. Retrieved from https://www.businessinsider.com/why-black-americans-still-face-obstacles-to-voting-at-every-step-2020-6.

Schwartz, G. L., and Jahn, J. L. 2020. "Mapping Fatal Police Violence Across US Metropolitan Areas: Overall Rates and Racial/Ethnic Inequities, 2013–2017." *PLOS ONE* 15, no. 6: e0229686. https://doi.org/10.1371/journal.pone.0229686

Stephens, B. 2015. "Social Media Helps Black Lives Matter Fight the Power." Wired. https://www.wired.com/2015/10/how-black-lives-matter-uses-social-media-to-fight-the-power/

JACKIE AINA AND YOUTUBE: INFLUENCERS, CULTURAL CRITICISM, AND SOCIAL MEDIA

CHRISTIANA DILLARD earned her master's degree from the Department of Media Studies and Production in the Klein College of Media and Communication at Temple University. She is a freelance writer.

INTRODUCTION

Guy Debord's book *The Society of the Spectacle* (1977; originally published in 1967) uses critical Marxist theory to assert that capitalist societies encourage materialistic consumption via the technologies of the media spectacle. *The spectacle* is Debord's term for the everyday manifestation of capitalist-driven phenomena: advertising, television, film, and celebrity. Debord defines *the spectacle* as the "autocratic reign of the market economy."

Further, he posits that the motivation behind a buyer's acquiring an item for its usefulness is often overshadowed by the buyer's desire to *acquire the image* that an item will provide them. Today, this spectacle plays out frequently on social media, where celebrities, influencers, and even people without a significant following or a high socioeconomic standing bring attention to what they deem as the positive aspects and acquisitions of their lives, including material goods. This is even true on the video-sharing platform YouTube, where "vlogs" (video blogs) give viewers an inside look at the life of their creator(s). This reading will examine the spectacle as it plays out on YouTube and how it is evidenced in the social media practices of YouTube beauty vlogger and influencer Jackie Aina, who incorporates cultural commentary into her videos. However, her cultural commentary also affects the way that she approaches her influencer practices.

BACKGROUND

Born in 1931, Guy Debord was a French philosopher who wrote *The Society of the Spectacle* in the spirit of German philosopher Karl Marx. Marx penned the pamphlet *The Communist Manifesto* (1848) and the book *Das Kapital* (1867), both of which are celebrated texts within the socialist movement. Using Marxist theory as a foundation for *The Society of the Spectacle* was not unusual, as Debord was a founding member of the Situationist International collective, a group of artists, intellectuals, and political activists whose aim was to fight against capitalism by rejecting the systems of production. The opening thesis of *The Society of the Spectacle* references the opening lines of Marx's *Das Kapital*, which Debord reworks to fit his theory of the spectacle (Morgan and Purje 2016), which he later defines loosely as being copies of original actions and activities. However, these are not images themselves, but "a social relation among

184

people, mediated by images" (Debord 1977, para. 4[1]). Though Debord's focus shifts throughout *The Society of the Spectacle*, he makes it clear in later theses in the book that the spectacle is contingent on the constant materialistic consumption in post–World War II societies—consumption that was fueled by capitalist forces and the proliferation of media images promoting the consumer lifestyle.

Today, it can be argued that spectacle does not need to be changed. However, the use of spectacle must be revised, in much the same way that Debord "updated" Marx's ideas. Debord's work has been referenced in several studies about how social media has made the spectacle an even greater phenomenon (Mihailidis and Viotty 2017; Stratton 2020). Social media is changing attitudes about collective activities that range from careers to democracy to protest, but it has a more apparent focus on egocentricity (Ventriglio and Bhugra 2017; Swigger 2013).

VLOGGING TECHNOLOGY AND THE SPECTACLE

Advancing media technologies provide endless opportunities and ways to see what it looks like to live a lifestyle that affords the acquisition of higher-end goods. With the advent of mobile technology, people became able to use portable devices such as video cameras, tablets, laptops, and cell phones as recording devices to document their daily lives. This kind of content became known as "vlogs" and surged in popularity after the creation of YouTube, which is now the world's largest video sharing platform.

YouTube makes it easy for vloggers to participate in the spectacle because of its design. Audiences on the platform are not forced to act as passive spectators who are only provided information without adding some input or insight of their own, which was the case before the creation of the internet and its capabilities for video streaming. Instead, they have the option to "like" videos, comment under videos, and subscribe to channels or creators whom they want to follow. Arguably, active viewers are making a social connection to their favorite vloggers by using these YouTube engagement features. These tools can help vloggers on YouTube determine how they will produce future content: by checking these metrics, they can gauge whether their viewers are into what they are doing. YouTube vloggers even use metadata of their own by putting particular words in the titles of their videos or using thumbnail images for their videos that convey extreme emotions like shock or disgust so that viewers can find their content and watch that content.

YouTube contains so many genres and formats of videos that it is practically impossible to design academic studies using samples of videos that accurately represent the makeup of the platform's content (Kavoori 2015). This means scholars have yet to understand the impact that such a collection of videos has on developing social communities within and outside of the platform. The never-ending proliferation of images—literal images and images in the sense of the spectacle—conveyed in vloggers' videos shows that there are several ways to approach creating content that appeals to viewers.

Vloggers' ability to present other messages to their audiences using the tools at their disposal is evidence of media convergence between external hardware (webcams, professional cameras, cell phone cameras), video editing software, and YouTube. This media convergence allows anyone with access to these tools to become a YouTube vlogger. Consequently, accessibility is one of YouTube's defining features, which helped it distinguish itself as the most popular platform. By uploading a public vlog that viewers can interact with through YouTube engagement features, vloggers are indicating that their content is more than just a creative project—instead, their output is worthy of some interaction or discussion, or even a subscription to their YouTube channel.

Another result of the mixing of technological media is that the editorial choices vloggers make to put together their vlogs can communicate plenty of additional information to their viewers. This is particularly true with conversational vloggers, whose choices to use technologies that have varying video quality or to position themselves in a certain way on video can affect what additional messages, besides the primary content of the video, audiences take away from their content (Aran, Biel, and Gatica-Perez 2014).

---

1   Revised version (1977): https://www.marxists.org/reference/archive/debord/society.htm.

JACKIE AINA: A UNIQUE APPROACH TO SOCIAL MEDIA INFLUENCE

Very few vloggers and social media content creators can make a living on their work, because they must have a large enough audience or generate enough income from advertisement revenue or partnerships. The term *influencer* is used to describe social media content creators like vloggers who can produce their work professionally. With more than 3.5 million subscribers on YouTube (at the time of this writing), Jackie Aina is among the most visible beauty vloggers and influencers, especially as a Black woman. Not only is Aina known for her industry-specific commentary, but she is also outspoken about popular culture and social justice issues (Payne 2018).

Aina's commentary and humor have allowed her to ascend within the world of YouTube vlogging and social media influence. She started her YouTube channel in 2009 as a means of connecting with others who had a similar interest in beauty, which helped relieve some of the stress she was experiencing in other aspects of her life (Jackson 2019). As an independent creator, she realized that she enjoyed making and putting out her content. She depended on her then-small YouTube community to keep her motivated and inspire her to get better at both her video production and her beauty tutorial abilities. Additionally, her audience's support contributed to the success of her channel: without their engagement, it would have been difficult for others to discover her content.

Aina has navigated the intersectionality of her various identities so that she can express herself in the most accessible ways possible (Delgado and Stefancic 2017). As a social media influencer who is also a Black woman, she has had to figure out how to balance all of her identifiers without them interfering with one another. Aina has said that she "advocates for viewers with skin tones like her own" in her work (Jackson 2019): her father is Nigerian and emigrated to the United States and her mother is African American (Kwarteng 2021), and Aina is a dark-skinned woman. Although there are other Black women influencers, her upbringing, which involves two Black parents who are from different locations in the African diaspora, is unique. In Aina's role as an influencer, this distinctive backstory allows her to stand out in an oversaturated pool of influencers on YouTube and other social media platforms.

YouTube, which is known for its racial controversies, among other things, was a natural platform for Aina to speak out against discrimination (Payne 2018). Aina has even spoken out against individual vloggers for what she sees as their bigoted remarks or actions, which has put some strain on her influencer relationships (Payne 2018). One of the most public examples of this was her exchanges with fellow YouTube beauty influencer Jeffree Star, who repeatedly used offensive and racist language. After she made a decision not to support his work any longer, he allegedly called her a "gorilla" among other racially charged insults (Payne 2018). This undoubtedly would have made any future collaborations between the two influencers hard to achieve—and certainly would disrupt any financial gain they could receive from such a collaboration.

Outside of vlogging circles on YouTube, Aina has used various platforms to speak out against what she deems as discriminatory practices. Her success on YouTube has enabled her to garner a large audience on other platforms—705,000 followers on Twitter and 1.7 million on Instagram at the time of this writing. On Instagram, Aina became a vocal advocate of the "Pull Up or Shut Up" campaign. The social media campaign was launched on June 3, 2020, by UOMA Beauty founder Sharon Chuter during antiracism and anti–police brutality protests in the summer of 2020. The purpose was for brands that posted messaging about supporting the Black community to provide more information about how they support Black people economically through career placement. Therefore, the campaign wanted the brands to publicize the number of Black employees in corporate and executive positions within their company. Until the brands satisfied the request, the campaign called on consumers to abstain from purchasing from them for seventy-two hours (Krause 2020). Aina released an Instagram video reading a statement from the campaign that made her support clear; it demonstrated her ability as an influencer to successfully navigate and use various social media platforms not only for financially incentivized purposes but also for issues related to cultural commentary and social justice.

Aina's vocal stances on social justice issues could put her into the "angry Black woman" trope (Ferguson

2019). The negative stereotype deems any Black woman who speaks up about something they disagree with or believes to be unfair as angry, and that anger is weaponized against them to make them appear as a villain (Ferguson 2019). However, that has not deterred Aina from speaking out and she continues to strategically critique institutions and individuals in her social media content (Ferguson 2019). Her approach appears to be working in her favor, as she still has financial partnerships and maintains a large social media following.

YOUTUBE INFLUENCERS AND THE SPECTACLE

However, the bottom line for influencers, no matter how outspoken they are, is whether they can make a living from their work. Therefore, YouTube vloggers like Aina must use both their personality and their personal beliefs, along with their *mastery of the spectacle* through the medium of video. Using video to relay their interests and give a certain impression about themselves falls in line with Marshall McLuhan's observation that "the medium is the message," with the medium taking on even more importance than the message it conveys (Eudaimonia 2016). The use of video and video editing tools to blog—an intimate yet usually highly strategic method of communication—communicates to viewers that what they are watching is both a lifelike representation of someone else's life but also one that maintains an air of superiority because it is on display and ready to be viewed at any point. Aina's use of humorous editing techniques (like meme videos to emphasize the points she makes in her dialogue) and quick cuts in between commentary keeps her viewers engaged. However, her videos are still a manipulated representation of her personality, especially when she incorporates sponsorships from beauty brands into her videos to serve the needs of her brand partnerships.

Although Debord believes we are participants in maintaining the spectacle as a way of life, he also thinks that we are being manipulated by those, like advertisers, who have the most capital and make the majority of marketing decisions (1977, para. 70). Because the spectacle convinces us that our lives are incomplete without the appearances that commodities afford us, it affects how we view those with the power to create and disseminate their brand or commodity. In the case of YouTube vlogging, businesses use vloggers as endorsers for their products or services (Munnukka, Maity, Reinikainen, and Luoma-Aho 2019), which likely affects how viewers feel about that business. If viewers feel that a vlogger they enjoy is connected in some way with a given product or a brand, that product or brand would be more likely to make a positive impression on the viewer.

This arrangement also pays off for vloggers: if they garner a larger viewership, they can see significant financial gain. The highest-paid YouTubers of 2019 were vloggers, and some of them have amassed millions of dollars based on their YouTube content (McKeever 2019). A significant portion of vloggers' revenue comes from partnering with companies that give them sponsorships. The partnerships between sponsors and YouTubers are made possible by the YouTube Partner Program, which allows YouTubers to receive compensation for monetized videos through Google AdSense. Vloggers' commitments to their sponsors requires them to recognize those sponsors explicitly; if they do not, they will not get paid. There are even rules dictating what vloggers can say during the main content of their videos, and if they violate those rules, there is a strong possibility that those videos will be demonetized (YouTube Partner Program n.d.).

Similarly, Aina portrays herself as having made an affluent living from her YouTube content. She must maintain an allegiance to one brand or another to garner partnerships and advertising revenue, meaning that upholding the capitalistic values of the spectacle capitalism plays a large part in her appeal. However, she has found a way for her work to combine her genuine concerns over social justice issues with the celebration of her accomplishments through purchasing and showing off luxury acquisitions (Kwarteng 2021). While she hardly divests from capitalism, she has found a way to criticize some of its components while still maintaining a successful business model.

Outside of Aina, these connections and partnerships create a community not only between vloggers and companies but also between those companies and viewers. When vloggers dedicate screen time or space in their vlog descriptions to highlight the brands that they partner with, viewers are sure to pay attention. So the community that, at one point, was almost surely built between viewers, subscribers to a vlogger's channel, and the vlogger now has to make room for an additional, capitalistic element: businesses. Although participatory culture exists alongside capitalism, at first it may seem intrusive for businesses to work their way into participatory enthusiast groups like those on YouTube. However, because consumerism thrives in capitalist economies, maybe this addition of businesses that want partnerships would be welcomed by vloggers and participants alike. It would be fair to say that Debord would find that the business-vlogger-audience arrangement plays directly into the cyclical nature of the spectacle—and influencers like Aina make up a key part of that revenue-generating relationship.

REFERENCES

Aran, O., Biel, J., and Gatica-Perez, D. 2014. "Broadcasting Oneself: Visual Discovery of Vlogging Styles." *IEEE Transactions on Multimedia* 16 (1). https://doi.org/10.1109/TMM.2013.2284893.

Debord, G. 1977. *The Society of The Spectacle* (Rev. ed.) [PDF file]. Translated by Black & Red. https://www.marxists.org/reference/archive/debord/society.htm.

Delgado, R., and Stefancic, J. 2017. *Critical Race Theory: An Introduction* (3rd ed.). New York: New York University Press.

Eudaimonia. 2016. *The Medium Is the Message by Marshall McLuhan*. Animated book review [Video file]. https://www.youtube.com/watch?v=gCr2binb4Fs.

Ferguson, A. 2019. "Jackie Aina May Teach You Makeup Skills, but Really, She's Crusading for Black Women." *Washington Post*, April 21, 2019. https://www.washingtonpost.com/arts-entertainment/2019/04/21/jackie-aina-may-teach-you-little-makeup-really-shes-crusading-black-women/.

Jackson, L. 2019. "The Work Diary of Jackie Aina, Beauty Influencer." *New York Times*, November 26, 2019. https://www.nytimes.com/2019/11/26/business/jackie-aina-work-diary.html.

Kavoori, A. 2015. "Making Sense of YouTube." *Global Media Journal* 13 (24).

Krause, A. 2020. "A Beauty Brand Owner Is Asking People to Stop Supporting Companies for 72 Hours Until They Reveal How Many Black People Are in Leadership." *Insider*, June 4, 2020. https://www.insider.com/beauty-brand-owner-starts-challenge-on-instagram-2020-6.

Kwarteng, A. 2021. "Jackie Aina Blew Up 'The Good Immigrant Daughter' Narrative—You Really Think She Cares What the Haters Say?" *Cosmopolitan*, February 24, 2021. https://www.cosmopolitan.com/entertainment/celebs/a35523393/jackie-aina-profile-interview-2021/.

McKeever, V. 2019. "This Eight-Year-Old Remains YouTube's Highest-Earner, Taking Home $26 Million in 2019." *CNBC*, December 20, 2019. https://www.cnbc.com/2019/12/20/ryan-kaji-remains-youtubes-highest-earner-making-26-million-in-2019.html.

Mihailidis, P., and Viotty, S. 2017. "Spreadable Spectacle in Digital Culture: Civic Expression, Fake News, and the Role of Media Literacies in "Post-Fact" Society." *American Behavioral Scientist* 61 (4): 441–454. https://doi-org.libproxy.temple.edu/10.1177/0002764217701217.

Morgan, T., and Purje, L. 2016. "An Illustrated Guide to Guy Debord's 'The Society of the Spectacle.'" *Hyperallergic*, August 10, 2016. https://hyperallergic.com/313435/an-illustrated-guide-to-guy-debords-the-society-of-the-spectacle/.

Munnukka, J., Maity, D., Reinikainen, H. and Luoma-Aho, V. 2019. "'Thanks for Watching': The Effectiveness of YouTube Vlog Endorsements." *Computer in Human Behavior* 93: 226–234. https://doi.org/10.1016/j.chb.2018.12.014.

Payne, T. 2018. "Jackie Aina Just Called Jeffree Star Out for His 'Racist Behavior.'" *Teen Vogue*, October 2. https://www.teenvogue.com/story/jeffree-star-racist-jackie-aina.

Stratton, J. (2020). "Death and the Spectacle in Television and Social Media." *Television & New Media* 21 (1). https://doi.org/10.1177/1527476418810547.

Swigger, N. (2013). "The Online Citizen: Is Social Media Changing Citizens' Beliefs about Democratic Values?" *Political Behavior* 35 (3).

Ventriglio, A., and Bhugra, D. 2017. "Social Media and Social Psychiatry." *International Journal of Social Psychiatry* 63 (3). https://doi.org/10.1177/0020764017691552.

YouTube Partner Program. n.d. "Overview and Eligibility." Google. https://support.google.com/youtube?#topic=9257498.

THANOS AND THE AVENGERS: ENVIRONMENTAL ADVOCACY AMID THE SPECTACLE

KELLY BARTSCH is a student in the Klein College of Media and Communication at Temple University. Bartsch is a career ecological activist and has directed campaigns for national nonprofits, including Environment America and the Public Interest Research Group.

Individualism has long been exalted in Western ideology. American pop culture is imbued with signifiers and threaded with cultural artifacts that have been manufactured to enforce the absolute agency of the individual. Whatever happened to the utilitarian creed of American patriotism? When have the needs of the individual grown to subsume the needs that incur the sum of the greatest good? The collective ethos of humanity is inextricably bound to the structural integrity of the natural world. If humankind continues to surrender the spans and quality of nature to the realms of hyper-reality and consumerism, our species and civilization may well perish, as prophesied by several Hollywood eco-dystopian films.

The future may harbor our bones as they lie sunken under the remnants of cities, suburbs, and the tangled steel of industry. Our flesh will mingle with the remains of the plants and animals we reduced to ash in martyrdom of our empire-building. We will decay beneath the stage of our own spectacle, indistinguishable from the viscous fossils we once extracted to fuel enlightened conquests. If nature and humanity cannot coexist, our species and civilization will fall. Can we—as activists, citizens, and members of the human species—prevent this apocalyptic destruction by our own hand? Where is Thanos when we need him?

THANOS'S PLAN

In the movies, villains are the bearers of dark prophecies that the villains themselves often coax to fruition. The stark deciders of good and bad, right and wrong, they endorse the hegemony of binary worldviews. In the film *Avengers: Infinity War*, the Avengers are the good guys— the heroes, protecting the realms of humans from the impending evil of a large purple villain named Thanos. Thanos is on a divine mission to save all of the species of the universe from extinction. This extinction is being proliferated by resource scarcity, resulting from overpopulation and mass consumption.

Thanos's goal is fairly uncomplicated and unarguably ethical: save all life. However, his method of executing this plan is ethically murky, to say the least. To save the universe, Thanos wants to cut the population in half. Essentially, his goal is to end the existence of half of all life, which would in turn preserve the existence of the other half. Thanos's genocide is a utilitarian martyrdom forced upon individualist ideology—*some* life must cease so that *all* life may persist. The Avengers, being sentient beings with human bonds and emotional attachments, want to stop him. Here I would like to pause and ask you to permit the similarities between the plot of *Avengers: Infinity War* and the plight of humanity. Overpopulation is happening. Species are going extinct every day due to deforestation and climate change. So, clearly, the movie framed Thanos as a villain, but I challenge you to ask: the villain of whom?

HOT MEDIA SPECTACLE

Having spent years of my professional life working on issue-based environmental campaigns, I consider myself an activist. And, as an environmental activist, I perceive Thanos to signify the preservation of nature and long-term ecological sustainability *at any cost*. We are all part of an intricately connected planetary system, and humans are disrupting the complex ecologies of the natural world. In the film, the Avengers were framed as the heroes, but from a very anthropocentric lens. Because who did they save? Their stance was that humans (and sentient life) were the most important elements of existence. This is also the lens of hot ego-media, which almost exclusively supports the dominant ideology of anthropocentrism. It is the ritual of humans looking at other humans—emphasizing the view that *we* are the center of the universe.

Through the technologies of hot ego-media, humanity entertains the spectacle of its own hubris and grandiosity. According to Guy Debord, the "spectacle" is the result of several stages of techno-economic evolution:

> The first stage of the economy's domination of social life brought about an evident degradation of *being* into *having*—human fulfillment was no longer equated with what one was, but what one possessed. The present stage, in which social life has become completely occupied by the accumulated productions of the economy, is bringing about a general shift from *having* to *appearing*—all "having" must now derive its immediate prestige and its ultimate purpose from appearances. At the same time all individual reality

has become social, in the sense that it is shaped by social forces and is directly dependent on them.[1] (Italics in original.)

Debord thought that capitalism had distorted the values of society and had lulled people away from creativity for the sake of passive consumption and living for appearances. I believe that his prediction has proved prophetic, except that the media consumption is now *active* and often *antagonistic*, bent upon protecting the dominant ideologies. Each day, we watch as more of our reality succumbs to the mediation of technology. Zoom meetings, Facebook threads, likes, tweets, selfies, comments, Instagram pics, and TikTok videos have replaced the lived experience of their users. We are abandoned by tangibility, left to stare, cheer, and yell at each other through screens. We are shouting out into the yawning abyss of the hyperreal. In the spectacle, the consumer *is* the commodity. Your own fervor, grief, pride, and all other features of your identity are packaged, and their reflection is sold to you. And you buy it. We all buy it.

Under the conditions of spectacle, image and appearance become the dominant value in society. Consumption of image is preferred to actual lived experience. So, the problem facing environmental activists is this: How do you run an environmental campaign that can defeat this binary? How can you use media tech not only to inform people, but also to inspire them to take direct, unmediated action? How can media tech help to defy the conditions created by that same media tech? In a world where representation has subsumed reality, how do you use image and the act of "viewing" to convince people to defy their apathy and *do* something to fix a real-world problem? Is it possible to use the politics of spectacle to turn "viewing" into "doing"?

Several social movements born alongside the controversial Trump administration have faceted tangible results from hyperreal movements. The #MeToo campaign founded a hashtag that actualized in justice for the victims of sexual abusers. The origin story of Harvey Weinstein's imprisonment begun with two words—"Me

---

1   Guy Debord, *Society of the Spectacle*, (Berkeley: Bureau of Public Secrets), 2014, pp. 5–6; original edition published in Paris by Editions Buchet-Chastel, 1967.

too"—spoken through a screen. The testimony[2] of victims penetrated its own virtual echo chamber, clamoring for collective recognition that would ultimately result in systemic change.

The Black Lives Matter (#BLM) movement used new media tech to obtain and disseminate images of police brutality against black and brown bodies. Accompanying this dissemination was a raucous outrage, an obstreperous rebellion against systemic inequities. In cities across the country, police budgets were slashed, no-knock warrants were banned, and the very ideology of retributive justice began to dissolve once subjected to scrutiny. People spoke in semiotics; they organized atop platforms constructed atop the incorporeal. Specters of revolution manifested in physicality, leaving reality to reconcile with their dialectic. Signifiers on screens across the world transmitted a recondite code that could transcend the borders of the hyperreal. Existing as allegory for Neo in *The Matrix*, the messages crafted by these activists revealed their formula: the transmutation of virtual content into physical action. These signs, these hashtags—they *changed* the world.

The Climate Strike too has drawn attention that may someday translate into action. But the transnational systemic changes that would be required to produce any impactful change have, so far, proved too stolid to persuade and too strong to breach. What can environmental activists learn from the blueprint gifted to us from #MeToo and #BLM? How can we weaponize the ideologies of media tech built to fundamentally commodify each message when commodification is one the problems contributing to the issue we seek to solve?

CLICKTIVISM AND ECHO CHAMBERS

New technology introduces new opportunities for social organization and new modes of perception. Marshall McLuhan once made the analogy that cars are an extension of the foot. Following this allegory, digital media like the internet are an extension of seeing and, in some

ways, an extension of existing. So, they have changed the material conditions for visibility in environmental politics. One way of interacting with these conditions is through clicktivism. Clicktivism is the practice of supporting a political or social cause via the internet through mediums like social media or online petitions, and it is typically characterized as involving little effort or commitment. Clicktivism and e-activism involve tactics like liking or sharing social media posts, online petitions, photo petitions, and hashtags.

These hyperreal tactics have become indispensable organizing tools for environmental campaigns. They allow a message to transcend what reality limits to a primary audience. But, although clicktivism extends the range of a message, it provokes a problem presented by these novel forms of e-activism. Tension arises between the medium, the message, and the viewers who are left to interpret the semiotic intent that imbues the signifier with meaning and ideology. Each virtual artifact is a vehicle for the hegemony endorsing its existence. Real-world issues like climate change are transposed to suit a hyperreal platform and are presented to viewers alongside nonissues like Hollywood gossip, selfies, memes, celebrity breakups, advertisements, and alternative facts.

Real-world issues are forced to compete for the viewer's attention, fighting their way through echo chambers resounding with the glittering fetishization of imagery. Hot media and the rapid succession of events atop a virtual platform obfuscate the tangible reality of things like climate change. Dire environmental issues should, by default, have an exalted status within the virtual hierarchy. Hot media exploits images of polar ice melting, species dying, and ocean levels rising. Yet, the profundity of their crisis is strewn about carelessly by algorithms, submerged in a sea of grandiose content.

These images of crisis are commodified through the media tech entrusted to convey them and are consumed for their entertainment value. The medium removes them from the temporal world and reduces them to images consistent with the spectacle of consumer culture—the same consumer culture that is ideologically responsible for their perpetuation. Everything seems to be of moral equivalence when subjugated to

---

2   Tanya Pai and Constance Grady, "Harvey Weinstein Has Been Sentenced to 23 Years in Prison," Vox, March 11, 2020. https://www.vox.com/2020/3/11/21174920/harvey-weinstein-sentence-23-years.

the judgment of dehumanized algorithms. Essentially, the medium overtakes the message. Considering this ideological conflict, the problem for activists becomes this: How do you use the politics of spectacle to communicate an important issue? Can you successfully communicate a real-world problem atop a hyperreal platform and, through that communication, persuade people to confront an issue like climate change?

ECO-ACTIVISM: BARBIE, CHICKEN SUITS, AND RONALD MCDONALD

Greenpeace is an environmental advocacy group that has largely perfected the art of spectacle-based campaigning by utilizing social media. In 2011, Greenpeace organizers transposed a real-world problem into a rhetorical exigence that they addressed through a YouTube video adorned with performativity, satire, and gorilla campaign tactics. The campaign was targeted at Mattel (the parent company of Barbie) in response to their sourcing cardboard toy packaging from trees logged from endangered rainforests.

Greenpeace activists produced a YouTube video that featured a litany of spectacle—some containing elements of the absurd. Activists daringly scaled the walls of Mattel's corporate headquarters to hang large banners with kitschy campaign slogans. Most slogans insinuated Ken's displeasure with Barbie's environmental indifference. Meanwhile, an activist in a Barbie costume drove a pink bulldozer around the company parking lot, the bulldozer prominently displaying a bumper sticker of a chainsaw hovering above the word "barbaric." Most protesters got arrested, with the publicity of the arrests only adding to the success of the campaign.

Greenpeace created a spectacle out of the issue of deforestation. This spectacle placed a lot of unwanted attention on the corporate practices of Mattel that supported deforestation. After this video went viral, Mattel released a global policy that established strict environmental standards for their paper suppliers. This policy was necessary in order for Mattel to maintain its public image and ensure the continued success of its product. Greenpeace moralized the debate and mobilized consumers to pressure Mattel to change its corporate environmental policies. The campaign worked, inverting the conditions of spectacle by inverting its politics, turning the spectacle in on itself.

Another campaign I want to offer as an example of spectacle is one that I had the pleasure of taking part in. It was an Environment Texas and Mighty Earth initiative called the "McWholeFoods" campaign. McDonald's and Whole Foods source their meat from Tyson and Cargill, two of the largest agricultural polluters in the United States. Simply put, we wanted them to shift their supply chain to exclusively include producers with responsible environmental standards. As established by a Mighty Earth industry report, Tyson and Cargill are responsible for the majority of deforestation in the Midwest and for the dead zone in the Gulf of Mexico.[3] The Dead Zone is a section of the gulf where nothing can live because the fertilizer runoff from industry farming has made it dense with toxic plumes of red algae. So, we gathered ninety thousand petition signatures, dressed our intern up as a chicken, and marched over to Whole Foods corporate headquarters in Austin to bring democracy to their doorstep and inform them of the concerns of their consumers.

Despite our attempts, Whole Foods and McDonald's refused to schedule a meeting with activists and ignored the concerns of their consumers.

So, we came back with Ronald McDonald himself (another intern in costume, waving a chainsaw menacingly at several cardboard trees we had brought as props). Since Ronald is a celebrity, the local news outlets all came out to interview him and ask him why he was aggressively cutting down fake trees with a chainsaw. Ronald took the opportunity to tell the public all about his passion for deforestation and agricultural pollution. But, he said, at least he didn't green-wash the branding of his products like Whole Foods did. And, although no

---

3 Jennifer Nastu, "Big Brands Are 'Flunking the Planet,' Mighty Earth Proclaims," *Environment + Energy Leader*, October 10, 2018, https://www.environmentalleader.com/2018/10/big-brands-are-flunking-the-planet-mighty-earth-proclaims/; Lucia von Reusner, "Mystery Meat II: The Industry Behind the Quiet Destruction of the American Heartland," Report for Mighty Earth, August 2017, https://www.mightyearth.org/wp-content/uploads/2017/07/Meat-Pollution-in-America.pdf.

one wants to argue with a clown holding a chainsaw, the public was brave enough to admonish Ronald for the McDonald's company's enthusiasm for environmental destruction. Hundreds of citizen activists showed up to protest in front of Whole Foods corporate headquarters in Austin and in front of McDonald's headquarters in Chicago. They wrote letters, sent emails, made phone calls, and let those powerful corporate giants know exactly where their consumers stood.

THREE STEPS IN DIGITAL ECO-ACTIVISM

After using the politics of spectacle to gain visibility for agricultural pollution, Environment Texas and Mighty Earth convinced McDonald's to issue sustainability standards for its meat suppliers. Despite this victory, the McWholeFoods campaign endures to this day. So far, it has been only partially successful. It takes a long time to liberate corporate machinery from the hegemonic rust that adorns it. Leverage, time, and tactics are essential for coaxing the correct gears to spin. Successful digital campaigns move people toward engagement in three steps: *Alert, Amplify, and Engage.*

1. **Alert (*Viewing* the issue):** Naming something has power. Digital media have the capacity to shape the public sphere by influencing opinions and winning hearts and minds. Identifying and defining an issue is an important first step to solving it. The words we choose to describe and communicate things have a huge impact on the way we perceive them. For example, "swamp" is often thought of as something gross and dirty that should be drained or removed. In contrast, "wetland" refers to nature, biodiversity, and something that should be protected and celebrated.

2. **Amplify (*Sharing* or talking about the issue):** Increasing the number of people who encounter the message helps to build influence. Grassroots power comes with sheer numbers of concerned citizens. This puts pressure on decision-makers. Amplification works by creating a buzz or going viral to increase the number of people who hear the message.

3. **Engage (*Doing* something about the issue):** Empowering people to take collective action will inspire them to plant the seeds of widespread social change. This is the tough one. This gauges how effective your communication tactics were. For example, citizens engaged on an issue will take direct action. This can mean organizing or participating in a rally, calling or writing to a legislator, or submitting a "letter to the editor" to a newspaper.

NARCOTIZING DYSFUNCTION

There are many challenges that accompany moving people from the "alert" stage toward "engagement." One that is particularly unique to hot media and spectacle is called narcotizing dysfunction. Narcotizing dysfunction is a theory that as mass media or social media inundates people with news of a particular issue, the people become apathetic to the issue, substituting knowledge for action. It is suggested that the vast supply of communication Americans receive elicits only a superficial concern about the problems of society.

The overwhelming flow of hot ego-media and spectacle has caused the populace to become more passive in their social activism, though there are some notable exceptions, including BLM, #MeToo, and the March for Science. These grassroots movements were able to use digital media to build a movement in which people took direct, unmediated political action to produce tangible changes despite resistance from hegemonic societal structures.

The most existential threat of narcotizing dysfunction is the ideological shift it injects into the public sphere. Under these new ideological conditions, viewing something or knowing something takes the place of *doing* something to fix a problem. People get stuck in the "alert" or "amplify" keyboard warrior stage. Educating people about an issue is an important first step, but knowledge is useless when it's not accompanied by a corrective action or behavior change. These new viewer-centric ideologies ensure that their audience remains imprisoned by apathy. Narcotizing dysfunction occurs when the recipients of this knowledge fail to go forth and implement what they've learned to make the world a safer and more equitable place. Engagement requires the application and weaponization of fact to initiate widespread social change. But, with so many things vying for monetized attention, what are the ethics of commodifying an important issue so that its entertainment value can compete within the sphere of hot ego-media? Grandiosity and catastrophizing specifically run the risk of desensitizing people, invoking the effects of narcotizing dysfunction.

NIMBY

Another obstacle in moving people from "alert" to "engage" is NIMBYism. NIMBYism (Not In My BackYard) is the ultimate case of anthropocentrism. It is an individualist mentality that extends the concern of an individual only to the specific circumstances that have a direct effect on that same individual. People look at climate change like it's some obscure problem in a faraway land that does not have a direct implication upon their lives. By the time it progresses far enough to where the people in power start to personally experience its consequences, it will be too late to fix it. Hot media and spectacle often fail to convey the relevance and immediacy of problems whose immensity defies their capacity for transmission. How can we get people to realize that they are all part of the same planetary system? How can we reframe ecological problems to inspire people to think not only as individuals but also as members of an interdependent species? This is an ideological problem requiring a shift in cultural values and perception.

THANOS AND ECOLOGICAL CHOICE

In *Avengers: Infinity War*, Thanos is a jeremiad, a voice for the autonomous creatures whose language denies them any refutation of the anthropocentrism destroying their habitat. They are part of the sublime enigma behind the ecology connecting us all. They do not speak in semiotics. They cannot communicate in hashtags. Their enduring cause is a specter that haunts the realms of men. Thanos speaks for those who lament in foreign semantics, echoing from the wild abyss of forest and sea. Thanos's goal is to save all species (sentient and insentient) from the overconsumption of natural resources. The Avengers' goal is to save their planet and their friends. The heroes make zero mention of how they intend to remedy the resource scarcity problem that Thanos is trying to address. Anthropocentric individualism is framed as the moral imperative. Collectivism, self-sacrifice, and necessary martyrdom are vilified.

In Western ideology, we worship the absolute autonomy of choice. If half of all beings in *Avengers: Infinity War* had given consent to exchange their lives for the greater good, the victims would become the heroes, the heroes would become the villains, and the villain would simply be the agent initiating the means of change. The Avengers would have lost their footing atop the lofty peak of the moral high ground. But, in individualist ideology, the end never justifies the means.

And this is where we remain socially. We have to make a consistent choice to purposefully defy the ideologies that keep us docile and complacent. Corporations use the spectacle to fetishize commodities through advertisements so they can sell us things we do not need. The excessive consumption of these products devalues environmental quality and social equity for the sake of the material wealth of the producers and for the instant gratification of the consumers. Entertainment and spectacle are employed to distract us from the deteriorating conditions of our environmental and social ecosystems.

THE CLOCK IS TICKING

While humanity continues its great performance, Planet Earth beneath our stage slowly fossilizes in stoic resignation. Scientists warn that our consumer society is causing the sixth great extinction.[4] Often, their warning

---

4 Elizabeth Kolbert, *The Sixth Extinction: An Unnatural History* (New York: Picador, 2015).

is lost amid the cacophony of content vociferating from our screens in neon lights. The general rate of species extinctions is accelerating, driven by five factors: land use, hunting or exploiting wildlife, climate change, pollution, and introducing invasive species. These are collective problems. They are being perpetrated not by any one individual, but by the human race as a whole. And, without the intervention of a nature-loving super-villain wielding magical infinity stones, it's likely going to require the effort of the entire human race to fix them.

Planet Earth is the original territory, and it is being exploited in dangerous ways for new maps of consumption and apathy. As environmental activists and advocates, we need to find a way to weaponize these new digital technologies and turn the exploiters' ideologies against them. We need to actively defy our anthropocentric nature and denounce the mindless consumptive pleasure of individualism. We need to make a conscious choice to recognize the sublime at the heart of humanity—inextricably fusing all of us to the enigma of Gaia's complex systems. Within this ongoing global drama of humankind's subordination of nature, we need to unitedly ask ourselves these questions: What do we stand for? Who are our villains? Who are our heroes? And do each of them deserve to be?

THE WILD ONE (1953)

GIRL (Peggy Maley): Hey, Johnny!

What are you rebelling against?

JOHNNY (Marlon Brando): Whaddya got?

FAHRENHEIT 451 (1966)

CLARISSE (Julie Christie): People who vanished. Some were arrested and managed to escape. Others were released. Some didn't wait to be arrested. They just hid themselves away. Up in the farm country; the woods and the hills. They live there in little groups. And the law can't touch them. They live quite peaceably and do nothing that's forbidden. Though, if they came into the city, they might not last long. MONTAG (Oskar Werner): But how can you call them Book People if they don't do anything against the law? CLARISSE: They are books. Each one, men and women, everyone, commits a book they've chosen to memory, and they become the books. Of course, every now and then, someone gets stopped, arrested. Which is why they live so cautiously. Because the secret they carry is the most precious secret in the world. With them, all human knowledge would pass away.

FIGHT CLUB (1999)

Tyler Durden: I see all this potential, and I see squandering. God damn it, an entire generation pumping gas, waiting tables; slaves with white collars. Advertising has us chasing cars and clothes, working jobs we hate so we can buy shit we don't need. ... We've all been raised on television to believe that one day we'd all be millionaires, and movie gods, and rock stars. But we won't. And we're slowly learning that fact. And we're very, very pissed off.

CHAPTER SEVEN

CAPITALISM AND CONSUMPTION

Exploiting Humanity's Cosmic Narcissism and Our Need for Art, Design, and Identity

By Barry Vacker and Colby Chase

COLBY CHASE served as the research assistant for the second edition of this book. This introduction includes passages from her work on that edition. Colby received her MA in Media Studies from Temple University and her BA in Creative Writing from Emerson College. Her research explores the effects of the consolidation of media ownership as well as the commercialization of countercultural movements.

"THE CULT OF INDIVIDUALITY"

I've had a handful of denim jackets in my lifetime—from college student to dropout to college graduate to corporate worker to grad student to professor and artist. My all-time favorite denim jacket is the Ziggy from "Cult of Individuality," a brand name designed by Ron Poisson, who is headquartered in Los Angeles (one of my favorite cities). Ron is a creative artist and seems like a nice guy, though I only know him from Instagram. I hashtagged his brand to my pic wearing the jacket at the Grand Canyon and we soon followed each other. The jacket is perfect for the chilly or breezy nights on my road trips through the American deserts. Along with the design and subtle paintlike layers to the fabric, I also like the perceptive irony in the name.

FIGURE 7.0.1   Pocket Button on "Cult of Individuality" Denim Jacket. Photo by Barry Vacker, 2021

No one wants to think they are not unique, not special, not an individual with some significance to their existence. That's understandable. But, the concept of "individualism" has become cultlike and is wildly confused with

- Egotism (I am important!)
- Exhibitionism (Look at me!)
- Hedonism (I want pleasure and instant gratification! Now!)
- Tribalism (I stand out, yet I belong!)
- Consumerism (Look at what I buy, own, and wear!)

Of course, the cult of individuality rests on the foundations of cosmic narcissism. That's the existential stance that one (or one's tribe) is super-special and exists at the center of everything, the center of all value, purpose, and meaning, often with a perceived special and central destiny in the universe. Like theologies and political ideologies, capitalism and consumption tap into this narcissism and its many related drives with brands, logos, advertising, influencers, and a host of other tactics. Of course, this narcissism and the "cult of individuality" are also fueled by the hot ego-media technologies in our planetary media ecologies (chapter 1).

THE SIMULACRA OF INDIVIDUALISM

The original philosophical meaning of individualism was a broad combination of intellectual integrity, thinking for oneself, and a kind of spiritual and creative independence, free from the dominant regimes of tribe, church, state, monarchy, aristocracy, and so on. In effect, individuals should be "free" to peacefully create their goals and shape their lives and lifestyles in hopes of self-realization while respecting the rights of others to do the same. Yet, the "individualists" should also see their *deep connection* to the human species and life on Earth, especially in light of contemporary science—genetics, biology, ecology, and cosmology. It takes a certain individualism and independence of thought to step outside of one's self, outside one's immediate interest, and think long-term for our species, to see our natural diversity (cultural and ecological), to see the need for more equality, more equity, more sustainability, and a universal narrative and shared destiny. In other words, individualism and collectivism are not inherently oppositional.

Yet, the "territories" of individualism have been utterly overtaken by the "maps," which simulate individualism via making selections among a nonstop parade of consumer and entertainment choices presented in the spectacle. What we see in the "cult of individuality" is the *simulacra of individualism*, manifest in the proliferation of narcissism, exhibitionism, and tribalism, all of which collectively function to limit our vision in developing a true universal narrative and shared destiny for our species.

Capitalism celebrates the cult of individuality as the dominant imperative marked by endless consumption, with brands and designs targeted to our self-perceived identities. The cult of capitalist individuality presents endless consumption as the universal narrative for our species. No one is immune to this narrative. That's because art, tech, design, fashion, and aesthetics are all intrinsic to the human species and important for our individual and collective identities, on a daily basis and a long-term basis.[1] Capitalism did not create these drives. Evolution did.

Critics of capitalism assume that these desires are merely byproducts of advertising and commercialism, but many are actually inherent to our species, residing deep in our evolutionary psyche. Just as we appreciate art at the gallery, museum, or movie theater, we need artistic design that inspires us and products and services that we will use and can respect, as Apple founder Steve Jobs understood all too well. In principle, there is nothing profane about product consumption in such contexts. *It becomes a problem when satisfying the desires leads to hyperconsumption and obscene levels of narcissism, tribalism, pollution, and ecological destruction.* We are not

---

1   Ellen Dissanayake, *Homo Aestheticus: Where Art Comes From and Why* (New York: The Free Press, 1992); Frederick Turner, *Beauty: The Value of Values* (Charlottesville: University Press of Virginia, 1992); Philip Shaw, *The Sublime* (London: Routledge, 2006).

merely warming the planet; we are also disrupting the ecosystems on a massive scale and creating our own fossil layers, such that we have effected a new epoch on Planet Earth (chapter 8).

Capitalism perfectly taps into these evolutionary drives. So does the existential stance of ego-media. The merger of capital and ego are perfectly expressed in Apple's iPod, iPhone, and iPad.

APOLLO AND APPLE: NIHILISM AND NARCISSISM

Founded in the 1970s (in the wake of the Apollo moon landings), Apple has coevolved with media culture to express the consumer narcissism that attempts to counter the cosmic nihilism revealed by Apollo's views of Earth from space. Apollo 8's and Apollo 11's views of Earth from space rocked the world in 1968 and 1969. Earth floating in the cosmic void, looking like a blue marble with the oceans and swirls of clouds on a borderless planet, with very clear limits to the resources and atmosphere. There is only one meaning to those images—we humans are tiny, yet brainy and creative, a diversity of peoples who exist as a single species on a planet from which we evolved and share the ecosystems with all other life-forms. Along with technologies like the Hubble Space Telescope, we have discovered a vast and wondrous universe in which we are insignificant and our existence is perhaps inconsequential and meaningless.

Yet, it seems that most of humanity is still in denial, with the narcissism and tribalism fueling hate, war, racism, fascism, violence, religious conflicts, and ecological destruction. All that's a fact. If that hits your hot button, that's the power of memes.

No products better signify the cosmic narcissism than Apple's iPhones—the aptly named devices that let every user pretend to be the center of everything, the center of the universe, with an app for every need and whim, an app to keep you glued to the screen and away from the stars.

This is not a naive indictment of Apple or of Apple users (I have been using Apple products since the mid-1980s) but merely the observation that Apple perfectly mirrors the dominant secular and consumer narratives since Apollo. With no chance for journeying into space and no self-evident meaning for human existence as seen from outer space and the Hubble Space Telescope, the only option that secular culture has provided (so far) is to consume more products and migrate to cyberspace and online existence to gaze upon ourselves and each other with love, hate, anger, and humor. Capitalism is taking over for the lapses in secular philosophy.

APPLE AND AMAZON

If any two corporations typify twenty-first-century "individuality" and consumerism, it is Apple (ranked #1 with a market value $2.2 trillion) and Amazon (ranked #3 at $1.6 trillion). Since its founding in the 1970s, Apple has long tapped into the individualist (I am unique) and aesthetic (form + function and elegance + efficiency) drives of humanity, which is one reason it is at the top in market value. As for the endless and instant consumption, Amazon has tapped into that drive, while also capitalizing on the effects of the COVID-19 pandemic.

Apple has profited from humanity's deep-seated cosmic narcissism and desire for existential centrality and significance. As of 2019, Apple sold over 1.5 billion iPhones and is fast approaching 2 billion. Apple reports that there are now over 1 billion active iPhones on Planet Earth.[2] Apple made $140 billion off iPhone sales in 2019 alone. No wonder Apple keeps raising its prices for incremental software and hardware improvements powered by Moore's Law (chapter 2). I wonder what happened to the hundreds of millions of iPhones that are no longer active? Recycled or in landfills?

---

2   Jacob Kastrenakes, "Apple Says There Are Now Over 1 Billion Active iPhones," *The Verge*, January 27, 2021, https://www.theverge.com/2021/1/27/22253162/iphone-users-total-number-billion-apple-tim-cook-q1-2021.

APPLE'S PROFITS VERSUS NASA'S BUDGET

Consider this. In the fourth quarter of 2020, Apple's sales were $114 billion, with profits of $28 billion.[3] In contrast, NASA's annual budget for 2020 was $22.6 billion. *That's right: Apple's fourth-quarter profit exceeded NASA's annual budget.* That alone tells you the existential priorities of American consciousness.

INDUSTRIAL CAPITALISM: GOODS AND DESIRES

In *Society of the Spectacle*, Guy Debord explained that as human civilization evolved, we have gone from lives of *being* to *having* to *appearing*. That's still true today. Technological civilization, mass production, and industrial capitalism have moved us from being and having, to a state where *being is having* and consuming on a massive scale. With the rise of electronic media and the spectacle, we have also entered the realm where *being is appearing*, which proliferates in the realms of advertising and social media. In fact, being-is-having and being-is-appearing in the spectacle correlate with the evolving demands for goods, desires, attention, and engagement.

In the wake of the Apollo moon landings, capitalism and contemporary society have largely followed the trajectories of technology, production, and consumption. In effect, the economics of *scarcity* have dramatically evolved with the introduction of new technologies and changing demographics—from mass production to mass entertainment to mass surveillance, from scarcities of *goods* to *desires* to *attention*.

By the time the Apollo program arrived, industrial capitalism was highly efficient in making most *goods* abundantly available, so buying products to satisfy *needs* was superseded by consuming products to satisfy *desires*. Products and services were branded and customized to satisfy consumer society's new scarcity: *desires and identities*. By the 1950s, General Motors dominated the automobile market by offering multiple vehicle designs and colors aimed at a diversity of desires and unique preferences (Ford was slow to follow such innovations). Credit cards were also introduced and fiercely marketed by Madison Avenue (as cleverly shown in the hit series *Mad Men*).

With the proliferation of radio and television, Western society saw the rise of cultural and consumer tribalism, beginning with the Beats in the 1950s, the mods and hippies in the 1960s, then the punks, rappers, New Wavers, and urban cowboys in the 1970s and 1980s, followed by a succession of yuppies, preppies, goths, gangstas, grungers, grrls, geeks, gamers, techies, hipsters, fashionistas, metrosexuals, and so on. In the 1960s, Coke gave birth to Sprite and Tab, and eventually to Diet Coke and Coke Zero. Blue jeans came in preshrunk, bell bottoms, and women's styles, then stonewashed, loose fit, boot cut, and skinny cut. Levi's was challenged by Lee and Wrangler before Calvin Klein, Jordache, Guess, Gap, Diesel, and Lucky arrived on the scene, followed by numerous other brands.

By the 1970s, cable introduced specialized TV programming, followed in the 1990s by the explosion of the internet and the ever more tribalized and personalized social media of the twenty-first century—which encourage a daily existence immersed in the 24/7 spectacle of media and consumption. Twenty-first century capitalism has evolved into new kind of digital and technological capitalism in which the commodities are information and entertainment—"infotainment" produced and distributed on a global scale. The multibillion-dollar mergers (in the 1990s) of firms like Microsoft and NBC and Time-Warner and Turner Broadcasting are now dwarfed by the market values of firms like Apple, Amazon, Netflix, and Facebook. Of course, the cable service providers like Comcast are key sites for accessing the internet and the various social media platforms, such as Facebook, Instagram, YouTube, and TikTok. Layers and layers of media technologies, through which tsunamis of "infotainment" flow in our planetary media ecologies (chapter 1).

---

3   Dominic Rushe, "Apple Records Most Profitable Quarter Even as Sales Soar Amid Pandemic," *The Guardian*, January 27, 2021, https://www.theguardian.com/technology/2021/jan/27/apple-profits-latest-quarter-surge-pandemic.

SURVEILLANCE CAPITALISM: ATTENTION AND ENGAGEMENT

With proliferating and miniaturizing media technologies, electronic capitalism was poised to satisfy the next scarcity: *attention and engagement*. Television merged with microprocessors in the creation of the personal computer. This was followed by the internet, which connected computers around the world. The World Wide Web provided a way for computers to "communicate," which soon led to social media, linking people via cyberspace.

We were invited to explore a range of internet aggregators (Yahoo, Google, Amazon, YouTube) and *attention*-consuming social media (Facebook, Twitter, Snapchat, Instagram), accompanied by *engagement* phenomena (blogging, fan cultures, microcelebrities, binge viewing, status updates). Consumer products complement these trends, including craft breweries, artisan coffeehouses, and restaurants and supermarkets offering locally grown produce, grass-fed beef, and organic poultry. By purchasing these various items and products, we subsequently purchase the tribal identities they represent, all designed to make us feel hip and super-special. In post-Apollo culture, we have gone from mass production to mass customization to mass participation, under the imperative of satisfying more desires and creating "unique" and "authentic" identities while consuming endless products and entertainment—the worlds of the iTribes. And we talk nonstop about these tribal worlds on the internet and in the 24/7 media spectacle.

Most of these technologies are hot ego-media, which makes them perfect for a predatory practice of what Shoshana Zuboff calls "surveillance capitalism," a system in which our labor (posts, images, likes, tweets, videos, streams, uploads, downloads, etc.) creates data that are harvested by social media firms. In this system, democracy is simulated as economic and political power flow up and down the system, to enrich the capitalists, engage the influencers, and entice the users to keep playing the game. Is this Orwell's worst nightmare, or is it just more twenty-first-century Huxley, an online world of selling dreams and delusions to keep us distracted and entertained?

DREAMS AND NIGHTMARES: HUXLEY, ORWELL, AND ADVERTISING

In contrast to George Orwell's dark vision of totalitarian domination, capitalist consumer society provides an optimistic dream world of individualist and self-actualizing seduction. At the heart of the seduction are the spectacle and advertising. Consider the following:

- Over $700 billion was spent on total global advertising in 2021 and is projected to surpass $850 billion by 2024.[4] Can we doubt it will pass $1 trillion by 2030?
- Digital advertising worldwide will reach $389 billion in 2021 and is projected to reach $526 billion by 2024.[5] Considering that digital advertising did not exist 30 years ago, can we doubt that it too will surpass $1 trillion in the near future?

Advertising sells us hopes and dreams (and some fears)—all day, every day, every year. Cars, homes, clothes, foods, beverages, music, and everything else, all sold to you based on what the advertisers think we desire from their endless supply of desire-satisfying goods and services. Does advertising *make* consumers buy things? No.

---

4 Ben Bold, "Coronavirus Impact on China Leads eMarketer to Marginally Downgrade Adspend Growth," *Campaign*, March 20, 2020. Total advertising includes TV, radio, newspapers, magazines, out-of-home (billboards, etc.), directories, and all digital advertising (as described below in note 6).

5 Ethan Cramer-Flood, "Global Digital Ad Spending Update," Insider Intelligence/eMarketer website, July 6, 2020. "Digital advertising" includes advertising that "appears on desktop and laptop computers, as well as mobile phones, tablets and other internet-connected devices; includes classifieds, display (banner/static display, rich media, sponsorships and video, including advertising that appears before, during, or after digital video content in a video player), search (paid listings, contextual text links and paid inclusion), in game advertising, newsletter advertising and email."

But, like Hollywood, TV shows, and music videos, advertising sells consumer lifestyles and worldviews which are baked into our minds from childhood. In effect, it's the idea that you can self-actualize through consumption to express your "individualism" and "freedom of choice."

The cult of individuality runs deep in advertising. Advertising promises the products that allow you to be you, or be like someone you like, or at least pretend to be very cool. This world is not unlike the metropolis of the Capitol in *The Hunger Games*, where everyone seems so hip, chatty, and fashionable, happily enthralled by their seductions. In this sense, our current consumer society and *The Hunger Games* resemble the contours of the dystopian world presented by Aldous Huxley in *Brave New World*.[6]

TABLE 7.0.1 SOCIAL CONTROL: DOMINATION AND SEDUCTION

	Orwell	**Huxley**
Book	*1984*	*Brave New World*
Control via	Domination	Seduction
Shape your	Nightmares	Dreams
	Fears	Desires
Lifestyles	Poverty	Luxury
	Sacrifice	Indulge
	Few luxuries	Massive debt
Organization	State	Corporation
Messages	Propaganda	Advertising
Sound bites	"Two minutes of hate"	Fifteen-second ads
Loyalties	Patriotism/Nationalism	Consumerism/Brands
Your "choice"	Vote	Buy
Symbols	Flags	Logos
Metaphor	Stick	Carrot

In the Orwellian vision, the people are dominated by their fears and nightmares, which are shaped by the state and propaganda. In the Huxleyian vision, the people are seduced by their dreams and desires, which are shaped by corporations and advertising. Orwell's vision speaks of control via sacrifice, hate, and patriotism, while Huxley's vision promises luxury, indulgence, and consumption. It's vote or buy, nations or brands, flags or logos, sticks or carrots. See Table 7.0.1

So what is the best way for governments and corporations to maintain their hegemony and power structures? What is the best way to control the rebels who might want to challenge the system and structures? Put 'em in jail or put 'em in debt? Cells or cell phones? Give 'em a fine or give 'em another credit card? The best way is to sell the would-be individualists all the signs and symbols of individualism that can be conceived in the spectacle. Tell them they can be free. Today. Now. If not, then tell them to rebel. Make movies about rebellion with cool rebel heroes—Morpheus and Trinity, V and Evey, Katniss and that dude named Peeta. Well, at least Katniss is cool. Above all, make rebellion look cool, fun, and available via a credit card.

---

6 Aldous Huxley, *Brave New World* (New York: Harper Perennial, 2006). First published in 1932.

WHY DO MEDIA AND CAPITALISM CELEBRATE REBELS?

In the 1953 classic movie *The Wild One*, Marlon Brando plays the leader of a motorcycle gang that has invaded a small California town. While Brando is standing at the jukebox, a girl, dancing with one of his buddies, asks, "Hey, Johnny! What are you rebelling against?" Brando sneers, "Whaddya got?" And so begins a long line of famed actors playing cool counterculture rebels in Hollywood films (see Table 7.0.2). Some rebels are "individualist" rebels, seeking no larger social movement. Other movie rebels actually try to overthrow the dominant regimes, at least, the regimes in the films.

Hollywood, media culture, and global capitalism have made counterculture and rebellion seem cool, very cool. In fact, rebels rival superheroes in coolness, with the coolest superheroes being those who seem like rebels, such as Batman and some of the X-Men. In my view, Professor Xavier of the X-Men is cool. But being a professor myself, perhaps I am just happy to see a cool professor in a movie!

Hollywood and Madison Avenue have merged rebels and cool into a lifestyle, a consumer choice, a mode of being. Of course, as with anything in the age of the spectacle and hyperreality, there are *real* rebels and *real* cool, and there are the signs and symbols of rebels and cool—the hyperreal rebels and hyperreal cool. There are a lot more signs and symbols of rebellion than there is real rebellion.

TABLE 7.0.2   COOL REBELS IN HOLLYWOOD

Actor	Rebel Character	Film	Year
Marlon Brando	Johnny Strabler	*The Wild One*	1953
James Dean	Jim Stark	*Rebel Without a Cause*	1955
Julie Christie	Clarisse	*Fahrenheit 451*	1966
Paul Newman	Luke Jackson	*Cool Hand Luke*	1967
Dennis Hopper and Peter Fonda	Billy and Wyatt	*Easy Rider*	1969
Jeff Bridges	Flynn	*Tron*	1982
Geena Davis and Susan Sarandon	Thelma and Louise	*Thelma and Louise*	1991
Brad Pitt and Edward Norton	Tyler Durden and Jack	*Fight Club*	1999
L. Fishburne, C. A. Moss, and K. Reeves	Morpheus, Trinity, and Neo	*The Matrix*	1999
Hugo Weaving and Natalie Portman	V and Evey	*V for Vendetta*	2005
Jennifer Lawrence	Katniss	*The Hunger Games*	2012
Britt Robertson	Casey	*Tomorrowland*	2015
Charlize Theron	Imperator Furiosa	*Mad Max: Fury Road*	2015
Daisy Ridley and John Boyega	Rey and Finn	*Star Wars: The Force Awakens*	2016
Emma Watson and John Boyega	Mae and Ty	*The Circle*	2017
Tye Sheridan	Wade	*Ready Player One*	2018
Anya Taylor-Joy	Beth	*The Queen's Gambit*	2020

CAPITALISM AND THE REBEL LIFESTYLE

In essence, Karl Marx was correct about the alienation of labor and commodity fetishism in an economic world of mass production and mass consumption. Workers become alienated and bored in meaningless jobs with meaningless tasks, not to mention tedious "service" to customers in the food service, tourism, and hospitality industries. To subdue the alienation and entertain the boredom, industrial capitalism produced an unprecedented abundance of goods and desires, all manifest in the media and consumer cultures found on television and in malls. So it is natural that workers also become consumers and learn to fetishize commodities in hopes of deriving personal identity from consumer products, especially products branded in special ways via advertising. The economic and cultural goals of capitalism were to stimulate demand to meet accelerating production while outproducing industrial communism in the Cold War. Thus was born the consumer society and a world of brands (which spread like memes via networks as part of the spectacle).

Born of industrial mass production, the mass societies of capitalism and communism were no longer ideal by the late 1960s. In other words, the mass societies and mass cultures of the Cold War were fragmenting in the "society of the spectacle." At the same time in the democratic West, capitalism evolved into new forms with new media technologies, including radio, television, computers, and theme parks. Entertainment capitalism began supplanting industrial capitalism in pop culture, creating a world of consumption and mass reproductions, the spectacle emerging from television and electronic media.

Mark Zuckerberg is one of the most famous internet capitalists on the planet. Zuckerberg's "entrepreneurial" networking skills were featured in the 2010 Oscar-winning film *The Social Network*, directed by David Fincher (better known for *Fight Club*). While the film does not reveal much about the many meanings of social media and Facebook, it does take moviegoers "behind the scenes" to see the founding of an epic media empire, at least so far. In showing the capitalist drive to earn huge profits by providing something of value to users and audiences, *The Social Network* follows in the steps of *Network* and *Quiz Show*, films that critiqued the capitalist imperative in corporate media.

What is Facebook's number one product? You. Who is Facebook's number one labor force? You. That's right: you (and 2.7 billion other people) are the product of and the labor force for Facebook and most social media. Are you gonna be a rebel now?

Apple, Google, Comcast, Disney, Fox, Viacom, Time-Warner, Reddit, Twitter, and Marvel Studios—like Facebook, these are multibillion-dollar media, film, and technology companies. They rely on you to consume and/or produce the content they produce and/or distribute on a global scale. Do they care if you are a rebel or not, as long as you produce and consume their content, even the content targeted to "rebels"?

Since the 1950s, mass culture has always yielded a counterculture with rebels—the Beats, hippies, rappers, new wavers, punk rockers, grunge bands, dotcoms, social media activists, and the populace of *Portlandia*. Corporate culture has its so-called young counterculture rebels—Steve Jobs started out that way and Mark Zuckerberg was perceived that way. So were many other internet entrepreneurs. During the same time period, capitalist media and mass society have fragmented into an ever-expanding kaleidoscope of television channels, lifestyle tribes, and endless forms of counterculture and rebellion.

Though the spectacle and consumer society allow anyone to purchase the signs of resistance, the truth is that these signs are not always akin to actual resistance. In the 1960s, it was bell-bottom pants, flowery shirts, and long hair. In the 1980s, it was black skinny-legged jeans, T-shirts with band logos, leather jackets, and dyed hair or mohawks. In the 2010s and 2020s, it is tattoos, body piercings, manly beards, the V mask, and all the signs and symbols of previous images of resistance and rebellion. It's one thing to be the rebel in a movie theater or a video game; it's another to develop an alternative ideology and take actions toward the rebellion suggested by the new worldview.

Are these rebel images and ideologies just another lifestyle sold in the capitalist consumer marketplace? Has rebellion entered the hyperreal, where we substitute the signs of rebellion for rebellion, to give us a tribal persona and a rebel lifestyle that make us feel a little better while living in a world we are unable to significantly change? Perhaps the proliferating countercultural lifestyles liberate "rebels" and "outlaws" from servitude to the brand narratives of corporations and the grand narratives of cosmology. After all, why contemplate the larger questions of human existence and our place in the universe when everything can be mass-customized to create personal identity?

CAN THE SPECTACLE BE CULTURE JAMMED?

The global media networks are used to disseminate images of rebellion and resistance, images that become commodities exchanged in the marketplace to create profits for the corporations and personas for consumers. As the founder of *Adbusters*, Kalle Lasn believes that capitalist culture and consumer society can be countered via "culture jamming." In the first reading in this chapter, Lasn explains how the signs of consumption can be turned back on consumption to generate a countercultural rebellion and a liberating freedom of expression. For Lasn, this is nothing less than meme warfare.

But is it that easy? Can the spectacle be jammed? Or is culture jamming merely the way another niche audience reflects their ideas back to themselves or to the social media overlords and their big data? Is culture jamming for rebels what Carl Sagan's *Cosmos: A Personal Voyage* (1980) and Neil deGrasse Tyson's *Cosmos: A Spacetime Odyssey* (2014) were for science geeks? As discussed in appendix B ("Media and Pseudoscience"), the 2014 *Cosmos* series tried some "science jamming" aimed at the dumbed-down media and decreasing scientific literacy in America. The ratings suggest the series was only partially successful. Similarly, will culture jamming be a pastime for those who want to rebel against social injustice and corruption while remaining ignored by the rest of the society?

Lasn is right that culture jamming represents meme warfare. So does Brian Cox's *Wonders of the Universe*, Christopher Nolan's *Interstellar* (2014), and Neil deGrasse Tyson's and Ann Druyan's *Cosmos: Possible Worlds* (2020). In the technocapitalist media spectacle, are "rebellion" and "science" mere lifestyle choices and intellectual stances sold to niche audiences who want to see and buy the symbols of their world and worldviews? Are rebellion, science, and freedom trapped in the spectacle of memes and the hyperreality of endless reproductions, where the signs of science and rebellion prevail over real scientific literacy and real rebellion?

FIGHTING THE FUTURE IN *FIGHT CLUB*

For many students of the twenty-first century, *Fight Club* is a film that deeply resonates and repels, often at the same time. Many reasons contribute to these simultaneous feelings, three of which are relevant here: the rebels who are seeking to overthrow the system, the critique of consumer society, and the overall dystopian vision of the future.

IS TYLER DURDEN A REAL REBEL?

One of the key challenges in the twenty-first century is to discern the real rebels from the hyperreal rebels in our 24/7 media environments.[7] Cool movie rebels may offer salient criticisms of media and culture, but that does not

---

7   Those who are using media technologies to bravely rebel against inhumane conditions and unjust governments in hopes of personal and social opportunity in a freer, more enlightened world of tomorrow deserve much support and encouragement. This includes recent marches and protest movements like MeToo, Black Lives Matter, the Climate Strike, and the March for Science. But those who want to rebel in taking societies backward to some imaginary "golden age" of superstition, censorship, repression, patriarchy, or premodern laws—then, speaking for myself, their movements are not worthy of support, at least not from anyone who desires a future civilization that is socially and politically organized around principles like those in the First Amendment and the UN Universal Declaration of Human Rights.

mean their main cause or end goal is desirable. Consider Tyler Durden (Brad Pitt), the rebel leader in *Fight Club*. Durden has many insightful witticisms and cultural criticisms. From among many, here are a few:

> Advertising has us chasing cars and clothes, working jobs we hate so we can buy shit we don't need. We're the middle children of history, man. No purpose or place. We have no Great War. No Great Depression. Our Great War's a spiritual war ... our Great Depression is our lives. We've all been raised on television to believe that one day we'd all be millionaires, and movie gods, and rock stars. But we won't. And we're slowly learning that fact. And we're very, very pissed off.
>
> We're consumers. We are by-products of a lifestyle obsession. Murder, crime, poverty, these things don't concern me. What concerns me are celebrity magazines, television with five hundred channels, some guy's name on my underwear. Rogaine, Viagra, Olestra.
>
> You are not your job. You're not how much money you have in the bank. You're not the car you drive. You're not the contents of your wallet. You're not your fucking khakis.
>
> The things you own end up owning you.

So is Tyler a real rebel? You decide. *Fight Club* comes from a long line of efforts to resist mass society via the quest for authenticity and autonomy. Beginning with the beatniks of the 1950s, there have been numerous efforts to resist mass culture and consumer society, to create a revolutionary counterculture, including hippies and leftists, punks and fundamentalists, goths and gangstas, and so on. The new struggle is a war on homogeneity, seeking authenticity in a culture of mass production, seeking identity in a culture of mass mediation, seeking roots in a culture of rapid acceleration.

While all these countercultural groups claim to have escaped the mass hive mind, their efforts to resist or revolt seem to have provided more markets for capitalism, be it corporate or entrepreneurial capitalism, apparently ever-ready to create and manufacture the lifestyles of the proliferating countercultures. To satisfy these new markets of "resistance," capitalism has evolved from mass-production to mass-customization to mass-simulation, cloning and copying all possible lifestyles for experiential consumption.

TAKING DOWN CONSUMER SOCIETY

Without doubt, *Fight Club* offers a trenchant critique of the consumer culture celebrated by the media and the advertising industries of the world. Indeed, consumer society has run amok, selling us prepackaged identities and "new and improved" lifestyles while trashing the planet with its supersized excess, embodied in malls, obesity, grande lattes, Hummers, McMansions, credit cards, government debt, and the deficit financing of an entire consumption lifestyle—"The things you own end up owning you." So consume now, pay later, and f*ck the future.

At the beginning of the twentieth century, the great economic fear was that industrial capitalism would not provide enough goods and wealth to the workers who produced the goods in the factories. Since it seemed that only the wealthy (those who owned or controlled the factories) would have decent lifestyles, many people thought industrial communism was the answer. By 1991, industrial communism had collapsed in the former Soviet Union, leaving the ever-evolving consumer capitalism to spread unchecked around the world. Now, at the beginning of the twenty-first century, capitalism is charged with providing too much production and too many goods at prices too cheap, thus leaving a bloated society and a polluted planet.

Can we do without the mechanized, mass-produced, consumer lifestyle? Tyler and the space monkeys would shout, "Hell, yes!" Or maybe it would be "Fuck, yeah!" followed by a punch to my face.

Of course, we must learn to do without the excess, bloat, and hyperconsumption, but targeting our rebellion is not quite that easy. Should we rebel against electricity? Indoor plumbing? Medicine? Science? Art? Design? Fashion? When you think about it, humans are much more than mere economic producers and consumers, as instilled into our intellectual culture by economists, business leaders, and the shallow talking heads on TV. Since the earliest beginnings of society and civilization, humans have been producing objects for reasons directly related to aesthetics, identities, and cosmologies—be they personal or cultural or universal. The designs for fashion, products, furniture, homes, buildings, bridges, factories, skyscrapers, skylines, and even rocket ships came about based on aesthetic reasons, often to generate feelings of beauty, awe, and wonder.[8] To utterly do away with design, machines, or mass production would eliminate most of the art and aesthetics of the cultural world, the very things that speak to us as human beings. Just as we need food, shelter, and knowledge, humanity needs aesthetics (in its many forms), and that need is wired into the evolution of the species.[9]

In fact, the mass production of modernism sought to create the unity of form and function in the aesthetics of design. That's why Jack's detonation of his IKEA-decorated condo in *Fight Club* suggests more than a rebellion against conformity and consumer society, for the goods destroyed were derivatives of designs born of modernism. After all, the specialty of IKEA is a derivative modernism, a modernism made cozy and comfy. For most furniture consumers, the simulacra of IKEA is the closest they will ever get to sitting in designs by the real modernist or futurist architects such as Le Corbusier, Frank Lloyd Wright, Buckminster Fuller, Zaha Hadid, or Frank Gehry.

The conceptual understanding of *modern* architecture and furniture is largely absent in cities around the world, leaving millions of people unable to distinguish between intellectual appreciation for modernism and the simulation of taste that fuels shallow and trendy consumerism—the very intellectual condition facing Jack. In this domestic void, we find chains like IKEA offering low-cost simulacra that look cheap and often feel spiritually empty—like copies of derivatives of knockoffs of originals. The overwhelming majority of consumers have rejected domestic modernism anyway, opting for the mass-produced crafts and simulated authenticity of Home Depot or the mass-produced styles of Martha Stewart, where devolutionary traditionalism is masked as domestic perfectionism. IKEA, Home Depot, and Martha Stewart are the three design concepts that fill the American home, and only one is a distant derivative of modernism, the one detonated in *Fight Club*.

None of this is a defense of the status quo, massive consumer excess, and accelerating trash and pollution. As humans, we need aesthetics and design, but as a civilization, we need to immediately realize that more and more stuff from IKEA, Martha Stewart, or Home Depot will not fill the voids in our personal and cultural identities. Neither will a Hummer, a McMansion, or a pair of Manolo Blahnik shoes, as glamorized in *Sex and the City*. Filling the voids is a task for art, nature, theory, philosophy, and understanding.

REBELS OF THE FUTURE-PAST?

Such understanding is where secular philosophy and civil society have fallen far too short, surrendering the meaning of existence to "cool hunters," *Mad Men*, Hollywood, and Silicon Valley, not to mention the New Agers and age-old televangelists. That's why the deepest issues in the 24/7 culture are not mere left versus right or communism versus capitalism, for they are indeed "spiritual," as Tyler exclaims in the quote above. These "spiritual" issues are ultimately cosmic. Consider two scenes featuring Jack:

1. Jack stands at a copy machine in the film *Fight Club* and says, "With insomnia, nothing is real. Everything's far away. Everything's a copy of a copy of a copy. When deep space exploration ramps up, it'll be the corporations that name everything: the IBM Stellar Sphere, the Microsoft Galaxy, Planet Starbucks."

2. After detonating his condo and wandering the edge of the exploded hole in the side of the building fifteen stories up, Jack offers the following thoughts: "Go to the edge of the floor, fifteen stories above the parking lot, and look at the city lights and stars, and you're gone. It's all so beyond us. Up here, in the miles of night between the stars and the Earth."

In the first passage, we see Jack's expression of hyperreality, where "nothing is real" in the world of copies of copies of copies. But Jack simultaneously expresses the conditions of the vast cosmos revealed by modern

8   David E. Nye, *American Technological Sublime* (Cambridge, MA: MIT Press, 1994).
9   Ellen Dissanayake, *Homo Aestheticus: Where Art Comes From and Why* (New York: Free Press, 1992).

science—"Everything's far away." Looking into the sky from his destroyed condo, he realizes that his previous identity is gone, for the stars are "all so beyond us." These lines reinforce a key idea in this book: the challenge for secular philosophy and global civilization is to provide a sense of meaning, beauty, purpose, and destiny in the universe *revealed by our most powerful media technologies*. In *Slugging Nothing*, I wrote:

> As it is in *Fight Club*, so it is around the world. Fundamentalists and terrorists of all stripes are waging wars with the perceived ills of the modern project. ... Modern production filled the cultural universe with material things, but modern science revealed a cosmic universe of vast voids and no self-evident meaning. Precisely as science and technology reveal a complex and expanding universe, fundamentalists and terrorists seek a return to technological simplicity and spiritual purity in a shrinking cultural world, sort of like the Big Bang being countered by the Big Crunch. At a deeper level, Project Mayhem and Fight Club were not merely battling modernity but were waging war against one of the key space-time parameters of the modern project—the idea of an optimistic and enlightened future. Tyler Durden and the space monkeys were fighting the future, struggling to hasten the end of the future, to effect a reversal of the trajectory of tomorrow, symbolized by getting humanity to "go all back to zero."[10]

Yearning for the reset button, the clean slate, the chance to get back to zero—that's why Tyler Durden's vision of the future is a radical reversal, a return to preindustrial civilization. In Tyler's future,

> You'll hunt elk through the damp canyon forests around the ruins of Rockefeller Center and dig clams next to the skeleton of the Space Needle leaning at a forty-five-degree angle. ... Imagine stalking elk past department store windows and stinking racks of beautiful rotting dresses and tuxedos on hangers; you'll wear leather clothes that will last you the rest of your life, and you'll climb the wrist-thick kudzu vines that wrap the Sears Tower. Jack and the beanstalk, you'll climb up through the dripping forest canopy and the air will be so clean you'll see tiny figures pounding corn and laying strips of venison to dry in the empty carpool lane of an abandoned superhighway stretching eight lanes wide and August-hot for a thousand miles. This was the goal of Project Mayhem, Tyler said, the complete and utter destruction of civilization.[11]

This sounds romantic and adventurous until you realize it would be horrible and terrifying. Tyler's vision is little different from the "anti-industrial" future idealized by the Unabomber, the professor-turned-terrorist who mail-bombed engineers and scientists in the 1980s and 1990s in America.[12] In fact, it would be little different from the future-pasts idealized by radical Luddites and radical fundamentalists, who want to return to antitechnological or anti-intellectual civilizations that would only bring about a patriarchal, premodern world of death and destruction, ignorance and endless tribal warfare. In this future-past, billions of humans would die off almost immediately due to starvation, disease, and the battles for the few remaining foods in the absence of refrigeration and electricity. Literally, the Dark Ages would return, and the few survivors could gaze up at the now-starry skies and wonder what went wrong.

For these future-pasts, forget the internet, human rights, and modern civilization. Forget art, science, media, movies, and medicine, not to mention margaritas, chips and salsa, and a plate of sizzling fajitas. As I wrote,

---

10 Barry Vacker, *Slugging Nothing: Fighting the Future in Fight Club* (Philadelphia: Theory Vortex Books, 2009), 39. This slender monograph was previously published in Read Mercer Schuchardt, ed., *You Do Not Talk About Fight Club* (Dallas: Benbella Books, 2008), 175–206.

11 Chuck Palahniuk, *Fight Club* (New York: Owl Books, 1996), 116.

12 FC, *The Unabomber Manifesto* (Berkeley, CA: Jolly Roger Press, 1995).

This is the future idealized in *Fight Club*, a premodern culture roaming amidst the ruins of the modern and postmodern worlds. The space monkeys are the noble savages of the non-information age, the next humans of the non-future, the hunter-gatherers glorified in *The Unabomber Manifesto*. In this cultural reversal, the skyscraper metropolis is replaced by the urban rain forest, the metrosexual by the space monkey, the superhighway by the walking trail, the fast food burger by the drying venison, the five-star restaurant by the campfire cookout, the joystick by the bare fist, and the Enlightenment by the fight club.[13]

Modern civilization surely has many, many flaws, mostly caused by humans and their continued lack of social and cultural evolution—imperialism, racism, fascism, nationalism, nuclear weapons, mindless consumerism, climate change, ecological destruction, massive pollution, grotesque inequalities, total surveillance, media spectacle, and far too many McMansions, to name a few. Along with the "cult of individuality," all of these deserve to be rebelled against and their worldviews overthrown. There are no easy solutions, no one thing that fixes all things. Taming narcissism will prove to be a huge challenge, precisely because it is supported by our smart phones (and tablets and laptops) and powers all the simulacra of individualism—egotism, exhibitionism, hedonism, tribalism, and consumerism.

But modern civilization also shows some of the great things human can do when they cooperate using art, science, technology, and the best of our humanist social ideals—books, museums, medicine, electricity, indoor plumbing, jetliners, the internet, widespread access to art and education, affordable clothing and fashion, human rights and democratic elections, national parks and wilderness areas, the great buildings and skyscrapers, walking on the moon, and the Hubble Space Telescope, to name a few. For me, a future without fashion, wilderness, diversity (cultural and ecological), medicine, great architecture, space telescopes, and margaritas on the rocks (with real lemon, lime, tequila, triple sec, and salt) is not a future worth having.

---

13 Vacker, *Slugging Nothing*, 73–74.

"THE REVOLUTIONARY IMPULSE" AND "DEMARKETING LOOPS"
from *Culture Jam*

KALLE LASN is an author, activist, and founder of *Adbusters*, the magazine which helped inspire the Occupy Wall Street movement. His most recent books include *Meme Wars: The Creative Deconstruction of Classical Economics* (2012).

In his book *Lipstick Traces*, American cultural critic Greil Marcus fixes The Sex Pistols' Johnny Rotten squarely in the tradition of the rebel seer. Rotten was a gleeful anarchist who used the word "fuck" on television and sang like he meant to change the world—or at least explode the dreamy, Beatles-fueled optimism of the day, and stick a fork into classic rock. He somehow rose above the obvious joke of The Pistols—the naked commercialism and hype of a band without much talent—and created something vital.

It's not clear whether Rotten knew anything about the Situationist International. But The Sex Pistols and the SI were most definitely on the same page, philosophically. Their song "Anarchy in the U.K." espoused, in crudely poetic form, the philosophy of the movement. The Pistols wanted to live "not as an object but as a subject of the story," as Marcus puts it. That's about as good a working definition of the culture jammers' ethos as you'll ever find.

Marcus recalls watching Johnny Rotten shouting madly over the band's guitars in front of the Berlin Wall and understanding that "his aim ... was to take in all the rage, intelligence and strength in his being and then fling them back at the world; to make the world notice; to make the world doubt its most cherished and unexamined beliefs." I think culture jammers can learn a lot from the original punks. They were one of the first to feel

the nihilism and to rail against a world that offered no future—and for a few years their rage shook the world.

The punks, like the hippies, yippies, beats, anarchists, Dadaists, surrealists, automatistes, fluxists and any number of other disaffected visionaries, represented an age-old spirit of spontaneous defiance toward the established order. But it was the Situationists who first applied that spirit of anarchy to modern media culture. They were the first to understand how the media spectacle slowly corrodes the human psyche. They were, in a sense, the first postmodern revolutionaries.

The Situationists were originally just eight artists and writers, most of them European, who sat down one July day in 1957 in the little town of Cosio d'Arroscia, Italy, to have a little fun together over Gauloises and absinthe. Though a reasonably short-lived group (by the '70s, most everyone had forgotten about them), they generated an anarchic drive that a generation of students, artists and radicals recognized as the real thing.

The Situationists declared a commitment to "a life of permanent novelty." They were interested only in freedom, and just about any means to it were justified. The creativity of everyday people, which consumer capitalism and communism had weakened but not killed, desperately needed to find expression. Down with the bureaucracies and hierarchies and ideologies that stifled spontaneity and free will. To the Situationists, you are—everyone is—a creator of situations, a performance artist, and the performance, of course, is your life, lived in your own way. Various stunts were concocted to foster spontaneous living. Situationist members suggested knocking down churches to make space for children to play, and putting switches on the street lamps so lighting would be under public control.

The Situationists believed that many times a day, each of us comes to a little fork in the path. We can then do one of two things: act the way we normally, reflexively act, or do something a little risky and wild, but genuine. We can choose to live our life as "a moral, poetic, erotic, and almost spiritual refusal" to cooperate with the demands of consumer culture.

The Situationists spoke often of the "spectacle" of modern life. The term encompassed everything from billboards to art exhibitions to soccer matches to radio and TV. Broadly speaking, it meant modern society's "spectacular" level of commodity consumption and hype. Everything human beings once experienced directly had been turned into a show put on by someone else. Real living had been replaced by prepackaged experiences and media-created events. Immediacy was gone. Now there was only "mediacy"—life as mediated through other instruments, life as a media creation. The Situationists used the term "kidnapped": The spectacle had "kidnapped" our real lives, co-opting whatever authenticity we once had.

I think this helps explain the strong visceral reaction so many people had to Nike's use of the Beatles tune "Revolution," and, later, to Apple's appropriation of Bob Dylan and The Gap's (posthumous) mugging of Jack Kerouac. Nostalgic, griping yuppies may not have been able to articulate it perfectly, but they understood that some fundamental part of their lives had been stolen.

In the Richard Linklater film *Before Sunrise*, the young hero, played by Ethan Hawke, has an existential crisis: He suddenly grows sick to death of his own company. Every party he goes to, there he is. Every bus he rides, every class he attends, he runs into … himself. For him, even his own identity had somehow become a spectacle. Here Linklater is staring into the Situationist abyss, and finding it a little terrifying. To paraphrase Situationist leader Guy Debord: Where the self is by proxy, it is not. This may also explain why one of the juiciest consumer target groups is the man or woman known as

the "emulator." Emulators look for products that make them feel like somebody else—someone more important. Since no product can help you fully escape your old identity, frustration mounts, a credit card is produced and the cycle of alienation deepens. (Situationists might point to emulators as proof of a devolution in the state of living: from "being" to "having," and then from "having" to "appearing to have.")

Debord remains a largely unheralded visionary. Derided in his later years, nearly canonized in France immediately following his suicide in 1967 and then gradually forgotten, Debord is only now enjoying a little posthumous fame—especially in France, where a group calling themselves the "Perpendiculaires" have positioned themselves as spiritual progeny of the Situationists. They maintain that culture ought to be spread laterally (through salon-type discussions) rather than vertically (through TV and the Internet).

In some ways, Debord was even more of a pioneer of the mental environment than his high-profile coeval, Marshall McLuhan. Where McLuhan only described the mass-culture trance, Debord developed some effective ways to break out of it. One way was the *dérive*. Literally "the drift," the *dérive* was an idea borrowed from the Dadaists. The Situationists defined it as "locomotion without a goal." As a *dériviste*, you float through the city, open to whatever you come in contact with, thus exposing yourself to the whole spectrum of feelings you encounter by chance in everyday life. Openness is key. You embrace whatever you love, and in the process, you discover what it is you hate.

The Situationists believed the *dérive* could largely replace the old twin occupations of work and entertainment, and become a model for the "playful creation" of a new way of life. The *dériviste* is a drifter in the best possible sense, not someone down and out but up and beyond, living outside the stifling roles society prescribes for us. Living well, Debord said, involves the "systematic questioning of all the diversions and works of a society, a total critique of its idea of happiness."

Another of the Situationists' favorite tropes was *détournement*, which Debord proposed as a way for people to take back the spectacle that had kidnapped their lives. Literally a "turning around," *détournement* involved rerouting spectacular images, environments, ambiences and events to reverse or subvert their meaning, thus reclaiming them. With its limitless supply of ideas, ranging from rewriting the speech balloons of comic-strip characters, to altering the width of streets and the heights of buildings and the colors and shapes of doors and windows, to radically reinterpreting world events such as the 1965 Watts riots in Los Angeles, the *Internationale Situationniste*—the journal the Situationists published between 1958 and 1969—was a sometimes profound, sometimes absurd laboratory of provocation and *détournement*. Once, Debord altered a famous drawing of Lenin by placing a barebreasted woman on his forehead with the caption "The Universe Turns on the Tips of Breasts." Debord had his book *Mémoires* bound in heavy sandpaper so that when it was placed on the shelves of libraries, it would destroy other books. One famous *détournement* happened in the Notre Dame cathedral on Easter Sunday in 1950. With thousands of people watching, a Lettrist provocateur dressed as a Dominican monk slipped onto the altar and delivered a sermon accusing the Catholic Church of "the deadly diversion of the force of life in favor of an empty heaven," and then solemnly proclaimed that "God is dead." It was with this spirit of *détournement* that the Situationists invaded enemy territory and tried to "devalue the currency of the spectacle."

* * *

Demarketing. The whole concept lends itself to satire, possibly because it seems so foreign to most of us. The word has a sinister ring to it. Whatever else demarketing is, it's certainly un-American.

Advertising and marketing are so deeply embedded in our culture now that it's hard to imagine a time when product placement and network logo "burns" and "bugs" weren't everywhere you looked, when our lifestyles and culture weren't predicated on consumption. But that pre-marketing era was not so long ago: only two generations. Demarketing is about restoring a little of the sanity we enjoyed back then. It's about uncooling our consumer culture, reclaiming the real, recovering some of what has been lost since consumerism became the First World's new religion.

The other day, in a moment of guy-to-guy candor, a friend challenged me on my demarketing philosophy and my whole outlook on life. "Kalle," he said, "you complain about advertising, you complain about the big, bad media, you bitch about how much we consume and how we govern ourselves and how corporations are ruining America. You say you want a radically different way of life—a revolution. But would you really want to live in the kind of world you're proposing?"

I asked him to be more specific.

"Isn't the live-fast, die-hard lifestyle you can't stand the very thing that makes it so much fun to be American? Living large is our inheritance. It's what we fought for and won. We have the highest standard of living in the world because we earned it. We did it by taking risks and being inventive and working our butts off. So now maybe I want to drive fast, and rattle the windows with my music, and have sex with my wife in our backyard swimming pool, and watch *Monday Night Football* while burgers grill on the barbecue. And I want to be able to do these things without having to listen to your sanctimonious objections."

My friend had just returned from New York, which he sees as an exciting microcosm of America. "Sure it has problems. It's big, it's loud, it's congested, you can step on a dirty needle in Central Park and the cab driver may be too scared to take you to Harlem. But I'll bet if you asked most New Yorkers they'd tell you they wouldn't want to live anywhere else. If you sanitized New York, it wouldn't be New York. It'd be Baltimore. And if you sanitized America, it wouldn't be America. It'd be Sweden or Canada. Life wouldn't be worth living."

"You just don't get it," I told him. "I'm not trying to sanitize America. The world I'm proposing isn't some watered-down, politically correct place. It's wilder and more interesting than your world in every way. It's open TV airwaves where meme wars, not ratings wars, are fought every day. It's radical democracy—people telling governments and corporations what to do instead of the other way around. It's empowered citizens deciding for themselves what's 'cool'—not a society of consumer drones suckling at the corporate teat. It's living a life that's connected to the planet, knowing something about it, caring for it and handing it down to our children in some kind of decent shape.

"What I'm saying is that the American dream isn't working anymore, so let's face that reality and start building a new one."

I noticed my friend roll his eyes a couple of times as I spoke. In many ways he is the typical North

American—ambitious, competitive, successful. If he could convince me that he really is happy and alive, I'd have to concede that his way, though it's not my way, is perfectly valid. But I just don't see it. The supersize American lifestyle generates at least a little guilt in every marginally thoughtful person who pursues it. There's a lot of dirty laundry in my friend's life that he can't ignore, no matter how far under the bed he shoves it. He sees me as a disgruntled Lefty pissing on the American parade; I see him as a man in upper-income-bracket denial, getting what he can while the going is good even as his world is collapsing around him. Of one thing I am sure: His hyperconsumptive lifestyle isn't cool anymore. The old American dream is dying. Change is coming.

One of the great secrets of demarketing the American dream is *détourning* it, in the public imagination, with a dream that's even more seductive. What's better than being rich? *Being spontaneous, authentic, alive.*

The new American dream is simply to approach life full-on, without undue fear or crippling self-censorship, pursuing joy and novelty as if tomorrow you'll be in the ground. The Situationists called this impulse "the will to playful creation," and they believed it should be extended "to all known forms of human relationships." There's no one more alive than the person who is openly, freely improvising—which is why the best stand-up comics love hecklers, and why the best hosts love wild-card dinner guests, and why the most electric political figures love deviating from their prepared scripts on live TV. There's no other way to discover what's at your core. This is what the new American dream is all about, and this is the kind of person the culture jammer aspires to be: someone who, to paraphrase Ray Bradbury, "jumps off cliffs and builds his wings on the way down."

UNCOOLING CONSUMPTION

On the most basic level, demarketing is simply about not buying. An anticonsumerist lifestyle flat-out repudiates the whole idea of marketing. When you don't buy, you don't buy in to consumer culture. When you don't buy in, corporations lose their hold on you.

One increasingly visible group of people have embraced this idea as a faith. They have looked hard at the way we do things in this country and decided it's no longer their way. Somewhere between the time Faith Popcorn coined the term "cashing out" and the time actor Sherry Stringfield walked away from the TV show *E.R.* (to rediscover the true meaning of life, a.k.a. leisure time and her partner), the downshifting movement took off. Thousands of Americans now call their lifestyle "voluntary simplicity" (after Duane Elgin's 1981 book of the same name). Some of these downshifters left high-powered jobs and took drastic pay cuts in order to make more time for family, friends, community, meaningful work. Others were wage slaves who simply decided to improve what Vicki Robin and Joe Dominguez, in *Your Money or Your Life*, call their "joy-to-stuff ratio." Away with frantic living, they have declared. Away with the acquisitive, secular culture that causes even the most sensible souls to drift out of plumb. Too much work, too much clutter, too much distance between expectation and outcome, between investment and payoff, between head and heart will spell the end of us. The downshifters concluded that a higher goal than to amass wealth is to concentrate on culture as Alexander Solzhenitsyn defined it: "the development, enrichment and improvement of non-material life." They understand intuitively what statistics bear out: The aggregate level of American life fulfillment peaked in 1957, and with a couple of brief exceptions, it's been downhill from there.

We hear many dramatic downshifting stories: the eight-figure bond trader who, while getting his shoes shined, picks up a copy of *The Tightwad Gazette* or *Living Green* ("Live simply, that all may simply live"), has an epiphany, bails out of the modern contest and flees to the country to farm hogs or write murder mysteries. But this kind of down-shifter is hardly the norm.

Many downshifters had no choice in the matter; they were canned, and that proved to be the best thing that ever happened to them. Alice Kline, whom Juliet Schor describes in *The Overspent American*, was a merchandising director for a high-fashion company. When she was wooed to return to lucrative full-time work after being laid off, Kline insisted on her own terms: chiefly, a four-day workweek. Priceless to her was the freedom to pad around dreamily in her slippers on Friday mornings. Downshifters like Kline cling to the promise of three things: more time, less stress and more balance. It's a fairly uncapitalistic brew, and to my knowledge only one advertiser has ever tried to sell it. In a network TV ad for the Mormon Church some years ago, a little boy walks tentatively into a board-meeting-in-progress, a tableful of men in suits. He shuffles over to the fellow at the end of the table, peers up and says, "Dad, is time really worth money?" The room falls silent. The boy has his father's attention. "Why yes, Jimmy, it is." Whereupon the kid plunks his piggy bank down on the table. "Well, I'd like to play ball after dinner."

Culture jammers are different from all of the downshifters thus far described. They aren't just trying to get themselves off the consumer treadmill and make more time for their kids. They dissent because they have a strong gut feeling that our culture has gone scandalously wrong and they just can't participate in it anymore. The old American dream of endless acquisition sickens them; it enervates them. For jammers downshifting is not simply a way of adjusting our routines; it's adopting a lifestyle of defiance against a culture run amok, a revolutionary step toward a fundamental transformation of the American way of life.

In *Small Is Beautiful*, a key book in the downshifting canon, E. F. Schumacher sets up an exquisitely sensible template for living. The point of life, he says, is "to obtain the maximum of well-being with the minimum of consumption." This idea is so profoundly simple that it may well become the credo—the cool—of the twenty-first century. It applies in all areas of culture, from food to cars to fashion. "It would be the height of folly … to go in for complicated tailoring when a much more beautiful effect can be achieved by the skillful draping of uncut material," Schumacher writes. By this reasoning, it's cooler to ride a bike than cruise around in an air-conditioned BMW. Or to wear a plain white T-shirt than, say, a $125 Ashcroft Freddy Couples golf shirt. It's true, of course. And the truly cool have always known it.

UNCOOLING FAST FOOD

Buying and eating food has, like any act of consumption, political and even moral implications. "Every decision we make about food is a vote for the kind of world we want to live in," wrote Frances M. Lappé in her classic little book, *Diet for a Small Planet*. Every purchase of a can of Coke or a trucked-in Chilean nectarine initiates

a multinational chain of responses that we simply can't afford to ignore.

Even when we exercise some discretion—watch what we eat when we can, pay attention to whether we're buying Maxwell House coffee (a Philip Morris brand) or Nescafé or whole coffee beans from Sumatra—we can still be duped at the supermarket level. That's because we have allowed our eating habits to be shaped by transnational agribusiness. In the heavily concentrated food industry, the likes of Archer Daniels Midland ("supermarket to the world"), Cargill (the world's largest agribusiness) and Philip Morris (one of the world's largest food corporations) are framing our choices.

Food corporations are formidable opponents because so much of what they do is invisible. One of the things they do is cut us off from the source of our food—a concept known as "distancing."

Distancing is a nasty bit of business, but it shouldn't surprise us. As Brewster Kneen, author of *Invisible Giant*, puts it, we are "distanced" from our mother's breast the moment a baby bottle is inserted into our mouth. "From that moment on, corporate America gets involved, hawking processed 'junior' foods and baby foods that contain lots of salt, sugar and chemicals. Thus we become eager consumers of Kentucky Fried Chicken, Doritos, Pizza Hut and Pepsi (all the same company) later in life." Eventually, we find ourselves participating in the ultimate act of distancing: eating a genetically altered tomato whose mother plant does not even exist.

The average pound of food in America travels 1,300 miles before it reaches a kitchen table. That's inefficient and unsustainable. Demarketing food involves closing the gap between the source and the plate. It means turning away from fast foods and superstores and embracing farmers' markets and the family kitchen; away from hothouse tomatoes and toward your own local supplier, and eventually, perhaps, your own garden plot. These decisions will change your life, if you have the appetite for the journey.

The commitment involves cutting, bit by bit, the food megacorporations out of your life. This is not so different from weaning yourself off a destructive yet magnetic relationship with another human being. Every time you change your mind and don't slip into McDonald's for a quickie, every time you squirt some lemon into a glass of water instead of popping open a Coke, every time you decide to put that jar of Maxwell House coffee back on the shelf, you strike the gong of freedom.

When a groundswell of people train themselves to do all of these things, to demarket on a daily, personal level, we are applying the bottom jaw of the Strategic Pincer. The top jaw of the pincer is a series of radio and TV campaigns that ridicule the fast/junk-food industry. Working from both ends—bottom up and top down—the pincer will transform the way America, and the world, eats.

Junk food is one of the most frequently advertised products on TV: that makes it a big target. Today, food jammers take on the junk-food corporations the way antismoking activists locked horns with the tobacco industry in the 70s. They try to "contaminate" junk food in the public mind. Every time an antijunk-food ad ("Fact: Over 50 percent of the calories in this Big Mac come from fat") airs, a replicating meme is planted. Every time an uncommercial appears on TV attacking those companies, their brands are a little bit uncooled.

Suppose one day a car full of teenage kids drives by the Golden Arches and everyone wants to stop for a bite. But one kid, inspired by a TV subvert he saw the night before, makes a crack about the McDonald's employee standing over the 900-degree french-fry cooker, wearing the funny hat, making minimum wage and saying, "Somebody remind me again why I'm not selling drugs?" His friends chuckle. And maybe they all still stop at McDonald's for that meal. But now they're thinking about McDonald's in a new way. The oppositional meme has been planted.

In the nutrition wars, change is afoot. People are rethinking their food and where it comes from. The idea is catching on that each of us should "have" a personal farmer, the way we now have a doctor, lawyer or dentist, a single individual we can trust to supply us with healthy, safe, flavorful produce. So are farmers' markets where regional producers (and only regional producers) are invited to sell their wares. So are community "box schemes" where hampers of fresh fruit and vegetables—whatever's in season—are delivered direct from local farms to consumers' doors. Out with Wonder Bread from megamarkets, in with community-supported agriculture, say the new food seers. Down with policies that encourage industrial, irradiated, bioengineered food

production to the detriment of everybody but agribusiness. Up with flavor! Up with nutrition! Up with local control!

UNCOOLING CALVIN

When fashion and cosmetics advertisers market our very physiognomies as renewable, reinventable commodities, we are dehumanized. We are used up and discarded. In the semiotics of advertising, we are "cut." The young woman made to feel insecure about her sexuality stops behaving authentically. She either comes on like a virago or, conversely, starts staying home Friday nights to compose sad poetry from her black heart. Likewise, a young man made to feel insecure about his sexuality either withdraws or grows angry and aggressive and starts taking what he wants.

As no other company in the last fifteen years, Calvin Klein has commodified sex, and in the process brutalized our notions of sexuality and self-worth. The man at the head is a pioneer. He's credited with creating the ad strategy of moving fashion ads from magazines to outdoor billboards and bus cards, and of trumpeting the era of the commercial nude.

Most people remember his 1995 campaign in which young models were crudely filmed in cheesy wood-paneled basements as an adult voice called instructions from the wings. The ads reeked of chicken-hawk porn. *Advertising Age's* Bob Garfield called it "the most profoundly disturbing campaign in TV history." The spots so offended public sensibility that they prompted an investigation by the U.S. Justice Department to determine if the models were underage or child-porn laws were violated.

When I saw those ads I felt an animal rage stirring inside me. This was an affront much worse than simple Skinner-box behaviorism. Calvin wasn't just trying to program young people's choice of jeans, he was down in the subbasement of consciousness, where the very rudiments of identity are formed.

I could imagine Mr. Klein rubbing his hands with glee. Here he was exploiting one of our final taboos and milking the controversy he created for all it was worth. From a marketing perspective, he was in a win-win situation and the more controversy the better.

Imagine, for a moment, that the logo cK were the man, Calvin Klein. Would we feel any differently about the way he goes about his business? Calvin Klein is very interested in your teenage daughter. You see him flirting with her. He propositions her. He unzips her pants. He touches her. He sleeps with her. Finally, he prostitutes her. He degrades her sexuality for his profit and then, when she has paid out—literally and figuratively—he dumps her.

If you discovered someone had done this to your daughter, you'd probably call up a couple of your big-armed friends and pay the sonofabitch a visit. Yet what's the difference, in the end, between the cK ads and imagery exploiting her and Calvin doing it himself? Psychically speaking, a hole is still a hole, whether it was made with an auger or a billion drops of water.

The first stage of demarketing our bodies involves realizing the true source of our self-esteem problems. It's important to understand that we ourselves are not to blame. Body-image distortions, eating disorders, dieting and exercise addictions—these are intensely personal issues, fought with therapy and lonely sessions of clandestine vomiting after dinner. They're our responsibility, *but they are not our fault.* The issue is primarily a cultural and a corporate one, and that's the level on which it must be tackled. We must learn to direct our anger, not inwardly at ourselves, but outwardly at the beauty industry.

Can the almighty fashion industry be uncooled? In some ways, its dependence on fads and trends makes it exceptionally vulnerable. Targeting one company—one man—is a good beginning. Cutting significantly into Calvin Klein's sales will effectively launch the crusade to take back our bodies. Uncooling Calvin will send a shock wave through the whole industry; it will rattle the cosmetics companies, which now account for the largest individual product group (with the highest markups) in most big department stores; and it will affect women's magazines, which have generated enormous profits by convincing women they are sexual machines. It will send a powerful message that the pageant is over, and that from now on beauty will no longer be defined by the likes of Mr. Klein—or any other Mister.

The jammer's best strategy is to plant antifashion memes on popular TV shows such as CNN's *Style with Elsa Klensch* and its Canadian knockoff, *Fashion File.* I hear fear in network executives' voices every time I try to buy airtime for our "Obsession Fetish" campaign on the big three networks or CNN. These executives practically do contortions trying to explain why they won't sell us the airtime; they know that Calvin Klein and indeed the whole fashion industry would significantly cut back their TV advertising budgets as soon as our campaign started. The fashion industry is already held in disdain by many. The only thing that keeps its bubble aloft is this uncontested billion-dollar presence in women's magazines and on the airwaves. When we win the legal right to buy airtime and challenge the industry on TV, that bubble will burst. And then it will be Calvin's and the industry's turn to feel insecure.

UNCOOLING THE CAR

Jammers are now targeting automobiles as the next pariah industry. We want to sever the intimate connection between people and their cars, just as we cut the intimate connection between people and cigarettes. We want auto executives to feel just as squeezed and beleaguered as tobacco executives. We want them to have a hard time looking their kids in the eye and explaining exactly what they do for a living.

Resistance to private cars is already building. In San Francisco thousands of bicyclists roll out of the Embarcadero district, snarling traffic; a few hold up a giant effigy of Willie Brown, the mayor who labeled cyclists "terrorists." In Portland, Oregon, the city council experiments with an Amsterdam-style system of free commuter bicycles, which can be borrowed and returned at various points downtown. In Canada, jammers air anticar ads, breaking the automobile industry's uncontested, uninterrupted fifty-year run on TV.

Across the First World, pressure mounts for more bike lanes on urban streets. Several high-profile architects and planners weigh in with striking visions of the ecofriendly cities of the next era. Some big oil corporations, British Petroleum among them, finally accept some responsibility for global warming and pledge to sink money into research to develop cleaner petroleum products. Around the world a half dozen companies compete to produce commercially viable fuel cells that will power cars at highway speeds with fewer harmful by-products. Seth Dunn of the WorldWatch Institute likens what's happening now to a full-circle return, one century later, to "engineless carriages."

On a strategic level, however, much work remains to be done.

More than any other product, the car stands as a symbol of the need for a true-cost marketplace, wherein the price you pay for a car reflects *all* the costs of production and operation. That doesn't just mean paying the manufacturing cost plus markup, plus oil, gas and insurance. It means paying for the pollution, for building and maintaining the roads, for the medical costs of accidents and the noise and the aesthetic degradation caused by urban sprawl. It means paying for traffic policing and for military protection of oil fields and supply lines.

The true cost of a car must also include the real but hard-to-estimate environmental cost *to future generations* of dealing with the oil and ozone-depletion and climate-change problems the car is creating today. If we added up the best available estimates, we'd come to a startling conclusion: The fossil fuel–based automobile industry is being subsidized by unborn generations to the tune of hundreds of billions of dollars every year. Why should they have to pay to clean up our mess?

In the true-cost marketplace of the future, no one will prevent you from driving. You will simply have to pay the real cost of piloting your ton of metal, spewing a ton of carbon out of the tailpipe every year. Your private automobile will cost you, by some estimates, around $100,000. And a tankful of gas, $250.

Moving gradually over a ten-year period toward true-cost driving (giving the global automakers clear signals for long-term planning) would force us to reinvent the way we get around. When the majority of people can no longer afford to drive, enormous public demand for monorails, bullet trains, subways and streetcars would emerge. Automakers would design ecofriendly alternatives: vehicles that recycle their own energy, human and fuel-powered hybrids, lightweight solar vehicles. Citizens would demand more bike lanes, pedestrian paths and car-free downtowns. And a paradigm shift in urban planning would ensue.

About five or so years into the transition period, personal automobiles would become more trouble than they're worth. People would start enjoying their calmer lifestyles and the new psychogeography of their cities. The rich car owner still cruising through town belching carbon would become the object of scorn and mockery.

In many ways the true-cost marketplace is the ultimate, all-purpose demarketing device. Every purchase becomes a demarketing loop. Every transaction penalizes the "bad" products and rewards the "good." Jammers envision a global, true-cost marketplace in which the price of *every* product tells the ecological truth. The price of a pack of cigarettes would include the extra burden it places on the health care system; the price of an avocado would reflect the real cost of flying it over thousands of miles to your supermarket; the cost of nuclear energy (if indeed we can afford it) would include the estimated cost of storing the radioactive waste in the Earth's crust for up to tens of millions of years.

True cost is a simple but potent way to redesign the global economy's basic incentives in a relatively uncharged political atmosphere. Conservatives like the idea because it's a logical extension of their free-market philosophy. Progressives like it because it involves a radical restructuring of the status quo. Governments like it because it gives them a vital new function to fulfill: that of calculating the true costs of products, levying ecotaxes and managing our bioeconomic affairs for the long term. And environmentalists like it because it may be the only way to achieve sustainability in our lifetimes.

UNCOOLING THE SPECTACLE

Demarketing and the true-cost economy are the metamemes that bring the culture jammers' revolution together. It all sounds pretty ambitious, but the first steps are straightforward. Using a methodical, systematic social marketing campaign, we start at the personal level and grow in scope. We begin by demarketing our bodies, our minds, our children. Then we join with like-minded jammers to demarket whole systems. We go after our chief social and cultural rituals, now warped beyond recognition by commercial forces, and try to restore their original authenticity. Mother's Day, Easter,

Halloween, Thanksgiving, Christmas: All are ripe for demarketing. All can be reclaimed.

Students insist on ad-free learning environments. Voters demand that election advertising be replaced with televised town hall–type meetings in which the candidates face the electorate directly. Athletes refuse to endorse unethical companies. Fans insist that stadiums be named after their heroes, not corporations. Reporters make sure that advertorials are not part of their job descriptions. Artists, writers and filmmakers work on product marketing as well as social marketing campaigns. Families get food from their gardens and "therapy" from each other, from friends, neighbors and community.

We reverse the spin cycle. We demarket our news, our entertainments, our lifestyles and desires—and, eventually, maybe even our dreams.

WHAT IS SURVEILLANCE CAPITALISM?

SHOSHANA ZUBOFF is the Charles Edward Wilson Professor emerita, Harvard Business School. She is the author of In *The Age of the Smart Machine: the Future of Work and Power* and *The Support Economy: Why Corporations Are Failing Individuals and the Next Episode of Capitalism*. She received her PhD from Harvard University and her BA from the University of Chicago. For more information see: ShoshanaZuboff.com.

Surveillance capitalism's successful claims to freedom *and* knowledge, its structural independence from people, its collectivist ambitions, and the radical indifference that is necessitated, enabled, and sustained by all three now propel us toward a society in which capitalism does not function as a means to inclusive economic or political institutions. Instead, surveillance capitalism must be reckoned as a profoundly antidemocratic social force. The reasoning I employ is not mine alone. It echoes Thomas Paine's unyielding defense of the democratic prospect in *The Rights of Man*, the polemical masterpiece in which he contested the defense of monarchy in Edmund Burke's *Reflections on the Revolution in France*. Paine argued for the capabilities of the common person and against aristocratic privilege. Among his reasons to reject aristocratic rule was its lack of accountability to the needs of people, "because a body of men holding themselves accountable to nobody, ought not to be trusted by any body."[1]

Surveillance capitalism's antidemocratic and antiegalitarian juggernaut is best described as a market-driven coup from above. It is not a coup d'état in the classic sense but rather a *coup de gens:* an overthrow of the people concealed as the technological Trojan horse that is Big Other. On the strength of its annexation of human experience, this coup achieves exclusive concentrations of knowledge and power that sustain privileged influence over the division of learning in society: the privatization of the central principle of social ordering in the twenty-first century. Like the *adelantados* and their silent incantations of the *Requirimiento*, surveillance capitalism operates in the declarative form and imposes the social relations of a premodern absolutist authority. It is a form of tyranny that feeds on people but is not of the people. In a surreal paradox, this coup is celebrated as "personalization," although it defiles, ignores, overrides, and displaces everything about you and me that is personal.

"Tyranny" is not a word that I choose lightly. Like the instrumentarian hive, tyranny is the obliteration of politics. It is founded on its own strain of radical indifference in which every person, except the tyrant, is understood as an organism among organisms in an equivalency of Other-Ones. Hannah Arendt observed that tyranny is a perversion of egalitarianism because it treats all others as equally insignificant: "The tyrant rules in accordance with his own will and interest ... the ruler who rules one against all, and the 'all' he oppresses are all equal, namely equally powerless." Arendt notes that classical

---

1   Thomas Paine, *The Life and Works of Thomas Paine,* ed. William M. Van der Weyde (New Rochelle, NY: Thomas Paine Historical Society, 1925), 6:97.

political theory regarded the tyrant as "out of mankind altogether ... a wolf in human shape. ..."[2]

Surveillance capitalism rules by instrumentarian power through its materialization in Big Other, which, like the ancient tyrant, exists out of mankind while paradoxically assuming human shape. Surveillance capitalism's tyranny does not require the despot's whip any more than it requires totalitarianism's camps and gulags. All that is needed can be found in Big Other's reassuring messages and emoticons, the press of the others not in terror but in their irresistible inducements to confluence, the weave of your shirt saturated with sensors, the gentle voice that answers your queries, the TV that hears you, the house that knows you, the bed that welcomes your whispers, the book that reads you. ... Big Other acts on behalf of an unprecedented assembly of commercial operations that must modify human behavior as a condition of commercial success. It replaces legitimate contract, the rule of law, politics, and social trust with a new form of sovereignty and its privately administered regime of reinforcements.

Surveillance capitalism is a boundary-less form that ignores older distinctions between market and society, market and world, or market and person. It is a profit-seeking form in which production is subordinated to extraction as surveillance capitalists unilaterally claim control over human, societal, and political territories extending far beyond the conventional institutional terrain of the private firm or the market. Using Karl Polanyi's lens, we see that surveillance capitalism annexes human experience to the market dynamic so that it is reborn as behavior: the fourth "fictional commodity." Polanyi's first three fictional commodities—land, labor, and money—were subjected to law. Although these laws have been imperfect, the institutions of labor law, environmental law, and banking law are regulatory frameworks intended to defend society (and nature, life, and exchange) from the worst excesses of raw capitalism's destructive power. Surveillance capitalism's expropriation of human experience has faced no such impediments.

The success of this *coup de gens* stands as sour testimony to the thwarted needs of the second modernity, which enabled surveillance capitalism to flourish and still remains its richest vein for extraction and exploitation. In this context it is not difficult to understand why Facebook's Mark Zuckerberg offers his social network as *the* solution to the third modernity. He envisions a totalizing instrumentarian order—he calls it the new global "church"—that will connect the world's people to "something greater than ourselves." It will be Facebook, he says, that will address problems that are civilizational in scale and scope, building "the long-term infrastructure to bring humanity together" and keeping people safe with "artificial intelligence" that quickly understands "what is happening across our community."[3] Like Pentland, Zuckerberg imagines machine intelligence that can "identify risks that nobody would have flagged at all, including terrorists planning attacks using private channels, people bullying someone too afraid to report it themselves, and other issues both local and global."[4] When asked about his responsibility to shareholders, Zuckerberg told CNN, "That's why it helps to have control of the company."[5]

For more than three centuries, industrial civilization aimed to exert control over nature for the sake of human betterment. Machines were our means of extending and overcoming the limits of the animal body so that we could accomplish this aim of domination. Only later did we begin to fathom the consequences: the Earth overwhelmed in peril as the delicate physical systems that once defined sea and sky gyrated out of control.

Right now we are at the beginning of a new arc that I have called information civilization, and it repeats the same dangerous arrogance. The aim now is not to dominate *nature* but rather *human nature*. The focus has shifted from machines that overcome the limits of bodies to machines that modify the behavior of individuals, groups, and populations in the service of market objectives. This global installation of instrumentarian power overcomes and

2 Hannah Arendt, *Between Past and Future: Eight Exercises in Political Thought* (New York: Penguin, 2006), 99.
3 Mark Zuckerberg, "Building Global Community," February 16, 2017, https://www.facebook.com/notes/mark-zuckerberg/building-global-community/10154544292806634.
4 Karissa Bell, "Zuckerberg Removed a Line About Monitoring Private Messages from His Facebook Manifesto," *Mashable*, February 16, 2017, http://mashable.com/2017/02/16/mark-zuckerberg-manifesto-ai.
5 Heather Kelly, "Mark Zuckerberg Explains Why He Just Changed Facebook's Mission," *CNNMoney*, June 22, 2017, http://money.cnn.com/2017/06/22/technology/facebook-zuckerberg-interview/index.html.

replaces the human inwardness that feeds the will to will and gives sustenance to our voices in the first person, incapacitating democracy at its roots.

The rise of instrumentarian power is intended as a bloodless coup, of course. Instead of violence directed at our bodies, the instrumentarian third modernity operates more like a taming. Its solution to the increasingly clamorous demands for effective life pivots on the gradual elimination of chaos, uncertainty, conflict, abnormality, and discord in favor of predictability, automatic regularity, transparency, confluence, persuasion, and pacification. We are expected to cede our authority, relax our concerns, quiet our voices, go with the flow, and submit to the technological visionaries whose wealth and power stand as assurance of their superior judgment. It is assumed that we will accede to a future of less personal control and more powerlessness, where new sources of inequality divide and subdue, where some of us are subjects and many are objects, some are stimulus and many are response.

The compulsions of this new vision threaten other delicate systems also many millennia in the making, but this time they are social and psychological. I am thinking here of the hard-won fruits of human suffering and conflict that we call the democratic prospect and the achievements of the individual as a source of autonomous moral judgment. Technological "inevitability" is the mantra on which we are trained, but it is an existential narcotic prescribed to induce resignation: a snuff dream of the spirit.

We've been alerted to the "sixth extinction" as vertebrate species disappear faster than at any time since the end of the dinosaurs. This cataclysm is the unintended consequence of the reckless and opportunistic methods, also exalted as inevitable, with which industrialization imposed itself on the natural world because its own market forms did not hold it to account. Now the rise of instrumentarian power as the signature expression of surveillance capitalism augurs a different kind of extinction. This "seventh extinction" will not be of nature but of what has been held most precious in human nature: the will to will, the sanctity of the individual, the ties of intimacy, the sociality that binds us together in promises, and the trust they breed. The dying off of this human future will be just as unintended as any other.

SURVEILLANCE CAPITALISM AND DEMOCRACY

Instrumentarian power has gathered strength outside of mankind but also outside of democracy. There can be no law to protect us from the unprecedented, and democratic societies, like the innocent world of the Tainos, are vulnerable to unprecedented power. In this way, surveillance capitalism may be viewed as part of an alarming global drift toward what many political scientists now view as a softening of public attitudes toward the necessity and inviolability of democracy itself.

Many scholars point to a global "democratic recession" or a "deconsolidation" of Western democracies that were long considered impervious to antidemocratic threats.[6] The extent and precise nature of this threat are being debated, but observers describe the bitter *saudade* associated with rapid social change and fear of the future conveyed in the lament "My children will not see the life that I lived."[7] Such feelings of alienation

---

6 Pippa Norris, "Is Western Democracy Backsliding? Diagnosing the Risks," Harvard Kennedy School, March 2017, https://www.hks.harvard.edu/publications/western-democracy-backsliding-diagnosing-risks; Erik Voeten, "Are People Really Turning Away from Democracy?" (SSRN Scholarly Paper, Rochester, NY: Social Science Research Network, December 8, 2016), https://papers.ssrn.com/abstract=2882878; Amy C. Alexander and Christian Welzel, "The Myth of Deconsolidation: Rising Liberalism and the Populist Reaction," *Journal of Democracy*, April 28, 2017, https://www.journalofdemocracy.org/sites/default/files/media/Journal%20of%20Democracy%20Web%20 Exchange%20-%20Alexander%20and%20Welzel.pdf; Ronald Inglehart, "The Danger of Deconsolidation: How Much Should We Worry?" *Journal of Democracy* 27, no. 3 (2016), https://www.journalofdemocracy.org/article/ danger-deconsolidation-how-much-should-we-worry; Roberto Stefan Foa and Yascha Mounk, "The Signs of Deconsolidation," *Journal of Democracy* 28, no. 1 (2017); Ronald Inglehart and Christian Welzel, "Democracy's Victory Is Not Preordained. Inglehart and Welzel Reply," *Foreign Affairs* 88, no. 4 (2009): 157–59; Roberto Stefan Foa, "The End of the Consolidation Paradigm—a Response to Our Critics," *Journal of Democracy*, April 28, 2017.
7 Bart Bonikowski, "Three Lessons of Contemporary Populism in Europe and the United States," *Brown Journal of World Affairs* 23, no. 1 (2016); Bart Bonikowski and Paul DiMaggio, "Varieties of American Popular Nationalism," *American Sociological Review* 81, no. 5 (2016): 949–80; Theda Skocpol and Vanessa Williamson, *The Tea Party*

and unease were expressed by many people around the world in a thirty-eight-nation survey published by Pew Research in late 2017. The findings suggest that the democratic ideal is no longer a sacred imperative, even for citizens of mature democratic societies. Although 78 percent of respondents say that representative democracy is "good," 49 percent also say that "rule by experts" is good, 26 percent endorse "rule by a strong leader," and 24 percent prefer "rule by the military."[8]

The weakening attachment to democracy in the United States and many European countries is of serious concern.[9] According to the Pew survey, only 40 percent of US respondents support democracy and *simultaneously* reject the alternatives. A full 46 percent find both democratic and nondemocratic alternatives to be acceptable, and 7 percent favor only the nondemocratic choice. The US sample trails Sweden, Germany, the Netherlands, Greece, and Canada in its depth of commitment to democracy, but other key Western democracies, including Italy, the UK, France, and Spain, along with Poland and Hungary, fall at or below the thirty-eight-country median of 37 percent that are exclusively committed to democracy.

Many have concluded from this turmoil that market democracy is no longer viable, despite the fact that the combination of markets and democracy has served humanity well, helping to lift much of humankind from millennia of ignorance, poverty, and pain. For some of these thinkers it is the markets that must go, and for others it is democracy that's slated for obsolescence. Repulsed by the social degradation and climate chaos produced by nearly four decades of neoliberal policy and practice, an important and varied group of scholars and activists argues that the era of capitalism is at end. Some propose more-humane economic alternatives,[10] some anticipate protracted decline,[11] and others, repelled by social complexity, favor a blend of elite power and authoritarian politics in closer emulation of China's authoritarian system.[12]

These developments alert us to a deeper truth: just as capitalism cannot be eaten raw, people cannot live without the felt possibility of homecoming. Hannah Arendt explored this territory more than sixty years ago in *The Origins of Totalitarianism*, where she traced the path from a thwarted individuality to a totalizing ideology. It was the individual's experience of insignificance, expendability, political isolation, and loneliness that stoked the fires of totalitarian terror. Such ideologies, Arendt observed, appear as "a last support in a world where nobody is reliable and nothing can be relied upon."[13] Years later, in his moving 1966 essay "Education after Auschwitz," social theorist Theodor Adorno attributed the success of German fascism to the ways

and the Remaking of Republican Conservatism (New York: Oxford University Press, 2016), 74–75.

8 Richard Wike et al., "Globally, Broad Support for Representative and Direct Democracy," *Pew Research Centers Global Attitudes Project,* October 16, 2017, http://www.pewglobal.org/2017/10/16/globally-broad-support-for-representative-and-direct-democracy.

9 As democracy scholar and author of the "democratic recession" thesis Larry Diamond puts it, "It is hard to overstate how important the vitality and self-confidence of U.S. democracy has been to the global expansion of democracy. ... Apathy and inertia in Europe and the United States could significantly lower the barriers to new democratic reversals and to authoritarian entrenchment in many more states." See Larry Diamond, "Facing Up to the Democratic Recession," *Journal of Democracy* 26, no. 1 (2015): 141–55, https://doi.org/10.1353/jod.2015.0009.

10 Naomi Klein, *The Shock Doctrine: The Rise of Disaster Capitalism* (New York: Picador, 2007); Erik Olin Wright, *Envisioning Real Utopias* (London: Verso, 2010); Wendy Brown, *Edgework: Critical Essays on Knowledge and Politics* (Princeton, NJ: Princeton University Press, 2005); Gerald F. Davis, *Managed by the Markets: How Finance Re-shaped America* (New York: Oxford University Press, 2011).

11 Immanuel Wallerstein et al., *Does Capitalism Have a Future?* (Oxford: Oxford University Press, 2013); Erik Olin Wright, *Envisioning Real Utopias* (London: Verso, 2010); Naomi Klein, *This Changes Everything: Capitalism Vs. the Climate* (New York: Simon & Schuster, 2015); Wendy Brown, *Edgework: Critical Essays on Knowledge and Politics* (Princeton, NJ: Princeton University Press, 2005); Davis, *Managed by the Markets;* Wolfgang Streeck, "On the Dismal Future of Capitalism," *Socio-Economic Review* 14, no. 1 (2016): 164–70; Craig Calhoun, "The Future of Capitalism," *Socio-Economic Review* 14, no. 1 (2016): 171–76; Polly Toynbee, "Unfettered Capitalism Eats Itself," *Socio-Economic Review* 14, no. 1 (2016): 176–79; Amitai Etzioni, "The Next Industrial Revolution Calls for a Different Economic System," *Socio-Economic Review* 14, no. 1 (2016): 179–83.

12 See, for example, Nicolas Berggruen and Nathan Gardels, *Intelligent Governance for the 21st Century: A Middle Way Between West and East* (Cambridge: Polity, 2013).

13 Hannah Arendt, *The Origins of Totalitarianism* (New York: Schocken, 2004), 615.

in which the quest for effective life had become an overwhelming burden for too many people: "One must accept that fascism and the terror it caused are connected with the fact that the old established authorities ... decayed and were toppled, while the people psychologically were not yet ready for self-determination. They proved to be unequal to the freedom that fell into their laps."[14]

Should we grow weary of our own struggle for self-determination and surrender instead to the seductions of Big Other, we will inadvertently trade a future of homecoming for an arid prospect of muted, sanitized tyranny. A third modernity that solves our problems at the price of a human future is a cruel perversion of capitalism and of the digital capabilities it commands. It is also an unacceptable affront to democracy. I repeat Thomas Piketty's warning: "A market economy ... if left to itself ... contains powerful forces of divergence, which are potentially threatening to democratic societies and to the values of social justice on which they are based."[15] This is precisely the whirlwind that we will reap at the hands of surveillance capitalism, an unprecedented form of raw capitalism that is surely contributing to the tempering of commitment to the democratic prospect as it successfully bends populations to its soft-spoken will. It gives so much, but it takes even more.

Surveillance capitalism arrived on the scene with democracy already on the ropes, its early life sheltered and nourished by neoliberalism's claims to freedom that set it at a distance from the lives of people. Surveillance capitalists quickly learned to exploit the gathering momentum aimed at hollowing out democracy's meaning and muscle. Despite the democratic promise of its rhetoric and capabilities, it contributed to a new Gilded Age of extreme wealth inequality, as well as to once-unimaginable new forms of economic exclusivity and new sources of social inequality that separate the tuners from the tuned. Among the many insults to democracy and democratic institutions imposed by this *coup des gens*, I count the unauthorized expropriation of human experience; the hijack of the division of learning in society; the structural independence from people; the stealthy imposition of the hive collective; the rise of instrumentarian power and the radical indifference that sustains its extractive logic; the construction, ownership, and operation of the means of behavior modification that is Big Other; the abrogation of the elemental right to the future tense and the elemental right to sanctuary; the degradation of the self-determining individual as the fulcrum of democratic life; and the insistence on psychic numbing as the answer to its illegitimate quid pro quo. We can now see that surveillance capitalism takes an even more expansive turn toward domination than its neoliberal source code would predict, claiming its right to freedom *and* knowledge, while setting its sights on a collectivist vision that claims the totality of society. Though still sounding like Hayek, and even Smith, its antidemocratic collectivist ambitions reveal it as an insatiable child devouring its aging fathers.

Cynicism is seductive and can blind us to the enduring fact that democracy remains our only channel for reformation. It is the one idea to have emerged from the long story of human oppression that insists upon a people's inalienable right to rule themselves. Democracy may be under siege, but we cannot allow its many injuries to deflect us from allegiance to its promise. It is precisely in recognition of this dilemma that Piketty refuses to concede defeat, arguing that even "abnormal" dynamics of accumulation have been—and can again be—mitigated by democratic institutions that produce durable and effective countermeasures: "If we are to regain control of capital, we must bet everything on democracy. ..."[16]

Democracy is vulnerable to the unprecedented, but the strength of democratic institutions is the clock that determines the duration and destructiveness of that vulnerability. In a democratic society the debate and contest afforded by still-healthy institutions can shift the tide of public opinion against unexpected sources of oppression and injustice, with legislation and jurisprudence eventually to follow.

---

14   Theodor Adorno, "Education after Auschwitz," in *Critical Models: Interventions and Catchwords* (New York: Columbia University Press, 1966).
15   Thomas Piketty, *Capital in the Twenty-First Century* (Cambridge, MA: Belknap Press, 2014), 571.
16   Piketty, *Capital in the Twenty-First Century*, 573. For a wise and elegant defense of democracy, see also Wendy Brown, *Undoing the Demos: Neoliberalisms Stealth Revolution* (New York: Zone, 2015).

SOYLENT GREEN (1973)

Set in a dystopian New York City of tomorrow, the film presents a future of rampant pollution and shortages of energy and food resources. The food shortages are met in a very special way, thus leading to one of most famous last lines in film history. Note the cool 1970s video game and the role of media.

Director: Richard Fleischer
Starring: Charlton Heston and Leigh Taylor-Young

THE CHINA SYNDROME (1979)

The nuclear power industry resorts to intimidation and cover-ups to conceal a nuclear accident and near meltdown. This film famously anticipated the 1979 nuclear accident at Three Mile Island in Pennsylvania, which happened shortly after the release of the film. Note the role of news media.

Director: James Bridges
Starring: Jane Fonda, Jack Lemmon, and Michael Douglas

THE DAY AFTER TOMORROW (2004)

In this eco-apocalypse, the Earth's climate turns against humans, all as a metaphor for global warming and climate change. Unfortunately, the special effects overwhelm the science midway through, but the film's message remains clear: the climate is changing and we are major contributors. Note the roles of media and media technologies.

Director: Roland Emmerich
Starring: Dennis Quaid and Jake Gyllenhaal

WALL-E (2008)

This film is set in a dystopian future, where Earth is covered with garbage and humans live inside a media metropolis masking as a cruise ship amid the stars. WALL-E cleverly critiques humankind's rampant consumption and pollution, along with a vision of hyperreality today: the signs of nature have replaced nature.

Director: Andrew Stanton
Starring: The voices of Ben Burtt and Elissa Knight

AVATAR (2009)

The top box office film of all time, *Avatar* is set on a distant planet in the future, where humans have extended their imperialism and ecological destruction. Created in computers, the forests of Pandora are stunning. The plot is cliché, but the messages are clear. Note the roles of media technologies.

Director: James Cameron
Starring: Sam Worthington and Zoe Saldana

CHAPTER EIGHT

MEDIA AND EARTH'S ECOLOGY

Gaia, the Anthropocene, and Planetary Consciousness

By Barry Vacker and Kelly Bartsch

"HELLO FROM THE CHILDREN OF PLANET EARTH"

Greta Thunberg and the Golden Record—they have much in common though they are separated by forty-two years and fourteen billion miles. Greta gave voice to millions of eco-minded youth in the Climate Strike on Planet Earth, while the Golden Record is hurtling through the Milky Way with greetings in dozens of languages, including one child's voice that says, "Hello from the Children of Planet Earth." That's right, the idea of youth speaking for the future of Earth is not new, no matter how much it triggers the dudes in power and their political supporters.

FIGURE 8.0.1 "Hello from the Children of Planet Earth," Mixed media with acrylic and pumice on stretched canvas; Hubble Deep Field image. 4 feet x 5 feet. Full-size replica of the NASA Voyager Golden Record. Concept by Julia Hildebrand and Barry Vacker, canvas by Barry Vacker and Liza Samuel. June 2019. Photo: Barry Vacker, 2019.

Greta's message to the youth echoed in the global media networks of 2019, while the greetings from Earth are encoded on the Golden Record attached to the *Voyager 1* and *Voyager 2* spacecraft, launched in 1977. Both Greta and the Golden Record are products of their eras, but are connected by their dire messages and the emergent planetary consciousness they represent. "Hello from the Children of Planet Earth" and the Climate Strike are voices born of two different apocalyptic fears—the Cold War and Climate Disruption. Importantly, the "Hello" greeting is part of an emerging planetary consciousness on Earth—*the idea that humanity needs to think as a species to prevent self-destruction on its tiny planet in the majestic universe.*

It's as if the artwork tapped into the emerging planetary consciousness symbolized by the Golden Record—and now Greta Thunberg. Conceived by Julia M. Hildebrand and myself, the artwork was called "Hello from the Children of Planet Earth" and was part of our mixed-media installation entitled "Media(S)cene," hosted by the Media Ecology Association at the University of Toronto, June 27–29, 2019. The artwork and installation was inspired by our *Medium* essay "Hot and Cool in the Media(S)cene," which sketches out a radically new media theory for our species living on Planet Earth and in the Anthropocene (see chapter 1).[1] Written for the youth of the world and for those who realize we need new media theory for the radical conditions we face, the essay presents the parameters of a massive media theory to connect our layers of media technologies to life on Planet Earth—to the Anthropocene, to our emerging planetary consciousness, and to the long-term future of the human species.

THE MESSAGE OF THE GOLDEN RECORD

Eight years after the optimistic triumph of Apollo 11 in 1969, humanity sent a dire message into the cosmic void. Mounted on both *Voyager 1* and *Voyager 2* is the famous Golden Record, a gold-plated copper disk containing an electronic compilation of life on Earth, encoded with 117 photographs, greetings in fifty-four languages, ninety minutes of music from around the world, and a selection of sounds from nature and culture, such as animals, symphonies, and a rocket launch. Included was a needle to play the record, with instructions on the record cover and the playing speed of 16 rpm listed in the binary code of ones and zeros. There was also a statement from US president Jimmy Carter:

> We cast this message into the cosmos. It is likely to survive a billion years into our future, when our civilization is profoundly altered and the surface of the Earth may be vastly changed. Of the 200 billion stars in the Milky Way galaxy, some—perhaps many—may have inhabited planets and space-faring civilizations. If one such civilization intercepts Voyager and can understand these recorded contents, here is our message:
>
> This is a present from a small distant world, a token of our sounds, our science, our images, our music, our thoughts, and our feelings. We are attempting to survive our time so we may live into yours. We hope someday, having solved the problems we face, to join a community of galactic civilizations. This record represents our hope and our determination and our goodwill in a vast and awesome universe.[2]

Though President Carter was referencing the fears of the Cold War, the basic message is not that different from Greta's—a message of warning and hope. Voyager was the next voice of the emergent planetary consciousness that first appeared with NASA's Apollo moon program.

Voyager was a continuation of that planetary consciousness in 1979, as was the Hubble Space Telescope in 1991, as are the internet and social media in the twenty-first century—at least on certain occasions for the internet and social media, such as the Climate Strike, Women's March, and the March for Science.

---

1   The essay won an international award—the 2019 John Culkin Award for Outstanding Praxis in the Field of Media Ecology, awarded by the Media Ecology Association.
2   Jimmy Carter, Voyager Spacecraft Statement by the President. Online by Gerhard Peters and John T. Woolley, The American Presidency Project, https://www.presidency.ucsb.edu/node/243563.

AN EMERGING PLANETARY CONSCIOUSNESS

Since our emergence and evolution in Africa, humanity has been migrating and globalizing for at least seventy thousand years. At first on foot, then via horse, boat, train, car, and plane—along with the evolution of communication and media networks, oral, written, electronic, and digital. Via our planetary media ecologies, we have effected an emergent planetary consciousness. Beneath all our diversity is the existential universal—all 7.7 billion humans share 99.5 percent of the same DNA and are made of the most common elements of the cosmos (primarily oxygen, hydrogen, carbon, and nitrogen). We humans are a single species with billions of computers, laptops, tablets, and phones, all linked in the layers of media networks that span the globe. As shown in the recent global strikes and protest marches, the planetary consciousness is showing an ability to organize—not merely to trade and wage war, but to rally for human rights, racial justice, scientific knowledge, and ecological sanity.[3]

Of course, these global networks and platforms also encourage a virulent tribalism that often seems to divide more than it unifies, precisely as individuals seek identities in the tribes of the spectacles they inhabit. *That's why this emerging planetary consciousness needs a coherent worldview, a new philosophy for human civilization—one that fully embraces our true existential conditions in the universe.* Rants and tribes are nowhere near enough. After all, it's still possible that our planetary consciousness could devour itself in narcissism and nationalism, given that there are twelve thousand nuclear weapons on Earth and more than $1 trillion is spent on the military every year. Imagine if that money was spent on research for sustainable energy and protecting the environment. Sooner or later—before it's too late—we must embrace a common understanding of life on Earth and our role in protecting it.

SPACESHIP EARTH AND GAIA

Just as we have an emerging planetary consciousness, we also have an emerging understanding of a planetary ecology. Most people do not realize that media technologies have utterly transformed how we understand ecology and our impact on the ecosystems of "Spaceship *Earth*." Marshall McLuhan observed that *Sputnik*'s encirclement of Earth placed the planet within a technological and mediated environment. Launched by the former Soviet Union, *Sputnik* was the first satellite put into orbit around our planet. McLuhan states,

> When *Sputnik* went up on October 4, 1957, it put the planet inside a man-made environment for the first time. Spaceship *Earth* has no passengers, only crew. *Sputnik* transformed the planet into Spaceship *Earth* with a program problem. Ecology became the name of the game from the moment of *Sputnik*. Nature ended. The planet became an art form inside a manned capsule, and life will never be the same on this planet again. Nature ended and art took over. Ecology is art.[4] (italics in original)

This statement means that global electronic media have transferred evolution from biology to technology by providing a mediated environment through which humans now perceive and model the world. Through technology, we can now shape evolution (though we would be fools to think we can control it entirely). We can see that our planetary spaceship—traveling through the universe—is our home and is the life support system for all living species. In fact, Spaceship *Earth* is a living system, or what is called Gaia.

---

3   Like life on Earth, these issues are deeply connected. Bill McKibben, "Racism, Police Violence, and the Climate Are Not Separate Issues," *The New Yorker*, June 4, 2020, https://www.newyorker.com/news/annals-of-a-warming-planet/racism-police-violence-and-the-climate-are-not-separate-issues.
4   Marshall McLuhan, *Understanding Me: Lectures and Interviews* (Cambridge, MA: MIT Press, 2003), 242.

Around the time of McLuhan's observation, James Lovelock posited the Gaia hypothesis, or the concept of the Earth as a single living organism. While working for NASA at the Jet Propulsion Laboratory in the 1960s, Lovelock was inspired by the photos of Earth from space, including those taken by Apollo 8, which helped inspire the idea of Spaceship *Earth*, or a single spacecraft floating through space without an instruction manual for how to pilot it. Lovelock marveled at "the awe with which astronauts with their own eyes and we by television have seen the Earth revealed in all its shining beauty against the deep darkness of space."[5] In the Gaia hypothesis, Earth is viewed as a singular living system, a megasystem in which its own evolution as well as that of life are tightly integrated, producing a self-regulating system for the biosphere over the eons of ancient time.

In effect, the Gaia hypothesis is the simple notion that the ecological, geological, oceanic, and atmospheric systems are all part of a complex system from which the living biosphere on Earth emerged. Aided by increasing computer power, Lovelock's Gaia hypothesis has proven effective for modeling climate change, including global warming and the effects of carbon emissions from burning fossil fuels to power our culture and our industrial-consumer-information society. In his more recent books, *The Revenge of Gaia* (2006) and *The Vanishing Face of Gaia* (2009), Lovelock suggests that humans face an ecological apocalypse that endangers the fate of technological civilization.[6]

As if anticipating Lovelock's fears, Roland Emmerich depicts an all-out climatic apocalypse in *The Day After Tomorrow*. The ecological science is plausible in the beginning of the movie, before the film veers off the radar screen into freezing hurricanes and instant ice ages. Despite all the scientific impossibilities, Emmerich delivers the message that global warming is a problem that must be addressed by humankind. According to Chris Mooney and Sheril Kirshenbaum, one study suggests that those who had seen *The Day After Tomorrow* were "significantly more worried about global warming than those who had not and were significantly more convinced that global warming could trigger specific weather and climatic impacts."[7] These are very strange cinematic and cultural conditions, where scientific impossibilities meet scientific illiteracy yet combine to increase awareness of some real scientific issues.

One can only wonder about the long-term effect of *WALL-E*, *The Day After Tomorrow*, *An Inconvenient Truth*, or any of the films described in Stephen Rust's reading "Hollywood and Climate Change." Surely, the filmmakers had some noble intentions. But do moviegoers care? Do they want to be merely entertained? Or do they want to be enlightened enough to realize that our civilization must make massive changes in its use of energy and resources?

If James Lovelock is correct, there are no easy solutions—and perhaps *no* solutions at all. If trends continue, it is an energy and ecological suicide. Since Apollo 8 and the "Earthrise" image, there has been a global increase in ecological awareness. However, we need to learn to live *within the means* of the planet and not merely live *on* the planet. Despite what is suggested as we face our electronic screens, we are not separate from the planet and biosphere that made us possible. We are part of Gaia. But is Gaia just another worldview destined to be absorbed into the spectacle of media images?

HUMANITY'S DEADLINE

Human lives are linear. We plan our days anticipating the predictions of clocks. Clocks exist in objectivity—simulacra for the vast abstraction of time. Clocks mediate eternity, reducing its incomprehensible spans to the cyclical ticktock of dials, gears, and numbers. They serve as existential maps, extending our tenuous grasp on reality's

---

5   James Lovelock, *Gaia: A New Look at Life on Earth* (Oxford: Oxford University Press, 2000), xv-xvi.

6   James Lovelock, *The Revenge of Gaia: Earth's Climate Crisis and the Fate of Humanity* (New York: Basic Books, 2006); and James Lovelock, *The Vanishing Face of Gaia* (New York: Basic Books, 2009).

7   Chris Mooney and Sheril Kirshenbaum, *Unscientific America: How Scientific Illiteracy Threatens Our Future* (New York: Basic Books, 2010), 93.

true nature. We find our footing in the infinite by synchronizing our moments with the overlapping moments of other people. What humanity cannot quantify, it reifies through the signs and symbols of the real.

THE DOOMSDAY CLOCK

In 1947, a concerned group of atomic scientists created the "Doomsday Clock" to represent the nuclear threat posed by nuclear annihilation during the Cold War. With midnight symbolizing "Time's up!" or "the end" of the day, the Doomsday Clock imparted a sober warning about the terror of nuclear war, the unwinnable war that would utterly destroy civilization in a few hours.

Though the Cold War is over (we hope), the Doomsday Clock is still in use, now offering a warning about the encroaching threat of global catastrophe. In contrast to nuclear war taking a mere few hours, these catastrophes happen over years and decades. Each year, the group of scientists and thinkers reassesses our vulnerability to catastrophe, manifesting from nuclear weapons, disruptive technology and biotechnology, and climate disruption. To this day, the Doomsday Clock stands as a simulacrum of the autocannibalistic nature of humanity. In 2021, the Doomsday Clock is set at 100 seconds till midnight.

LIMITS TO GROWTH

Spaceship *Earth* and Gaia are two discourses about our planet and ecology, along with visions of "wilderness," "noble savages" living in a state of nature, "limits to growth" and resource depletion, and the Promethean idea that we can manage the environment and use technological innovation for endless consumption. These narratives are deeply engrained in media, advertising, and Hollywood films.[8] Is all this really possible?

Human population has exploded around the planet, powered by the spread of industrial, electrified, and mediated civilization, along with modern medicine, antibiotics, and vaccines that have saved perhaps billions of lives (see figure 8.0.2).

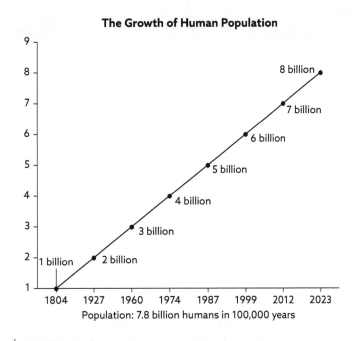

The Growth of Human Population

Population: 7.8 billion humans in 100,000 years

| FIGURE 8.0.2   The Growth of Human Population

8   Patrick D. Murphy, *The Media Commons: Globalization and Environmental Discourses* (Urbana: University of Illinois Press, 2017).

Given this population growth, the current levels of energy and resource consumption described in chapter 7 likely cannot be sustained over the long haul, at least not in their current forms. As shown in the following figure, humanity dominates Planet Earth and we are altering the atmosphere and overtaking the remaining wildernesses. Gaia will have something to say about us altering the atmosphere and oceans. It's no wonder the Doomsday Clock is at 2 minutes and the Climate Clock is ticking.

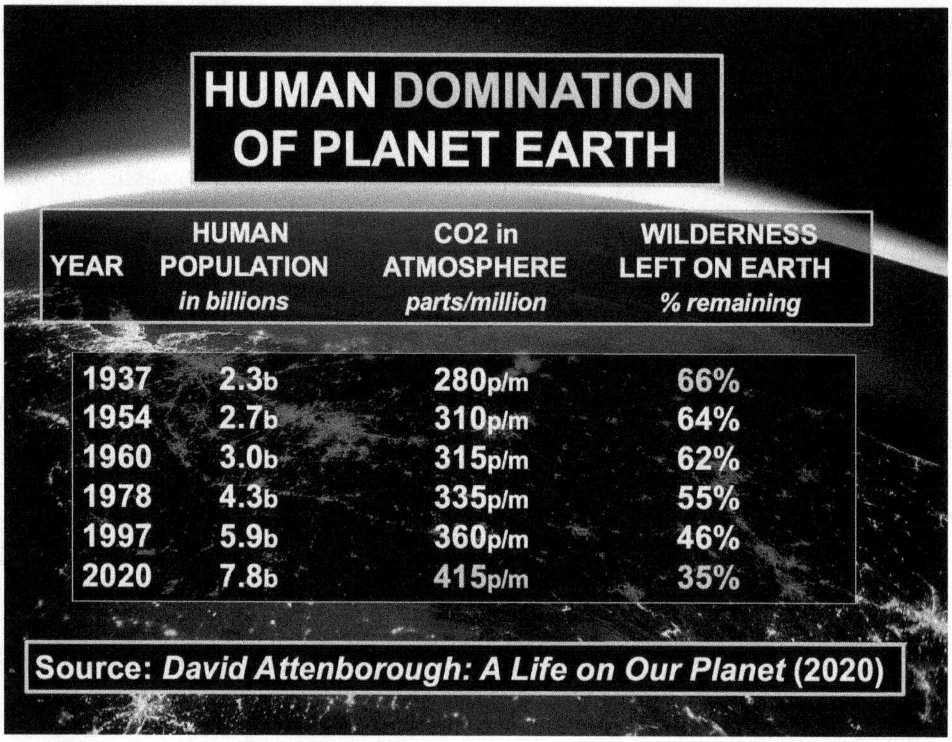

HUMAN DOMINATION OF PLANET EARTH

YEAR	HUMAN POPULATION in billions	CO2 in ATMOSPHERE parts/million	WILDERNESS LEFT ON EARTH % remaining
1937	2.3b	280p/m	66%
1954	2.7b	310p/m	64%
1960	3.0b	315p/m	62%
1978	4.3b	335p/m	55%
1997	5.9b	360p/m	46%
2020	7.8b	415p/m	35%

Source: *David Attenborough: A Life on Our Planet* (2020)

FIGURE 8.0.3   Human Domination of Planet Earth. Table created by Barry Vacker, 2021.

THE CLIMATE CLOCK

Proliferating from this simulacrum of ecological destruction is another apocalyptic time-teller: the Climate Clock. The trope of the Climate Clock has proliferated across the globe. New York City, Berlin, and Paris are just a few of the cities adorned with the clock's looming red and green numbers. The green number depicts the growing percentage of global energy derived from renewable resources. The red number quantifies the time we have left to reduce carbon emissions so as to limit global temperatures to the maximum increase of 1.5 degrees Celsius. Planet Earth's "lifeline" and "deadline" are reified in this digital numeric medium. The Climate Clock allows humanity to collectively bear witness to our own prophecy of destruction. Instead of mapping an enlightened march forward into eternity, the Climate Clock mediates a final countdown into the silent abyss of the naught.

A new coherent worldview needs to evolve from the detritus of humankind's grandiosity—one that can provide humanity with some philosophical recourse that can shield it from the nihilistic prophecy of the Doomsday Clock and the Climate Clock. The most important number in the world is not GDP. It is not the number of empires we build, the amount of capital we produce, nor the rate of our national deficit. These numbers represent the darkest realm of the hyperreal—that which will continue to propel our own ruin.

Among the most important numbers in the world are the numbers ticking down upon the Climate Clock. In reddened semiotics, it shows the painful fact that we are running out of time. Eternity was never promised to humankind. We are the keepers of our own fate. Ensuring our longevity is a feat that is contingent upon preserving the fragile ecosystems of our planet, our spaceship spinning through the cosmos, with its own living systems powered by the nearby star.

ECOLOGICAL CHALLENGES WE FACE AS A SPECIES

Films like *WALL-E* and *Interstellar* pose numerous questions and challenges regarding the future of media, society, and the ecosystems upon which all life depends. Like the tourists on the *Axiom* in *WALL-E*, we sit in front of our screens and gaze upon the carnival of humanity as our species consumes products and devours resources. Let's consider three questions and challenges.

WHAT ARE WE DOING ABOUT CLIMATE DISRUPTION AND GLOBAL WARMING?

So far, despite the urging of Al Gore's Oscar-winning documentary *An Inconvenient Truth* (2006), it looks like what we're doing is not much or not enough. We can certainly work to eliminate fossil fuels and develop alternative energies, especially solar power. Frankly, we should be pouring hundreds of billions of dollars into solar research, but we are too busy waging war (which gets higher TV ratings than news about a breakthrough in solar power). We should be focusing on new engines and energy for our trucks and cars, rather than mindlessly converting them into mobile media entertainment systems that function as little more than vehicular extensions of iTunes and Netflix. Would you be surprised if we soon see a supersized SUV with a mini-IMAX screen on the inside roof?

WHAT ABOUT THE AMOUNT OF TRASH ON THE LAND?

The totals are mind-boggling. For every person on the planet, one metric ton of trash is generated, and less than 25 percent is recycled. Scientist Chris Impey writes this:

> In the US the discarded trash includes 50 million computers, 100 million cell phones, and 3 billion batteries a year. This rapidly growing electronic detritus contains lead, cadmium, chromium, mercury, and polyvinyl chlorides, which have toxicological effects ranging from brain damage and kidney disease to mutations and cancers. Not as toxic, but a headache for the planet nonetheless, are the 3,600,000 metric tons of junk mail, 22 billion plastic bottles, and 65 billion soda cans discarded a year.
>
> Americans are the world champion wasters, with 5 percent of the population but 40 percent of the trash. When we get rid of our trash, it doesn't totally go away. In a landfill some of the toxins leech [*sic*] into the groundwater and in an incinerator some escape into the air. The US Environmental Protection Agency keeps track of 1300 of the worst toxic waste sites, but the so-called Superfund that pays for cleanup has been bankrupt for years despite the intention from the original legislation that the polluter should pay.
>
> At the nation's 120 nuclear waste sites, the decontamination problem is huge. There are 245 million metric tons of mine tailings from uranium ore, 45,000 metric tons of highly radioactive spent fuel from commercial and defense reactors, and over 340 million liters of high-level waste left over from plutonium processing.[9]

Is the e-waste ever mentioned in the ads for Apple? Is the plastic waste ever mentioned in the ads for Pepsi? Of course, Apple and Pepsi are not responsible for the polluting habits of their consumers, but such firms should take a much more active and visible role in trying to reduce pollution caused by their products. To be sure, almost no

---

9   Chris Impey, *How It Ends: From You to the Universe* (New York: Norton, 2010), 80–81.

one cares about nuclear waste unless there is a meltdown. When the meltdown is on the other side of the planet, most people soon ignore it, too. Witness Fukushima.

WHAT ABOUT THE HEALTH OF OUR OCEANS?

Around the world, we treat the seas as our pantry and toilet, harvesting the fish while dumping our refuse in the water. The Great Pacific Garbage Patch in the Pacific Ocean is horrifying. Apparently, there is a Texas-sized patch of plastic garbage and plastic particulates floating just beneath the ocean surface. The garbage patch includes billions of tons of floating bottles, lids, bags, plates, disposable lighters, plastic particles, and anything else plastic that will float. The trash comes from cruise ships, military ships, and the cities of the world, where humans discard plastic on the streets, which then enters the sewers, followed by streams and rivers, and eventually the currents of the oceans. The garbage is decomposing into tiny particulates the size of sand grains and entering the ocean food system, killing birds and fish and destroying the ecosystems. The origins and effects of this ecological catastrophe are explained in Angela Sun's documentary film *Plastic Paradise* (2014).

Satellite imagery reveals other garbage patches in the oceans, including one in the Atlantic Ocean. Studies suggest the plastic trash in the oceans has increased a hundredfold over the past forty years.[10] Apparently, the largest floating garbage patch is now the size of Alaska.[11] Meanwhile, we are overharvesting the fish populations, bulldozing the ocean floors for the leftover fish, and acidifying the oceans with our CO_2 emissions, thus endangering coral reefs and the food chains of the oceans.[12] As shown in the documentaries *Blackfish* (2013) and *The Cove* (2009), humans are harvesting dolphins and capturing whales to entertain us in aquariums, marine parks, and theme parks like SeaWorld, where "nature" is experienced as spectacle and hyperreality.

How can these levels of waste, trash, and resource depletion be considered remotely sane? There is no one to blame but lazy humans, who imagine themselves at the center of everything, without regard for the planet from which they emerged. What are the roles of the news media and entertainment industries in addressing current and future ecological challenges? On Netflix and YouTube, you can find all sorts of ecological documentaries and ecovideos, but the viewership is tiny compared to the entertainment programming that dominates movies, television, and the internet. Is there no hope for a more enlightened media worldview regarding Gaia and the ecology of the future?

ARE *WALL-E* AND *INTERSTELLAR* COMING TRUE?

When we think of environmental films, we might immediately think of documentaries such as Al Gore's *An Inconvenient Truth*, Angela Sun's *Plastic Paradise: The Great Pacific Garbage Patch*, or *Before the Flood*, narrated by Leonardo DiCaprio. However, fictional films have played a key role in critiquing our impact on the environment and our misuse of natural resources. Not too long after Apollo 8's "Earthrise" image helped reboot environmentalism and spawn Earth Day in 1970, Hollywood began producing films about the environment and the planet's ecosystems, as explained by Stephen Rust in chapter 8. At the beginning of the chapter some of the films that fit this anthology, showing not only our impact on the planet but also humanity's misuse of technology, including media technology.

This tradition is continued in recent films such as *WALL-E* and *Interstellar*. Clever and funny, *WALL-E* was a box office smash starring cute robots who help humans return to an ecologically destroyed Earth. A visual and sci-fi masterpiece, *Interstellar* depicts brave scientists and astronauts (and a cool robot) helping humanity find

---

10   Thomas M. Kostigen, "The World's Largest Dump: The Great Pacific Garbage Patch," *Discover*, July 10, 2008; "Plastic Trash Altering Ocean Habitats, Scripps Study Shows," *Scripps News*, May 8, 2012.
11   David Meyer, "The World's Biggest Floating Garbage Dump Is Now Bigger than Alaska," *Fortune*, March 23, 2018.
12   Sylvia Earle, "My Wish: Protect Our Oceans," TED2009 Talk, February 2009.

a new planet because the food systems on Earth have collapsed. Despite being very different films, *WALL-E* and *Interstellar* share a common theme about our future: we might well trash our planet such that it will become utterly uninhabitable.

WALL-E and *Interstellar* are clever and powerful in their own ways, each capturing elements of our current culture. *Interstellar* shows some of the antiscience and conspiracy culture of today, while *WALL-E* depicts the prevailing cultural conditions in the electrified metropolises around the world—humans sitting in front of glowing screens all day while their waste and trash destroy the ecosystems of the planet. In addition, the film shows the dominance of the spectacle and hyperreality as modes of daily existence. On the *Axiom* space cruise ship, the signs of the real have replaced the real as humans cast their gaze inward, away from the starry skies just outside their windows. We could easily think of the *Axiom* as a stand-in for Spaceship *Earth*, hurtling through the cosmos with its passengers staring at screens and burning up resources and fossil fuels while tossing trash all over the planet. In that sense, *WALL-E* might be less a sci-fi film of the future than a documentary of the present moment. In fact, *WALL-E* and *Interstellar* coincide with the emergence of the Anthropocene.

EFFECTING THE ANTHROPOCENE

We live in a dual system of existence: Civilization's electrified metropolises have erased nature and the cosmos from our consciousness, producing a kaleidoscopic carnival of daily events while divorcing us from our impact on the planet and our origins in the universe. The universe and nature are "out there" somewhere. Meanwhile, we're "in here," in the glow of our electrified metropolises and 24/7 media spectacle. Humanity has transformed the biosphere of our planet with the global embrace of industrial civilization powered by fossil fuels, from advanced agriculture to the consumer society to the 24/7 media spectacle. Technologies, consumption, urban sprawl, and resource depletion have been accelerating since the 1950s and the birth of the global consumer society.[13] While there are many cultural benefits to a global-planetary civilization, a consumer society operating on steroids is not one of them. Immersed in hot media, we are not only warming the oceans; we are also heating and transforming the planet.

The technocultural acceleration of consumer society is quite possibly triggering the sixth extinction event in Earth's history, with our pollution and detritus now generating its own fossil layer.[14] According to Jan Zalasiewicz, the human species is creating a new geological and ecological epoch on Earth: what scientists call the Anthropocene. As explained by Zalasiewicz, here is the moment marking the popular emergence of the term:

> The idea was born in Mexico, in the year 2000. It was pure improvisation, by Paul Crutzen, one of the world's most respected scientists. ... In Mexico he was listening to experts discuss evidence for changes in the global environment that had occurred throughout the Holocene, a distinct epoch that geologists say began 11,700 years ago and continues today. Growing visibly more frustrated, he burst out: "No! We are no longer in the Holocene. We are in"—he paused to think—"the Anthropocene!"

Zalasiewicz elaborated on the striking moment:

> The room went silent. The term had apparently hit home. And it kept coming up, again and again, for the rest of the meeting. That year Crutzen co-wrote an article with Eugene Stoermer (since deceased), a specialist in microscopic algae called diatoms who had independently coined the term "Anthropocene" some years earlier. ... Spurred by Crutzen's prestige and vivid, persuasive

---

13   J. R. McNeill and Peter Engelke, *The Great Acceleration: An Environmental History of the Anthropocene* (Cambridge, MA: Belknap Press of Harvard University, 2014).
14   Elizabeth Kolbert, *The Sixth Extinction: An Unnatural History* (New York: Picador 2014); Jeremy Davies, *The Birth of the Anthropocene* (Berkeley: University of California Press, 2016).

writing, the concept spread rapidly among the thousands of scientists in the International Geosphere-Biosphere Program, which had sponsored the Mexico meeting. "The Anthropocene" began to appear in scientific papers around the world.[15]

Thus was born the concept of the "Anthropocene." As the scientific and environmental evidence mounts from all over the planet, the Anthropocene seems destined to become a permanent part of the philosophical and cultural discourse.[16] How we handle this challenge will mark the success or failure of our civilization.

Climate disruption is merely one part of the Anthropocene, along with polluted air, nuclear waste, species extinction, sprawling landfills, human-created rocks from asphalt and concrete, chemical pollution of the rivers and water tables, and the plasticized and acidified oceans—all destined to be fossilized across the eons. Four billion years of strata show us that new mountains will rise and current deltas will sink. According to Zalasiewicz,

San Francisco, pushed up by tectonic forces, seems destined to be weathered away. Sinking New Orleans, Shanghai, and Amsterdam, however, will leave ample traces of their massive, complex structures, together with aluminum, plastic, ceramics—and skeletons with metal-filled teeth and artificial hips. When these strata are ultimately pushed up high by tectonic forces, millions of years from now, the newly minted cliffs will reveal a distinctive Anthropocene layer. ...

The meteorite strike that ended the Cretaceous period was instantaneous; the immediate shock wave was over in hours. But its effects reshaped biology for millions of years, and the reverberations are still with us today. Without that meteorite we might not be here now; dinosaurs might still be ruling the earth. Humanity's impact, swift though not that sudden, could likewise change the planet in ways that will be felt long after we disappear.[17]

We are just beginning to grasp the long-term planetary effects of the Anthropocene. What kind of civilization—if any—will evolve out of the Anthropocene remains to be seen. One thing is for certain: cute robots and brave astronauts will not save us on Spaceship *Earth*. We are the meteor hitting Earth. Will we be the newest version of the dinosaurs?

THE ULTIMATE STATUS UPDATE: EXTINCTION EVENT

Could the ecological visions in *WALL-E*, *Interstellar*, and *The Hunger Games* come true? In the news, there are stories of pollution, global warming, nuclear meltdowns, ecological destruction, the anthropogenic transformation of the planet. There are the growing fields of "disaster communications" and "disaster journalism," or the practice of reporting in the aftermath of natural and human-caused disasters.[18] So it's no surprise that our culture is filled with apocalyptic films and doomsday scenarios, especially in Hollywood films and TV series.

Obviously, there is a complexity of reasons for so many doomsday scenarios, reasons that stretch beyond the scope of this book. But one thing seems certain: there is a correlation between the Anthropocene, acceleration of consumer society, climate disruption and global warming, and the possible "sixth extinction" event. There

15   Jan Zalasiewicz, "A History in Layers: What Mark Will We Leave on the Planet?" *Scientific American* 315 (September 2016): 31–37.
16   J. R. McNeill and Peter Engelke, *The Great Acceleration: An Environmental History of the Anthropocene Since 1945*, (Cambridge, MA: Harvard University Press, 2014); Jeremy Davies, *The Birth of the Anthropocene* (Berkeley: University of California Press, 2016).
17   Zalasiewicz, "A History in Layers," 37.
18   George D. Haddow and Kim S. Haddow, *Disaster Communications in a Changing Media World* (Oxford, UK: Butterworth-Heineman, 2008); Mervi Pantti, Karin Wahl-Jorgensen, and Simon Cottle, *Disasters and the Media* (Bern: Peter Lang, 2012).

have been five apocalyptic mass extinctions on Earth, and 98 percent of all species that have lived on our planet have perished.

Could it happen to humanity because of our narcissism and our sense that we are invincible? Theorist Annalee Newitz believes that humankind will survive by scattering, adapting, and remembering our past. Because of these skills, Newitz sees possibilities for a new, postapocalyptic future in which humans will survive and possibly flourish.

We know that when early humans were threatened with extinction they fanned out across Africa in search of new homes, many of them leaving the continent entirely. This urge to break away from home and wander has saved us before and could save us in the future. If we colonize other planets, then we will be imitating the survival strategy of our ancestors. Scattering to the stars echoes our journey out of Africa—and it could be our best hope for lasting through the eons.[19]

Perhaps this explains why *Star Wars* and *Star Trek* have remained popular (chapter 10). To survive long-term, we know we must eventually leave the planet and venture into the vast cosmos. After all, *Star Trek* opens with the classic line "Space: the final frontier." This view also underlies Elon Musk's quest to colonize and terraform Mars. You might be a fan of Musk, but driving Tesla cars and colonizing Mars are not going to save Earth in your lifetime. Unless we take better care of this planet, we might well face the ultimate status update.

YOUR CHILDREN WILL LIVE INTO THE TWENTY-SECOND CENTURY

Consider this: if you decide to have children, they will likely live past the year 2100 and into the twenty-second century. What kind of planet do you want to leave them and their children? The planet of *WALL-E* and *Interstellar*? Or something better? It seems we need to ensure that we are worthy ancestors to the children who will inherit our civilization and planet.

CREDITS

Fig. 8.0.1a: Source: NASA.

Fig. 8.0.2: Source: https://en.wikipedia.org/wiki/Population_growth.

Fig. 8.0.3: Source: https://commons.wikimedia.org/wiki/File:NASA_astronaut_Scott_Kelly_captured_this_sunrise_over_the_US_East_Coast_01.jpg.

19 Annalee Newitz, *Scatter, Adapt, and Remember: How Humans Will Survive a Mass Extinction* (New York: Doubleday, 2013), 10.

HOW *AVATAR* DISTURBS GLOBAL MEDIA ECOSYSTEMS

ANTONIO LÓPEZ, PhD has a research focus on bridging ecojustice with media literacy. His most recent book is *Ecomedia Literacy: Integrating Ecology into Media Education* (Routledge). He is Associate Professor of Communications and Media Studies at John Cabot University in Rome, Italy. Resources and writing are available at: https://antonio-lopez.com/

According to original definitions, an *avatar* is the manifestation of a deity on Earth or the individual embodiment of a philosophy. In current vernacular usage, it refers to a computer-generated icon that represents a user in online forums or videogames. Combining all three usages is the avatar for Earth, which comes in the form of a portrait photographed by the crew of the Apollo 17 spacecraft in 1972. Often referred to as "The Blue Marble," the image doesn't just represent Earth but is a manifestation of a unique technological and cultural reality. It has the dual nature of being produced by the most advanced military-technology complex in world history while simultaneously responding to the desires of a latent planetary environmental movement.

As a gestalt image for the twentieth century, it has been repurposed across social sectors, ranging from signifying globalization on credit cards to representing the goddess Gaia by back-to-nature groups. Likewise, Pandora, the fictional planet of James Cameron's 2009 film *Avatar*, is an expanded and updated manifestation of the sensibility triggered by the image of Earth from space. While it may not be exactly the paradigm-shifting moment that "The Blue Marble" invoked fifty years ago, Avatar's $2.7 billion in global box office earnings shows that it tapped into some kind of zeitgeist that is undeniably significant.

Like the NASA image of Earth from space, *Avatar* demonstrates how symbolic resources circulate in the global media ecosystem in complex and contradictory ways. On the surface, *Avatar* is a typical product of the culture industry. Its production, marketing, product tie-ins, and normal hype that accompanies blockbuster films point to it being just another Hollywood spectacle appropriating social anxieties for profit. In particular, the film was criticized as a simplistic New Age fantasy that demeans and stereotypes indigenous cultures. Yet audiences reacted profoundly to the movie.

The film visualizes a war of opposing knowledge systems: one based on the commodification of natural resources and the other a sophisticated ecoculture struggling against colonial forces of extraction and destruction. The former is represented by corporate colonial forces attempting to conquer what they view as a lifeless planet, and the latter is the planet's native inhabitants, the Na'vi, who are connected to Pandora as an entity that is animate and alive. As a melodrama about the conflicts between anthropocentric and ecocentric values, *Avatar* likely resonates with global audiences because of how it dramatizes a struggle that is ongoing and real on contemporary Planet Earth.

There is tension between the film as passive spectacle and the film as something that can invoke ecological activism. Experiencing the film within the high-tech milieu of modern cinema, some audiences were in awe of the Na'vi and empathized with their plight, perhaps reflecting Cameron's description of Pandora's natives as avatars of our "higher selves." But some eco-critics also wondered if the film is just another cathartic spectacle that channels our ecological desires but does little to actually solve real problems like the Climate Crisis.

True enough, most culture-industry products hardly qualify as paragons of ecology. Filmmaking can be resource-intensive and damaging to the environment, and historically it does ideological work that reinforces the status quo. After all, Hollywood cinema is, first and foremost, an industry in the business of selling cultural commodities. So when it comes to environmental issues, Pietari Kääpä (2013) notes that even the best-intentioned Hollywood films reinforce an "ecological Panoptic," normalize the frameworks of the current geopolitical and geo-economic order, and reinforce Western hegemony.

By reflecting unexamined and assumed values, such films don't fundamentally challenge the power and hegemony at the source of ecological problems. "Feel-bad" cinema acknowledged problems but turns them into spectacles for consumption, often stereotyping and generalizing "Others" for Western viewers through an Orientalist gaze. The assumed audience of "greenbusters" like *Avatar* is primarily Western, so it will take some effort to recognize the possibility that *Avatar* offers a significant ecological moment in pop culture for transnational audiences that expands Hollywood's normal market segmentation. Like the Earth image, *Avatar* has the capacity to disturb global media ecosystems.

AVATAR'S SPECIAL AFFECT

Avatar's paradox is that in order for the film to connect viewers to an ecological paradigm that challenges consumerism and criticizes technology, it must do so as a vehicle of the culture industry. The film is a commodity that requires the price of a ticket as well as earning income from licensing for ancillary products, such as action figures and fast-food tie-ins. Additionally, as a 3D megaspectacle *Avatar* is another step in the progression of the "technological sublime" (Nye 1994) in which films

(and other entertainment products) increasingly amp up nerve stimulus while simultaneously veiling their deeper ideological work to move us away from directly experiencing nature as a source of awe and wonder.

Moreover, Jacques Ellul (1964) argued that technology is a result of technique, a way of thinking and categorizing the world that is based on the need for greater efficiency. Any tool designed by this mindset ultimately furthers and reinforces efficiency as an end unto itself. In media logic you can see this played out in the theory of the creeping cycle of desensitization. According to this model, in order to rise above the normalization of common aesthetic practices (standing out to gain audience share), media products become faster and louder, and more violent, sexualized, and shocking. If you compare a James Bond trailer from 1963 with one from 2020, you will see vastly different aesthetic practices, all enabled by more efficient imaging and filmmaking technologies that artists and producers have at their disposal.

Avatar's 3D and motion-capture technology creates a quandary. In order for the film to connect alienated viewers to nature, it must use the technology of the system that it critiques. Ironically, Pandora's human miners deploy 3D imaging to map and exploit the world, while the film uses the same technology to exploit the apparent contradiction between technology and nature. This thereby produces the curious effect of a 3D simulated world within a 3D simulated world, all the while offering an ecological allegory for the "real" world inhabited by the audience (see "Simulations of the Simulacra" by Baudrillard).

In *Avatar* there are also echoes of Marshall McLuhan's idea that media serve as extended prosthetics of our nervous system. Different examples of technological prosthetics include the violent machinery of the RoboCop variety deployed by the colonial military force, and then there is the *Avatar* Project, which allows humans to control biologically engineered clones in order to infiltrate Pandora's natives. The film itself serves as a prosthetic of our enlarged senses. Like us, the film's avatars are digital natives.

Ecologically speaking, *Avatar* as pure spectacle is problematic. But the relationship between media and ecology in the twenty-first century is dynamic. Audiences still retain some inherent desire to feel connected to nature. Indeed, as Ursula K. Heise (2008) asserts, the internet is often used in popular culture as a synecdoche for planetary connectivity, to signal an ongoing yearning for community and connectivity that is out of sync with the prevailing dogma of individualism promoted by neoliberal ideology. In *Avatar*, Pandora is itself a kind of organic internet where its native inhabitants "jack in" like the cyberpunk cowboys of William Gibson's prescient sci-fi novels of the 1980s and 1990s.

Not surprisingly, ecological themes are pervasive in sci-fi films and often challenge taken-for-granted views of the world. *Avatar*, along with other zeitgeist movies like the *Matrix* series, provokes audiences to imagine the world differently. Subsequently, many fans of the film ended up experiencing a form of Post-*Avatar* Depression Syndrome—a sense of loss and alienation because they believe they can never live in a place like Pandora or be like the Na'vi.

MEDIA OBJECTS, INTERTEXTUALITY, AND SYMBOLIC RESOURCES

Like Etienne Wenger's (1998) concept of a boundary object, a media object such as a film like *Avatar* has mutually agreed-upon properties, but it changes significance according to its perceived purpose and social utility. *Avatar* will mean different things depending on whether you are an actor, a director, a film crew, a producer, a theater owner, a streaming network executive, an audience, a film critic, an eco-activist, or a remixer.

Media objects that deal specifically with ecological issues have the dual condition of being "images of ecology" while also being part of an "ecology of images," that is, an ecology of meaning systems: "the social and industrial organization of images" and the "ecological arguments to be made about those processes" (Ross 1995, 172). Cox and Pezzullo (2017) assert that media are a form of "symbolic action" in which the media object not only says something, but also does something. As Carey (2009) proposes, media objects are both of and for something, like, for example, an architectural blueprint, which is a drawing of a house (a literal map of the house)

but is also for use in building the house. A media object like *Avatar* is a map of and for culture.

The elasticity of a media text like *Avatar* is partially explained through a look at its intertextuality (when a text refers to another text). As a kind of sci-fi version of a "cowboys and Indians" movie, *Avatar* plugs and plays a number of tropes from a long history of popular culture—including films like *Dances with Wolves*, *Last of the Mohicans*, *FernGully*, and Disney's *Pocahontas*—that trigger a kind of "genre literacy" in the audience (Gray 2006). Humorous mash-ups on the internet even went as far as intercutting audio from *Avatar* with sequences from *Pocahontas*.

But genre conventions are also didactic. When the Na'vi symbolize pan-indigenous peoples (such as their stylized blend of both plains Native American and East African tribal motifs), audiences can draw upon preexisting symbol maps to form an updated mythology. This is not without its traps. On a superficial level we have an updated version of the "white messiah" (Sam Worthington as Jake Sully) violently intervening to resolve a conflict between "noble savages" and a colonial war machine. Stereotypes like these remain hurtful to Native Americans, so such blatant associations in *Avatar* were not universally celebrated. On the other hand, the film's machines—as cartoony as they are—are literal world eaters, visually depicting the very system that exists on our planet right now, be they rain forest–consuming corporations or imperial invasions.

Ultimately, media's affective economy moves through audiences and interpretive communities (Gray 2006). *Avatar* catalyzed mash-ups, memes, discussion boards, online communities, and solidarity movements, mirroring participatory cultural practices described in Henry Jenkins's (2006) *Convergence Culture*. Since it exists in a digital world, *Avatar* can be copied, remixed, shared, and interacted with in ways that are unpredictable. Activists can take the movie and recontextualize it with real-life examples that others can connect with emotionally as "symbolic expressions of solidarity" (Gilland and Pickeral, [quoted in Hansen 2010, 62]).

For example, at the time of *Avatar*'s release an indigenous group in India, the Dongria Kondh, were fighting the mining operation of Vedanta Resources. Their situation closely paralleled that of the Na'vi, which got the attention of Survival International, an NGO that helps protect indigenous peoples. In a published appeal directed to James Cameron, Survival International directly framed the tribe's struggle against the British mining concern in the following terms:

> *Avatar* is fantasy ... and real.
>
> The Dongria Kondh tribe in India are struggling to defend their land against a mining company hell-bent on destroying their sacred mountain.
>
> Please help the Dongria.
>
> We've watched your film—now watch ours ...
>
> (Survival International 2010)

Survival International produced an accompanying short documentary and sent demonstrators in blue makeup and Na'vi prosthetics to protest in London outside the mining concern's headquarters. The strategy worked. Vedanta Resources canceled its project in India, and the Dongria Kondh's land was saved.

Curiously, before *Avatar* hit the global stage, Survival International released a photo taken from an airplane of an uncontacted tribe in the Amazon, which circulated through the twenty-four-hour media cycle because the image hauntingly struck a chord among commentators that there still remained "prehistoric" humans in our world. Are such images appealing because they offer us avatars of our latent ecological selves?

For indigenous people to insert their struggles into a global context (and hence to get attention for their causes), they have to contend with preexisting symbolic resources that are markers for planetary citizenship and ecology. Nick Couldry (2006, 92) asserts that the global media ecosystem serves as the main theater of action, because media are "the site of reality construction." Couldry advocates for the redistribution of "symbolic resources" to redress the misrepresentation or absence of actors who also make up the world's population, but whose presence is unknown in the same way that, post-9/11, many in the West lacked any understanding or awareness of the countries that were being invaded by Western powers.

Colonized people have long recognized that survival requires mastering the visual and written language of the oppressors. Consequently, battles over land and human rights often are also semiotic struggles, as Alf Hornborg (2001) demonstrates in his discussion of the Mi'kmaq fight for land rights in Nova Scotia, Canada. He notes that Native American activists needed to dress in traditional attire during court appearances to make the claim that their land is sacred. In Western culture, in the public arena someone dressed like a lawyer cannot claim a religious right to the land, but someone who "looks Indian" can.

Likewise, the simple tropes and genre mash-ups of *Avatar* took a similar role to make the ecological morality play obvious and digestible within established pop culture conventions. As Gilland and Pickeral argue, "'Being global' is less about building formal connections between international groups and far more about re-scaling the meaning of local actions to a global audience. This is achieved primarily by articulating a form of imaginal solidarity, while simultaneously maintaining the importance of domestic issues" (quoted in Hansen 2010). To this end, we can expect to see more blue beings appearing on Earth in the very near future.

CONCLUSION

Though *Avatar*'s message is often criticized as contradictory, global environmentalism is a mix of art, science, political activism, and media. The space opened by the film enabled local struggles in India, Brazil, Ecuador, and the Middle East to be newly contextualized as global political concerns that otherwise lacked previous semiotic expression in the planetary media ecosystem. In the case of *Avatar*, pop culture can make visible on a global scale the latent desire to solve environmental problems. The example of *Avatar* shows how a media object disturbs different media ecosystems.

If we are to analyze the film solely in terms of its function as a commodity, then it certainly belongs to the industrial media ecosystem we call Hollywood. But when it's remixed and shared, it enters into other media ecosystems—be they activist webs, social media networks, or postcolonial genre critiques—to become something global and participatory. Just as the avatar of the Earth image from space has come to serve different social purposes, films like *Avatar* tap into the spirit of our age to disturb the preexisting order and to produce something new. As Neil Postman (1998, para. 16) argued, "Technological change is not additive; it is ecological. ... A new medium does not add something; it changes everything." To some, *Avatar* changed and disturbed the world.

REFERENCES

Carey, J. T. 2009. *Communication as Culture, Revised Edition: Essays on Media and Society.* New York: Routledge.

Couldry, N. 2006. *Listening beyond the Echoes: Media, Ethics, and Agency in an Uncertain World.* (Boulder, CO: Paradigm Publishers.

Cox, R., and Pezzullo, P. C. 2015. *Environmental Communication and the Public Sphere,* 5th ed. Los Angeles: SAGE.

Ellul, J. 1964. *The Technological Society.* New York: Knopf.

Gray, J. 2006. *Watching with The Simpsons: Television, Parody, and Intertextuality.* New York: Routledge.

Hansen, A. 2010. *Environment, Media and Communication.* London: Routledge.

Heise, U. K. 2008. *Sense of Place and Sense of Planet: The Environmental Imagination of the Global.* New York: Oxford University Press.

Hornborg, A. 2001. *The Power of the Machine: Global Inequalities of Economy, Technology, and Environment.* Lanham, MD: AltaMira Press.

Jenkins, H. 2006. *Convergence Culture: Where Old and New Media Collide.* New York: New York University Press.

Kääpä, P. 2013. "Transnational Approaches to Ecocinema: Charting an Expansive Field." In *Transnational Ecocinema: Film Culture in an Era of Ecological Transformation,* ed. P. Kääpä and T. Gustafsson, 21–44. Bristol, UK: Intellect.

Nye, D. E. 1994. *American Technological Sublime.* Cambridge, MA: MIT Press.

Postman, N. 1998. "Five Things We Need to Know About Technological Change." March 28, 1998. https://samim.io/dl/Five_Things_We_Need_to_Know_About_Technological_Change_by_Neil_Postman.pdf

Ross, A. 1995. *The Chicago Gangster Theory of Life: Nature's Debt to Society.* Brooklyn, NY: Verso.

Survival International. 2010. "Tribal People Appeal to James Cameron." February 8, 2010. https://www.survivalinternational.org/news/5529

Wenger, E. 1998. *Communities of Practice: Learning, Meaning, and Identity.* Cambridge, UK: Cambridge University Press.

HOLLYWOOD AND CLIMATE CHANGE

from *Ecocinema Theory and Practice*

STEPHEN RUST is a Post-Doctoral Fellow at the University of Oregon where he teaches film history and media aesthetics. His publications explore the intersections of media, culture, and the environment, and have appeared in such journals as *Film & History*, *ISLE*, and *Jump Cut*.

Tipped off by a phonecall to the office, a National Weather Service employee turns on the Weather Channel and sees that an unprecedented storm front has suddenly descended upon Los Angeles. He immediately calls his supervisor for authorization to issue a severe weather alert. Cut to the supervisor who answers the call, turns on his television, and walks to his bedroom window to witness a funnel cloud form on a nearby hillside. Cut to paleo-climatologist Jack Hall (Dennis Quaid) and his team of researchers as they walk into the White House situation room, which is filled with televisions tuned to Fox News coverage of a tornado destroying the Hollywood sign. Cut back to the supervisor as he drives into downtown LA, steps out of his car, and watches several more funnels destroying the city's skyscrapers. Cut to the employee watching television who suddenly sees his boss standing directly in the storm's path. Cut to the boss who answers a phone call from the employee and

gets in his car to flee. Cut to the employee who watches as a funnel picks up a city bus and drops it directly on the supervisor's car. Cut to a Fox News reporter who has been tracking the "only this is the real thing!" he shouts into the camera just before being smashed by the wall of a building, flung by a global warming super-tornado in this sequence from Hollywood blockbuster film *The Day After Tomorrow*.

Released in 2004, *The Day After Tomorrow* earned more than $500 million at the global box office and is often mentioned alongside former Vice President Al Gore's *An Inconvenient Truth* (2006) as a touchstone moment in the history of environmental cinema.[1] The timely release of these films occurred during the same period that a significant majority of Americans came to recognize climate change as a phenomenon that will impact not only the planetary atmosphere but every aspect of social life.[2] Responding to what Yale public

---

1 See for example Kamienski, Sheldon and Michael E. Kraft. "Forward." In Joseph DiMento and Pamela Doughman (eds.) *Climate Change: What it Means for us, Our Children, and Our Grandchildren*. Cambridge, MA: MIT Press, 2007; Murray, Robin and Joseph Heumann. *Ecology and Popular Film: Cinema on the Edge*. Albany: State University of New York Press, 2009; and Willoquet-Maricondi, Paula, Ed. *Framing the World: Explorations in Ecocriticism and Film*. Charlottesville and London: University of Virginia Press, 2010.

2 For public opinion polling data confirming this shift see: "Sea Change in Public Attitudes Toward Global Warming Emerge: Climate Change Seen as Big a Threat as Terrorism." Yale Center for Environmental Law and Policy (February 27, 2008). http://opa.yale.edu/news/article.aspx?id=4787. Additionally, between 2003 and 2006, "false balance" (i.e. reporting the issue as a scientific debate rather than consensus) almost completely disappeared from major US newspapers, decreasing from 16.6 percent of coverage in 2001 to 3.1 percent in

opinion researchers have described as a "sea change" in American public attitudes toward global warming between 2004 and 2007, this reading provides a brief historical survey of climate change cinema and analyzes how *The Day After Tomorrow* and *An Inconvenient Truth* uniquely demonstrate that cinematic texts can and do reflect hegemonic environmental perceptions as well as the ways in which those prevailing hegemonies have shifted over time. That is, they offer a window into what I term the "cultural logic of ecology," and epitomize the pronounced shift in American popular discourse about the relationship between human beings and the Earth that is taking shape in the early twenty-first century.

Climate change is not the only global environmental risk exploited by Hollywood in recent years: consider nuclear war (*Terminator 2: Judgment Day*, 1991), deforestation (*Fern Gully*, 1992), bioterrorism (*28 Days Later*, 2002), species extinction (*Earth*, 2009), and population growth (*Slumdog Millionaire*, 2008), for example.[3] Yet, climate change films also deserve sustained ecocritical analysis because over the coming decades the phenomenon is expected to exacerbate existing environmental problems and to present new challenges.

By 2050, based on mid-range scenarios, climate change alone is expected to globally displace up to 200 million people and to ensure that between 15 and 37 percent of the world's terrestrial fauna are "committed to extinction."[4] Already strained by the forces of globalization, developing nations can expect to endure the most immediate and severe impacts.[5] At the most recent round of UN climate talks, held in Durban, South Africa in late 2011, more than 180 nations signaled their continued willingness to take action on climate change by voting to extend the 1997 Kyoto Protocol through 2015.[6] Meanwhile, the United States—the world's top per capita energy consumer and greenhouse gas emitter—continues to sit on the sidelines, hampered by deep-seated political and ideological divisions.[7] Nevertheless, this reading demonstrates that between 2004 and 2008 *The Day After Tomorrow* and *An Inconvenient Truth* played a crucial role in American culture by drawing sustained media attention to the issue, raising awareness among viewers, and signaling a popular shift in the cultural logic of ecology.

2006. Boykoff, M. T. "Flogging a Dead Norm? Newspaper Coverage of Anthropogenic Climate Change in the United States and United Kingdom from 2003 to 2006." *Area* 19.4 (2007): 470–481.

3 See for example, Cubitt, Sean. *EcoMedia*. New York: Rodopi, 2005; Chris, Cynthia. *Watching Wildlife*. Minneapolis: University of Minnesota Press, 2006; and Lu, Sheldon and Jiayan Mi, eds. *Chinese Ecocinema*. Seattle: University of Washington Press, 2010.

4 In the Western Hemisphere, Lawyer, et al., predict a minimum extinction rate of 10 percent for all fauna by 2100 even if carbon emissions are severely restricted, and note that extinction could reach 90 percent in some geographic areas. Lawyer, Joshua, et al., "Projected Climate-Induced Faunal Change in the Western Hemisphere." *Ecology* 90.3 (2009): 588–97; Thomas, Chris D., et al. "Extinction Risk from Climate Change." *Nature* 427 (January 8, 2004): 145–8; and Wynn, Gerard. "Climate Change Forces New Migration Response-Study." *Reuters* (June 10, 2009). http://www.reuters.com/article/ idUSLA 1045416

5 Smith, Mark D. *Just One Planet: Poverty, Justice and Climate Change*. Warwickshire, UK: Intermediate Technology Publications, 2006.

6 Importantly, however, those nations did not include China and the United States, respectively the world's top overall energy consumers and greenhouse gas emitters. Canada also used the occasion to officially withdraw from the treaty, citing economic cost as its primary reason. Samuelsohn, Darren. "Durban Climate Conference Ends with Deal for More Deal Making." *Politico* (December 11, 2011). www.politico.com/news/stories/1211/ 70252.html

7 President Clinton signed the Kyoto Protocol in 1998 but Congress refused to ratify it. President George W. Bush (2001–9) refused to endorse the treaty. In 2009, after the election of President Obama, the Democrats passed a climate bill (dubbed "cap and trade") in the House of Representatives on a Republicans united to prevent 57 Democrats and 2 Independents from ending debate on the bill, effectively killing the measure. The Senate's move prompted the Obama administration to postpone any efforts on federal climate legislation until after the 2012 presidential election. The administration has also cited China's unwillingness to agree to binding emissions targets as a reason for its decision not to endorse international agreements. Wasserman, Lee. "Four Ways to Kill a Climate Bill." *New York Times*. July 26, 2010: A23.

A BRIEF HISTORY OF CLIMATE CHANGE CINEMA

In a sense, all cinema is a form of climate cinema because anthropogenic warming of the climate was already underway by the time Edison and the Lumière Brothers made their first films. For thousands of years prior to 1750, carbon dioxide in the earth's atmosphere averaged around 280 parts per million (ppm) by volume.[8] Yet by 1957, when Charles Keeling began measuring carbon dioxide concentrations at the National Oceanic and Atmospheric Administration's Mauna Loa Observatory in Hawaii, levels had risen to 310 ppm.[9] In 2010 the total volume of carbon dioxide in the earth's atmosphere surpassed 393 ppm, an increase of 40 percent over the preindustrial era.[10]

Increased levels of carbon dioxide and other greenhouse gases in the atmosphere amplify "the greenhouse effect," a natural process that traps the sun's heat at the earth's surface. The increased carbon released through the burning of fossil fuels is acting "like a thermal blanket to keep the earth warmer than it would otherwise be."[11] As James Hansen, director of NASA's Goddard Institute, explained to Congress in 2008: "Warming so far, about 2°F over land areas, seems almost innocuous,

being less than day-to-day weather fluctuations. But more warming is already 'in-the-pipeline', delayed only by the great inertia of the world ocean."[12] Although it is impossible to accurately predict the effects of sea level rise and shifting weather patterns, it is clear that these issues demand serious and immediate attention.[13]

Interestingly, 1896 was a touchstone year in the intertwined histories of cinema and climate change. That year, Swedish chemist Svante Arrhenius first calculated that doubling the amount of carbon dioxide in the atmosphere would cause average global temperatures to rise between 5 and 6°C (9 to 11°F), a result "remarkably similar to current projections."[14] Expecting population and energy consumption to remain relatively consistent, however, Arrhenius estimated that it would take nearly 3,000 years for the volume of carbon dioxide in the atmosphere to reach 500 ppm, a level we may potentially reach by 2050.[15] Also in 1896, Lumière cinematographers began traveling the globe and filming events for local audiences.[16] Among the first cinematographers was Kamill Serf, who traveled to the oil fields of Baku, Azerbaijan, and shot a 30-second film of burning oil wells.[17] In the film, flames billow from two tall derricks and a plume of smoke covers the sky at the top of the frame. The scale of the spectacle is emphasized by a small human figure walking away from the center

8   Kluger, Jeffrey. "What Now for Our Feverish Planet?" *Time* (April 3, 2007).
9   Doyle, Alistair. "C02 at New Heights Despite Economic Slowdown." Reuters (March 15, 2010). www.reuters.com/article/idUSTRE62E2KJ20100315?feedType=RSS&feedName=environmentNews&utm_source=feedburner&utm_medium=feed&utm_campaign=Feed%3A+reuters%2Fenvironment+%28News+%2F+US+%2F+Environment%29>; and "Atmospheric C02 at Mauna Loa Observatory." National Oceanic and Atmospheric Administration. Accessed October 15, 2011. www.esrl.noaa.gov/gmd/ccgg/trends/co2_data_ mlo.html
10   McKibben, Bill. "The Science of 350, the Most important Number on the Planet." *Treehugger* (October 6, 2009). www.treehugger.com/files/ 2009/10/the-science-of-350-the-most-important-number.php
11   Leiserowitz, Anthony A. "Global Warming in the American Mind." University of Oregon. Environmental Science Dissertation, 2003: 2–5.
12   Hansen, James. "Twenty Years Later Tipping Points Near on Global Warming." *Guardian* (June 23, 2008). www.guardian.co.uk/environment/2008 /jun/23/climatechange.carbonemissions
13   Spotts, Peter S. "Earth Nears Tipping Point on Climate Change." *Christian Science Monitor* (May 30, 2007). www.csmonitor.com/2007/0510/p02s01-wogi.html
14   Leiserowitz, "Global Warming": 6.
15   Caldiera, Ken. "C02 Emissions Could Violate EPA Ocean Quality Standards Within Decades." *Earth Observatory*. National Aeronautics and Space Administration (September 19, 2007). http://earthobservatory.nasa.gov/ Newsroom/view. php?id=33395
16   As film historian Charles Musser has discussed, the differing technologies used by each film company reflects their differing ideological (and ecological) approaches. Musser, Charles. "At the Beginning: Motion Picture Production, Representation and Ideology at the Edison and Lumiére Companies." In Lee Grievson and Peter Kramer (eds.) *The Silent Cinema Reader*. New York: Routledge, 2004: 15–30.
17   Searight, Sarah. "Region of Eternal Fire: Petroleum Industry in Caspian Sea Region." *History Today* 5.8 (2000): 46.

derrick and out of the frame, as if this is all just business as usual.

Intended primarily to astound rather than persuade audiences, Serf's actuality film falls under film historian Tom Gunning's description of the early "cinema of attractions."[18] When considered from a modern ecocritical perspective, however, as Murray and Heumann suggest, the film's meaning shifts from spectacle to catastrophe, especially when considered alongside material consequences, such as *Lessons of Darkness* (1992) and *There Will Be Blood* (2007).[19] These changing meanings of spectacle and catastrophe are also present in films that feature automobiles. While Henry Ford, chief engineer at Edison Illumination Company, completed work on his first gasoline-powered automobile, the "Quadricycle" in 1896,[20] between the 1930s and 1950s gangster films (*Scarface*, 1932), war films (*Pittsburgh*, 1943), teen films (*Rebel Without a Cause*, 1956), and other genres of this era illustrate that in the Western world the automobile is the dominant form of transportation, oil is the primary source of energy, and the United States is the dominant military and economic power.[21] By the 1960s, suburbia, car culture, fast food, and other consumerist images that would later be associated with America's growing carbon footprint had become the central motifs of Hollywood cinema.[22] The fact that, as modern viewers, we are compelled to reinterpret historical images of oil, cars, and their related military-industrial complexes through the lens of global environmental risk underscores the degree to which cinema and its viewership can provide a useful glimpse into the shifting nuances that mark the cultural logic of ecology.

Modern environmentalism is often said to begin with Rachel Carson's bestselling *Silent Spring* in 1962. As Greg Garrard points out in his book *Ecocritiasm* (2004), Carson's title operates on one level as an allusion to the loss of birdsong due to the overuse of pesticides, and on another "as a synecdoche for a more general environmental apocalypse."[23] In 1968, biologist Paul Ehrlich also made headlines with *The Population Bomb*, in which he predicted that unchecked population growth would lead to mass starvation and global food shortages by the end of the century.[24] This period also witnessed the formation of environmental organizations such as Greenpeace, the first Earth Day in 1970, and passage of the Endangered Species Act in 1973.

As David Ingram and Pat Brereton have discussed at length, during the 1960s and 1970s, environmental perspectives found their way into popular film through a new generation of filmmakers.[25] In such films as *Born free* (1966), *Omega Man* (1971), and *Silent Running* (1972), the nonhuman world is no longer imagined merely as a reflection of the characters' inner psychology, as in the classical Hollywood style, but as a character with its own agency.

Concurrent with a rapid increase in fossil fuel consumption, scientific understandings of climate change also began to shift during the 1960s and 1970s, signaled by the publication of a 1956 paper by Roger Revelle and Hans Seuss of the Scripps Institute of Oceanography. "Human beings," they argued, "are now carrying out a large-scale geophysical experiment of a kind that could not have happened in the past nor be reproduced in the future."[26] A year later, the first version of what became

---

18   Gunning, Tom. "The Cinema of Attractions: Early Film, Its Spectator and the Avant-Garde." In Thomas Elsaesser and Adam Barker (eds.) Early *Film*. London: British Film Institute, 1989: 56–62.
19   Murray and Heumann, *Ecology and Popular Film*: 19–35.
20   Clymer, Floyd. *Treasure of Early American Automobiles*. New York: Bonanza Books, 1950: 58.
21   See for example, Duffield, John S. *Over a Barrel: The Costs of US Dependence on Foreign Oil*. Stanford, CA: Stanford University Press, 2008; Friedman, Thomas. *Hot, Flat, and Crowded*. New York: Farrar, Straus and Giroux, 2008; and Zakaria.
22   Ehrlich, Paul and Anne Ehrlich. *The Dominant Animal: Human Evolution and the Environment*. Washington, DC: Island Press, 2008.
23   Garrard, Greg. *Ecocriticism*. London: Routledge, 2004: 6.
24   Repeating the same basic argument made by Thomas Malthus in 1789 that unchecked population growth would eventually outstrip food production, Ehrlich went so far as to call for the sterilization of men in over populated (i.e. non-Western) countries and was roundly criticized for his alarmist and Eurocentric positions. Ibid. 93–95.
25   Ingram, David. *Green Screen: Environmentalism in Hollywood Cinema*. Exeter, UK: University of Exeter Press, 2000; and Brereton, Pat. *Hollywood Utopia*. Bristol, UK: Intellect, 2005.
26   Leiserowitz, "Global Warming": 6.

known as the Keeling Curve (a graphic representation of atmospheric carbon levels from 1958 to the present) was published. Reeling's measurements disproved current scientific assumptions that the oceans were absorbing excess carbon and proving the greenhouse effect.[27] During the 1970s, as Carl Sagan explains in his 1980 television documentary *Cosmos*, the scientific community generally agreed that fossil fuels were causing a buildup of carbon dioxide in the atmosphere but had yet to reach a consensus on global warming.

It makes sense, then, that the first film to directly portray global warming would be a post-apocalyptic science-fiction film set in the future. *Soylent Green* (Richard Fleisher, 1973) stars Charleton Heston and Edward G. Robinson as detectives on the case of a murdered food-industry executive. The film is set in New York in the year 2022, a time when 41 million inhabitants are enduring a permanent heat wave, there are no longer plants or animals, and a single corporation controls half of the world's food supply.[28] Detective Thorn (Heston) solves the mystery by figuring out that the executive arranged his own murder after realizing that the Earth's penultimate source of food—plankton—has gone extinct. While a few rich elites enjoy fresh food grown in greenhouses, the masses have no choice but to eat Soylent Green, a cracker made out of people. The film's aesthetics (including an opening in which still photographs are used to narrate the history of industrialization), morally ambiguous hero, stark themes, and unfixed ending quickly made it a cult classic.[29]

With its uncanny foreshadowing of present concerns *Soylent Green* is important to the development of ecocinema studies. Ingram, for example, reads the film as an articulation of the myth of "the total city and the end of nature."[30] In the film's final shot, Thorn's upraised finger dissolves into a field of tulips as the credits roll, accompanied by Beethoven's *Symphony No. 6* ("Pastoral"). This postmodern ending leads Ingram to argue that the film's "formulation of ecological crisis as already total, and of corporate and state power as monolithic, leaves little space for the formulation of a convincing politics of resistance."[31] Understood historically, however, the final image of the film's hero—his fist raised in protest as he takes his dying breath—remains a poignant reminder of the challenges facing the environmental movement by the mid-1970s, as the era of mass public demonstration was coming to an end. Further, in light of recent estimates by global health experts that as many as 50 million climate refugees may need to find new places to live by as soon as 2020, the film's depiction of food shortages and riots have become increasingly relevant from an environmental justice perspective.[32]

Through the late twentieth-century, as the science of global warming solidified, the energy industry and conservative think tanks led a concerted effort in the mainstream media to frame the issue as a theoretical debate rather than a practical concern, as Alison Anderson documents in *Media, Culture, and Environment* and Julia Doyle in *Mediating Climate Change*.[33] By the time global warming reemerged in cinema during the late 1980s and early 1990s, "a majority of scientists [had become] convinced that global warming was occurring."[34] Opinion polls also demonstrate growing awareness of the issue among the general public. In a 2007 research article

---

27 Ibid: 7.

28 The film is loosely based on Harry Harrison's 1966 novel *Make Room! Make Room!* but references to global warming and cannibalism are original to the film. [...]

29 *Soylent Green* was available on VHS throughout the 1980s and 1990s, was released on DVD in 2003, and is expected to become available on Blu-Ray in 2012 in anticipation of a forthcoming remake. "Soylent Green (Remake)." *New York Times* (April 2, 2010). http://movies.nytimes.com/movie/444298/Soylent-Green-remake-/overview

30 Ingram, *Green Screen:* 143, 154.

31 Ibid: 155.

32 The figure of 50 million environmental refugees was cited by University of California, Los Angeles, professor of Global and Immigrant Health Cristina Tirado at the 2011 meeting of the American Association for the Advancement of Science. Zelman, Joanna. "50 Million Environmental Refugees by 2020, Experts Predict." *Huffington Post* (February 22,2011). www.huffingtonpost.com/ 2011/02/22/ environmental-refugees-50_n_826488.html

33 Anderson, Alison. *Media, Culture, and Environment.* New Brunswick, NJ: Rutgers, UP, 1997; and Doyle, Julia. *Mediating Climate Change.* London: Ashgate, 2011.

34 Leiserowitz, "Global Warming": 8–9.

detailing 20 years of public opinion polling on the issue, Mathew Nisbet and Teresa Meyers explain that the percentage of people who had heard about global warming increased dramatically over the period, from 39 percent in 1986 to 58 percent in late 1988 and upwards of 80 percent by the early 1990s.[35] Dr. Hansen's 1988 congressional testimony on global warming and concerns over ozone depletion had even led *Time* magazine to forgo its typical "Person of the Year" award and name Earth its "Planet of the Year" in 1989. However, there were only a few passing references and allusions to climate change in Hollywood films during the 1980s and 1990s, demonstrating that the issue was generally perceived as lacking relevance to the concerns of daily life.

For example, in Spike Lee's *Do the Right Thing* (1989), the only character to discuss global warming is an old wino who is laughed off as making it up, and the excessive heat wave portrayed in the film is used primarily as a metaphor to comment upon the era's heightened racial tensions. In *Batman Returns* (1992), the Penguin jokingly decides to run for office on the slogan "Stop Global Warming! Start Global Cooling!" Released the summer after the culture wars propelled the Republican Party into majority control of Congress for the first time in 40 years, *Waterworld* (1995), a post-apocalyptic film starring Kevin Costner, which visualizes the polar ice caps melting in its opening sequence, is considered one of the decade's biggest flops.[36] The Charlie Sheen vehicle *The Arrival* (1996), which blames global warming on an alien invasion, and Steven Spielberg and Stanley Kubrick's *A.I.* (2001), which is also set in a dystopic future beset by global warming, also performed below expectations at the American box office. And while the success or failure of any film depends on many factors, it is clear that at the beginning of the twenty-first century climate change had yet to emerge as a rival to such risks as nuclear war and terrorism in the cultural imagination.[37]

ENVIRONMENTALITY IN *THE DAY AFTER TOMORROW* AND *AN INCONVENIENT TRUTH*

A compilation of peer-reviewed science that drew carefully on old and new research, the United Nations Intergovernmental Panel on Climate Change (IPCC), represented the early twenty-first century scientific consensus on climate change.[38] The most recent IPCC report (2007) states: "Human induced warming of climate system is unequivocal" and there is "very high confidence" that human industrial activities are to blame.[39] Additionally, a comprehensive survey of American climate scientists conducted in 2007 found that "belief in human-induced warming has more than doubled since the last major survey of American climate scientists in 1991 … Eighty-four percent now say they personally believe human-induced warming is occurring.[40] Yet in early 2004, when *The Day After Tomorrow* was released, global warming policy remained notably absent from the public agendas of the federal government and the

---

35   Nisbet, Mathew C. and Teresa Myers. "The Polls—Trends: Twenty Years of Public Opinion about Global Warming." *Public Opinion Quarterly.* 71.3 (Fall 2007): 450.

36   *Waterworld* was the most expensive film produced to date at an estimated cost of $175 million but took in only $88 million at the US box-office and struggled to break even worldwide. *A.I.* performed well internationally but was widely panned by critics in the US where it earned only $75 million. Bishop, Tim. "What Makes a Film Flop?" *BBC News Online* (April 13, 2004). http://news.bbc.co.Uk/2/hi/entertainment/3621859.stm

37   Beck, Ulrick. *World at Risk.* London: Polity, 2008.

38   Although the IPCC's findings were somewhat tainted in 2009 by the leaking of questionable emails written by climate scientists at East Anglia University in Britain (an event dubbed "Climategate"), three independent investigations concluded in 2010 that no data had been tampered with. See, for example, Palin, Sarah. "Sarah Palin on the Politicization of the Copenhagen Climate Conference." *Washington Post* (December 9, 2009). www.Washingtonpost.com/wp-dyn/content/article/2009/12/08/AR2009120803402.html

39   Pachauri, R. K. and Reisinger, A. (eds.). "Contibution of Working Groups on Climate Change." Geneva: United Nations Intergovernmental Panel on Climate Change, 2007.

40   Lichter, Robert S. "Climate Change Scientists Agree on Warming, Disagree on Dangers, and Don't Trust the Media's Coverage of Climate Change." Statistical Assessment Service (STATS). George Mason University. (April 24, 2008). http://stats.org/stories/2008/global_warming_survey_apr23_08.html

mainstream media. Behind the scenes, the White House was busy censoring sensitive government reports and preventing Dr. Hansen and other scientists from sharing their findings with the public, despite the fact that the US military was already incorporating climate change into its long-term strategic planning.[41]

Given the lack of sustained media attention to the issue, coupled with the lackluster performance of writer/director Roland Emmerich's previous film *Godzilla* (1998), executives at 20th Century Fox had good reason to worry if the studio would recoup *The Day After Tomorrow*'s $125 million budget.[42] Yet, in a strange twist of corporate synergy—enabled by the horizontal integration of Rupert Murdoch's News Corporation—in March 2004 Fox News launched an aggressive television and internet campaign to attack the accuracy of the film's depiction of abrupt climate change.[43] Although evidence does not suggest that this move was planned from the top down by News Corp, the 2007 documentary *Everything's Cool* shows how media outlets like CNN, MSNBC, and ABC News quickly responded to Fox and stories about the film spread virally across television, print, and the internet.[44] Endorsements of the film by leading environmental advocates like Robert F. Kennedy, Jr. and Al Gore also fanned the flames. Describing "all the hoopla" and "media feeding frenzy" that developed in anticipation of the film's exaggerated portrayal of climate change, the editors of

Discover decided that the magazine would join the growing list of nationwide publications (*including Greenpeace, National Geographic, Newsweek, Science,* and *Time*) to dedicate extensive coverage to global warming and its depiction in the film in the weeks before and after the film's release.[45] Along with the controversy, the studio's massive advertising campaign, saturation booking in 3,435 domestic movie theaters, and Emmerich's cultural cachet as the director of the smash hit *Independence Day* (1996) helped *The Day After Tomorrow* open to an $85 million Memorial Day opening weekend in the US.[46]

The Day After Tomorrow's plot follows Jack's exploits as he struggles to keep his family together while convincing the US administration that a long-term climate shift is underway. Jack's story intensifies when the film introduces a climate "tipping point." In the world of Emmerich's disaster genre film, neither scientific consensus nor increasing weather anomalies inspire the government or the public to begin mitigating global warming in time to avert disaster. Only when Americans finally *see* climate change and *feel* its direct impact within the United States, the film argues, will they accept responsibility for causing global warming and begin to take action in response to it.

But, in a disaster film this moment of recognition—the turning point in the narrative when the characters begin to act—is signaled to the audience as being

---

41 Bowen, Mark. *Censoring Science.* New York: Dutton, 2008; and "Hot Politics." *Frontline,* Public Broadcasting, 2007. www.pbs.org/wgbh/pages/frontline/hotpolitics/

42 See for example, Clark, Mike. "The Day After Tomorrow': Cloudy, Chance of Frosty Reception." *USA Today* (May 27, 2004). Accessed April 2009. www.usatoday.com/life/movies/reviews/2004-05-27-day-after-tomorrow_x. htm; and Jowit, Julliette and Robin McKie. "Cool Reception for Ice-Age Movie." The *Observer* (April 25, 2004). Accessed September 2009. www.guardian.co.uk/environment/2004/apr/25/film.theobserver

43 Milloy, Steven. "Global Warming: The Movie." *Fox News* (March 26, 2004). Accessed September 2009. www.foxnews.com/story/0,2933,115203,00.html

44 "Hollywood Flick Generates Political Interest." *CNN* (May 25, 2004); and Tapperland, Jake and Toni L. Wilson. "Are the Latest Political Movies Propaganda?" *ABC News* (June 17,2004). http://abcnews.go.com/WNT/story? id=131720

45 Lemly, Brad. "A New Ice Age?" *Discovery* (May 22, 2004). http://discover magazine.com/2004/may/a-new-ice-age-day-after-tomorrow; Lovgren, Stefan, "'Day After Tomorrow' Ice Age Impossible, Researchers Say." *National Geographic* (May 27, 2004). http://news.nationalgeographic.com/news/2004/05/0527_040527_DayAfter. html; "We Have to Think of the Future." *Newsweek* (May 25, 2004). www.newsweek.com/2004/05/25/ we-have-to-think-of-the-future.html; Hansen, Bogi, et al. "Already the Day After Tomorrow." *Science* 305.5686 (August 2004): 953–954; and Grossman, Lev. "Hollywood's Global Warming." *Time* (May 17, 2004). www.time.com/time/magazine/article/ 0,9171,638411,00.html

46 Like *Godzilla,* attendance for *The Day After Tomorrow* dropped off dramatically after its opening weekend. However, although the film's revenues dropped more than 58 percent during the second weekend, the film is considered a blockbuster because it went on to make more than $400 globally. Box-office data available at BoxOfficeMojo.com.

too late to avoid catastrophe. Satisfying the generic demands of disaster films, global warming triggers a killer storm that sends North America into an ice age over the course of a few days. Recalling the "revenge of nature" film cycle that began with *Jaws* in the mid-1970s, Harold Klosser's score employs a two-note leitmotif that creates a character out of the storm according to a "symbolic attributive process."[47] As the storm descends on Los Angeles and New York, the low register of the motif is accented by the downbeat of the second note and thus suggests large size and power while imbuing the storm with agency and menace.

While scientists were quick to point out the film's flaws, particularly its shift in meaning of the phrase "climate tipping point" from geological time (decades) to cinematic time (minutes), the film's popularity offered the scientific community a rare opportunity to directly communicate their views with the public. *USA Today* reported that although climate scientists and environmental groups generally regarded the film's science as "bunk, most applauded it for bringing the global warming debate to Americans' attention."[48] Despite the film's narrative closure in a melodramatic space of innocence—highlighted by the restoration of the hero's nuclear family and Becker's *mea culpa* speech about the perils of ignoring humanity's impact on the environment—the government's decision to evacuate comes too late to save much of the nation, leaving hundreds of millions dead or displaced to Mexico. Exploiting the digital technologies whose manufacture, development, and use are enabled by globalization, and adapting the science of climate change to fit the conventions of the disaster film, *The Day After Tomorrow* drew widespread public attention by providing a spectacular hyperbole of the cataclysmic social and ecological impacts of global warming.

In a unique reception study completed the year the film was first released, researchers coordinated a global research survey of *The Day After Tomorrow*'s audiences. In his report on the film's American reception, Anthony Leiserowitz concludes:

> *The Day After Tomorrow* had a significant impact on the climate change risk perceptions, conceptual models, behavioral intentions, and even voting intentions of moviegoers ... These results demonstrate that the representation of environmental risks in popular culture can influence public attitudes and behaviors.[49]

Leiserowitz further notes that the film's impact on perceptions of climate change were felt more keenly in the United States than in Europe and Japan where the public was not so skeptical of climate science. Based on the results of a survey conducted three weeks after the film opened, researchers determined that, "across the board, the movie appears to have had a strong influence on watchers' risk perceptions of global warming" yet also concluded that the film's reception had not (in and of itself) produced a major shift in the culture.[50]

On the one hand, the media attention the film garnered "paled in comparison to either *Fahrenheit 9/11* or *The Passion of the Christ.*" On the other hand, Leiserowitz notes, "Some commentators had predicted that the film would bring more public attention to the issue of global warming than the publication of most scientific articles, reports, or congressional testimonies, and this prediction appears to have been correct."[51] In *Hollywood Science*, physicist Sidney Perkowitz argues that "despite its imperfections [the film] and for illustrating the conflict that can and does occur when scientific findings clash with government policies or agendas."[52] *The Day After Tomorrow* may not have been the first commercial film to portray global warming, but unlike *Soylent Green* it was able to draw sustained media attention to the issue.

47   Wingstedt, Johnny, Sture Brändström, and Jan Berg. "Narrative Music, Visuals, and Meaning in Film." *Visual Communication.* 9.2 (2010): 196.

48   Bowles, Scott. "'The Day After Tomorrow' Heats Up a Political Debate." *USA Today* (May 26, 2004). www. usatoday.com/educate/college/firstyear/ articles/20040530.htm

49   Leiserowitz, Anthony A. "Before and After *The Day After Tomorrow*: A U.S. Study of Climate Change Risk Perception." *Environment* 46.9 (November 2004): 36.

50   Ibid: 31.

51   Ibid: 34.

52   Perkowitz, Sidney. *Hollywood Science: Movies, Science, and the End of the World.* New York: Columbia, 2007: 208.

As hyperbolic as a film like *The Day After Tomorrow* may appear in its rendering of a serious issue like anthropogenic climate change into mass entertainment, key moments in the film, like the scene described at the beginning of this reading, have the potential to prompt viewers into a conceptual/sensual consideration of the relationships between human culture and the global environment. Such moments as those described at the beginning of this reading reflect the film's "environmentality," a term Lawrence Buell employs in *The Future of Environmental Criticism* to describe the diverse means by which literary and audiovisual artworks engage explicitly and implicitly with environmental and ecological concerns.[53]

In the scene described at the beginning of this reading, the repeating visual motif of the Fox News logo calls viewers' attention to their prior contextual knowledge of Fox News as pervasively skeptical of global warming science. This particular scene thus resonates with environmentality, prompting Roger Ebert to describe the film as "ridiculous, yes, but sublimely ridiculous," and demonstrating that, *The Day After Tomorrow* reaches for something a little beyond the lowest common denominator, a pejorative film critics commonly attach to Hollywood's audiences. On its own hyperbolic, and "sublimely ridiculous," *The Day After Tomorrow* may not have produced a significant shift in the cultural logic of ecology, but its impact did set the stage for this shift, most prominently by inspiring the production of *An Inconvenient Truth*.

At a New York City premiere party for *The Day After Tomorrow* organized by the liberal political action and media organization MoveOn.org, media producer and National Resources Defense Council trustee Laurie David recognized the potential for Hollywood to help bring about a tipping point in public awareness of climate change. She reportedly approached Al Gore and quipped, "We all know one disaster film is worth 1,000 environmental speeches." Also sensing the buzz building around the release of *The Day After Tomorrow*, Gore was on hand to deliver his well-traveled global warming slide show to the audience gathered in New York. While Gore spoke about the issue and praised Emmerich's movie as "extremely enjoyable and exciting" and "honest fiction," David claims she devised the idea of turning Gore's presentation into a feature-length documentary film.[54] Director Davis Guggenheim was brought on board to craft Gore into an image of intellectual and ethical authority on global warming. Inspired by Emmerich, who had personally invested $200,000 to purchase carbon offsets for *The Day After Tomorrow*, David also sought to make the production of *An Inconvenient Truth* carbon neutral.[55] While the project moved through preproduction, Gore simultaneously worked on a companion book (which would itself become a bestseller). The film's reception was also bolstered by the unprecedented box office success of Michael Moore's *Fahrenheit 9/11* (2004) and Luc Jacquet's *March of the Penguins* (2005), which set new theatrical earnings records for documentary films, $119 and $77 million respectively, and demonstrated the form's viability in the market.

As the development and production context of *An Inconvenient Truth* demonstrates, by the end of 2005 publicity and media interest generated by *The Day After Tomorrow* had clearly played a tangible role in reframing the media coverage of climate change. In a press release dated May 12, 2004, in order to promote itself as the "weather authority" for *The Day After Tomorrow*, The Weather Channel formally acknowledged that global warming is real, that human activities are contributing to it, and that it had recently hired climatologist Dr. Heidi Cullen in order to inform the public about the impacts of climate change on weather patterns.[56] Dr. Cullen starred in her first leading role in the half-hour

53   Buell, Lawrence. *The Future of Environmental Criticism: Environmental Crisis and Literary* com/press/LA 26.html

54   David repeats her claim that the idea for a film version of *An Inconvenient Truth* came at the premier party on the film's DVD audio commentary track.

55   Corbett, Charles J. and Richard Turco. *Sustainability in the Motion Picture Industry.* University of California Institute of the Environment. Sacramento: State of California Integrated Waste Management Board, 2006.

56   "Nation's Weather Provider Hires Leading Climate Expert, Presents New Climate Programming, Serves as Weather Authority for Upcoming Twentieth Century Fox Movie 'Day After Tomorrow'." The Weather Channel. Press release. *Greenwire* (May 12, 2004). Accessed November 2009. www.heatisonline.org/contentserver/objecthandlers/index.cfm?id=4567&method=full

special *Extreme Weather Theories* which aired May 27, 2004, as part of "Extreme Weather Week," to coincide with the premier of *The Day After Tomorrow.*

When Hurricane Katrina struck New Orleans in August, 2005—resulting in massive flooding, billions of dollars in damage, and more than 1,800 deaths—the storm became bound up in the media with concerns about the looming effects of global warming. Pundits and scientific authorities on CNN, MSNBC, Fox News, and the Weather Channel devoted considerable airtime to discussions of whether or not the storm's devastating fury was a sign of the increasingly tangible effects of global warming.[57] In *Everything's Cool,* Cullen explains that the unusually powerful series of hurricanes that hit the coast that year were consistently linked to climate change in coverage of the event in print media, television, and the internet, resulting in a significant increase in her own airtime during the second half of 2005.

Coverage of Katrina and the impact of *The Day After Tomorrow* helped David generate buzz for *An Inconvenient Truth,* which was picked up for distribution by Paramount after it received a standing ovation at its premier at the 2006 Sundance Film Festival.[58] Paramount opted to open the film on four screens to heavy promotion, recording for the highest per-screen box office take for a Memorial Day Weekend opening. The film was then released in multiplex theaters and went on to earn $50 million at the global box office. In 2007 it earned an Academy Award for Best Documentary. It has since been rented, downloaded, purchased, and viewed millions of times, caused debates over its screening in thousands of public schools and universities around the world, helping to transform an erstwhile American politician into a global media superstar.[59]

Gore has since appeared in political cartoons with penguins and polar bears, had his documentary adapted as an opera, made guest appearances on popular sitcoms and talk shows, continued traveling the world to deliver technology contests, addressed international gatherings of the scientific community, and testified before Congress on climate change. He hosted *Live Earth* (2007), the largest "concert for a cause" ever held, shared the 2007 Nobel Peace Prize with the several thousand scientists serving on the United Nations Intergovernmental Panel on Climate Change, and has written another book: *Our Choice: A Plan to Solve the Climate Crisis* (2009).[60]

Like its fictional and documentary precursors, *An Inconvenient Truth* employs melodramatic affect to present a persuasive argument on the science of global warming. The film opens with images of a river as Gore speaks in voiceover about his feelings of renewal through nature. His suffering over the 2000 presidential election and his son's automobile accident invite viewers to suture themselves to his point of view as a heroic figure reemerging to fight another day. As Gore's explanations of climate science and political wrangling build toward a plea for why we must act now, affective vignettes situate him visiting his parents' farm and building a case for climate change as a moral/familial issue. These moments, including animated images of drowning polar bears, frame the issue melodramatically.

As with the disaster film, it is not just that emotion is being used to convey science, but that scientific realism is being used to enhance the weight of the film's moral charge. Gore's apocalyptic tone is punctuated by documentary images of melting glaciers but tempered with moments of humor, nostalgia, and an emotive soundtrack composed by Michael Brook. Videos, photographs, scientific graphs, satellite images, computer climate models, a scissor-lift, and Simpsons-style animation were all incorporated into the film's production. These techniques

57 Daniel Gold and Judith Helfand (directors). *Everything's Cool.* (2007).
58 Booth, William. "Al Gore, Sundance's Leading Man." *The Washington Post* (January 26,2006). www.washingtonpost.com/wp-dyn/content/article/2006/01/25/AR2006012502230.html
59 See, for example, Libin, Kevin. "Gore's Inconvenient Truth Required Classroom Viewing?" *National Post,* Canada, (May 19, 2007). Accessed June 2011. www.canada.com/nationalpost/ story.html?id=27a24986-008e-4a55-al8c-fb3fb7acf0e9&k=0; Leask, David. "All Secondary Schools to See Gore Climate Film." *The Herald,* Scotland, (January 17, 2007). www.heraldscotland.com/all-secondary-schools-to-see-gore-climate-film-1.838142; "German Government Defends Gore: 'Inconvenient Truth' to Continue Airing in Schools." Spiegel Online (October 13, 2007). www.spiegel.de/ international/germany/0,1518,511325,00.html
60 See, Tierney, John. "The Aria of Prince Algorino." *The New York Times* (June 17, 2008). Accessed June 2009. www.nytimes.com/2008/06/17/science/earth/17tier.html

were designed to make the science palatable to general audiences and to heighten the film's emotional impact.[61] It is worth noting, however, that although climatologists are generally skeptical of popular media, in a 2007 survey they ranked *An Inconvenient Truth* as the most accurate mainstream representation of their research.[62]

The film exemplifies the ability of melodrama to inhabit the cultural logic of capitalism, to speak directly to the individual consumer and instill in us the sense that we each have the power and obligation to act. As Linda Williams explains, "melodrama offers the hope that it may not be too late ... that virtue and truth can be achieved in private individuals and individual heroic acts rather than, as Eisenstein wanted, in revolution."[63] Cut to Melissa Ethridge's Oscar-winning song, "I Need to Wake Up," *An Inconvenient Truth* concludes in the space of hope, reframing the "too bigness" of climate change in terms of an individual's power to enact changes that matter to the entire planet: recycling, driving less, planting a tree, turning down the thermostat. Noting the degree to which Americans' feelings about climate change had inspired a "dramatic shift in the business community's attitude toward the environment" around the time of the film's release, Dan Etsy, director of the Yale Center for Environmental Law and Policy, explains: "It's clear that the public is not waiting for the government to take the lead. Americans no longer think it's entirely the domain of government to solve environmental problems. They expect companies to step up and address climate change and other concerns."[64] Although Gore has been roundly criticized for presenting his viewers with easy answers that fail to address the systemic nature of climate change, his move highlights the fact that although the government has yet to act, consumers have.[65]

Of course, with this consumerist attitude, the closer American society has come to enacting a sustained shift in the cultural logic of ecology in the years since the release of *An Inconvenient Truth*, the more daunting the task has become. In an interview with David and Gore about An *Inconvenient Truth* on May 31, 2006 National Public Radio interviewer Robert Siegel asked, "What would be evidence of the American public taking on board the message of this film, that you could point to and say, 'That's what I hoped would happen'?" They responded in turn:

> **Laurie David:** My focus is media and how do you permeate popular culture with this issue ... so I'm already thinking that this is a huge success.

> **Al Gore:** I have a single objective, and that is to move the United States of America past a tipping point ... beyond which the overwhelming majority of the American people demand that their political leaders and their business leaders put this climate crisis in the number one priority position.[66]

Although a case cannot yet be made that American society has reached the cultural tipping point Gore describes, it can be said with certainty that *The Day After Tomorrow* and An *Inconvenient Truth* inspired media producers to permeate the mediascape with images of global warming as David suggests. Influenced by the success of Emmerich and Gore's films, between 2006 and 2009 more than 40 television, independent, and studio documentary and feature films were released between 2007 and 2008 that explicitly or implicitly reference global warming, including such

61 See Sean Cubitt's chapter in this collection for a detailed analysis of Gore's use of data visualization.
62 Lichter, "Climate Change Scientists Agree on Warming ..."
63 Williams, Linda. "Melodrama Revised." In Nick Browne (ed.) *Refiguring American Film Genres*. Berkeley: University of California Press, 1998: 77.
64 "Sea Change," Ibid.
65 Ecocritic Timothy Luke, for example, argues, "At best, Gore's work seems essentially to 'greenwash' existing networks of corporate organization and expert tech-nocracy with renewed institutional legitimacy." Luke, Timothy W. "The Politics of True Convenience or Inconvenient Truth: Struggles over how to Sustain Capitalism, Democracy, and Ecology in the 21st Century." *Environment and Planning* 40 (2008): 1811–1824.
66 "Al Gore Sounds Global Warming Alert." *All Things Considered,* National Public Radio (May 31, 2006). www.npr.org/templates/story/story.phplstoryld=5441976

diverse films as: *Category 7: At the End of the World, Planet in Peril* (2007); *Encounters at the End of the World* (2007); *The 11th Hour* (2007); *The Day the Earth Stood Still* (2008); *Flow: For the Love of Water* (2008); *Quantum of Solace* (2008); *Wall-E* (2008); *Whatever Else* (Woody Allen, 2009); and the highest-grossing motion picture of all time, *Avatar* (2009).[67]

Commenting on the impact of Al Gore's efforts alone, Gallup pollster Frank Newport argues that during the period of the film's theatrical run and DVD release, an increasing number of Americans came to perceive that the effects of global warming would begin to occur within their lifetime (from 56 percent in 2004 to 65 percent in 2008), which is "in line with what one might have expected given the high level of publicity on the topic."[68] In a global internet poll conducted by Nielsen and Oxford University which returned 26,000 responses, "Sixty-six percent of viewers who claimed to have seen *An Inconvenient Truth* said the film had 'changed their mind' about global warming" and "three out of four (74 percent) viewers said they changed some of their habits as a result of seeing the film."[69] Although Gore's film did not produce the immediate changes he was hoping for, audience surveys show that enough viewers did change their habits to suggest that the film did inspire a form of collective action.

CONCLUSION: THE CULTURAL LOGIC OF ECOLOGY

While environmental problems created by human beings are typically thought of as disruptions to the natural order of things, climate change, as these films suggest, is a phenomenon which upends traditional notions of "nature" and "culture" as separate and oppositional. By the end of the eighteenth century, as Western society developed a more ecologically complex relationship with the planet—due to such factors as the spread of science and technology, secular humanism, and market capitalism—nature came to be understood as some inert *thing*, entirely independent from human culture.[70] As a result of this ideological shift, capitalism has flourished by enabling individuals and corporations to exploit the planet's resources without any sense of moral obligation. By foregrounding moral appeals in their use of verbal and visual rhetoric, climate change films suggest that "nature" can no longer be used to refer to a material world that exists outside the sphere of human influence. As such, they echo the sentiments expressed by Bill McKibben in *The End of Nature* (1989), the first book on the topic written for general audiences: "We have produced the carbon dioxide—we are ending nature."[71] Ultimately then, these cinematic narratives, hyperbolic though they may be, present themselves not as prophecies of apocalyptic doom but as prescient calls for humanity to alter its deeply dysfunctional relationship with the planet before it is forced to do so by the planet itself.

A reframing of Fredric Jameson's concept of the "cultural logic of late capitalism," the cultural logic of ecology—as evidenced by these films and how they shape *and* are shaped by the world around them—describes society's dominant perceptions of the relationships between humans, other organisms, and their shared environments. In "Postmodernism, or The Cultural Logic of Late Capitalism," first published in 1984, Jameson writes:

> In modernism, some residual zones of "nature" and "being," of the old, the older, the archaic, still subsist; culture can still do something to that nature and work at transforming that "referent." Postmodernism is what you have

67   Schechner, Sam. "March of the Inconvenient Truths." *The Wall Street Journal* (August 17, 2007): W2.
68   Pollster Frank Newport contends that Gore's efforts had an impact on global warming polling until 2008. *Gallup* (March 11, 2010). www.gallup. com/poll/126560/americans-global-warming-concerns-continue-drop.aspx
69   Psychological research has also determined that certain segments of the film were particularly suited to encouraging feelings of "motivation" and "empowerment" in viewers. Beattie, Geoffrey. "Making an Action Film." Global Warming Cause: Nielsen Survey." (July 7, 2007). http://hk.nielsen. com/news/20070707.shtml
70   See Merchant, Carolyn. *The Death of Nature: Women, Ecology, and the Scientific Revolution.* New York: Harper & Row, 1980; and Williams, Raymond. *Keywords.* Revised Edition. New York: Oxford University Press, 1985.
71   McKibben, Bill. *The End of Nature.* New York: Random House, 1989: 41.

when the modernization process is complete and nature is gone for good.[72]

While Jameson is correct to assert that "this whole global, yet American, postmodern culture is the internal and superstructural expression of a whole new wave of American military and economic domination throughout the world," his theory nevertheless rests on the faulty assumption that nature could ever be gone for good. "Nature," as Adrian Ivakhiv reminds us, "if by that we mean the ecological and biological fabric of life on this planet, has neither ended nor gone away ... even if it is increasing modified and interlaced with human activities."[73]

In his 2008 article, "Stirring the Geopolitical Unconscious: Toward a Jamesonian Ecocriticism," Ivakhiv argues that Jameson's methodology of reading "products of culture as heralding, reflecting, and responding to the latest stage in the development of capitalism" highlights the means by which "commodification has been extended, albeit unevenly, to all levels of social and biological life." However, as Ivakhiv rightly suggests, Jameson's "political-economic" approach to cultural production must be complimented by a "political-ecological" one because "uneven development and global inequality are directly related to the ways advanced industrial capitalism both commodifies and thoroughly transforms the natural world and our relationship with it."[74] Economics, after all, offers a society merely the means of organizing and carrying out its broader perceptual and physical relationships with its ecological surroundings.

As this reading demonstrates, climate change cinema illuminates the Zeitgeist of a society slowly coming to terms with the reality of global environmental change. Despite the global economic recession that began in September 2008, in 2010 "over 90 percent of Americans said that the United States should act to reduce global warming, even if it has economic costs."[75] However, as sociologist Anthony Giddens explains in his 2009 book *The Politics of Climate Change*, "[S]ince the dangers posed by global warming aren't tangible, immediate or visible in the course of day-to-day life ... many will continue to do nothing of a concrete nature about them. Yet waiting until they become visible and acute ... will be, by definition, too late."[76]

Giddens' Paradox is underscored in the United States by the fact that just as public awareness of the issue has risen sharply over the past few decades so too has the nation's carbon footprint. Amidst the melodramatic narratives and heightened realism of these cinematic texts, global warming becomes something that audiences can grasp onto and wonder if perhaps this is what their world might actually look like in the not-too-distant future. In their melodramatic narratives, climate change films also articulate an awareness that traditional forms of collective action are being unhinged in a postmodern era of globalization. Whether or not capitalism (and by extension Hollywood) is capable of surviving the transition to a new cultural logic remains an important question for scholars to discuss. But if these films make anything clear, it is that more and more people are becoming aware that new ways of imagining the relationship between people and the planet are not only possible, but necessary.

ACKNOWLEDGMENTS

Special thanks to Michael Aronson, Patrick Bartlein, and Louise Westling for their feedback on previous versions of this reading.

72   Jameson, Frederick. *Postmodernism, or The Cultural Logic of Late Capitalism*. Durham, NC: Duke University Press, 1991: ix.
73   Ivakhiv, Adrian. "Stirring the Geopolitical Unconscious: Toward a Jamesonian Ecocriticism." *New Formations* 64 (2008): 98.
74   Ibid: 99.
75   Leiserowitz, Anthony, Edward Maibach, and Connie Roser-Renouf. *Climate Change in the American Mind: Americans' Climate Change Reliefs, Altitudes, Policy Preferences, and Actions.* Yale Project on Climate Change and George Mason University Center for Climate Change Communication, 2009.
76   Giddens, Anthony. *The Politics of Climate Change*. Cambridge, UK: Polity, 2009: 2.

INTERSTELLAR, ECOCIDE, AND RESISTANCE: ECO-CRITIQUING URBAN EXPANSION WITH TRADITIONAL CHINAMPA FARMING IN MÉXICO

ADRIÁN GARCÍA holds an MA in Visual and Critical Studies from the School of the Art Institute of Chicago. He is a Mexican filmmaker, musician, writer, and visual artist interested in the intersections of art and science. He is an adjunct professor at the School of Humanities and Education at Tecnológico de Monterrey, León Campus, in Mexico.

MATEO PAZZI holds a BA in Communication from the Universidad de León. Previously, he worked as a translator and copy editor for UNESCO in Paris, France. Currently, he lives and works in San Miguel de Allende, Guanajuato, Mexico, where he holds the position of editorial director of the Guanajuato International Film Festival (GIFF). He is an adjunct professor at Tecnológico de Monterrey, León Campus, in Mexico.

Christopher Nolan's sci-fi epic *Interstellar* is haunting. Like a black hole, it swallowed an entire semester of my attention in grad school. The task: to write a paper that, among other things, looked at the film's depiction of an American-centered space exploration and where this idea puts the rest of the world when leaving Earth becomes crucial for survival. The result: equal parts love and hate for the film.

BREATHTAKING BEAUTY

When *Interstellar* premiered in 2014, it took a couple of runs at the movie theater to actually let the awesomeness of the work sink into the conscious mind. The film was simply mind-blowing. The most striking aspect of *Interstellar* is, obviously, its visuals: the awe-inspiring rendering of deep space and deep time; the thrilling and downright beautiful portrayal of complex ideas such as higher dimensions, alien worlds, and wormhole interstellar travel; and, of course, the utter respect for scientific accuracy—at least of our current understanding of physics.

Interstellar really does its work in stimulating our wildest imagination, the kind of spirit that set the goal to put humans on the surface of the moon decades ago, when our technological means were, in comparison to now, far less advanced.

Today, our means seem just as archaic, especially when we're talking about the heavy stuff that drives the plot of the film: five-dimensional beings and relativistic and interdimensional space travel. This film is less about what we can do now than it is about the desire to keep learning, discovering, inventing, moving forward—a mindset similar to that which launched the original space race.

Interstellar wouldn't be misplaced if put shoulder to shoulder with Stanley Kubrick's *2001: A Space Odyssey* and Carl Sagan's *Cosmos: A Personal Voyage* in terms of how brilliant and affective their celebrations of logic and scientific understanding of the universe are, without forgetting how much there still is to know, how we shouldn't disregard our earthly origins and human condition, and even the things that are (and probably will always be) beyond our comprehension. They share a sense of spirituality that comes not from fear or ignorance, but from knowledge.

Another point in *Interstellar*'s favor, almost lost in the near-three-hour run of the film, is the subtle school sequence where Cooper (an expert pilot himself) pushes back against the negationist narrative from the educators who saw the Apollo moon landing as a hoax.

School directives are backed up by questionable official textbooks, as a way to build a case for the unimportance of scientific development and research for space exploration, thus taking the budget away from them and putting it into farming subsidies instead. Are schools really necessary in this apocalyptic scenario—where, in the end, conspiracies are the backbone of "education"?

This excerpt is as brief as it is powerful and meaningful. *Interstellar* takes place in a deteriorated environment, a Planet Earth soon to be hostile to life as we know it. An Earth like this would need understanding, both (1) respecting the environment, meaning dignifying it, or to put it simply, leaving it alone to be, and (2) understanding it through a scientific viewpoint, to fully grasp the extent of its complexities and how we play a role in the vast network of connections, negotiations, constructions, and destructions that make life here possible.

Enough praising. Let's get to the murky details.

THE UNSEEN DISASTER

The source of Earth's downfall is fairly unclear throughout the plot: a blight has wiped out all major edible crops, and corn is the only one remaining. That's where we land during the first act of the film, a complete collapse of the global food system, subsequently and naturally leading to a series of crises (political, social, and so on) that, really, are absent from the film's immediate perspective. The world outside Cooper's surroundings is, most probably, absolutely devastated. This absence from the frame, and what it could mean, is frankly horrifying. Billions must have died by famine, thirst, disease, and resource wars, so things are as we see them in the film.

According to Kip Thorne's grade of plausibility for scientific facts behind *Interstellar*, the blight falls under the category of speculation (other categories are truth and educated guess).[1] This, of course, means at least a possible scenario of what the end of life might look like given our current knowledge of biology.

A pathogen spreading across the globe, jumping from one species to another, is no longer part of an apocalyptic sci-fi blockbuster, we know for sure. But a blight both deadly and highly contagious—like the one in the film, capable of wiping out all edible crops within a human lifespan—although not impossible, remains a long shot. Yet, however slim, the possibilities for something similar happening to our food system stems from the very nature of our current way of producing it.

Cooper's world is one that has reversed from a global highly technological civilization to a small agrarian society. Here and there, the film does its best to remind us about that lost world. Automatic harvesters do labor on the fields; old abandoned military drones still patrol the skies, wandering until they break down and fall; and people like Cooper scavenge them for the precious solar panels and batteries to fuel other appliances. *Interstellar* faces us with our own possible downfall: humans capable of surviving but at the mercy of a broken, unpredictable, dying world.

Society went from stockbrokers to farmers, and food is paramount in *Interstellar*'s world, as it should be to ours too. But even on the brink of total collapse, farms like Cooper's still present the vast monotonous

---

1 K. Thorne, *The Science of* Interstellar (New York: W.W. Norton, 2014).

landscape of single-crop agriculture. We've known for years now how degrading these practices are to the soil, keeping ground from fixing nitrogen and other vital nutrients, eroding the uppermost layers and thus favoring desertification. But in a capitalist-kidnapped food market, knowledge is an inconvenience. The saddest thing (and spoiler alert): even on board of Cooper Station at the end of the film, all you can see are blocks of monocrops traveling through deep space to settle in a new world, as if to say "Forget Earth, let's rape the next planet."

There's a reason why our industrial food system came to be. Grasses like corn, rice, and wheat are relatively cheap and easy to grow because of their simple reproductive cycle, dependent on air instead of insects; also, they are high in nutrients for us and our livestock. However, these crops are very demanding on fertilizers, and the degraded soils wouldn't be able to sustain them without the artificial help from agrochemicals.

Interstellar's total food production collapse really becomes an ominous cautionary tale when we realize that these three varieties of crops sum up half of our dietary input globally. As a matter of fact, from the three hundred thousand edible plants we know of on Earth, only 0.6 percent are actually farmed and consumed en masse.[2] In a warming world where climate is becoming unpredictable, our future food security looks, by contrast, certainly precarious.

Interstellar apart, here on Earth, in real life, the stakes are gradually reaching a similar level of urgency. There has been an undeniable warming trend in global temperatures, supported by strong evidence gathered by land-, sea-, and space-based research since the 1980s, linked to human activity. The result is a continuous increase of temperature with ever-breaking records for the past seven years.[3]

Climate change means unstable conditions around the world, both hot and cold in the extremes. We have just started to witness what such events may cause. The rise of human civilization has benefited from the relative stability of weather patterns since we left the last glacial period behind. And even while *The Day After Tomorrow* and *Interstellar* scenarios are pretty far-fetched, the collapse of the climate systems as we know them will definitely pose a very real threat to our long-term survival on this planet.

EXPLORERS OR CARETAKERS?

Interstellar's journey is accompanied by a secondary plot line that keeps us on Earth, where Professor Brand tries to figure out a way to save the remains of humanity by mastering gravity and putting a humongous spaceship into orbit with everyone on it—and by "everyone" I mean the few American moon-landing-denying monoculture-farmers we actually see on board Cooper Station at the end. But the bottom line is to *leave broken Earth*. Earlier, when asked to join a (very possibly fatal) mission to find other habitable planets, Cooper declines in order to stay with his family. This makes his infamous line all the more dissonant when he finally commits to the idea of going full hero mode: "We've forgotten who we are: explorers, pioneers, not caretakers."

Aren't we, Cooper? Aren't we?

Interstellar is about relations: fathers and daughters, family at large, lovers, the kinship that binds us all as a species. This last relation is actually what makes Cooper change his mind: he's faced with the realization that humanity, his family included, will certainly die if the opportunity offered by the five-dimensional beings is ignored. Two notes here:

First, there's value in thinking in terms of species rather than individually. When stakes are high and endeavors are challenging, humans will need cooperation beyond national or political (or any other kind of) divisions. It has happened before: the Montreal Protocol, signed in 1987, to stop and reverse the depletion

---

2   L. Plitt, "¿Por qué sólo consumimos el 0,06% de las 300.000 plantas que podríamos comer?" BBC Mundo (August 10, 2015), https://www.bbc.com/mundo/noticias/2015/08/150723_plantas_comestibles_cosechas_lp#:~:text=El%20hecho%20es%20que%20de,%3A%20ma%C3%ADz%2C%20arroz%20y%20trigo.

3   K. Brown, "2020 Tied for Warmest Year on Record, NASA Analysis Shows," NASA (2021), https://www.nasa.gov/press-release/2020-tied-for-warmest-year-on-record-nasa-analysis-shows.

of the ozone layer is still an example of international collaboration; the ozone layer is expected to recover by mid-century, through our placing limits on the production and consumption of damaging substances.[4] We need that kind of commitment to fight global warming now.

Second, even when science is key to resolve the problem that is posed, the way it turns out in *Interstellar* is rather touching. Cooper understands that the only way to reach out to Murph (his daughter and future scientist) and deliver the information required to solve the gravitational conundrum is through a significant object, a token of his presence, which, fittingly, is a watch that Cooper gives to Murph when leaving and introducing her (and the audience) to the relativistic effects of light-speed traveling and time dilation. Memory and affection become metaphors for time travel—"Now we're just here to be memories for our kids," says Cooper; loss crystallizes in a hopeful fable for the future. But again, however compelling and humane this may be, there's still a blind spot: regard for our home planet.

EXHAUSTING LAND

As these lines are typed, Guanajuato, where we live and work, is on the brink of an emergency declaration for water scarcity. Throughout the years, the state's economy has changed dramatically. Guanajuato used to be known as one of the country's most productive agricultural centers, with fertile soils across its territory feeding on the runoff from mountain rains. After the ratification of the North American Free Trade Agreement in 1994, however, motor vehicle assembly plants cascaded and urban centers grew rapidly and practically without planning. The economy was industrialized, and contamination has increased ever since.

Those fertile terrains have been swallowed. Real estate speculators and construction firms built on top of them, chopping down vast amounts of mesquite trees, a native species with huge capabilities for nutrient fixation. Soils are buried beneath concrete platforms, making practically impossible for water to infiltrate and replenish the underground reserves.

Contamination, desertification, depletion of resources, loss of fertility; luckily, destiny will find us in our fancy suburban mass-produced homes. The death drive of capitalist progress.

Land as property, as simply an object on which to exert our will, is precisely the blind spot of *Interstellar*. There's a lack of recognition of the complexities and relations with the nonhuman, a defining element of western sci-fi that replicates colonial expansion.[5] As described above with regard to growing cities in Guanajuato, the process mimics the colonizer sense of entitlement to the land, as well as the film does when planting a flag on a foreign planet. It's all about shaping the environment to fit our desires, rather than adapting ourselves to survive in balance with the conditions that nature offers.

The reluctance to concede failure and work with our surroundings has shaped the world radically. Soon after the conquest of Tenochtitlán, Spanish settlers started damming, tubing, and draining the five-lake hydrographic system that covered around 442 square miles of today's Mexico City. Less than 2% of the ancient lakes remain, sometimes heavily polluted.[6]

The biggest megalopolis in Latin America, home to over twenty million people, is only possible thanks to an engineering complex that keeps the rain from replenishing the lake and flooding the city. Water is still pumped out from decreasing underground supplies, so the soil, mainly clay, retains less and less humidity, resulting in a sinking city (in some parts up to 4 cm yearly). One would think that water scarcity isn't an issue here, but there's not enough liquid to sustain the growing population. In the last eighty years, the city has built two gargantuan dam systems to bring fresh water, sometimes over 60 km away from other river networks that, in turn, grow insufficient to fulfill the needs of their

---

4   UN Environment Programme, "About Montreal Protocol," *Ozonaction* (October 29, 2018), http://www.unep.org/ozonaction/who-we-are/about-montreal-protocol.
5   L. Cornum, "The Space NDN's Star Map," *The New Inquiry* (January 26, 2015), https://thenewinquiry.com/the-space-ndns-star-map/.
6   Ivan Carrillo (2016). Axolotl: Un dios en peligro de extinción. *National Geographic En Español, 39*(03), 83–99.

immediate surroundings.[7] Guanajuato's water scarcity has its roots here.

Ancient Tenochtitlán was forced to fit a more European urban configuration. Mexico City (and the country at large) has, systematically, ostracized native configurations of living and relating to nature. Tubed rivers and streams are ubiquitous all over the country; we need them yet we trash and condemn them to invisibility.[8]

OTHER KNOWLEDGE, OTHER THINKING

South of Mexico City there's a remnant of the past lakes, Xochimilco. There, a handful of farmers still grow food as Mexicans did before the conquest. The chinampa is a unique agricultural system, a farm over the waters, built layer by layer of sediments from the lakebed. The mud is shoveled from the bottom and accumulated over the edges of the chinampa; the farmers compact it by stepping on it, slowly growing and expanding it. Tenochtitlán island was surrounded by chinampas.

This nutrient-enriched sediment nourishes the milpa, a diverse crop system that contains maize, beans, and squash along with several other varieties of edible plants. Milpa is an ecosystem itself, built on relations. The benefits of chinampa agriculture expand to the water system: layered sediments filter water, cleaning it in the process. Native fish, crustaceans, and amphibians flourish in the pristine fluid, keeping plagues controlled in return.[9]

However, degradation and pollution have disjointed the fine-tuned network, as these practices and the culture that keeps them alive are close to disappearing. The city keeps growing, further fragmenting the already degraded landscape and exploiting the few remaining resources. Also, the proximity to the city and the opportunities it offers draw the young away from their heritage to pursue studies and careers that are tailored to urban needs. There might be no next generation of chinamperos: this is cultural ecocide.

Is there a bright side? That will come when we heal the severed bonds with the land and nature, with the consciousness of interconnectedness.

Back in Guanajuato, the Billion Agave Project seeks to fight desertification, air pollution, soil degradation, water scarcity, and even unemployment by looking to the ancient knowledge of the land and the natural interactions of native species that help restore the ecosystem.[10] Mexico City, too, is finding solace in hearing what the ancestral practice of chinampa farming has to offer to rebuild the lost richness of the lakes and fight the environmental crisis of the capital.[11]

Interstellar's message that love transcends time and space, rather than serving some utilitarian purpose, might be a nice way to begin. We need to dismantle our utilitarian metrics of productivity, dismantle our systems of consumption and exploitation. Ironically, by pursuing the veneer of an ever-growing economy, we terminate Earth's natural production potential. We need to prioritize the intrinsic value of nature as it is, rather than commodifying it to the point of exhaustion. We need to reconcile with the caretakers that we really are.

7   Canal Once, *Sobre el agua* series, "Las fuentes de abastecimiento" episode (June 3, 2013), https://www.youtube.com/watch?v=Wo7OmxotSF4&list=WL&index=20&ab_channel=CanalOnce.

8   L. F. Lazos Murrieta, "Reminiscencias del Agua," Medium (March 7, 2021), https://medium.com/@galimatias.mx/reminiscencias-del-agua-4182303b1380.

9   DW Español, "Un sistema agrícola único en el mundo" (November 26, 2020), https://www.youtube.com/watch?v=xvjYspF3PxA&list=WL&index=19&ab_channel=DWEspa%C3%B1ol.

10   Regeneration International, "Billion Agave Project," retrieved February 15, 2021, from https://regenerationinternational.org/billion-agave-project.

11   Iván Carrillo, *Axolotl: Un Dios Azteca en Peligro de Extinción* (2016).

2001: A SPACE ODYSSEY (1968)

A mind-bending masterpiece, *2001* tells the epic story of humankind's origins and destiny, from apes to astronauts to star children, from Stone Age to space age. Featuring cinema's single most influential vision of computers, artificial intelligence, and ambient media networks, *2001* also offers a warning about the dangers of total surveillance. The monolith and radio signal change human destiny forever, allowing us to explore these questions: Are we alone? What is the role of technology? And what is our destiny as a species?

Director: Stanley Kubrick
Starring: Keir Dullea and Gary Lockwood

CONTACT (1997)

An extraterrestrial civilization is discovered using a laptop connected to the Very Large Array of radio telescopes in New Mexico. Inspired by Carl Sagan's novel, this film tells the story of humans making "contact" with an extraterrestrial civilization and building the machine to transport a human to meet them. In this film, media technologies change the course of human destiny. Given the recent discoveries of the Kepler Space Telescope, will the humans listen to the message of the cosmic media technologies?

Director: Robert Zemeckis
Starring: Jodie Foster and Matthew McConaughey

GRAVITY (2013)

Astronauts are repairing the Hubble Space Telescope when an exploded satellite disrupts their mission. The Hubble and space shuttle are destroyed, along with the International Space Station. Sandra Bullock's journey back to Earth is not scientifically possible, but the filmmakers want the film to symbolize a message for humans. If so, what is this film really saying about media technology and human destiny?

Director: Alfonso Cuarón
Starring: Sandra Bullock and George Clooney

INTERSTELLAR (2014)

With Earth's resources destroyed and food supply diminishing, humanity must find another planet to inhabit if it wants to survive as a species. Courageous astronauts venture through wormhole and black hole to save humanity and find another habitable planet. A film masterpiece that offers hope and bravado, with a clear warning for humanity.

Director: Christopher Nolan
Starring: Matthew McConaughey, Anne Hathaway, David Gyasi, and Michael Caine

CHAPTER NINE

MEDIA AND SCIENCE
Technology and Our True Place in the Universe

By Barry Vacker

THE LARGEST INTERNATIONAL DARK SKY RESERVE ON PLANET EARTH

In the remote regions of far west Texas and northern Mexico, plans are underway to create the "Greater Big Bend International Dark Sky Reserve"—which will be the largest International Dark Sky Reserve on Planet Earth. The Big Bend Dark Sky Reserve will span approximately *18,000 square miles* of Texas and Mexico.[1] That's almost the collective size of Vermont, Connecticut, and Rhode Island. This will be the largest area to combat the effects of skyglow and light pollution.

Of course, this may seem like an irrelevant topic to the 90 percent of humanity living in the electric skyglow, far removed from the starry skies that surround our planet. After all, how can views of the radiant Milky Way help solve our seemingly intractable problems—nationalism, racism, fascism, border walls, climate disruption, and proliferating conspiracy theories and antiscience worldviews, all happening amid a global pandemic?

Yet, these very issues point to why the world's largest International Dark Sky Reserve is an important signpost for a species lost in the skyglow of its 24/7 electric civilization. This Dark Sky Reserve brings together nature and science, ecology and cosmology, and peaceful cooperation along a contentious border—all quietly pointing toward a new transborder narrative and a new philosophy for the human species. In a culture filled with despair about the future, this gives me hope.

AWE AND WONDER IN THE TEXAS DESERT

In far west Texas, the light pollution threatens the dark skies essential to the Big Bend National Park, the Big Bend Ranch State Park, and the McDonald Observatory (no connection to the McDonald's hamburger chain). The Big Bend National Park is one of the largest and most spectacular national parks in America, featuring 801,000 acres of the Chihuahuan Desert ecoregion Administered by the Texas Parks and Wildlife Department. The Big Bend Ranch State Park is the largest state park in Texas and also features spectacular desert landscapes. Combined with the Chinati Mountains Natural Area, the Big Bend Ranch State Park Complex contains 355,000 acres. Already

---

1   Carlos Morales, "West Texas Observatory Shoots for the Stars to Preserve Night Skies," Marfa Public Radio, February 22, 2021; Big Bend Sentinel, "Greater Big Bend Dark Sky Reserve Plans Virtual Town Hall Meeting," Big Bend Sentinel, February 17, 2021.

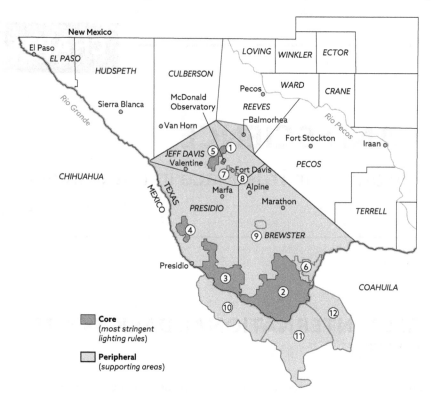

Greater Big Bend International Dark Sky Reserve

FIGURE 9.0.1 Map provided by the McDonald Observatory (2020). *(1) The University of Texas McDonald Observatory (2) Big Bend National Park 3) Big Bend Ranch State Park (4) Chinati Mountains State Natural Area (5) Davis Mountains Preserve (The Nature Conservancy) (6) Black Gap Wildlife Management Area (7) Davis Mountain State Park (8) Chihuahuan Desert Research Institute (9) Elephant Mountain Wildlife Management Area (10) Área de Protección Flora y Fauna Cañon de Santa Elena (11) Área de Protección Flora y Fauna Ocampo (12) Área de Protección Flora y Fauna Maderas del Carmen*

designated as "Dark Sky Parks" by the International Dark-Sky Association (IDA), the two Big Bend Parks and the Observatory will be the central core of the International Dark Sky Reserve.

Efforts to protect the dark skies from light pollution are being led by Bill Wren at the McDonald Observatory and Amber Harrison at Big Bend State Park, along with leaders at Big Bend National Park and the Big Bend Conservation Alliance. As shown in figure 9.0.1, these organizations are seeking to create the largest International Dark Sky Reserve, which will have to be officially designated by the IDA. The designation will require a great deal of coordination across the Big Bend and border areas. There has been a very high degree of interest from partners in Mexico, including the Áreas de Protección de Flora y Fauna in Maderas, Ocampo, and Santa Elena.

COOL MEDIA AND THE COSMIC SUBLIME

Directly experiencing the stars and nearby galaxies from both a scientific and an aesthetic perspective is thrilling and inspiring. It's like what I have directly experienced at McDonald Observatory in the desert mountains of far west Texas. Owned and operated by the University of Texas at Austin, the McDonald Observatory is one of the premiere astronomical facilities in the world and home to the Hobby-Eberly Telescope, the fourth largest optical telescope in the world. Many kinds of epic research are conducted at the facility, among them studying the expansion rate of the universe caused by dark energy and searching for habitable exoplanets. You might think such discoveries have no relevance for our lives, but I think it speaks to a new philosophy for our species, as does the Greater Big Bend International Dark Sky Reserve. Cool media (exo-media) direct our gaze away from humanity to tell a very different story than we hear from the hot (ego-media) that permeate our daily lives.

Seeing the dark skies filled with the radiant Milky Way has enabled me to experience the cosmic sublime and transcendent moments in which I am connected to a narrative much larger than the human-centered narratives that dominate the 24/7 media spectacle. Once you embrace the content of cool media, you will never forget the "explosion of awareness." It's the same as when you view *2001: A Space Odyssey* with open eyes: you'll see a new view of human existence and the universe, as explained in the final reading in this chapter.

During my many visits to McDonald Observatory's "star parties" (where visitors are permitted to look at the stars, planets, and galaxies through very powerful telescopes), I have gazed upon the Andromeda and Whirlpool Galaxies, neighbors of the Milky Way. Andromeda is over two million light-years from the Milky Way, while the Whirlpool Galaxy is at least fifteen million light-years away. Imagine seeing the tilted spiral of Andromeda, with photons from one trillion stars traversing the voids of the cosmos at the speed of light for two million years—light leaving that galaxy long before any human walked on Earth! On one particular visit, it occurred to me while I was gazing through one telescope that, after eons of space traveling, the starlight I was witnessing was passing through the telescope's lenses and into my own eyes, where photons from the Andromeda Galaxy were actually converting into bioelectrical patterns in my brain.

Andromeda's photons merged with my neurons. In that existential moment, my consciousness was reconnected with the cosmos, and a tiny fragment of the universe was directly aware of itself on a grand scale—connecting the infinite and the infinitesimal. Though I'm tiny in relation to the cosmos, I felt the exaltation and affirmation of human existence, the power of human reason to grasp what I was seeing and sensing. It is likely I have never felt more inspired and at peace in the same moment. That's the power of cool media and the cosmic sublime. Mind blown!

RADICAL WONDER

In the sublime moment, we have the simultaneous sense of awe and wonder while feeling connected to the vastness and majesty of the universe. The *radical wonder* of the sublime is the universal experience that (1) connects us to each other and (2) connects us to our origins and destiny to nature and the universe from which we evolved.

THE EYES OF THE HUBBLE SPACE TELESCOPE

Over the decades, the film industry has produced thousands upon thousands of science fiction films. Most of them are dystopian or apocalyptic, with monsters, mad scientists, and implausible science.[2] That's one reason so few have won Oscars. At the 2014 Academy Awards ceremony, Alfonso Cuarón won the Oscar for Best Director, thus becoming the first director to win for a science fiction film. Of course, the film was the 3D marvel and box office hit *Gravity*. Lost amid all the discussion of the stunning special effects and Sandra Bullock's performance (she was nominated for Best Actress) were the possible meanings suggested by the plot of the film. It was as if the spectacle of special effects and space locale overwhelmed the apocalyptic meanings.

Gravity begins with Bullock and George Clooney portraying scientists and astronauts whose task is to upgrade the Hubble Space Telescope. The apocalypse begins when Russia shoots down one of its satellites, leaving a debris field hurtling around the planet in space. The space shuttle and Hubble Space Telescope crash into the debris, destroying both. Clooney floats to his frozen death in deep space, and Bullock comes crashing down to Earth under the force of gravity. By the end of the film, the International Space Station and Russia's *Soyuz* spacecraft have been destroyed, along with NASA's space shuttle and the Hubble.[3]

---

2   Chris Mooney and Sheril Kirshenbaum, *Unscientific America: How Scientific Illiteracy Threatens Our Future* (New York: Basic Books, 2010); see "Hollywood and the Mad Scientists," 81–95.
3   Of course, some of these events were implausible because the craft involved are at different altitudes and they orbit on different trajectories.

Metaphorically, the utter destruction of some of humankind's greatest technological achievements, including the most powerful and profound exo-media technology ever—the Hubble Space Telescope—illustrates a seeming disenchantment toward space exploration felt by much of the world's population and many citizens in America. In the opening scenes of *Gravity*, Sandra Bullock's character is upgrading the Hubble Space Telescope. That's what make the apocalyptic collisions in *Gravity* so tragic. It is as if humanity's most powerful eyes have been blinded.

In effect, the Hubble's first eyes were blinded. When the Hubble was launched into space in 1990, the original mirror was slightly defective—2.2 thousandths of a millimeter out of shape. Thus, the images of the universe were blurry and ruined. Designed to be the most perfect mirror ever constructed, the original mirror could not be replaced: its vision could only be corrected. This required NASA to launch, in 1993, the most complex repair job in human history. The shuttle *Endeavor* carried astronauts to the Hubble Space Telescope, with the task of refitting the telescope with new corrective equipment.[4]

Bullock's character in *Gravity* is based on real NASA astronauts such as Story Musgrave, who led the team that corrected and upgraded the Hubble. Musgrave describes what his experience with the Hubble meant:

> Majesty and magnificence of Hubble as a starship, a spaceship. To work on something so beautiful, to give it life again, to restore it to its heritage, to its conceived power. The work was worth it—significant. The passion was in the work, the passion was in the potentiality of Hubble Space Telescope.[5]

Over the past thirty years, the Hubble Space Telescope has exceeded its potentiality as originally imagined. It has transformed our understanding of the cosmos, especially in size and scale. As we extend these powerful exo-media technologies outward from our senses and consciousness, they, in turn, shape our consciousness and change our view of the universe and society. Or at least they should, if our eyes are open and our consciousness embraces what it sees. It's a wondrous universe offering us a cool future—as in the chill of cool media.

FIGURE 9.0.2 Two of humanity's most powerful eyes. The Hubble Space Telescope and the James Webb Space Telescope; background is one of the "Hubble Ultra Deep Field" (June 3, 2014) images. This image created by Barry Vacker from images provided by NASA (2021). All NASA images are in the public domain.

---

4   Brian Cox, *Wonders of the Universe* (London: Harper Design, 2011), 52–53.
5   Cox, *Wonders of the Universe*, 53.

EXO-MEDIA AND THE EPIC COSMOS

There are many topics that could be discussed with regard to science and the universe. But, easily the most profound is the discovery of the expanding universe, made possible by exo-media technologies, which always chill us down with a cool gaze.

Cool media cast their gaze into the cosmos, away from humans and human events on Earth. In doing so, they reveal profound things about our species and the universe. As Hildebrand and Vacker explain in chapter 2,

> In the cool gaze, events slow, attention spans grow, reflection trumps reaction, the species supersedes the tribe, borders and wars become artificial and absurd. Micro-particularities and hot affective conditions are not visible, but large-scale patterns, movements, and locations become more apparent. The more distant, aerial, and heightened perspective—beyond the thick, hot, reactive layers closer to us—opens up larger views and visions. ... Thrust apart by ever-expanding voids of space, the universe is expanding in all directions, likely forever, across trillions of trillions of years, toward thermodynamic exhaustion, zero energy. Voids, holes, and emptiness in outer space and our philosophies become visible. We are the center of nothing. Nihilism and enlightenment are the challenge. The universal over the tribal. *Terrestrial heat replaced by the cosmic chill.* There are no widely accepted politics or political narratives in the cool. Hot politics freeze in the cosmic background temperature.

Powered by exo-media, a new cosmology has emerged that explains our place in the cosmos and is supported by an ever-growing "galaxy" of evidence provided by our most advanced exo-media technologies. This cosmological meme is known as the "big bang" and the expanding universe. And it is an epic cosmos in which we are not the center of anything. Is that why so many people prefer *Dancing with the Stars* on television over watching the stars in a telescope?

Galileo's telescope and the Hubble Space Telescope show why media technologies are not neutral. As media technologies increase in power, they change our view of humankind's place on the planet and in the cosmos. Across the past five centuries, we have extended exo-media technologies ever further out into space and time, and in doing so we have transformed our view of the cosmos, culture, and consciousness. Media technologies shape how we think and what we believe. That is what McLuhan's phrases mean: the medium is the message and the medium is the massage (as we discussed in the introduction to chapter 2).

Cool media and curious minds have discovered a vast and ancient universe of staggering size and scale, far larger and older than anyone could have previously imagined. Simply put, we live in an epic cosmos. These discoveries are made possible by the most powerful telescopes on Earth along with the Hubble and Kepler telescopes in space. As Brian Cox explains in "Mapping the Milky Way,"

> Observing the night sky with the naked eye can only take us so far on our journey to discover and understand the wonders of the universe. Advances in technology have brought us crafts that can take humans on expeditions beyond our planet, but also sophisticated equipment that has changed our view of the universe entirely.[6]

WE ARE NOT THE CENTER OF THE UNIVERSE

Brian Cox's "sophisticated equipment" is exo-media technology such as the Hubble Space Telescope, which orbits at 370 miles in space, beyond the distortion effects of the Earth's atmosphere. We know that our planet orbits a typical star situated in an arm of the Milky Way, a spiral galaxy with at least 200 billion to 400 billion stars and a

---

6   Brian Cox and Andrew Cohen, *Wonders of the Universe*, p. 50. Copyright © 2011 by HarperCollins Publishers and HarperCollins UK. Reprinted with permission.

width of one hundred thousand light-years (100,000 × 6 trillion!). Most of these stars have planets, meaning that the number of planets in the Milky Way is in the billions. At the center of the Milky Way, a supermassive black hole is believed to exist, estimated to contain at least 4.1 million times the mass of the Sun. Wow. Think about that for a moment. Black holes like Gargantua in *Interstellar* likely exist.

Given that the observable universe is 13.7 billion years old, that Earth is about 4.5 billion years old, and that life on our planet emerged about four billion years ago, we are newcomers—appearing on the scene in the most recent moment in cosmic time. The human species has existed for about two hundred thousand years, and our brains have been largely the same size for about fifty thousand years. These brains have provided us a civilization, evolving from simplicity to complexity for five thousand years. For us, those are massive time spans. But for the universe and our planet, our existence is a mere moment in time. If the 13.7 billion years were spread across twelve months of a "cosmic calendar," humans do not appear until the last moments of December 31.

You can see a visual representation of some of the vastness of the universe in the opening sequence of the film *Contact* (1997), or in *The Known Universe* (2009), a beautiful six-minute video created by the American Museum of Natural History. Available on YouTube, *The Known Universe* is based on the most accurate mapping of the universe at that time.

From our minds, we have extended a complex information and communications network around the planet, throughout the solar system, and now beyond the solar system. We have also extended endo-media technologies throughout our bodies, including deep into our DNA and neurons. With our endo- and exo-media technologies, we can map the movement of distant galaxies and the innermost regions of our cells and neural networks, home to our consciousness, reason, emotion, curiosity, creativity, and the desire for meaning in our existence.

Rather than seek meanings for specific groups or tribes of humans, exo-media theory looks to discover meanings that are *universal to all humans*. The product of an exploding star, the solar system and everything in it—including you—is comprised of star stuff in its always-evolving forms. To borrow from Carl Sagan, we are self-aware star stuff. In the final paragraph of *Wonders of the Universe*, Brian Cox explains:

> But that doesn't make us insignificant, because life is the means by which the Universe [*sic*] can understand itself, if only for an instant. This is what we've done in our brief moments on Earth: we have sent space probes to the edge of our solar system and beyond; we have built telescopes that can glimpse the oldest and most distant stars, and we have discovered and understood at least some of the natural laws that govern the cosmos. This, ultimately, is why I believe we are important. Our true significance lies in our continuing desire to understand and explore this beautiful Universe—our magnificent, beautiful, fleeting home.[7]

If humans quit waging war and destroying the planet, then we might have value to the cosmos in this way: humans are how the cosmos knows and reflects upon itself in this small area of the universe.

YOU ARE SPINNING THROUGH THE UNIVERSE AND ORBITING A BLACK HOLE

Chill on this. Our planet is spinning at 932 miles per hour on its axis as it orbits the Sun at 67,000 miles per hour, and our solar system is orbiting the supermassive black hole in the center of the Milky Way at 492,000 miles per hour. And the Milky Way is hurtling through the cosmos at more than one million miles per hour. Yes, right now, as you read this book, you and everything on Earth are moving through space at speeds exceeding one million miles per hour. And it still takes us 225 million years to complete an orbit of the Milky Way![8]

---

7 Cox, 241.
8 Cox, 204–205.

More strangely, scientists estimate that the edges of the universe are expanding at one billion miles per hour. This model of an expanding, accelerating universe is a mind-boggling narrative, and it offers further proof that as exo-media technologies increase in power, they change our view of the cosmos and our place in it.

BIG BANG THEORY

The Hubble Deep Field images suggest the Milky Way is just one of at least two trillion galaxies in the known universe, each with many *billions* of stars.[9] Our telescopes and computers have revealed that the universe emerged from a cosmological eruption known as the "big bang." You might immediately think of *The Big Bang Theory*, the hit sitcom that has aired for eleven seasons (so far). It's often a funny show, but I'm referring to the "big bang" referenced in the opening stanza of *The Big Bang Theory*'s theme song:

> Our whole universe was in a hot, dense state
>
> Then nearly fourteen billion years ago expansion started, wait
>
> The earth began to cool, the autotrophs began to drool
>
> Neanderthals developed tools
>
> …
>
> Math, science, history, unraveling the mysteries
>
> That all started with the big bang! Hey!

It's true that the observable universe began expanding from a hot, dense state in a small region of space-time about 13.7 billion years ago. We don't know what existed before, or why, but we know the observable universe stretches across one hundred billion light-years and contains two trillion galaxies, each with billions of stars and untold numbers of planets, black holes, and possible life-forms. Our knowledge of this immense universe began with the telescope—perhaps the most important media technology of all time, precisely because it removed us from the center of the universe.

From Galileo's telescope to the Hubble Space Telescope, our media technologies empower us to peer across the depths of the universe to discover our true place in the universe. Our discovery of humanity's cosmic origins might be our greatest achievement as a species: through our media technologies, we have discovered a vast and majestic universe in which we are utterly insignificant. That's a meme that's both empowering and humbling.

The telescope was the technological "big bang" that knocked us off center stage, forcing us to rethink our origins and destiny by showing we're not the center of everything, not the center of the universe. The big bang and our noncentrality are memes still shaking our world, because our species still seems in denial, almost always acting like it's the center of all meaning, value, and purpose. Look at how we've trashed our planet while causing so many species to go extinct. And now some of the most popular futurists on the planet want to trash Mars.

MARS AND ELON MUSK

> *When faced with a totally new situation we tend always to attach ourselves to the objects, to the flavor of the most recent past. We look at the present through a rear-view mirror. We march backwards into the future.*

> —Marshall McLuhan

---

9   Cox, 26–27, 55.

Since the founding of SpaceX in 2002, Elon Musk has been viewed in popular culture as a space "visionary"—one of the billionaire pioneers to lead humanity off the planet by terraforming and colonizing Mars in the twenty-first century. Ridley Scott's hit film *The Martian* (2015) was a movie-length advertisement for colonizing and terraforming Mars into a mirror of Earth. After all, the "Martian" in the film title was a human.

To stamp his futuristic status, Musk and his partner Grimes (the pop singer) have given their baby boy a futuristic name: X Æ A-12. That's kinda cool and fine with me. Of course, "Elon Musk" is a catchy name. So is "Tesla," named after one of the pioneers of electricity, a name surely more futuristic than Toyota "Prius" and Nissan "Leaf." But, is Musk really the "cool dude of the future," especially when it comes to venturing into space? It's more than ironic that the first thing SpaceX launched beyond Earth and into the solar system was a Tesla car piloted by the "Starman"—a dummy. Prophetic?

Elon Musk is a charismatic salesman of "the future." After all, Musk has thirty-four million Twitter followers, and thousands of them quickly signed up for the Mars One colonization plan. To terraform Mars for colonization, Musk has proposed that we launch thousands of nuclear weapons to heat the planet, melt the ice caps, and release CO_2, all supposedly to trigger a runaway greenhouse effect to make Mars habitable. This is definitely not a "cool media" future.

Even though NASA says we can't terraform Mars with today's technology (or any time soon), we can pretend it might be possible to terraform Mars enough to fully colonize the Red Planet—just to compare different models for how we might treat Mars. The central question this section poses is: *Why can't art, science, and ecology be our messengers into the universe, the high-marks of enlightenment for our civilization?*

THE MIRROR OF GAZE

Marshall McLuhan's quote summarizes today's so-called futurism, trapped in rearview mirror visions. Into which mirror should we cast our gaze? Is it the *rearview mirror* of nuclear destruction, followed by resource exploitation and pollution on celestial bodies? Is it the mirrors that always reflect human narcissism, nationalist competition, technological fetishism, and tribal warfare?

Or should we embrace the mirrors of the world's telescopes, especially the Hubble Telescope and Webb Telescope? The most profound media technology of all time, telescopes reveal humans to be a single species on a tiny planet in a vast and majestic universe. Telescopes show that the human species can be brainy, curious, and truly creative, so why not embrace the obvious message? *Why not venture off this planet as a united and cooperative species, with humility and respect for the beautiful worlds we will visit, explore, and admire?*

TESLA'S STARMAN: TRAPPED IN THE REARVIEW MIRROR GAZE

One of SpaceX's most famous launches has been the Tesla piloted by the Starman, supposedly a testament to the cool space future that awaits humanity. Or maybe the Tesla Starman is merely a stellar work of pop art or the greatest car ad of all time. Or perhaps the Tesla Starman is another example of consumption and pollution, now being extended into space by our cosmic narcissism? After all, space junk already rings our planet, just like the star-light pollution of Starlink.

Tesla's Starman is symbolic of the dominant space philosophies. We're all dressed up and ready to go, but we're on autopilot, with cruise control speeding us backward to the nineteenth- and twentieth-century industrial consumer model. We are trapped in the gaze of the rearview mirror, all being celebrated in the tweets of the twenty-first-century media spectacle. We don't need to terraform Mars, we need to *transform* our worldviews on Earth—before we go anywhere off this planet.

THE "VALUE" OF MARS

Elon Musk champions the Mars One colonization of the Red Planet, along with possibly terraforming Mars into a mirror of Earth. What follows is the inevitable industrialization and destruction of ancient landscapes, not unlike the dominant philosophies prior to the rise of national parks and ecological protections in the twentieth century.

We are sending into space the very things that cause horror and warfare on Planet Earth: resource exploitation, industrial pollution, nationalist rivalry, economic greed, and eventual military conflict. It doesn't have to be this way. There are two different ways we can "value" Mars:

1. Industrial-consumer-narcissistic values
2. Aesthetic-scientific-species values

INDUSTRIAL-CONSUMER-NARCISSISTIC VALUES

The industrialization model leads directly to the consumer society, where everything of value is based in material objects for consumption and images for entertainment. Think Disney Mars. Absent a different model, Mars colonization will echo what's happened on Earth, where human narcissism reigns supreme. As for colonizing the Red Planet, let's not merely think of some cool "biosphere" with brave human explorers, as first prototyped at Biosphere 2 in Arizona and celebrated in the 2015 film *The Martian*.

In the early 1990s, the internet provided a new and untouched world, which some thinkers thought would be an electronic utopia for human consciousness—until the rest of humanity arrived, colonized it, and polluted it with hate, nationalism, and endless advertising. Absent a counter to the rearview mirror model, it'll be the same with Mars. As with Earth and the internet, China and Russia will have their territories on the Red Planet. Maybe India and Japan, too. Any resource or product brought back to Earth for consumption will not make life better on Earth. It will only end up in a landfill.

AESTHETIC-SCIENTIFIC-SPECIES VALUES

Fortunately, there is another model we could follow, where we think and act as a single species. This model is hopeful and optimistic, offering something much different than consumerism and industrial conquest. That Mars has untouched landscapes does not mean it is "empty" and valueless, ready for us to "fill it" with our cultural baggage. Mars is already "full"—as it is, a planet filled with extraordinary beauty and sublimity. That's its most profound and enlightened value, along with the scientific discoveries we might make. As with the Grand Canyon, we don't need to fill Mars with anything. Let's visit it, study it, admire it, and protect it from our blind and greedy selves.

Following the National Park and Wilderness models, why not protect Mars (and the moon) as "Celestial Wildernesses" for visits by artists, scientists, thinkers, and space tourists? That's what is implied in the moon scenes in *2001*. Similarly, let's set aside tiny fractional parts of Mars and the moon for scientific study and habitation, but leave the remaining parts untouched for aesthetic appreciation—just as we do with national parks and wilderness areas on Earth.

To be clear, this recommendation is not about setting aside a few patches of "park land" on Mars and the moon while the rest of the territories are polluted, terraformed, strip mined, and colonized by industrial workers, tourists visiting "Disney Mars," and bloated space consumers in McDonald's and Starbucks. Can't you just see the Golden Arches glowing atop a Martian mesa? How about electronic billboards lining the rim of a crater, creating a Mars Times Square?

The idea of protecting Mars as a site for aesthetics and science may seem naive or impractical—until we consider that on Earth we have already created a huge tourist economy based on the aesthetics of nature, vastness, and the sublime. That's the ultimate basis for all the national parks in America and around the world. In 2018, over twenty million people visited the national parks in the desert southwest of America. It's a massive multibillion-dollar industry.

Earthlings go to national parks and wilderness areas for a variety of reasons, but they mostly center on seeking and experiencing some combination of the following:

*   Natural beauty
*   Amazing experiences of sublimity and immensity: forests, mountains, oceans, deserts, and canyons made possible by eons of biological, geological, and celestial evolution

- Solitude and remoteness away from civilization
- Ancient landscapes and ecosystems untouched by humans (or at least mostly untouched)

Let's imagine that the aesthetic-science model ensures that all but *0.001 percent of Mars* is completely set aside for ecological protection, available only for scientific study, philosophical inquiry, and aesthetic appreciation. Given that Mars has about fifty-five million square miles of surface area, 0.001 percent would still leave 550 square miles for minimal human development scattered among select spots on Mars.

These areas would be set aside for human usage and habitation, such as biospheres, astronomical observatories, museums (with artifacts from the planet), art galleries (with artwork based on the planet or the cosmos), outdoor art installations, and sites for space tourism (hotels, campsites, and hiking trails). How amazing would it be to hike along the Valles Marineris canyon, which stretches almost four thousand kilometers and has depths that reach almost seven kilometers? Space hotels could orbit Mars, while the rest of the Red Planet would remain untouched.

Imagine visiting great artworks, museums, or observatories on Mars (or the moon), with celestial artworks and science exhibits that tell the story of our cosmic origins and neighborhood.

REASONS WHY MARS AND THE MOON SHOULD BE PROTECTED AS CELESTIAL PARKS AND WILDERNESS AREAS

1. Mars and the moon are objects of truth, beauty, and wonder: sites for scientific discovery and space tourism.

   —Humans should protect 99.999 percent of Mars and the moon for the same reasons we protect nature and wilderness areas on Earth: beauty, science, solitude, ecological protection, and to place humans in a larger planetary and cosmic narrative.

   —Mars and the moon have been around about 4.5 billion years longer than humans; thus, we have no intrinsic right to plunder, pillage, or own either of these celestial bodies.

   —We should think of Mars and the moon as "celestial museums" for art and science—sites for aesthetic appreciation, scientific understanding, and existential solitude.

   —Humans should visit Mars and the moon: study them, admire them, explore them, camp on them, and even build hotels on them or space hotels that orbit them. But we should not pollute them. We should respect them.

2. Mars and the moon should not be a part of human consumption.

   —Humans should not mine Mars or the moon for energy and minerals that we will use on Earth and then just spew into the atmosphere and toss into landfills. We would thus be polluting Mars, the moon, and our own planet while literally putting Mars and the moon into our landfills.

3. Mining Mars or the moon will not improve the human condition.

   —Extracting resources from Mars and the moon will not make a better society or better species; it will only make some people rich, create some jobs, and produce more pollution.

—The same goals (wealth and jobs) could be attained by tapping into the so-called battery in the sky: the Sun and its 4.7-billion-year life span of solar energy.

4. We do not want to pose a threat to celestial objects and extraterrestrial species.

    —Pillaging and polluting Mars and the moon show that *we are a threat* to extraterrestrial species and other planets, not a worthy and enlightened cosmic civilization.

5. As a species and civilization, we will become greater and more celestial if we refrain from polluting and ravaging other planets and moons.

    —It's time to give up the pre-Copernican narcissism. From the moon, Earth is a borderless planet traversing the voids of space and time. From Mars, our planet is just a tiny speck of light. That we know this confirms our greatness *and* our insignificance simultaneously. To admire and respect other planets confirms our wisdom and our right to exist as a space-faring and cosmic civilization.

MUSK: SIMULACRUM OF THE SPACE FUTURE

Elon Musk is not the human to lead Earthlings into space, not if we are the enlightened species we claim to be. Like most high-tech billionaires, Elon Musk has absorbed the surrounding intellectual culture—good and bad—and cleverly capitalized on a few technological trends to become fabulously wealthy. As philosopher Jean Baudrillard explained, we live in the era of the simulacrum, where the copy has replaced the original in our mediated culture—a world of signs and symbols, clones and copies, fakes and facades. Perhaps more poetically, the mediated maps have overtaken the territories they were supposed to represent. On these maps, we see celebrities playing presidents, talk show hosts posing as philosophers, and nineteenth-century space visions pretending to be twenty-first-century visions. *Elon Musk is the simulacrum of the future, the copy of yesterdays past that look like the new tomorrows to come—but are not.* As best I can tell, the Tesla Starman's eyes are locked on the rearview mirror, gazing upon a future that is past, a tomorrow that should remain as yesterday. Otherwise, we are the species that poses the threat to other life-forms off this planet.

ARE WE ALONE?

In the summer of 2018, I was scrolling through my Facebook feed the night before I headed on a four-week road trip and vacation—much needed after completing the anthology *Black Mirror and Critical Media Theory*. I came across a link to a *New York Times* article entitled "Suspicious Minds: Mingling with Wariness and Wonder at a Conference Devoted to 'Ancient Aliens.'" Located in the Style section of the newspaper, the article took the reader on a journey through a conference with three thousand attendees along with photos of the outlandish fashions and discussions with the leading "Ancient Alien theorists" who star on the long-running series *Ancient Aliens*. Then, with massive surprise, I came across the following passage:

> Another critique, posted to *Medium* by Barry Vacker, a professor at Temple University, argued that since the Apollo 11 mission, Americans have lacked a popular narrative to explain the vast cosmos and our origins and destiny within it.

"In *Ancient Aliens*, we can see philosophy's mediated corpse," writes Mr. Vacker, who called the show "an attack on logic, rationality, and the nature of evidence."[10]

My jaw dropped, then I laughed out loud. The *New York Times* never contacted me; apparently, the author found my essay on *Medium*.[11] Imagine a philosophical media theorist being cited in the Style section of the *New York Times* among high fashion models, Broadway plays, and *Ancient Alien* believers. It's all absurd, yet a perfect indicator of our culture.

ANCIENT ALIENS

Kevin Burns, the producer of *Ancient Aliens*, says I am a "naysayer" who adds little to the discussion. No wonder: I actually rely on logic, science, real evidence, and exo-media technologies. The cited essay is an excerpt from my book *Specter of the Monolith*, which was inspired by *2001: A Space Odyssey* and offers a new philosophy for the human species to fill the void left in the wake of the Apollo moon landings. My "Ancient Aliens" essay is my second-most-read essay on *Medium*, trailing only my "Apollo Hoax" essay—both of which have had thousands of readers. Of course, that is a tiny audience compared to the millions of believers in ancient aliens. The spectacle reigns supreme.

HIJACKING THE NARRATIVES OF NASA AND *2001*

As mentioned earlier, 35 percent of Americans believe ancient aliens visited Earth. Not surprisingly, there exists the long-running television series *Ancient Aliens*, which has utterly hijacked the cosmic narratives of NASA and *2001: A Space Odyssey* by claiming that "ancient astronauts" have visited Earth and advised humans. The ancient-astronaut theory draws upon two valid cosmological concepts: (1) the reality of the immensity of space and time and (2) the possibility of advanced civilizations somewhere in the cosmos. Given that the scale of the observable universe is immense and that the Kepler Telescope suggests there may be billions of planets in the Milky Way, there is almost certainly life elsewhere in the cosmos, perhaps including intelligent civilizations. Given that the observable universe is 13.7 billion years old and it took four billion years for intelligent life to emerge on Earth, then it is possible that the remaining nine billion years produced civilizations that may have existed for millions or billions of years. If so, they may have developed space travel technologies that allow them to traverse the great distances with relative ease. (At least that is the "wormhole" scenario depicted in *Contact* and *Interstellar*.)

Ancient Aliens has aired for ten seasons and over ninety episodes. In various episodes, the ancient-astronaut theorists assert that ancient visitors did the following:

- Consulted on the Mayan calendar
- Inspired Plato's Atlantis
- Made possible the Great Pyramids
- Designed ancient megaliths and temples
- Caused floods, plagues, pandemics, and assorted apocalypses
- Consulted with Leonardo da Vinci
- Advised America's Founding Fathers
- Contacted cowboys and Native Americans in the Old West
- Worked with Nikola Tesla in developing electricity
- Gave hints about relativity to Albert Einstein

---

10   Steven Kurutz, "Suspicious Minds: Mingling with Wariness and Wonder at a Conference Devoted to 'Ancient Aliens,'" *New York Times*, July 21, 2018. A link to my essay was embedded in the word "writes."
11   Barry Vacker, "Ancient Aliens: Evidence of Stephen Hawking's Claim that 'Philosophy Is Dead,'" Medium, February 26, 2017.

- Helped design Nazi weapons
- Advised NASA on how to put humans on the moon
- Left behind clues to the "God particle" allegedly discovered by the Large Hadron Collider at CERN

The above assertions are among the most ludicrous and illogical interpretations of human artifacts made by the ancient-astronaut theorists, and all are wholly unproven. In many ways, the series is an attack on logic, rationality, and the nature of evidence. That *Ancient Aliens* has been on television for seven seasons suggests there are sizable audiences who are quite gullible, unable to think logically, and scientifically illiterate. Plus, there are irresponsible and intellectually bankrupt television programmers, but that is nothing new either.

In *Ancient Aliens*, virtually all of the so-called evidence and arguments provided by the theorists are myth, superstition, hearsay, anecdotal, or involve an inference or conclusion that is fallacious, implausible, or unknowable. The "evidence" and arguments also contain inaccuracies, mistaken assumptions, unrelated facts, and false similarities. The few remaining pieces of "evidence"—which are a tiny fragment of the absurd claims—are simply mysteries yet to be solved or mysteries that will *never* be solved. That an advanced extraterrestrial civilization would be so interested in the fate of human civilization is a rather narcissistic take on the importance of humanity.

Virtually all the claims of extraterrestrial influence made on *Ancient Aliens* assume that human consciousness and civilization have little creativity, originality, or ability to innovate. The general idea is that without assistance from the ancient astronauts, humans would be helpless and could never build such great structures or make profound scientific discoveries. Plus, the show assumes there is no room for chance, surprise, emergence, singularities, or any of the insights of chaos theory and complexity theory. In the end, the series represents an assault on rationality and scientific methods, not unlike all other paranormal movies and television shows.

A VIABLE POSSIBILITY: PANSPERMIA

Far more likely than ancient aliens is the possibility that life was carried to our planet via a comet or a meteor. That's called panspermia, and it is possible. The famed Murchison meteorite contains traces of the amino acids necessary for life, traces that are visible and decipherable only because of endo-media technologies such as microscopes.

In the universe, there exists the possibility of trillions of suns with planetary systems and, quite possibly, numerous planets with life. Thanks to the astounding discoveries of the Kepler Space Telescope, NASA estimates that there may be one hundred billion *planets* in the Milky Way alone, with perhaps tens of billions of them being habitable and earthlike.[12] If one out of eight planets in our solar system has life, then how many could have life out of one hundred billion? The answer is12.5 billion. E.T. may take many forms and phone many homes.

The possibilities for discovering panspermia and populated planets are more examples of the effect of exo-media technologies. The human mind is a very large space in a very small place. That is why we should feel proud that we possess the potential to grasp our cosmic conditions and that we are just beginning to understand our true place in the cosmos as passengers on Spaceship *Earth*.

If we are not alone, exo-media technologies may soon let us know. Exo-media power the work of the SETI (Search for Extraterrestrial Intelligence) Institute, the organization dedicated to answering the question "Are we alone?" So far, the Kepler Space Telescope shows that billions of stars in the Milky Way have orbiting planets, with many likely suitable for life in its many forms—from bacteria to creatures with brains. Though not confirmed yet, possibilities for life elsewhere in the universe seem 99 percent certain. The idea that we are alone in the universe seems more implausible every time we build a more powerful telescope to peer into the universe.

---

12   "The Milky Way Contains at Least 100 Billion Planets According to Survey," *HubbleSite: Newscenter*, January 11, 2012.

CONTACT AND COOL MEDIA

The existence of an advanced civilization is at the heart of Robert Zemeckis's *Contact*. Jodie Foster plays Ellie Arroway, an astronomer who uses radio telescopes (cool, exo-media) and her laptop to discover "contact" with an extraterrestrial civilization. Foster's character is based on Jill Tarter, the real-life astronomer who pioneered work in this field. This film never fails to mesmerize students in my courses, and it always generates much discussion and curiosity.

As explained by Neil deGrasse Tyson in "Our Radio Bubble," the extraterrestrial civilization detects our television signals (which travel at the speed of light) and sends the signals back to us. Humans soon learn the signal's encoded with blueprints for building an interstellar transportation machine that would permit humans to visit the civilization, even though it is many trillions of miles away. The television signals from Earth had made it to the star system known as Vega, from which they are sent back by the civilization.

Since the discovery is made at the Very Large Array facility (radio telescopes in New Mexico), masses of people converge to reveal the absurdity of the human carnival on Spaceship *Earth* as it floats through the cosmos. There are people waving American flags, people dressed like Hollywood aliens, people wearing homemade space suits with headphones and antennae, people selling UFO abduction insurance, and Native Americans chanting and dancing. Hot air balloons are adorned with various messages ("Vega or Bust" and "This Way to Oz"), and an Elvis impersonator proclaims "Viva Las Vegas." Pop songs about "one-eyed" aliens, wanting "to be a spaceman," and going up to "the spirit in the sky" abound.

Eventually, nations and their scientists and politicians organize and build the massive interstellar transportation machine, which resembles the famed symbol for an atom—three rings encircling the nucleus (and its surrounding void). Arroway is seated in a pod during the journey, though she is also wearing a video headset to record the events. The machine's swirling rings generate a powerful electromagnetic field into which the pod is dropped, sending Arroway hurtling through a series of wormholes, all surrounded by spectral patterns of light.

The pod then hurtles through another wormhole before hovering over a spiral galaxy, aglow in a brilliant spectrum of colors. Floating in the pod, Arroway speaks into her headset in a breathless whisper:

> Some celestial event. No! No words! No words to describe it! Poetry! They should have sent a poet. It's so beautiful, beautiful. So beautiful! So beautiful! I had no idea.

This is said while her eyes are *wide* open, without blinking, in awe, experiencing the cosmic sublime. Here the film is perceptive; the universe as revealed by science and cosmology has infinitely greater beauty and grandeur than anything on Earth.

During Ellie's journey, the film loses its philosophical energy and veers toward a mostly Hollywood ending, all while trying to remain mysterious. Pay attention to Ellie's video camera and flat screen in the pod. The static on the screen is background radiation left over from the big bang and the expansion of the universe. The screen ends up functioning as "exo-media" and proves Ellie's scientific explanation of the events on her journey.

2001, *Contact*, and *Arrival* (chapter 1) are the most intelligent films about a possible encounter with an extraterrestrial civilization, mainly because the extraterrestrials are not presented as monsters who want to wipe out humanity. Unless we adopt a cool media philosophy, we will extend our hot media hyperreality into space to show that we are the threat to other planets and celestial bodies, other life-forms and possible civilizations.

THE EXPLODING POWER OF EXO-MEDIA

As can be seen in the graphic below (figure 9.0.3), the size and power of exo-media are exploding dramatically. Peering across the universe are optical and radio telescopes—the Hubble Space Telescope, the Very Large Telescope, the Gran Telescopio Canarias, and the Event Horizon Telescope Array, which joins telescopes spread across three continents. The Event Horizon Telescope Array enabled Katie Bouman's team to capture the first imagery of a black hole. Coming soon is the Square Kilometre Array, which will span the Pacific Ocean, from the Australian outback to southern Africa. Also coming are the Giant Magellan Telescope and the European Extremely Large Telescope, both located in the Atacama Desert in the Andes mountains of Chile. In fact, Chile has become a sort of telescope utopia, with its clear dark skies and dry air on remote mountaintops.

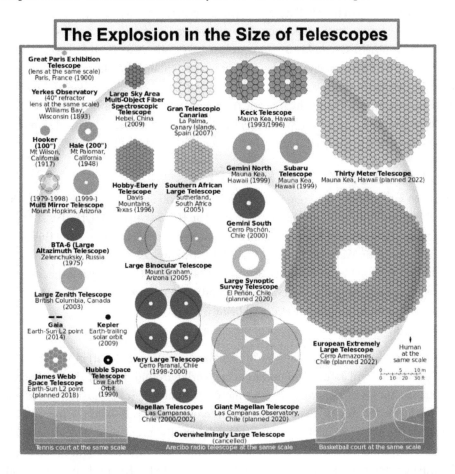

FIGURE 9.0.3 Graphic from Sidney C. Wolff, *The Boundless Universe: Astronomy in the New Age of Discovery* (Tucson, AZ: Rio Nuevo Publishers, 2016), p. 67.

Figure 9.0.3 uses tennis courts and basketball courts as references to the sheer size of the mirrors in these telescopes. The addition of a smartphone, laptop, and flat-screen TV next to the human pictured above the basketball court would further illuminate the scale because these objects would be specks. Like the tiny human, who is almost an afterthought when pictured alone, the technologies would provide a dramatic contrast with the size and power of the two-decade old telescopes.

As for the use of various colors for the telescopes in the graphic, that choice may be more pleasing to the eye. However, these mirrors are just that—mirrors—with various tints depending on the material used in the surface. It would be more accurate if the table displayed the colors of the mirrors themselves. For example, the mirrors in the James Webb Space Telescope are tinted bright gold, not dark gray as seen in the graphic. Using a silver color to stand for the mirrors would reinforce the reflective power of the telescopes.

Scientists, astronomers, and cosmologists almost always refer to telescopes as *instruments* and *tools*. Rightly so, for these telescopes are extremely intricate instruments for observing deep into the universe. In that sense, these massive telescopes are indeed tools of science and astronomy. Yet, this terminology lacks any reference to telescopes as *media technologies* and thus they are routinely excluded from discussions of media theory. In effect, scientists and astronomers are seen as doing *science*, while media theorists focus on the media in the hands of citizens and their social effects. This separation of media technologies is deeply flawed and misguided, precisely because it neglects the deeply related effects of these many media technologies. The explosion in the size and power of telescopes, as seen in the graphic, needs to be complemented by an explosion in the scale of media theory.

As explained in "Hot and Cool in the Media(S)cene" in chapter 1, media technologies exist on a spectrum, each with a different direction of gaze. Endo-media peer into things, ego-media allow humans to gaze upon humans, eco-media look down up territories, and exo-media (telescopes) look away from humans and Earth, peering deep into the cosmos. Different gazes have different effects, best explained by the hot-cool spectrum developed by Hildebrand and Vacker in chapter 1. Grasping the chilling effect of telescopes is key to understand their full effects—what we call cool media. That's why it's time to include telescopes in any model and theory for understanding the power of twenty-first century media technologies. The effects are extended into the International Dark Sky movement discussed in the final reading in this book, "Dark Skies Philosophy."

THE JAMES WEBB SPACE TELESCOPE

It's likely that the most famous new telescope will be the James Webb Space Telescope (JWST), the successor to the Hubble Space Telescope.[13] Currently slated to be launched on Halloween in 2021, the JWST was built by NASA and the European Space Agency. JWST has more than one hundred times the power of the Hubble Telescope. In a talk at the Perimeter Institute (in Waterloo, Ontario, Canada), astrophysicist Amber Straughn explained the design and functions of the JWST.[14] Don't be intimidated. Straughn's talk was outstanding and she clearly explained the details of the telescope, complemented with many photos and video images. As you can see from figure 9.0.4, the design of the JWST is visually striking, futuristic, and beautiful.

According to Straughn, here are the highlights of the design:

- The JWST will be parked one million miles from Earth, at a stationary location known as Lagrange Point 2 (or L2). The telescope will actually follow Earth in its orbit around the Sun. That's amazing!
- Regarding its size, the JWST's mirror will be 6.5 meters in diameter, in contrast to the Hubble's 2.4 meters. Of course, the larger the mirror, the more light that can be gathered—and the more light, the more we can learn about the universe. The JWST telescope will have light- and heat-deflecting shields measuring about the size of a tennis court, while the Hubble's tubular structure was about the size of a school bus.
- The JWST will be primarily an infrared telescope, in contrast to the Hubble being an optical telescope. In a nutshell, the infrared lens allows the space telescope to peer through the massive dust clouds that are sites for star formation and that also block out other parts of the universe.

---

13   There is increasing pressure for NASA to rename the space telescope. Here's why. As explained by Chanda Prescod-Weinstein, Sarah Tuttle, Lucianne Walkowitz, and Brian Nord: "James Webb, a career civil servant whose time at the Department of State under Truman included advancing the development of psychological warfare as a Cold War tool, was later the NASA administrator who oversaw the Apollo program. When he arrived at NASA in 1961, his leadership role meant he was in part responsible for implementing what was by then federal policy: the purge of LGBT individuals from the workforce. When he was at State, this policy was being carried out by men who worked under Webb." The evidence suggests that Webb clearly supported these governmental policies. Webb also participated in "making psychological warfare a tool of the military industrial complex." Though Webb did great things for NASA during the 1960s, his overall legacy of homophobia and support of psychological warfare makes his name the wrong name for the space telescope that follows the Hubble. Chanda Prescod-Weinstein, Sarah Tuttle, Lucianne Walkowitz, and Brian Nord, "NASA Needs to Rename the James Webb Space Telescope," *Scientific American*, March 1, 2021.
14   Amber Straughn, "A New Era in Astronomy: NASA's James Webb Space Telescope," presentation at the Perimeter Institute for Theoretical Physics, Waterloo, Ontario, Canada, March 2, 2017. Video available in YouTube, https://www.youtube.com/watch?v=S4td1hZLP8w.

FIGURE 9.0.4 Using a crane, NASA engineers lifted the mirror of the James Webb Space Telescope and moved it inside a clean room at the Goddard Space Flight Center (Greenbelt, Maryland). NASA website, April 25, 2017.

According to Straughn, here are the main astronomical research goals of the space telescope:

- To seek out the "first light" and earliest galaxies in the universe, peering back across 13.5 billion years (Just think: The light has been traveling for 13.5 billion years, 9 billion years before the Earth was even formed);
- To get a better grasp on how galaxies form, including our own Milky Way;
- To study the birth of stars and planetary systems; and
- To study exo-planets orbiting other stars, and to look for signatures of life in their atmospheres.

There are three hundred billion to four hundred billion stars in the Milky Way, and statistically there is at least one planet for each star. That's a lot of land and water that life could emerge from. The discovery of life off of Planet Earth will easily be one of the top two discoveries of all time, right up there with the overall discovery of the expanding universe and its trillions of galaxies. By peering into the "first light," the JWST will be extending the edges of the observable universe, and who knows what discoveries might emerge with this exo-media power. Finally, the JWST just looks damn cool, as do the Giant Magellan Telescope and others.

DISCOVERIES THAT JUSTIFY OUR FUTURE EXISTENCE

Through the power of exo-media, look at what we've discovered. An epic and wondrous universe—trillions of galaxies, black holes galore, billions of planets in the Milky Way, a cosmic web of galaxies and vast voids stretching across one hundred billion light-years.

Closer to home, our solar system is about five billion years old, and the Sun is a flaming ball of hydrogen and helium with eight planets and trillions of asteroids in its gravitational field. And the icy moons around Jupiter and Saturn may host microbial life-forms. These are just the broad brushstrokes. But not bad for our species, the advanced simians who migrated out of Africa one hundred thousand years ago and eventually colonized the continents before casting their gaze to the starry skies—armed with telescopes to see what the hell is out there!

Physically, our species is utterly insignificant and might well be meaningless. But two things are certain: We are stardust and we are one way the universe is aware of itself. To me, those two facts philosophically justify our continued existence and the quest for an enlightened future.

MILKY J AND "HUBBLE GOTCHU"

In 2010, "Milky J" (portrayed by comedy writer and actor Bashir Salahuddin) did a skit on *Late Night with Jimmy Fallon* called "Hubble Gotchu."[15] Milky J said to Fallon,

> Your show is good. As a matter of fact, your show is great. But you know what's greater? The exquisite interstellar photography you get with the Hubble Space Telescope!"

Milky J talked and sang about the awesome Hubble images and how they dwarfed everyday life in New York City. A few years later, Milky J went to NASA to check out the new James Webb Space Telescope while singing of his love for the Hubble.[16] It's all funny. And intellectually provocative. The subtext to "Hubble Gotchu" is that "Hubble GotUsConfused" about what we're doing on Planet Earth. Milky J points right to the philosophical heart of the matter.

BRIAN COX'S "UNIVERSAL" TOUR

In 2019, Brian Cox took his "Universal" live lecture tour to the theaters in major cities in the United States. I saw his presentation in the Kimmel Center in downtown Philadelphia, just three blocks from my urban cliff dwelling—a high-rise of lofts. Discussing cosmology and black holes in swank theaters tells us how far the scientific universe has reached into segments of popular consciousness, powered in part by the new phenomenon of celebrity scientists—such as Neil deGrasse Tyson, Brian Cox, and Amber Straughn, who appears in Milky J's "Hubble Gotchu" video.

Though enlightening and visually compelling, Cox's presentation fell short on providing any "universal" meaning outside of scientific discovery, which leaves us in awe. That's important, but far, far more is needed. Like Milky J, Tyson, and Straughn, Cox seems cool and charming, but his "Universal" presentation was philosophically lacking. Being cool is not enough, for cool media demand an entirely new philosophy for human existence.

CREDITS

---

15 Milky J, "Hubble Gotchu," *Late Night with Jimmy Fallon*, April 15, 2010. Video available in YouTube, August 15, 2014.

16 Milky J, "JWST Gotchu," *Late Night with Jimmy Fallon*, September 21, 2010. Video available in YouTube, March 21, 2014.

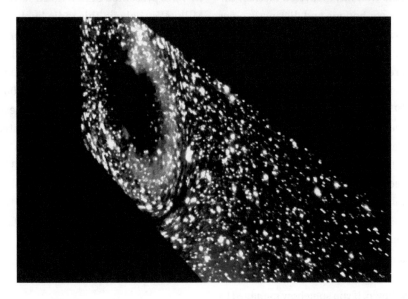

FIGURE 9.0.5, 9.0.6 and 9.0.7   Top photo: Brian Cox on stage in front of electrified Earth; middle photo: website and social media for the Universal tour; bottom photo: dynamic giant image of a black hole, a crowd-pleasing image for sure! Photos by Barry Vacker (2019).

OUR RADIO BUBBLE

from *Death by Black Hole*

NEIL DEGRASSE TYSON is an astrophysicist with the American Museum of Natural History and director of the world-famous Hayden Planetarium. Author of numerous articles and books, his most recent book is *Space Chronicles: Facing the Ultimate Frontier* (2013). He was the host for the 13-part documentary series, *Cosmos: A Spacetime Odyssey* (2014).

For the opening scene to the 1997 film *Contact*, a virtual camera executes a controlled, three-minute zoom from Earth to the outer reaches of the universe. For this journey, you happen to be equipped with receivers that enable you to decode Earth-based television and radio broadcasts that have escaped into space. Initially, you hear a cacophonous mixture of loud rock music, news broadcasts, and noisy static as though you were listening to dozens of radio stations simultaneously. As the journey progresses out into space, and as you overtake earlier broadcasts that have traveled farther, the signals become less cacophonous and distinctly older as they report historical events that span the broadcast era of modern civilization. Amid the noise, you hear sound bytes in reverse sequence that include: the *Challenger* shuttle disaster of January 1986; the Moon landing of July 20, 1969; Martin Luther King's famous "I Have a Dream" speech, delivered in August 28, 1963; President Kennedy's January 20, 1961, inaugural address; President Roosevelt's December 8, 1941, address to Congress, where he asked for a declaration of war; and a 1936 address by Adolf Hitler during his rise to power in Nazi Germany. Eventually, the human contribution to the signal disappears entirely, leaving a din of radio noise emanating from the cosmos itself.

Poignant. But this scroll of acoustic landmarks would not unfurl exactly as shown. If you somehow managed to violate several laws of physics and travel fast enough to overtake a radio wave, then few words would be intelligible because you'd hear everything replayed backward. Furthermore, we hear King's famous speech as we pass the planet Jupiter, implying Jupiter is as far as the broadcast has traveled. In fact, King's speech passed Jupiter 39 minutes after he delivered it.

Ignoring these facts that would render the zoom impossible, *Contact*'s opening scene was poetic and powerful, as it indelibly marked the extent to which we have presented our civilized selves to the rest of the Milky Way galaxy. This radio bubble, as it has come to be called, centers on Earth and continues to expand at the speed of light in every direction, while getting its center continuously refilled by modern broadcasts. Our bubble now extends nearly 100 light-years into space, with a leading edge that corresponds to the first artificial radio signals ever generated by Earthlings. The bubble's volume now contains about a thousand stars, including Alpha Centauri (4.3 light-years away), the nearest star system to the Sun; Sirius (10 light-years away), the brightest star in the nighttime sky; and every star around which a planet has thus far been discovered.

Not all radio signals escape our atmosphere. The plasma properties of the ionosphere, more than 50 miles up, enable it to reflect back to Earth all radio-wave frequencies less than 20 megahertz, allowing some forms of radio communication, such as the well-known "short wave" frequencies of HAM radio operators, to reach thousands of miles beyond your horizon. All the broadcast frequencies of AM radio are also reflected back to Earth, accounting for the extended range that these stations enjoy.

If you broadcast at a frequency that does not correspond to those reflected by Earth's ionosphere, or if Earth had no ionosphere, your radio signals would reach only those receivers that fell in its line of "sight." Tall buildings give significant advantage to radio transmitters mounted on their roofs. While the horizon for a 5'8" person is just 3 miles away, the horizon seen by King Kong, while climbing atop New York City's Empire State Building, is more than 50. After the filming of that 1933 classic, a broadcast antenna was installed. An equally tall receiving antenna could, in principle, be located 50 miles farther still, enabling the signal to cross their mutual 50-mile horizon, thereby extending the signal's reach to 100 miles.

The ionosphere reflects neither FM radio nor broadcast television, itself a subset of the radio spectrum. As prescribed, they each travel no farther on Earth than the farthest receiver they can see, which allows cities that are relatively near each other to broadcast their own television programs. For this reason, television's local broadcasts and FM radio cannot possibly be as influential as AM radio, which may account for its preponderance of politically acerbic talk shows. But the real influence of FM and TV may not be terrestrial. While most of the signal's strength is purposefully broadcast horizontal to the ground, some of it leaks straight up, crossing the ionosphere and traveling through the depths of space. For them, the sky is not the limit. And unlike some other bands in the electromagnetic spectrum, radio waves have excellent penetration through the gas and dust clouds of interstellar space, so the stars are not the limit either.

If you add up all factors that contribute to the strength of Earth's radio signature, such as the total number of stations, the distribution of stations across Earth's surface, the energy output of each station, and the bandwidth over which the energy is broadcast, you find that television accounts for the largest sustained flux of radio signals detectable from Earth. The anatomy of a broadcast signal displays a skinny and a wide part. The skinny, narrow-band part is the video carrier signal, through which more than half the total energy is broadcast. At a mere .10 hertz wide in frequency, it establishes the station's location on the dial (the familiar channels 2 through 13) as well as the existence of the signal in the first place. A low-intensity, broadband signal, 5 million hertz wide, surrounds the carrier at higher and lower frequencies and is imbued with modulations that contain all the program information.

As you might guess, the United States is the most significant contributor among all nations to Earth's global television profile. An eavesdropping alien civilization would first detect our strong carrier signals. If it continued to pay attention, it would notice periodic Doppler shifts in these signals (alternating from lower frequency to higher frequency) every 24 hours. It would then notice the signal get stronger and weaker over the same time interval. The aliens might first conclude that a mysterious, although naturally occurring, radio loud spot was rotating into and out of view. But if the aliens managed to decode the modulations within the surrounding broadband signal they would gain immediate access to elements of our culture.

Electromagnetic waves, including visible-light as well as radio waves, do not require a medium though which to travel. Indeed, they are happiest moving through the vacuum of space. So the time-honored flashing red sign in broadcast studios that says "On the Air" could justifiably read "Through Space," a phrase that applies especially to the escaping TV and FM frequencies.

As the signals move out into space they get weaker and weaker, becoming diluted by the growing volume of space through which it travels. Eventually, the signals get hopelessly buried by the ambient radio noise of the universe, generated by radio-emitting galaxies, the microwave background, radio-rich regions of star formation in the Milky Way, and cosmic rays. These factors, above all, will limit the likelihood of a distant civilization decoding our way of life.

At current broadcast strengths from Earth, aliens 100 light-years away would require a radio receiver that was fifteen times the collecting area of the 300-foot Arecibo telescope (the world's largest) to detect a television station's carrier signal. If they want to decode our programming information and hence our culture, they will need to compensate for the Doppler shifts caused by Earth's rotation on its axis and by its revolution around the Sun (enabling them to lock onto a particular TV station) and they must increase their detection capacity by another factor of 10,000 above that which would detect the carrier signal. In radio telescope terms, this amounts to a dish about four hundred times Arecibo's diameter, or about 20 miles across.

If technologically proficient aliens are indeed intercepting our signals (with a suitably large and sensitive telescope), and if they are managing to decode the modulations, then the basics of our culture would surely befuddle alien anthropologists. As they watch us become a radio-transmitting planet, their attention might first be flagged by early episodes of the *Howdy Doody* show. Once they knew to listen, they would then learn how typical human males and females interact with each other from episodes of Jackie Gleason's *Honeymooners* and from Lucy and Ricky in *I Love Lucy*. They might then assess our intelligence from episodes of *Gomer Pyle*, *The Beverly Hillbillies*, and then, perhaps, from *Hee Haw*. If the aliens didn't just give up at this point, and if they chose to wait a few more years, they would learn a little more about human interactions from Archie Bunker in *All in the Family*, then from George Jefferson in *The Jeffersons*. After a few more years of study, their knowledge would be further enriched from the odd characters in *Seinfeld* and, of course, the prime-time cartoon *The Simpsons*. (They would be spared the wisdom of the hit show *Beavis and Butthead* because it existed only as a nonbroadcast cable program on MTV.) These were among the most popular shows of our times, each sustaining cross-generational exposure in the form of reruns.

Mixed in among our cherished sitcoms is the extensive, decade-long news footage of bloodshed during the Vietnam war, the Gulf wars, and other military hot spots around the planet. After 50 years of television, there's no other conclusion the aliens could draw, but that most humans are neurotic, death-hungry, dysfunctional idiots.

* * *

Rather than let aliens listen to our embarrassing TV shows, why not send them a signal of our own choosing, demonstrating how intelligent and peace loving we are? This was first done in the form of gold-etched plaques affixed to the sides of the four unmanned planetary probes *Pioneer 10* and *11* and *Voyager 1* and *2*. Each plaque contains pictograms conveying our base of scientific knowledge and our location in the Milky Way galaxy while the *Voyager* plaques also contain audio information about the kindness of our species. At 50,000 miles per hour—a speed in excess of the solar system's escape velocity—these spacecraft are traveling through interplanetary space at quite a clip. But they move ridiculously slow compared with the speed of light and won't get to the nearby stars for another 100,000 years. They represent our "spacecraft" bubble. Don't wait up for them.

A better way to communicate is to send a high-intensity radio signal to a busy place in the galaxy, like a star cluster. This was first done in 1976, when the Arecibo telescope was used in reverse, as a transmitter rather than a receiver, to send the first radio-wave signal of our own choosing out to space. That message, at the time of this writing, is now 30 light-years from Earth, headed in the direction of the spectacular globular star cluster known as M13, in the constellation Hercules. The message contains in digital form some of what appeared on the *Pioneer* and *Voyager* spacecraft. Two problems, however: The globular cluster is so chock full of stars (at least a half-million) and so tightly packed, that planetary orbits tend to be unstable as their gravitational allegiance to their host star is challenged for every pass through the cluster's center. Furthermore, the cluster has such a meager quantity of heavy elements (out of which planets are made) that planets are probably rare in the first place. These scientific points were not well known or understood at the time the signal was sent.

In any case, the leading edge of our "on-purpose" radio signals (forming a directed radio cone, instead of a bubble) is 30 light-years away and, if intercepted, may mend the aliens' image of us based on the radio bubble of our television shows. But this will happen only if the aliens can somehow determine which type of signal comes closer to the truth of who we are, and what our cosmic identity deserves to be.

MAPPING THE MILKY WAY GALAXY

from *Wonders of the Universe*

BRIAN COX is a physics professor at the University of Manchester, as well as a researcher on one of the most ambitious experiments on Earth, the ATLAS experiment on the CERN Large Hadron Collider. His most recent book is *Wonders of Life* (2013), which is also a BBC documentary. Cox was also a keyboardist in the UK pop band D:Ream in the 1990s.

ANDREW COHEN

Our galaxy, the Milky Way, contains somewhere between 200 and 400 billion stars, depending on the number of faint dwarf stars that are difficult for us to detect. The majority of stars lie in a disc around 100,000 light years in diameter and, on average, around 1,000 light years thick. These vast distances are very difficult to visualise. A distance of 100,000 light years means that light itself, travelling at 300,000 kilometres (186,000 miles) per second, would take years to make a journey across our galaxy. Or, to put it another way, the distance between the Sun and the outermost planet of our solar system, Neptune, is around four light hours—that's one-sixth of a light day. You would have to lay around 220 million solar systems end to end to cross our galaxy.

At the centre of our galaxy, and possibly every galaxy in the Universe, there is believed to be a super-massive black hole. Astronomers believe this because of precise measurements of the orbit of a star known as S2. This star orbits around the intense source of radio waves known as Sagittarius A* (pronounced 'Sagittarius A-star') that sits at the galactic centre. S2's orbital period is just over fifteen years, which makes it the fastest-known orbiting object, reaching speeds of up to 2 per cent of the speed of light. If the precise orbital path of an object is known, the mass of the thing it is orbiting around can be calculated, and the mass of Sagittarius A* is enormous, at 4.1 million times the mass of our sun. Since the star S2 has a closest approach to the object of only seventeen light hours, it is known that Sagittarius A* must be smaller than this, otherwise S2 would literally bump into it. The only known way of cramming 4.1 million times the mass of the Sun into a space less than 17 light hours across is as a black hole, which is why astronomers are so confident that a giant black hole sits at the centre of the Milky Way. These observations have recently been confirmed and refined by studying a further twenty-seven stars, known as the S-stars, all with orbits taking them very close to Sagittarius A*.

Beyond the S-stars, the galactic centre is a melting pot of celestial activity, filled with all sorts of different systems that interact and influence each other. The Arches Cluster is the densest known star cluster in the galaxy. Formed from about 150 young, intensely hot stars that dwarf our sun in size, these stars burn brightly and are consequently very short-lived, exhausting their supply of hydrogen in just a couple of million years. The Quintuplet Cluster contains one of the most luminous stars in our galaxy, the Pistol Star, which is thought to be near the end of its life and on the verge of becoming a supernova [...]. It is in central clusters like the Arches and the Quintuplet that the greatest density of stars in our galaxy can be found. As we move out from the crowded galactic centre, the number of stars drops with distance, until we reach the sparse cloud of gas in the outer reaches of the Milky Way known as the Galactic Halo.

In 2007, scientists using the Very Large Telescope (VLT) at the Paranal Observatory in Chile were able to observe a star in the Galactic Halo that is thought to be the oldest object in the Milky Way. HE 1523-0901 is a star in the last stages of its life; known as a red giant, it is a vast structure far bigger than our sun, but much cooler at its surface. HE 1523-0901 is interesting because astronomers have been able to measure the precise quantities of five radioactive elements—uranium, thorium, europium, osmium and iridium—in the star. Using a technique very similar to carbon dating (a method archaeologists use to measure the age of organic material on Earth), astronomers have been able to get a precise age for this ancient star. Radioactive dating is an extremely precise and reliable technique when there are multiple 'radioactive clocks' ticking away at once. This is why the detection of five radioactive elements in the light from HE 1523–0901 was so important. This dying star turns out to be 13.2 billion years old—that's almost as old as the Universe itself, which began just over 13.7 billion years ago. The radioactive elements in this star would have been created in the death throes of the first generation of stars, which ended their lives in supernova explosions in the first half a billion years of the life of the Universe.

*   *   *

THE HUBBLE TELESCOPE

The naked eye can only allow us to travel back in time to the beginnings of our species; a mere 2.5 million light years away. Until recently, Andromeda was the furthest we could look back unaided, but modern, more powerful telescopes now enable us to peer deeper and deeper into space, so that we can travel way beyond Andromeda, capturing a bounty of messengers laden with information from the far distant past.

In the history of astronomy, no telescope since Galileo's original has a greater impact than the eleven-tonne machine called Hubble. The Hubble Space Telescope was conceived in the 1970s and given the go-ahead by Congress during the tenure of President Jimmy Carter, with a launch date originally set for 1983. Named after Edwin Hubble, the man who discovered that the Universe is expanding, this complex project was plagued with problems from the start. By 1986, the telescope was ready for lift off, three years later than planned, and the new launch date was set for October of that year. But when the Challenger Space Shuttle broke apart seventy-three seconds into its launch in January 1986, the shutters came down not only on Hubble, but on the whole US space programme. Locked away in a clean room for the next four years, the storage costs alone for keeping Hubble in an envelope of pure nitrogen came to $6 million dollars a month.

With the restart of the shuttle programme, the new launch date was set for 24 April 1990 and, seven years behind schedule, shuttle mission STS-31 launched Hubble into its planned orbit 600 kilometres (370 miles) above Earth. The promise of Hubble was simple: images from the depths of space unclouded by the distorting effects of Earth's atmosphere. A new eye was about to open and gaze at the pristine heavens, but within weeks it was clear that Hubble's vision was anything but 20:20. The returning images showed there was a significant optical flaw, and after preliminary investigations it slowly dawned on the Hubble team that after decades of planning and billions of dollars, the Hubble Space Telescope had been launched with a primary mirror that was minutely but disastrously misshapen. Designed to be the most perfect mirror ever constructed, Hubble's shining retina was 2.2 thousandths of a millimetre out of shape, and as a result its vision of the Universe was ruined.

Such was the value and promise of Hubble that an audacious mission was immediately conceived to fix it. This was possible because Hubble was designed to be the first, and to date only, telescope to be serviceable by astronauts in space. A new mirror could not be fitted, but by precisely calculating the disruptive effect of the faulty mirror, NASA engineers realised that they could correct the problem by fitting Hubble with spectacles.

In December 1993, astronauts from the Shuttle Endeavour spent ten days refitting the telescope with new corrective equipment. In charge of the repairs, by far the most complex task ever undertaken by humans in Earth orbit, was astronaut Story Musgrave. Already a veteran of four shuttle flights, a test pilot with 16,000 flying hours in 160 aircraft types, ex-US Marine and trauma surgeon with seven graduate degrees, Musgrave is quite an extraordinary example of what people can do if they put their minds to it. He is a metaphor for the space programme itself; in Musgrave's own words, this is what restoring sight to Hubble meant. 'Majesty and magnificence of Hubble as a starship, a spaceship. To work on something so beautiful, to give it life again, to restore it to its heritage, to its conceived power. The work was worth it—significant. The passion was in the work, the passion was in the potentiality of Hubble Space Telescope.'

On 13 January 1994, NASA opened Hubble's corrected eye to the Universe and opened the eyes of our planet to the extraordinary beauty of the cosmos. A decade late and costing around $6 billion dollars, it has proved to be worth every cent.

*　*　*

HUBBLE'S MOST IMPORTANT IMAGE

For almost two decades the Hubble Space Telescope has captured the faintest lights and enabled us to rebuild these spectacular images, providing a window onto places billions of light years away and events that happened billions of years ago. These are places forever beyond our reach. However, there is one Hubble image that has done more than any other to reveal the scale, depth and beauty of our universe. Known as the Hubble Ultra Deep Field, this shot was taken over a period of eleven days between 24 September 2003 and 16 January 2004. During this period Hubble focused two of its cameras—the Advanced Camera for Surveys (ACS) and Near Infrared Camera and Multiobject Spectrometer (NICMOS)—on a tiny piece of sky in the southern constellation, Fornax. This area of sky is so tiny that Hubble would have needed fifty such images to photograph the surface of the Moon.

From the surface of Earth this tiny piece of sky is almost completely black; there are virtually no visible stars within it, which is why it was chosen. By using its million-second shutter speed, though, Hubble was able to capture images of unimaginably faint, distant objects in the darkness. The dimmest objects in the image were formed by a single photon of light hitting Hubble's camera sensors every minute. Almost every one of these points of light is a galaxy; each an island of hundreds of billions of stars, with over 10,000 galaxies visible. If you extend that over the entire sky, it means there are over 100 billion galaxies in the observable Universe, each containing hundreds of billions of suns.

However, there is something more remarkable about this image than mere scale, due to the slovenly nature of the speed of light compared to the distances between the galaxies. The thousands of galaxies captured by Hubble are all at different distances from Earth, making this image 3D in a very real sense. But the third dimension is not spatial, it is temporal. As we stare at Hubble's masterpiece we are looking back in time; deep time, time beyond human comprehension. Just as an ice core leads us back through layer after layer of Earth's history, so the Hubble Ultra Deep Field transports us back through the history of the Universe.

The photograph contains images of galaxies of various ages, sizes, shapes and colours; some are relatively close to us, some incredibly far away. The nearest galaxies, which appear larger, brighter and have more well-defined spiral and elliptical shapes, are only a billion light years away. Since they would have formed soon after the Big Bang, they are around twelve billion years old. However, it is the small, red, irregular galaxies that are the main attraction here.

There are about 100 of these galaxies in the image, and they are among the most distant objects we have ever seen. Some of these faint red blobs are well over twelve billion light years away, which means that when their light reaches us it has been travelling for almost the entire 13.75-billion-year history of the Universe. The most distant galaxy in the Deep Field, identified in October 2010, is over thirteen billion light years away—so we see it as it was 600,000 years after the beginning of the Universe itself.

It is hard to grasp these vast expanses of space and time. So, consider that the image of this ancient galaxy was created by a handful of photons of light; when they began their journey, released from hot, primordial stars, there was no Earth, no Sun, and only an embryonic and chaotic mass of young stars and dust that would one day evolve into the Milky Way. When these little particles of light had completed almost two-thirds of their journey to Hubble's cameras, a swirling cloud of interstellar dust collapsed to form our solar system. They were almost here when the first complex life on Earth arose and within a cosmic heartbeat of their final destination when the species that built the Hubble first appeared.

The story hidden within the Hubble Ultra Deep Field image is ancient and detailed, but how can we infer so much from a photograph? The answer lies in our interpretation of the colours of those distant, irregular galaxies.

* * *

Each day we awake to the rhythm of our planet as it spins at over 1,500 kilometres (932 miles) an hour, relentlessly rolling us in and out of the Sun's glare. Earth's ceaseless motion beats out the tempo of our lives with unerring repetition. A day is the twenty-four hours it takes Earth to rotate once on its axis; the 86,400 seconds it takes for anyone standing on the Equator to be whipped around the 40,074-kilometre (24,901-mile) circumference of our planet. This is the most obvious rhythm of the Earth, which comes about because of the spin rate of our rocky, iron-cored ball that was laid down somewhere in Earth's formation and 4.5-billion-year history.

Travelling at 108,000 kilometres (67,108 miles) an hour, we move through space in orbit around our star. Racing around the Sun at an average distance of 150 million kilometres (93 million miles), we complete one lap of our 970-million-kilometre (600-million-mile) journey in 365 days, five hours, 48 minutes and 46 seconds, returning regularly to an arbitrarily defined starting point. As we sweep through this place in space relative to the Sun, we mark the beginning and end of what we call a year.

Everywhere we look in the heavens we see celestial clocks marking the passage of time in rhythms. Our moon rotates around Earth every 27 days seven hours and 43 minutes, and because it is tidally locked to Earth it also takes almost exactly the same amount of time to rotate on its own axis: 27 Earth days. This means that the Moon always presents the same face to Earth. Further out in the Solar System, a Martian day is very similar to our own, lasting one Earth day and an additional 37 minutes. But because Mars is further from the Sun, a Martian year lasts longer with the red planet taking 687 Earth days to complete an orbit. In the farthest reaches of the Solar System, the length of a year gets progressively greater, with distant Neptune taking over 60,000 Earth days or 165 Earth years to make its way around its parent star. In September 2011, Neptune will have completed its first full orbit of the Sun since it was discovered in 1846.

As we look deep into space, the clockwork of the cosmos continues unabated, but as the distances extend, the cycles become grander, repeating on truly humbling timescales. Just as Earth and other planets mark out the passing of the years as they orbit the Sun, so our entire solar system traces out its own vast orbit. We are just one star system amongst at least 200 billion in our galaxy, and all these star systems are making their own individual journeys around the galactic centre. We are all in orbit around the super-massive black hole that lies at the heart of the Milky Way. It is estimated that it takes us about 225 million years, travelling at 792,000 kilometres (492,125 miles) per hour to complete one circuit, a period of time known as a galactic year. Since Earth was formed four and a half billion years ago, our planet has made 20 trips around the galaxy, so Earth is 20 galactic years old. Since humans appeared on Earth a quarter of a million years ago, less than one-thousandth of a galactic year has slipped by. In Earth terms, that is the length of a summer's afternoon.

This is an immense amount of time; difficult to comprehend when we speak of the entire history of our species as the blink of a galactic eye. We live our lives in minutes, days, months and years, and to extend our feel for history across a galactic year is almost impossible. Yet here on Earth there are creatures that have existed for lengths of time that span these grandest of rhythms.

* * *

A VERY PRECIOUS TIME

The fact that the Sun will die, incinerating Earth and obliterating all life on our planet, and that eventually the rest of the stars in the Universe will follow suit to leave a vast, formless cosmos with no possibility of supporting any life or retaining any record of the living things that brought meaning to its past, might sound a bit depressing to you. You might legitimately ask questions about the way our universe is put together. Surely you could build a universe in a different way? Surely you build a universe such that it didn't have to descend from order into chaos? Well, the answer is 'no', you couldn't, if you wanted life to exist in it.

The arrow of time, the sequence of changes that will slowly but inexorably lead the Universe to its death, is the very thing that created the conditions for life in the first place. It took time for the Universe to cool sufficiently after the Big Bang and for matter to form; it took time for gravity to clump the matter together to form galaxies, stars and planets, and it took time for the matter on our planet to form the complex patterns that we call life. Each of these steps took place in perfect accord with the Second Law of Thermodynamics; each is a step on the long road from order to disorder.

The arrow of time has created a bright window in the Universe's adolescence during which life is possible, but it's a window that won't stay open for long. As a fraction of the lifespan of the Universe, as measured from its beginning to the evaporation of the last black hole, life as we know it is only possible for one-thousandth of a billion billion billionth, billion billion billionth, billion billion billionth of a per cent.

And that's why, for me, the most astonishing wonder of the Universe isn't a star or a planet or a galaxy; it isn't a thing at all—it's a moment in time. And that time is now.

Around 3.8 billion years ago life first emerged on Earth; two hundred thousand years ago the first humans walked the plains of Africa; two and a half thousand years ago humans believed the Sun was a god and measured its orbit with stone towers built on the top of a hill. Today, our curiosity manifests itself not as sun gods but as science, and we have observatories—almost infinitely more sophisticated than the Thirteen Towers—that can gaze deep into the Universe. We have witnessed its past and now understand a significant amount about its present. Even more remarkably, using the twin disciplines of theoretical physics and mathematics, we can calculate what the Universe will look like in the distant future and make concrete predictions about its end.

I believe it is only by looking out to the heavens, by continuing our exploration of the cosmos and the rules that govern it, and by allowing our curiosity free reign to wander the limitless natural world, that we can understand ourselves and our true significance within this Universe of wonders.

In 1977, a space probe called Voyager 1 was launched on a 'grand tour' of the Solar System. It visited the great gas giant planets Jupiter and Saturn and made wonderful discoveries before heading off into interstellar space. Thirteen years later, after its mission was almost over, Voyager turned its cameras around and took one last picture of its home. This picture is known as the Pale Blue Dot. The beautiful thing, perhaps the most beautiful thing ever photographed, is the single pixel of light at its centre; because that pixel, that point, is our planet, Earth. At a distance of over six billion kilometres (3.7 billion miles) away, this is the most distant picture of our planet that has ever been taken.

The powerful and moving thing about this tiny, tiny point of light is that every living thing that we know of that has ever existed in the history of the Universe has lived out its life on that pixel, on a pale blue dot hanging against the blackness of space.

As the great astronomer Carl Sagan wrote:

'It has been said that astronomy is a humbling and character-building experience. There is perhaps no better demonstration of the folly of human conceits than this distant image of our tiny world. To me, it underscores our responsibility to deal mare kindly with one another, and to preserve and cherish the pale blue dot, the only home we've ever known.'

Just as we, and all life on Earth, stand on this tiny speck adrift in infinite space, so life in the Universe will only exist for a fleeting, dazzling instant in infinite time, because life, just like the stars, is a temporary structure on the long road from order to disorder.

But that doesn't make us insignificant, because life is the means by which the Universe can understand itself, if only for an instant. This is what we've done in our brief moments on Earth: we have sent space probes to the edge of our solar system and beyond; we have built telescopes that can glimpse the oldest and most distant stars, and we have discovered and understood at least some of the natural laws that govern the cosmos. This, ultimately, is why I believe we are important. Our true significance lies in our continuing desire to understand and explore this beautiful Universe—our magnificent, beautiful, fleeting home.

"EXPLOSION OF AWARENESS" KUBRICK, NIETZSCHE, HUBBLE, AND THE STARTING POINTS FOR A 21ST CENTURY PHILOSOPHY

Based on excerpts from *Specter of Monolith* (2017)

BARRY VACKER

Stanley Kubrick had it right—*2001: A Space Odyssey* showed the need for a 21st century philosophy, an entirely new cosmic worldview for the universe unveiled by science and technology. It's a vast universe of trillions of galaxies and giant stretches of emptiness, all sprawling across 100 billion light years of space. *2001* ranks as the greatest space film and one of the most philosophically profound films of all time, precisely because it embraces such a universe and envisions our place in it. In *2001*, Kubrick depicts a past and future in which humans have evolved from apes to astronauts via science and technology, along with an assist from a mysterious black monolith—all primed to propel an enlightened species into a massive and majestic universe in which we are not alone. The black monolith is the blank slate for a new philosophy for the human species. We have yet to write that philosophy, but we have made an impressive start.

That's the message of hope in *2001*, with the Star-Child appearing against the blackness of the cosmos, our planet in its gaze as the film ends. Seeing Earth from space has profoundly affected numerous astronauts, who experience deep feelings of awe, self-transcendence, and a primal connection to the universe, while sensing that humanity has gone awry on the planet below them. ***Apollo 14 astronaut Edgar Mitchell poetically described the experience as an "explosion of awareness."***

This "explosion of awareness" is felt in the "cosmic sublime"—the only direct human experience to unite our braininess and insignificance by connecting us and our species to a larger narrative directly related to the immensity of existence. This "explosion of awareness" provides an exciting and existential basis for a 21st century philosophy—for the future of the human species in space and on Earth. A new philosophy tells us not only where we're going, but 1) what will we be doing, 2) what does it mean, and 3) what can we hope for. It gives us the chance to be the enlightened species we claim to be.

WHY THE NEED FOR A NEW PHILOSOPHY?

Here's why: we're still pretending to be the center of the universe, the center of all value, meaning, and purpose. *Why else do we believe we have the cosmic right to strip-mine the moon or terraform Mars in the image of Earth?* Our cosmic narcissism suggests we'll send into space many of the worst features of humanity: greed, pollution, strip-mining, weaponization and militarization, and the usual narcissistic antics of our 24/7 media spectacle on Earth. We're set for war, mayhem, and planetary destruction in space. An epic fail. An alternative vision is needed. In the words of Ann Druyan: "What is coming of age but realizing that you are not the center of the universe?"

So far, a new philosophy worthy of *2001* and the Hubble Space Telescope is nowhere in sight, which is why Stephen Hawking says "philosophy is dead" and the *Ancient Aliens* TV series is creating a new space theology to explain our origins and destiny. *Ancient Aliens* has hijacked the *2001* narrative by filling the void in the search for human meaning in the universe. But, we've found no aliens, just like we've found no gods and no universal meaning for human existence. Zero, nada, zip. Oh sure, we've created stuff to fill the voids—gods, aliens, war, tribalism, nationalism, family, politics, consumption, celebrities, superheroes, sports teams, selfies, social media, all of which reflect and reinforce our need to feel special, central, and participants in a larger and meaningful narrative. Terraforming Mars, strip-mining moon, and militarizing space are part of the same efforts to fill the void. (For the record, I wish highly advanced and enlightened extraterrestrials would arrive today and jolt us out of our cosmic narcissism.)

If there is any cosmic justification for our existence—perhaps as self-aware stardust, as one way the universe knows itself in a tiny part of one galaxy—then we should start acting like wise, knowledgeable, and enlightened beings we claim to be. Simply put, contemporary secular philosophy has yet to produce a widely-embraced cultural cosmology that accounts for **the human species** in a vast and ancient universe, a universe in which we are very brainy, but utterly insignificant and not the center of anything—just smart specks on a tiny planet in a remote part of one galaxy. That's the philosophical and existential abyss in *2001*, which is why the film riffs off Nietzsche's famed book, *Thus Spoke Zarathustra* (1891).

That's why the ultimate challenge of the 21st century space age is to develop a universal philosophy that spans the abyss by connecting the human species to the cosmos from which it emerged—to reconcile our cosmic irrelevance with a shared destiny of hope, peace, meaning, and discovery. Perhaps then we can begin transcending our current ideologies and creating a vision for a space-faring civilization that is sane and humane, ecological and technological, optimistic and inspiring, meaningful and beautiful, respectful of other planets and life forms, and grounded in the art and science of the cosmos as best we know it.

"A ROPE OVER AN ABYSS": NIETZSCHE AND HUBBLE

In *Thus Spoke Zarathustra*, Nietzsche explores the death of God, the eternal recurrence (the endless recycling of world events), and the possible rise of the Ubermensch (the "Overman" or "Superman"). Nietzsche speculated that since humans are the superior species that evolved from apes, there might be an equally greater species that would evolve from humans—what he termed the Ubermensch or Superman:

> "What is the ape to man? A laughing-stock, a thing of shame. And just the same shall man be to the Superman: a laughing-stock, a thing of shame."[1]

Nietzsche suggested the next stage of human evolution could occur if we accepted our place on Earth—in the material world—rather than looking to otherworldly Gods for meaning and purpose. Far from naive about the wonders of modernity, Nietzsche knew that the death of God presented a huge philosophical challenge for the human species:

---

1   Friedrich Nietzsche, *Thus Spoke Zarathustra: A Book for Everyone and No One*, 26.

"man is a rope stretched between the animal and the Superman—a rope over an abyss."[2]

TABLE 9.3.1   TEN MEANINGS OF 21ST-CENTURY COSMOLOGY

TRIUMPH FOR OUR SPECIES

1. Our discovery of the epic universe represents the greatest intellectual triumph for the human species, bar none.
2. Through science and reason, we now know that humanity emerged from the "star stuff" of the universe, thus revealing the power of the universe to know itself and increase this knowledge.

THE FUTURE

3. The epic universe provides us with an endless amount to explore and countless planets to potentially visit in the near and distant future.
4. The evolution of 21st-century cosmology shows that our knowledge of the universe will always be expanding and evolving.
5. As our knowledge expands, so will our ignorance, thus posing continuing challenges for science and philosophy.

PHILOSOPHY

6. Knowledge of the epic universe has destroyed all previous narratives for human existence, suggesting instead our cosmic non-centrality and utter insignificance, further intensifying the issue of cosmic nihilism.
7. Because the universe is accelerating away from us in all directions—toward the "big crunch," "big chill," or "big rip"—it's creating celestial vanishing points that also destroy all previous narratives.
8. The epic universe presents the opportunity for artists, filmmakers, and philosophers to come up with a new space philosophy that embraces the cosmic sublime.
9. Our shared celestial origins with the universe might be the only way for us to find cosmic meaning for the human species.

HISTORY

10. If humans become extinct in the not-too-distant future, then the universe will have lost knowledge of itself, at least in this tiny portion of the Milky Way.

---

2   Ibid.

In the 1920s, Edwin Hubble expanded Nietzsche's abyss with the twofold discovery of *other galaxies* outside the Milky Way and *the expanding universe* in which the galaxies are moving away from each other. Since then, the Hubble Space Telescope and other telescopes have revealed a mind-blowing universe of two trillion galaxies and three sextillion stars along with untold numbers of moons, planets, supernovas, and black holes, all organized around supervoids and gigantic galaxy clusters that stretch for billions of light years. The energy of this universe is destined to last for trillions upon trillions of years.

Nothing symbolizes Nietzsche's abyss better than the Hubble Deep Field images, where the Hubble telescope peers into empty spaces in the night sky and finds thousands of galaxies located billions of light years away from Earth. *The universe of Hubble and the Hubble telescope—that's the abyss upon we have yet to develop the philosophical and existential rope.* So far, we are nowhere near fulfilling the vision of *2001: A Space Odyssey*, precisely because we don't have a 21st century philosophy, a cultural cosmology to complement the science and the mind-bending technological discoveries.

The Hubble telescope and the discovery of the vast universe is truly an epic human achievement. This image is one of the many "Ultra Deep Field" images from the Hubble Space Telescope. Each speck of light is a galaxy with billions of stars. Courtesy: NASA.

THE PARADOX OF OUR GREATEST ACHIEVEMENT

We are an amazing and paradoxical species. We are advanced simians that emerged from Africa's savannas and evolved into humans, apes who became astronauts, spear throwers who became space farers. We have the genius to extend our consciousness across 100 billion light years of a universe dotted with webs of galaxies located amid vast voids of space and dark energy. The Hubble telescope shows we're the center of nothing, yet we pretend that we're the center of everything—the center of all value, meaning, and purpose.

Consider this: Do we really, honestly believe that hydrogen atoms evolved for billions of years so that a single species on a tiny planet in a remote part of the cosmos could pretend it was the center of the universe, when in fact that species was the center of nothing and nothingness? Yet, we act as if we're the center of all worth seeing, doing, and knowing—*or so we think*—when it comes to our own consciousness and the 24/7 electronic media spectacle extending from that consciousness. Of course, this pretense to cosmic centrality is a delusion. It's as if Galileo and Hubble never existed. It's what I call the "pre-Copernicanism" of post-Apollo culture.

No doubt our discovery of the vast cosmos and our non-centrality ranks as our greatest triumph and poses our most important philosophical challenge. *We face the paradox of having discovered a sublime universe, and yet we are insignificant and our existence might be meaningless.* In this magnificent achievement and mind-blowing universe are the greatest opportunities for human enlightenment. As illustrated in Table 9.3.3, the future is wide-open for art, science, human discovery, and a new philosophy based on our our place in space and the universe.

Since the Apollo program, space and the universe as sources of philosophical insight about human living on Earth have been largely abandoned in popular discourse. Sure, there are the *Star Trek* and *Star Wars* movie franchises and films like *Interstellar*, which warns of ecological doom in the human future. But outside the realm of planetary ecology, outer space is largely viewed as:

1. a place where telescopes reveal cool images with no relevance to human life or meaning on Earth;
2. a place where Elon Musk and a bunch of rich guys can send their toys for fanboys living out sci-fi fantasies while terraforming and strip-mining planets.

It's as if the vast universe and a philosophy for living on Earth are billions of light-years apart. As a species, we are still coming to terms with the meaning of Apollo's views of Earth from space—a tiny planet in a vast and ancient cosmos.

KUBRICK AND LYOTARD: "MOMENTARY MICROBES" AND "SPASMODIC SMILES"

The paradox of our greatest achievement—discovering a vast universe in which we are insignificant—posed challenges for Stanley Kubrick and the philosopher Jean-Francois Lyotard. That challenge is *nihilism* and the apparent universal meaninglessness and irrelevance of human existence in the vast universe. About the humanity's existence, Kubrick said:

> If man merely sat back and thought about his impending termination, and his terrifying insignificance and aloneness in the cosmos, he would surely go mad, or succumb to a numbing sense of futility. Why, he might ask himself, should he bother to write a great symphony, or strive to make a living, or even to love another, when he is no more than a momentary microbe on a dust mote whirling through the unimaginable immensity of space?[3]

Since our sun is destined to die out in 4.5 billion years and expand to consume Earth and all human thought and artifacts left on our planet, Lyotard observes:

> This arrangement is transitory—lasting a few billion years more or less. Lunar years. Not a long time on a cosmic scale. The sun, our earth and your thought will have been no more than a spasmodic state of energy, an instant of established order, a smile on the surface of matter in a remote corner of the cosmos.[4]

---

3 Norden, "Playbook Interview: Stanley Kubrick," 47–74; and Patrick Murray and Jeanne Schuler, "Rebel Without a Cause: Stanley Kubrick and the Banality of the Good," in *The Philosophy of Stanley Kubrick*, ed. Jerold Abrams (Lexington: University Press of Kentucky, 2009), 144.
4 Jean-Francois Lyotard, *The Inhuman: Reflections on Time*, 10.

Lyotard knew these conditions ultimately *annihilate* and render absurd the passions that consume society, with its wars, borders, politics, economics, and belief that the "smile on the surface of matter" actually matters to the cosmos. In the eyes of Kubrick and Lyotard, the cosmos permits us to exist but does not care if we exist. *Because of this existential condition amid the majesty and vastness, Lyotard believed the sublime is "the sole serious question to face humanity today" and "everything else seems insignificant."*

And it is against this vision of nihilism that Kubrick directed *2001*, with its hopeful vision of human origins and destiny, going from simians to space-farers. Kubrick countered nihilism with the sublime, a vision of awe and wonder, culminating in the "explosion of awareness"—symbolized by Dave's cosmic journey through the Star-Gate and beyond and back to Earth.

THE COSMIC SUBLIME: "EXPLOSION OF AWARENESS"

Astronaut Edgar Mitchell is spot on when he described the sublime as triggering an "explosion of awareness." Having experienced the sublime numerous times when looking through the telescopes at the McDonald Observatory in Texas, I can attest to the poetic and philosophical power of Mitchell's phrase. Seeing galaxies such as Andromeda and Whirlpool directly through the telescopes is at once awe-inspiring, humbling, and empowering. And the feeling one gets is indeed an "explosion of awareness." You realize you are a small part of something massive and majestic—you are the infinitesimal amid the infinite. But rather than feel merely tiny and hopeless, you transcend your insignificance to feel empowered.

If you've gazed at the Milky Way in dark sky areas far from the city lights, you have likely experienced the cosmic sublime—the awe and wonder of the vastness. In fact, you might have experienced a bit of fear or horror because of the sense of your mortality beneath the starlight eternity. It's the same with the Hubble telescope images—awe, wonder, and perhaps a tinge of terror. Your experience is the cosmic sublime—and

it is the singular aesthetic experience that connects us (the infinitesimal) to the universe (the infinite). It's the "explosion of awareness" shared as members of the human species, the only species on our planet to have this aesthetic experience of the vast universe we have discovered.

Borrowing from Kant, Lyotard, and other thinkers, here is what I mean by the cosmic sublime: We encounter the cosmic sublime when there's a tension between our perceptions and our reason, when our senses are *overwhelmed*, yet our minds can still order the percepts into *knowable*, *pleasurable*, and *terrifying* concepts. The features of the vast universe—immense scales of space and time; dynamic systems of stars, galaxies, supernovas, and black holes; limitless arrangements of energy and matter; sprawling voids and seeming emptinesses; immeasurable realms of cosmic destruction and renewal—confront and stimulate our imaginations in awe-inspiring experiences. In such we grasp the *affirmation* of human rationality and *annihilation* of our centrality, our *exaltation* before the cosmos in tandem with the *extinction* of our species' dominant narratives, and the sense of human *freedom* in conjunction with our *void in meaning*. In our infinitesimalness, we can feel connected to the universe or crushed by its infiniteness.

The sublime moment is poignant with emotional, cognitive, and aesthetic overload—the **"explosion of awareness."** We realize we are no physical match for nature and the cosmos, yet we're confident of our ability to tackle the intellectual challenge of exploring them via science and technology. Because the sublime affirms humanity's right to exist at the same time that it draws attention to the inevitability of our own extinction, it evokes paradoxical emotions in us that coexist, side by side, such as pleasure and pain, attraction and repulsion, and power and fear. The sublime is not a mystical or religious experience; it's a profoundly existential aesthetic experience.

Art historian Elizabeth Kessler explains the phenomenon of the cosmic sublime perfectly in her book *Picturing the Cosmos*, describing how the images from the Hubble Space Telescope:

> invoke the sublime and ... encourage the viewer to experience the cosmos visually

TABLE 9.3.2 EXPERIENCING THE COSMIC SUBLIME

The paradoxical feelings and experiences we have when observing the vast universe.

PERCEPTS OF COSMIC VASTNESS, IMMENSITY, LIMITLESSNESS, EMPTINESSES, ETC.

Ordered via human reason—Overwhelmed senses and perceptions

FEELINGS

Pleasure —	Pain
Pain —	Repulsion
Power —	Fear
Awe —	Terror

WHAT HUMAN REASON AND REFLECTION GRASP OR CONFIRM

Affirmation of human reason —	Annihilation of our significance
Exaltation before the cosmos —	Extinction of our previous narratives
The infinite —	The infinitesimal
Human freedom —	The void of meaning
Connection to the Universe —	Crushed by the universe

From Chapter 4 of *Specter of the Monolith*. These meanings reveal the philosophical power of cool media.

and rationally, to see the universe as simultaneously beyond humanity's grasp and within reach of our systems of knowledge.[5]

THE SOCIAL-PSYCHOLOGICAL EFFECTS OF AWE

Rather than denying or ignoring our insignificance in the vast universe, perhaps we should be finding ways to experience *the sublime* more often. Recent psychological studies suggest that experiencing awe can inspire people to situate themselves in larger narratives and engage in what some researchers call "pro-social behavior." By experiencing things that are vast or infinite, humans

develop a sense of what researchers term the "small self" (the infinitesimal). Awe and vastness also make people feel more connected to a universal narrative for their species. As explained by the authors of one study:

> Awe involves positively valenced feelings of wonder and amazement. Awe arises via appraisals of stimuli that are vast, that transcend current frames of reference, and require new schema to accommodate what is being perceived. Although many stimuli can inspire awe, from beautiful buildings to elegant equations, the prototypical awe experience, at least in Western cultures, involves encounters with natural phenomena that are immense in size, scope, or complexity, e.g. the night sky, the ocean. However elicited, experiences of awe are unified by a core theme: perceptions of vastness that dramatically expand the observer's usual frame of reference

5   Elizabeth A. Kessler, *Picturing the Cosmos: Hubble Space Telescope Images and the Astronomical Sublime* (Minneapolis: University of Minnesota Press, 2012), 5.

in some dimension or domain. ... Taken together, these studies suggest that awe directs attention to entities vaster than the self and more collective dimensions of personal identity, and reduces the significance the individual attaches to personal concerns and goals.[6]

In their article entitled "The Overview Effect: Awe and Self-Transcendent Experience in Space Flight," Yaden et al. (2016) state:

> The overview effect, as the experience is called, refers to a profound reaction to viewing the Earth from outside its atmosphere. A number of astronauts have attributed deep feelings of awe and even self-transcendence to this experience.[7]

The authors explain there are several features that contribute to the astronauts' experience of awe: (a) the experience of cosmic vastness, (b) the totality of seeing Earth as a complete system, and (c) the juxtaposition of Earth's features against the black voids of space. In other words, the overview effect and the experience of awe combine vastness, totality, and the voids of space, resulting in a transcendent experience that connects astronauts to much larger narratives of cosmic unity.

These astronauts and cosmonauts come to the realization that human narratives on Earth are deeply flawed. Altered perceptions of Earth's existential value are among the most important psychological effects of space flight, which "seems to be one of the few endeavors that can be a true source of collective inspiration." In conclusion, Yaden et al. (2016) state:

> Awe and self-transcendence are among the deepest and most powerful aspects of the human experience: it should come as no surprise that they emerge as we gaze upon our home planet and our whole world comes into view.[8]

These "awe studies" support my explication of the cosmic sublime, particularly the simultaneous experience of the infinite (immensity, totality) and infinitesimal ("small self"), the exaltation before the cosmos, and the extinction of our narratives (the need for new schema and a new frame of reference). It is the sublime moment that inspires humans to "transcend current frames of reference" and have "altered perceptions of Earth's existential value." The sublime can be a unifying experience that *connects humans to the cosmos and larger narratives for our species*. That's why the sublime is key to developing a cosmic and space narrative for the human species

THE ROPE, THE MONOLITH, AND THE SUBLIME

The sublime experience is the way we experience the infinite and infinitesimal, the way we transcend awesomeness and nothingness. The sublime is the "explosion of awareness"—the first moment we toss the rope over the abyss. That's the symbolic significance of the black monolith in *2001: A Space Odyssey*. What follows are some starting points for a 21st century philosophy, accompanied by two tables from my new book, *Specter of the Monolith* (2017).

A SHARED DESTINY. Collectively, the sublime experience connects the infinite and infinitesimal in us—as individuals and a species—and suggests a *shared destiny* for a diverse humanity on our tiny planet. *Borders, nations, and tribal warfare become absurd in the sublime and in any sane philosophy.* In my view, it is the sublime that unites and connects a diverse

---

6   Paul K. Piff, Matthew Feinberg, Pia Dietze, Daniel M. Stancato, and Dacher Keltner, "Awe, the Small Self, and Prosocial Behavior," *Journal of Personality and Social Psychology*, vol. 108, no. 6 (June 2015), 883-99, 884.
7   David B. Yaden, Jonathan Iwry, Johannes C. Eichstaedt, George E. Vallant, Kelley J. Stack, Yukun Zhao, and Andrew Newberg, "The Overview Effect: Awe and Self-Transcendent Experience in Space Flight," *Psychology of Consciousness: Theory, Research, and Practice*, vol. 3, no. 1 (March 2016), 1-11.
8   Ibid.

humanity to it evolutionary-cosmic origins as members of a single species.

UNIVERSAL RIGHTS AND ENLIGHTENMENT. In the sublime experience, our reason and freedom are stimulated, which provides an existential basis for pursuing *secular enlightenment* (via art, science, and philosophy) and *universal human rights on Earth and all other celestial bodies.* This also means we recognize the same rights for the extraterrestrial life forms and civilizations we encounter.

SPACE ECOLOGY AND PROTECTING PLANETS/ MOONS. Our insignificance should generate humility before the grandeur of the universe, thus inspiring us to *protect the ecosystems on Earth and beyond,* especially reverence for those planets and celestial bodies we visit. That we can travel to Mars or the moon in the future does not mean we have the cosmic right to plunder and pollute them. We should study them, admire them, and protect their beauty.

UNITED IN OUR GREATNESS AND INSIGNIFI-CANCE. Informed by scientific knowledge, the sublime enables us to directly experience and deduce a *universal narrative* for our species, a narrative directly experienced as we transcend our individual experience—we're the infinitesimal connected with the infinite. It's a narrative that unites our greatness as thinkers and our insignificance as humans in the immense universe we have discovered. Of course, this is only a sketch of the sublime, the mere starting point for a 21st century philosophy.

OUTLINE FOR A NEW PHILOSOPHY

The table on the left outlines a new narrative for space exploration, one that embraces scientific discovery, philosophical inquiry, ecological protection for the places we visit, the aesthetics of beauty and the sublime, and global cooperation among nations, peoples, and corporations. Let's call this the **Science Philosophy Ecology Aesthetic Cooperative (SPEAC)** model for space exploration. We should develop this narrative and let it *speak for our species* in the universe!

What's needed is a philosophical launch directly into the cosmic sublime—smack dab, dead on, right into celestial nothingness and everything massive, beautiful, and terrifying in the universe. As dramatized in *2001,* let's touch the monolith, toss the bone, zoom through the Star-Gate, probe deeper into the dark skies, and turn our neurons on to a new narrative and philosophy for our species. If we don't do the philosophical launch, we'll never reach the space odyssey of *2001* because we'll still be battling on the *Planet of the Apes.*

After our philosophical launch, our "explosion of awareness" might extend into all fields of human endeavor and into our understanding of our role in the universe. We might evolve into our own Ubermensch, a much more intellectually advanced human species with a new philosophy for the universe we have discovered. Or maybe not. We may end up enlightened, exterminated, or existentially meaningless, but we will have experienced the awe and wonder of the cosmos on scales that previous humans and all other Earthly animals could have never known. Regardless of our eventual failure or success in the cosmos, using the "explosion of awareness" to launch us into the universe would be a cosmic gesture for which our species can be proud.

TABLE 9.3.3 OUR CELESTIAL ORIGINS: THE EX-ISTENTIAL GROUNDS FOR A PHILOSOPHY FOR THE HUMAN SPECIES

(These are the conditions revealed by our cool, exo-media technologies.)

1. **Hydrogen atoms evolved across 13.7 billion years to produce our galaxy, the sun, our planet, and all life on Earth.**
   Meaning: We are the product of a vast and ancient universe that permits us to exist.

2. **All humans are made of the most common elements of the cosmos (hydrogen, nitrogen, oxygen, carbon, etc.) and share 99.9% of the same DNA.**
   Meaning: We are star stuff; the universe is in us, and we are of the universe. We are members of one species sharing one planet with millions of other species.

3. **We are the only species on Earth that creates art, science, and philosophy to understand the universe and represent it to ourselves.**
   Meaning: We are self-aware stardust and one way the cosmos knows itself. Our consciousness has built an impressive body of knowledge about the universe, which shows that we are capable of being an enlightened species.

4. **We are the center of nothing amid the immensity and majesty of the cosmos.**
   Meaning: Cosmic non-centrality is our starting point as enlightened space voyagers who travel in peace, seek more knowledge and wisdom, cherish beauty and sublimity in the universe, and share our art, science, and technology with other civilizations we encounter.

5. **We embrace the cosmic nihilism and the sublime.**
   Meaning: We are a species humbled—but not terrified—by our possible cosmic meaninglessness and extinction; we simultaneously grasp tne infinitesimal (us) and the infinite (the cosmos) as we search for our meaning and destiny in the awe-inspiring universe.

From Chapter 4 of *Specter of the Monolith*.

TABLE 9.3.4 OUTLINE FOR A 21ST-CENTURY SPACE PHILOSOPHY

The Science, Philosophy, Ecology, Aesthetics, Cooperative Model of Space Exploration (SPEAC)

1. SCIENTIFIC DISCOVERY
   — Our scientific exploration of the universe should continue, but with much more funding. We should send more telescopes into space, more robots to planets and moons, and humans to Mars and elsewhere in the quest to discover extraterrestrial life and ecological knowledge to prevent our planet from becoming like Mars (a planetary desert) or Venus (a runaway greenhouse).

2. PHILOSOPHY
   — If we claim to be an enlightened species, then we need to determine the philosophical meaning (if any) of our scientific and cosmological discoveries. Is nihilism all we can expect from the cosmic sublime?
   — As shown by Apollo's *Earthrise* and the Hubble images, there is no self-evident meaning to human existence in the universe. The only path out of post-Apollo culture is the development of a *universal narrative* to give us hope for a meaningful destiny in a cosmos in which we are not central or important.

3. ECOLOGY
   — Since we have no cosmic right to lay waste to other planets and moons, we should extend our ecological protections to all the planets and moons we explore. How can we not want to protect the beauty and sublimity of such celestial objects?
   — Destroying landscapes of other celestial objects shows we are a threat in the universe and invite future retribution from any advanced extraterrestrials we encounter.

4. AESTHETICS
   — As illustrated by the national parks and wilderness areas of the United States, many people want to experience natural beauty along with solitude and the sublime of ancient topographies, panoramic landscapes, and the Milky Way in the dark skies of remote locales.
   — Obviously, the untouched wildernesses will be available in much greater scale on other planets and moons while providing unlimited opportunities to experience the cosmic sublime amid the stars.
   — In our embrace of the sublime lies the greatest chance to counter nihilism and develop a universal human narrative.

5. COOPERATION
   — If we claim to be an advanced civilization, then the combination of science, philosophy, ecology and aesthetics should make us realize the inherent wisdom of cooperating as nations and peoples when venturing into space.
   — Our planetary cooperation is already celebrated by the original *Star Trek*, put into practice at the International Space Station, and supported in films such as *The Martian*. Similarly, NASA shares its discoveries with the world, and the European Space Agency represents many countries.
   — In the end, we are a single species exploring the universe from which we emerged, while the universal awe felt toward tne Milky Way and the cosmos tells us we should cooperate.

From Chapter 1 of *Specter of the Monolith*.

This book was inspired by the science-fiction masterpiece, *2001: A Space Odyssey*. Though these passages were written before Julia Hildebrand and I developed the hot-cool media theory (Chapter 2), they perfectly expresses how *cool media* should shape a new cosmic narrative grounded in the universe as it is, not as we wish it was. That's the power of cool media, to provide the technological basis for a new philosophy for the human species.

BLACK MIRROR (2011–)

Brimming with existential angst toward the technological future, the *Black Mirror* anthology series has established itself as *The Twilight Zone* of the 21st century. Each episode is a stand alone film exploring the near-future in which humans are dominated by the technologies they worship, with the merger of media and human behavior presenting a full array of spectacles, hyperrealities, and bizarre visions of tomorrow.
Creator: Charlie Brooker

THE HUNGER GAMES: CATCHING FIRE (2013)

After winning the 74th Hunger Games with Peeta, Katniss becomes the symbol inspiring rebellion in the various districts of Panem. President Snow tries to force Katniss into turning her defiance into a love story about her and Peeta, before declaring a special Hunger Games involving past winners, with the goal of silencing Katniss and subduing the spirit of the rebellion. The film ends with the outcome uncertain.
Director: Francis Lawrence
Starring: Jennifer Lawrence and Josh Hutcherson

TOMORROWLAND (2015)

A science-oriented teenager and a former boy-genius inventor embark on a journey to discover whether the future will be better world filled with hope and optimism or a dystopian world filled with despair and destruction. Along the way, they find themselves traveling with a robot from the 1964 World's Fair and a plenty of questions about what makes the future. A surprisingly thoughtful film from Disney.
Director: Brad Bird
Starring: George Clooney, Britt Robertson, Hugh Laurie, and Raffey Cassidy

BLADE RUNNER 2049 (2017)

The long-awaited sequel to Ridley Scott's masterpiece, *Blade Runner* (1982), *Blade Runner* 2049 presents a future that is at once beautiful and barren, stunning to look at, yet absent much hope for a better humanity. Set in the Los Angeles and Las Vegas of the future, our technologies and hyperrealities have continued to advance, while we have plundered the lands and the seas levels continue to rise. It seems we'll be able to make better copies of people, but not necessarily better people.
Director: Denis Villeneuve
Starring: Ryan Gosling, Harrison Ford, and Robin Wright

BLACK PANTHER (2018)

The Marvel superhero gets a stellar Hollywood treatment that makes "Black Panther" a household name and catapults *Black Panther* into the all-time top 10 at the box office, grossing $1.3 billion. Not only does T-Challa became a superhero of global fame, but the nation of Wakanda presents a striking vision of the future, where tradition and technology merge into a utopian vision that offers hope, optimism, and progress in a better tomorrow.
Director: Ryan Coogler
Starring: Chadwick Boseman, Michael B. Jordan, Angela Bassett, and Lupita Nyong'o

CHAPTER TEN

POSSIBLE MEDIA FUTURES
Hot and Cool, Hope and Diversity, Dystopia and Dark Skies

By Barry Vacker

DREAMING HOT AND COOL

Inspired by a strange dream and the "Hot and Cool" essay/art installation I cocreated with Julia Hildebrand, I wrote the following passages six weeks after having cancer surgery in March of 2020.

High temperatures, hot planet, hotter tempers. Corona fever, global warming, flame wars. Spiraling dreams, screening delirium. It's all connected. Deeply.

It's a world of screens, filled with high densities of image, information, and energy. Phone gets hot in my hand, laptop heats on my desk. Screens are instant proximity to all events, getting hotter every moment. Corona spreading, death count climbing, some claim hoaxing. Hot screens, hot takes, hot planet. System overload.

I scroll through my Twitter and Insta feeds. NASA and the world's telescopes bring deep space into my eyes. Nebulae, galaxies, the expanding universe. Everything is far away. My mind cools, wanders, wonders. So I chill on our tiny rock in a big universe, while stuck at home in a pandemic on a hot planet.

I dream hot and cool in the time of Corona.

In my loft in downtown Philadelphia, I wake up before sunrise. I get my coffee and sit on my balcony. The streets are quiet, a few birds chirp. I see the skyglow in which we all live at night, the orangish orb of electric light that blocks out the stars, effecting a 24/7 civilization that never sleeps— but is always dreaming, often in delirium. Meanwhile, our civilization has altered the ecosystems and surfaces of Earth, ushering in the Anthropocene, the human epoch on a hot planet.

Soon my hand grabs the phone, my fingers scroll, my electronic eyes roam the planet. Packed with tribes, fans, and feuds. Day after day, it never ends.

On my screens, everything is an all-at-once "reality." Signs and symbols, clones and copies, fakes and facades. Echo chambers. Implosion. There is no future to see. It is an endless now.

Is there no exit? Am I trapped in Jean-Paul Sartre's fictional hotel room, where I cannot shut my eyes and cannot turn off the electric lights? Am I stuck in the hell of delirium?[1]

---

1   Eventually, I published the passages as part of a "spoken word" essay, curated in the Poetry section of *Medium*: Barry Vacker, "Dreaming Hot and Cool in the Time of Corona," Medium, May 12, 2020.

CAN WE UNPLUG FROM AN IMPLODING FUTURE?

A year later, I am cancer-free, feeling fit and strong.[2] But it's also a year later in America, a nation neither fit nor strong, seemingly trapped in hot media conditions and imploding into a largely dystopian future that is right before our eyes. We can change that, but it requires new modes of seeing and thinking.

As I write these words in 2021, I feel the same as I did a year ago, trapped in the hell of hot media delirium. Maybe you feel the same, maybe not. Surely there has to be a way out of the delirium and accelerating feedback loops of hot media. Doesn't there? To borrow from Julia Hildebrand, can we "unplug" from this endless now that is our terminal future? Can't we greenlight better futures?

GREENLIGHTING FUTURES

Matthew McConaughey's *Greenlights* reached #1 on the *New York Times* best-seller list because it tapped into a deep existential need. As shown in the *Greenlights* passages in chapter 1, we all need a vision of hope and optimism for our lives, no matter how many red and yellow lights are flashing. As McConaughey writes, "It's a matter of how we see the challenge in front of us and how we engage with it. Persist, pivot, or concede. It's up to us, our choice every time."

As a long-time professor at Temple University in Philadelphia, where I teach a large lecture course called Introduction to Media Analysis (formerly called Media and Society), I know today's college students desperately want to be hopeful about their future and the human future. They may not say it up front, but deep down, they want an optimistic vision of things to come. Amid the various apocalyptic scenarios of our current culture—systemic racism, proliferating ignorance, climate disruption, plastic-filled oceans, the apparent sixth extinction, the new Anthropocene epoch, and the possible death of democracy in America—it is no surprise that students and millennials are seeking hope for a better future, a far more just, inclusive, hopeful, and sustainable tomorrow.

That's the reason we need a *common narrative* than spans from city to nature to the night skies, a vision of a shared destiny that gives us meaning in our collective origins and futures. And, we should not forget that we need to be good ancestors, for your children will live beyond the year 2100 and perhaps far into the twenty-second century.

YOUR FUTURE

Your future. What will it be? After you graduate, for you personally, for your family, for your relatives, and for your extended family—the human species? Obviously, that's a complex question, precisely because there will be many futures unfolding over the remainder of the twenty-first century, which is the remainder of your life.

Obviously, you have taken charge of your future by devoting four to five years of your life to earn an undergraduate degree. That's a smart move. That's an example of long-term thinking at the personal level. We also need that kind of thinking, but on a far greater scale, spanning our cities, nations, plant life, and species. About the shared future we all will inhabit, there are two things we can learn from this book is that are absolutely certain—*there will be two different speeds for tomorrow, moving along two different trajectories in space and time.*

THE HOT FUTURE

One future trajectory will be coming at you very fast: the implosion and acceleration of hot, ego-media—further wiring you inside hives and tribes of the global village, surrounded by the proliferation of consumption, spectacle,

---

2   I was lucky: the cancer was caught early via a blood test (endo-media). I am fortunate and privileged, as my job as a professor provided me with the suddenly needed major medical benefits. I am deeply humbled and grateful for all the scientific skills and compassionate empathy displayed by the doctors, nurses, and technicians at the University of Pennsylvania Hospital in Philadelphia. Some of the doctors and nurses are very witty and funny, too!

and hyperreality. We already know that future; it's at the Apple store, it's delivered to us by Amazon, it's the apps on our phones, it's the spectacle of Twitter and TikTok, it's the hyperreality of Vegas, Hollywood, and the Super Bowl. Of course, hot conditions are prevalent in the racism and police brutality on display in America, the anti-science denialism of climate disruption, and COVID-19.

It's a future with much of the stuff in chapters 1–7: endless transient enthusiasms and continual conflict inside our 24/7 media environments. And just like hot media, the planet gets hotter and more polluted, while conspiracy theories of denial fuel ever more ignorance, growing ever more arrogant. Like the Climate Clock in chapter 8, the future is ticking, seemingly ever faster, ever hotter. As discussed at the end of this introduction, Elon Musk's Starlink satellite network is polluting the night sky and may make astronomy extremely difficult, and thus make observatories obsolete—a case of hot, ego-media rendering exo-media irrelevant and making the cool, chill gaze impossible to experience.

THE COOL FUTURE

If possible, the other future trajectory will be much, much slower: the chill of cool media—our space telescopes that peer across one hundred billion light years. The existential effect is to connect us to the universe and get us to think long-term, to think as members of the human species, our extended family with a shared destiny on a tiny planet in a vast universe. That future is where we chill out, and its key signposts include the continued explosion of exo-media, the Greater Big Bend International Dark Sky Reserve spanning the border of Texas and Mexico, and a Dark Skies philosophy to connect us to the planet and the universe. Here, Julia Hildebrand's "Unplugging" takes on even larger significance. Will we have the willpower and foresight to unplug our daily ideologies from the heat and embrace the chill?

FILMS AND THE FUTURE

When films try to project a vision of the future, almost all are dystopian, apocalyptic, and/or filled with some kind of doom and dread. Films such as *Blade Runner 2049, Interstellar, Gravity, WALL-E, Avatar, World War Z, Fight Club, The Hunger Games, Tomorrowland, Black Panther,* and the many *Stars Wars* movies are very popular with audiences. So are television series such as *The Walking Dead* and *Black Mirror,* the latter with its devious scenarios involving media technologies and the future. For us all, the dystopian future seems a *fait accompli.*

Super-popular are the superhero films, featuring an array of superbeings busy saving humans from their apocalyptic demise or fighting against injustice, exploitation, and domination. Many people draw meaning from superheroes, who function like secular gods, as do celebrities. The *Avengers* series boasts three of the top 10 all-time films in terms of international box office revenues, with *Avengers: Endgame* at #1. Batman, Wonder Woman, Black Panther, and the Avengers—superheroes who save us to show we still are worthy of existence, despite our warfare and trashed planet. Isn't that why we invented superheroes—because deep down, we know that we and our leaders have no answers and no solutions, and we all seem unwilling to significantly alter our tribal-con-sumer-nationalist behavior? *That these superhero films are both hugely popular and utterly apocalyptic suggests something awry in how we imagine the future—as we munch popcorn and dream of superhero saviors.*

The *Stars Wars* films have always suggested we will extend into space the same ideologies that dominate life on Earth—namely, tribalism and warfare, along with some individualist rebels battling evildoers. Perhaps that's why the films are so popular: they do not require a change in our thinking or behavior. You may love the *Star Wars* films, but they do not offer very optimistic futures. War is never an optimistic future, unless you've never been in a war. Even the recent *Star Trek* films, which are generally considered optimistic, have many elements of doom and destruction.

Gravity presents an apocalyptic future in which some of humankind's very greatest technological achievements are destroyed. After all, the Hubble Space Telescope is our most powerful and profound media technology—an extension of the human eye across 13.7 billion light-years of space and time to reveal a universe of staggering size and scale. The universe is massive and humans are tiny, but our brains are powerful, and the discoveries of cosmology and the Hubble Telescope are among the very greatest of human achievements. If these exo-media technologies are destroyed in an Oscar-winning film, what does that say about our vision of tomorrow?

Rather than humanity being destroyed, in *Interstellar* our exo-media technologies help save us. The massive universe and our powerful brains are featured; brave scientists and astronauts venture through wormholes and black holes to find habitable planets and save the future for the human species. Why do we need a new planet? Because we have so messed up our planet that the food systems have collapsed and we can longer live on Earth (as discussed in chapter 8).

In the superhero film *Black Panther*, the cosmic metal vibranium powers Wakanda and its utopian Afrofuturist city, while the media technologies empower the citizens of Wakanda. Holograms, virtual reality, wireless communication, and all kinds of advanced technologies ensure the economic and social future of Wakanda. Like *Tomorrowland*, *Black Panther* presents a hopeful and optimistic media future.

In contrast, will we descend into barbarism and anti-intellectualism, as depicted in *The Walking Dead*? Will we accept the ecological and political fate of *The Hunger Games*, where the seas have risen to flood coastal regions, people in the districts are dominated via entertainment, and the people in the capitol wear wacky beards and watch reality TV shows about struggles to survive? Will we just delude ourselves and mess with each other via our media technologies, as shown in *Black Mirror*? Will we wage war on Earth or above Earth, as imagined by America's new "Space Force" to be run by the Pentagon? Are *Star Wars* and *Star Trek* desirable futures? In the readings in this chapter:

- Devon Powers integrates futurism into cultural studies as a way to take control of our imagined tomorrows and manifest more diverse visions in our mediated futures;
- Stephen Hawking explores the optimistic future suggested by the *Star Trek* television series (not the recent films);
- Abigail Moore provides a provocative spin on the deeper meaning of superheroes and their popularity;
- Osei Alleyne explains the proliferating art and philosophy of Afrofuturism and its role in shaping the superhero blockbuster *Black Panther* (2018);
- Antonio López details the multiple levels of meaning in *Blade Runner 2049* (2017), the acclaimed sequel to the 1982 masterpiece *Blade Runner*; and
- Barry Vacker outlines a unique philosophy based in cool media and the International Dark Sky movement.

All of these essays help us decode the many ways these films depict our mediated and technological futures.

THE HUNGER GAMES: ARE TERROR AND ENTERTAINMENT OUR FATE?

Set in the future, *The Hunger Games* is a warning for the present. *The Hunger Games* presents a postapocalyptic world in which the various districts are ruled by the Capitol and the kinglike dictator President Snow. Given plenty of food, fashion, entertainment, and reality TV, most citizens of the Capitol seem willing to accept their status and the prevailing cultural conditions. Could the Hunger Games happen—if not literally, then metaphorically? Perhaps the games are happening right now, as the films show some possible media futures for the coming decades. In the spirit of Orwell's doublethink (chapter 7) and the "Mockingjay" (a genetic hybrid of a mockingbird and blue jay that becomes the symbol of revolution in *The Hunger Games*), let's consider the possible futures. Yeah, we can have some intellectual fun yet be serious at the same time.

1. **"Domitainment."** *The Hunger Games* cleverly and creatively presents a world where the dystopian visions of George Orwell and Aldous Huxley have merged in the fictional nation of Panem. Orwell's *1984* explains how a society can be dominated by an all-powerful state that uses media technologies to control the fears and nightmares of the citizens. Meanwhile, Huxley's *Brave New World* shows that society can be "programmed" by its ruling institutions, which use technology and entertainment to control the dreams and desires of the citizens. *Panem is where domination meets entertainment—a future of Domitainment.*

In *The Hunger Games*, Panem combines the entertainment spectacles of *American Idol*, *Survivor*, and the Super Bowl with the violent barbarism of cage fights and the Ultimate Fighting Championship matches. *The Hunger Games* also captures the media celebration of violence and crime along with war news, war movies, and teen slasher films. Mixed throughout is the fascination with fame and the worship of celebrity culture. Such media spectacles help the government preserve its power as it maintains total surveillance and domination amid an endless war. As Huxley explains in *Brave New World*, entertainment and a dumbed-down society are central to government-corporate domination, while Orwell demonstrates that fear in a paranoid society is crucial to maintaining political power, too. Thus, there is the fear of an uprising in *The Hunger Games*, a fear that justifies the Capitol's power.

Millions in America and Britain tune in to *American Idol*, *Britain's Got Talent*, the Super Bowl, the World Cup, Netflix, and TikTok feeds, while their governments subvert civil liberties, attack freedom of the press, perpetuate racial and social injustice, and wage war with drones and propaganda. Is Domitainment happening now? What do you think?

If much of our society and its worldviews have entered the spectacle and hyperreality, as argued by Guy Debord and Jean Baudrillard, then why not the very concepts of freedom, democracy, liberation, revolution, and enlightenment? Perhaps future rebellions and revolutions will be less real than hyperreal. Is it possible? What do you think?

2. **"Liberlightenment."** We always have the choice to try to change these our conditions and try to end the stupidity, or we can keep viewing reruns of *The Matrix*, *V for Vendetta*, and *The Hunger Games*. We can also try to clean up our disastrous impact on the ecosystems of the planet, or we can watch *WALL-E* and *Avatar*, cheering the robots and Na'vi. We can try to eliminate unjust economic and social conditions, as illustrated by Occupy Wall Street and various other protest movements of recent years. Centuries of tribalism and human ignorance can be countered by existential truths for our species, as shown in the documentaries *Cosmos: A Spacetime Odyssey* and *Wonders of the Universe*.

There is an explosion of art and scientific knowledge happening around the world, much of which can make for a more knowledgeable, peaceful, and enlightened civilization. We can use the media to access this art and science, or we can remain dumbed down by our own choosing. *Cosmos* shows how we can begin making ourselves smarter and wiser about our place in the cosmos and our impact on the planet. Will this happen in reality, a liberation inspired by enlightenment—a future of "Liberlightenment"? It's possible. Is it likely? What do you think?

BLADE RUNNER AND THE NEXT TECHNOFUTURES?

Directed by Denis Villeneuve (who also directed *Arrival*), *Blade Runner 2049* is situated on a long trajectory of dystopian technofutures and urban cities in science fiction film. Dystopian sci-fi cities are animated by themes of megacities, overpopulation, regimentation, dehumanization, nuclear warfare, ecological destruction, and endless forms of hot media technology and artificial intelligence running amok. *Blade Runner 2049* is the long-awaited sequel to Ridley Scott's masterpiece *Blade Runner.* Both films are very complex, and what follows is only a summary of key points related to media, society, and the future.

In the *Blade Runner* futures, there is no new idea for any meaning, purpose, or happiness for actual humans. Set in a Los Angeles that is packed with skyscrapers and surrounded by a polluted wasteland and rising sea levels, *Blade Runner 2049* suggests that hot media technologies and surveillance will proliferate, within which we'll have hologram lovers, very cool fashions, and some sleek buildings, along with dirty streets, polluted air, drone warfare, and a likely police state. Corporate titans will be building humanlike replicants (genetically engineered robots) as slave laborers to keep the consumer-media machine running while companies strip mine various planets, home to the "off-world" colonies. In contrast to *Her,* where the artificial intelligence is entirely inside the network, in *Blade Runner 2049* the artificial intelligence takes the form of holograms and the replicants that exist among the humans.

In *Blade Runner 2049,* the only place we see "nature" is in a virtual reality simulation featuring trees and insects. Can we doubt that outside Los Angeles and California there is a massive extinction event? The replicant K (Ryan Gosling) visits massive wastelands and landfills. We see decaying factories where children and/or replicants are exploited as a cheap labor force. Though we see mirrored solar farms, they must be ineffective, given all the air pollution—apparently caused by fossil fuel consumption. Climate disruption and rising sea levels must be happening, as there is a giant seawall to keep the ocean from flooding Los Angeles. But we'll look great in all the cool clothes.

Blade Runner 2049 presents an awe-inspiring and strangely beautiful future, but it is also a very bleak world—utterly disconnected from nature and the universe. Cool media play zero role in the *Blade Runner* future. In other words, humanity's long-term *collective future* seems mostly messed up, at least if you care about the future of the human species and the other species and ecosystems on Earth. Antonio López explores the multiple futures on display in *Blade Runner 2049.*

A BETTER TECHNOFUTURE IN *TOMORROWLAND*?

As a counter to these dystopian futures, Walt Disney Pictures tried to imagine an optimistic, techno-utopian world to come in *Tomorrowland.* Though it's not a great film, Disney and director Brad Bird have created a thoughtful and entertaining film that provides action while posing important questions with no easy answers. Why are there so many doomsday scenarios in our culture and movies? And why are some people so pessimistic toward the future, while others remain highly optimistic? Why is doom prevailing over success in imagining the human future on Planet Earth?

In *Tomorrowland,* George Clooney plays Frank, a cynical inventor who believes that humans are doomed. Why does he believe that? Frank lives in a run-down house on the outskirts of a small town, where he sits in a room all day glued to multiple electronic screens, all showing apocalyptic news and imagery from around the world. War, famine, pollution, catastrophe, and climate disruption are starring in the media spectacle on his screens. Frank has even designed a Doomsday Clock that calculates the odds of the end of the world based on the levels of destruction on our planet.

In contrast to Frank, there is Casey (Britt Robertson), a young woman who optimistically believes that science, technology, and some clear thinking will enable humans to solve their problems and build a better future. In *Tomorrowland,* not unlike in *Interstellar,* the robots and artificial intelligence are our friends and work to help humanity. As the plot plays out, we see that the future of humanity is in the hands of technology and its users. In a key scene, the film explains that scientists, artists, and thinkers have long been *warning* humans that their current behavior—war, endless consumption, and ecological destruction—cannot continue without dire consequences for the future of humanity and life on Earth. Yet rather than pay heed to the warnings and change our behavior, we line up at the box office and consume more apocalypses along with our soda and popcorn.

Meanwhile, a "Tomorrowland" does exist, where an optimistic future is possible for humanity. The challenge the film poses: Are we humans ready for it? Are we too trapped in old models of behavior? Or do we deserve a new future? Yes, but only if we become more optimistic about what science, technology, logic, and diversity can do for the future. It's an optimism that must begin with the youth of the world, precisely because they are the humans who will inhabit the future and will shape the world left to their children and future generations. The optimistic and futuristic city of *Tomorrowland* is in direct contrast to the dystopian Los Angeles of *Blade Runner*.

BLACK MIRROR AND HUMAN EXISTENCE

With its strange plots and mind-blowing endings, Charlie Brooker's *Black Mirror* is one of the most philosophically challenging television series of all time. In my courses, students enjoy discussing the episodes and writing their critical media theory papers on episodes of *Black Mirror*. But while it's fun to discuss the plots and storylines, what are the deepest messages of *Black Mirror* for our future?

In the conclusions to "USS Callister" and "White Christmas," we see two of the most bizarre endings in science fiction history. These endings counter the warrior myths of *Star Trek* and *Star Wars* while revealing a deep truth about our place in the universe as revealed by media technology. *Black Mirror* has always been very clear about its stance on humans and technology: the electronic screens are where humans collide with each other and their existence on a tiny planet, with the vast universe somewhere else beyond.

In the universe of *Black Mirror*, there is nothing of value, meaning, and purpose outside the technologies we inhabit in our electrified metropolises—screens and lights aglow 24/7 as our planet hurtles through the cosmic void. Nature and the night skies are irrelevant. Electric light illuminates our civilization, turning night into day, a media technology for security against the starry skies beyond—the distant lights that force us to contemplate our destiny as a single species on a tiny planet in the cosmic vastness.

"USS CALLISTER"

As should be obvious to gamers and science fiction fans, "USS Callister" is ripping into toxic masculinity, obsessive fan culture, and the tribal warrior mentality among many gamers, all set in a video game parody of the original *Star Trek*. First airing two years after *The Twilight Zone* (1959–1964) ended its run, the original *Star Trek* (1966–1969) reflected the space-age optimism of the Apollo era, when going to the moon was celebrated as a great human achievement, not as a search for a site for strip mining. As discussed above, *Star Trek* suggested that our meaning was to be found in the quest for discovery and knowledge, with humans uniting in their diversity to boldly explore "the final frontier"—as an enlightened single species. Not so in "USS Callister," where "space" is just another site to war with people—to degrade, exploit, and humiliate other humans.

As in *Star Trek* and *Stars Wars*, the same in "USS Callister." The beauty and wonder of the cosmos serve no purpose other than as a backdrop for tribal warfare on an intergalactic scale. It's all about us and our conquests! As shown in "USS Callister," there is no Captain Kirk or Mr. Spock to save us from our insignificance in an infinite universe. But we can have the video game *Infinity* to explore deep space, to escape from the cubicles of office existence. But even in *Infinity* we encounter Captain Daly (as in the kind of jerk you might meet in *daily* life). A demented version of Captain Kirk, Captain Daly (Jesse Plemons) plays out his fanboy fantasies by torturing coworkers in his bogus space adventures. Nanette (Cristin Milioti) and crew turn the tables on Daly, striking a blow for female empowerment in a triumph of heroism over a wannabe masculine hero—a dude who has no idea how to be masculine or a hero.

THE ENDINGS OF "USS CALLISTER" AND "WHITE CHRISTMAS"

Captain Daly is left alone forever in the black void of deep space, the very universe revealed by our exo-media technologies. Alone in the void with no one to battle but himself, Daly's existential fate is ours for now, at least symbolically. The universe is mostly empty, vast voids populated by distant galaxies stretching toward infinity. As far as we know, we're alone in our part of the Milky Way. Outside of space movies and video games, our civilization will not be battling with "evil aliens" any time soon. It's just us, battling among ourselves, Twitter gods on a tiny planet.

In "White Christmas," Matt (Jon Hamm) faces a similar existential fate. As payback for his social media voyeurism, law enforcement officials activate the electronic "Zed-Eyes" to block Matt from seeing anyone or anyone seeing Matt. All Matt sees are the outlines of other people, while others see only his outline. Their electronic outlines are filled with pixelated white space dotted with black and gray specks. The strange imagery is not unlike the static on television screens tuned to a dead channel. What most people do not realize is the static is produced by cosmic background radiation that confirms the expansion of the universe. Instead of gazing upon people, Matt is fated to gaze upon origins of the vast universe we have discovered with cool media technologies. That's the trippy meaning of that bizarre ending.

Without a new philosophical narrative for the human species in the Hubble universe, we can't block out the cosmic static forever and hope to survive, no matter how much we surround ourselves with electric light and black mirrors. In the end, *Black Mirror* shows there is no one to save us but ourselves—and a new philosophy for the twenty-first century universe. Isn't it time to grow up?

THE FUTURES IN *STAR TREK* AND *STAR WARS*

Rey's line—"I need someone to show me my place in all this"—in *Star Wars: The Last Jedi* perfectly echoes the void in contemporary philosophy. What's the void? It's the absent answer to "What's my place and destiny in this freaking gigantic universe?" It's the *missing secular narrative* that provides hope and meaning in the vast and ancient cosmos revealed by science—the universe in which humanity is insignificant and *perhaps* meaningless amid two trillion galaxies. Oh, I'm sure there are other meanings to Rey's line in her quest, but that's the ultimate meaning. Like Katniss (*The Hunger Games*) and the recent Wonder Woman, Rey (Daisy Ridley) is a strong female role model, but we can't overlook the existential messages of the films in which they appear. Or is the *Star Wars* saga so sacred that its deepest meaning is beyond critique? One of humanity's deepest problems is that it finds meaning and purpose in war and in the conquest of other humans, not to mention the species we are rendering extinct.

Of course, *Star Wars* films are proliferating. Perhaps most famous is *Star Wars: The Force Awakens*, which is the top-rated box office film of all time in the United States and number four worldwide, at least according to Box Office Mojo. Of course, the *Star Wars* and *Star Trek* franchises have roots that stretch back decades, with the *Star Trek* films having origins in the *Star Trek* television series of the Apollo era and *Star Wars* films having origins in the first *Star Wars*, now retitled *Star Wars: A New Hope*. Given the new subtitle and the global popularity of the two film series, it is reasonable to ask: What can we hope for? What can we hope for human destiny in space and for our future on Spaceship *Earth*? Of course, the media technologies continue to evolve in the films (along with the special effects), but what about the ideologies and worldviews represented in some of Hollywood's most popular visions of the future?

THE ORIGINAL *STAR TREK* FUTURE

Space: the final frontier. These are the voyages of the starship Enterprise. Its five-year mission: to explore strange new worlds, to seek new life and new civilizations, to boldly go where no man has gone before.

In the famous introduction in the original *Star Trek* series, William Shatner's voice-over references President Kennedy's "New Frontier" of Apollo and space exploration, but the space-age visuals say even more. The design aesthetic central to the Space Age features curvilinear forms, giving the impression of both *acceleration and elevation*. Speed and uplift are needed for attaining the altitude and escape velocity that are needed not only to reach the moon, planets, and the rest of the cosmos but also to zoom into the future. That's why the *Enterprise* always looks like it is taking off even when it is stationary. Even the logo on the *Star Trek* crew members' shirts—an arrowhead pointing upward—gives a sense of acceleration and elevation.

The original *Star Trek* worldview professed that not only would science and technology evolve onward and upward, but so would human consciousness and philosophy via a more enlightened view of humanity and the cosmos. *Star Trek* does not present a utopian world of perfected humans, but rather a *utopian worldview* that expresses hope for progress, inclusion and diversity, and the overall transformation of human consciousness. In reviews of the 2009 *Star Trek* film, reviewers Stephanie Zacharek and Manohla Dargis cleverly summarized this worldview. Writing in *Salon*, Zacharek said,

> For kids of the '60s and '70s, "Star Trek" offered a vision of the future that suggested we had something to look forward to, not just in terms of groovy space travel, but in the sense that citizens of the coming centuries would share the same civic values. ... Initially appearing in 1966, the original "Star Trek" is a utopian fantasy of the first order, a vision of the enlightened future in which whites, blacks, Asians and one poker-faced Vulcan are united by their exploratory mission ("to boldly go"), a prime directive (no intervention) and the occasional dust-up.[3]

That's why the overall technology, design, and architecture evident throughout the series suggest movement into the future—*faster, forward, upward*. From the beginning, *Star Trek* launches us into a new cosmology, a new cosmic narrative for the human species, one that some expected to emerge with Apollo. In chapter 10, Stephen Hawking sees *Star Trek* as providing a comfortable world of social progress and technological evolution:

> *Star Trek* shows a society far in advance of ours in science, in technology, and in political organization. (The last might not be difficult.) There must have been great changes, with their accompanying tensions and upsets, in the time between now and then, but in the period we are shown, science, technology, and the organization of society are supposed to have achieved a level of near perfection.

Hawking likes this vision and is not afraid to admit that it might be naive and unrealistic:

> The future of science won't be like the comforting picture painted in *Star Trek*: a universe populated by many humanoid races, with an advanced but essentially static science and technology. Instead, I think we will be on our own, but rapidly developing in biological and electronic complexity.

Hawking is correct, but *Star Trek* represents more than a society of "near perfection." More importantly, *Star Trek* also represents the evolution of the Enlightenment project and the very notion of social, cultural, and material progress for humans, powered in part by advances in science, technology, and human intellect. Can that combination make a better world?

Much has been written about the meaning of the original *Star Trek* TV series and the space-age optimism it represented during the Apollo era—a confident vision of the human world of tomorrow, both culturally and technologically. *Star Trek* represents an *enlightened* future, where the ethnically diverse crew of the *Enterprise*

---

3   Stephanie Zacharek, "Star Trek," *Salon*, May 8, 2009.

serves as an example of humans having put aside centuries of tribal, religious, and nationalist warfare to unite as a secular and democratized civilization on Planet Earth. In the original *Star Trek*, humans were recognized as *one species* with common origins and destinies, not the competitive tribes that have dominated human society. Further, technology had eliminated economic scarcity such that equality trumped inequity, while money, greed, and conspicuous consumption were not dominating passions.

The *Star Trek* introduction expresses a confident, committed, yet open-minded and rational epistemology that has proven best for gaining new knowledge, for building a better world, and for understanding ourselves and the universe around us. Is this worldview overly optimistic? Sure. But if this worldview does not make a better world and more hopeful future, then whose fault is that?

STAR WARS AND THE FUTURES PAST[4]

In 1977, a mere eight years after Apollo 11, the *Voyager 1* space probe and the *Star Wars* film franchise were launched, with *Voyager 1* leaving for the outer planets and *Star Wars* arriving in the multiplexes. Though launched with much media fanfare, *Voyager 1* and its scientific discoveries would end up largely ignored by most of society. Meanwhile, *Star Wars* and its spectacle of apocalyptic warfare and hero journeys are revered throughout popular culture, providing meaning and hope for hundreds of millions of people. Of course, *Star Wars* features a complexity of other themes, too—the importance of friendships, our relationship with machines, the control of one's destiny, the battle between good and evil, and the resurrection of endless warfare as an inevitable or desirable future.

The *Star Wars* saga hurtled filmgoers into the technological future while retreating into the cultural past, celebrating all the tropes of medieval yesteryear—beautiful princesses (Leia), reluctant heroes (Luke Skywalker), virtuous knights (the Jedi), evil rulers (Darth Vader), civil wars (the Rebel Alliance versus the Galactic Empire), and wise old wizards (Obi-Wan Kenobi). In the wildly popular reboot, *Star Wars: The Force Awakens* (2015), Leia is no longer a princess but a "general." Within the patriarchal military narrative of society, that's surely cultural and feminist progress. But within the larger cosmic narrative for the human species, "General Leia" represents a *simulation* of progress—she's merely showing that feminist babes can kick ass and wage war like their macho-men counterparts. Both General Leia and Katniss Everdeen from *The Hunger Games* series (2012–2015) represent the same basic notion—feminist progress is possible amid a regressive and militaristic vision of the future.

As many movie fans know, George Lucas was heavily influenced by the work of mythology expert Joseph Campbell, who wrote extensively about myths and the journey of the hero. It's true that every culture needs stories of heroines and heroes. Yet why must we consistently explore the cosmic sublime via ancient myths and age-old war? Do we really need more stories that celebrate militarized conflict and religious warfare? Can't we imagine space heroes and a human future *beyond* tribal and religious warfare?

That *Star Trek* of the 1960s was eclipsed by *Star Wars* of the 1970s and 1980s is very telling. The mere titles—*Star Trek* and *Star Wars*—say it all: a "trek" for discovery, a "war" for death. "Live long and prosper" was replaced by "May the Force be with you." The science of *Star Trek* was replaced by the endless warfare of *Star Wars*.

WHAT CAN WE HOPE FOR?

In one sense, *Star Trek* and *Star Wars* are secular religions, not unlike the superheroes who serve as secular gods in the movies. Like the Hollywood superheroes, the *Star Wars* and *Star Trek* warriors are a damn sexy bunch with some flashy threads, but they're still trapped in very unattractive worldviews and philosophies. That's because *Stars Wars* has always been *Hollywood propaganda for more tribal warfare and a vague cosmic religion*, presented in the guise of epic hero/heroine journeys along with brave "rebels," evil villains, and endless cool effects, all set in the future past.

---

4   Much of the following discussion of *Star Wars* and *Star Trek* is based on select passages in Barry Vacker, *Specter of the Monolith* (Philadelphia: Center for Media and Destiny, 2017).

In the end, the films of *Star Trek* and *Star Wars* present failed futures—worlds of tomorrow where science and technology have progressed but the warfare, bloodshed, tribalism, and superstition continue. Can't we imagine a more enlightened future and a more evolved human species precisely because we are inspired by a vast universe that silently asks us to seek our meaning and destiny via knowledge and exploration? That's the secular and cosmic hope offered in *2001: A Space Odyssey*.

2001 AND EARTHWORKS—"RADICAL WONDER" AND "UNPLUGGING"

Science and media technologies have revealed an awe-inspiring and wondrous universe, which is precisely why we need art and philosophy to connect us to the universe as it is, not as we wish it was. We need radical wonder to connect us, and we need art to help us "unplug" from the hot media conditions that dominate our daily existence, as suggested by Julia Hildebrand in chapter 4. Two examples of such art are *2001: A Space Odyssey* and "Earthworks," the term that describes monumental artworks built into the deserts of the American Southwest and elsewhere on Planet Earth.

2001

Without doubt, *2001: A Space Odyssey* is the greatest and most profound science-fiction movie ever made. In fact, it's one of the greatest works of art of the twentieth century. *Star Trek* and *Star Wars* fans beware: *2001* features no light sabers, no space battles, and no galaxies to conquer. As explained by Barry Vacker in "Explosion of Awareness," the main challenge in *2001* is philosophical and existential. The key philosophical icon of the film is not the HAL 9000 artificial intelligence program, but rather the "black monoliths" that guide the trajectory of the film and lead us to our greatest philosophical challenge.

As *2001* makes clear, the sleek black monoliths are crafted works of art, with the first monolith inspiring apes to invent technology and thus accelerate their evolution into the human species. *2001* poetically shows that we are an evolutionary species capable of great things. Inspired by the black monolith, humans evolved from apes to artists to astronauts, from simians to scientists and spacefarers. Inspired and seduced by the black monolith, we created a technological civilization capable of exploring the stars and seeking to understand its origins and destiny via art, science, and philosophy. This film is mostly a cool media experience, symbolized by the monoliths and astronaut Dave Bowman's journey through the Star Gate. The chill stance is in striking contrast to the hot conflicts that drive the *Star Trek* and *Star Wars* film franchises.

EARTHWORKS

We've all heard of national parks with beautiful scenery, often located in more remote areas with awe-inspiring vistas and dark night skies. Spending a few nights in a national park or a wilderness area is one way to practice what Julia Hildebrand calls "unplugging" (chapter 4). There is also an international art movement that taps into natural beauty and remote locations, giving "art tourists" the chance to unplug with a synthesis of art and nature on a grand scale. Tapping into the ancient traditions of megalithic art around the world, "Earthworks" are massive artworks built into the natural landscapes and environments, which is why they often described as Land Art. The goal of Earthworks is to inspire us to look away from ourselves and our the skyglow of our electric civilization, to connect with Earth, nature, wilderness, and the universe. Like the International Dark Sky movement, Earthworks also represent a movement that has spread around the world. Most Earthworks are another form of cool media.[5]

Classic, modern, and contemporary artworks mostly look at us or inside us, with objectivity and/or subjectivity. We gaze at each other or inward into ourselves. Abstraction expressionism is hot; Earthworks are cool. Galleries are mostly hot, desert spaces, and night skies are cool. The closer the proximity, the hotter the art. The farther away, the cooler the art. The smaller the negative space, the hotter the art. That's the gallery wall. The larger the negative space, the cooler the art. That's the desert spaces and night skies. Though Earthworks are spreading and have been created in many countries, several of the most famous Earthworks are in America. Over the years, I have had the good fortune to personally visit several these sites. Each is located in a remote location, far from the skyglow of our electric media environments.

Double Negative. Cut into the rim of a mesa north of Las Vegas, Michael Heizer's *Double Negative* (1969) comprises two empty trenches (together about 1,500 feet long) that directly pose the challenge of the philosophical void in the surrounding desert and cosmos above. Like *Spiral Jetty, Double Negative* is experienced by looking into the empty space within each trench and away into the empty space beyond—toward the skies or the desert basin running beside the mesa. Negative space surrounds the sculpture and the viewer, forcing one to situate oneself on Planet Earth, yet within nature and the universe. (For more, google "Double Negative" or look up the videos in YouTube.)[6]

FIGURE 10.0.1   Photo *of Double Negative* from Wikicommons [https://commons.wikimedia.org/wiki/File:Michael_Heizer,_Double_Negative,_1969_(7841453092).jpg]. Use of image permitted under the Creative Commons 2.0; original source: http://doublenegative.tarasen.net/double-negative. This image is better than my personal photo.

---

5   Parts of this section are drawn from the essay by Barry Vacker, "Chill Out: Land Art, Dark Skies, and Cool Media," in the forthcoming *Bloomsbury Encyclopedia of New Media Art* (London: Bloomsbury, 2022).
6   See also http://doublenegative.tarasen.net/double-negative.

Spiral Jetty. Set on the edge of the Great Salt Lake in Utah, Robert Smithson's *Spiral Jetty* (1970) is a 1,500-foot spiral of dirt and boulders that references the Milky Way above, while salt crystals show emergence and entropy over time. (For more, google "Spiral Jetty" or look up the videos in YouTube.) This Earthwork is experienced by looking at it and looking away toward the horizon and the sky. *Spiral Jetty* is framed by a vast realm of negative space. The canvas is the Great Salt Lake, the daytime sky, and the starry sky at night.[7]

| **FIGURE 10.0.2** *Spiral Jetty*. Photo by Barry Vacker (2016).

Sun Tunnels. Set in the flat emptiness of northern Utah, Nancy Holt's *Sun Tunnels* (1976) are four giant concrete cylinders aligned with the summer and winter solstices; the cylinders are nine feet in diameter and eighteen feet in length. The holes on the tops of the cylinders align with various constellations. *Sun Tunnels* is an exo-medium that encourages us to look away from ourselves, while the artwork collectively forces us to situate ourselves in the vastness of the negative space of sky, stars, and desert. (For more, google "Sun Tunnels" or look up the videos in YouTube.)[8]

---

7   See also https://www.diaart.org/visit/visit-our-locations-sites/robert-smithson-spiral-jetty.
8   See also https://www.diaart.org/visit/visit-our-locations-sites/nancy-holt-sun-tunnels.

FIGURE 10.0.3 and 10.0.4 Top photo: the *Sun Tunnels* in the day time. Bottom photo: the *Sun Tunnels* during the summer solstice, with the sun setting "inside" two of the aligned tunnels. Photos by Barry Vacker (2016).

Star Axis. Built into the edge of a spectacular mesa in northern New Mexico, Charles Ross's *Star Axis* (begun in 1973 and only now nearing completion) is a giant steel and stone sculpture designed to be a naked-eye observatory aimed at the North Star; *Star Axis* will be accurate for thousands of years. During my tour of *Star Axis*, led by Ross, photos were not permitted. This is in keeping with the philosophy that Earthworks are best experienced in-person, but the limits on photos will be impossible once the site is open for visitors on a daily basis. (For more, google "Star Axis" or look up the videos in YouTube.)[9]

Roden Crater. I have yet to visit *Roden Crater*, but it deserves mention here precisely because it is a cool medium, naked-eye observatory, and exo-media installation. Located in a dormant volcano east of the Grand Canyon, James Turrell's *Roden Crater* (begun in 1979 and still in development) contains a series of his "skyspaces" and several naked-eye observatories. According to Turrell, "In this stage set of geologic time, I wanted to make spaces that engage celestial events in light so that the spaces perform a 'music of the spheres' in light." Recently, Kanye West

---

9   See also https://www.staraxis.org.

donated several million dollars to help complete the project and obtained permission to film a music video inside *Roden Crater*. (For more, google "Roden Crater" or look up the videos in YouTube.)[10]

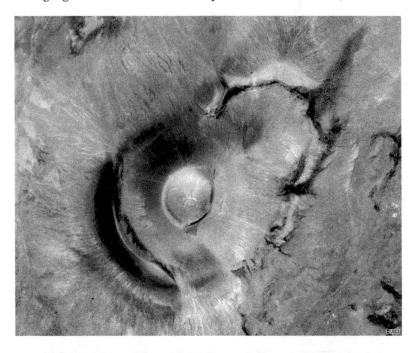

FIGURE 10.0.5   *Roden Crater* (2007). Photo from Wikicommons [https://commons.wikimedia.org/wiki/File:Roden.jpg]. This image is in the public domain in the United States because it contains only materials that originally came from the U.S. Geological Survey, an agency of the United States Department of the Interior.

Of course, these artworks are not easy to visit. That's part of what make them special, just like the remote national parks around the world. But what is most important are the ideas embedded in all the artworks. The goal is to get us out of our narcissism, to experience art and aesthetics in the context of nature and the universe. Except for *Roden Crater*, I have visited all of these Earthworks and I can say they inspire a different view and worldview, one that is optimistic and hopeful about the enlightenment of the human species in a long-term future with a shared destiny. Chill out. The dark skies are fantastic!

But will the dark skies survive Elon Musk?

STARLINK: HOT FUTURES OVERTAKE COOL FUTURES?

Perhaps nothing illustrates our planetary consciousness better than the view of Earth at night from space, where we see our glowing electrified cities, where night becomes day and the starry skies are erased from our consciousness. Electric light illuminates our planetary civilization and is a media technology for enlightenment, entertainment, and emotional security against the starry skies beyond—the very distant lights that force us to confront our destiny as a single species.

The *black mirrors* that surround us in our homes are like the night skies that surround our planet. We fill these screens with bright lights to provide us with hope and meaning amid the night skies, once filled with stars that twinkle impersonally and perpetually against the infinite blackness. Now we stare at our *black mirrors* in

---

10   See also https://rodencrater.com.

the glowing orbs, where the full spectrum of artificial light is deployed to secure us from having to face our true destiny—individually and collectively—in the dark voids of the cosmos.

STARLINK'S NIGHT SKY POLLUTION

Powered by Moore's Law (chapter 2), the dark skies are soon to be cluttered with satellites. Beginning with the first satellite in 1957 (*Sputnik*) and up to 2019, there were approximately four thousand satellites in orbit around Earth. That number is expected to explode in the coming decade, increasing by at least a factor of five (and maybe even ten or more). By 2025, more than one thousand satellites could be launched every year. With approval from the FCC, Elon Musk's Starlink plans to launch twelve thousand satellites (and likely thirty thousand more) in low Earth orbit by 2027.[11] Apparently, the main goal of Starlink is to provide high-speed bandwidth for 4K video on a global basis, surely a worthy endeavor for those who live in remote places or underserved locations and are unable to access the internet. Of course, Starlink expects to make a hefty profit. Other firms planning to compete with Starlink include Amazon (thirty-two thousand satellites) and OneWeb, a UK-based company planning on launching 650 satellites. All of the above means that we could go from four thousand satellites in 2019 to over forty thousand in the coming decade, an increase by a factor of ten.

Of course, why should you care? More satellites mean more bandwidth, better Zoom meetings, improved streaming of Netflix, and ever more videos to watch via YouTube, TikTok, or whatever comes next. After all, you likely live in a metropolis or city trapped in the skyglow bubble and the night skies seem utterly irrelevant. After all, 80 percent of Americans have never seen—"experienced" is a better word—the Milky Way directly with their eyes. However, consider the image of Starlink satellites against the nights sky.

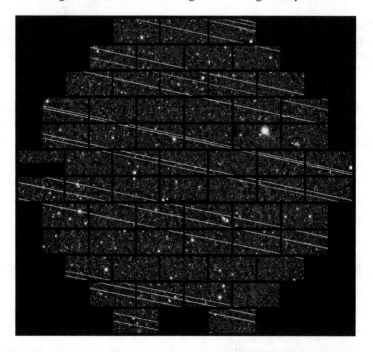

FIGURE 10.0.6   Streaks in night sky imagery caused by Starlink satellites (2019). Image in public domain, Wikicommons [https://commons.wikimedia.org/wiki/File:Astro.jpg]. Image from Blanco 4-meter telescope at the Cerro Tololo Inter-American Observatory (CTIO), 333 seconds-exposure image by astronomers Clara Martínez-Vázquez and Cliff Johnson.

---

11   Tate Ryan Mosley, Erin Winick, and Konstantin Kakaes, "The Number of Satellites Orbiting Earth Could Quintuple in the Next Decade," *MIT Technology Review*, June 26, 2019.

Scientists and astronomers have already lodged complaints about the first Starlink satellites, because the satellites are reflecting light back down to Earth and interfering with dark skies needed at the observatories around the world.[12] Musk is far less visionary than many believe (chapter 9), and he and his crack team of engineers did not have the foresight to design the satellites to be unreflective. Starlink has pledged to address the matter, though they are still launching the reflective satellites. As reported by Brian Resnick, here is the story behind the above image:

> In the predawn hours of November 18, 2019, Northwestern University astronomer Cliff Johnson noticed a huge swarm of unfamiliar objects streaking across the sky.
>
> That night, Johnson was surveying the Magellanic Clouds—two very dim dwarf galaxies that orbit our own Milky Way galaxy—with the telescopes at the Cerro Tololo Inter-American Observatory in Chile. These galaxies are teaching scientists how stars form, and what happens when two galaxies pass near one another. Johnson was watching them remotely, through a webcam at Fermilab outside of Chicago. "All of a sudden," he says, "we just start seeing these streaks come across the webcam view. I've never seen anything like that."
>
> The streaks weren't from the heavens. They were from Earth.
>
> Over five minutes, a train of 19 satellites had crossed into the telescopes' view, scarring the observation with bright parallel marks, and degrading their scientific value. It didn't take Johnson and his colleagues long to figure out whose satellites they were: A week earlier, Elon Musk's SpaceX had launched 60 small satellites into low Earth orbit. Johnson's colleague, astronomer Clarae Martínez-Vázquez, who was also working that night, vented her frustration on Twitter.[13]

Here is the tweet from Martínez-Vázquez:

> Wow!! I am in shock!! The huge amount of Starlink satellites crossed our skies tonight at @cerrotololo. Our DECam exposure was heavily affected by 19 of them! The train of Starlink satellites lasted for over 5 minutes!! Rather depressing ... This is not cool!

Martínez-Vázquez has every right to be shocked, as you might be, too. As for now, Starlink's pollution is not an issue addressed in the United Nations Outer Space Treaty or current status of international space law. Here are two other forms of pollution of the night skies:

> In 2018, a New Zealand company called Rocket Lab launched the "Humanity Star," which was basically a disco ball in low Earth orbit. Talk about ego-media and humanity's cosmic narcissism! Fortunately, the Humanity Star had faulty design and crashed back to Earth, perhaps a form of space graffiti foreshadowing our own demise in space.[14]

---

12 Loren Grush, "SpaceX Continues to Blast Satellites into Orbit as the Space Community Worries," The Verge, January 14, 2020, https://www.theverge.com/2020/1/14/21043229/spacex-starlink-satellite-mega-constellation-concerns-astronomy-space-traffic; Stuart Clark, "Are Elon Musk's 'Megaconstellations' a Blight on the Night Sky?" *The Guardian*, September 12, 2020, https://www.theguardian.com/science/2020/sep/12/stars-astronomy-spacex-satellite-elon-musk.
13 Brian Resnick, "The Night Sky Is Increasingly Dystopian," Vox, January 29, 2020, https://www.vox.com/science-and-health/2020/1/7/21003272/space-x-starlink-astronomy-light-pollution.
14 Alison Kiesman, "The Demise of (the) Humanity (Star)," Astronomy, March 23, 2018, https://astronomy.com/news/2018/03/the-demise-of-the-humanity-star.

A Russian firm called RocketStart "plans to use a hundreds-strong constellation of CubeSats, each equipped with a reflective sail, to display ads, and perhaps emergency and event-based messages."[15] Imagine the night sky turned into a horizon-to-horizon carnival of billboards, an aerial Times Square glowing ever larger and brighter to reflect our consumer selves back to our selves.

LOSS OF THE COOL GAZE: FOR TELESCOPES AND OUR NAKED EYES

By stating that Starlink's sky pollution is "not cool," Clarae Martínez-Vázquez is spot-on in more ways than one, for this is a clear example of hot ego-media overtaking the territories of cool exo-media. Starlink's global web of satellites further illustrates the layers of media presented in the "Hot and Cool" essay in chapter 1. As with the Anthropocene, we are creating layers of our Media(S)cene.

The reflective pollution of the Starlink satellites *reflects* a stunning lack of foresight from Musk and SpaceX, who are largely unchallenged in their roles as space visionaries. As discussed in chapter 9, Musk is much more a simulacrum of the future. The lack of foresight is also indicative of the unchecked hubris and cosmic narcissism of the human species, wedded to unchecked technological proliferation—from electric lights to fossil fuels to global webs of satellites. Caitlin Casey, an astronomer at the University of Texas at Austin, poetically summarizes the issue:

> The fact that one person, or one company, can take control and completely transform humans' experience of the night sky, and not just humans, but every organism on Earth ... that seems profoundly wrong. [The night sky is] the one thing that all humans have had in the past 200,000 years, millions of years, it's always been there. ... My whole attachment to science and pursuing this as a career dates back to seeing the night sky as a child and being mesmerized. Astronomy is a unique science: we can't tinker with things in a lab, experimenting on stars. The entire science is looking up at the sky, and losing that would be tragic.[16]

When are we going to wake up?

Starlink's sky pollution involves more than astronomy. Under dark skies, there are somewhere between four thousand and six thousand stars visible to the naked eye. Currently, the Starlink satellites are brighter than most stars! Under current plans to reduce the reflection, the satellites will still be as bright as many stars. Imagine forty thousand satellites roaming across the sky every night, like ants crawling across an ant-bed stretching from horizon to horizon, illustrative of our planetary hive-mind. Lost will be the cool gaze that has existed for the human species since its emergence on Planet Earth. Prior to light pollution and Starlink, every human being and every civilization that has ever existed was able to bask in the radiance of the Milky Way. We are litterly polluting our connection to our cosmic origins, for we are made of the stardust we see in the Milky Way.

For me, it would be no surprise to see our ego-media networks utterly trash the night sky for exo-media, just as we have polluted the lands, rivers, and oceans. Ego trumps exo; hot trumps cool. We can change that, but it requires a different philosophy.

---

15 Sarah Scoles, "Space Billboards Are Just the Latest Orbital Stunt," *Wired*, January 10, 2020, https://www.wired.com/story/space-billboards-are-just-the-latest-orbital-stunt/.
16 Resnick, "The Night Sky is Increasingly Dystopian."

CHILL OUT: THE DARK SKY MOVEMENT

According to a recent study of light pollution, 99 percent of Europeans and Americans live under heavily light-polluted skies, such that 80 percent of Americans can't even see the Milky Way. Around the world, 80 percent of humans live under light-polluted skies.[17] As artificial light spreads, so will the light pollution. Given these totals and trends, it's not hard to imagine a near future in which most everyone will never see the Milky Way with their own eyes. That's why the International Dark-Sky Association exists and is now a movement that spans our planet.

Protecting the night skies is like protecting the wilderness areas. In effect, the thousands of stars we see (with our naked eyes) in the Milky Way represent the nearest edge of the celestial wilderness that is the universe. Just as the *untouched* wilderness is important for the psychology and philosophy of our species, so too the *unpolluted* Milky Way is important for our cosmology and experience of the sublime. This idea is at the heart of the amazing "Skyglow" project developed by time-lapse filmmakers Harun Mehmedinovic and Gavin Heffernan. Google it: the images are incredible, and you'll want to go to those places.

If the Milky Way and dark skies could be returned to human consciousness on a regular basis or become easily accessible in national parks and dark-sky reserves, then this might help inspire the development of planetary systems of value and a new cosmic narrative for our species. That's the unstated narrative in the Earthworks and International Dark Sky Reserve. In the final reading of this book, Barry Vacker outlines the contours of a "Dark Skies Philosophy."

Time to gaze far. Think long-term. Chill.

CREDITS

---

17 Michelle Z. Donahue, "80 Percent of Americans Can't See the Milky Way Anymore," *National Geographic*, June 10, 2016; Bahar Gholipour, "Most of Us Can't See the Milky Way Anymore. That Comes with a Price," *Huffington Post*, July 1, 2018.

TOWARDS A FUTURIST CULTURAL STUDIES

DEVON POWERS is an associate professor of advertising at Temple University. She is the author of *Writing the Record: The Village Voice and the Birth of Rock Criticism* and coeditor of *Blowing Up the Brand: Critical Perspectives on Promotional Culture*.

TOWARD A FUTURIST CULTURAL STUDIES

In November 2019, *New York* magazine invited writers to speculate about the year 2029. The result was a wide-ranging series of essays and vignettes, covering everything from artificial intelligence to Frankeneating, plastics to Xi Jinping, TikTok to Ava DuVernay. As imaginative and thought-provoking as the articles proved to be, the magazine did not offer a panorama of the future—at least not exactly. Rather, its target was the long present: examining how the current moment suggests a world that might be while marveling in disbelief over the world that is. In that sense, the 'uncanny shimmer of future weirdness' (*New York* magazine, 2019) that percolates through our times is better understood as a tangle of hopes, confusions, and uncertainties about where all this is leading. What future are we driving toward? What will happen when we arrive there? And how much of the journey is under our control?

The journalists, fiction writers, critics, and creatives who contributed to *New York*'s Future Issue are not alone in grappling with these questions. Imagining tomorrow has long been a central, if under-appreciated, facet of cultural studies. Work within the field considers the implications of cultural developments (Abidin, 2018;

Banet-Weiser, 2012, 2018; John, 2017; Lotz, 2018), raises alarms about technological, political, and economic shifts (Andrejevic et al., 2015; Benjamin, 2019; Couldry and Mejias, 2019; Zuboff, 2019), and ponders how evolving sociocultural dynamics might extend or challenge power relations (Beer, 2016; Lash, 2007). The future itself has also been an object of inquiry within cultural studies. Representations of the future, from science fiction to World Expos, serve as cultural texts which illuminate expectations and assumptions about futures (Bacon-Smith, 2000; Hubbert, 2017; Wang and Chan, 2020; Wood et al., 2019). Scholars endeavor to theorize the role of the future in everyday life and thought, intersecting in various ways with work on temporality, memory, and the relationship of technology to both (Alper, 2019; Szpunar and Szpunar, 2016). And in works like John Urry's 2016 *What is the Future?*, the future is understood as a crucial terrain for the contestation of power. Urry thus implores his readers to reclaim the future as within our domain, since 'a key element of power is thus power to determine—to produce—the future, out of the many ways it is imagined, organized, materialized and distributed' (2016: 11, 17).

In addition to the aforementioned pursuits, which get at the heart of the 'culture' of cultural studies, cultural studies scholars also mind the future of the subfield. There are regular debates about what direction the field should go and how it might get there (Grossberg, 2010; Hartley, 2009). As Larry Grossberg argues in his 2010 book *Cultural Studies in the Future Tense*: 'Cultural studies matters because it is about the future, and about some of the work it will take, in the present, to shape the future' (2010: 1). Grossberg views cultural studies as a political project that 'takes contestation for granted, not as a reality in every instance, but as an assumption necessary for the existence of critical work, political opposition, and even historical change' (2010: 8–9). It is not, in his view, enough to study or decipher culture, not enough to analyze cultural texts in terms of meaning and power. The duty of cultural studies, for him and many others, is to effect change within and beyond the academy. To do otherwise is to become irrelevant or complicit (Grossberg, 2010: 7).

Yet despite these investments in the future, cultural studies has yet to embrace futurism—the systematic study of the future—in a meaningful way. Futurological literature has been around since the mid-20th century, but cultural studies does not engage with it, except at the fringes. We flirt with futurist language (such as 'futuring' and 'futures') and methods (such as trends, scenarios, and pattern recognition), though usually only by accident. In cultural studies, it is common to make predictions and deliver warnings, but it is rare to find scholars who identify as futurists or who consider the purpose and implications of future speculation. Moreover, like the *New York* magazine contributors, our considerations of the future often speak more to current anxieties and obsessions than they do to plausible shifts or practical outcomes. And while there is certainly utility in envisioning desirable futures or lamenting the slide toward unwelcome ones, cultural studies is at constant risk of making future speculation more about hubris and ideology than humility and curiosity. Rigid beliefs sound righteous but can limit one's ability to see the world as it is or might be (Tetlock and Gardner, 2015: 71–2). And despite our constant handwringing, the sky is not always falling.

The contemporary moment presents challenges and opportunities that should push cultural studies toward clearer perception. In his book *Futures Past: On the Semantics of Historical Time*, Reinhart Koselleck argues that the 'weight of the future' intensifies during certain epochs, '[forcing] upon its inhabitants ever briefer intervals of time in which to gather new experiences and adapt to changes induced at an ever-increasing pace' (2004: 3). One can certainly argue over whether and for whom the pace of time has demonstrably increased (Sharma, 2014); we nonetheless find ourselves within one of these heavy moments, where discussion of the future is frequent and deliberate, and the demands of the future necessitate conversation and action. As it stands, elite interests—often with the aid of futurist professionals—are making decisions about the future on behalf of the rest of us, without our input or knowledge (Powers, 2019). The kinds of questions that drive cultural studies could bring much-needed critical awareness to future imaginaries, but it will require endowing cultural studies with more robust methods and theories for thinking, acting, and making change. In short, we need a futurist cultural studies. Futurism can increase our efficacy; cultural studies can increase futurism's humanity.

Mandating 'change' has been an operating assumption of cultural studies since its inception. In its quest to engage in critique—of power; of class, race, and gender relations; of totalizing narratives of all kinds—cultural studies is praxis aimed at refashioning society toward progressive goals (Hartley, 2003; Johnson, 1986). Cultural studies likewise is dedicated to changing itself: flexibility, reflexivity, and experimentation are its bulwarks against stasis, conservatism, or obdurate institutionalization. As Johnson influentially wrote, what defines cultural studies is 'its openness and theoretical versatility, even self-conscious mood … cultural studies is a process, a kind of producing useful knowledge; codify it and you might halt its reactions' (1986: 38). These characteristics have made cultural studies at times paralyzingly solipsistic. At the same time, they have also ensured that cultural studies questions its founding assumptions and tests out new ways of doing things.

A constitutional commitment to change links cultural studies to the future as both a concept and a temporality. Cultural studies tends to conceptualize the future as a contest between change and the status quo, where change signifies a progressive political project that blends empowerment of the *demos*, radical equality, and critical awareness. The status quo, on the other hand, is often regressive, marginalizing, and discriminatory. Thus, the future cultural studies desires is often implicitly (and sometimes explicitly) deemed possible only within democratic socialism, though there have been moves over cultural studies' history to realize emergent elements of that future, especially through the embrace of the revolutionary aspects of popular culture (Webster, 2006: 579). The future thus exists as the current struggle as well as an ideal temporality that will be achieved only once certain forms of revolution are actualized. Taken together, these dual notions of the future perform the rhetorical and theoretical work that makes cultural studies possible.

But what if the future of cultural studies never arrives? An impossible question. One way to make it manageable is to ask what happens if cultural studies does not achieve the equity, emancipation, and empowerment that are its expressed goals. Take for example the wild disciplinary success of cultural studies since its inceptions—the classes, departments, journals, conferences, students, faculty. On the one hand, this flourishing can be read as evidence that cultural studies sallies forth toward the future incrementally, even if its utopian vision remains unrealized. On the other hand, one might argue that the formalization of cultural studies is evidence of its connivance—proof that the project of cultural studies has failed to critique systems, to interrogate and unmask power, so much so that it has become part of the machine. In both scenarios, and dozens of others we could conjure, cultural studies remains intact, on the one hand thanks to its acceptance, on the other because its project is incomplete. Change, it seems, can go in many different directions—ironic considering the subfield's dedication to 'radical progress.'

Let's pose the question of the future of cultural studies in a different way. How should the field make sense of the futures that compete with cultural studies—the utopian futures upon which other philosophies depend, the tomorrows they are striving towards? How can cultural studies contend with the fact that the future is not solely ours to imagine, but involves competition and cooperation between ways of thinking and being that not only transcend what we believe and know, but directly challenge it? There are a few ways to respond to this question. First, it reminds us that cultural studies has not been very good at considering perspectives that do not see its aims as progress. Another important point of response is that like the present and the past, the future exists in multiple layers. The world is full of temporal configurations that don't drive toward the future in any progressive sense, but which rather experience time as multidirectional, discontinuous. The push toward progress, however that progress is defined, always comes from a limited vantage point, and always ignores other epistemes.

Futurism is a useful beginning for engaging with such multiplicity. For sure, futurism has many embodiments and its own internal contradictions—even the word 'futurism' is a gauntlet to those who identify with futurology, future studies, or some other term. Yet for the sake of argument, here I use futurism as an umbrella term to refer to the field of study devoted to the future—both analyzing future signals and influencing future outcomes. The discipline of futurism, like cultural studies, made inroads during the 1960s and 1970s, a time during when the social sciences erupted with new paradigms for understanding the world. Futurism, like cultural studies, embraced change as its organizing concept and, in certain manifestations, possessed idealized notions of how change might unfold. Both traditions, then, are interested in how human beings can influence the world around them and bring about their preferred futures.

Cultural studies and futurism share meaningful connections, but much separates them as well. A major distinction concerns futurism's acceptance of uncertainty: less concerned with 'knowing' the future than with influencing how it unfolds (Powers, 2019). Especially in later manifestations—where futurism took shape within corporate rather than academic settings—this comfort with uncertainty frequently manifested in a laissezfaire attitude toward those future directions, where the goal was simply to gain advantage no matter the future. For example, within strategic foresight, a branch of futurism especially popular among military, intelligence, and government entities, forecasting involves determining the likelihood of possible outcomes, not to alter those outcomes per se but to plan suitable tactics (Tetlock and Gardner, 2015). In the corporate arena, capitalizing on uncertainty translated into staying adaptable in the present, which generally has not pushed for big, systemic change so much as the kinds that are easily marketized (Powers, 2019).

Practical and professional versions of futurism have had influence despite the field's relative obscureness.

Similarly, academic futurism remains a niche discipline across much of the globe. Even so, as Andersson explains, futures research gave rise to the 'expertise, methods, and technologies that have become part of governmentality of the contemporary' (2018: 6)—futurism helped make strategic management of the future a present-day concern. The irony is that the use of these tools by powerful interests has tended to limit the capacity for humans to shape their future, and instead compelled many of us to give in to powerful dynamics and accept developments that feel beyond our control.

This is all starting to change, however. Futurism is beginning to expand beyond its confines in military and corporate strategy, becoming an activist tool or a generalized method for future speculation. And in light of climate change, environmental degradation, polarizing nationalisms, rising inequality, and major geopolitical and public health crises with enormous human costs, futurism is increasingly necessary as a means not simply to react to the onslaught of problems but to imagine beyond the despair and create solutions that dispense with old ways of thinking. For example, while we can say that major technology platforms are increasingly powerful and intrusive, a futurist approach transcends critique to plot how political, social, economic, and behavioral trends might shape how those powers develop, and how that in turn might suggest different critical interventions.

It is at this moment that cultural studies and futurism need one another most.

Critical future studies, for example, offers a playbook for cultural studies to adopt. Critical future studies may be defined as an interdisciplinary field of study that 'investigates the scope and constraints within public culture for imagining and debating different potential futures' and 'interrogates imagined futures founded—often surreptitiously—upon values and assumptions from the past and present, as well as those representing a departure from current social trajectories' (Godhe and Goode, 2018: 109). The aim of this work is to enhance public debate about the future. Godhe and Goode accurately recognize that 'in terms of shaping society's capacity to imagine and deliberate on potential futures (and therefore to steer towards or away from specific scenarios), we are always and unavoidably dealing with matters of culture' (2018: 111).

That is, the tendency within future studies to instrumentalize the future needs to be balanced against the ends that instrumentalization has traditionally served, the cultures of futuring it has supported and the ones it has not. Cultural studies has much to contribute in this regard, to help to understand the future as more than a zone of capitalist strategy, but rather one of democratic possibility.

Too often, the future is a handy signifier—a word we use to mean surprising, distant, or different. Or 'future' gets used promotionally, to give our thinking the appearance of foresight or specialness. But the future is too important to be embraced merely as rhetoric. Instead, we must think of the future as a zone to be occupied, fought over, theorized, envisioned, and possibly emancipated, if our imaginations and our best thinking will allow.

FUNDING

The author received no financial support for the research, authorship, and/or publication of this article.

REFERENCES

Abidin C (2018) *Internet Celebrity: Understanding Fame Online.* Bingley, UK: Emerald Publishing.

Alper M (2019) Future talk: Accounting for the technological and other future discourses in daily life. *International Journal of Communication* 13: 715–735.

Andersson J (2018) *The Future of the World: Futurology, Futurists, and the Struggle for the Post-Cold War Imagination.* New York: Oxford University Press.

Andrejevic M, Hearn A and Kennedy H (2015) Cultural studies of data mining: Introduction. *European Journal of Cultural Studies* 18(4–5): 379–394.

Bacon-Smith C (2000) *Science Fiction Culture.* Philadelphia, PA: University of Pennsylvania Press.

Banet-Weiser S (2012) *Authentic TM: The Politics of Ambivalence in a Brand Culture.* New York: New York University Press.

Banet-Weiser S (2018) *Empowered: Popular Feminism and Popular Misogyny.* Durham, NC: Duke University Press.

Beer D (2016) *Metric Power.* London: Palgrave Macmillan.

Benjamin R (2019) *Race after Technology: Abolitionist Tools for the New Jim Code.* Malden, MA: Polity.

Couldry N and Mejias UA (2019) Data colonialism: Rethinking big data's relation to the contemporary subject. *Television & New Media* 20(4): 336–349.

Godhe M and Goode L (2018) Critical future studies: A thematic introduction. *Culture Unbound: Journal of Current Cultural Research* 10(2): 151–162.

Grossberg L (2010) *Cultural Studies in the Future Tense.* Durham, NC: Duke University Press.

Hartley J (2003) *A Short History of Cultural Studies.* London: Sage.

Hartley J (2009) From cultural studies to cultural science. *Cultural Science Journal* 2(1): 1–16.

Hubbert J (2017) Back to the future: The politics of culture at the Shanghai Expo. *International Journal of Cultural Studies* 20(1): 48–64.

John NA (2017) *The Age of Sharing.* Medford, MA: Polity.

Johnson R (1986) What is cultural studies anyway? *Social Text* 16: 38–80.

Koselleck R (2004) *Futures Past: On the Semantics of Historical Time.* New York: Columbia University Press.

Lash S (2007) Power after hegemony: Cultural studies in mutation? *Theory, Culture & Society* 24(3): 55–78.

Lotz AD (2018) *We Now Disrupt This Broadcast: How Cable Transformed Television and the Internet Revolutionized It All.* Cambridge, MA: MIT Press.

New York magazine (2019) The weirdness is coming: An issue about the future. 11–24 November. Available at: https://nymag.com/tags/the-future-issue/ (accessed 9 March 2020).

Powers D (2019) *On Trend: The Business of Forecasting the Future.* Champaign, IL: University of Illinois Press.

Sharma S (2014) *In the Meantime: Temporality and Cultural Politics.* Durham, NC: Duke University Press.

Szpunar PM and Szpunar KK (2016) Collective future thought: Concept, function, and implications for collective memory studies. *Memory Studies* 9(4): 376–389.

Tetlock PE and Gardner D (2015) Superforecasting: *The Art and Science of Prediction.* New York: Crown.

Urry J (2016) *What Is the Future?* London: Polity.

Wang X and Chan SCK (2020) Introduction: Imagining the future in East Asia. *Cultural Studies.* Available at: https://www.tandfonline.com/doi/abs/10.1080/09502386.2019.1709090? (accessed 9 March 2020).

Webster D (2006) Pessimism, optimism, pleasure: The future of cultural studies. In: Story J (ed.) *Cultural Theory and Popular Culture: A Reader.* New York: Pearson, pp. 571–585.

Wood R, Litherland B and Reed E (2019) Girls being Rey: Ethical cultural consumption, families and popular feminism. *Cultural Studies.* Available at: https://pure.hud.ac.uk/en/publications/girls-being-rey-ethical-cultural-consumption-families-and-popular (accessed 9 March 2020).

Zuboff S (2019) *The Age of Surveillance Capitalism: The Fight for a Human Future at the New Frontier of Power.* New York: Public Affairs Books.

OUR FUTURE? *STAR TREK* OR NOT?

from *The Universe in a Nutshell*

STEPHEN HAWKING is the former Lucasian Professor of Mathematics at the University of Cambridge. His first book, *A Brief History of Time* (1988) sold nearly 10 million copies in 40 languages and inspired the popular science documentary, *A Brief History of Time* (1991). His most recent book is *The Grand Design*, which he co-authored with Leonard Mlodinow.

The reason *Star Trek* is so popular is because it is a safe and comforting vision of the future. I'm a bit of a *Star Trek* fan myself, so I was easily persuaded to take part in an episode in which I played poker with Newton, Einstein, and Commander Data. I beat them all, but unfortunately there was a red alert, so I never collected my winnings.

Star Trek shows a society that is far in advance of ours in science, in technology, and in political organization. (The last might not be difficult.) There must have been great changes, with their accompanying tensions and upsets, in the time between now and then, but in the period we are shown, science, technology, and the organization of society are supposed to have achieved a level of near perfection.

I want to question this picture and ask if we will ever reach a final steady state in science and technology. At no time in the ten thousand years or so since the last ice age has the human race been in a state of constant knowledge and fixed technology. There have been a few setbacks, like the Dark Ages after the fall of the Roman Empire. But the world's population, which is a measure of our technological ability to preserve life and feed ourselves, has risen steadily, with only a few hiccups such as the Black Death.

In the last two hundred years, population growth has become exponential, that is, the population grows by the same percentage each year. Currently, the rate is about 1.9 percent a year. That may not sound like very much, but it means that the world population doubles every forty years.

Other measures of technological development in recent times are electricity consumption and the number of scientific articles. They too show exponential growth, with doubling times of less than forty years. There is no sign that scientific and technological development will slow down and stop in the near future—certainly not by the time of *Star Trek*, which is supposed to be not that far in the future. But if the population growth and the increase in the consumption of electricity continue at their current rates, by 2600 the world's population will be standing shoulder to shoulder, and electricity use will make the Earth glow red-hot.

If you stacked all the new books being published next to each other, you would have to move at ninety miles an hour just to keep up with the end of the line. Of course, by 2600 new artistic and scientific work will come in electronic forms, rather than as physical books and papers. Nevertheless, if the exponential growth continued, there would be ten papers a second in my kind of theoretical physics, and no time to read them.

Clearly, the present exponential growth cannot continue indefinitely. So what will happen? One possibility is that we will wipe ourselves out completely by some disaster, such as a nuclear war. There is a sick joke that the reason we have not been contacted by extraterrestrials is that when a civilization reaches our stage of development, it becomes unstable and destroys itself. However, I'm an optimist. I don't believe the human race has come so far just to snuff itself out when things are getting interesting.

The *Star Trek* vision of the future—that we achieve an advanced but essentially static level—may come true in respect of our knowledge of the basic laws that govern the universe. [...] There may be an ultimate theory that we will discover in the not-too-distant future. This ultimate theory, if it exists, will determine whether the *Star Trek* dream of warp drive can be realized. According to present ideas, we shall have to explore the galaxy in a slow and tedious manner, using spaceships traveling slower than light, but since we don't yet have a complete unified theory, we can't quite rule out warp drive.

On the other hand, we already know the laws that hold in all but the most extreme situations: the laws that govern the crew of the *Enterprise*, if not the spaceship itself. Yet it doesn't seem that we will ever reach a steady state in the uses we make of these laws or in the complexity of the systems that we can produce with them. It is with this complexity that the rest of this reading will be concerned.

By far the most complex systems that we have are our own bodies. Life seems to have originated in the primordial oceans that covered the Earth four billion years ago. How this happened we don't know. It may be that random collisions between atoms built up macromolecules that could reproduce themselves and assemble themselves into more complicated structures. What we do know is that by three and a half billion years ago, the highly complicated DNA molecule had emerged.

DNA is the basis for all life on Earth. It has a double helix structure, like a spiral staircase, which was discovered by Francis Crick and James Watson in the Cavendish lab at Cambridge in 1953. The two strands of the double helix are linked by pairs of bases, like the treads in a spiral staircase. There are four bases in DNA: adenine, guanine, thymine, and cytosine. The order in which they occur along the spiral staircase carries the genetic information that enables the DNA to assemble an organism around it and reproduce itself. As it makes copies of itself, there are occasional errors in the proportion or order of the bases along the spiral. In most cases, the mistakes in copying make the DNA either unable or less likely to reproduce itself, meaning that such genetic errors, or mutations, as they are called, will die out. But in a few cases, the error or mutation will increase the chances of the DNA surviving and reproducing. Such changes in the genetic code will be favored. This is how the information contained in the sequence of DNA gradually evolves and increases in complexity.

Because biological evolution is basically a random walk in the space of all genetic possibilities, it has been very slow. The complexity, or number of bits of information, that is coded in DNA is roughly the number of bases in the molecule. For the first two billion years or so, the rate of increase in complexity must have been of the order of one bit of information every hundred years. The rate of increase of DNA complexity gradually rose to about one bit a year over the last few million years. But then, about six or eight thousand years ago, a major new development occurred. We developed written language. This meant that information could be passed from one generation to the next without having to wait for the very slow process of random mutations and natural selection to code it into the DNA sequence. The amount of complexity increased enormously. A single paperback romance could hold as much information as the difference in DNA between apes and humans, and a thirty-volume encyclopedia could describe the entire sequence of human DNA.

Even more important, the information in books can be updated rapidly. The current rate at which human DNA is being updated by biological evolution is about one bit a year. But there are two hundred thousand new books published each year, a new-information rate of over a million bits a second. Of course, most of this information is garbage, but even if only one bit in a million is useful, that is still a hundred thousand times faster than biological evolution.

This transmission of data through external, nonbiological means has led the human race to dominate the world and to have an exponentially increasing population. But now we are at the beginning of a new era, in which we will be able to increase the complexity of our internal record, the DNA, without having to wait for the slow process of biological evolution. There has been no significant change in human DNA in the last ten thousand years, but it is likely that we will be able to completely redesign it in the next thousand. Of course, many people will say that genetic engineering of humans should be banned, but it is doubtful we will be able to prevent it. Genetic engineering of plants and animals will be allowed for economic reasons, and someone is bound to try it on humans. Unless we have a totalitarian world order, someone somewhere will design improved humans.

Clearly, creating improved humans will create great social and political problems with respect to unimproved humans. My intention is not to defend human genetic engineering as a desirable development, but just to say it is likely to happen whether we want it or not. This is the reason why I don't believe science fiction like *Star Trek*, where people four hundred years into the future are essentially the same as we are today. I think the human race, and its DNA, will increase its complexity quite rapidly. We should recognize that this is likely to happen and consider how we will deal with it.

In a way, the human race needs to improve its mental and physical qualities if it is to deal with the increasingly complex world around it and meet new challenges such as space travel. Humans also need to increase their complexity if biological systems are to keep ahead of electronic ones. At the moment, computers have the advantage of speed, but they show no sign of intelligence. This is not surprising, because our present computers are less complex than the brain of an earthworm, a species not noted for its intellectual powers.

But computers obey what is known as Moore's law: their speed and complexity double every eighteen months. It is one of those exponential growths that clearly cannot continue indefinitely. However, it will probably continue until computers have a complexity similar to that of the human brain. Some people say that computers can never show true intelligence, whatever that may be. But it seems to me that if very complicated chemical molecules can operate in humans to make them intelligent, then equally complicated electronic circuits can also make computers act in an intelligent way. And if they are intelligent, they can presumably design computers that have even greater complexity and intelligence.

Will this increase of biological and electronic complexity go on forever, or is there a natural limit? On the biological side, the limit on human intelligence up to now has been set by the size of the brain that will pass through the birth canal. Having watched my three children being born, I know how difficult it is for the head to get out. But within the next hundred years, I expect we will be able to grow babies outside the human body, so this limitation will be removed. Ultimately, however, increases in the size of the human brain through genetic engineering will come up against the problem that the body's chemical messengers responsible for our mental activity are relatively slow-moving. This means that further increases in the complexity of the brain will be at the expense of speed. We can be quick-witted or very intelligent, but not both. Still, I think we can become a lot more intelligent than most of the people in *Star Trek*, not that that might be difficult.

Electronic circuits have the same complexity-versus-speed problem as the human brain. In this case, however, the signals are electrical, not chemical, and travel at the speed of light, which is much higher. Nevertheless, the speed of light is already a practical limit on the design of faster computers. One can improve the situation by making the circuits smaller, but ultimately there will be a limit set by the atomic nature of matter. Still, we have some way to go before we meet that barrier.

Another way in which electronic circuits can increase their complexity while maintaining speed is to copy the human brain. The brain does not have a single CPU—central processing unit—that processes each command in sequence. Rather, it has millions of processors working together at the same time. Such massively parallel processing will be the future for electronic intelligence as well.

Assuming we don't destroy ourselves in the next hundred years, it is likely that we will spread out first to the planets in the solar system and then to the nearby stars. But it won't be like *Star Trek* or *Babylon 5*, with a new race of nearly human beings in almost every stellar system. The human race has been in its present form for only two million years out of the fifteen billion years or so since the big bang.

So even if life develops in other stellar systems, the chances of catching it at a recognizably human stage are very small. Any alien life we encounter will likely be either much more primitive or much more advanced. If it is more advanced, why hasn't it spread through the galaxy and visited Earth? If aliens had come here, it should have been obvious: more like the film *Independence Day* than *E.T.*

So how does one account for our lack of extraterrestrial visitors? It could be that there is an advanced race out there which is aware of our existence but is leaving us to stew in our own primitive juices. However, it is doubtful it would be so considerate to a lower life-form: do most of us worry how many insects and earthworms we squash underfoot? A more reasonable explanation is that there is a very low probability either of life developing on other planets or of that life developing intelligence. Because we claim to be intelligent, though perhaps without much ground, we tend to see intelligence as an inevitable consequence of evolution. However, one can question that. It is not clear that intelligence has much survival value. Bacteria do very well without intelligence and will survive us if our so-called intelligence causes us to wipe ourselves out in a nuclear war. So as we explore the galaxy we may find primitive life, but we are not likely to find beings like us.

The future of science won't be like the comforting picture painted in *Star Trek*: a universe populated by many humanoid races, with an advanced but essentially static science and technology. Instead, I think we will be on our own, but rapidly developing in biological and electronic complexity. Not much of this will happen in the next hundred years, which is all we can reliably predict. But by the end of the next millennium, if we get there, the difference from *Star Trek* will be fundamental.

AVENGERS IN THE VOID
NIETZSCHE, NIHILISM, AND WHY WE NEED SUPERHEROES

ABIGAIL MOORE received her masters student from Temple University. She studies superheroes as a cultural phenomenon. Her research is focused on the intersections of popular culture, media studies, and philosophy.

INTRODUCTION: THE RED CAPES ARE COMING

Twenty-three big-budget superhero movies and twenty-six new television series with at least two seasons each have come out since 2001.[1] That's around two superhero movies per year and more than nineteen superhero episodes a week. Three of the top ten highest-grossing films of all time are superhero films. In 2018, the top three highest-grossing films of the year are all Marvel superhero films. Team-up movies, origin stories, spin-off series, sequels, and prequels flood the media market. Popular superheroes are ubiquitous in mainstream culture, but even the lesser-known ones generate enough revenue to warrant a $50-million-dollar budget per Netflix season (e.g., *Daredevil*, *Iron Fist*, *Luke Cage*, and *Jessica Jones*).[2] When it's impossible to flip channels or go to the movie theater without seeing a superhero movie, movie trailer, TV show, video game, or ad for superhero merchandise, it's time to start wondering why this particular genre has such a powerful hold on our collective cultural psyche.

Superheroes are our modern mythology, a renewed pantheon of secular gods and goddesses modeled after pantheonic religions. Myth figures are constant staples for any culture. They have familiar origins—Arthur pulls Excalibur from the stone and becomes king, Peter Parker is bitten by a spider and becomes Spider-Man, Heracles performs his labors to redeem himself. What happens after the origin changes depends on who's telling the story and when that story is being told, and it doesn't matter that much. Superheroes are the gods and heroes of our modern media mythology. They demand our attention as sacrifice, and we gladly give it. You could look closely at any superhero and figure out exactly what type of worshipper they attract, but even this doesn't explain *why* we're seeing such a glut of superhero media right now, at this moment in history.

To explain this trend, we must look back to the original superhero. It's not Superman, if that was your guess.

---

1 "All Time Worldwide Box Office Grosses," Boxofficemojo.com, 2018.
2 Ryan Fleming, "Marvel's Netflix Bound TV Shows To Cost A Whopping $200 Million," *Digital Trends*, February 17, 2014.

Friedrich Nietzsche's "Übermensch" is often translated as "superman," but better translations include "overman" or "beyond man." Nietzsche theorized that under the right societal conditions, humanity would be forced to continue to evolve and grow. The Übermensch would be a philosophically powerful man whom people would look to for leadership, security, and as a moral role model.

The well-known comic book hero Superman was in fact based on Nietzsche's Übermensch. Originally, he was designed as a villain to match the anti-German sentiment of the time, but the character was so incredibly powerful that the idea of having him as a villain was dismissed as too terrifying, and he was instead rewritten as a hero. At the time, he was a hero who was sorely needed. With the Great Depression and a world war as their nursery, the age of superheroes as we know them now began. When many people lined up in the cold for the dole, stood in unemployment lines day after day in the hopes of getting a job that wasn't there, the cultural backdrop for superheroes was just right. They provided a bright-colored, distracting world where the good guys always won in a time when people needed that hope most.

Following a distinct slowdown in the eighties and nineties, the Hollywood superhero exploded back onto the screen in the 2000s. There is no doubt that the terrorist attack on September 11, 2001 played a part in rebooting the superhero industry back into high gear. Fear of instability, fear of future attacks, and worry about a new war in the Middle East are obvious reasons for people to want to escape into fantasy worlds. However, this doesn't explain why we're still seeing *growth* in superhero media. What is it about the world right now that is driving audiences to superheroes? What are these caped vigilantes really saving us from?

As the trend towards more superhero media has gone increasingly up, a few other societal factors have changed in the exact ways that Nietzsche predicted to necessitate a world that would need an Übermensch. Superheroes exist to provide us with the fantasy of safety and security in place of the failing traditional institutions of order as well as to stave off the existential panic that comes from a loss of identity.

TRUST ME, I'M A POLITICIAN

Nietzsche introduces the concept of the Übermensch in *Thus Spoke Zarathustra*, in which the main character, Zarathustra, hears a wise man (whom Zarathustra later mocks for his folly) speaking to a crowd. The "wise" man says, "Honour to the government, and obedience, and also to the crooked government! ... How can I help it, if power like to walk on crooked legs?"[3] This is a sentiment shared by many modern American citizens who have never even heard of Nietzsche, and it is one that contributes to our need for superheroes.

The Pew Research Center has marked a steady, significant decline in trust for the government since 1958.[4] As seen in the chart, one of the only increases in trust occurred just after the terrorist attack on September 11, 2001. However, this surge of trust was short-lived and dropped back down very quickly afterwards. This leaves many people with a sense of fear that further fuels the worry about the state of the whole world. A sense of identity is often derived from nationality, and if you believe that your nation is crooked, it doesn't leave you much.

People, in general, do not like to believe that they are "crooked" or evil, even if they are. This leaves people unable to identify with their nations if they believe that their government can't be trusted. This is another key point at which nihilism can be glimpsed: by losing a sense of national identity, people cling harder to their heroes, using them as a substitute, as parts of their identity. Although they may have no reason to identify with America, Captain America is a character who embodies only the best parts of what is thought of as "American." He's brave, he's strong, he's smart, he's an unfailing moral compass, and he's not afraid to break rules to do the right thing. Compared to a government that makes a majority of its people think of men in suits making suspicious deals behind the scenes, it's almost impossible

---

3 Friedrich Nietzsche, *Thus Spoke Zarathustra* (Chemnitz: Ernst Schmeitzner, 1891), 32.
4 No author listed, "Trust in government: 1958–2015," Pew Research Center, November 23, 2015.

to come up with a reason why people *wouldn't* identify more with Cap.[5]

Superheroes are almost always vigilantes acting of their own accord, *outside* the system, and this is why we trust them. An excellent, if terrifying, example of this is the 2016 presidential election. The two most fanatically loved candidates both presented themselves as anti-establishment, and one of them is now the president. Although Bernie Sanders did not win the Democratic primary, he had the same kind of appeal that Trump did. He branded himself as outside the system, and because "government official" is practically synonymous with "suspicious sneak," people were passionate that he really could change things. Donald Trump's victory is primarily a victory of the TV spectacle in society, but he too branded himself this way: an outsider, someone with hands clean of sketchy government dealings who promised to "drain the swamp."[6]

In a time when concern about police shootings is soaring and confidence in all three branches of government is dropping regardless of party affiliation, a president as unstable and unpredictable as Donald Trump is the last thing that America needs, but he won anyway.[7] Is it because, like our superheroes, he promised to act outside the system, as a vigilante of sorts? Is it because the only comforts left to us are entertainment? Perhaps the only laudable skill Trump has is that he is an excellent reality TV star. Is this familiarity what drew the country to him?

Regardless, instead of placing its confidence in our systems—the institutions we have trusted for so many years to keep peace and order—we have turned to pinning our hopes on comic book heroes. Of course, we know that they won't actually save us from any real-world danger (the existential dread is another story), but the delusion of safety is addictive and distracting enough to serve as a balm against the frightening political madness that is largely outside the average person's control at this point.

CRIME ON THE BRAIN

According to polls conducted by Gallup and *Time* magazine, adults' worries about violent crime rates increase every year, in an almost perfect mirror of the *decrease* in actual violent crime every year.[8] There are many different, good explanations for this disparity between perception and reality.[9] In his book *The Culture of Fear*, Barry Glassner discusses this in depth, describing the ways in which news media as well as fiction contribute to the way that Americans view the world as far more violent than it really is.[10]

One of the ways that people cope with living in a world they perceive to be this violent is via superhero stories, and it is affecting the superheroes that are growing in popularity versus the heroes who are less popular. People turn to superheroes because they, unlike the government, have one simple but powerful claim: they care about *you*. We don't really care if our superheroes are flawed or amoral as long as they care about us more than anything else in the world. By placing us at the center over and over, they give us a sense of meaning in a world increasingly filled with evidence for the arguments of nihilism, and they provide us with a sense of safety. Of course, we know that they're not real, but the fantasy of having an ultimate protector who will stand up to crooked governments, terrorists, and supervillains is a powerful dream. In fact, it's a dream fueling a multibillion-dollar entertainment genre.

Within the larger trend towards superheroes in general, there's a marked increase in "gritty," darker heroes. We've lost interest in Superman, and it's not because he's not powerful: it's because we don't think Superman can handle our world. To the average American, our cities are much more like Batman's Gotham. We think that everywhere is as dangerous and the government as deeply corrupt as in Batman's city. This is why we need Batman—who is equipped to handle a world as awful as ours, and not Superman, who knows only his utopian Metropolis—to save us from it. It is these darker,

5   Ron Elving, "Poll: 1 in 5 Americans Trusts The Government," NPR, November 23, 2015.
6   Robert Zaretsky, "Trump and the 'Society of the Spectacle,'" *New York Times*, February 20, 2017.
7   Justin McCarthy, "Americans Losing Confidence in All Branches of U.S. Gov't," Gallup, June 30, 2014.
8   Alyssa Davis, "In U.S., Concern About Crime Climbs To 15-Year High," Gallup, April 6, 2016.
9   Josh Sanburn, "Why Americans Are Increasingly Worried About Violent Crime," *Time*, April 7, 2017.
10 Barry Glassner, *The Culture of Fear* (New York: Basic Books, 1999).

grittier heroes who speak to us now. They are not only more human and more relatable; they are also better equipped to handle the world we think we're living in.

It's easy to see which heroes we think can handle our world. Go simply by sales: pick out which heroes make the most money and garner the most success. Sure, Iron Man flies around in a metal suit, but he is still relatable to us because he's flawed in ways that make him suited to the corrupted world we see around us. He was a war profiteer for years before becoming a hero, and his fight for good hinges on his desire for redemption of his past wrongs. Iron Man could stop ISIS bombings with his fabulous technology and knowledge of terror cells. Batman, with his experience with corrupted governments like the one in Gotham, could watch over our corrupted government and try to keep it in line. Despite the fact that they're both billionaires, heroes like these make sense to us. They live in a world like ours, a terrifying world that they are shown beating back in sequel after sequel. They understand our world, and they've proven that they can save us from it.

GOD'S NOT QUITE DEAD

An interesting paradox exists in America in regards to religion. The number of Americans classified as "nones" grows every single year, at an unprecedented rate since the late sixties[11]. Many who do identify with an organized religion are nominal believers at best. Gallup has marked a nearly inverse rate of believers who state that they still have a "great deal" or "quite a lot" of confidence in the church or organized religion as an institution.[12]

Religion is, by any measure, not nearly as important to Americans as it has been in the past. At the same time, American politics has witnessed a growth in religious activism. Antiscience movements against the most irrefutable data, such as evolution, along with many other issues, are increasingly loud in the public sphere. Christian fundamentalist movements grow stronger and louder as well, in contrast to an increasingly ambivalent general populace.

In Nietzsche's book *Thus Spoke Zarathustra*, he makes his most famous proclamation: "God is dead! God remains dead! And we have killed him!"[13] An atheist, Nietzsche did not mean that there had been a God who had literally died but that the idea of God was no longer needed. Science—Darwin, specifically—existed to explain natural phenomena, to order the universe. Philosophy had shown that governments could be organized by the consent of the governed rather than by religious rules and morality and that a ruler could be elected democratically rather than assuming control by "divine right." This has only become truer in the 130 or so years since he published this iconic phrase. Our science advances every single day. Our deep-space telescopes have revealed millions and millions of planets to us, many of which may be habitable. Every day, our medicine creates more ways for us to cheat death. Philosophers and democratic thinkers have mapped out secular ways to examine ethics and morality. Humanity has never been so privileged: never before in history have so many had so much. We have outgrown our need for God, and every day that our science, technology, philosophy, and culture advances, we bury him deeper. We don't need God to explain thunder to ourselves: we have Google. We don't need shamans or spiritual healers: we have doctors armed with antibiotics. Though there are many who insist that God gives their lives meaning, more and more people are finding their individual purpose through secular means.

Less religion in people's lives means two things, mainly. For one, people have one less way to construct their identities. While, of course, many nones do construct their identities around their lack of religious affiliation and find community in secular or humanitarian societies, many others just don't think about it that much. Their lack of religion is not so much a conviction based on thought and research as it is a blank space. It's not terribly important to them one way or another. Rather than being *secular thinkers*, they are simply *not*

---

11   Heidi Glen, "Losing Our Religion: The Growth of the 'Nones,'" NPR, January 23, 2013. "Nones" are classified as people who do not identify with any organized religion. This includes agnostics, atheists, and anyone who does not follow any *specific* religious teaching, even if they self-describe as "spiritual."
12   Lydia Saad, "U.S. Confidence In Organized Religion At Low Point," Gallup, July 12, 2012.
13   Friedrich Nietzsche, *Thus Spoke Zarathustra* (Chemnitz: Ernst Schmeitzner, 1891), 20.

religious, either because they weren't raised with religion or because it became irrelevant to their lives. In a country like America, where "atheism" is still a filthy word in many places despite our history of separating church and state, the vast majority of nones are left without a community. They are, in many regions, unable to talk to other like-minded people, and so their lack of religious affiliation becomes a quiet, stifled thing in their lives, losing its importance. What this does is create a void in their identities and leaves people searching for something else to define themselves around.

The other effect of religion's decline in America affects the remaining believers as well as the nones. Nonreligious people have no illusions that a deity will come and intervene in their lives. If they believe they live in a dangerous world, they have no hope that any god will swoop in to stop them from being mugged, for example. In that way, the lack of religion only adds to people's "mean world" worries. However, even the believers who argue that God has a plan or that "everything happens for a reason" are not immune to Mean World Syndrome. They, too, become pulled into the spiral of negative thinking and confirmation bias. They are faced with a constant barrage of evil in the world, which they must reconcile with their notions of an all-powerful, all-good God. One must wonder if they ever look around at their world and question if God exists, and if so, if he would even bother to save them, should they need him.

THE AVENGERS: MORALITY, "FREEDOM," AND A NEW SECULAR PANTHEON

Marvel's *The Avengers* marks a crucial point in the surge of superhero films, the key plot point on the exponential curve marking the explosion of superheroes that our media is currently saturated with. Up to 2012, Marvel Studios had strategically built up momentum with the first two installments of the wildly successful *Iron Man* franchise, with *Thor*, and with *Captain America, The First Avenger*. Each of these films did well at the box office on its own. *The Avengers* brought together every

single one of these movie franchises in the first superhero "team-up" film of note, and it did so in a way that appealed to both the die-hard comic fan as well as the casual moviegoer. It is one of the top five domestic box office hits of all time, grossing $1.52 billion in the US and abroad.[14]

The story centers on Thor's adopted brother, Loki. After discovering his true parentage in the film *Thor*, Loki feels as if he has been cheated out of his chance to be king and comes to Earth with a powerful weapon and an alien army; his intent is to take over and rule as king. His goal is to subjugate humanity entirely to his will, a goal he proudly declares many times throughout the film. In his first scene, he states, "I come with glad tidings of a world made free." When questioned about what he intends to free the world from, Loki answers, "Freedom. Freedom is life's great lie. Once you accept that in your heart, you will know peace." He's very simply a tyrant wannabe, and it takes no effort beyond this to make the audience respond to the buzzword "freedom" and launch straight into hating him. Although he's painted as a very sympathetic villain (almost entirely due to the influence of Tom Hiddleston's portrayal), there is no question that his motives are completely, to-the-core evil. However, he's also the most honest voice in the film.

The Avengers fight the good fight for "freedom," and while this is as literal as it sounds for the citizens of this fictionalized version of New York City, it's not so true for the real-life audience watching their film. Nietzsche viewed worshipping God as an act of self-enslavement, and although superheroes aren't religious figures, their function in society has become that of secular gods. The creators of these films know and even reference this: in the second *Avengers* movie, the ending credit sequence is overlaid on a carved marble statue of the Avengers mid-fight. At first glance, it could easily be mistaken for a statue of Greek gods and goddesses. The difference between actual religions and the "worship" of superheroes is that superheroes demand nothing of their worshippers except viewership (and maybe the purchase of merchandise). There are no rules to follow, no commitments outside what each viewer wants to give. However, by kneeling before them, they affirm,

---

14 "All Time Domestic Box Office Results," Boxofficemojo.com, 2016.

with the same power as religious figures, that human lives have meaning.

When Loki says, "It's the unspoken truth of humanity, that you crave subjugation. The bright lure of freedom diminishes your life's joy in a mad scramble for power, for identity. You were made to be ruled. In the end, you will always kneel," he's not entirely wrong. The mad scramble for identity is one that occurs in almost every moment of human lives, both fictional and real. Choosing a favorite Avenger is no different than any other ultimately meaningless consumer choice, but by pledging allegiance to these fictional heroes, an audience can feel a deep sense of belonging and, therefore, a shared identity. The siren call to claim this easily adopted identity is difficult to resist. Obviously, not every person identifies as a superhero fan, but enough people do that American culture is being absolutely flooded with hundreds of variations of heroes, so there's one for every fan.

Perhaps the most important scene in the film occurs at the climax of the battle between Loki's alien army and the Avengers. New York City is besieged as the alien army comes pouring into the city via a wormhole in the sky. The police are wildly outmatched, their guns and training rendered entirely useless (although the Black Widow's pistols seem to work just fine against the aliens), and the Avengers are the only ones capable of helping. As Manhattan comes under attack, the Avengers do their best to hold off the fight and evacuate as many people as possible. However, the World Security Council makes a call to Nick Fury, the head of SHIELD, the government agency responsible for putting together the Avengers team. Instead of letting the Avengers fight the good fight, the World Security Council decides to cut their losses and nuke Manhattan, civilians included. Confident in his misfit team and voicing serious moral issues with a nuclear strike against a civilian population, Nick Fury refuses to acknowledge their orders. A rogue pilot follows the Council's orders anyway and fires a nuclear missile at Manhattan. As this happens, Iron Man gets a brilliant idea. He flies under the missile and holds on, redirecting it into the wormhole that the alien army is still coming through, and the nuke flies into the alien mothership.

It's a moment of celebration—the civilians have been saved, the aliens all died *Phantom Menace*–style when their mothership was bombed, and the Avengers have triumphed—but the event has serious, terrifying implications that are never addressed. A security council representing all the world nations unanimously agreed to a nuclear strike against the island of Manhattan? Without question or a second thought? This moment of fiction is accepted without a moment's hesitation by its viewers, perfectly representing the cultural distrust of their government and even showcasing a disdain for their assumptions of government morality.

The Avengers spend a great deal of time in their film rescuing random civilians rather than focusing their energy on taking down the big bad guy, which says that you, random citizen, are deeply important, maybe more important than anything else. Audience members leave with absolutely no reservations about the assumption that their safety is top priority. When a constantly decreasing amount of Americans feel that their government would protect them the same way, that feeling of safety is highly prized. The consequences of this effect are part of the reason that superhero media is saturating culture to the degree it is. They make us feel safe in a turbulent world, and they give us meaning on an increasingly crowded planet, surrounded by an ever-expanding universe of largely empty space.

THE DARK KNIGHT: NIHILISM, ABSURDISM, AND ORDER

The second film in Christopher Nolan's *Batman* trilogy, *The Dark Knight* remains as the sixth most successful domestic box office hit, ranking just one spot below Marvel's *The Avengers*. It is regarded as one of the most thoughtful superhero films to date and has won multiple Academy Awards as well as a Golden Globe. Heath Ledger posthumously won countless awards for his show-stealing performance as the Joker. *The Dark Knight* is very similar to *The Avengers* in that they are both culturally ubiquitous films, regardless of people's interest in superheroes.

The Dark Knight's main villain, the Joker, is possibly the most obvious representation of nihilism in any superhero movie yet. Unlike in *The Avengers*, where freedom is the purported goal of the heroes, freedom is the villain's aim in *The Dark Knight*. The Joker doesn't mean just your usual First Amendment stuff, either; his goal is freedom *from* everything—total anarchy. While a world with no rules or systems of governance is not inherently a bad one, in a world filled with the kinds of sinister characters who live in Gotham, it would mean instant chaos. Like *The Purge*, but every single day. Needless to say, it would be a terrifying world to live in.

The most interesting part of Nolan's Joker (aside from Heath Ledger's outstanding performance) is his seeming lack of intent. At one point, he describes himself as "a dog chasing cars. I have no idea what I'd do if I actually got one." Unlike Loki, who desires power, authority, and respect—the trappings of monarchy—or the mobsters of Gotham, who are all after money, the Joker isn't interested in any of that. He's not after a girl; he's not after respect; he doesn't even want vengeance. As Batman's assistant Alfred puts it, "Some men aren't looking for something rational, like money. Some men just want to watch the world burn." Someone like this is scary for the obvious reasons: the Joker can't be reasoned with, bought, or threatened, which means that his chances of seeing that global bonfire are significantly higher than your average thug's.

He's also terrifying on an altogether different level. The Joker represents the destruction of systems, and even when our governing systems are as corrupt as they are in Gotham, they are one of the few reliable things that give us security, both physical and existential. There's no reference whatsoever to any sort of religious belief in Gotham,[15] and the place is generally seen as godforsaken, in most understandings of the word. The government is so corrupt that even the police lieutenant's right-hand woman is buyable. With no hope that a religious figure will save the city and dwindling hope in what remains of the governing structures, Batman exists to provide the citizens of Gotham with a sense of safety.

There have been many discussions on what Batman represents and what he means, but I would argue that what he represents, above all else, is *order*. Batman might argue that he represents "justice," but that's not true. He prioritizes the people he personally cares about over what is technically "fair" or "just" all the time. This isn't a bad thing, necessarily; he's a human, and he's not perfect. That's part of the reason we love him so much. The Joker, who is inarguably his antithesis, says "I'm an agent of chaos. The thing about chaos? It's fair." And in a way, this is true as well. The Joker doesn't seek out particular victims—he picks on everyone, at random. In this twisted way, the Joker is more "fair" than Batman. He's chaos at its purest, anarchy personified. His opposite, Batman, doesn't stand for what's fair. Batman represents order, the *systems* of justice. His desire to right wrongs and punish wrongdoers is not about justice. It is about balance. The architecture of his lab is an excellent example of this: clean, white, open space, and above, a gridded, glowing ceiling. The Wayne Enterprises building is built in a similar image: it's modern, logical. His building has square edges and square windows—clean, simple lines. Bruce Wayne surrounds himself with order and spends most of his time inside a chart-style room.

Although he knows more than anyone how corrupt the governing systems in Gotham are, Batman upholds them. He seeks to clean them, straighten out the crooked parts until the system is once again functional. The Joker, on the other hand, wants to rip the systems apart. In possibly one of the most famous scenes from the movie, the Joker burns a massive pile of cash with a smile. "It's not about the money," he says. "It's about sending a message. Everything burns." His goal isn't just to destroy Gotham. It's to point at the absurdity of the systems themselves. While both the Joker and Batman stand outside these systems, the Joker attempts to demonstrate the pointlessness of attempting to control the world, Batman attempts to strengthen the city's ability to control the world.

This is a possible explanation for why the Joker is so rampantly popular. People are increasingly more aware of the corruption of the institutions they had previously put their faith in. Priests are found to have molested children, government officials are caught embezzling money, and these stories only multiply across the front pages of newspapers. We know that things are eroding, and it makes us more likely to latch onto a villain who recognizes something we see as truth. It also explains

---

15 Gotham is generally agreed upon to be a more dystopian model of Chicago. If we model Gotham's religiosity on Chicago's, it still is weak enough that it doesn't really matter.

the reason we crave a hero like Batman: he knows the systems are corrupt, but he promises to uphold and fix them for us.

The battle between Batman and his nemesis is not necessarily just a battle between good and evil; it's a battle between meaning and meaninglessness. The Joker's nihilism is modeled most closely after Albert Camus's absurdism (though notably without his positive attitude), which was best explained in his essay *The Myth of Sisyphus*.[16] Absurdism is best defined as the conflict between the human desire for life to have inherent meaning and the simple fact that life does not inherently have meaning. While Camus argues this is an opportunity for beauty—a chance to create our own meaning—the Joker puts a far more negative twist on it. In Gotham, this is best seen in Batman's attempt to control his city in a way that makes it, in his view, better—more meaningful. The Joker exists to counteract this attempt to instill inherent meaning in human life. He even says to Harvey Dent at one point, "I try to show them how pathetic their attempts to control things are." This moment is one of the most direct attacks on meaning, and it's the reason we're so desperate for him to lose. If the Joker wins, then life is absurdly, hilariously meaningless. Everything is chaos, and there is no reason for anything. If Batman wins, the world is still fighting an uphill battle against entropy, but the fact that he keeps fighting means that the systems are worth saving, optimism is a view worth having, and human existence is ultimately meaningful. Even if the battle lasts forever, that's fine—because the fight itself gives us meaning, too.

WONDER WOMAN: ONE FOR THE GIRLS

Wonder Woman (2017) was met with overwhelming praise, scoring a 92 percent on Rotten Tomatoes. Although men tended to review the film a full point (out of ten) lower than women, the film was overall agreed upon to be one of the DC Extended Universe's (DCEU) best films so far—though many don't view that as a particularly high bar to clear. Written by Zack Snyder and Patty Jenkins and directed by Patty Jenkins, the film has the same "villain problem" that most of the DCEU has: one-dimensional baddies who, honestly, don't diverge enough from their cardboard-cutout comic book origins to justify their existence on the big screen. However, Patty Jenkins recognized the hugely underserved audience of female fans and gave them what they'd been asking for. Her Wonder Woman is strong and smart, and she refuses to give casual chauvinism as much as a second thought. She wears her traditional outfit, but despite the costume's origins, the film is shot without the male gaze that American viewers are accustomed to seeing. [17] We get no awkward up-the-skirt angles. Diana does not coquettishly bend over for things, and although there's a whole scene dedicated to her changing outfits, there's not a single "oopsie" shot meant to sexualize her. It's great—a big step forward for a genre that has been famous for catering to the male power fantasy. But does it really change anything, philosophically? Does her film say anything radically different than these other superhero films? It doesn't seem like that's the case.

Wonder Woman confirms the existence within the DCEU of the actual Greek pantheon of gods. Diana grows up on Themyscira, the mythical home of the Amazons, sheltered from time itself as they prepare endlessly to defeat Ares, the Greek god of war. After centuries of peace, a spy crash-lands a plane in the water nearby, bringing with him a battling group of soldiers armed not with spears and swords but with the far more advanced weaponry of World War I. Diana learns from the spy about the ongoing "war to end all wars." Diana is sure that this bloodshed is the work of Ares and sets out with the spy to kill him, wanting to end the fighting and save lives. She is exposed to all the horrors of war and ultimately does find and kill the god Ares, in the process realizing that she is not just an Amazon but also a child of Zeus.

Not only does Diana physically act out Nietzsche's famous "we have killed God"; she goes one step further and *replaces* God herself. There can be no better visualization of the death of old religious institutions and their being replaced with a new pantheon than in *Wonder Woman*. Diana literally kills Ares, the last of the old gods, and takes her place in the Justice League,

16 Albert Camus, *The Myth of Sisyphus and Other Essays* (New York: Knopf, 1955).
17 Jill Lepore, "The Surprising Origin Story of Wonder Woman," *Smithsonian Magazine*, October 2014.

the pantheon of new gods. In her battle with Ares, she commits to protecting human life, even though Ares points out that the humans in her film are largely undeserving of her protection. "It's not about deserve," she says to him, "It's about what you believe. And I believe in love." Sure. Love works, but what this really signifies is dedication. In order for Diana's power as a mythic goddess-heroine to be reassuring and comforting as opposed to terrifying, she promises, as does Thor, our other god-hero, that her truest purpose is to protect human lives, even at great personal cost or when they don't necessarily warrant saving.

Wonder Woman is a nice break from the veritable deluge of male heroes and provides a much-needed, refreshingly feminist take on what heroism can look like on the big screen. Philosophically, however, it doesn't do anything new. Wonder Woman exists to combat nihilism in the face of institutional collapse by insisting on the uniquely special and worth-saving qualities of humanity. She may claim to stand for love, but like the other heroes in our new pantheon, Wonder Woman provides us not with love but with a sense of security in an existentially fraught time. The only addition to the superhero landscape is a new altar for goddess worship. Let's hear it for the ladies.

BLACK PANTHER: UTOPIA IN WAKANDA

To say that *Black Panther* was well received might be like saying that Bill Gates has some money. The film surpassed *Titanic* as the third highest-grossing film of all time in the US and had the fifth-largest opening weekend in history, making it one of Marvel's most successful films to date.[18] The release of *Black Panther* was a movement, an argument in and of itself for why media representation matters. There are countless studies on how positive representation in media can change the way that people, especially kids, think about themselves and their potential. One man even started a GoFundMe to send

Black children to see the film in theaters.[19] In this new age of mythic hero-gods, it's more important than ever that children are given the opportunity to experience seeing themselves as superheroes. So far, our pantheon of superheroes has been alarmingly homogenous: mostly straight white men named "Chris." If we're going to continue upholding the superhero as the ultimate vision of human perfection, it's vital that our superheroes are more than just a bunch of ripped white guys.

Black Panther stands out for more than just its addition of Black characters to the Marvel universe. Wakanda, the home country of T'Challa, who is the Black Panther, is a technological utopia. Hiding under the guise of being nothing more than a poor farm country in Africa, Wakanda is a super-advanced, wealthy society that has kept its perfection largely due to its lifelong isolationist foreign policy. This is unorthodox for superhero films, wherein we usually don't get visions of utopia. The idea of a utopia is more alien to us than Krypton. Our world is one that seems to us to be far more dystopian, and our heroes have had to shift to fit that perception. *Black Panther* goes further than other superhero films because of its exploration and critique of the inherent assumption we carry that utopias couldn't really work.

The antagonist of the film, Erik Killmonger, is a Wakandan who grew up in Oakland, California. With his father's stories about the beauty and perfection of Wakanda as a comparison to the oppression of Black people that he witnessed every day, Killmonger began to hatch a plan to take over the Wakandan government so he could use their resources and technology to arm oppressed people around the world. His methods are brutal and violent, but his ultimate goals are deeply sympathetic. Killmonger harshly criticizes Wakanda for its lack of intervention around the world. Though they had the technology and resources, they never provided aid to other countries, no matter what, to preserve their secrecy. In the Marvel Universe, Wakanda borders Kenya, Ethiopia, Uganda, and South Sudan. Wakanda has medical technology that can heal severed spines and nearly unlimited amounts of wealth, but they didn't intervene when one of their close neighboring countries

---

18   Alissa Wilkinson, *"Black Panther* Just Keeps Smashing Box Office Records," *Vox*, April 20, 2018.
19   Clarisse Loughrey, "There's a GoFundMe to Help Children in Harlem see *Black Panther," The Independent*, January 11, 2018.

endured a genocide that killed millions. Killmonger doesn't mention Rwanda by name, though he does point out injustices against "people who look like us" many more times throughout the film, to which T'Challa never has a good answer. Knowing that despite his good intentions, Killmonger's success would mean worldwide calamity, T'Challa fights him for the right to be king. He argues that Killmonger can't just arm thousands of people without creating world war, but ultimately, he ends up taking some of Killmonger's ideas and creating Wakandan outreach centers around the world.

It's novel that our hero actually learns something from the villain, but more interesting is that Wakanda is allowed to remain a utopia by the end of the film. It's not because of the government system or anything inherent to the people of Wakanda themselves: it's because of who is king. During Killmonger's brief stint as king, Wakanda proves itself to be a place like any other: prone to corruption, easily tainted by the destructive urges of the outside world. However, with T'Challa, a superhero, as king, Wakanda resumes its place as a utopian society, now an even more idyllic place that strives to improve not only itself but the world around it.

Nietzsche wrote about the Übermensch in exactly this way. The Übermensch was meant to be a leader, a philosopher-king who would recreate morality in accordance with his own will. Despite our perceptions of corruption and violence in the world around us, Wakanda can still make sense as a utopia because all of the power there belongs to a myth figure we trust. Unlike any other governing body or person we are capable of imagining in fictional films, T'Challa *can* create a utopia because he's not just any king: he is a modern Übermensch.

CONCLUSION

When most people (including many media scholars) think about superhero films, often their reflex is to think of them as shallow media artifacts. At most, they're viewed as only analyzable through a feminist lens as male power fantasies or artifacts of fanboy nostalgia. The misconception that superhero films are not worthy of analysis is unfounded and ignorant of the power these films have. That they have financial power is indisputable within two minutes of research, but their sociocultural power is just as evident.

These films are influencing our society by filling cultural voids. For one, they present the world as violent as we already believe it to be, which makes them feel real to us. They give us a world just like ours but with an ultimate hero, a perfect protector, to fantasize about in order to feel a little better about the world around us. Especially when trust in government has never been lower in this country, it is a comforting fantasy to imagine heroes with perfect moral compasses who will always make the right choice, even if the "officials" tell them not to. In a time when religion in America has never been less prevalent, superheroes provide us with a secular pantheon before which to kneel. This provides us with the same sense of community that religions boast, and with the same existential protection. These "solutions" might make us feel better about the problems we face, but it is troubling that we are choosing to handle our existential problems via escapist fantasy.

Superhero films comprise one of the most prevalent, profitable genres of film at this moment in time. To assume that they do not affect culture or society and to deny them study is naïve. At the same time that caped vigilantes dominate the box office, they dominate our minds, and it is important to ask what happens when they do. What other effects do these new mythological figures have? What other messages do these media carry? Are these a helpful coping mechanism for a culture feeling adrift? Or are they pure escapism, a way of letting us feel as if we have worked to solve problems without any of the hard work required to actually do it?

As long as trust in the institutions that organize our society continues to remain low or continues to sink, I think it is likely that these caped heroes will remain with us. They may change form, shifting from comic book heroes to gritty TV antiheroes, as some scholars believe.[20] Or they may stay as they are for a while longer: bright spots of color and larger-than-life personalities that cloud out an otherwise dark and existentially threatening world.

---

20   Spencer Nitkey, *Simulating Sisyphus: Tracing Camus's Absurd Hero Through Contemporary Television Antiheroes*, manuscript in preparation.

AFROFUTURISM IN *BLACK PANTHER*: COUNTERNARRATIVES AS KEYS TO ALTERNATE FUTURES

OSEI ALLEYNE is a double-major PhD and former post-doc in Anthropology & Africana Studies at the University of Pennsylvania. He is now Assistant Professor at the Department of Media Studies and Production in the Lew Klein College of Media and Communication at Temple University. Alleyne writes on global urban music subcultures, Afro-diasporic religions and art-movements such as Afrofuturism.

Afrofuturism challenges the Western stereotype of African backwardness and the notion of Africa as dystopia. The habitual exclusion of people of African descent from discourses regarding technology and the future is the result of intimidating and pessimistic predictions of the African social reality in the decades to come.

Adriano Ellia, 2014

Black people live the estrangement that science fiction writers ... talk about. All those stories about alien abduction ... and alien spaceships taking subjects from one planet to another ... they've already happened. How much more alien do you think it gets than slavery ... than entire mass populations moved, genetically altered [and] forcibly dematerialized. It really doesn't get much more alien than that!

Kodwo Eshun, 1996

It's after the end of the world ... don't you know that yet?

Sun Ra, 1974

Smashing box office records and setting off a firestorm of affective African American jubilation, Disney's cinematic mounting of Marvel Comics's *Black Panther* has not only effectively launched a Black superhero into the global consciousness, but it has achieved the near-impossible balancing act of generating both massive ticket sales and streams and a notable measure of critical acclaim. Importantly, director Ryan Coogler's *Black Panther* has also significantly contributed to a once-obscure and yet growing Afrofuturist arts movement—one invested in centering the experience of Afro-diasporans within speculative fiction. Resplendent in its rendition of a technologically superior African nation and its warrior king, and yet probing in this fictive nation's haunted relationship with its African American diaspora, Coogler's vision speaks volumes to themes of counternarrative and transcendence, but also alienation and fugitivity that are foundational to Afrofuturism.

The term *Afrofuturism* was coined by literary critic Mark Dery to describe the marginalization of African American life-worlds within mainstream science fiction. Dery (1994) observed that "African American voices have other stories to tell about culture, technology and things to come." Immediately thereafter, scholars such as Allondra Nelson, Greg Tate, Reynaldo Anderson, Kodwo Eshun, John Akomfrah, and DJ Spooky

337

have richly theorized the term, recognizing in the work of early-twentieth-century and emerging Afro-diasporic artists an underrecognized and yet compelling engagement with the worlds of science, technology, and speculative fiction. Quite counter to both real-world and sci-fi mainstreams, which generally rendered nonwhite bodies as marginal to society and largely invisible in projected future worlds, African American and Afro-diasporic creators have seized upon speculative fiction as imaginative spaces within which to rethink problematic pasts and to author redemptive and liberatory futures.

Much of the reflexive scholarship on Afrofuturism labors to capture the philosophical breadth that its canonical and contemporary artists convey in their oeuvres. Indeed, in many ways Afrofuturism is in part a revisionist movement, retrospectively mining the works of W.E.B DuBois, Ishmael Reed, Ralph Ellison, and authors of the Black Radical tradition for foreshadows of Afrofuturist thought. Another branch of the movement celebrates, curates, and critiques the work of contemporary artists, linking these to their progenitors in the Harlem Renaissance, Negritude, and Black Arts movements of the twentieth century. The perhaps more slowly accreting contemporary Afrofuturist movement manifests itself today as a more fragmented, decentralized, networked discursive space in the contemporary social media age—graphic artists, game designers, and visual artists projecting their speculative visions on Instagram, Facebook, YouTube, and other platforms.

Indeed, Afrofuturism is a broad and flexible category. It requires a consideration of the ideological and epistemological innovations of its key proponents to unearth the philosophic backbone upon which Afrofuturist visual, textual, and musical worlds hinge. This lineage generally positions Le Sony'r Ra, also known as Sun Ra (born Herman Poole Blount, lived 1914–1993), at its origin point—if not for his outright conception of the Afrofuturist movement (Sun Ra's work predates the coining of the term), but for his embodiment on stage, in recordings, and in film of Afrofuturism's most abiding principles, philosophic outlooks, and aesthetics. Claiming to be an alien from Saturn, Sun Ra infused his Arkestra jazz ensemble's performances with an idiosyncratic and metaphysical creed that sought to waken his audiences to the cosmic possibilities he believed lay dormant within them. Garbed in phantasmagoric

costume, Sun Ra would lead his commune of musicians in extended renditions of his recorded material for rapt audiences. In the campy and yet penetratingly philosophical short film *Space Is the Place* (1974), Sun Ra etches out these protocols, pitting his alien alter ego against earthly pimp characters and state agents, as he attempts to rescue the souls of lost inner-city youth.

Other musicians follow in Sun Ra's tradition, notably Parliament-Funkadelic band leader George Clinton, whose stadium stage-shows featured Clinton emerging from his own landed starship *The Mothership Connection*, the vehicle within which Clinton would transport his funk audiences to their true homes in outer space. "Free your ass and your mind will follow!" and "Paint the White House black"—as Clinton's more directly political mantras would ring. Pioneering Jamaican reggae producer and audio-engineer Lee Scratch Perry, who wrote and produced some of Bob Marley's early discography, would invoke the sensations of both endless abyss and yet limitless possibility through his reverb-drenched and hauntingly remixed reggae music instrumentals—in many ways achieving with dub reggae what Sun Ra had with jazz and what Clinton later engaged with P-Funk—that is, an exploration of the future through music.

At the dawn of hip-hop culture, Afrika Bambaataa would take up Sun Ra's and Clinton's caped regalia, infusing early hip-hop with esoteric African American religiosity and drawing into his Zulu Nation formulation the symbolic systems of the Five-Percent Nation, the Moorish Nation, the Nuwabians, the Nation of Islam, and others (Branson 2018). Indeed, Afrofuturists would draw as easily on ancient Egyptian symbolism as they would on the syncretic religious practices of the Black Atlantic—Vodun, Santeria, Candomblé (Brooks 2018)—and southern US practices of root-working (Barber 2018), reapplied to alternate futures. The southern Black Christian Church of the US tradition also has been theorized by some as an interstellar vehicle of sorts—transporting, transformative, recuperative, and transcendental in its uniquely ecstatic and embodied practices of worship—indeed, a sweet chariot swinging low, coming forth to carry the faithful home (Rollins 2018).

Hip-hop progenitor Bambaataa and his seminal release *Planet Rock* (1982) would later influence X Clan, the Native Tongues collective, Digital Underground, Kool Keith, MF Doom—and, importantly, OutKast, whose albums *ATLiens* and *Aquemini* stand as something of Afrofuturist tomes within hip-hop culture. Taking the torch from OutKast's André 3000, the alternative-musician most closely associated with Afrofuturism today is Janelle Monáe. Monáe's *Metropolis: Suite 1* (2007) and *The Archandroid* (2010) concept albums featured a narrative in which the artist embodied a twenty-second-century android, Cindi Mayweather. Upon falling in love with a human, and thereby transgressing strict social codes, Mayweather is castigated, ostracized from her community, and forced to flee disassembly. According to Monáe in an interview in 2011, "I date only androids" and "I speak about androids because I think the android represents the new other." By rereading historic racial boundaries as applicable to a future dystopic human/artificial intelligence divide, Monáe's necessarily racialized android both takes up and pushes Donna Haraway's (1991) gender nonbinary cyborg feminism as well as the "deracinated images of robots and cyborgs" in the celebrated Afrofuturist novelist Octavia Butler's *Xenogenesis* trilogy (1987–1989). According to Lisa Yaszek (2002), Butler uses android figures to explore "the appropriations of black labor in the name of ... global progress."

AFROFUTURISM IN CONTEMPORARY CINEMA

Notable in the realm of more recent cinema is the latest edition of the Gene Rodenberry saga, *Star Trek Discovery*. This seventh Star Trek teleseries seemingly responds to the implicit Afrofuturist critique of early sci-fi—that is, the high body count and premature killing-off of already obscure Black characters in twentieth-century narrative schemes. Instead, *Discovery* launches its leading character, Michael Burnham, played with subtlety and urgency by actor Sonequa Martin-Green, on a trajectory from fugitive officer to a messianic Red Angel figure and ultimately into the captain's chair. In this manner, *Discovery* expands on what progressive cache the broader series had accumulated with actor Nichelle Nichols's Lt. Uhura character in the late 1960s—centering, as its narrative, on an ultimately redemptive Black female experience.

Immediately foreshadowing the excitement of *Black Panther* was Jordan Peele's lauded (2018) *Get Out*. In this admittedly more horror-oriented bit of cinema, a young Black male protagonist, once hypnotized and hurled into the depths of the "sunken place" by his new white girlfriend's psychoanalyst mother, very nearly has his body snatched—appropriated and auctioned by an avaricious coven of wealthy elderly white suburban folk. In "Jig-a-boo," perhaps the most exciting episode of the more recent Peele-produced (2019) teleseries *Lovecraft Country*, the character Ruby Baptiste is rescued from street-harassment by a white male figure, who later seduces the vulnerable woman—offering her the power to take on the embodiment of an upper-class white lady and with it a respite from the daily racial aggression she faces. After Ruby finds her new reality to be equally unacceptable and involuntarily molts her newly acquired white skin, her lover later shape-shifts, revealing himself to be Christina-Braithwaite, daughter of the Grand Wizard of the Society of the Ancient Dawn—a malevolent figure who has plotted Ruby's entrapment all along.

Of special note is Damon Lindelof's (2019) HBO teleseries remix of the DC Comics–originating (1986) *Watchmen*. Fronted by notable African American actors Regina King and Yahya-Abdul Mateen II, this retake on the original Alan Moore and Dave Gibbons narrative draws poignantly on the real-world 1921 Tulsa Race Riot, in which white mobs burn to a cinder the enviable Black Wall Street—a fledgling oasis of Black commerce in the Jim Crow South. In the world of *The Watchmen*, heroic Oklahoma police agents, the most talented among whom is Regina King's "Sister Night" character, don vigilante masks in order to effectively combat the Seventh Cavalry, a white supremacist criminal organization that has long infiltrated the highest ranks of the local police force. Notable in this remix is Mateen's portrayal of the *Watchmen's* post-human, godlike, and transformative figure Dr. Manhattan—a blue-skinned, near-omnipotent figure whom the Calvary intend to melt down for his quantum powers. Here, Mateen captures well Dr. Manhattan's existential contradictions as an alien stowaway on Earth—a character who is nether-worldly in his ability to inhabit various time-scapes simultaneously and yet is radically naive and ultimately susceptible to human political intrigue. Drawing on a tradition that hails John Sayles's (1984) *The Brother from Another Planet* and John Akomfrah's (1996) documentary *The*

Last Angel of History as low-budget and yet theoretically groundbreaking Afrofuturist tomes, these pieces frame the contemporary moment within which *Black Panther* has emerged.

COUNTERNARRATIVES AS KEYS

Afrofuturist work is driven at its core by counternarratives that intervene against the Enlightenment and industrial-era thrust of Euro-American-centered notions of progress and of (H)istory—notions of modernity founded in, for example, the German philosopher Georg Wilhelm Hegel's (1807) *Phenomenology of Mind*. Here Hegel invokes a highly teleological and linear reading of history, in which, for example, the West, having rapidly advanced through lower stages of civilization and having acquired superior reason, stands as the pinnacle of human progress and freedom, a chronotype at the other end of which the indigenous and African mind remains static, out of time, in a perpetual state of unconscious savagery and as such justifiably enslavable—doomed to be involuntary conscripts to Rudyard Kipling's (1899) poem "White Man's Burden," and dragged kicking and screaming into Western futures.

In response to, but also transcending, these Eurocentric framings, Afrofuturists author counternarratives that center the epistemologies of Afro-diasporic peoples, and further marginalized groups among them: a bottom-up history designed to artfully upstage the histories of the dominant order. Novelists, filmmakers, graphic artists, gamers, and other visual artists draw on precolonial African and indigenous symbolic systems of antiquity and reapply these to the protagonists who populate their futurist worlds. Importantly, according to literary critic Kodwo Eshun, the most compelling Afrofuturists go beyond crudely Manichean inversions of the twentieth-century racial order that seek to simply supplant a White for a Black Supremacy (Eshun 2003). Critical Afrofuturists center histories that challenge racialized as well as gendered, classed, sexualized, and ableist supremacies altogether. Here the intersectional critical lenses of Black femme

Afrofuturists offer additional tools with which to unmask more deeply layered and less immediately discernible circulations of power.

It is through these counternarratives, these radical rereadings/reinterpretations of deep time and space, that Afrofuturists project and launch their own (dys)utopic futures—visions that either implicitly or explicitly critique the present, real-world, sociopolitical, economic, and racial orders. Additionally, it is an Afrofuturist penchant for ironic interpretations of space-time—an embrace of its elliptical rather than linear propensities—that allows artists such as the jazz futurist Sun Ra and Parliament Funkadelic's George Clinton, for example, to don the headdress and symbols of Kemetic Egypt and Ancient Nubia in live performance, even as they embody advanced, interstellar heroic aliens from the future—self-charged with rescuing Black, brown, and otherwise entrapped earthlings from the chains of mental slavery.

Classic Afrofuturists thereby engage an ancient-alien theory in which, unlike its popular History Channel iteration, indigenous peoples are, in actuality, the original aliens (predictably wiped from Eurocentric history texts), who have in antiquity ceded earthly populations with technology and who are justified in their return, through Afrofuturist imaginaries, to redeem their mistreated descendants. Here, I picture pseudo-archaeologists Erich Von Daniken and George Tsoukalas arriving on yonder native shores with camera crew behind them, imploring the indigenous people to "Take me to your ancient alien leader"—when in fact it is the very natives before them who have in antiquity authored the so-called "extraterrestrial" genius that these self-styled academics so crave to rediscover.

But this inability of nineteenth- and early twentieth-century scientific-racist frames to recognize the antecedent genius of indigenous cultures is not new to Afrofuturists. These artists generally read, in the experience of kidnap, chattel slavery, and genocidal racial terror, the very definition of alienation and othering. Afrofuturists read in the modernist project itself—the engineering of the New World, the generation of a racialized lumpen proletariat, the arbitrary harvesting of which is an integral part of the imperial project—a racial violence that, the Afropessimist school agues, has at its center the ontological binary of white supremacy and anti-Blackness. Far more pressing than the wistful speculations into extraterrestrial intelligence, Afrofuturists contend, is the bodies of descendants of the world's oldest cultures that today have been relegated to alien status—"othered" by the dominant order. It is in the inclination of the Afrofuturist, then, to resurrect the enslaved, who having experienced the world from its margins—its slave dungeons, slave skiffers, plantations, and salt mines—are morally equipped to be reincarnated as the enlightened extraterrestrial: ominous in power, agency, and influence and yet morally motivated by a wisdom of the ages.

COUNTERNARRATIVES IN *BLACK PANTHER*

It is squarely Afrofuturist counternarrative that lies at the center of *Black Panther*'s fictive nation, Wakanda—a space whose highly localized history runs diametrically opposite to the general thrust of the transatlantic slave trade, the European "Scramble for Africa," and the continent's subsequent colonization. Uniquely fortunate, or perhaps especially fated that it might wield such power, Wakanda is in its antiquity smitten by a meteor shower drenched in Vibranium—a manna from the heavens of a sort—a singularly indestructible and yet highly malleable ore, one upon which Wakanda will build its technologically and morally advanced civilization. Through its internal Vibranium industries, Wakanda launches itself into to an orbit safely beyond the reach of Euro-American (neo)colonization and global geopolitics.

That this vision of Wakanda was first authored by two Jewish-American comic book authors, some six months before the emergence of the real-world, Oakland-originating Black Panther Party in 1966, is perhaps more a testament to the global news mediation of guerilla-styled anticolonial struggle on the African continent in the moment—of Mau sniffers rebels fighting the British in the colonial Kenyan hills—than it is to an unencumbered moment of cross-cultural exchange, though there is a notable history of civil rights movement solidarity and coordination among these groups. Still, some argue that Stan Lee and Jack Kirby's launching of Marvel's first

Black superhero as continentally African rather than African American offered itself as a way to circumvent the immediate racial powder keg of the period—particularly as such politics shifted from the nonviolent civil disobedience of Dr. Martin Luther King toward the Black Power exhortations of Stokely Carmichael and the arms-bearing, second-amendment right-asserting Panther movement of Huey Newton and Bobby Seale.

And yet Lee and Kirby's sketchings of Wakanda as a superior global nation, with a moral and technologically gifted warrior king, remains a resonant symbol of inversion in contemporary popular culture, reinfused as it has been by later African American auteurs Reginald Hudlin and Ta-Nehisi Coates, and most recently the director Ryan Coogler. These contributions to the Panther mise-en-scène have generally been to realign the Wakandan hero with the concerns of African American superheroes, with Hudlin going as far as to marry the Panther to the Black woman-warrior Storm of the X-men in one of his authored sequences. Hudlin also closely allies T'Challa to the bulletproof Black American hero figure Luke Cage in others. For his part, Coogler scores points for his cinematic reimagination of T'Challa's royal guard, the Dora Milaje—women-warriors whose acuity on the battlefield often surpasses that of the Panther himself. Indeed, General Okoye could likely do more damage than could T'Challa in a Panther suit. And herein lies the rub: Could not Okoye herself reign, given her greater clarity of focus and equal battle prowess?

FEMINIST AND POSTCOLONIAL YEARNINGS IN *BLACK PANTHER*

In one moment within the action-laced swell of the film's climactic battle scene, Okoye presses her estranged lover and traitor Lieutenant W'Kabi into abject submission at the end of a spear on the battlefield, inverting dominant tropes of greater masculine prowess at arms. When implored by her partner as to whether she should indeed kill her love if he would not submit, Okoye responds, "For Wakanda, without question!"—embodying the kind of abstracted altruism and dedication to national duty that normally is reserved for heroic male cinematic figures of yore. And while some critics have pointed out that such inversions serve only to reproduce violent masculine performatives in Black woman-face, actors Lupita Nyong'o, Danai Gurira, and Letitia Wright infuse these characters with intellectual clarity and palpable agency.

Within the trajectory of these framings lies a resistant, if potentially revolutionary, rethinking of a global space and people as being technologically and morally advanced, in an unbroken genealogy with their ancient and precolonial traditions of self-governance—rather than being the unwitting subjects of colonization, human trafficking, and institutional slavery. This is a notable, if fantastical, part-Afrocentric, part-postcolonial reading of Africa and Afro-diasporic people that continues to resonate with cinema-goers the world over—the retention of royalty and bloodline, perhaps differing from the more Marxist-infused anticolonial struggles across the real-world continent of the 1960s and 1970s. Nonetheless, the conception that is Wakanda turns author Joseph Conrad's (1899) *Heart of Darkness*, and its literary inauguration of the Dark Continent in Western literature, on its head. Rather than finding ever more degenerate and cannibalistic tribes as Conrad's white male protagonist travels up the Congo River and into the heart of Black Africa, instead Marvel's Wakanda is a reimagination of a timeline—one in which an African nation avoids cultural disintegration in the face of colonialism, as in, for example, Nigerian author Chinua Achebe's (1992) *Things Fall Apart*, first published in 1958. Untouched, Wakanda and its king must instead descend from the nation's own moralist repose to rescue the world from a self-generated crisis.

The vibranium-generated wealth of *Black Panther*'s Wakanda also operates as an inversion of the African resource-curse, an Afro-pessimist 1980s media discourse within which resource-rich African nations (gorged with diamonds, lithium, quartz, oil, and bio-diversity) remain nonetheless cursed—doomed to have their fledgling national projects ever-undermined by their former colonial masters and the predatory mining corporations and private armies that the old crowns and global governing bodies enable. Here, Coogler's resource-rich T'Challa runs counter to, for example, the lowly fisherman Solomon Vandy, the character played by Djimon Honsou in the 2006 box office hit *Blood Diamond*, who is forcibly interned into diamond mining by marauding rebel armies in Sierra Leone—his only escape the blood-conflict diamond that he uncovers while under duress. If only Sierra Leone was in fact resource-poor, Vandy might have avoided enslavement altogether. As for Wakanda, this fictive holy city is able, through its vibranium-laced legacy, to remain cloaked to the rest of the global community, flying under the radar of the international global speculators and geopolitics.

ALIENATION AND FUGITIVITY

Despite such a moving construction of a transcendental and redemptive Afrofuturist space, classically Afrofuturist themes of alienation and fugitivity abound in *Black Panther*—particularly where the film takes up the struggle between its hero and its villain: the reigning Wakandan king T'Challa and his bastardized, orphaned, estranged, and outlawed African American cousin and potential claimant to the throne, Killmonger. Indeed, the stark contrast in ontological positionality between the two characters heightens an already tenuous real-world diasporic relationship in which continental and diasporic Africans confront, in each other, the traumatizing specters of the Middle Passage—each from different sides of the Black Atlantic (Gilroy 1995). This conflict is poignantly captured at the very end of the film's climactic battle: the already impaled villain Killmonger, dying in the arms of the hero T'Challa, gasps, "Just bury me in the ocean ... with the ancestors who jumped from the ships. Because they knew that death was better than bondage."

Indeed, it is in the chronotypic drama of this narrative thread that the film is most captivating to Afro-diasporic and otherwise progressive audiences, riveting moviegoers to the point of ecstatic exuberance. This has been captured in so many viral YouTube clips: moments of cultural nationalist dress and both staged and spontaneous performance in the foyers of so many North America and continental African cinema chains—corporate spaces reappropriated, if only momentarily, for public displays of affective community. Indeed, it is in the pregnant and yet precarious possibility of this confrontation between continental and diasporic kin (in T'Challa and Killmonger or, better here, N'Jadaka)—this renegotiation of accountability and culpability, of claims and counterclaims—that African communities at home and abroad glimpse the potential in their own futures. Coogler's *Black Panther* seems to suggest—that is, it is only through a calling to account of the circumstances under which colonial domination had come to ravage Africa and its diaspora—that a genuine pathway forward could be devised.

While T'Challa's initial inclination is to withhold vibranium from an unfit world and thereby assure Wakanda's secrecy, national security, and supremacy, Killmonger's is to reappropriate and redeploy Wakanda's ore deposits for the military liberation of subject peoples the world over—"by any means necessary," as the Malcolm X–attributed phrase borrowed from existential philosopher and psychologist Frantz Fanon would assert. That the villain's ideological bent and mission remains immediately more morally compelling and politically radical than the hero's is a notable narrative paradox that places *Black Panther* squarely within a critical Afrofuturist frame—one willing to confront internal African demons even as it slays old colonial dragons. In this imaginary, the recently crowned king and heir to the Panther super suit is forced by his nemesis, on pain of death and dissolution, to clarify his ideological orientation, recalibrate his moral compass, and reassess his self-narrative as hero. For what cause and for whose benefit does the Black Panther fight? For the exceptionalist, isolationist, and conservative Wakandans exclusively? Or for oppressed peoples broadly? Could, for example, the cause of the fictitious Black Panther match the urgent resolve of the real-world Panther party?

That ultimately even Coogler's progressive *Panther* narrative vanquishes Killmonger, and with him the more radical approach to liberation, speaks volumes to the film's embeddedness within Western liberal entertainment and finance markets—assemblages that require narrative resolutions that deliver on blockbuster-styled marketing protocols. Here even Coogler's critical inner narrative gives way to a conciliatory ending in which Wakanda realigns with Western forces, embodied in American CIA agent Everett Ross, to defeat Killmonger. Indeed the naive T'Challa, moved by Killmonger's revealed life story of abandonment as scorned son of an expatriate Wakandan dissident, only belatedly readjusts his nation's mission—on the one hand crushing Killmonger's attempted coup, and on the other hand setting up an NGO-style outreach science program deployed in Oakland's inner-city neighborhoods. This is a move that some critics have said is arguably as paternalistic to Black American communities as any Euro American aid NGOs are to spaces on the African continent (Derkson 2018). And yet, the very idea that a continental African community could take up such a cause on American soil is the very stuff of Afrofuturist projection. In many ways, jazz musician Sun Ra presented himself, in performance with his Arkestra ensemble, as having returned from outer-space to engage in projects of metaphysical outreach, rescue, and recovery for lost earthlings.

THE DISNEYFICATION OF *BLACK PANTHER*

Whether or not this narrative resolution is the (un)conscious work of the Walt Disney Company and its Marvel Cinematic Universe machines to privilege the least Western-threatening among these competing models of liberation is for critical audiences to determine. Whatever the takeaway, the ramification of Disney's juggernaut cultural power in, for example, its recent acquisition of the *Star Wars* and Marvel intellectual catalogs—even appending Beyoncé's (2020) *Black Is King* to its recent *Lion King* reboot—remains necessarily vested in the radical commodification of even the most particular of indigenous legends and arcane tracts of folklore—the most radical narratives of anticolonial warfare—and to exploit such cultural capital. For this is the stuff of Hollywood cinema, is it not? The effective teleporting of working-class audiences, black and brown people among them, into the vicariously reenacted embodiments of often politically sanitized historic and imaginary heroic figures of yore—or so the Frankfurt School might contend. Nonetheless, the tension between Coogler's ambitious diasporic drama and Disney's ultimate framing produce, in *Black Panther*, a compelling if somewhat vulnerable work of Afrofuturist imagination, driven by the very Hollywood financing that produced Disney's early-twentieth-century sambos, imperialist

Donald Ducks, and docile damsels in distress—and yet searching to rethink African trauma as a path to Afrofutures, as in *Black Panther*. Has Hollywood by now appropriated one of the as-yet most probing artistic explorations of African diaspora? Or have Afrofuturists like Coogler successfully stormed the barricades of corporate finance and bent the very markets, within which African bodies were once sold, to the will of the dispossessed? But I digress.

Awed by T'Challa's sublime moment of triumphant arrival in the ghetto after vanquishing his enemy, young Black Oakland teens ogle at his uncloaked spaceship, as the king instructs his sister and science minister in her new task of outreach in the inner city. Here, T'Challa's Wakanda eschews Killmonger's radicalism for a Western-aligned and evolutionary approach to change—in many ways reaffirming the order that the superhero, or the revolutionary figure, might lash out against. And this begs the question of whether our contemporary comic book–derived superheroes, literary figures that they are, could be equated with revolutionary figures. Given the thrust of history, it would appear that for Afro-diasporic peoples this is a must—that our futurist protagonists must at the very least be born with a veil, be gifted with second sight, and wield a Du Boisian "double-consciousness"—a lens through which to interpret and act in the world, a lens informed by the historic position of the Black experience.

THE AFTERLIVES OF AFROFUTURISM

Actor Chadwick Boseman's highly private battle with colon cancer (which he must have suffered while on set) and far too premature transitioning have rightfully vaulted him into the realm of not only cinematic but also real-world, if posthumous, superhero. Indeed, Boseman's riveting on-screen embodiments of cultural and political icons Jackie Robinson, Thurgood Marshall, and James Brown remain a poignant reminder of how fragile and precious African American models of excellence remain in our culture. By now muralized and memorialized in a fashion similar to the recent passings of hip-hop artist Nipsey Hussle and superathlete Kobe

Bryant—Boseman's departure has added a layer of poignancy, if not outright legend (the kind Disney could never engineer), to the *Black Panther* project—one that is indeed worthy of further deconstruction. Disney's corporate entanglements notwithstanding, and the thespian's legacy considered, it is not difficult for the Afrofuturist purveyor to imagine Boseman now piloting Clinton's Funkadelic Mothership into the cosmic horizon, en route to rendezvous with Sun Ra to take up his position as icon and ancestor—there to beckon us to fearlessly create the Afrofutures that we dare imagine.

REFERENCES

Achebe, C. 1992. *Things Fall Apart*. New York: Alfred A. Knopf.

Adriano, Elia. 2014. "The Languages of Afrofuturism." *Lingue Linguaggi* no. 12, 83–96. https://doi.org/10.1285/i22390359v12p83

Akomfrah, J., dir. 2016. *The Last Angel of History*. Icarus Films.

Anderson, Reynaldo, and Jennings, John, eds. 2018. *Cosmic Underground: A Grimoire of Black Speculative Discontent*. Chicago: Cedar Grove Publishing.

Barber, Tiffany. 2018. "Root Working's Recursions in the Black Imagination." In *Cosmic Underground: A Grimoire of Black Speculative Discontent*, edited by John Jennings and Reynaldo Anderson. Chicago: Cedar Grove Publishing.

Beyoncé. 2020. *Black Is King*. Null/Parkwood Entertainment/Disney.

Branson, Ryan. 2018. "Out of the Night, into the Night: The Moorish Effect on the Enlightened and Modern Worlds. In *Cosmic Underground: A Grimoire of Black Speculative Discontent,* edited by John Jennings and Reynaldo Anderson. Chicago: Cedar Grove Publishing.

Brooks, Kinitra. 2018. "Ontologies of Orisha Technology: West African Spirituality Afrofuturistic Visions." In *Cosmic Underground: A Grimoire of Black Speculative Discontent,* edited by John Jennings and Reynaldo Anderson. Chicago: Cedar Grove Publishing.

Butler, Octavia. 1987. *Dawn*. New York: Warner Books.

Conrad, Joseph. 2006. *Joseph Conrad's Heart of Darkness*. New York: W. W. Norton. First published 1899.

Däniken, E, and Burns, K. 2010. *Ancient Aliens: Season 1*. Prometheus Entertainment/A&E Networks.

Derkson, Kyle. 2018. "Racism and Capitalism in *Black Panther*." *Journal of Religion and Film*, 22 (1): Article 40.

Dery, Mark, ed. 1994. "Black to the Future: Interviews with Samuel R. Delany, Greg Tate, and Tricia Rose." In *Flame Wars: The Discourse of Cyberculture*. Durham, NC: Duke University Press.

Du Bois, W.E.B. 2014. *The Souls of Black Folk*. New York: Library of America. First published 1903.

Eshun, Kodwo. 2003. "Further Considerations on Afrofuturism." *CR: The New Centennial Review 3*, no. 2: 287–302. http://www.jstor.org/stable/41949397.

Gilroy, Paul. 1995. *The Black Atlantic: Modernity and Double-Consciousness*. Cambridge, MA: Harvard University Press.

Haraway, Donna J. 1991. "A *Cyborg Manifesto*: Science, Technology, and Socialist-Feminism in the Late Twentieth Century." In *Simians, Cyborgs, and Women: The Reinvention of Nature*. New York: Routledge, 149–181.

Hegel, Georg W. F. 1967. *The Phenomenology of Mind*. Translated by J. B. Baillie. New York: Harper Colophon. First published 1807.

Kipling, Rudyard. 2020. "The White Man's Burden: A Poem." In *The Poems of Rudyard Kipling: Poetry for the Ages*. Independently published. First published 1899.

Lindelof, Damon. 2020. *Watchmen*. Warner Bros. Television.

Majors, J. 2021. *Lovecraft Country: The Complete First Season*. Warner Bros. Television/HBO.

Monáe, J. 2010. *The Archandroid*. Atlanta, GA: Wondaland Studios.

Peele, Jordan. 2017. *Get Out*. Universal Pictures.

Posada, Tim. 2019. "Afrofuturism, Power, and Marvel Comics's *Black Panther*." *Journal of Popular Culture* 52, no. 3: 625–644. https://doi.org/10.1111/jpcu.12805.

Reed, Ishmael. 1972. *Mumbo Jumbo*. YouTube.

Rollins, A. 2018. "The Oddities of Nature: Bishop Charles H. Mason and the Realm of the Supernatural." In *Cosmic Underground: A Grimoire of Black Speculative Discontent*, edited by John Jennings and Reynaldo Anderson. Chicago: Cedar Grove Publishing.

Sayles, John. 2020. *The Brother from Another Planet*. Swank Motion Pictures.

Semel, D. 2018. *Star Trek Discovery: Season One*. Paramount Pictures.

Sun Ra, Joshua Smith, and Jim Newman. 1974. *Space Is the Place*.

Yaszek, Lisa. 2002. *The Self Wired: Technology and Subjectivity in Contemporary Narrative*. New York: Routledge.

Zwick, Edward. 2006. *Blood Diamond*. Warner Bros. Pictures.

BLADE RUNNER 2049: CLI-FI AND FUTURE EARTH SCENARIOS

ANTONIO LÓPEZ, PhD has a research focus on bridging ecojustice with media literacy. His most recent book is *Ecomedia Literacy: Integrating Ecology into Media Education* (Routledge). He is Associate Professor of Communications and Media Studies at John Cabot University in Rome, Italy. Resources and writing are available at: https://antonio-lopez.com/

Is the following scenario real or science fiction? A planet is suffering ecological breakdown. Climate chaos, biodiversity loss, ocean acidification, drought, soil degradation, deforestation, and water contamination generate threat multipliers like economic crises, war, famine, pandemics, and forced migration, and hence a manifold, global political, economic, and social crisis. You would be forgiven if you mistook our world for a dystopian science fiction film. But this is our reality.

Rarely a day goes by without a major headline about catastrophic weather events (hurricanes, floods, droughts, fires, etc.), new scientific studies raising the alarm of dangerous climate temperatures, the decline of regional ecosystems (deforestation, topsoil loss, permafrost thawing, melting glaciers, fires, new diseases, animal die-offs, biodiversity loss, extinction, etc.), or human-made ecological disaster (oil spills, plastic pollution, nuclear contamination, toxic algae blooms, etc.). It's hard not to be shell-shocked by pervasive, dreadful news about the environment. But given that the political system seems to be doing little about it, it's often up to artists—in particular, filmmakers—to make sense of it all so we can process what is happening with our planet's ecosystems.

So, though it's cliché to say that science fiction is never about the future, but the present, eco-apocalyptic cinema is especially directed toward current environmental trends. It's also true, to paraphrase Susan Sontag, that sci-fi is always about disaster. Such is the case of *Blade Runner 2049*, a futuristic postmodern film *par excellence* that explores the disastrous present. Unlike the original *Blade Runner* film from 1982, the loss of an ecologically coherent world is an especially stark theme in *2049*.

This fits within an emerging genre of literature and film called cli-fi (climate fiction), which grapples with the consequences of our rapidly heating atmosphere and what a future Earth might look like.

IT'S EASIER TO IMAGINE THE END OF THE WORLD (THAN TO STOP CLIMATE CHANGE)

End-of-the-world spectacles are often about scenario testing, warning, or catharsis. They process general anxieties about the future while also offering utopian possibilities, even if these are not obvious in the plot line. By amplifying (and even exaggerating) the negative consequences of current trends, they also point to ideals that we can be drawn on to fix current trends. As Pat Brereton (2004, 185) argues, "'Nature' and its co-present ecological sensibility can evoke a potentially subversive, even utopian, presence as opposed to the 'cultural logic' of contemporary Hollywood film." Novelist Margaret Atwood (known for *The Handmaid's Tale* and her cli-fi trilogy *MaddAddam*) notes, "Within each utopia, a concealed dystopia; within each dystopia, a hidden utopia" (quoted in Kaplan 2016, 13).

Since the 1960s there has been an increase in disaster, zombie, and postapocalyptic films that point to some generalized angst about an impending end of the world. When it comes to sci-fi, there is a long tradition of movies dealing with prevailing anxieties that are the "dispirit of the age." In the 1970s, *Soylent Green* and *Logan's Run* offered scenarios related to a panic about overpopulation. In the 1980s, fears of nuclear warfare and oil wars gave us *The Day After* and the *Mad Max* series. Terrorism become a central plot device for action movies of the 1990s. By the 2000s, we arrive at pandemics and climate change as prominent anxieties, best expressed by *The Day After Tomorrow* and *Contagion*.

There is a well-known phrase that "it's easier to imagine the end of the world than the end of capitalism." If you accept that our environmental troubles are connected to our economic priorities (such as promoting endless growth, consumerism, and unquestioned technological progress at the expense of devastating the environment), then imagining and scenario-testing the consequences of this behavior becomes one of the ways that cinema responds to social crisis. Popular culture is better adept at incorporating and processing whatever angst is being experienced about the world than it is at actually trying to change it. By managing social anxieties, films can also perform closure and catharsis. It puts potential catastrophe into the safe container of cinema so we don't have to live it in real life.

To explain this creeping foreboding about the future, media theorist Richard Grusin (2004) postulates that media "premediate" the future by preparing the public for potential disasters or future technological developments and practices. *Blade Runner 2049* prepares us to deal with not just an environmentally bleak future, but also a future in which the only manifestation of the state is the police, and biopolitics are dominated by a single company called Wallace Corporation. The film presents fears about GMO foods, robotics, algorithmic artificial intelligence, and climate change. Movies about pandemics perform a similar function, although no film could really prepare us to deal with COVID-19. Thus, there are limits to the ability of cinema to fully premediate the future.

More recent ecocinema scholarship talks of pre-trauma disorder: fears about the future, especially the climate, are already traumatizing us in the present (Kaplan 2016). But with the exception of natural disasters, the effects of most environmental problems are slow and gradual. Even though extreme weather events are increasing, the worse effects of climate change are long-term and may not be experienced in our lifetimes. Translating geological time to media's fast-paced, condensation of time, is no easy task.

Which begs several questions. Can the climate crisis be represented cinematically? Can cli-fi change our behavior? Some ecocinema scholars argue that Hollywood spectacles allow us to "feel" and "see" something that is otherwise intangible to our senses. Other scholars believe that spectacle films are just that, and they end up only entertaining us without leading to further action (see this volume's discussion of *Avatar*). But by scenario-testing (asking "What if?" questions), cli-fi cinema offers us a future we can contemplate. We can visualize our future selves and how we might respond under such conditions.

PK DICK'S POSTMODERN PROPHESY

Blade Runner 2049 has its origins in Philip K. Dick's 1968 novel *Do Androids Dream of Electric Sheep?* Dick was a preeminent sci-fi writer who explored the schizophrenia of modernity, probing the increasing difficulty for people to navigate a world full of environmental threats, income inequality, social breakdown (violence, cults, terrorism), technological control of multinational capitalism, and the loss of spirituality and religion. In his stories there are often ominous, unseen conspirators controlling reality. His characters experience confusion over what is real and what is constructed, the loss of a stable or objective reality, simulacra, and alternate universes. They often confront existential issues, such as what constitutes an authentic human.

That Dick would be a sage of postmodern sci-fi is reflected in the number of movies based on his stories: *Screamers, Paycheck, Impostor, The Adjustment Bureau, Next, The Crystal Crypt, Minority Report, Total Recall,* and *A Scanner Darkly*. TV series include *The Man in the High Castle* and *Philip K. Dick's Electric Dreams*. Dick's stories also presaged the dark paranoia of the *Black Mirror* Netflix series.

In the original *Blade Runner* novel, the natural world has largely been wiped out by a nuclear war. Real animals are rare and are considered prized status symbols. Genetic engineering and robotics have advanced to the point that androids ("replicants") are made to perform as slaves. A group of elite Nexus-6 replicants go rogue and it's the job of the detective and bounty hunter ("blade runner") Rick Deckard to track down and eliminate them. The inability to distinguish between replicants and humans is one of the core themes of the book. A test to find if they experience empathy (especially concerning animal welfare) is the only way to probe the difference.

Ridley Scott's 1982 film adaption of the book, set in 2019, captures the main themes of the novel but departs substantially from the plot. The film's design and style led it to becoming one of the most celebrated cult sci-fi films of the twentieth century. David Harvey's (1989) *The Condition of Postmodernity* outlines how both the aesthetics and the politics of *Blade Runner* represent the nexus of postmodern themes of the 1980s.

It was set in a time when in the United States and other rich nations were transitioning to postindustrial economies that farmed out manufacturing to countries like Mexico and China. It marked the visibility of an increasingly globalized and stratified economy and multicultural society, with the film's location, Los Angeles, serving as the quintessential poster child of a degraded world and future shock. Megacities are a common motif of this genre (*WALL-E, Judge Dredd, Elysium*), so Los Angeles serves as a perfect setting for the film's themes. Ironically, film companies first settled in Hollywood due to stable weather, climate, and light so that they could film year-round. Perhaps as a sign for the failure of modernity's utopian project, the destruction of Los Angeles (and the Hollywood sign in particular) is a constant trope in disaster films.

Blade Runner's opening sequence features a polluted nighttime cityscape of acid rain, gas explosions, and smoke. It shows a completely artificial environment composed of synthetic light. Its claustrophobic atmospherics gives the sense that its inhabitants are trapped. Their only escape is to the off-world colonies of Mars, which are advertised on giant floating video billboards.

The film's streets are filled with video ads and neon in multiple languages, all markers of consumer capitalism in a postindustrial, globalized world. Class stratification and income inequality are reflected in architecture and spatial relations, with the uber-aristocracy occupying monumental buildings fashioned after Mesoamerican pyramids, perhaps nodding to past civilizational collapse. The city reflects the rise of gated communities by showing us a world where the super-rich are separated from the rest of society. Unlike the shiny white surfaces typical of futuristic sci-fi films, in *Blade Runner* working-class and poor people live in postindustrial urban decay.

Built by the Tyrell Corporation, replicants are dubbed to be "more human than human." They are indistinguishable from humans in appearance, but they possess deadly, superhuman strength. Replicants have implanted memories and fake family photos, so they believe they have had "real" childhoods. This reflects two important postmodern themes. First, what is real is based on that which is mediated, such as photos offering "proof" that memories exist. Second, identity is unstable, since it is not grounded in real experience or history. Without a stable identity, people just have roles to play (such as having your destiny predetermined by the Tyrell Corporation). They (like us) live in a fragmented and discontinuous world.

Being parentless represents the idea of a free-floating signifier. Without a direct connection to its origins (the chain of signification), a sign has no basis in the "real." To be born (as opposed to being made) is to have a soul. In this case, replicants have no actual history. They are hyperreal beings that have replaced natural humans, and therefore they have no ecological identity that ties them to the natural world. Unlike "original nature," to replicants time and space have no integrity.

It is this last point that makes *Blade Runner*'s ecological messaging so urgent. As argued by Fredric Jameson (1984), under the postmodern condition of late capitalism there is no alienation, because there is no coherent self to be alienated from. For environmental action, the sense of alienation caused by the loss of nature is a powerful motivating force. But if you do not know what you have lost, how can you fight for something you don't know?

Interestingly, *Blade Runner*'s highly derided first commercial release (the vastly improved director's cut was released many years later) closes with Deckard and his replicant love interest, Rachael, fleeing LA to a green forested region, symbolizing a return to some green utopia, the classic Western environmental trope of a "return to nature." *Oikos* ("home" or "household" in Greek) is the root of "ecology" (and "economics"). In the universe of *Blade Runner*, there is no "home" and hence no ecological integrity.

THE *2049* ECO-REBOOT

What *2049* captures differently than the first *Blade Runner* film is ecological catastrophe. *2049* reveals the radiation zone and devastated natural world of the original novel—there are no forests to flee to. To the south of the city is a zone made entirely of trash. And in a nod to the actual devastating impacts of e-waste, we see a massive sweatshop filled with orphaned children hammering away at circuit boards to mine precious metals (again note the theme of parentless children).

Climate change is represented by the massive seawall guarding LA from the rising ocean caused by global heating. It's always overcast or raining, indicating that weather is no longer stable. There is also a shortage of potable water.

In many ecoscience fiction narratives, organic vegetation is greatly prized in such synthetic or ecologically wasted worlds. This is definitely a common theme in *Blade Runner 2049*, which depicts highly industrialized agriculture. The only green vegetation we see is in the virtual reality constructed by the replicant memory designer, Dr. Ana Stelline. But rather than a farmer of organic matter, she is manufacturer of digital worlds. Ecological agency is characterized by the manipulation of signs.

Otherwise, the landscape is comprised of charred soil, dead trees, perspex-canopied greenhouses, and solar arrays. In the opening sequence, an original Nexus-6 replicant, now a farmer, is cooking with fresh garlic, which Agent K has never smelled before. The image of a replicant farmer—even if it's aquafarming GMO worms—recalls the more nostalgic and authentic vision of ecology, at the same time showing a glimpse of post-human agriculture (Brereton 2019, 109).

Loneliness leads to a dependence on media (such as holographic companions) to provide companionship and escape in an otherwise claustrophobic environment. In the *Blade Runner* films (and other postmodern cinema), media are not just prosthetics but spaces that are inhabited.

Like the first film, in *2049* the central character is a blade runner, Agent K (Ryan Gosling). Throughout the film Agent K questions his identity and origins. He's not sure if he is a replicant or if his memories are real. Due to a prior nuclear event, most records of the past were wiped out. Data are therefore unreliable.

His only possible connection to being an authentic human is a carved toy horse made from real wood. This is a rare and coveted item because living trees no longer exist. Possessing organic (authentic/pure) matter signifies the ultimate prize of the "real." This ties to the importance of maintaining an ecological identity through connection to nature, the only thing that is true and authentic.

The primary biopolitical conflict to be resolved in *2049* has to do with whether replicants can reproduce themselves through birth. In our world (the "real world") the inability to reproduce is actually the marker of extinction, which is the death of birth. The power of life or death is determined by corporations that own the replicants, or the police who patrol the boundaries between real and fake humans. Even Agent K's girlfriend, Joi, which is an AI hologram, can exist only if the technology that maintains her can be sustained.

FUTURE FEARS (AND HOPES)

The aim of modernity is liberation from the material constraints of the environment. But the quest to transcend the limits of the physical and material world leads to disaster. Modernity is a project of progress, technology, and bettering humanity through the combination of philosophy, science, and art. Modernity is also predicated on clear divisions between humans and nature, and mind from body, which makes humans distinct and exceptional. Postmodernism marks an epistemological crisis that shatters these divisions. It asks, What is valid knowledge, and How do we know what we know? The *Blade Runner* series points to this rupture.

The films demonstrate the death of the modern subject: we are not rational or autonomous but constructed, best represented by the replicants. With no fixed points of reference or origins (who are the parents?), the past (and nature) is unreachable. Thus, postmodernism marks the demise of history. And without truth or foundational knowledge, it also indicates the end of metaphysics.

Another postmodern theme is that signs and symbols are unstable: they change meaning according to context, and knowledge is produced under conditions of power. In *Blade Runner*, the lack of a basic knowledge of one's own history—as demonstrated by the orphaned children or replicants with no real childhood—is like broken signifiers.

The break from nature is the ultimate loss of an authentic connection to the real. Only the wooden horse can genuinely reconnect the characters to history and nature. Ironically, the film is in fact connected to the real. The greenhouses were filmed in Spain, the junkyards are in Hungary, and the dark polluted dronescapes were shot in Mexico City.

To summarize, *Blade Runner 2049* denotes a number of fears about the future. Ecocide is represented by the scorched earth and trashed wastelands, best expressed by the young prostitute who states, "I've never seen a tree before." The lack of real animals signifies a wider extinction (when Agent K encounters a dog, he asks, "Is the dog real?"). The lack of fresh food and the synthetic farming are another indicator of ecological (and economic) collapse. Curiously, the memory maker, who is the first replicant/human hybrid, has environmental sensitivity, and must live in a hermetically sealed, sterile dome.

But the flipside of these fears are hopes. As indicated, one of the primary themes of the *Blade Runner* franchise is the question of what makes us human. The test is empathy, and the loss of empathy leads to ecocide.

Humanity is also linked to animal welfare. Without real animals, humans are alone and incomplete. The loss of a coherent environment creates a kind of homelessness. Bees and trees represent that which is real and should be cared for (bees, which are fundamental to pollination, are threatened in real life by the industrial use of pesticides).

The optimistic strand of postmodernism is the problematization of binaries that we inherited from modernity. Creating a wall between humans and nature, and between humans and machines, points to the problem of how much these concepts are actually cultural constructs. By the end of the film, we find that the characters that express the most humanity are not even human. So, if nature and humanity are constructs, they can be reimagined.

The postapocalyptic sci-fi film *Mad Max: Fury Road* asks the question, Who killed the world? *Blade Runner 2049* tells us. Ecocide is entirely the fault of humans. But there are glimmers of hope where the sublime can be invoked. During the opening segment, Agent K finds a small yellow flower at the base of a dead tree. Later in the film he discovers hives and marvels at the bees, which represent the return of life. Flashes like this for our future selves can reconnect the chain of signification back to the home planet.

REFERENCES

Brereton, Pat. 2019. *Environmental Literacy and New Digital Audiences*. London: Routledge.

Brereton, Patrick. 2004. *Hollywood Utopia: Ecology in Contemporary American Cinema*. Portland, OR: Intellect Ltd.

Grusin, Richard. 2004. "Premediation." *Criticism* 46 (1): 17–39. https://digitalcommons.wayne.edu/criticism/vol46/iss1/3.

Harvey, David. 1989. *The Condition of Postmodernity: An Enquiry into the Origins of Cultural Change*. Cambridge, MA: Blackwell.

Jameson, Fredric. 1984. "Postmodernism, or the Cultural Logic of Late Capitalism." *New Left Review* 1 (146).

Kaplan, E. Ann. 2016. *Climate Trauma: Foreseeing the Future in Dystopian Film and Fiction*. New Brunswick, NJ: Rutgers University Press.

DARK SKIES PHILOSOPHY

BARRY VACKER

FIGURE 10.6.1   The Milky Way above the Rio Grande River and Big Bend Ranch State Park in far west Texas. Photo by Morteza Safataj, Big Bend Conservation Alliance website.

This reading was originally published in *Curious* (November 14, 2020), a publication inside *Medium*.

LOOKING OUT AND AWAY

What if the "Dark Skies" movement might be the most important long-term idea for our civilization and life on Planet Earth? What if a new philosophy can generate new dreams, desperately needed amid the waking nightmares haunting our lives and civilization: climate disruption, environmental destruction, antiscience worldviews, conspiracy theories, and racism and nationalism? What if Dark Skies is the natural light we need, if only we will look out and away from ourselves, away from our species?

As seen in the Milky Way image above (figure 10.6.1), we can gaze upon the starry skies with awe and wonder, contemplating about the deeper meaning silently embedded in the dark skies at night. However, this is not true of 80 percent of people living inside skyglow cities have not seen the Milky Way in its radiant beauty. Think about it—80 percent of humans have never seen the image above, which is the source of Earth and every living thing on it, including humans. Having lived without ever seeing our origins: that makes me sad.

One of the reasons so few people have seen the Milky Way is because it is getting harder to find night sky locations free of artificial light. Most of our state and national parks are tainted with light pollution—but not all of them. This photo of the Milky Way was taken on the border of Texas and Mexico, with the Rio Grande seen running along the right of the two-lane highway.

On the left side of the highway is the edge of the Big Bend Ranch State Park. Nearby is the Big Bend National Park, and both parks are among the largest in America in addition to being very remote. El Paso is five hours by car from where this photo was taken, while hipster Austin is a nine-hour drive. To get to these dark sky parks, you really have to want to go. Most everyone in hipster Austin would rather spend nine hours taking selfies and looking for celebrities at the annual SXSW event rather than drive nine hours for star gazing! That's not to say Austin is alone in that—it's true of every city.

The image of the car's bright headlights on the highway is striking and philosophically revealing. No matter how remote the locale, we have extended our lights and technologies to lead us—and also trap us. Like the headlights that guide our night drive, our overall vision is trapped within the urban and mediated realms of artificial light, which contain our vision inward upon our species and ourselves. Thus, we are existentially removed from nature and the night skies. Of course, we cannot all get to remote areas. That's why we need to bring the dark skies closer to our cities and ourselves. Technology need not separate us from the universe, unless we remain fully wedded to the spectacle and hyperreality that dominate our cities and homes.

The absence of the Milky Way in our daily lives makes the Dark Skies movement seem irrelevant to ourselves, cities, and societies. Yet, hidden beyond the skyglow are the Milky Way and dark skies, suggesting our consciousness look away from Earth for a starting point for a new human philosophy. After all, all our bodies and brains are made of stardust—so perhaps it makes sense to look to the stars and Dark Skies for new answers to human problems, both ancient and contemporary.

"Dark Skies" refers to the worldwide movement (see https://www.darksky.org/) to protect the Milky Way from light pollution, efforts that have many practical benefits for humans and wildlife. To me, the Dark Skies movement suggests much more, precisely because its effect is to *re-orient our civilization* within nature and the universe and reestablish the human connection to the starry skies. Dark Skies is about looking out and away from humanity, casting our gaze into the Milky Way and beyond. Hidden in this change of gaze is a very different philosophy for our species.

Picture in your mind's eye the skyglow of our cities and the radiant Milky Way. In the contrast between the two is an opening, a space, a void—a chance to create a new philosophy for human civilization going forward in the twenty-first century and the still-new millennium. We have to start somewhere. Notably, this philosophy is grounded in science and aesthetics, combining our rationality with the emotions we feel toward the starry skies and our true place in the universe. Of course, there are serious implications for politics, economics, and consumer society, but those are not the starting points. This philosophy represents a worldview anchored in our scientific understanding of the universe and the sublime feeling beneath the dark skies, which combine to ground *a shared experience and universal narrative for the human species.*

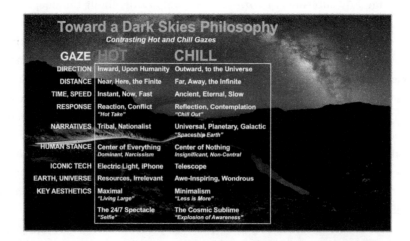

FIGURE 10.6.2 Table created by Barry Vacker, 2020. This reading draws from "Hot and Cool in the Media(S)cene," a 2018 *Medium* essay I authored with Julia Hildebrand. The essay won the John Culkin Award, an international award given annually by the Media Ecology Association, and inspired our art exhibit at the University of Toronto.

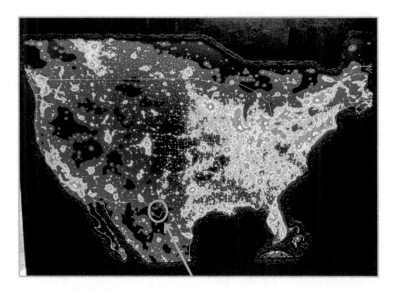

FIGURE 10.6.3 Map of light pollution in North America. (Note: The blue circle was added here to locate the International Dark Sky Reserve in Texas and Mexico.) This image is a section of "Electric Vanishing Points," a mixed-media installation currently in development; acrylic, pumice, and printed image, 6 feet × 8 feet. Barry Vacker, 2021. Printed on the canvas, the light pollution in North America is mapped in a spectrum of colors, which are simultaneously beautiful and horrifying. The beauty works to mask the effect of electric lights, which is to trap civilization in a spectral glow, as if we exist separate from nature. At the same time, the sprawl of the skyglow stretches across the continent in a perfect illustration of the Anthropocene—the human epoch in which we have transformed and disrupted the ecosystems of the Planet Earth (See Chapter 8).

Let's call this the "Dark Skies" philosophy, and it all begins with understanding the differences between the hot and chill gazes. "Chill gaze" is the philosophy illustrated in the Milky Way image within the table below (figure 10.6.2). Of course, the table does not present a complete philosophy, which is beyond the scope of this essay. However, the outline presented is a starting point for bringing the Milky Way down to Earth and stimulating our consciousness in new directions. Our cosmic origins ground a universal narrative and shared destiny for the human species, a concept which hides in the Milky Way pictured above the remote lands of Texas and Mexico.

WORLD'S LARGEST DARK SKY RESERVE

A profoundly hopeful border project is underway in the deserts of far west Texas and northern Mexico. The goal is to create the largest "International Dark Sky Reserve" on Planet Earth. The Dark Sky Reserve will span approximately fifteen thousand square miles in Texas and Mexico (see figure 10.6.3). As I have written in *Medium*:

> The world's largest International Dark Sky Reserve is an important signpost for a species lost in the skyglow of its 24/7 electric civilization. This Dark Sky Reserve brings together nature and science, ecology and cosmology, and peaceful cooperation along a contentious border—all quietly pointing toward a new philosophy for the human species.

This transborder project gives me hope for our species precisely because it directs and positions humanity's gaze away from itself. ***Changing the direction of the gaze changes our philosophy of existence.*** The Dark Sky Reserve allows humanity to see itself in terms of its true origins and place in the universe, thus providing an existential stance and universal narrative that are missing from the nationalistic and narcissistic worldviews that dominate our culture.

ORIGINS AND BENEFITS OF THE DARK SKIES MOVEMENT

The Dark Skies movement has its origins in Arizona. In the 1950s, to protect the dark skies for the Lowell Observatory, Flagstaff became the first city to pass ordinances to limit light pollution. By the 1970s, similar policies were enacted in Tucson to protect the night skies for the nearby Kitt Peak Observatory.

Tucson is home to the International Dark Sky Association (IDA), which was founded in 1988 to protect the dark skies and educate the public about the many practical benefits from reducing light pollution. These benefits include

- Lower energy costs for outdoor lighting;
- Health benefits for humans, including reduced risk of cancer;
- Reduced impact on wildlife and our planet's ecosystems;
- Increased tourism for towns and national parks that promote "astrotourism," where visitors come to see the Milky Way (and often bring their own telescopes);
- Protecting the dark skies for observatories and astronomical studies; and
- Making it possible for people to see the deep beauty of dark skies and feel connected to the universe.

To realize and expand these benefits, the IDA started the "International Dark Sky Places" program in 2001. The program honors proper stewardship of the night skies and includes Dark Sky Communities, Dark Sky Parks, Dark Sky Sanctuaries, and Dark Sky Reserves.

THE HOT GAZE: SKYGLOW AND SPECTACLE

Electric light is a media technology that has utterly transformed the modern world and human consciousness. Electric light has produced a 24/7 planetary civilization that displaces the Milky Way with an electric galaxy of light bulbs, streetlights, neon signs, and LED lights. Electric light also powers our glowing televisions, computers, laptops, tablets, and smartphones. These lights collectively create a skyglow civilization, networks of cities existing inside domes and spectra of light.

"Hot take" and "chill out"—these are two different responses to events, expressing two radically different existential stances toward the universe. In these two stances are two different philosophies oriented in two different gazes—hot and cool. The hot gaze is filled with artificial lights and glowing screens, while the cool gaze looks toward the natural light of dark skies and twinkling stars. Here, I will be referencing "Hot and Cool in the Media(S)cene," the international award-winning essay I authored with Julia Hildebrand (mentioned above with the table outlining Dark Skies Philosophy in figure 10.6.2).

THE 24/7 SPECTACLE

In our cities and towns, the hot gaze is dominant and directed ***inward*** upon our species, the endless antics of our 24/7 spectacle—filled with high densities of image and information, powered by electric energy. Smartphones get hot in our hand, laptops heat on our thighs. Screens offer instant proximity to all events, getting hotter every moment. Events coming at us, colliding and rubbing against one another, generating fission and friction. Acceleration, quick reactions, short attention spans, instant feedback loops. Temperatures are higher, tempers are hotter.

The 24/7 spectacle is a realm of mediated images and events, commodified into the exchange values of clicks, emojis, ratings, downloads, subscribers, and trillions of dollars for global media firms. In the skyglow and spectacle, we humans ***appear*** to be the center of the universe—the center of all value, purpose, and meaning.

Everything is near and now. Swipe right, scroll down, click here. Instant gratification. Circulation, replication, memes going viral. Siri and Alexa, Androids and iPhones. Apps galore.

In the spectacle, we dominate this planet. Tribalism, nationalism, and reality-TV stars reign supreme. Sexism, racism, fascism, and antiscience are on the march. Protests rise to resist, #MeToo, BLM, the Climate Strike, the March for Science. Conflict, consumption, and entertainment—all day, every day. Rants and rage, likes and love. Celebrities, footballers, billionaires, influencers, YouTube videos, and TikTok dancers. Fakes, facades, fast food, fast fashion, and faster connections. Streaming, bingeing, buying. Netflix, Twitter, Facebook, Instagram, Times Square, Las Vegas. Bright lights, big data, 5G, and 152″ plasma screens in our McMansions. Meanwhile, the COVID consumer society flows through Amazon and the fossil fuel CO_2 still spews into the atmosphere. We're living large.

Hot gaze, hot takes, hot planet. System overload. Relax and take a selfie.

THE CHILL GAZE

We know what happens to temperatures when the sun sets and the stars come out. The air gets cooler as the skies darken. Outside the city skyglow, we can direct our gaze toward the Milky Way. Like the cooling air, our gaze begins to chill. The chill gaze is grounded in the naked eye and telescopes, the ***cool media*** technologies that counter the heat of electric light and screens. Cool media are any technology that casts the human gaze away from itself, such as telescopes, space probes, and satellites that look away from Earth. Telescopes are the most radical media technology, precisely because they removed humanity from the center of the universe and ushered in science as a means for knowing our true origins on Earth and true place in the cosmos.

The chill gaze is an outward view, looking away from the instant of the spectacle, toward the distant and infinite of dark skies—the stars, planets, nebulae, and galaxies. Above is the Milky Way, below is Spaceship Earth, spinning on its axis as it orbits a nearby star. In the chill gaze, we are travelers in space and time. The universe is ancient, time seems eternal.

The chill gaze confronts lower densities, lower friction, and more remote events. Temperatures are lower, tempers are cooler. In the darkness, there is less artificial light and more natural light. Our eyes open wider, our minds wander and wonder. We see we're not the center of the universe, not the center of everything. We're the center of nothing. That's the big chill for human narcissism.

In the chill gaze, events slow, attention spans grow, reflection trumps reaction, borders and wars become artificial and absurd. Hot conditions are not visible. Large-scale patterns, movements, and locations become more apparent. Our eyes see planets and constellations—Saturn, Jupiter, Vega, Betelgeuse, Orion, and the Big Dipper. We see meteor showers and shooting stars, ending their billion-year journeys as burnt embers in the Earth's atmosphere.

Our most powerful telescopes map supernovas, black holes, and the cosmic web of two trillion galaxies—in a vast and ancient universe stretching across one hundred billion light years. Voids, holes, and emptinesses in outer space and in our philosophies become visible. Nihilism meets enlightenment. The universal over the tribal. Terrestrial heat replaced by the cosmic chill. There are no widely accepted political narratives in the cool. Hot politics freezes in the cosmic background temperature, tending toward absolute zero.

Chill out.

THE COSMIC SUBLIME

Wow! Awesome! Amazing! Incredible! Breath-taking! If you've seen the Milky Way in truly dark skies, then you know the feelings, which are almost indescribable. Modern philosophers call it the sublime.

If the spectacle is the heart of the hot gaze, then the sublime is at the heart of the chill gaze. The sublime simultaneously grounds our experience of the universe and our consciousness, the outer universe and inner being—***the starry skies and the aesthetic laws within.***

In the chill gaze, the infinitesimal and the infinite merge in our eyes to trigger the sublime—the deep feelings of awe, wonder, and reverence for the universe and our existence in it. The sublime is the singular transcendent experience that connects us (the infinitesimal) to the universe (the infinite), and it is shared by all of humanity—the only species on our planet to knowingly have the aesthetic experience of the majestic universe we have discovered. That's why ancient peoples had elaborate rituals and celebrations beneath the starry skies. We need new versions of these rituals, celebrations that unite the ancient and the futurist sensibilities. Astrotourism and Star Parties (see below) are mere first steps.

We experience the sublime when there's a tension between our perceptions and our reason, when our senses are ***overwhelmed*** yet our minds can still order the percepts into ***knowable*** and ***pleasurable*** concepts (concepts that are terrifying for some people). The sublime is what we feel when viewing the Grand Canyon, walking among the California redwoods, or looking up at the Milky Way.

Our naked eyes and telescopes are cool media, chilling us as we peer into the vast universe—immense scales of space and time; dynamic systems of stars, galaxies, supernovas, and black holes; sprawling voids and seeming emptinesses; and immeasurable realms of cosmic destruction and renewal. These distant objects and patterns stimulate our imaginations in awe-inspiring and wondrous experiences. Let's call this experience the *cosmic sublime.*

"STAR PARTIES"—ARRIVING AS INDIVIDUALISTS, LEAVING AS MEMBERS OF A SPECIES

Directly experiencing the stars and nearby galaxies from both a scientific and an aesthetic perspective is thrilling and inspiring. It's like what I have directly experienced at the McDonald Observatory (no connection to the hamburger chain) in the desert mountains of Texas. The dark skies are filled with the radiant Milky Way and have enabled me to experience the cosmic sublime and transcendent moments in which I am connected to a narrative much larger than the human-centered narratives that dominate the 24/7 spectacle.

Owned and managed by The University of Texas at Austin, the McDonald Observatory is the site for "Star Parties" every Tuesday, Friday, and Saturday night. Peering into very powerful telescopes, visitors view planets in our solar system, various phenomena in the Milky Way, and even other galaxies far beyond. During my many visits to the Star Parties, I have gazed upon the Andromeda and Whirlpool Galaxies, neighbors of the Milky Way. Andromeda is over two million light-years from the Milky Way, while the Whirlpool Galaxy is at least fifteen million light-years away.

Imagine seeing the tilted spiral of Andromeda, with photons from one trillion stars traversing the cosmic voids at the speed of light for two million years, light leaving that galaxy long before any human walked on Earth! On one particular visit, it occurred to me while I was gazing through one telescope that, after eons of space traveling, the starlight I was witnessing was passing through the telescope's lenses and into my own eyes, where photons from the Andromeda Galaxy were actually converting into bioelectrical patterns in my brain.

In that existential moment, my consciousness was connected with the cosmos, and a tiny fragment of the universe was directly aware of itself on a grand scale—connecting the infinite and the infinitesimal. Though tiny in relation to the cosmos, I felt the exaltation and affirmation of human existence, the power of human reason to grasp what I was seeing and sensing. It is likely I have never felt more inspired and at peace in the same moment. Mind-blown!

Visitors arrive at the Star Parties at sunset as individualists. As the Milky Way rises above, the individuality dissipates beneath the dark skies. Gazing at the Milky Way in wonder, peering through the telescopes and having their minds blown, visitors are quietly transformed into members of a species—the human species. The cosmic sublime is not a mystical or religious experience; it's a profoundly aesthetic, existential, and transcendent experience. That's the power of the cosmic sublime, that's the shared experience everyone feels, that's the effect of cool media and the chill gaze.

In the experience of awe, we can feel deeply connected to the universe or crushed by its infiniteness. In the sublime, we are rational and free, we feel exaltation and wonder before the stars, and we know we are tiny, yet brainy, creative, and curious. Science shows that our origins are in stars, that our destiny is to live and die, that species thrive and go extinct, and that our dominant narratives are wrong for our civilization and the planet. We know we face the paradox of our greatest intellectual achievements—we have discovered a vast and majestic universe in which we are insignificant and perhaps meaningless as a species. Or are we?

PLANETARY MINIMALISM

If there is one guiding aesthetic in the 24/7 spectacle, it is *maximalism* on all fronts. Increased consumption, larger screens, brighter images, bigger data, taller skyscrapers, faster speeds, greater populations, more stuff everywhere, more everything all the time. It's living large ... with plenty of bling!

The Dark Skies philosophy is not a call to return to a mythical past, to some quaint notions of living in villages or small towns of yesteryear. Rather, it is a call to embrace a different aesthetic vision to guide our civilization, a different system of values, a different visual narrative to guide our species, daily and long-term.

The Dark Skies philosophy implicitly reflects an embrace of *minimalism*, the aesthetics of less clutter and less ornament, with overall spareness and empty space. Minimalism is the aesthetic of *less is more*. At night, the world is minimalist and monochromatic, illuminated by the moon and the Milky Way. Inside our bright skyglow, we all stand out as individuals, as part of

Appendix A
Doublethink America

INTRODUCTION

Situated on our tiny planet, we are not gods. Neither are we fools. (Well, let's ignore our Twitter feeds for a few moments and stick to philosophy and science.) In an Alt-Fact America, where science and rationality are dismissed or under assault in our networks of echo chambers, it is important to understand how knowledge evolves and why some theories are indeed facts. And why some "alt-facts" are not equally true, but are fact-free falsehoods utterly unsupported by evidence or logic or clear reasoning.

First, it's important to realize that Alt-Fact America did not begin with the Trump–Pence administration, MAGA, or QAnon. Far from it. It began in the wake of NASA's Apollo moon landings. As historian Matthew Tribbe posits in *No Requiem for the Space Age*, when the Apollo era came to a close, "America [was] taking its first steps to nowhere, as its Space Age visions of progress and mastery of the universe succumbed to cultural forces that even the earth-shaking rockets of the Apollo era could not overcome."[1] Tribbe explains how the triumphs of Apollo were followed in the 1970s by a reactionary rebirth of old-time religion, New Age mysticism, and all kinds of pseudoscientific magical thinking.[2] The cool media perspective of Apollo was negated and denied, in no small part because secular philosophy did not develop a widely embraced narrative to counter the age-old tribalism and superstitions. It's clear the educational and cultural systems have failed to instill widespread scientific literacy and clear reasoning skills among the populace in the wake of the Apollo triumphs and the majestic universe unveiled by NASA and the world's astronomers.

Spanning pop culture and the popular consciousness, all kinds of antiscience and pseudoscience are circulating in the spectacle and the hyperreal—Bigfoot, Flat Earth, alien abductions, antivaxxers, "wellness" quackery, "New Age" nonsense, fake moon landings, climate change denialism, televangelists selling faith healing, celebrities hawking miracle cures, and creationists preaching a six-thousand-year-old universe. Doublethink is everywhere.

Growing up in Texas, I personally saw this happening in high school, in college, and all over the Lone Star State. I saw evolution and genetics routinely dismissed, mocked, or ignored, as were NASA's scientific discoveries. Sure, the space shuttle was semipopular, but the expanding universe not so much—13.75 billion years of cosmic evolution does not fit into the biblical timelines. It's hard to keep the Young Earth and Flat Earth at the center of everything in a universe stretching across 100 billion light-years. Time for some red lights.

SPECIAL EFFECTS FOR THE MIND

Like the coronavirus in the body, doublethink is sophisticated in how it operates in the brain, essentially creating special effects for the mind—cognitive illusions for a pop consciousness untethered from reality. Throughout pop culture, ignorance is celebrated as strength, whether it is measured by pleasure, by profits, or by popularity. Also celebrated is blind allegiance to ideology, no matter the facts or the evidence. That's why there are a lot of people in America who confuse

---

1 Matthew Tribbe, *No Requiem for the Space Age* (New York: Oxford University Press, 2014), 117.
2 Tribbe, *No Requiem*, 157–217.

1. Hedonism and narcissism with freedom,
2. Ignorance with individualism,
3. Profits with truth, and
4. Political and cultural truths with the party line.

Doublethink is always dangerous. This is especially true in the pandemic, where COVID-19 does not care what fantasies anyone believes and will use these people as *hosts* to spread the virus to everyone nearby. As with memes and hot media viruses, so it is with COVID-19, a deadly virus.

Most people think the main message of George Orwell's *1984* is the warning about a totalitarian surveillance society controlled by the all-powerful "Big Brother." What's overlooked is that Big Brother maintains his infallible godlike status only because of the power of "doublethink." Doublethink is the method of "thinking" in which people accept and believe that two opposite and contradictory propositions are both true at the same time and in the same respect. Orwell explains:

> *Doublethink* means the power of holding two contradictory beliefs in one's mind simultaneously, and accepting both of them. The Party intellectual knows in which direction his memories must be altered; he therefore knows that he is playing tricks with reality; but by the exercise of *doublethink* he also satisfies himself that reality is not violated. The process has to be conscious, or it would not be carried out with sufficient precision, but it also has to be unconscious, or it would bring with it a feeling of falsity and hence of guilt. ... To tell deliberate lies while genuinely believing in them, to forget any fact that has become inconvenient, and then, when it becomes necessary again, to draw it back from oblivion for just so long as it is needed, to deny the existence of objective reality and all the while to take account of the reality which one denies—all this is indisputably necessary. ... By a fresh act of *doublethink* one erases this knowledge; and so on indefinitely, with the lie always one leap ahead of the truth.[3]

Doublethink is a form of thought control. But those under control *must believe they are exercising their highest freedoms*, especially those people in politics and media. Any contradictions between reality and thought must be resolved and embraced in the mind of the follower and true believer. The doublethinker must not only accept two opposite propositions as being true—the doublethinker must also *feel good* about it, even take a certain *pride* in standing beside such cognitive contradictions. Doublethink would be impossible without this cognitive contentment.

IT'S MORE THAN LYING AND HYPOCRISY

Doublethink is not mere hypocrisy, for it is the flouting of reason and logic and an attack on the very nature of reality and human thought. Doublethink eventually leads to a complete madhouse, where 2 + 2 = 5 and scientific truths are obscured or obliterated—from evolution to archaeology to astronomy. Thus, pseudoscience and conspiracy theory proliferate, constantly undermining the ability of people to grasp reality and know what is true or false, precisely as they believe they possess great and mysterious truths. *Doublethink is one way that the meanings of cool media are countered by hot media and pretenses to cosmic centrality.*

Doublethink is not merely lying, it is form of magical thinking, a special effect for the special mind—which sees itself liberated from the constraints of reality or any laws of existence. The greatest doublethinkers possess the arrogant self-assurance to stand astride empirical reality and evidence-free delusion, to stand astride the cool and the hot and believe they are equivalent. The "universe" and "reality" become endless distortion fields where anything can be true or false as needed, now or at any time, past or future, to maintain the existing social order or the dominant belief systems.

---

3 George Orwell, *1984* (New York: Plume Books, 1983), 176–177.

Across the planet, the greatest doublethinkers convey a magical worldview to their followers, who gaze in awe and wonder while cheering the epic achievements of their Great Leaders. Logic, science, ethics, and solid education, these things are not needed in the promised worlds of the gods and Great Leaders. Meanwhile, society regresses in a real world of prejudice, corruption, incompetence, and perpetual shortages, all while history and reality are rewritten by the moment to support the illusion of progress. As the world collapses, the world is being made great again every day, every hour, every moment. Only *gods* can accomplish such feats and still be worshipped by their followers.

DOUBLETHINK AND CULTURAL DIVIDES

In our twenty-first-century world of scientific understanding, it is doublethink that fuels some of the deepest cultural and political divides. For example, it is doublethink

- To stand on the rim of the 6-million-year-old Grand Canyon and see rocks and layers that are up to 1.8 billion years old—and believe that Earth is 10,000 years old[4];
- To learn that humans share 99 percent of our DNA with bonobos and chimpanzees—and believe that human evolution on Earth is not true[5];
- To learn that all humans on average share 99.5–99.9 percent of the same DNA—and believe in any kind of gender, ethnic, identity, or class superiority; or believe in denying universal human rights for all individuals and peoples, regardless of gender, ethnicity, identity, ability, or class[6];
- To learn that humanity and its galaxy share 97 percent of the most common elements (carbon, hydrogen, nitrogen, oxygen, phosphorus, and sulfur) of the universe—and believe that our cosmic origins and evolution are not true[7]; and
- To learn that the observable universe may have 2 trillion galaxies stretching across 100 billion light-years—and believe that we humans are cosmically significant and central to the universe.[8]

If any of these doublethink examples hit your hot button, that's the power of memes. *Memes do not care what you believe, only that you believe.* That's why it is important to ground our beliefs in the best available evidence and best methods for discerning what is true and what is false. Trapped in the heat of denial, doublethink and Alt-Fact culture put our future in peril. Gaslighting on a grand scale.

THE PURPOSE OF THIS APPENDIX

The purpose of the chapters in this appendix is not to refute every conspiracy theory or pseudoscientific claim; that would require numerous books and feature-length documentaries, and still probably be impossible. For the believers, it likely would not matter anyway. No matter how much they were proven wrong or

---

4 "Geology," Grand Canyon National Park, U.S. National Park Service, 2021, https://www.nps.gov/grca/learn/nature/grca-geology.htm.
5 Ann Gibbons, "Bonobos Join Chimps as Closest Relatives," *Science*, June 13, 2012, https://www.sciencemag.org/news/2012/06/bonobos-join-chimps-closest-human-relatives.
6 "Whole Genome Association Studies," National Human Genome Research Institute, 2021, https://www.genome.gov/17516714/2006-release-about-whole-genome-association-studies.
7 Elizabeth Howell, "Humans Really Are Made of Stardust, and a New Study Proves It," *Space.com*, January 10, 2017, https://www.space.com/35276-humans-made-of-stardust-galaxy-life-elements.html.
8 Lindsay Brooke, "A Universe of Two Trillion Galaxies," Phys.Org, January 16, 2017, https://phys.org/news/2017-01-universe-trillion-galaxies.html.

shown to have unsubstantiated beliefs, the true believers would invent new reasons to dismiss the evidence or critique. I know.

In my youth, I believed that UFOs were piloted by extraterrestrials and there must be a government cover-up of some kind, even though I knew my belief never really added up. Eventually, I fully realized that I was wrong. Are there UFOs? Sure, there are "Unidentified Flying Objects," things and phenomena in the sky that we are unable to identify. Are ETs in the pilot's seat? No. For details, see appendix C.

The goal of this appendix is rather modest. The aim is to show some of the reasons for antiscience and conspiracy beliefs, how and why they replicate in our media environments, and some of the dangerous effects they have. In my view, it is time for media studies to take a stand against conspiracy theory, pseudoscience, and Alt-Fact culture. Of course, my intellectual stand will only prove to many believers that conspiracy is real, greenlighting the perception of me as just another "academic" and professor defending the power system status quo. Of course, if you read this book, you can see that that is far, far from the truth. But, memes do not care.

COUNTERING GASLIGHTING WITH GREENLIGHTING

How can all the pseudoscience and conspiracy madness not require a massive red light? Flashing red lights across America and on a planetary scale. In fact, pseudoscience and conspiracy theory are gaslighting the popular consciousness, making us think we are crazy while true believers get away with murdering reality—Jean Baudrillard's "perfect crime." To counter the gaslighting and death of the real, we need to be greenlighting science literacy programs and logical thinking courses (studying the numerous logical fallacies all over our media) in our educational systems—before it is literally too late, if it is not already. This and other major efforts are summarized in appendix C, "UFO-JFK-X-NEO-Q: The Alpha Omega of Conspiracy Theory."

Appendix B
Media and Pseudoscience

"WHAT'S YOUR SIGN?"

"Aquarius"—that's my sign. When I was a little boy, my parents had the classic 1960s album *The Age of Aquarius*, by the Fifth Dimension, that featured the song "Aquarius," which had peaked at number one for six weeks on the Billboard charts in the spring of 1969. For several years, my mom played that song on my birthday. Good memories. I loved that song, still do. It's a powerful meme in my consciousness.

Featuring the celestial voices of Florence LaRue and Marilyn McCoo, "Aquarius" began with the lines "When the moon is in the Seventh House / And Jupiter aligns with Mars / Then peace will guide the planets / And love will steer the stars." The rest of the band joined in on the chorus: "This is the dawning of the age of Aquarius." With television, satellites, hippies, pop art, rock music, Motown, mod fashions, the civil rights movement, and the Apollo moon landings, it seemed a new age was indeed emerging on Planet Earth.

That "Aquarius" topped the charts in 1969 is no coincidence, for that was the year of the Apollo 11 moon landing. Featured on television, Apollo 11 was by far the top program, reaching one billion viewers on the day of the moonwalk. On July 20–21, people gathered with friends and families to watch events unfold on the moon, as televised around the world. Imagine that: one billion people simultaneously contemplating their first steps on another celestial object, while also gazing at Earth floating in space. A billion people suddenly contemplating our origins and destiny as a single species on Planet Earth.

When Neil Armstrong stepped on the moon and said, "One small step for a man, one giant leap for mankind," it seemed like anything was possible for the human species venturing into the stars. Many believed that Apollo's views from Earth would inspire peace around the world, echoing the "Aquarius" song. Yet, since 1969, we've seen a parallel massive rise in both pseudoscience and conspiracy theory. These beliefs are complex memes and metamemes that keep replicating and proliferating, getting green lights from across the cultural spectrum. This appendix offers yellow and red lights. As Matthew McConaughey wrote in *Greenlights*,

> We don't like yellow and red lights. They slow us down or stop our flow. They're hard. They're a shoeless winter. They say **no**, but sometimes give us what we need.

As discussed in chapter 1, memes replicate regardless of whether they are true or false. Memes do not care about truth; they only need fans, followers, and believers to keep giving the greenlights. To stop or even slow down the falsehoods, it's up to us to provide the flashing red lights! If any of the following critique in this appendix hits your hot buttons, welcome to the power of memes. Here, evidence gets the greenlights.

ZODIAC NASA: HOT COUNTERS COOL

In 2019, Silicon Valley venture capitalists invested $5 million in Co–Star, an online astrology firm with this stated philosophy:

> Our powerful natural language engine uses NASA data, coupled with the methods of professional astrologers, to algorithmically generate insights about your personality and *your future*.

Astrology puts our temporary bodies in context with the universe's vastness, allowing irrationality to invade our techno-rationalist ways of living.

Co–Star also provides an "A.I. powered astrology app" featuring real-time horoscope updates along with "cutting edge personalization." Online astrology is booming, and Co–Star is on the cutting edge.

So, what should we make of Co–Star and the other astrology apps proliferating in iTunes? Does astrology work? Is it based in science? Are capitalists merely exploiting hopes, fears, and pseudoscience for profit—like so many Hollywood films and TV shows? Is Co–Star's techno-irrational philosophy merely an ironic play for hipster angst and millennial love-seekers? Or is Co–Star filling the philosophical void for living in NASA's vast universe? Perhaps Co–Star is a "sign" of the times for a species lost in space.

FIVE REASONS FOR THE POPULARITY OF ASTROLOGY

Astrology and astronomy used to be the same thing. That ended with the invention of the telescope, the media technology that fueled our modern understanding of the stars, the planets, the universe, and our origins in that cosmos. That's the power of cool exo-media. Astrology is how cool media are countered by hot media, exo-media countered by eco-media.

That's why astrology remains popular. The same is true for much of pseudoscience. The purpose of this discussion is not to refute the "science" of astrology, which has been done elsewhere (most extensively by Phil Plait at the Bad Astronomy website). Rather, the goal is to show that the increasing popularity of astrology is the result of five parallel and paradoxical trends in pop culture, most of which are overlooked when experts explain cultural trajectories and the meaning of science in the twenty-first century:

1. The inherent drive to feel connected to the stars and universe, from which we emerged and evolved as a species

2. The ever-increasing tsunami of memes, images, and information flooding through our screens, promising to make us super-special if we buy all the products and buy into all the ego-centric ideologies

3. The challenge posed to human narcissism by the ever-increasing size and scale of the universe, as revealed by cool media technologies like the Hubble Space Telescope—to counter the cool with the hot, the exo with the ego

4. The rise of religious nonbelief in the aftermath of the Apollo space program, a void that is being filled in part by astrology and pseudoscience

5. The near-complete failure of art and philosophy to develop a meaningful and widely embraced narrative for the human species in the vast and majestic universe unveiled by NASA and astronomers around the world—*the very things promised by Co–Star and its clever app*

Top-selling books like *Greenlights* perfectly illustrate point 5. Celebrities and superheroes are the dominant philosophers now, precisely because art, science, and secular philosophy have dropped the ball. And Co–Star is filling the voids, too.

ASTROLOGY IS NOT SCIENTIFIC, BUT IT FILLS A VOID

The above trends are powered by the 24/7 spectacle and the apocalyptic backdrop of climate disruption, species extinction, and the Anthropocene—on a planet hurtling through a cosmos of trillions of galaxies and giant stretches of voids and emptinesses, all sprawling across one hundred billion light-years (that's one hundred billion times six trillion miles, the distance that light travels in a year). *Humans are a species that needs a worldview, a model of the universe, a sense of connection to their origins and destiny in the cosmos.* And life must have meaning, for we cannot tolerate meaninglessness, no matter what Nietzsche said.

Belief systems will fill the vastness and the voids. For Earthlings who are not attracted to theology and are more oriented toward science or secularism, the option might well be astrology. As illustrated by Co–Star, it is online astrology that connects our telescopes to our telephones, to turn meaninglessness in a vast universe to meaningfulness on Planet Earth, to shrink light-years to lights on our screens.

Though astrology is 100 percent not scientific, it is tapping into the cosmic and philosophical voids revealed by NASA and the Hubble Telescope. Our species is still grappling with our cosmic noncentrality, seemingly unable to handle a narrative that does not have us as the stars and warriors of the universe—the ultimate meaning of *Star Wars*. Absent a new secular philosophy that meaningfully connects Earthlings to the Hubble universe, astrology will continue to exist and thrive, filling the void with the poetics of stars and planets—even if it is scientifically bogus.

"JUPITER AND MARS" AND THIS BOOK

Having read a lot of Jean-Paul Sartre and Carl Sagan and seen *2001: A Space Odyssey* far too many times, my existentialist and scientific orientation shows me astrology is not true. Cool media prevail for me. The alignment of "Jupiter and Mars" when I was born had zero impact on my destiny or the topics of this book, precisely because the gravity of those planets had less impact than the gravity of doctors and nurses who helped my mom give birth to me. Though Jupiter and Mars are larger than the doctors and nurses, the planets were far away and the doctors and nurses were much closer. They were actually handling my little body. Since I was born inside a hospital, the sunlight reflecting off Mars or Jupiter was blocked out, too.

That said, we can see how the movement of stars and planets appeals to deep human needs. Trapped in the skyglow of the electric cities, most people have never really seen the night skies, the radiant Milky Way bursting with stars. But most know the stars and universe are still out there, as shown by NASA and movies like *Interstellar*.

Astrology pretends to provide the planetary dope on our daily destinies and long-term fates—the hoped-for success in our careers, the meanings of our hookups and love affairs, and the crazy quest for a happy and meaningful life in our temporary and transient existence on Planet Earth. Astrology and theology both tap into humanity's deep-seated narcissism and the desire to feel cosmically super-special, even if we rationally know we're not that super, not that special. That's why we crave a plan, especially if it seems ordained or celestial. *It's in the stars!*

So, while astronomy shows that the stars are far away, astrology says we can still be "co-stars" with the stars. Just download the Co–Star app! After all, astrology is still fun, especially on a first date to a concert or a first dance in a rave or nightclub: "Hey, what's your sign?"

WERE THE APOLLO MOON LANDINGS FAKED?

It happens every year. One or more students ask me if I think the Apollo moon landings were a hoax. I teach Critical Media Studies at Temple University in downtown Philadelphia, where the diverse collection of urban students is street-smart, open-minded, and hardworking. This is not an indictment of students in my classes. I'm sure it happens at other colleges and universities. Frankly, it's not surprising that some American college students wonder about the Apollo 11 moon landings, given that polls and surveys show 24 percent of Americans believe NASA faked the moon landings.[1]

The internet and YouTube are littered with zillions of claims that NASA masterminded an Apollo hoax. Some even assert that NASA hired *2001* director Stanley Kubrick to stage it and film it. Christopher Nolan's *Interstellar* (2014) depicts this issue in the scene where Cooper (Matthew McConaughey) confronts the future educators who believe the moon landings were a NASA hoax perpetrated to bankrupt the former Soviet Union, America's rival

---

1   Chapman University, "What They Aren't Telling Us: Chapman Survey of American Fears," October 11, 2016.

during the Cold War. Why are there so many attacks on the great achievements of Apollo? One reason is because of the rise of pseudoscience in media and popular culture.

SIX REASONS WHY THE MOON LANDINGS COULD NOT HAVE BEEN FAKED

In 1969, the video and television technologies weren't advanced enough to stage and fake the moon landing in any plausible way. NASA didn't have anything like CGI or Photoshop back then. The TV cameras were primitive compared to the cameras of 2017, with HD and 360-degree perspectives. Though the fake-moon-landing claims have been debunked many times on the internet, here are some of the most obvious reasons the Apollo moon landings could *not* have been faked.

1. 842 Pounds of Moon Rocks

The astronauts on the six Apollo missions retrieved 842 pounds of moon rocks that were brought to Earth and shared with scientists around the world. If the rocks were from our planet and not from the moon, the scientists would surely have realized that and called NASA on its trickery. NASA still loans out sample moon rocks to educators and scientists. Could they all be in on the hoax across fifty years?

2. The Soviet Union Knew Apollo 11 Happened

The United States and the former Soviet Union were in a "space race" to get to the moon first, supposedly to show the superiority of their socioeconomic systems. The Soviet Union could have easily tracked the Apollo spacecraft traveling to the moon with its telecommunications satellites and picked up both the Apollo radio transmissions to Mission Control and all of the television broadcasts. The Soviets possessed such technologies, because they too sent spacecraft to the moon in the 1960s (sans cosmonauts). If NASA didn't really send astronauts to the moon, the Soviet Union would have certainly known it and taken the opportunity to embarrass the United States on the world stage at the height of the Cold War. The possibility of the Soviets going along with such a hoax is far below zero (lower than the winter temperatures in Siberia!). Moscow's *Pravda* newspaper even acknowledged the Apollo 11 moon landing with a front-page story.

3. Reflectors Left on the Moon

The Apollo 11 and Apollo 14 astronauts left behind mirrorlike prisms (the Lunar Laser-Ranging RetroReflector array that is targeted with lasers by scientists at the McDonald Observatory in Texas) on the moon. The lasers accurately determine the distance from Earth to the moon, which is moving away from the Earth by about 3.8 cm per year. Could all the astronomers at the McDonald Observatory be in on the NASA hoax?

4. Tracks on the Moon

The *Lunar Reconnaissance Orbiter* has provided images of the Apollo landing sites, including astronaut tracks, moon buggies and their tracks, and the descent part of the lunar modules. In the twenty-first century, could the world's scientists and astronomers be fooled by trick photos from NASA?

5. **Could Four Hundred Thousand Scientists Be Tricked?**

Approximately four hundred thousand scientists, engineers, and technicians worked on the Apollo project for over a decade. They came from many countries and from all over the United States. It is patently absurd to think they were all somehow tricked or were part of a NASA hoax.

6. **Why Land on the Moon Five More Times?**

The United States made six visits to the moon. Let's consider for a moment that the visits were all staged. If the first "hoax" was successful, the United States would have defeated the Soviets in the race to the moon. *Why risk faking five more visits and thus increase the chances of slipping up and getting caught by 500 percent?* NASA would have had to fake the famed Apollo 13 mission, which was aborted on the way to the moon because of an onboard explosion; it was freaking scientific genius that enabled the Apollo 13 astronauts to orbit the moon and return safely to Earth. If NASA faked the moon landings, one time would have been enough. Along with the other reasons listed above, that's why we can be certain Apollo landed on the moon and returned to Earth six times.

REBELS WITHOUT EVIDENCE: PSEUDOSCIENCE IN THE GUISE OF SKEPTICISM

The students skeptical of the Apollo moon landings are often those who fashion themselves as rebels, anti-authoritarians, and challengers to the American cultural orthodoxy. It's the same with QAnon believers. Of course, being skeptical of the US government is understandable in general. Like *all other political systems* throughout history, the US government has lied, is currently lying about something, and will lie again in the future. Though governments are often lying about something, they also tell the truth about many things as well. It's rather obvious the US intelligence agencies are still hiding something about the Kennedy assassination, but there is zero doubt that NASA sent humans to the moon. Governments, corporations, and many institutions often lie or bend the truth, but that does not mean they lie about everything. The COVID pandemic is real. So is climate disruption.

It saddens me that youthful rebellion and much-needed skepticism are channeled into pseudoscientific nonsense—not unlike the "ancient-astronaut theorists" celebrated in the long-running *Ancient Aliens* (2010–) series, which is repeatedly aired on the History Channel in the United States. Like those who deny the Apollo moon landings, the ancient-astronaut theorists present themselves as rebels against the mainstream orthodoxy of modern science and archaeology. They offer nothing other than an endless stream of bogus "evidence" for the scientifically illiterate and well-intentioned skeptics such as the students who ask me about Apollo. (See the introduction in chapter 9). Also, there are the deluded charlatans who think Earth is flat or that Bigfoot is roaming the Pacific Northwest. And the National Geographic Channel gives the Bigfoot hunters an entire television series (*Bigfoot: The Evidence*) to wander the woods and claim to hear Bigfoot in the darkness.

THE EROSION OF SCIENCE IN MEDIA AND SOCIETY

That 30–40 percent of Americans would not wear a mask (for whatever reason) during a global pandemic shows one profound thing: There has been a massive cratering of the scientific, ethical, and educational systems in the United States—at least for the 100+ million people who arrogantly and belligerently do not care enough for the safety of their fellow humans to wear a mask (a properly fitted N95-level mask) to prevent the spread of a highly contagious and often deadly virus. Or those who believe the pandemic is a hoax or a conspiracy.

That's why we see "patriots" berating nurses battling COVID-19 and people not wearing masks screaming at retail workers and flight attendants, claiming their rights are being violated. That's why we see people claiming it is tyranny to care enough about your neighbors to protect them from the disease you may be carrying. "Freedom" and "democracy" now mean never heeding the facts, or the evidence, or the rights of people nearby in the grocery store. COVID-19 has revealed a deep-seated and toxic narcissism that spans society and the political spectrum, right to left, from evangelicals to conspiracy theorists to New Age believers.[2]

The antiscience culture has left a smoking crater, a descent happening for decades. In the wake of the Apollo triumph, there has been a steady increase in all forms of antiscience culture in America—pseudoscience, ancient aliens, antivaxxers, medical quackery, fake moon landings, alien abductions, climate change deniers, and endless conspiracy theories. TV and Hollywood have produced zillions of shows and movies to celebrate these beliefs, along with televangelists selling faith-healing and celebrities hawking miracle cures. It's clear the educational and cultural systems have failed to instill widespread scientific literacy and clear reasoning skills among the populace in the wake of the Apollo triumphs.

As Stephen Hawking explains in chapter 10, scientific knowledge is exploding, revealing stunningly beautiful new insights into the evolution of life on this planet and the life of the cosmos. The empirical truths of science are all around us:

- Been to the doctor? Science was there. Science helps doctors treat us, operate on us, and mend our broken bones. The endo-media technologies of X-rays, blood tests, and anaesthesia all help keep us alive. Science helped me survive cancer in 2020 and live cancer-free, at least so far.
- Ever received a tetanus shot or any other shot to prevent infection or disease? Science was there. Science and medical technologies can cure diseases and help prevent them from spreading—such as using genetic sciences to create the vaccine for COVID-19.
- Ever been to the dentist? Science was there. Science and technology make going to the dentist mostly painless, while the dentists and technicians repair or straighten our teeth. Science can even make our teeth supernova white, if we prefer to create a blinding glare on the dance floor when we smile.
- Ever driven a car, rode on a train, or flown on a plane to a fun vacation spot? Science was there. Science and technology make possible our cars, trains, jet airliners, and the entire global transportation system.
- Ever used a computer or the internet? Science was there. Science and technology make possible our laptops, desktops, and mobile phones, along with all the apps, videos, and websites.
- Ever taken a selfie or made a TikTok video? Science was there.
- Ever turned on the heater or the air conditioner? Science was there.
- Ever opened the fridge to get an ice-cold drink? Science was there.
- Ever turned on a light? Science was there.

Science and technology are the environments for our civilization, with all the wonders we take for granted. How spoiled we are.

Yet, many millions believe the science of vaccines is a vast conspiracy. Think about it: The world's scientists, doctors, and nurses would all have to be in on the cover-up. All those shots we receive are just to fake us out. And all the global prevention of polio, measles, smallpox, and tuberculosis is just bogus history. The longer life spans since the invention of vaccines must be bogus, too.

It's the same with climate disruption: The world's climate scientists and meteorologists would all have to be in on the scam. Literally, this would involve hundreds of thousands of scientists. Why would they devote their entire careers to a lie?

It's the same with Flat-Earthers, Young-Earthers, and Apollo 11 moon landing deniers. To them, NASA is just one big Hollywood studio bent upon tricking humanity with special effects—across sixty years! Most of the world's universities have science departments, with experts in geology, cosmology, astronomy, and astrophysics. They

---

2 Apollo Love, "How COVID Exposed New Age Narcissism," *Elephant Journal*, December 19, 2020.

too would all have to be in on the conspiracy. All the observatories of the world are just sites for more fakery. No evidence is sufficient to dislodge the narcissists from their pretenses to cosmic centrality.

WILLFUL IGNORANCE AND FAILING EDUCATIONAL SYSTEMS

Of course, you don't have to be in college to be exposed to this knowledge. Most of this scientific knowledge is easily accessible via the internet. So are pseudoscience, conspiracy theories, and Alt-Fact worldviews. And many people are *willfully not choosing* a basic scientific worldview for understanding life, how things work, and our place in the universe. When huge percentages of the population choose not to wear properly fitted masks and to believe the COVID-19 pandemic is overblown, then it is clear that our media and education systems are failing.

The same is true for the plague of systemic racism in America, where the educational systems have failed or been overwhelmed by the creationist, antiscience, and antihumanist views that underlie racism, prejudice, patriarchy, and White supremacy—all clearly and completely refuted by the fact that the human species shares 99.5 percent of the same DNA and all of our brains and bodies are made of the most common elements of the cosmos (hydrogen, nitrogen, oxygen, carbon, and so on). Again, we humans are one species sharing one tiny planet in a vast and majestic universe, and we all should have equal and universal human rights (as explained in the introduction to this book).

SCIENCE ILLITERACY

In their book *Unscientific America*, Chris Mooney and Sheril Kirshenbaum show how the decline of scientific literacy is reaching epidemic proportions in America, fueled, in part, by Hollywood and the media industries.[3] This decline correlates with the deterioration of intellectual standards in America, as detailed by Susan Jacoby, who sees television and electronic media playing a central role in the decay.[4]

The United States has been at the center of the global explosion of the internet over the past three decades, yet there is *little evidence that most Americans* are getting smarter, even with all that knowledge at their fingertips. The academic rankings of American teenagers have dropped to fourteenth in reading, twenty-fifth in math, and seventeenth in science in comparison to other developed nations.[5] Mooney and Kirshenbaum report that for every five hours of cable news programming, one minute is devoted to science news, while the number of American newspapers with science sections has declined by two-thirds in the past thirty years. For example, newspapers like the *Boston Globe* and the *Washington Post* have eliminated their science sections to save money, even though Boston is a central location for the biotech industry and Washington, DC, is the seat of the US federal government. CNN has also cut its entire science, space, and technology unit.[6]

In sum, there is hardly any attempt to cover science in television news or in most newspapers, other than with a few articles here and there. In contrast, there is unlimited coverage of sports, celebrities, and catastrophes. The coverage of science and science news has migrated to the highly specialized realms of science websites and science-oriented blogs. Though these websites and blogs serve important functions for those interested in science, they fail to reach the large part of the population who need to be more informed about science and the way the world actually works.

No wonder America is filled with scientifically illiterate politicians and people. While the educational systems fail, the entertainment industries profit. As prophesied by *The Howard Beale Show* in the movie *Network* (1976), Hollywood and television provide an endless parade of movies and programs that celebrate every superstitious

---

3 Chris Mooney and Sheril Kirshenbaum, *Unscientific America: How Scientific Illiteracy Threatens Our Future* (New York: Basic Books, 2010).
4 Susan Jacoby, *The Age of American Unreason* (New York: Pantheon Books, 2008).
5 Jessica Shepherd, "World Education Rankings: Which Country Does Best at Reading, Maths, and Science?" The *Guardian*, September 7, 2010.
6 Mooney and Kirshenbaum, *Unscientific America*, 67–80.

and pseudoscientific meme, from electronic pulpits to celebrity "ghost stories" to psychic detectives to the apocalyptic prophecies of Nostradamus. According to various surveys about pseudoscientific beliefs among Americans:

- 75 percent of Americans have a paranormal belief
- 52 percent believe houses can be haunted
- 35 percent believe ancient aliens visited Earth
- 19 percent believe fortune tellers can foresee the future
- 16 percent believe Bigfoot is a real creature[7]
- 25 percent do not know the Earth orbits the Sun[8]
- 42 percent think astrology is "very scientific" or "sort of scientific" (among those aged 18–24, the total is 58 percent)[9]

The Chapman University surveys "Paranormal America 2017" and "Paranormal Beliefs" (see note 7) suggest that pseudoscientific beliefs seem to be increasing during the twenty-first century. Regarding the hot-button issue of evolution, only 33 percent of Americans believe in Darwinian evolution (i.e., evolution solely by natural processes, with no involvement of a Supreme Being).[10] Though the majority of Americans say they are very interested in new scientific discoveries,[11] they and the media are not doing a very good job of exploring the world of science and what it means to be a member of the human species in a vast and ancient universe.

THE INTERNET AND RELIGIOUS NONBELIEF

We are living amid an explosion of scientific knowledge, which is paralleled by increasing anti-intellectualism and by religious fervor among creationists and fundamentalists. In America, more people are going to college, and there is greater access to the internet—circumstances that parallel two trends that seem at odds (at least partially) with each other. On one hand, scientific illiteracy is increasing, and pseudoscientific beliefs remain popular. On the other hand, there has been a decline in religious affiliation. Obviously, these kinds of trends correlate with many cultural factors, such as socioeconomic conditions, changing demographics, varying lifestyles, and religious upbringing. Surely, the internet and media technologies are related to these trends, too.

As Stephen Hawking explains in chapter 10, scientific knowledge is exploding in our culture. Much of this knowledge is easily accessible via the internet. Is this accessibility impacting the cosmologies and increasing the religious nonbelief embraced by members of society? The past four decades have seen a steady rise in the number of Americans who have no religious affiliation. In 2012, the Pew Research Center reported that one in five American adults and a third of adults under age thirty are religiously unaffiliated, the highest percentages ever.[12] Religious nonaffiliation for first-year college students has risen from 8 percent to 25 percent since the 1980s.[13]

---

7   Chapman University, "Paranormal America 2017," October 27, 2017; Chapman University, "Paranormal Beliefs," October 11, 2016.
8   Michael Stone, "Science Literacy: 1 in 4 Americans Don't Know the Earth Orbits the Sun," *Patheos*, February 17, 2014.
9   National Science Foundation, "Science and Technology: Public Attitudes and Understanding," *Science and Engineering Indicators 2014*, chapter 7, pp. 25–26. By contrast, 92 percent of the Chinese population think astrology is not scientific. Brooks Hays, "Majority of Young Adults Think Astrology Is a Science," *UPI Science News*, February 11, 2014.
10   David Masci, "For Darwin Day: 6 Facts About the Evolution Debate," FactTank, Pew Research, February 10, 2017.
11   National Science Foundation, "Science and Technology: Public Attitudes and Understanding," Chapter 7 "Highlights."
12   "'Nones' on the Rise," *Pew Research: Religion & Public Life Project*, October 9, 2012.
13   Jessica Ravitz, "Is the Internet Killing Religion?" *CNN*, April 9, 2014.

Others report that from 1990 to 2010, the total number of Americans with no religious affiliation increased from 8 percent to 18 percent.[14] Surely, there is a complexity of factors. Computer scientist Allen Downey believes the internet is partly responsible.[15]

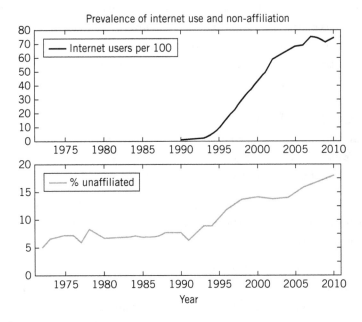

Prevalence of internet use and non-affiliation

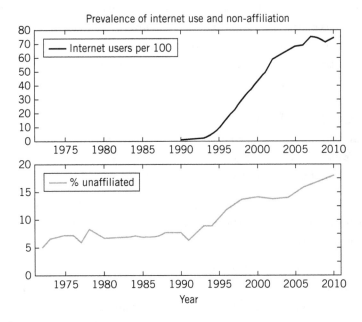

| FIGURE A.B.1   Trends in internet usage

The table above suggests a dramatic correlation between internet usage and religious affiliation. However, the issue is very complex. In a study of four decades of survey data trends regarding demographics, socioeconomics, religious affiliation, and internet usage, Downey concludes that:

- Religious upbringing increases the chance of religious affiliation as an adult. Decreases in religious upbringing between the 1980s and 2000s account for about 25 percent of the observed decrease in affiliation.
- College education decreases the chance of religious affiliation. Increases in college graduation between the 1980s and 2000s account for about 5 percent of the observed decrease in affiliation.
- Internet use decreases the chance of religious affiliation. Increases in internet use since 1990, from 0 to nearly 80 percent of the general population, account for about 20 percent of the observed decrease in affiliation.[16]

By 2018, the total number of nonbelievers had risen to 23 percent.[17] As explained in chapter 7, the proliferation of social media seems to correlate with increasing nonbelief, further supporting Downey's theory. Please keep in mind that "correlation" does not equal "causation." Correlations show patterns that we must connect to other knowledge, evidence, and observations. Downey's study also suggests that the single greatest influence on religious affiliation is parental upbringing—where, when, and how you were raised on this planet. If this study is accurate in its data and conclusions, then we can see the power of memes, showing that the single greatest factor in determining religious affiliation is chance, not choice—just like fan allegiance to football teams at the World Cup and the Super Bowl (chapter 1).

14   "How the Internet Is Taking Away America's Religion," *MIT Technology Review*, April 4, 2014.
15   Allen B. Downey, "Religious Affiliation, Education, and Internet Use," arXiv:1403.5534 [stat AP], March 21, 2014.
16   Downey, "Religious Affiliation."
17   Derek Thompson, "Three Decades Ago, America Lost Its Religion. Why?" *The Atlantic*, September 26, 2019.

MEDIA, SCIENCE, AND KNOWLEDGE

Situated on our tiny planet, we are not gods and neither are we fools. We are at once tiny and brainy—in terms of our size, scale, and consciousness in relation to the universe. As Barry Vacker explains in chapter 9, we might be tiny, but our brains give us enormous power to know the universe, to make a better world, and to unite as a single species that cooperates to protect the planet upon which all life depends. Yet we live in an "Alt-Fact" culture where science and rationality are under assault in our networks of tribes and our echo chambers. That's why it is important to understand how knowledge evolves and why some theories are indeed facts.

THE SCIENTIFIC METHOD

Science is not perfect, and it's not always correct. But science has a method of dealing with imperfections and incorrect conclusions. It's called evidence, logic, and the scientific method. Neil deGrasse Tyson poetically summarized this method in the first episode of *Cosmos: A Spacetime Odyssey*:

> Test ideas by experiment and observation, build on those ideas that pass the test, reject the ones that fail. Follow the evidence wherever it leads, and question everything. Accept these terms and the cosmos is yours.

As Carl Sagan explains in "Science and Hope," science is the best hope we have for understanding the world around us, even with the flaws of science, scientists, and scientific research.[18] Yet when science is combined with theory and art (including the humanities), we have a chance to expand our understanding to realms far greater than we might imagine. These three areas of human thought and creativity—art, science, and evidence-based theory—give us the best hope for a meaningful life in a better world.

Like memes, science and our cosmology evolve by replicating. In essence, science evolves by selecting *new* models and theories based on one of three factors: (1) the correlation of an *existing* model (or theory) with new evidence, (2) the correlation of a *new* model (or theory) with new evidence, or (3) the better correlation of a new model (or theory) with existing evidence. Much of the new evidence is gathered with the assistance of media technologies such as telescopes, microscopes, cameras, and computers. When new evidence warrants a new model or when a new model better explains existing evidence, a new model (or meme) is born. What refutes any particular scientific conclusion or theory is empirical data and further scientific investigation, not religions, feelings, politics, or hot takes after watching YouTube videos. Of course, science is not perfect and scientists may make mistakes and some scientists may not be good people—all of which is true for the rest of humanity.

WHY SOME MODELS AND THEORIES ARE FACTS

When the new model or theory is verified by additional evidence or additional tests, the model has survived and will be replicated. The model (or meme) is believed to be true precisely because it has not been falsified by other tests, models, or theories. Science builds on the models that prove to be true over time by their correlation with evidence and/or other proven theories. Meanwhile, those theories that are proven false—such as the geocentric and flat-Earth models—will fail to replicate, and they eventually die out. Sometimes, a new model or theory is so profound that it creates a new model of life or the universe, such as Charles Darwin's evolution, Albert Einstein's relativity, and Edwin Hubble's big bang.

That some theories become facts can no longer be disputed. For example, the Earth-centered universe began as a theory based on the limited powers of direct empirical observation without the aid of technology. To the naked eye gazing at the Milky Way at night, it seems the stars and universe are, indeed, orbiting around Earth. This cosmology reigned for millennia, until it was challenged by the technological innovation of the telescope—likely

---

18   Cark Sagan, "Science and Hope," in *The Demon-Haunted World: Science as a Candle in the Dark* (London: Headline Books, 1997), 27–42.

the most radical media technology of all time. Powered by the telescope, Galileo's observations removed Earth from the center of the universe, a fact that has since been confirmed by NASA at least a zillion times.

That the Earth goes around the Sun is an empirical fact and will be a fact until something knocks the Earth out of solar orbit or the Sun expands to scorch our planet and burn it to a cinder. *It is flat-out absurd to claim that Earth orbiting the Sun is not a fact and is only a theory.* The same goes for gravity, evolution, and the expansion of the universe—these theories are facts; they are true. The expansion of the universe has been confirmed in numerous ways, though we still do not fully understand the causes of the expansion or the so-called dark energy that is driving the galaxies apart. Yet, that the universe is expanding is a fact. Likewise, evolution has been overwhelmingly confirmed, as evidenced by the discoveries of the evolutionary, genetic, and biological sciences. Without the genetic sciences, there is no vaccine for COVID-19 or any other contagious disease.

EXPANDING THE KNOWN AND THE UNKNOWN

Science and philosophy can be embraced without a commitment to naive empiricism or empty relativism. We are not omniscient beings, and our methods of knowing have natural limits. Such limits are determined by evolution and the cosmos. Knowledge is asymmetrical, evolving, and open-ended. Like the cosmos from which we emerged, our models of the universe are always evolving and adapting to new evidence, new theories, and new technologies. It is natural that theory evolves, and such evolution does not mean that all knowledge and understanding is relative or can be instantly countered by an Alt-Fact Facebook feed.

The more we come to know, the more we realize there is more we don't know. That's why we have universities and why you are in college, to explore the known and realize there is a vast unknown yet to understood or discovered. Only a very small worldview claims that there is little more to know. Our sciences and technologies are producing more of the known and unknown at the same time.[19] That's a good thing, and it mirrors the universe we have unveiled with our technologies.

Because of the increasing power of media technologies, our knowledge of the universe is expanding rapidly, always evolving. The same with our knowledge of climate change, extinction events, and the Anthropocene—the evidence is massively mounting, and it is naive to remain in denial. The fact that science *evolves* is often used to question scientific evidence in matters of cosmic truth, but this is a flawed critique rooted in human yearnings for omniscience and eternal truths, mistakenly believed to be available to nonempirical, nonevidentiary modes of awareness. Science is not omniscient, and neither is any other field of human knowing.

THAT WE ARE NOT GODS DOES NOT MEAN WE ARE FOOLS

Human knowledge is evolutionary and open-ended, always subject to revision when presented with new facts, conditions, theories, and evidence from new media technologies. That's why some predictions prove to be correct and some prove to be false. That's why science is filled with surprising discoveries and big disappointments.

If knowledge, certainty, and prediction signify the complete grasp of every possibility in the entire universe, then we are left with the false alternatives of being either omniscient gods or ignorant fools. If certainty and prediction mean omniscience, then we must certainly be ignorant now and blind to the future. From the fact that we cannot know everything, it does not follow that we cannot understand anything—that we are not gods does not mean we are fools.

---

19   In *The Postmodern Condition* (1979), Jean-François Lyotard summarizes the philosophical challenges, which remain relevant today: "Postmodern science—by concerning itself with such things as undecidables, the limits of precise control, conflicts characterized by incomplete information, 'fracta,' catastrophes, and pragmatic paradoxes—is theorizing its own evolution as discontinuous, catastrophic, nonrectifiable, and paradoxical. It is changing the meaning of the word *knowledge*, while expressing how such a change can take place. It is producing not the known, but the unknown." Jean-Francois Lyotard, *The Postmodern Condition: A Report on Knowledge* (Minneapolis: University of Minnesota Press, 1984), 60. That I have cited Lyotard does not mean my ideas can be classified as "postmodern" or that I am a champion of postmodernism, which evolved into a deeply flawed philosophy. I am citing Lyotard because he provides a profound observation.

Appendix C
UFO-JFK-X-NEO-Q

THE ALPHA-OMEGA OF CONSPIRACY THEORY

COPIES OF COPIES OF COPIES

In conspiracy theory, the true believers are millions of copies of Neo, downing red pills as they break free from the Matrix. Copies of copies of copies. The new Neos were born in the desert near Roswell, shocked on the streets of Dallas, made heroic in Hollywood, validated on the History Channel, and now feeling empowered by the prophecies of Q—yearning to be born again in "the desert of the real," to quote from Morpheus in *The Matrix*.

"Flying saucers"—"single bullet theory"—"the truth is out there"—"the Matrix is everywhere"—"where we go one, we go all": these are concepts and slogans that accelerated conspiracy into pop consciousness over the past seven decades. There are many. Bigfoot exists. The Earth is flat. Nostradamus predicted 9/11. The moon landings were faked. UFOs prove ETs visit us. Area 51 has alien bodies. COVID-19 is a hoax. Stop the steal.

One of those conspiracy theories might be true. The rest, well, they are all memes and media viruses too. And they keep replicating. Like any popular media virus, QAnon has its memes and slogans. "The Storm." "The Great Awakening." "Where we go one, we go all." As in a stormy descent into sheer delusion and complete derangement, fueled by religious fervor, conspiracy worldviews, and scorching hot media conditions in our planetary networks and platforms.[1] The bigger the territory, the bigger the map, the bigger the conspiracy, the more the believers. As discussed in chapter 3, the maps are obliterating the territories they are supposed to represent and are now generating the replacement territories—and there is no better example than conspiracy theory and Q.

For many millions of people, on the left and the right, from New Age spirituality to age-old religion, conspiracy theory has become an entire worldview, with its own cosmology and structure that satisfy deep philosophical and psychological needs. After all, the "deep state" taps into deep fears. If you are a believer in Q or another massive conspiracy theory, there is little that can be said to persuade you otherwise. All I can say is I used to believe in a conspiracy theory that I now know was false. Which one? UFOs piloted by ETs!

Obviously, I am being playful with the letters alpha and omega. That's because the point of this appendix is not to refute the conspiracies, but to show the philosophical role that conspiracy theory plays in twenty-first-century culture and consciousness—and to have a little fun while we do it. After all, it does not matter how many times prophecies fail; the true believers will find another one to "predict" the future. It's like Nostradamus shows on the History Channel or the Bible's Book of Revelation, where the so-called prophecies never have to come true, for the viewers and believers will just move on to the next "prophecy." America is utterly whacked out on conspiracy, and Q is the new Nostradamus offering online Revelations for the true believers.

STOP THE STEAL: "REALITY" HAS BEEN HIJACKED

Long celebrated by Hollywood and the History Channel, the mainstream champions of pseudoscience and paranormalism, it's no surprise that conspiracy theory plays a key role in contemporary pop culture. The History Channel has long been intellectually bankrupt, with endless loops of conspiracy theories, ancient aliens, Nostradamus

---

1 Abby Ohlheiser, "Evangelicals Are Looking for Answers Online. They're Finding QAnon Instead," *MIT Technology Review*, August 26, 2020; Joel Rose, "Even if It Is 'Bonkers,' Poll Finds Many Believe QAnon and Other Conspiracies," NPR, December 30, 2020.

prophecies, and Revelation doomsday scenarios, all making claims about past or future apocalypses, when the real apocalypse in happening in the brains of the true believers—the destruction of reason and reality.

This issue has roots that are deeper and older than Facebook and Twitter. UFO-JFK-X-NEO-Q, that's the alpha and omega of twenty-first-century conspiracy theory, the origins for the alternative "reality" in the minds of millions. "Stop the Steal" should apply to reality, because reality has been hijacked and re-routed into an Alt-Fact worldview, a simulation of thinking powered by sacred scrolls and scrolling through Q and Twitter.

CONSPIRACY NARRATIVES: COUNTERING COOL MEDIA WITH HOT MEANING

"Alpha" is not only the first letter of the Greek alphabet; it is a word that stands for the first stage of product development—*when alpha prototypes are released for testing among consumers*. Twenty-first-century conspiracy theory was first prototyped with missing UFOs in Roswell and the Zapruder film of the JFK assassination, followed by the deep-state theories in Oliver Stone's *JFK*, Fox Network's *The X-Files*, Neo's journey in *The Matrix*, and Q's Revelation-like prophecies.

Conspiracy theory creates mythologies with *origins* and *destinies* to model an entire alternative reality or alternative history, to provide a sense of meaning and purpose to events on our speck of a planet in a NASA universe of two trillion galaxies. In contrast to NASA, the Hubble Space Telescope, and twenty-first-century cosmology, conspiracy theory offers a worldview in which the true believers are still central to everything, the center of all truth, value, purpose, and meaning. As with astrology and pseudoscience, conspiracy is one way to counter cool media with hot meaning.

The larger the universe unveiled by science, the larger the conspiracies needed to fill the vastness, exemplified by UFOs and *Ancient Aliens*. The larger the government, the larger the global systems of trade, and the larger the realms explained by science, the larger and more outlandish the conspiracies must be. Hence QAnon. Conspiracy theory provides grand narratives to order the chaos of events beyond the believers' control, to map a participatory construction of "reality"—free from the "fake news" of mainstream media, liberated from the classrooms of the Ivory Tower. For true believers, conspiracy theory is the challenge to the "elites" in media and academia.

THE ALPHA AND OMEGA OF CONSPIRACY

Wherever there is an *alpha*, there is an *omega*, the last letter in the Greek alphabet. For every beginning that is *hopeful*, there is an end that is *fearful* and must be fought. Together the alpha and omega of pop culture are welcomed by conspiracy theory, which functions to fill the voids in scientific meaning and secular philosophy. That's the existential and spiritual function of all major conspiracy theory—beginnings and ends, voids filled, and purpose and meanings saved.

THE ALPHA & OMEGA OF CONSPIRACY THEORY

	BIRTH *Origin Moment*	ALPHA *Origin Moment*	OMEGA *Ends and Fears*	VOIDS FILLED *Meanings Saved*
UFO	1947 Roswell	• two years after Hiroshima • origins of space age	• fears of atomic destruction • fears of human non-centrality	• saviors/demons from space fill voids in newly discovered vast universe • alien visit show humanity is special
JFK	1963 Dallas	• one year after Cuban Missile Crisis	• fears of Cold War, Soviets • end of "democracy"	• giant hole in JFK's blown out head • holes in Warren Commission Report • holes in Boomer idealism
X	1993 *The X-Files*	• two years after Cold War • three years after Hubble Space telescope	• deep-state, and of democracy • aliens taking control	• void left after demise of USSR • humans still central in vast universe • pseudoscience equal to science
NEO	1993 *The Matrix*	• coming new millennium	• end of millennium; Y2K • real replaced by hyperreal • deep state conspiracy; A.I.	• vastness of cyberspace • red pill fills void in secular philosophy • religious apocalypse fulfilled
Q	2017 Internet	• one year after first Black president & first female presidential candidate • first reality-TV president	• end to white rule/patriarchy • new global order • decline in religious believers	• Q is new Nostradamus, prophet for ideologies clinging to power/centrality in NASA's 21st century universe • Trump is celeb icon for conspiracy

FIGURE A.C.1 Chart by Barry Vacker, 2020.

CONSPIRACIES FILL VOIDS

Not unlike astrology, conspiracy theories fill massive philosophical and cultural voids, by providing huge narratives with beginnings and ends. The conspiracy theories function like creation myths and claim to reveal hidden patterns.

1. Across the decades, "labyrinthine conspiracy theories have morphed into massive creation myths, not unlike those in the theologies of the world."[2] For many, conspiracy theory is another religion, a myth without which the world would seem utterly chaotic, with "evil" forces lurking everywhere.

2. As a species, we evolved on a planet teeming with life-forms, when everyday life was a struggle to survive amid the tumble of seeming chaos. That's why our brains evolved powerful pattern-recognition skills: to find food, to hunt animals, to stay safe in the dark. Though we now live in a scientific world, we still yearn to know what's hidden, or what we imagine might be hidden—the unseen patterns that could be revealed with the right vision, technologies, or sources in a Facebook feed.

Add on our 24/7 media environments, and we see how maps generate territories, how media generate a hyper-reality—untethered to any underlying real reality.

We humans need a worldview that explains our origins and destiny, while giving us a sense of hope, meaning, and purpose. For me, I eventually anchored that worldview in art, science, and the existentialist philosophy presented in Jean-Paul Sartre's *Being and Nothingness*, where I learned that our highest responsibility is to develop our personal and collective meaning and purpose in the universe—as it is, not as we wish it was.[3] I have yet to encounter evidence or logic that refutes Sartre's philosophy as presented in *Being and Nothingness*, which also happens to mesh with twenty-first-century cosmology. That's also our biggest challenge, the biggest philosophical void we must fill. Enter UFOs and conspiracies.

---

2   Barry Vacker, "Lone Stars, Lost Amid the Big Bang," in Peter Granser, *Signs* (Stuttgart: Hatje-Cantz and Chicago Museum of Contemporary Photography, 2008), 10.
3   Jean-Paul Sartre, *Being and Nothingness* (New York: Citadel, 1956).

UFO

It's no coincidence that flying saucers exploded in pop consciousness after World War II, just at the earliest beginnings of the Space Age, while following on the heels of the nuclear annihilation of Hiroshima and Nagasaki by the US military. Three radical concepts were entering popular consciousness:

1. We now had the power to wipe out civilization, to completely self-destruct in a collective act of suicide. This is an omega point, an end that must be fought, even as humanity ramped up the nukes in the Cold War.
2. Humanity had the potential to develop rockets that could fly around the planet, into space, perhaps even to the moon or Mars.
3. The universe is much larger than we had long thought, as Edwin Hubble's discoveries of the expanding were filtering outside the scientific academies and the term *big bang* entered the popular vocabulary in 1950 (via science broadcasts on radio). This is an alpha point, a new beginning for humanity.

From these alpha and omega points, the UFO conspiracy emerged. Aliens could be our saviors or our destroyers. In NASA's universe of two trillion galaxies, stretching across one hundred billion light-years, with untold zillions of stars and planets, the science and evolutionary percentages strongly suggest that there are other life-forms out there—including intelligent beings and advanced civilizations. *That's why I think there's a 99.99 percent chance that intelligent life exists elsewhere in the cosmos.* But have the extraterrestrials visited Earth, a tiny speck of a planet orbiting an ordinary star in a remote part of a galaxy, one among trillions across billions of light-years?

The Milky Way is 100,000 light years across and a single light year is 6 trillion miles—which means that the distances between stars are immense, dwarfing our solar system and journey to the moon. Unless ETs have picked up our TV signals and tracked them back to Earth, there is a near-zero chance they would know we humans exist on our speck of a planet orbiting a typical medium-sized star, among four hundred billion in the Milky Way. Our planet is tiny, remote, and it's time we give up the cosmic narcissism. Outside of our arts and sciences, we merit little attention.

ROSWELL

In 1947, a rancher named William Brazel found a cluster of strange debris about thirty miles north of Roswell, New Mexico. According to various newspaper reports, the US Air Force stated it was a "flying saucer," only to flip-flop the next day and say it was a "weather balloon." Thus, the flying saucer or "UFO" conspiracy was born. Roswell is ground zero for UFO conspiracy theory and even has the UFO Museum, which draws visitors from around the world.

FIGURE A.C.2   The UFO Museum in Roswell. Photos by Barry Vacker, 2017.

HOLLYWOOD UFOS

It took Hollywood only four years to put the flying saucer on the big screen, with the classic *The Day the Earth Stood Still* (1951), still one of the coolest science-fiction films ever made. In the film, an extraterrestrial savior named Klaatu arrives to welcome humanity to join the other peaceful planetary civilizations, yet with a warning that we cannot extend our violence off the planet. If we do, Klaatu says Earth will be reduced to "a burned out cinder." Frankly, I am all in favor of this message and I deeply wish a Klaatu figure would arrive from deep space to shake us out of our cosmic narcissism and arrogance.

FIGURE A.C.3 Left: Gort, the robot, and Klaatu; movie still from trailer for *The Day the Earth Stood Still* (1951); right, scene from trailer for *Earth vs. the Flying Saucers* (1956); trailers before 1964 were not copyrighted and are in the public domain.

Five years after Klaatu came in peace, ETs arrived to wage all-out war in *Earth vs. the Flying Saucers* (1956). Endless alien and UFO movies have followed, with the extraterrestrials being enlightened saviors or evil destroyers. In Steven Spielberg's *Close Encounters of the Third Kind* (1977), the extraterrestrials are friendly and peaceful, while the government tries to cover up their existence. In contrast, in *Independence Day* (1996) the aliens are bent upon wiping out humanity.

FIGURE A.C.4 UFO photo, Passaic, NJ, 1952; US Air Force video footage released in 2020. Both images are in the public domain.

These images are not the same as empirical evidence. Every documentary I have seen on UFOs follows the same formula. There are world-weary truth-tellers showing us strange photos and blurry documents while narrating a tale of endless stories, rumors, speculations, and hearsay "evidence" from various sources, all claiming there is a deep-state conspiracy involving the most powerful governments of the world. The empirical, independently verifiable evidence is never provided. Recently, the Pentagon began using the term "UAP," which stands for "Unidentified Aerial Phenomenon." Yet, the US military still have not produced any empirical evidence of extraterrestrial visitors. All we have are stories and speculation. Billions of high-quality cameras have proliferated with our smart phones, yet not one clear photo of an extraterrestrial or alien spacecraft.

As the scientist Carl Sagan said about UFOs, we have "stories of things, but not the things in themselves." We have numerous blurry or unclear images in photos and videos, of mysterious lights in the sky, but not one shred of physical evidence. In a universe stretching of two trillion galaxies across one hundred billion light-years, are we so *special* to have been discovered, visited, monitored, assisted, or even abducted by advanced extraterrestrials? Extraordinary claims should require extraordinary proof.

Are there UFOs and UAPs? Sure, there are "Unidentified Flying Objects" and "Unidentified Aerial Phenomena," things and phenomena in the sky that we are unable to identify. Are ETs in the pilot's seat? No. Are the grainy UFO images proof that an extraterrestrial civilization is visiting us? No. We have invented the mythology to fill a void. It's the same with the *Ancient Aliens* TV series, which is discussed in chapter 9. What better way to fill the cool voids than to imagine aliens spying on us or giving us the secrets of our greatest inventions?

JFK

In 1962, the United States and the former Soviet Union almost triggered a full-scale nuclear war, which would have destroyed most of humanity and civilization. This omega moment was known as the Cuban Missile Crisis. The cool hand of president John F. Kennedy was central to preventing the atomic apocalypse, along with a few sane leaders in the Soviet Union. Peace prevailed. The world breathed a sigh of relief.

Tragically, a year later in 1963, President Kennedy was assassinated on the streets of Dallas, in broad daylight, in one of the most horrifying scenes ever caught on film. The JFK assassination conspiracy might never have been born were it not for Dallas businessman Abraham Zapruder, who, while filming the passing motorcade, captured the moments of the shots hitting Kennedy.

The Warren Commission provided the official government position by concluding that Lee Harvey Oswald acted alone as the sole assassin, firing three shots from behind while nested in the Texas School Book Depository building. The Warren Commission also presented the "single bullet theory," which claimed that the first bullet that struck Kennedy then struck Texas governor John Connally (seated in front of Kennedy). The bullet supposedly passed through Connally's shoulder and thigh, after which the pristine bullet was found on Connally's stretcher in Parkland Hospital. Completely absurd, but the single bullet theory was needed to maintain the coherence of the Warren Commission Report.

Though mass media provided frames of the Zapruder film, the frames with the fatal head shot were not shown to audiences. Nevertheless, many conspiracy books were soon published, such as *Rush to Judgment* (1966) and *Six Seconds in Dallas* (1976). A decade after the assassination, the first Hollywood movie was produced (*Executive Action*, 1973), wherein a small cabal of mysterious men orchestrated the killing of President Kennedy.

BLOWING HOLES IN MINDS AND TVS

In 1975, Geraldo Rivera and Dick Gregory screened a bootleg copy of the Zapruder film on late-night television, including the fatal head shot. The images shocked Americans, metaphorically blowing holes in minds across the United States and soon the world.

Kennedy's skull is literally blown wide open, his head jolting backward, with brain matter exploding in the air. Viewers in Geraldo's TV studio can be heard to gasp. I am sure gasps and screams were heard in living rooms across America, as if holes were blown in the TV screens. The clear implication was a conspiracy and coup d'état. Who did it? What did it mean? Was America still a democracy? Omega.

Such questions were like gaping voids, which must be filled. If democracy is in trouble, such ends must be resisted. In 1976, the House of Representatives formed the "Select Committee on Assassinations," which revisited the assassination evidence and concluded that a conspiracy was likely. Democracy seemed still alive.

By 1991, JFK conspiracy fever reached its apex with Oliver Stone's *JFK*, which presented a sprawling "deep state" version of the assassination. The expertly made film expressed Boomer angst and tarnished democratic ideals, with a message that seemed to fill some of the philosophical and political voids left by the holes blasted in Kennedy's head.

For the record, I think the Zapruder film clearly suggests there were two shooters in Dallas—thus, there was a conspiracy. But I think it was a very small group who did it (maybe just three or five people were involved), which makes it even more scary for the government and Americans.[4] In the end, the JFK assassination effectively marks *the omega point for Americans blindly trusting their government.*

X

The X-Files appeared at a unique moment in history, with profound alpha and omega moments. By 1991, the Cold War was over (omega) and a new era of space exploration was under way (alpha). The Hubble Space Telescope was launched in 1990, and after corrections were made to the mirror, the telescope began unveiling an epic universe to the curious Earthlings on a tiny rock in space. So far, Hubble has had little impact on the cultural and political narratives on Earth, other than it seems to have joined the internet and social media in contributing to the decline in religious beliefs.

"EVERYTHING IS CONNECTED"

By far the best produced of all conspiracy shows, *The X-Files* was a cult hit that aired on Fox Network from 1993 to 2001, and again in 2016 and 2018. The series also spawned two big-budget Hollywood films (*The X-Files: Fight the Future* in 1998 and *The X-Files: I Want to Believe* in 2008). In essence, *The X-Files* featured two FBI agents confronting a far-reaching deep-state conspiracy theory, buttressed by pseudoscience and paranormalism.

Every time agent Dana Scully (Gillian Anderson) presented a scientific explanation for mysterious events, it was countered by the pseudoscientific or paranormal version championed by agent Fox Mulder (David Duchovny). Throughout the series, it was made clear that pseudoscience was not merely a valid counter to real science, but the better and more magical worldview. In many ways, the show was a *direct attack on science and reason.*

In the *X-Files* narrative, everything was connected, with sprawling conspiracies orchestrated by a secret cabal, tucked away in the deep state of the American military-industrial complex. Building on the Roswell-UFO conspiracy theory, the story of "alien autopsies" played a key role in the overall narratives of *The X-Files*. So did UFOs and JFK's assassination, along with biowarfare and alien-human hybrids. Anything was possible, everything was connected in *The X-Files*, the televised precursor to QAnon. All that was needed for the transition from X to Q was Neo in *The Matrix*.

---

4   My full explanation is in this essay: Barry Vacker, "The Kennedy Assassination and Zapruder Film: Conspiracy Theories and Alt-Fact Worldviews," *Medium*, October 29, 2017.

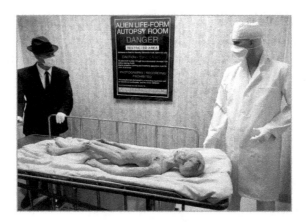

FIGURE A.C.5   Exhibit of "alien autopsy" in the UFO Museum; photo by Barry Vacker, 2017.

NEO

The Matrix exploded into pop consciousness in 1999, precisely as the new millennium dawned and fears of Y2K loomed at the end of the twentieth century. Alpha and omega mindsets were all over America and the world. Still are.

In the opening of the film, the title—THE MATRIX—emerges from a glowing cascade of numbers. With the camera slowly zooming in on a single digit—0—moviegoers are propelled through the zero, through the void, the mediated realm of nothingness, the virtuality of "the Matrix." At once, *The Matrix* presented an alpha and omega moment in our culture. Suddenly, young Neos were everywhere—and many who saw themselves as Trinity and Morpheus, too.

In *The Matrix*, humans are unknowingly wired into to a global computer network, where the mediated world has become the "real world" for everyone—except for Morpheus (brilliantly played by Laurence Fishburne) and his band of rebel hackers. *The Matrix* presents a deep-state conspiracy protected by artificial intelligence programs circulating throughout "the Matrix," a metaphorical version of the internet. The conspiracy here is not about a particular event, such as UFO sightings or JFK's murder, but rather a conspiracy about all of "reality." Of course, the only way one can know this conspiracy is to follow Neo (Keanu Reeves) and swallow the red pill provided by Morpheus.

HAVE ANY OF QANON'S RED-PILLERS READ NEO'S BOOK?

I wonder how many of the red-pilled rebels populating QAnon websites and rallies have bothered to read the only book featured in *the Matrix* trilogy. Maybe 1 in 10,000? 1 in 100,000? 1 in 1,000,000? As discussed in chapter 3, that one book is key to grasping the meaning of *The Matrix* and the red pill.

Early in *The Matrix*, Neo opens a green book called *Simulacra and Simulation* by media philosopher Jean Baudrillard, the central theorist of "hyperreality." The book is hollowed out to secretly store computer disks and other items. When Morpheus says, "the Matrix is everywhere," he is drawing from Baudrillard. For true believers of conspiracy theory, conspiracies are everywhere, just like in *The Matrix*.

For Baudrillard, there was no grand conspiracy, no secret puppet masters. Just the continual evolution of our technologies, coupled with our endless desire to reproduce the world in our own image in order to give us meaning. Media technology has ended the distinctions between the fictional and the authentic—between the symbol and what it stands for. We live in a world where the signs and symbols of the real have largely replaced the real. For more discussion, see chapter 3 and the reading "Welcome to the Desert of the Red Pill."

The deeper meaning of the red pill is that there are no easy exits, no surefire way to freedom, no backdoor escape from hyperreality, and no conspiratorial pathway to truth. Baudrillard thought there was no exit. Yet, screens in hand, the conspiracy true believers remain trapped in the Matrix, the existing system they fight to preserve, all the while wandering "the desert of the real" in search of salvation and redemption. It's a hyperreal religion, the simulacra of the future past. Enter Q.

Q

Born in hyperreality, QAnon is the next evolution of conspiracy theory, the next layer of simulacra. Copies of copies of copies. QAnon is nothing really new, other than that it resides on a new twenty-first century platform.[5] That platform is the internet.

For conspiracy theorists, the internet and social media function like Baudrillard's hyperreality coupled with humanity's narcissism—all on steroids. Spanning the globe, the ego-media networks and platforms are dense and complex. Images and information pour in from all over. Layer upon interlinked layer. The more one digs, the more one becomes immersed. The rabbit hole. Everything seems connected, deeper and deeper. Endless links, blogs, sources, websites, and YouTube videos. Political propaganda, government lies, corporate cover-ups, and now Photoshop and deep fakes. Maps overtaking territories, maps obliterating territories, maps becoming new territories. It's hard to tell what is true and what is false. Tribes galore, fans and followers, hives and swarms. TikTok, Instagram, Pinterest. Information overload. Hyperreality everywhere. *The Matrix*. Hot media. Chaos!

To keep the dominant ideological and theological systems intact, the chaotic vastness of cyberspace must be countered by a vastness of conspiracies. Thus the alpha-omega codes of UFOs, JFK, *The X-Files*, and *The Matrix* have all been amplified, along with Apollo 11 and 9/11 conspiracies, Flat-Earthers, Young-Earthers, and so on. But, that is not enough on Planet Earth. Many need a new fix. Q. Cue up the Q-tubers, who believe that the world is being run by a Satan-worshipping cabal of child-eating cannibals and that a celebrity billionaire president has been delivered by God to save America. If one believes in alleged prophecies of Nostradamus and Revelation, then one might well believe in QAnon, whose conspiracies function like unproven and unrealized prophecies.

Of course, there are many ludicrous conspiracies believed by Q followers in addition to the falsehood that the 2020 election was stolen from Trump. Two of my favorites are (1) that John F. Kennedy Jr. faked his death and would join Trump in the battle to save America and (2) that China used a weather machine to create and steer a severe winter storm over Texas in 2021. Never mind that meteorologists showed the "polar vortex" coming from the North Pole for days before its arrival or that such severe cold snaps have happened before in Texas. I know: I lived in Austin when a similar cold storm brought severe cold to Texas in the early 1990s.

"SECRET KNOWLEDGE"

The conspiracy structure is always the same, even with Q. There is "someone" with access to "secret knowledge" about the events of the world, able to see and reveal hidden causes. Maybe it's a renegade doctor, a turncoat scientist, a military expert, or a person with high security clearance—*à* la Q. As with Revelation, the secret and cryptic knowledge is to be shared, with followers adding their takes and spreading it far and wide, thus effecting a mass movement from what amounts to a massive media virus. Self-help becomes self-delusion, brainwashing masquerades as braininess, and memes and YouTube videos substitute for sound research and empirical knowledge. "Do your own research" becomes a mantra for ignoring all logic, reason, and evidence, precisely as Q followers simulate all three.

---

5 Charlie Warzel, "Is QAnon the Most Dangerous Conspiracy Theory of the 21st Century?," *New York Times*, August 4, 2020.

WHO IS Q?

It would not surprise me to learn that the name "Q" was based on the fictional character Q from *Star Trek: The Next Generation* (1987–1994). Q was an omnipotent, mischievous, manipulative, Machiavellian character who could alter space, time, and reality to serve mysterious purposes and to mess with various characters, especially for pure amusement.[6] In the series, Q was an antihero counter to Captain Jean-Luc Picard. Ultimately, it does not matter whether Q the conspirator was inspired by Q from *Star Trek: The Next Generation*.

In the final episode of *Q: Into the Storm*, the 2021 HBO documentary, director Cullen Hoback states that he strongly believes Q is Ron Watkins, who helped run the 8Chan and 8kun sites that host QAnon. Maybe so. But, in the end, it never did matter who Q is or was.

Q's intellectual and cultural function was to be a *contemporary Nostradamus*, an alleged prophet replicating throughout the layers of hyperreality. Q provided the narratives, the alpha-omega points for hundreds of millions of minds, deluded by decades of media-empowered creationism, doublethink, and pseudoscience, all free flowing in the networks and platforms of hyperreality. That's why the actual identity of Q is irrelevant. Just like the prophecies of Nostradamus, nothing has to be true; followers only need to believe. That's the power of memes. That's the power of hyperreality.

NOSTRADAMUS AND "A GAME THAT PLAYS PEOPLE"

Nostradamus was the most searched book the day after the terrorist attacks of September 11, 2001. Four days after the attacks, a book by Nostradamus was the top seller in Amazon and books about Nostradamus occupied spots 4, 5, 11, 12, and 25 on the list.[7] Of course, all this was *after* September 11. No one read Nostradamus and warned the world *before* the terrorist attacks or warned NYC with the specific passage and prophecy.[8]

That's because Nostradamus did not prophecy anything having to do with September 11 or anything else in the twenty-first century. Nostradamus was an astrologer from the sixteenth century, and his "prophecies" are just another myth, filling voids and claiming to reveal hidden patterns and secret knowledge. Yet, the History Channel frequently broadcast shows about Nostradamus. Imagine that—seeking a prophetic explanation for twenty-first-century events from a sixteenth-century astrologer!

Not surprisingly, Q also had a top-selling book in Amazon. As reported in an online documentary by *Vice*, the first appearance of Q was on Saturday, October 28, 2017. There was an anonymous post on the "4chan" message board, a post by someone claiming to be a "high-level government insider" with a prediction of a future event. The post was signed "Q."[9]

The Q meme was born, with rabbit holes replicating and accelerating like a deadly virus in a global pandemic, attacking reason, logic, and common sense around the world. As detailed by *Vice*, the Q worldview is filled with false predictions, racism and prejudice, and medieval claims of demonic control of the world. Just as COVID-19 is a deadly biological virus that gets our cells to replicate the virus, Q is a mind virus that replicates precisely as it *simulates* critical thinking. It's just like the doomsday cults with prophecies set to happen on certain dates, and when the prophecy does not happen, they just move the date back and re-do the prophecy.

---

6   As summarized in WikiLeaks, Q is "an extra-dimensional being of unknown origin who possesses immeasurable power over time, space, the laws of physics, and reality itself, being capable of altering it to his whim. Despite his vast knowledge and experience spanning untold eons (and much to the exasperation of the object(s) of his obsession), he is not above practical jokes for his own personal amusement, for a Machiavellian and manipulative purpose, or to prove a point. He is said to be almost omnipotent and he is continually evasive regarding his true motivations." See https://en.wikipedia.org/wiki/Q_(Star_Trek).
7   Janelle Brown, "Nostradamus Called It!," *Salon*, September 17, 2001.
8   Snopes Staff, "Did Nostradamus Predict the 9/11 Attacks?," Snopes, September 21, 2001.
9   "QAnon 101: The Search for Q," Vice, January 25, 2021. Video available on YouTube.

The Q posts are called "drops," which are cryptic messages just like the "quatrains" of Nostradamus or "prophecies" from Revelation. Mysterious puzzles that supposedly predict future events. Who doesn't like puzzles and games? Yet, as one game designer explained, Q is "a game that plays people."[10] Millions of Americans were played.

#WWG1WGA

For the true believers, Q signals the "Great Awakening" and "nothing can stop it." The "Storm" is also coming. Q believers are united: #WWG1WGA ("Where We Go One, We Go All"). Q is ripping families apart, precisely as the theories generate cultlike behavior that leaves parents and their adult children on opposite sides of an unbridgeable gulf.[11]

Q is replicating throughout the "Wellness" communities, inspiring COVID-19 and antivaxx conspiracies.[12] Q followers are now being elected to the US Congress. All of this is why Q is very dangerous for democracy and the health of the world.[13] Flashing red lights! This "Great Awakening" is both their dream and their delusion—emerging after the first Black president (Barack Obama) and the first female presidential candidate (Hillary Clinton), surely signs of the changing of the political guard in terms of race and gender. Kamala Harris as a Black female vice-president further illustrates the point.

As Adrienne LaFrance shows in "The Prophecies of Q," the QAnon believers are most often highly religious (not to say that all highly religious people are apt to believe in QAnon or conspiracy theories) and searching for Revelation-like prophecies of "End Times" to confirm their apocalyptic beliefs from sacred texts and TV sermons.[14] This correlates with the religious motivations of President Trump's insurrectionists, who merged evangelicalism and extremism in the efforts to violently seize political power.[15]

As revealed by the Q flags and Q T-shirts at the insurrection, many felt empowered by Q and President Trump's evidence-free conspiracy theory that the election was "stolen." With the "My Pillow" founder serving as one of the head cheerleaders, the promotional meme was "Stop the Steal." There is zero evidence to support this claim, and the Trump administration has had their legal challenges rejected by ninety-six judges.[16] Election officials in fifty states had verified the vote totals and found no evidence of any fraud that would have come close to overturning the winner in any state. As the Cybersecurity and Infrastructure Security Agency reported, "The November 3rd election was the most secure in American history."[17] Of course, to the Q believers, this proves the election was "stolen" by the "deep state."

---

10   Reed Berkowitz, "A Game Designer's Analysis of QAnon," Medium, September 30, 2020. See also Anna Merian, "The Conspiracy Singularity Has Arrived," Vice, July 17, 2020.
11   Greg Jaffe and Jose A. Del Real, "Life Amid the Ruins of QAnon: 'I Wanted My Family Back,'" Washington Post, February 23, 2021.
12   Shayla Love, "'Conspirituality' Explains Why the Wellness World Fell for QAnon," Vice, December 16, 2020.
13   Charlie Warzel, "Is QAnon the Most Dangerous Conspiracy Theory of the 21st Century?," New York Times, August 4, 2020.
14   Adrienne LaFrance, "The Prophecies of Q," The Atlantic, June, 2020.
15   Elizabeth Diaz and Ruth Graham, "How White Evangelicals Fused with Trump Extremism," New York Times, January 11, 2021; Michael Gerson, "Trump's Evangelicals Were Complicit in the Desecration of Our Democracy," Washington Post, January 7, 2021; Morgan Lee, "Christian Nationalism Is Worse Than You Think," Christianity Today, January 13, 2013; Paul Moses, "The Renegade Catholic Clerics Who Shamefully Backed Trump's Big Lie," CNN website, January 19, 2021.
16   Ann Gerhart, "Election Results Under Attack: Here Are the Facts," Washington Post, January 14, 2021. The ninety-six judges represent the total as of this writing on February 28, 2021. Jim Rutenberg, Nick Corasaniti, and Alan Feuer, "Trump's Fraud Claims Died in Court, but the Myth of Stolen Elections Lives On," New York Times, December 26, 2020.
17   "Joint Statement from Elections Infrastructure Government Coordinating Council and the Election Infrastructure Sector Coordinating Executive Committees," Cybersecurity & Infrastructure Security Agency, November 12, 2020.

JANUARY 6, 2021

On January 6, 2021, Q-inspired wannabe Neos—along with White Supremacists and Christian Nationalists—stormed the US Capitol in a violent insurrection, aiming to overturn a fair election and install a would-be authoritarian dictator. In reality, "Stop the Steal" was the actual conspiracy, a coordinated plot to enact a coup d'état in the United States, with millions of Americans apparently ready for an antidemocracy dictatorship.[18] It is what it is and we can no longer live in denial of the threats to American democracy.

As of this writing, many of the low-level insurrectionists are facing relatively minor charges for their role in the events of January 6, with a few "Proud Boys" facing stiffer charges. Yet, nothing has happened to any of the political ringleaders—Ted Cruz, Josh Hawley, Paul Gosar, Rudy Giuliani, Donald Trump Jr., former president Donald Trump, etc. The 147 Republicans who voted against certifying the election *after the attempted coup* are still in office, facing no penalties or repercussions for supporting the falsehood that that the election was stolen, for cheerleading the insurrection, for voting to overturn the election, or for still supporting the overall coup effort.

Rather, they have spent the past few months on TV and social media gaslighting America while they are seeking to restrict voter access to the polls in numerous states—all based on the hyperreal conspiracy myth that the election was stolen.[19] As if echoing the conspiracy table at the beginning of this chapter, Dallas-based insurrectionist Jenna Ryan recently tweeted the following with the hashtag #EndTimes: "Behold, I am coming soon! My reward is with me, and I will give to everyone according to what he has done. I am the Alpha and the Omega, the First and the Last, the Beginning and the End."[20] Indeed, just as the table says.

COVID-19 AND "THE PERFECT CRIME"

In the book *The Perfect Crime*, Jean Baudrillard wrote that media and hyperreality had killed "reality" and gotten away with it in "the perfect crime." Baudrillard wrote, "So the prophecy has been fulfilled: we live in a world where the highest function of the sign is to make reality disappear and, at the same time, to mask that disappearance."[21] We don't have to take that literally to see how much truth there is to the metaphor, especially with conspiracy and antiscience worldviews. *After all, isn't that what happened in much of America with the COVID pandemic, where hyperreality has led to the death of real people and an attempted coup d'état to install a dictatorship?*[22]

The Trump–Pence White House bungled the pandemic completely, powered by the hyperreal combo of Q, conspiracy theory, antiscience, and the repeated displays of doublethink and ignorance. President Trump even suggested injecting bleach disinfectants into the body to fight COVID-19 and "appeared to propose irradiating patients' bodies with UV light."[23] It's hard to believe those words were coming from the leader of the nation which

18   Ben Collins, "As Trump Meets with QAnon Influencers, the Conspiracy's Adherents Beg for Dictatorship," *NBC News*, December 22, 2020. Some believe that President Trump and his fervent followers represent the rise of fascism in America. Paul Krugman, "Appeasement Is What Got Us Here: It's Time to Stand Up to the Fascists Among Us," *New York Times*, January 7, 2021. The *Merriam-Webster* online dictionary defines *fascism* as "a political philosophy, movement, or regime (such as that of the Fascisti) that exalts nation and often race above the individual and that stands for a centralized autocratic government headed by a dictatorial leader, severe economic and social regimentation, and forcible suppression of opposition." Similarly, the online *Cambridge Dictionary* defines *fascism* as "a political system based on a very powerful leader, state control, and being extremely proud of country and race, and in which political opposition is not allowed."

19   Amy Gardner, Kate Rabinowitz, and Harry Stevens, "How GOP-Backed Voting Measures Could Create Hurdles for Tens of Millions of Voters," *Washington Post*, March 11, 2021. Alex Samuels, Elena Mejia, and Nathaniel Rakich, "The States Where Efforts to Restrict Voting Are Escalating," *FiveThirtyEight*, March 20, 2021.

20   Michelle Boorstein, ""A Horn-Wearing 'Shaman.' A Cowboy Evangelist. For Some, the Capitol Attack was a Kind of Christian Revolt," *Washington Post*, July 6, 2021.

21   Jean Baudrillard, *The Perfect Crime* (London: Verso, 1995), 6.

22   Marina Fang, "Trump Is 'The Largest Driver' of COVID-19 Conspiracy Theories, Study Finds," *HuffPost*, October 20, 2020.

23   "Coronavirus: Outcry After Trump Suggests Injecting Disinfectant as Treatment," *BBC News*, April 24, 2020; Meredith McGraw and Sam Stein, "It's Been Exactly One Year Since Trump Suggested Injecting Bleach. We've Never Been the Same," *Politico*, April 23, 2021.

produces the most scientific advances on Planet Earth, the country of NASA, the Apollo moon landings, the Hubble Space Telescope, and endless breakthroughs across the realms of science, medicine, and technology. Yet, those words again reveal the spectacle of the celebrity system and the power of hyperreality, where ignorance is presented as strength. Prior to the violent insurrection, Corporate America was happy with its tax breaks and remained largely silent about the antiscience policies and evidence-free worldviews replicating in America, from Main Street to the White House.[24]

Throughout much of the COVID-19 pandemic, more than one hundred million Americans chose to deny the science of vaccines and mask-wearing in the name of "freedom" and "strength"—no matter that they could pose a serious risk to the health of nearby family, neighbors, business owners and their customers, and the rest of their fellow American citizens. The argument was that being *required to wear a mask in public settings* was a violation of their constitutional rights and a sign of "weakness."

What about diners being required to wear shoes and shirts in restaurants? What about motorists being required to drive with headlights on at night? Are these requirements signs of "weakness" and a violation of constitutional rights? Or are they just common sense measures to ensure cleaner restaurants and safe driving for *everyone*? Imagine everyone driving at night with no headlights, such that it is almost impossible to see cars coming and going. How is this different than not wearing a mask, when no one knows who has COVID-19 among the people coming and going? Endless car crashes and COVID spreading are to be expected.

These Americans repeatedly shouted to the world that their antivaccine and mask-free stances showed they were being strong and patriotic, bent upon saving America from demise, with the superpowers to see through the alleged conspiracies surrounding the development of the vaccines. Perhaps they are patriots and internet tough guys in their Twitter feeds, Facebook updates, and YouTube videos, but they are not strong in the actual, empirical, and underlying scientific reality they inhabit with the rest of humanity. Hyperreality permits weaknesses to be presented as strengths, precisely because it presents an artificial map as the territory, replacing the actual reality.[25] Not getting a vaccine or not wearing a mask shows how the signs and symbols of strength replace actually being strong—the map overtaking and generating the territory it claims to represent. *Only in a hyperreal culture of endless Twitter feeds and YouTube videos can "not getting a vaccine" or "not wearing a mask" be signs of strength, precisely because it is the simulation of strength in its very absence.* Additionally, it assumes the YouTube vloggers know more than the world's scientists, doctors, nurses, and medical technicians, who are supposedly part of a global hoax involving millions of people with careers dedicated to science and medicine.

One factor in being strong is facing reality, the actual empirical reality of the world and the universe around us—as it is, not as we wish it was (especially in our childish, immature, and narcissistic fantasies). That means accepting and embracing the realities of evolution and NASA's cosmic discoveries, realities that challenge and refute our worldview, and even realities that are a hassle, inconvenient, and simply not fun.[26] Wearing a mask

---

24 Todd C. Frankel, Jeff Stein, Jena McGregor, and Jonathan O'Connell, "Companies Backed Trump for Years. Now They're Facing a Reckoning After the Assault on the Capitol," *Washington Post*, January 8, 2021.

25 The techno-enabled hyperreal worldview empowers YouTube Flat Earthers to deny that our planet is a sphere, empowers Young Earthers to deny that our planet is 4.7 billion years old, and empowers creationists to deny that our species is the product of billions of years of cosmic and biological evolution.

26 As a cancer survivor, I can speak to this firsthand, forced to do things that I had only read about happening to others. Upon my diagnosis, was I nervous and scared? Yes, absolutely. But, I placed my confidence in reason, medical science, and the expertise of the doctors, nurses, and technicians. My surgery also happened during the first surge of the COVID pandemic. Obviously, the surgeons and nurses wore masks all the time, though they would have anyway during the surgery. Somehow, I mustered the strength to do what I had to do. I am not special. I just faced reality, like millions of other cancer patients. The doctors, nurses, technicians, and patients do what is needed so the patient has the best chance of surviving. That's biological and cultural evolution working as a team—the will to survive plus technology, Darwin plus doctors and nurses. So far, I am cancer-free, thanks to the wonders of medical science, the expertise and compassion of healthcare workers, and the evolutionary drive to stay alive.

(properly fitted, with an N95 level of protection for the user and those nearby) is a hassle and not fun. Getting a vaccine is no fun, especially if you do not like needles.

No one in their right mind wants restaurants, retail stores, and various businesses to close down because of the pandemic. That's why wearing masks and social distancing were essential. Wearing masks and properly social distancing would have significantly reduced the severity, duration, and economic effects of the closures and "lockdowns." *Going mask-free amplified the economic problems it claimed to be opposing.* Patriotism has its simulacra and the faux patriots are proliferating across America (and the world). That's hyperreality!

These beliefs and worldviews helped wreck the economy and had deadly consequences. As of this writing (July 1, 2021), more than six hundred thousand Americans have died horrible, lonely deaths, suffocating from within because of COVID-19. For the dead, their freedom was indeed taken away, with their freedom of speech canceled forever. In their pretense to strength, the antivaxxers and antimaskers display a staggering indifference to helping prevent human suffering.[27]

As of this writing, America has 4 percent of the world's population, yet almost 15 percent of the deaths from COVID.[28] At the website for the Centers for Disease Control, the average number of flu deaths over the past decade is about thirty-seven thousand per year—that's with almost no one wearing masks during flu outbreaks in America. Imagine how many would have died from COVID-19 if no one had worn masks since the outbreak. *Currently, the one million dead are thirteen and a half times the average annual flu death rate (thirty-seven thousand).*

All because of conspiracy theory, toxic narcissism, antiscience worldviews, all replicating in hyperreal culture, where the maps have overtaken the territories. No political leader has been penalized in any way. None. Nada. Zero. Apparently, nothing gets in the way of the myths, not even mass death.[29]

Welcome to Baudrillard's perfect crime.

ARE THERE ANY SOLUTIONS?

American democracy is in deep trouble. It may not survive, except as a simulacrum of itself, fifty states united in hyperreality. After all, QAnon supporters are now getting elected to Congress and local elections. Unchallenged for decades, the forces of doublethink, pseudoscience, creationism, and conspiracy have merged in hot media and hyperreality. There are no simple solutions.

Unlike the findings of the Warren Commission, which studied the JFK assassination, there is no "single bullet theory" that can solve the massive conspiracy problem. It's a deep-state level of creationist consciousness, a false-flag neural network, a Roswell red pill worldview. Such deep-state beliefs are protected by the First Amendment, even if they are not supported by empirical evidence or reason and logic. The US government is not the arbiter of cosmic truth. Obviously, conspiracy theories, pseudoscience, and fact-free beliefs need to be confronted and refuted as often as possible. But, sadly, that has not stopped pseudoscience, creationism, and conspiracy theory from proliferating over the past seven decades, despite (or because of) the discoveries of science and technology.

There is no sign that Hollywood or the TV networks will stop producing films and shows that capitalize on pseudoscience and paranormalism. There are tons of pseudoscience and conspiracy videos on YouTube. When I did a Google search for UFOs, ads appeared for *Ancient Aliens*. The algorithms and maps keep generating the territories.

The only real solution is a long-term plan (and even this may not prevail). Here are a few steps:

---

27   Adam Geller and Janie Har, "Shameful: US Virus Deaths Top 400K as Trump Leaves Office," *AP News*, January 19, 2021.
28   World-o-meter cite
29   Robin Givhan, "Americans Are Stubbornly Unmoved by Death," *Washington Post*, March 23, 2021.

1. We need to massively increase science and critical-thinking education for every student in every public school—from kindergarten to the post-graduate level. By critical thinking, I do not mean hot takes in Twitter feeds. I mean the introduction to identifying fallacies and practicing logical thinking—from a logic textbook! Not some twelve-minute TED Talk with instant solutions.

2. Networks like the History Channel need to be discredited, as do Hollywood studios that produce movies celebrating paranormalism, pseudoscience, and conspiracy theories. Executives, producers, directors, writers, and actors should be called to account for their decisions to promote unproven claims and known falsehoods. This does not mean limiting their First Amendment rights, but it also does not mean that media platforms continually be provided to them so that their maps can steal the territories of reality for unwitting readers and viewers. The First Amendment does not require anyone be given a megaphone, a TV show, or a Twitter feed.

3. Artists and philosophers need to step up—big time! They need to collectively develop a widely embraced secular narrative that provides a sense of hope, purpose, inclusion, and common destiny for humanity, a species that shares a tiny rock in space yet remains philosophically lost amid two trillion galaxies.[30] Of course, that narrative must be ecologically sustainable, inclusive, and diverse, and it must include universal human rights for everyone—and that means *everyone* (as stated in the introduction to this book).

4. Filmmakers need to produce science-fiction films that tap into the *cool* meanings by inspiring awe and wonder, à la *2001: A Space Odyssey*. More documentaries need to be produced like Carl Sagan's *Cosmos* (1980), Neil deGrasse Tyson's *Cosmos: A Spacetime Odyssey* (2014), Tyson's and Ann Druyan's *Cosmos: Possible Worlds* (2020), Brian Cox's *Wonders of the Universe* (2011) and *Human Universe* (2015), and Jim Al-Khalili's many stellar science documentaries for the BBC.[31]

5. Celebrate that the cosmic truth—our evolution with the expanding universe, populated with untold numbers of stars, planets, supernovas, black holes, life-forms, and perhaps even advanced civilizations—is way cooler than conspiracy theory and creation myths. Schools and universities should mandate that every student complete a course on Introduction to Astronomy, among others.

There is an underlying reality in our world that can be explained by reason, science, technology, art, and philosophy. America's and the world's scientists and universities are still on the forefront of scientific discoveries in numerous fields, especially astronomy and cosmology. All of these discoveries should be greenlighted across our media and pop culture. Yet, such progress and discoveries are not celebrated in our popular culture or popular philosophies. For many, these triumphs are lost in a 24/7 spectacle of simulacra, celebrities, billionaires, superheroes, movie stars, televangelists, conspiracy theorists, and internet tough guys, all radiating across the hyperreal vectors of Hollywood, Disneyland, Times Square, and Las Vegas.

Welcome to the desert of the real.

CREDITS

Fig. A.C.1: Copyright © 2011 Depositphotos/Ivankmit.

Fig. A.C.4a: Source: https://commons.wikimedia.org/wiki/File:PurportedUFO2.jpg.

Fig. A.C.4b: Source: https://www.navair.navy.mil/foia/documents.

---

30   The contours of such a philosophy were outlined in *Specter of the Monolith* (2017), my book inspired by *2001: A Space Odyssey*.

31   Brian Cox and Andrew Cohen, *Wonders of the Universe* (London: HarperCollins and BBC, 2011); Brian Cox and Andrew Cohen, *Human Universe* (London: William Collins, 2015); Ann Druyan, *Cosmos: Possible Worlds* (Washington, DC: National Geographic, 2020).

Subject Index

Media Index

— these are referenced in the chapter introductions and many are mentioned in the essays for the chapters.

395

Printed in the USA
CPSIA information can be obtained
at www.ICGtesting.com
LVHW022038180823
755660LV00007B/26